COLLEGE OF ALAMEDA LIBRARY
WITHDRAWN

D0398483

V

KF
8742   Schwartz, Bernard,
S29   The ascent of
1990   pragmatism

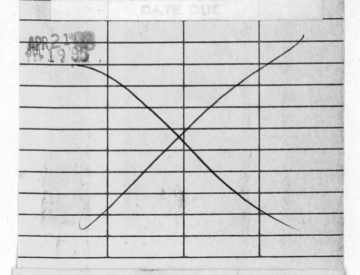

DATE DUE

APR 21
19 95

LENDING POLICY
IF YOU DAMAGE OR LOSE LIBRARY
MATERIALS, THEN YOU WILL BE
CHARGED FOR REPLACEMENT. FAIL-
URE TO PAY AFFECTS LIBRARY
PRIVILEGES, GRADES, TRANSCRIPTS,
DIPLOMAS, AND REGISTRATION
PRIVILEGES OR ANY COMBINATION
THEREOF.

R 3   '93

The Ascent of Pragmatism

The Ascent of Pragmatism
The Burger Court in Action

BERNARD SCHWARTZ

Addison-Wesley Publishing Company, Inc.
Reading, Massachusetts   Menlo Park, California   New York
Don Mills, Ontario   Wokingham, England   Amsterdam   Bonn
Sydney   Singapore   Tokyo   Madrid   San Juan

Library of Congress Cataloging-in-Publication Data

Schwartz, Bernard, 1923–
    The ascent of pragmatism : the Burger Court in action / Bernard
Schwartz.
        p. cm.
    Includes index.
    ISBN 0-201-51817-1
    1. United States. Supreme Court—History.   2. Burger, Warren E.,
1907– . I. Title.
    KF8742.S29   1990
    347.73'26—dc20
    [347.30735]   89-31627
                                                                        CIP

Copyright © 1990 by Bernard Schwartz

All rights reserved. No part of this publication may be re-
produced, stored in a retrieval system, or transmitted, in any
form or by any means, electronic, mechanical, photocopying,
recording, or otherwise, without the prior written permission
of the publisher. Printed in the United States of America. Published simultaneously in Canada.

Jacket design by Marge Anderson
Text design by Joyce C. Weston
Set in 11-point Sabon by G&S Typesetters, Inc., Austin, TX

ABCDEFGHIJ-DO-89
First printing, November 1989

As always, for Aileen

CONTENTS

SOURCES AND
ACKNOWLEDGMENTS

THIS BOOK is based on both oral and documentary sources. The oral sources consisted of personal interviews. I interviewed members of the Supreme Court and former law clerks, as well as others. Every statement not otherwise identified was made to me personally. I have tried to identify the statements of different people, except where they were made upon a confidential basis. In the latter case, I have given the position of the person involved, but not the name. This book could never have been written without the cooperation of those who shared their time and experiences so generously with me.

The documentary sources are conference notes, docket books, correspondence, notes, memoranda, and draft opinions. The documents used and their location are identified, except where they were made available upon a confidential basis. Most of these documents have never before been published.

The conferences themselves, at which cases are discussed and the votes taken on decisions, are, of course, completely private—attended only by the Justices themselves. The secrecy of the conference is, indeed, one of the great continuing Court traditions. I have tried to reconstruct the conferences in most of the cases discussed, including all the important cases decided by the Burger Court. The conference discussions are given in conversational form and the quotes are taken verbatim from notes made by a Justice who was present.

I have been afforded generous access to the papers of the Justices and gratefully acknowledge the help given by the Manuscript Division, Library of Congress and the Mudd Manuscript Library, Princeton. I also wish to acknowledge the efforts of my editor, Martha Moutray, the staff of Addison-Wesley Publishing Co., Marshall De-Bruhl for his editorial help, my literary agent, Gerard McCauley, the support of Deans John Sexton and Norman Redlich and the New York University School of Law, the work of my tireless secretary, Mrs. Barbara Ortiz, and the generous help of the Filomen d'Agostino and Max E. Greenberg Research Fund of New York University School of Law. Mere words cannot express my feelings about her to whom all my work is dedicated.

Chapter One

Chief Justice Burger and His Court

"DON'T LET them push you around." Chief Justice Burger once told me this was the principal advice given him by his predecessor, Earl Warren. But the leadership role of a Chief Justice depends more on his abilities than his position, and in the Supreme Court it is difficult for a Chief Justice to assert a *formal* leadership role. Aside from his designation as Chief of the Court and his slightly higher salary, the Chief Justice is not superior to his colleagues—and certainly is not legally superior.

The Justices themselves have always been sensitive to claims of Chief Justice superiority.[1] As Justice Tom C. Clark said, "The Chief Justice has no more authority than other members of the court."[2] And Justice Felix Frankfurter wrote "that any encouragement in a Chief Justice that he is the boss . . . must be rigorously resisted. . . . I, for my part, will discharge what I regard as a post of trusteeship, not least in keeping the Chief Justice in his place. . . ."[3]

The Chief Justiceship should not, however, be approached only in a formalistic sense. The greatest Chief Justices have known how to make the most of the extralegal potential inherent in their position. The Chief Justice may be only *primus inter pares;* but he is *primus.* Somebody has to preside, both in open court and in the even more important work of deciding cases in the conference chamber. The Chief Justice controls the discussion in conference; his is the prerogative to call and discuss cases before the other Justices speak. A great Chief Justice leads the Court with all the authority, all the *bravura,* of a great maestro.[4]

Yet even a strong Chief Justice is limited. The Supreme Court is a collegiate institution, which is underscored by the custom of the Justices calling each other "Brethren." The Justices can only be guided, not directed. As Frankfurter stated, "Good feeling in the Court, as in a family, is produced by accommodation, not by authority—whether the authority of a parent or a vote."[5]

The Court "family" is composed of nine individuals, who constantly bear out James Bryce's truism that "judges are only men."[6] "To be sure," Frankfurter once wrote, "the Court is an institution, but individuals, with all their diversities of endowment, experience and outlook determine its actions. The history of the Supreme Court is not the history of an abstraction, but the analysis of individuals acting as a Court who make decisions and lay down doctrines."[7]

In many ways, the individual Justices operate like "nine separate law firms." Justice Stewart told me that even Chief Justice Warren "came to realize very early . . . that this group of nine rather prima donnaish people could not be led, could not be told, in the way the Governor of California can tell a subordinate, do this or do that."

What Stewart says was particularly true when Warren Burger was appointed. The Court stars then were Justices Black, Douglas, Harlan, and Brennan—four of the greatest judges ever to serve on the highest bench, brilliant jurists, each a forceful personality. The first three were soon to leave the Court; but their replacements were also men of strong views. The Court was also divided into blocs representing polar views on the proper role of the Court in interpreting the Constitution. Their doctrinal differences made it most difficult for the Chief Justice to assert a strong leadership role—particularly since Burger himself was a strong adherent of one of the blocs.

BURGER ON OLYMPUS

Earl Warren brought more authority to the position of Chief Justice than had been the case for years, and the Warren Court bore his image as unmistakably as the earlier Courts of John Marshall and Roger B. Taney. The high bench was emphatically the *Warren* Court, and he and the country knew it.

This was plainly not as true under Warren E. Burger. The Burger tenure was not marked by strong leadership in molding Supreme Court jurisprudence.

Burger himself was cast from a different mold than Warren. Although, as a reporter pointed out, his "white maned, broad-shouldered presence on the bench is very reminiscent of his predecessor's,"[8] the men beneath the dignified exteriors were completely dissimilar. Burger's background was mostly in a law firm in St. Paul.

He had nothing like the spectacular career and broad experience in politics of Warren, although he had been active in the Republican party. He worked in Harold E. Stassen's successful campaign for governor, and in 1952 he was Stassen's floor manager at the Republican convention when Minnesota's switch supplied the necessary votes for Eisenhower's nomination.

After the election, Burger was appointed assistant attorney general in charge of the Claims Division of the Department of Justice. This experience led directly to one of his most noted opinions as an appellate judge.[9] It held that a government contractor might not be debarred from further government contracts without notice and hearing. Burger told me that the ruling was directly influenced by the many debarment orders that had come across his desk in the Justice Department—"issued in the name of the Secretary of the Navy; but the actual decision was made by some Lieutenant, J.G., way down the line."

In 1956, Burger was named to the U.S. Court of Appeals in Washington, D.C., where he developed a reputation as a conservative, particularly in criminal cases. He was sworn in as Chief Justice in June 1969 and headed the Court until 1986.

Burger's critics contend that he stood too much on the dignity of his office and was aloof and unfeeling. Intimates stress his courtesy and kindness and assert that the office, not the man, may have made for a different impression. "The Chief," says Justice Blackmun, who grew up with him, "has a great heart in him, and he's a very fine human being when you get to know him, when the tensions are off. One has to remember, too, that he's under strain almost constantly."[10]

Burger, not a person to develop intimate relations with colleagues, was as close to his law clerks as to anyone. And law clerks, in particular, speak of him with affection. One of them worked all day doing research for a conference that evening. She brought her work to the Chief Justice's home after 6:00 P.M. He asked her if she had eaten. "That's not important," she replied. "The main thing is to finish before the conference." At this Burger said, "You can't work if you don't eat." He brought in tomatoes from his garden and made her a sandwich. Later, just before the conference, Burger said, "You see, we finished on time."

Every Saturday at noon, Burger made soup in his tiny office kitchen for his clerks. Then Burger would sit and talk with them informally for hours, usually with colorful reminiscences about his career. The one rule was that no one could talk about the cases currently before the Court.

Another clerk recalls how one day Burger decided to eat in the Court cafeteria and after a few moments found himself posing for pictures with tourists and their children. "He seemed entirely comfortable, just like a politician, even though he never got his lunch."

Others picture the Chief Justice as a petty pedant, not up to the demands of his position and most concerned with minor details and the formal dignity of his office. Burger himself undertook the redecoration of the Supreme Court cafeteria and personally helped choose the glassware and china. He also redesigned the Court bench, changing it from a traditional straight bench to a "winged," or half-hexagon shape.

Burger was dismayed to find that his Supreme Court office was smaller than the one he had had at the court of appeals. Next door was the elegant conference room, which could serve admirably as a ceremonial office for the Court head. Burger did not go so far as to take over the conference room; instead, he placed an old desk in the room and moved the conference table to one side. Thus the conference room also became the Chief Justice's reception room.

Burger's use of the conference room irritated the others. Justice Hugo L. Black's wife noted in her diary that she was told "that C. J. Burger had decided to take the *Conference* Room for *his office!* Funny thing. Isn't that a kick! Hugo says he will not quarrel with him about such an insignificant matter but John Harlan called from Connecticut and was red-hot about it." [11]

Burger was also criticized for his treatment of those who disagreed with him. Lewis Powell at one time cast a critical fifth vote in an emotional criminal case. Burger tried hard to get Powell to change his vote, and, after resisting weeks of pressure, Powell told another Justice: "I'm resigned to writing nothing but Indian affairs cases for the rest of my life." [12] Or as Justice Blackmun said, "If one's in the doghouse with the Chief, he gets the crud." [13]

Yet Burger himself could wryly refer to his reputation in this respect. During one term, the Chief Justice had had a number of disagreements with John Paul Stevens. One of the Court secretaries was taking a course in cake decorating, and each week she brought in the fancy cake she had baked. At the end of the course, she made a cake in the shape of a bench, with realistic figures of the Justices. There was a chocolate Thurgood Marshall and a Stevens with bow tie and glasses. It was decided that the cake should be sent up to the Justices, but the clerks had eaten the Stevens figure. When the cake was brought in, the Chief Justice turned to Stevens and declared with mock solemnity, "You see what happens when you disagree with me!"

Burger's clerks often speak of his humor, which is rarely displayed in public. After Blackmun was appointed, Burger sent Harlan a newspaper clipping that read: "The new Chief Justice Warren Burger has his fellow Minnesotan, thus making it finally a dull Court." Under this, Burger had written, "Well, that's the way it is with people from Minnesota."[14]

Burger was always sensitive to what he perceived to be slights to his office and to himself; throughout his tenure he had an almost adversarial relationship with the press. According to one reporter, "He fostered an atmosphere of secrecy around the court that left some employees terrified of being caught chatting with us."[15] When a network asked permission to carry live radio coverage of the arguments in what promised to be a landmark case, the Chief Justice replied with a one-sentence letter: "It is not possible to arrange for any broadcast of any Supreme Court proceeding." Handwritten at the bottom was a postscript: "When you get the Cabinet meetings on the air, call me!"[16]

Burger was particularly concerned about leaks to the press. He once circulated a memorandum to the conference headed "*CONFIDENTIAL*" because a reporter had attempted to interview law clerks. "I have categorically directed," Burger declared, "that none of my staff have any conversation on any subject with any reporter. This directive was really not necessary since this is a condition of employment. I know of no one who is skilled enough to expose himself to any conversation with a reporter without getting into 'forbidden territory.' The reporter will inevitably extract information on the internal mechanisms of the Court, one way or another, to our embarrassment."[17]

The Chief Justice was deeply hurt by derogatory accounts about his performance, particularly in the best seller *The Brethren,* and was gleeful when he told me that copies of the book were remaindered at ninety-eight cents in a Washington bookstore. But all the Justices were sensitive to the effect of *The Brethren* on the public perception of the Court. In a memorandum to the others, Rehnquist urged that it would be unwise for the Court to take certain action, "especially . . . in light of the microscopic scrutiny which our actions are apt to receive for a while."[18]

Burger's critics often singled out his concern with food and attire. Author Lincoln Caplan quotes Burger as saying "that he himself should be in a wig and gown, and had been cheated out of it by Thomas Jefferson."[19] Early Supreme Court Justices did wear wigs and gowns, but the practice was soon abandoned, in part at least because of Jefferson's opposition.[20] Caplan does state that he "wasn't sure whether [Burger] was being humorous or not."[21]

It cannot be denied that, from his "Middle Temple" cheddar, made according to his own recipe,[22] to the finest clarets, Burger is somewhat of an epicure. One of the social high points of a 1969 British–American conference at Ditchley, Oxfordshire, was the learned discussion about vintage Bordeaux between Burger and Sir George Coldstream, head of the Lord Chancellor's office and overseer of the wine cellar at his Inn of Court. The Chief Justice was particularly proud of his coup in snaring some cases of a rare Lafite in an obscure Washington wine shop.

The effectiveness of a Chief Justice is, of course, not shown by his epicurean tastes. Indeed, the one Justice who was willing to talk to me frankly about Burger's professional performance was most uncomplimentary.

Burger, according to this Justice, "will assign to someone without letting the rest know, and he has five [votes] before the rest of us see it." The Justice also complained about the Burger conduct of conferences in criminal law cases. "If it's a case in which a warden is the petitioner, the Chief Justice goes on and on until the rest are driven to distraction."

The Chief Justice's votes were based upon his own scale of values, which were different from those that had motivated members of the Warren Court. When he considered a fundamental value to be at stake, Burger could be as stubborn as his predecessor. "Someone," he insisted to a law clerk, "must draw the line in favor of basic values and, even if the vote is eight-to-one, I will do it." As Douglas once put it, in a case on which the Chief Justice had strong views, "The CJ would rather die than affirm."[23]

Among the things the Chief Justice felt strongly about was the dignity of the legal profession. Despite the Court's acceptance of lawyer advertising, Burger constantly railed against it. He also was quick to condemn poor professional performance. In one case, he wrote to the others, "The petitioner's counsel was somewhat above mediocre but the State's case was *miserably* presented." Because of this, the Court should "at least appoint amicus curiae for California and begin our drive to force the States to abandon their on-the-job training of their lawyers in this Court."[24] In a case involving a doctor, he urged that the opinion should contain "a few well chosen (?) comments about the gross fraud perpetrated by this 'quack.'"[25]

The Chief Justice also complained about undue use of the courts. At a conference on a 1972 case,[26] Burger asserted that the case was "much ado about nothing by a do-gooder lawyer attacking what is really a social problem for the legislature."

But the Chief Justice also had his doubts about legislative attempts to cure social evils through massive regulatory schemes. A 1977 Burger letter speaks deprecatingly of the Occupational Safety and Health Act. "It may well be another one of those 'monsters' passed by Congress as an assumed response to some need. The response probably goes beyond need, but that is not our business." Then, with the wry humor that was too rarely displayed in public, he asserted: "I would be willing to give $1.00 to every one of the 535 who would certify under oath to having read this legislation before voting on it. It wouldn't cost me much."[27]

Burger was greatly offended when the Court reversed the conviction of a young man for wearing a jacket emblazoned with the words "Fuck the Draft" in a courthouse. The Chief Justice was particularly upset by the opinion's quoting the offensive four-letter word. He prepared a two-paragraph dissent, ultimately withdrawn, which, according to the covering memo, "is the most restrained utterance I can manage."[28] In the draft dissent, Burger wrote, "I, too, join a word of protest that this Court's limited resources of time should be devoted to such a case as this. It is a measure of a lack of a sense of priorities and with all deference I submit that Mr. Justice Harlan's 'first blush' was the correct reaction. It is nothing short of absurd nonsense that juvenile delinquents and their emotionally unstable outbursts should command the attention of this Court."

Even though the Chief Justice may have felt strongly about them, these were relatively minor matters. On more important concerns Burger came to the Court with an agenda that included a massive dismantling of the jurisprudential edifice erected by the Warren Court, particularly in the field of criminal justice. In large part, Burger owed his elevation to the highest judicial office to his reputation as a tough "law and order" judge. He had commented disparagingly on the Warren Court decisions on the rights of criminal defendants. As Chief Justice, he believed that he now had the opportunity to transform his more restrictive views into positive public law.

Burger expressed opposition during most of his tenure to *Mapp* and *Miranda*[29]—the two landmark criminal procedure decisions of the Warren Court—but he was never able to persuade a majority to cast those cases into constitutional limbo. The same was true of other aspects of Burger's anti-Warren agenda. No important Warren Court decision was overturned by the Burger Court. If Burger hoped that he would be able to undo much of the Warren "constitutional revolution," he was clearly to be disappointed.

Burger was more effective as a court administrator and as a representative of the federal courts before Congress than as a leader and molder of Supreme Court jurisprudence. Looking back at the Warren years, Byron White told me that, as far as relations with Congress were concerned, "Things have changed . . . for the better as far as I can see. . . . Chief Justice Warren did have such a problem with the civil rights thing, and with prayers and reapportionment. Congress was in such a terrible stew that his name was mud [there], which rubbed off on all of us." Under Burger the situation was different. Few Chief Justices have had better relations with Capitol Hill.

As for court administration, Burger played a more active role than any Court head since Chief Justice Taft. His administrative efforts ranged from efforts at fundamental changes, such as his active support of the creation of a new court of appeals to screen cases that the Supreme Court would consider, to attention to such petty details as the shape of the bench.

One must conclude that Burger was miscast in the role of leader of the Court—a harsh but fair description of a man who devoted so much of his life to the bench and worked as hard as he could to improve the judicial system and one who also could be warm and charming in his personal relationships. Yet his personality was, in many ways, contradictory—"at once gracious and petty, unselfish and self-serving, arrogant and insecure, politically shrewd yet stupid and heavy-handed at dealing with people."[30]

Of course it was more than these personality contradictions that damaged Burger's effectiveness as a leader of the Court. A major part of his failure may be attributed to the manner in which he presided at conferences and assigned opinions. But an important factor was his inadequacy as a judge. One who examines the decision process in important cases must reluctantly conclude that Burger was out of his depth. Although the picture in some accounts of his intellectual inadequacy is certainly overdrawn, most of his colleagues could run intellectual rings around the Chief Justice.

Burger's ineffectiveness as a judge was particularly striking in the *Nixon* case.[31] The Chief Justice's draft opinion was so inept that it had to be completely rewritten by the other Justices. The final opinion was described by a Justice as an "opinion by committee," instead of one written by its nominal author.

There was a comparable situation in the last important case decided by the Burger Court—*Bowsher v. Synar*.[32] The Burger draft opinion contained a far more expansive view of presidential power than the other Justices were willing to accept. It was only after the Chief Justice revised his draft in accordance with the Justices' suggestions that the draft could come down as the *Bowsher* opinion.

Similarly, in the *Swann* school-busing case,[33] the Chief Justice's opinion had to be substantially revised before it could come down as the opinion of the Court. His draft was not supported by the law or the rationale behind the decision itself. In *United States v. Johnson*[34] the Chief Justice's draft opinion contained so many statements that the others could not support that the opinion lost its conference majority and the case was dismissed without any decision.

BURGER AND THE *JOHNSON* CASE

A U.S. customs officer had ordered a "strip search" of the defendant at the Mexican border because, he stated, he was "suspicious." Heroin was, indeed, found hidden in the defendant's undergarments. The court of appeals had held that the search was illegal, ruling that such a search at the border had to be supported by "a 'real suspicion' . . . supported by objective, articulable facts."[35]

In the Supreme Court, the conference vote was six to three (Justices Douglas, Brennan, and Marshall) to reverse. The Chief Justice assigned the opinion to himself. Burger's typed draft opinion of May 26, 1971, according to one Justice, "ranked among the most ludicrous of his many ludicrous circulations of the year." The key to the case for Burger was the seriousness of the narcotics problem. The draft refers to the "factor [of] the gravity of the problem sought to be met by the government in terms of controlling a burgeoning illicit traffic in lethal and dangerous drugs such as heroin. . . . If reasonableness as a test is to be responsive to the need of the sovereign, the need in the control of dangerous drugs is at once apparent. . . . [A] sovereign's powers at its borders are broad and the advent of widespread international trade and travel increases rather than decreases the need for close regulation. . . ."

Burger, with his "tough-on-crime" approach, rejected the lower court requirement of "objective facts" as virtual folly. What an Associate Justice called the draft's "purple passage" on this point deserves quotation at length:

"There is an enormous range of decisions made in important areas by persons more highly trained and experienced in articulating thought processes and legal abstractions than are Customs Inspectors. A great chef, for example, may not be able to articulate his reasons why a sauce or a dressing needs a particular combination of spices or why he uses a particular quantity. A banker, far more accustomed to articulating his reasoning, cannot always articulate his basis for granting or denying credit; a personnel official in granting or refusing employment; the appraiser of jewels, paintings or horseflesh would often be hard pressed to articulate his basis for judgment. Often a physician or surgeon cannot fully articulate the basis of a diagnosis, or a decision to operate or not to operate, except to say that he 'had a hunch,' or he 'knew something was wrong.' The instinctive or intuitive—and articulable—reaction acquired by long experience or intensive training often proves more reliable than one elaborately articulated.

"A situation involving a search must be evaluated as it appears to a prudent, trained or experienced officer on the scene at the time. . . . Powers of observation become more acute with experience, and factors meaningless to the untrained eye enter automatically into the human brain 'computer,' so that a synthesis of numerous unarticulable factors accumulate to form a judgment."

In a June 2 Memorandum to the Conference, the Chief Justice also stressed the need to allow broad powers of search because of "the terrible urgency of the drug problem. . . . *Every* border entrant is, in a very real sense a potential 'suspect' because of the ease of concealing small packages on the person. In the internal or domestic setting a 'suspect' or person under observation by the police does not necessarily know of the surveillance. Border entrants on the other hand are well aware of the stringency of border searches. The 'guiltier' the entrant, the more he is on guard to conceal. With the 'amateur' this in itself may betray him, but those carrying drugs are not likely to be 'amateurs' but rather seasoned professionals."

The language in the Burger draft offended even those who had voted with him. Harlan persuaded him to omit the more extreme passages, and his redraft, circulated June 14, reflected this. Brennan circulated a draft dissent that argued that the search was contrary to customs regulations that required that strip searches have supervisory approval. This administrative law point appealed to White, who joined the dissenters.

At this point, the Chief Justice realized that his majority was evaporating. In a June 28 note, he said that the case "presents problems we ought not to have chiefly due to an incompetent prosecutor. There would be no case if he had asked just one more simple question: 'On what did you base your suspicions?'" Burger suggested that the case be set for reargument, and the others quickly agreed. Justice Brennan framed the question to be reargued on the administrative law point raised in his draft dissent. An order setting the case for reargument was issued the final day of the 1970 term, but early in the next term, before any reargument, the Court dismissed the *Johnson* case.[36]

Burger lost his strong majority because of the poorly written opinion. Instead of the leading case on border searches for which the Chief Justice had hoped, *Johnson* became not even a minor footnote in Supreme Court jurisprudence.

CONFERENCES AND ASSIGNING OPINIONS

Traditionally the most important work of the Supreme Court has been done in private, particularly in the conference sessions that take place after cases have been argued.[37] It is in the conference that the Court decides, and the primary role at the conference is exercised by the Chief Justice, who leads the discussion. He starts the conference by discussing the facts and issues involved. He then tells how he would vote. Only after his presentation do the other Justices state their views, in order of descending seniority.

The manner in which he leads the conference is the key to much of a Chief Justice's effectiveness. His presentation fixes the theme for the discussion that follows and, if skillfully done, is a major force in leading to the decision he favors.

The two strongest leaders of the conference during this century were Charles Evans Hughes and Earl Warren. Most students of the Court rank Hughes as the most efficient conference manager in the Court's history. He imposed a tight schedule on case discussions. Long-winded and irrelevant discourses were all but squelched; "no matter how long the Conference List," Justice Douglas recalls, "we were usually through by four-thirty or five. The discussions were short; Hughes's comments were always succinct."[38]

If Hughes was the most efficient, Warren may have been the most effective in presiding over the sessions—the "ideal" conference head, Justice Stewart said to me. His forte was his ability to present cases in a manner that set the right tone for discussion. He would state the issues in a deceptively simple way, one stripped of legal technicalities, and, where possible, relate the issues to the ultimate values that concerned him. Opposition based upon traditional legal-type arguments seemed inappropriate, almost pettifoggery. As Justice Fortas once told me, "Opposition based on the hemstitching and embroidery of the law appeared petty in terms of Warren's basic-value approach."

Conference notes show that when Warren sought to lead the Court in a particular direction, he was usually able to do so. Conference notes taken during the Burger tenure do not give the same impression. Burger did not have anything like the Warren ability to state cases succinctly, to lead the discussion along desired lines. Burger was too often turgid and unfocused, with emphasis upon irrelevancies rather than central points. It was said that Burger's discussion of cases at conference left the Justices with the feeling that he was "the least prepared member of the Court."[39] In a comment on Chief Justice William H. Rehnquist, Thurgood Marshall said, "He has no problems, wishy-washy, back and forth. He knows exactly what he wants to do, and that's very important as a chief justice."[40] There is little doubt that Marshall was contrasting the Rehnquist conference approach with Burger's.

More important was Burger's lack of leadership. The conference notes in hundreds of cases reveal how frequently the lead was taken by the Associate Justices—particularly so in the major cases. It was not the Chief Justice who usually played the crucial role in the decision process.

One must also fault him for his use of the power to assign the writing of opinions—aside from managing the conference, the most important function of the Chief Justice. In discharging it, a Chief Justice determines what use will be made of the Court's personnel; the particular decisions he assigns to each Justice in distributing the work load will influence both the growth of the law and his own relations with his colleagues.

The power of the Chief Justice to assign the opinions probably goes back to John Marshall's day.[41] During Marshall's early years, it is probable that he delivered the opinion of the Court even in cases where he dissented. Apparently the practice then was to reserve delivery of the opinion of the Court to the Chief Justice or the senior Associate Justice present on the bench and participating in the decision.[42] But as time went on, other Justices also began to deliver opinions. By Chief Justice Taney's day, the Chief Justice assigned each opinion.

In the early years of opinion assignment by the Chief Justice, he may well have assigned all opinions. It was not very long, however, before the Chief Justice's assigning power was limited to cases where he had voted with the majority. It is probable that this practice developed under Chief Justice Taney. In his authoritative history of the Supreme Court under Chief Justice Chase, Charles Fairman describes the procedure at the beginning of Chase's tenure: "The writing of opinions was assigned by the Chief Justice—save that if he were dissenting, the Senior Justice in the majority would select the one to write."[43]

Whether or not this procedure was firmly established then,[44] by the present century the Chief Justice's assigning power was limited to cases where he was not in dissent. The situation was summarized in 1928 by former Associate Justice Hughes: "After a decision has been reached, the Chief Justice assigns the case for opinion to one of the members of the Court, that is, of course, to one of the majority if there is a division and the Chief Justice is a member of the majority. If he is in a minority, the senior Associate Justice in the majority assigns the case for opinion."[45]

Chief Justice Burger did not always follow the established practice. According to an English comment, "Chief Justice Burger would sometimes vote against his instincts in order to preserve his prerogative of assigning the majority opinion."[46] In other words, Burger would vote with the majority in order to control the assignment of opinions.

The one Justice who was willing to talk to me frankly about Burger's assignment practice spoke of it in a most denigratory fashion. "The great thing about Earl Warren was that he was so considerate of all his colleagues. He was so meticulous on assignments." Now, the

Justice went on, "all too damned often the Chief Justice will vote with the majority so as to assign the opinion, and then he ends up in dissent."

Voting with the majority in this way certainly appears contrary to the spirit, if not the letter, of the Court's assignment practice. But Burger went beyond the letter of the tradition as well. A striking illustration is contained in the *Swann* school-busing case.[47] Burger assigned the opinion to himself even though he had supported the minority view at the conference. Another example is in *Roe v. Wade*.[48] The Chief Justice assigned the opinion to Justice Blackmun, though it was not clear that Burger was then part of the majority.

In *Roe*, Douglas circulated a strong memorandum that declared that Burger's assignment of the case was "an action no Chief Justice in my time would ever have taken. For the tradition is a longstanding one that the senior Justice in the majority makes the assignment." Hence, Douglas asserted, he, as senior member of the majority, should have assigned the case. "When, however, the minority seeks to control the assignment, there is a destructive force at work in the Court. When a Chief Justice tries to bend the Court to his will by manipulating assignments, the integrity of the institution is imperiled."[49]

Not long before, Douglas had written a memorandum to the Chief Justice complaining about the Burger assignment practice: "If the conference wants to authorize you to assign all opinions, that will be a new procedure. Though opposed to it, I will acquiesce. But unless we make a frank reversal in our policy, any group in the majority should and must make the assignment."[50]

Of course, Chief Justice Burger also made use of more traditional assignment techniques. He took many of the most important cases, such as the *Nixon* case,[51] since the Court in such cases should speak through its head; he assigned the more significant cases to his allies, such as Blackmun in his earlier years and Rehnquist more recently; and left lesser cases to his opponents on the Court, notably Brennan.

The Chief Justice also employed the technique of assigning a case to the most lukewarm member of the majority. An illustration can be found in a November 14, 1978, Burger letter to Justice Brennan: "Apropos your opinion (I believe at lunch Monday) whether Bill Rehnquist was an appropriate assignee of the above case, I had discussed this with Bill. He prefers his first choice disposition, i.e., no judicial review, but he was willing to write the holding to reflect the majority view otherwise. There were 8 to affirm and he fits the old English rule-of-thumb as the 'least persuaded,' hence likely to write narrowly."

THE APOSTATE

The Court that Chief Justice Burger was called upon to lead contained some of the most noted Justices in Supreme Court history. Two of them—Black and Harlan—retired after the second Burger term. But they both played such an important part in modern jurisprudence, and even in the Burger Court cases in which they sat, that something should be said about them.

The senior Justice was Hugo Lafayette Black—then in his eighty-second year and thirty-first term on the Court. By then the furor that had surrounded his appointment because he had once been a member of the Ku Klux Klan seemed like an echo from another world. Black had become the recognized leader of the Court's liberal wing—a position he continued to hold through the first decade of the Warren Court.

The Black who sat on the Burger Court, however, was no longer the leading liberal. The Alabaman's fundamentalist approach to the Constitution did not permit him to adopt an expansive approach toward individual rights. Black stood his constitutional ground where the rights asserted rested on specific provisions, such as the First Amendment or the Fifth Amendment privilege against self-incrimination; but when he could not find an express constitutional base, Black was unwilling to create one. Black's opposition to busing at the *Swann* conference[52] was, Justice Brennan remarked, because the word *bus* is not found in the Constitution.

Black's "apostasy" had become apparent during the last years of the Warren Court. He refused to join the Court in recognizing the new right of privacy because he could not find an express constitutional foundation for it.[53] He voted to uphold convictions of sit-in demonstrators, giving greater weight to the constitutional guarantees protecting property rights, including the owner's right to limit access to his property.[54] During the conference in the latter case, Black emotionally declared that he could not believe that his "Pappy," who ran a general store in Alabama, did not have the right to decide whom he would or would not serve.

In the Burger Court, Black continued to display the same restrictive posture. In the *Swann* case, he actually prepared a draft dissent, which was not issued so as to continue the tradition of unanimity in school segregation cases. In a covering letter, Black explained his position, asserting, "I do gravely doubt this Court's constitutional power, however, to compel a State and its taxpayers to buy millions of dollars worth of buses to haul students miles away from their neighborhood schools and their homes. Such an order by this Court appears not only to be 'bizarre,' . . . but actually unconstitutionally requiring the States to spend money." [55]

In *Palmer v. Thompson*,[56] the city of Jackson, Mississippi, had closed its municipal swimming pools after a declaratory judgment had been issued that they might not be operated on a segregated basis. In a February 16, 1971, letter, Black answered a Blackmun note asking whether an affirmance in an earlier case[57] did not indicate that the city should be compelled to reopen the pools. Black replied, "I joined in that affirmance and I can assure you that if I had ever entertained an idea that any part of the decision in that case would stand for the principle that the United States Constitution compels a State to tax its citizens to run public schools, I would never have voted to affirm the judgment. I cannot believe, for instance, that if the State of Minnesota should decide for any reason, good or bad, that the State no longer wanted to run public schools but depend on some other method of educating its people, that you or I would hold that a majority of the lifetime judges of this Court could compel the State to operate public schools."

Black wrote that *Palmer* itself was an even easier case, since it was up to the given government to decide "to tax its people to operate swimming pools." Indeed, Black's letter concluded, "There is no closeness or troublesomeness whatever in this case for me because I agree . . . that if the judgment here is reversed the city will be 'locked in' and must continue to operate swimming pools so long as a majority of our Court declines to let them free themselves from that burden."

Despite his eminent position, Black's appearance always indicated his origins in what he called a "God-forsaken" Alabama rural county.[58] With his drawl and often quaint manner of expression, he resembled a lively old southern farmer. In *Oregon v. Mitchell*,[59] where Congress had lowered the voting age to eighteen, the Court divided one-four-four. Black supplied the crucial fifth vote, agreeing on one aspect of the decision with one bloc of four and with the other four on another aspect. Black's opinion explaining his vote is usually considered the one that states the law laid down by the decision, even though it was concurred in by no other Justice. Coming off the bench after delivering his *Oregon v. Mitchell* opinion, Black commented to a law clerk that the case "reminded me of the hunts we used to have when I was a boy. We'd go out there with the dogs after some birds, and those old dogs would smell a rabbit and run all over the field after that rabbit—never mind the bird. Well, some of the opinions in these cases it just seemed to me that somebody had lost sight of the bird."

THE PATRICIAN

In appearance, there was no greater contrast than that between Justice Black and Justice John Marshall Harlan, the only descendant of a Justice to become a Justice. His grandfather was the Justice John Marshall Harlan who wrote the famous dissent in the 1896 case of *Plessy v. Ferguson.*[60]

Tall and erect, with sparse white hair, and conservatively dressed in his London-tailored suits, with his grandfather's gold watch chain, Harlan exuded the dignity associated with high judicial office. Yet underneath this dignified surface was a warm nature that enabled him to be close friends with those with whom he disagreed intellectually, notably Justice Black. Visitors could often see the two Justices waiting patiently in line in the Court cafeteria. The two were a study in contrasts: the ramrod-straight patrician with a commanding presence and his slight, almost wispy colleague who looked like an Alabama rube.

The term most frequently used to describe Harlan by those who knew him is *gentleman*. To the other Justices, Harlan was the quintessential patrician, with his privileged upbringing and Wall Street background. "I hear 'mi lord,'" reads a note from a Justice to Harlan, "that you have been under the weather. . . . Your Lordship should be more careful of your whiskey and your habits."[61]

Harlan took a cautious approach to the judicial function. When Burger took his seat, Harlan's was the Court's principal voice calling for judicial restraint, and the new Chief Justice had reason to expect support from him. He shared Burger's concern over "the 'horse and buggy' conditions under which the federal judiciary, and particularly this Court, are now operating"[62] and he had been the leading conservative in the last years of the Warren Court.

Harlan's conservative philosophy did not, however, permit him to go along with the Chief Justice's agenda vis-à-vis the Warren Court decisions. "Respect for the Courts," Harlan once wrote, "is not something that can be achieved by fiat."[63] He applied this principle to reflexive refusals to follow prior decisions with which he disagreed. The true conservative, Harlan believed, adhered to stare decisis, normally following even precedents against which he had originally voted.

The Harlan posture in this respect can be best seen in *Coleman v. Alabama*.[64] At issue was the right to counsel at a preliminary hearing, where the defendants were bound over to the grand jury. At the conference there were seven votes to affirm the conviction, with only Harlan voting the other way. The Justice had dissented from the Warren Court's landmark *Miranda* decision.[65] Despite this, Harlan said at the *Coleman* conference that *Miranda* was "still on the books" and it should be followed here since the preliminary examination was as critical a stage as the custodial interrogation involved in *Miranda*. Ultimately, the Court agreed with Harlan, holding that the conviction had to be reversed because defendants had not been assigned counsel.

Coleman shows better than anything the Harlan conception of a conservative judge. Such a judge is not to use "judicial fiat" to disregard a precedent any more than he is to establish the precedent by fiat in the first place. While the precedent is "still on the books," it is to be followed in cases to which it logically applies.

Harlan also had the true conservative's aversion to absolutes. During the first Burger term, the Court had to decide the constitutionality of a statute that permitted recipients of sexually offensive mail to require the Post Office to prohibit further mailings to them.[66] Chief Justice Burger drafted an opinion of the Court upholding the law, which was circulated April 21, 1970. It asserted a strong right of parents to control or censor their children's mail. Indeed, the Burger draft described this right as "absolute." The Chief Justice told Brennan that parents ought to exercise tight control over their children and their failure to have done so had led to the excesses of the present college generation.

Harlan, however, was taken aback by the categorical Burger language. "Your statement . . .," Harlan wrote in an April 23, 1970,

"Dear Chief" letter, "to the effect that parents have an 'absolute' right to control the reading of their children in the home makes me a little gun-shy. I have a distaste for absolutes and I can think of situations where a state might be able to enter the home in this realm, e.g., requiring children to read their report cards." The offending passage was deleted.

THE WARREN LIBERALS

In dealing with the other members of the Burger Court, we can start with a 1986 analysis by Justice Blackmun of the divisions within the Court. "I had always put on the left" Justices Brennan and Marshall, and "on the right" Chief Justice Burger and Justice Rehnquist. "Five of us," Blackmun said, were "in the middle"—Justices Stewart, White, Powell, Stevens, and himself.[67]

In the early Burger years, it was a Warren holdover, Douglas, who sat instead of Stevens, who was appointed after Douglas retired. Douglas must, of course, be put on the left with Brennan and Marshall, and those three constituted the liberal bloc on the early Burger Court.

William O. Douglas is, without a doubt, one of the famous names in modern Supreme Court history. He had overcome early polio and poverty to become a noted outdoorsman and legal light. Douglas' impressive physical vitality always seemed out of place in Parnassus. "The tradition here," he once complained, "makes one feel like a statue."[68] To the public Douglas was noted as much for his books describing his peripatetic wandering and mountain climbing as for his judicial work. In a birthday greeting, Black called him "Our Judge with wanderlust . . . Marco Polo Douglas."[69] Douglas reveled in exotic and dangerous travels that would have daunted his less adventurous colleagues.

The real Douglas was very different from his public image. He was the quintessential loner—a lover of humanity who did not like people. No one on the Court, neither among the Justices nor the law clerks, was really close to the strapping Westerner. The clerks particularly described Douglas as the coldest of the Justices. It was an event when Douglas stopped to say hello in the Court corridors. His severity toward his own clerks became legend. A recent description of a meeting with Douglas asserts that he "had compressed into 20 minutes more cold-eyed rudeness than I have ever since confronted in a long and varied life."[70]

There is no doubt that Douglas had a brilliant mind, but he was erratic. He could whip up opinions faster than any of the Justices and did almost all the work himself. But his opinions were too often unpolished, as though he lacked the interest for the sustained work involved in transforming first drafts into finished products. Lack of interest in the Court's work was, indeed, apparent in Douglas' whole attitude. During oral argument Douglas seemed to spend most of his time writing letters, and from time to time he would stop his scribbling and very ostentatiously lick an envelope from side to side and seal it. Every now and then he would lift his head and direct an acute question to counsel. As one of the Justices put it, "Bill could listen with one ear." Douglas apparently spent only three or four days a week on Court work,[71] and Chief Justice Warren, for one, felt that he devoted too much time to other things.

Douglas was the senior Associate Justice on the Burger Court, and although the public considered him the leader of its liberal wing he was not the one to play the leadership role. He was a maverick, an idiosyncratic loner who was least effective in the give-and-take required in a collegial institution.

The Douglas antithesis in this respect was Justice William J. Brennan, Jr., who had served as the catalyst for some of the most important decisions of the Warren Court. Brennan had become the most active lobbyist among the Justices, always willing to take the lead in trying to mold a majority for the decisions that he favored.

Before his 1956 appointment by President Eisenhower, Brennan had been a judge in New Jersey for seven years, rising from the state trial court to its highest bench. He was the only Justice to have served as a state judge before Justice O'Connor's appointment.

"One of the things," Justice Frankfurter once said, "that laymen, even lawyers, do not always understand is indicated by the question you hear so often: 'Does a man become any different when he puts on a gown?' I say, 'If he is any good, he does.'"[72] Certainly Justice Brennan on the supreme bench proved a complete surprise to those who saw him as a middle-of-the-road moderate. He quickly became a firm adherent of the activist philosophy and a principal architect of the Warren Court's jurisprudence. Brennan had been Frankfurter's student at Harvard Law School; yet if Frankfurter expected the new Justice to continue his pupilage, he was soon disillusioned. After Brennan had joined the Warren Court's activist wing, Frankfurter supposedly quipped, "I always encouraged my students to think for themselves, but Brennan goes too far!"

Brennan soon became Chief Justice Warren's closest colleague. The two were completely dissimilar in appearance. Brennan is small and feisty, almost leprechaun-like in appearance, yet he has a hearty bluffness and an ability to put people at ease. Brennan's unassuming appearance and manner mask a keen intelligence. He is perhaps the hardest worker on the Court. Unlike such Justices as Douglas, Brennan has always been willing to mold his language to meet the objections of his colleagues, a talent that would become his hallmark on the Court. Thus, it was he who suggested the compromise approach that characterized the decision in the landmark *Bakke* case,[73] as well as the intermediate standard of review that has governed in gender discrimination cases.[74]

After Warren's retirement, Brennan was no longer the trusted insider. Instead, he became the Justice who tried above all to keep the Warren flame burning and, as a consequence, Burger's leading opponent on the Court. Both Brennan and the Chief Justice accepted this over the years the two sat together. One year the Brennan law clerks were guests at a convivial Burger luncheon. The Chief Justice telephoned Brennan to tell him what fine gentlemen his clerks were. When they returned, the Justice reproved them. "You turncoats," he said, "what did you do over there?"

Brennan has always remained unceremonious and unassuming, despite his reputation as being perhaps the most influential Associate Justice during the past half century. He related to me with awe how, at a charity auction, someone once bid $2,000 to have lunch with him and Mrs. Brennan.

The third member of the liberal bloc in the Burger Court was Justice Thurgood Marshall. His career added a racial dimension to the American success story. The first black appointed to the Court, Marshall was the great-grandson of a slave and the son of a Pullman car steward. Blackmun tells how, "When we went up to Justice Marshall's native Baltimore for the ceremony in connection with the dedication of his statue up there in front of the Federal building, he and I were sitting next to each other and he said, 'Why do you think that fellow asked me what high school here in Baltimore I went to? Hell, there was only one I could go to!'"[75]

Marshall was the first head of the NAACP Legal Defense Fund's staff and chief counsel in the *Brown* school segregation case.[76] On the Court, he has always been a firm member of the liberal bloc. In the Burger Court he served as a virtual judicial adjunct to Brennan. The law clerks, it is said, took to calling Marshall "Mr. Justice Brennan–Marshall."

Marshall may not have been an outstanding Justice; but he has a gift for a succinct phrase that sometimes cuts to the heart of a case. When the Court was asked to apply an endangered species law to save a few obscure fish, even though it meant destruction of a dam costing hundreds of millions,[77] Marshall told the conference on the case, "Congress has the right to make a jackass of itself."

In the *Bakke* case,[78] Marshall put his finger on the dilemma presented by affirmative action programs. "You are arguing," he told Bakke's counsel, "about keeping somebody out and the other side is arguing about getting somebody in."[79]

"IN THE MIDDLE"

In the Blackmun lineup of the Justices,[80] five were placed "in the middle"—Stewart, White, Powell, Stevens, and Blackmun. Of these the most influential were Stewart, Blackmun, and Powell.

Potter Stewart was one of the youngest Justices (only forty-three when selected by President Eisenhower); at sixty-six he also was one of the youngest to retire. When he first took his seat, Stewart's youth and handsome appearance added an unusual touch to the highest bench, showing that it need not always be composed of nine old men. To those who knew him in those days, it was painful to see his physical decline before he died in 1985.

Before then, people who met Stewart were surprised by his vigor and clearly expressed views, which contrasted sharply with his public image as an indecisive centrist without clearly defined conceptions. Unlike Brennan and Rehnquist, Stewart never acted on the basis of a deep-seated philosophy regarding the proper relationship between the state and its citizens. When asked if he was a liberal or a conservative, he answered, "I am a lawyer," and went on to say, "I have some difficulty understanding what those terms mean even in the field of political life. . . . And I find it impossible to know what they mean when they are carried over to judicial work."[81]

Stewart was a moderate with a pragmatic approach to issues that polarized others. Under Chief Justice Warren, Stewart remained in the center as the Court moved to the left. In the Burger Court he continued as the leading moderate. His center role enabled him to play a pivotal role—particularly, in the *Swann* and *Nixon* cases.[82] The others tended to turn to Stewart because they trusted his judgment as a lawyer. Thus, in the *Swann* case, where he was the senior Justice in the conference majority, Douglas wrote at the time, "The case was obviously for me to assign, and I would have assigned it to Stewart."[83]

After Harlan retired, Stewart became the one most interested in the technical aspects of the Court's work. He insisted on legal niceties and, at times, was a stickler for legal technicalities. These propensities are illustrated by a January 28, 1971, letter to the Chief Justice on a Burger draft opinion in a self-incrimination case.[84] Stewart wrote, "Your opinion for the Court is basically excellent and I would like very much to join it." However, Stewart went on, "(1) I cannot subscribe to an opinion that says that the Fifth Amendment is directly applicable to the States. The provision of the Constitution applicable to this case is the Fourteenth Amendment, as it may have 'absorbed' or 'incorporated' a particular provision of the Fifth Amendment.

"(2) I cannot subscribe to an opinion that says the Constitution accords a privilege against self-incrimination. What the Constitution guarantees is a right against compulsory self-incrimination."

Not until Burger gave in and deleted the language saying that the Fifth Amendment directly applied to the States and changed the phrasing of the guaranty from a "privilege against self-incrimination" to a "right against compulsory self-incrimination" did Stewart join the opinion. Stewart recognized in his letter that such insistences on legal niceties "are considered no more than eccentricities by some of our colleagues"—"no more than semantic," he called it in another letter—but, he wrote, "to me they are of considerable importance."[85]

Stewart was best known for his comment in a 1964 obscenity case, "I know it when I see it"[86]—a phrase that he later lamented might well become his epitaph. Stewart's aptness for the pungent phrase helped make him the press's favorite Justice, and he was more accessible to reporters than any of his colleagues.

Of the other men "in the middle" in the Burger Court, it can be argued that Blackmun came to play the most important role himself. Harry A. Blackmun had served eleven years on the U.S. Court of Appeals for the Eighth Circuit. He went to grade school with Warren Burger, and the two remained close friends thereafter. He was best man at Burger's wedding. After graduation from Harvard Law School, Blackmun served as a law clerk in the court of appeals, spent sixteen years with a Minneapolis law firm, and was counsel to the Mayo Clinic for almost ten years.

Because of his work as Mayo counsel, the others tended to consider Blackmun a medical expert. Justice Harlan once wrote to him, "I am consumed with admiration for your mastery of the medical lexicon, and . . . I am perfectly content to leave my legal conscience in your careful hands on this score."[87] That may be one reason why he was given the opinion in *Roe v. Wade*[88]—the famous abortion case.

In his early years on the Court few expected Blackmun to be more than an appendage of the Chief Justice. He was then virtually Burger's disciple; they were on the same side in almost all cases. The press had typecast Blackmun as the subordinate half of the "Minnesota Twins," after the baseball team.

All this was to change. One can, indeed, see Blackmun's development during those years. The Blackmun opinion in *Roe v. Wade* sounded the first Blackmun declaration of independence from the Chief Justice. Blackmun wrote an opinion striking down the abortion law—first on limited grounds and then, in a revised draft, with a categorical holding on the right to an abortion during the early stages of pregnancy.

In the *Nixon* case,[89] Blackmun gave the final blow to Burger's hope to mold the Court opinion when he handed the Chief Justice a complete revision of the statement of facts in the case. Thereafter, the Chief Justice had to yield to a thorough rewriting by the Justices of the other parts of his original draft opinion. It is said that within the Court, the incident came to be known as the "Et Tu Harry" story.[90] "I am fairly positive," Blackmun himself says, "that [the Chief Justice] feels I have not been the supportive arm he would have liked me to be."[91]

By the later years of the Burger tenure, Blackmun was completely his own man. His opinions became increasingly as liberal as any that the Justices "on the left" might have written. One can also see an improvement in Blackmun's work. If we compare his hesitant first draft in *Roe v. Wade* with his more self-assured opinions in later cases, we see how the Justice grew with increasing experience and self-confidence. As a 1983 *New York Times* article put it, "Justice Blackmun's evolution as a jurist and prominence on the Court represent one of the most important developments in the judiciary's recent history."[92]

In many ways, the paradigm of the lawyer turned Justice was Lewis F. Powell, who was also one of those who, in the Blackmun phrase, "hold the center." But unlike Blackmun, Powell was more to its right. Powell came to the Court after private practice with one of Virginia's most prestigious law firms, a career that was capped by his term as president of the American Bar Association. Surprisingly few Supreme Court Justices have been drawn directly from the practicing bar. Indeed, during the past half century, only Powell and Justice Abe Fortas were in private practice when they were appointed.

Everyone who meets Powell is impressed by his innate gentility and soft-spoken manner. On and off the bench he remained the essential courtly Southerner. When a Brennan opinion noted that it had been foreshadowed by a Powell dissent and quoted from the latter, Powell sent a written note to Brennan, "Thank you so much. . . . You are a scholar and a gentleman—and a generous one!"[93]

Powell's pre-Court experience always played an important part in his judicial attitude, particularly his years on the Richmond school board. In a case involving a school desegregation plan that included a comprehensive and costly remedial education program,[94] Powell told the conference, "I've sat on a school board and the rest of you have not." What "bothers me," he said, is "putting the court in the seats of the school board. This is the most far reaching intrusion I've seen yet." And when Brennan asked Powell to modify his position in the *Bakke* case, Powell reminded his colleague of his extensive experience in educational administration and said, politely but firmly, that his views were fixed.[95]

In a case in which the authority of a school board over the contents of school libraries had been restricted by the lower court,[96] Powell asked the conference, "Are we going to enter a new era of intrusion into the democratic system?" He strongly opposed the judicial limitation upon the school board's authority, calling it "the most important case of overreaching by the federal judiciary since I came here."

On the bench, Powell was "a lawyer's Justice" and a pragmatic centrist who followed the measured approach developed by his thirty-five years of practice. He avoided doctrinaire positions and hard-edged ideological decisions and gained a reputation as a moderate, though he voted more often with Chief Justice Burger than some of the others in the center bloc. His quest for the middle ground is best illustrated by his most famous opinion—that in the *Bakke* case—where he cast the deciding vote. Though the Powell *Bakke* opinion was joined by no other Justice, it is considered by most commentators as the authoritative statement of law.

Powell was essentially a conservative whose judicial approach was reminiscent of that followed by Justice Harlan during the early Burger years. Like Harlan, Powell believed in following precedents of which he may have disapproved until they were overruled. Thus, he voted to decide cases in accordance with the *Mapp* and *Miranda* decisions,[97] even though he might well have voted against those decisions had he been on the Court. In the conference on a 1983 case,[98] Powell said, about a prior decision,[99] "It's bad law. I would want to limit it to its own facts, without overruling it in so many words."

Powell's conception of conservatism is perhaps best shown in his reception of the attempt in *Frontiero v. Richardson*[100] to treat sex as a "suspect" classification that would be subject to strict-scrutiny review. Brennan redrafted his *Frontiero* opinion to provide for such strict-scrutiny review in gender classification cases. Powell's opinion rejected the Brennan suspect-classification approach. In a March 2, 1973, letter to Brennan, he explained that he did so, in large part, because of the Equal Rights Amendment, which was then before the states. In Powell's view, the Brennan approach "places the Court in the position of preempting the amendatory process initiated by the Congress."

For the Court to act as the Brennan opinion would have it do would, Powell wrote, be for it to "have assumed a decisional responsibility (not within the democratic process) unnecessary to the decision of this case." Powell's judicial approach required him "to question the desirability of this Court reaching out to anticipate a major political decision which is currently in process of resolution by the duly prescribed constitutional process."

Throughout his judicial career, Powell displayed the true conservative's concern for upholding deeply felt traditional values, such as free speech, family life, and procedural safeguards. When the Court was faced with the Occupational Safety and Health Act, under which a fine may be assessed by a single hearing officer, with no right of appeal to the Commission,[101] Powell objected to this "serious procedural omission." "The net effect of the procedure under this Act," Powell asserted, "is to vest enormous power in a single individual, who may or may not be well qualified, without the procedural and other protections that are available in a court or in most administrative agencies."[102]

The other centrist Justices, White and Stevens, did not play as influential a role in the Burger Court. When he was appointed by President Kennedy in 1962, Byron R. White was certainly not the typical Supreme Court appointee. He was best known as "Whizzer" White— an all-American quarterback who became the National Football League rookie of the year in 1938.

As a Justice, White, like Stewart, has defied classification. He tends to take a lawyerlike approach to individual cases, without trying to fit them into any overall judicial philosophy, and is considered one of the more conservative Justices in the Burger Court's center, particularly in criminal cases. "In the criminal field," as Blackmun sees it, "I think Byron White is distinctly a conservative."[103]

In one area, however, White tended to vote with the liberal bloc— civil rights. "One gets into racial problems . . . ," says Blackmun, "and Byron is distinctly to the left of center. I think it's the old John F. Kennedy influence, if you like."[104] As Kennedy's deputy attorney general, White had personally gone to Montgomery, Alabama, to restore order during the Freedom Riders protest in May 1961. In a confrontation with the Alabama governor, when the Governor sarcastically asked, "Where are all those Freedom Riders?" White replied that they were in the hospitals to which the governor's men had sent them.[105] In the Burger Court, White tended to vote with the Brennan wing in civil rights cases, particularly in important cases such as *Swann*[106] and *Bakke*.[107]

It is fair to say that White is more respected among his colleagues than outside the Court—in part because of his gruff bluntness and no-nonsense manner. When loyalty-oath cases were still part of the Court's agenda, he curtly told a conference,[108] these oath cases are a "pain in the neck." When he did not think much of a case, he termed it "this pipsqueak of a case."[109] And when an attorney was doing a particularly bad job in oral argument, White was heard in a stage whisper, "This is unbelievable."[110]

Justice John Paul Stevens was a judge on the U.S. court of appeals when he was selected by President Ford, largely on the recommendation of Attorney General Levi. He was considered a moderate. It is, however, even harder to classify Stevens than the others on the Burger Court. "On a Court that everyone likes to divide into liberal and conservative, Justice Stevens has a list of labels all his own: enigmatic, unpredictable, maverick, a wild card, a loner." [111]

Statistically, Stevens was the Justice nearest the Burger Court's center, disagreeing equally with the Justices at the poles. In the 1981 term, Stevens disagreed with Justice Rehnquist in 35 percent of the cases and with Justice Brennan 33 percent of the time. [112]

Stevens is a loner like Douglas, to whose seat Stevens was appointed, and, like Douglas, Stevens makes little effort to win over other members of the Court. What a law clerk once said about Douglas applies equally to Stevens: "Douglas was just as happy signing a one-man dissent as picking up four more votes." Stevens writes more dissents than any other member of the Court; he is often a lone dissenter. A book on the Burger Court concludes that, while Stevens was once viewed as a potential leader of the Court, "the effect of his independence of mind often has been to fragment potential majorities and leave the state of the law indeterminate." [113]

In one case,[114] Stevens took issue with the reliance in a Powell draft on the absence of any evidence of rioting to support the conclusion that confinement of two prisoners in a small cell was not cruel and unusual punishment. "It is at least theoretically possible," wrote Stevens in an April 23, 1981, letter to Powell, "that prisoners in a truly barbarous concentration camp might be too intimidated to riot. Moreover, I would hesitate to send out a signal to a community of prison litigants that a few good riots would improve their litigation posture."

Over the years, Stevens has acquired something of the reputation of an iconoclast—albeit an idiosyncratic one. Stevens is idiosyncratic in more than his decisions. He hires only two law clerks instead of the usual four and drafts more of his own opinions than any of the others. He also deviates from the Court's unwritten conservative dress code; his constant bow tie (worn under the judicial robe) gives him a perpetual sophomoric appearance. In 1986, the Justices were hearing argument on whether Orthodox Jews, with their religious duty to wear yarmulkes, should be exempt from the military dress code's ban on hats indoors. Counsel for the government told the Justices, "It's only human nature to resent being told what to wear, when to wear it, what to eat."

"Or whether you can wear a bow tie?" chimed in Stevens.[115]

MR. RIGHT

In the Blackmun analysis of the Burger Court, Justice Rehnquist stood on the right with the Chief Justice. No one can doubt that this is the correct position. A *Newsweek* article on Rehnquist was titled "The Court's Mr. Right."[116] According to the *New York Times,* "William H. Rehnquist is a symbol. People who have trouble naming all nine Supreme Court Justices quickly identify him as its doctrinaire, right-wing anchor. . . . Justice Rehnquist is the Court's most predictably conservative member, using his considerable intelligence, energy and verbal facility to shape the law to his vision."[117]

The Rehnquist vision in this respect has always been a clear one. In a 1985 interview, he noted that he joined the Court with a desire to counteract the Warren Court decisions.[118] "I came to the court," Rehnquist said, "sensing . . . that there were some excesses in terms of constitutional adjudication during the era of the so-called Warren Court." Some of that Court's decisions, the Justice went on, "seemed to me hard to justify. . . . So I felt that at the time I came on the Court, the boat was kind of keeling over in one direction. Interpreting my oath as I saw it, I felt that my job was . . . to kind of lean the other way."[119]

By the time of his nomination as Chief Justice, Rehnquist had become the most influential member of the Burger Court, both because he stood out in a Court of generally bland personalities, which lacked a firm sense of direction, and because he was closely allied with the Chief Justice. During his early Court years, however, the majority remained largely unsympathetic to the Rehnquist entreaties from the right. It was then that he received a Lone Ranger doll as a gift from his law clerks, who called him the "lone dissenter" during that period. During his fourteen years as an Associate Justice, Rehnquist dissented alone fifty-four times—a Court record.

When asked about the origins of his conservatism, Rehnquist replied, "It may have something to do with my childhood."[120] He was raised in a modest house in a middle-class Milwaukee suburb. After World War II service in North Africa, he attended Stanford and its law school. He then served as a Supreme Court clerk to Justice Robert H. Jackson. Rehnquist wrote a memo on the *Brown* segregation case,[121] urging that the separate-but-equal doctrine, under which segregation had been upheld,[122] was "right and should be affirmed."[123]

The memo became an important factor in the Senate confirmation hearings on the nominations of Rehnquist, first to the Supreme Court and then as Chief Justice. Rehnquist maintained that the memo "was prepared by me at Justice Jackson's request; it was intended as a rough draft of a statement of *his* views at the conference of the justices, rather than as a statement of my views." [124] Rehnquist's version is inconsistent with a draft concurrence that Jackson prepared but never issued in *Brown*. In it, Jackson declared categorically, "I am convinced that present-day conditions require us to strike from our books the doctrine of separate-but-equal facilities and to hold invalid provisions of state constitutions or statutes which classify persons for separate treatment in matters of education based solely on possession of colored blood." [125] Would Jackson have written this if he had held the view stated in the Rehnquist memo?

Justice Rehnquist has since stated that his views have probably changed and that he accepts *Brown* as the law of the land. [126] But his votes in cases involving racial issues clearly placed him at the opposite extreme from the Brennan wing of the Court. On most other issues, too, Rehnquist has reflected his conservative Republican background, with years of private practice and active involvement in the Goldwater wing of the party in Arizona and a position as assistant attorney general in the Nixon Department of Justice.

Rehnquist has anything but the appearance of a Justice, much less a Chief Justice. Well over six feet tall, he still has the look of an over-age college student—lumbering around the Court in his thick brown glasses, mismatched outfits, and running shoes. Despite his robust appearance and weekly tennis with his law clerks, Rehnquist has had health problems. In 1982, he was hospitalized because of his back and underwent withdrawal symptoms, with a period of mental confusion and slurred speech, when the heavy dosage of a powerful pain killer, Placidyl, was reduced. In 1977, Rehnquist had written in reply to a letter comment on his draft opinion in a case: "It may be that my adverse reactions to your letter of March 7 are partially induced by my doctor's insistence that I take valium four times a day. . . ." [127]

Rehnquist was once called the Burger Court's "most self-consciously literate opinion writer." [128] He was the best legal stylist and phrase-maker on the Burger Court, though too much of his literary ability was overshadowed by the extreme positions which it supported. Rehnquist's literary talents are not limited to his opinion writing. A typical example is contained in a 1980 memo on a case involving a mandatory life sentence under a recidivist statute. The defendant had obtained $229 by fraud and forgery through his three criminal acts.[129] Rehnquist's draft opinion holding that the sentence did not constitute cruel and unusual punishment was disputed by a Powell draft dissent. Rehnquist took issue with the Powell view that, since the crimes were "properly related" and did not involve "violence," the sentence was unconstitutionally harsh. "The notions embodied in the dissent," Rehnquist wrote, "that if the crime involved 'violence,' see *post,* page 11, fn. 11, a more severe penalty is warranted under objective standards simply will not wash, whether it be taken as a matter of morals, history, or law. Caesar's death at the hands of Brutus and his fellow conspirators was undoubtedly violent; the death of Hamlet's father at the hands of his brother, Claudius, by poison, was not. Yet there are few, if any states which do not punish just as severely murder by poison (or attempted murder by poison) as they do murder or attempted murder by stabbing. The highly placed executive who embezzles huge sums from a state savings and loan association, causing many shareholders of limited means to lose substantial parts of their savings, has committed a crime very different from a man who takes a smaller amount of money from the same savings and loan at the point of a gun. Yet rational people could disagree as to which criminal merits harsher punishment. . . . In short, the 'seriousness' of an offense or a pattern of offenses in modern society is not a line, but a plane." [130]

In another memo, Rehnquist referred to *Buckley v. Valeo*.[131] The lower court had upheld congressional restrictions on campaign financing and expenditures. According to Rehnquist, "The Court of Appeals there, it seemed to me, appeared to say that in order to achieve the 'compelling state interest' of allowing everybody to be heard to some extent, Congress did not abridge the First Amendment by preventing some people from talking as much as they wanted. This seemed to me like something out of George Orwell, or like Rousseau's idea that people would be forced to be free." [132]

His extreme views have not prevented Rehnquist from being on good terms with the other Justices. Even his ideological opposites like Brennan comment on their cordial relations with the categorical conservative. To his colleagues, Rehnquist has been as well known for his good nature as for his rightist acumen. On a Court where, as Justice Blackmun once lamented, "There is very little humor," [133] Rehnquist stood out because of his impish irreverence and wit. When the Burger Court sat, one of Rehnquist's clerks would every now and then pass notes to the Justice. These were not legal memos but *Trivial Pursuit-*

style questions. Rehnquist would answer them and then hand them to Justice Blackmun for that Justice to try his hand.[134]

The Rehnquist wit was almost proverbial in the Burger Court. During the argument in the celebrated *Bakke* case,[135] the plaintiff's counsel, according to one Justice, "began his argument by explaining, at great length, that he was Alan Bakke's lawyer, and by summarizing all the steps that were taken to commence the lawsuit. After three or four minutes of these essential [*sic*] irrelevancies, Bill Rehnquist interrupted and brought down the house" with the observation, "But no one is charging you with laches here, Mr. Colvin."[136]

Another illustration may be seen in a 1973 Rehnquist memorandum: "In going over some material which had been stored for a long period of time in my present Chambers, I came across a manuscript poem entitled 'To a Law Clerk Dying Young,' written by someone named A. E. Schmaussman, or Schmousman[137] (the handwriting is not too good), who was apparently a law clerk here at one time." Rehnquist wrote, "I found the poem very moving and emotional, and thought that a public reading of it would be a suitable occasion for a gathering of present and retired members of the Court and their law clerks to toast a departing Term with sherry."

The Rehnquist memo concluded with what some considered a satiric allusion to the Burger obsession with Court-secrecy: "P.S. I debated circulating the actual text of the poem with this invitation, but decided that there was too great a chance that it might be leaked to the newspapers before the party."[138]

The Rehnquist sense of humor sometimes degenerated into practical jokes. On April Fool's Day 1985, the Chief Justice was the Rehnquist victim. Rehnquist had a life-size photo cutout of Burger produced and sent a street photographer to a corner outside the Court with a sign, "Have your picture taken with the chief justice, $1." To make sure he wouldn't miss Burger's reaction, the Justice called him at home, saying he needed a ride to Court on April 1. Rehnquist "was laughing like crazy" when he drove past the scene that day with the overdignified Chief Justice.[139]

THE FIRST SISTER

When the Supreme Court was first established, the author of an opinion was designated, "Cushing, Justice." In 1820, the form was replaced by "Mr. Justice Johnson" as opinion author. This style lasted over a century and a half. Then, in 1980, Justice White suggested to the conference that, since a woman Justice was bound to be appointed soon, they should avoid the embarrassment of changing the style again at that time. All the others agreed, and the manner of designating the author of an opinion became simply, "Justice Brennan."[140]

White's prescience was borne out the next year when Sandra Day O'Connor was appointed as what *Time* called "the Brethren's first sister."[141] Her career dramatically illustrates the changed place of women in the law. Though O'Connor graduated third in her class at Stanford Law School (Rehnquist had been first), only one California law firm would hire her; a Los Angeles firm offered her a job as a legal secretary. Ironically, Attorney General William French Smith, one of the partners in the firm that had refused to hire her as an associate, recommended O'Connor for the Supreme Court.[142]

After law school, O'Connor returned to Arizona, where she combined legal work with political activity. She became assistant attorney general and then a member, and ultimately majority leader, of the state senate. She was elected to the Superior Court, where she served for five years. In 1979, she was appointed to the Arizona Court of Appeals. O'Connor was the second Burger Court member (after Justice Brennan) to have served as a state judge.

The Justices used to jest among themselves about the effect a woman Justice would have. Tradition says that the junior Justice answers the conference door (one of them used to quip that he was the highest-paid doorman in the world). As rumors of a female appointment gained ground, the Justices joked, first to Rehnquist and then to the new junior Justice, Stevens, that when a woman came to the Court, he should be a gentleman and continue to answer the door. In the event, when O'Connor became the newest Justice, she assumed the doorkeeper's task without question. And the Justices continued to be called the Brethren even though a woman had joined their ranks.[143]

Soon after O'Connor took her seat, a *Time* headline read, "And Now the Arizona Twins; Justice O'Connor teams up with court Conservative Rehnquist."[144] There is no doubt that O'Connor has been more conservative than her predecessor, Stewart. "I think it is fairly clear," said Blackmun during the last Burger term, that O'Connor "is on the right."[145] She has typically voted opposite Rehnquist only about 10 percent of the time, while disagreeing with Brennan and Marshall in over 45 percent of the cases.[146]

It is not accurate to picture O'Connor as only a Rehnquist clone. She tends to be as conservative as the latter in criminal cases and was, in fact, the author of opinions limiting *Miranda*[147] during the last two

Burger terms.[148] She has also sided with her fellow Arizonian on the importance of recognizing state powers[149] and the need for judicial restraint vis-à-vis the legislature.[150] But she has been more moderate in a few areas—most notably (in view of her own experience with sex discrimination) in cases involving sexual bias,[151] but also in cases involving affirmative action[152] and the First Amendment.[153]

Even those who disagree with her recognize that O'Connor has been an above-average Justice, who has become an effective conservative voice. She has not been hesitant in expressing her views both in conference and from the bench.

O'Connor's opinions are characterized by clear analysis and focus upon the points at issue. But they are at times lightened by a little-credited gift for language. In a case involving the right of a defendant to represent himself, the O'Connor opinion noted, "We recognize that a . . . defendant may wish to dance a solo, not a *pas de deux*."[154] And, disagreeing with a decision that overruled a prior holding that the wages and hours of state employees were beyond the reach of congressional power, O'Connor, in dissent, asserted, "The Court today surveys the battle scene of federalism and sounds a retreat. . . . I would prefer to hold the field and, at the very least, render a little aid to the wounded."[155]

The O'Connor approach was perhaps shown at its best in a 1983 case in which the Court reaffirmed its commitment to *Roe v. Wade*.[156] The Court held that a state could ban abortions only after the point in pregnancy at which a fetus was "viable." In 1973, that point was considered to be no earlier than twenty-four weeks (six months) into a pregnancy. Thus, *Roe* held that a state could ban only third-trimester abortions.

In the decade since *Roe*, however, advances in medical science and technology had enabled doctors to keep alive, at least for hours or days, children born even earlier in pregnancy. Such advances raised the distinct possibility that the point at which a state could ban abortion would also move back earlier and earlier in pregnancy, curtailing the freedom initially set out in *Roe*.

None of the other Justices had noted this development. But O'Connor made it the basis of her 1983 dissent. Scientific advances, she urged, had put the *Roe* rationale "on a collision course with itself." In O'Connor's view, the *Roe* trimester approach may no longer be valid "because of . . . technological advancement in the safety of abortion procedure. The State may no longer rely on a 'bright line' that separates permissible from impermissible regulation, and it is no longer free to consider the second trimester as a unit." [157]

The *Roe* framework is thus no longer valid. "As the medical risks of various abortion procedures decrease, the point at which the State may regulate for reasons of maternal health is moved further forward to actual childbirth. As medical science becomes better able to provide for the separate existence of the fetus, the point of viability is moved further back toward conception." [158]

The O'Connor challenge is for the Court to rebuild the logical underpinnings of the *Roe* trimester framework, for which there is now "no justification in law or logic." [159] The alternative is for the legal landmark to be transformed into an anachronism by advances in medical science. [160]

JUNIOR SUPREME COURT

In a congratulatory letter to Justice Rehnquist, Justice Douglas wrote, "I realize that you were here before as a member of the so-called Junior Supreme Court." [161] Douglas was referring to service as a law clerk to Justice Jackson. Once upon a time, the Douglas characterization of the clerk corps might have been taken as one made wholly in jest, but that was no longer the case.

Over half a century ago, Justice Louis D. Brandeis stated, "The reason the public thinks so much of the Justices of the Supreme Court is that they are almost the only people in Washington who do their own work." [162] The legend that this remains true is still prevalent, and in his book on the Court, even Chief Justice Rehnquist tells us that "the individual justices still continue to do a great deal more of their 'own work' than do their counterparts in the other branches of the federal government." [163]

The Rehnquist-type account has been accepted both by the press and the public. "Alone among Government agencies," Anthony Lewis wrote in the *New York Times,* "the court seems to have escaped Parkinson's Law. The work is still done by nine men, assisted by eighteen young law clerks. Nothing is delegated to committees or ghostwriters or task forces." [164] In an earlier day, the law clerk would perform only the functions of an associate in a law firm, i.e., research for senior members and assistance generally in the firm's work. It may be doubted that Justices such as Holmes or Brandeis used their clerks as more than research assistants. More recently, however, the Justices have given their clerks an ever-larger share of responsibility, including even the writing of opinions.

Complaints against the clerks' role have been common, including a noted 1957 article in *U.S. News & World Report* by William H. Rehnquist himself.[165] Rehnquist stated that the Justices were delegating substantial responsibility to their clerks, who "unconsciously" slanted materials to accord with their own views. The result was that the liberal point of view of the vast majority of the clerks had become the philosophy espoused by the Warren Court.

A reply to Rehnquist was made, largely under Justice Frankfurter's instigation, by Alexander M. Bickel, a former Frankfurter clerk and a leading constitutional scholar. In a 1958 article in the *New York Times,* Bickel asserted that "the law clerks are in no respect any kind of a kitchen cabinet." Their job is only to "generally assist their respective Justices in researching the law books and other sources for materials relevant to the decision of cases before the Court." They also "go over drafts of opinions and may suggest changes."[166]

In the Burger Court, the truth was closer to the Rehnquist than the Bickel picture. "In the United States," notes a recent *London Times* article, "judges have 'clerks', i.e., assistants who prepare and frequently write judgments which their masters often merely adopt and which a qualified observer can easily recognize as the work of a beginner."[167]

An even harsher view of the clerk system was expressed the year after Chief Justice Burger retired by Professor Philip B. Kurland, a leading constitutional scholar. As he notes, the law clerks now exercise a major role in the two most important functions of the Justices: (1) the screening of cases to determine which the Court will hear and decide; and (2) the drafting of opinions. "I think Brandeis would be aghast."[168]

A few years ago, Justice Stevens publicly conceded that he did not read 80 percent of the certiorari petitions presented to the Court.[169] Instead his clerks prepare memoranda summarizing those cases and issues and recommending whether or not certiorari should be granted. The Justice reads only those where the granting of certiorari is recommended. The only member of the Burger Court who personally went over petitions for review was Brennan, who customarily shared the work with his law clerks. In a letter to Brennan, who was temporarily away from the Court, his clerks stated, "We are all fascinated by the certs and shudder to think that when you get back you may take some of them away from us. But if you're very nice we won't fight too hard." [170]

In the 1972 term, Powell urged that the Justices combine their efforts in the screening process by having their clerks work together in one "cert pool." [171] The petitions would be divided equally among all the clerks in the pool, and the cert memos prepared by them would be circulated to each of the Justices participating. The Chief Justice and White, Blackmun, Powell, and Rehnquist agreed to join in the cert pool. Douglas, Brennan, Stewart, and Marshall declined to participate—as did Stevens, who was appointed after Douglas resigned. [172]

While the Justices make the final decision on what certiorari petitions to grant, *the* work on the petitions is done by the law clerks. In the vast majority of cases, the Justices' knowledge of the petitions and the issues they present is based on the clerks' cert memos, and they normally follow the recommendations in the memos. Sheer volume, if nothing else, has made this the prevailing practice.

The Justices themselves have expressed qualms about this delegation of the screening task. In declining to join the cert pool, Douglas wrote to the Chief Justice: "The law clerks are fine. Most of them are sharp and able. But after all, they have never been confirmed by the Senate." [173] Some years earlier, Justice Frankfurter wrote to Justice Stewart, "The appraisal and appreciation of a record as a basis for exercising our discretionary jurisdiction is, I do not have to tell you, so dependent on a seasoned and disciplined professional judgment that I do not believe that lads—most of them fresh out of law school and with their present tendentiousness—should have any routine share in the process of disemboweling a record, however acute and stimulating their power of reasoning may be and however tentative and advisory their memos on what is reported in the record and what is relevant to our taking a case may be." Referring to a recent case, he told Stewart, "it is a striking illustration of which I have found many over the years, Term after Term, of the slanted way in which, through compassionate feelings and inexperienced predispositions, these . . . cases are reported to us on the strength of which, so predominantly, action is taken by the court." [174]

An even more important delegation to the clerks involves the opinion-writing process itself. "As the years passed," says Douglas in his *Autobiography,* "it became more and more evident that the law clerks were drafting opinions." [175] Even the better Justices have made more extensive use of their clerks in the drafting process than outside observers have realized. In the Burger Court, indeed, the routine procedure was for the clerks to draft virtually all opinions.

As one federal judge put it, "What are these able, intelligent, mostly young people doing? Surely not merely running citations in *Shepard's* and shelving the judge's law books. They are, in many situations, 'para-judges.' In some instances, it is to be feared, they are indeed invisible judges, for there are appellate judges whose literary style appears to change annually."[176]

The present Chief Justice has candidly described the opinion-writing process. "In my case," Rehnquist said, "the clerks do the first draft of almost all cases to which I have been assigned to write the Court's opinion." Only "when the case-load is heavy" does Rehnquist sometimes "help by doing the first draft of a case myself."[177] Rehnquist has continued this practice as Chief Justice,[178] but he concedes that the "practice . . . may undoubtedly . . . cause raised eyebrows." Still, the Chief Justice asserts, "I think the practice is entirely proper: The Justice must retain for himself control not merely of the outcome of the case, but of the explanation for the outcome, and I do not believe this practice sacrifices either."[179]

It is, of course, true that the decisions are made by the Justices—though, even with regard to them, the weaker Justices have abdicated much of their authority to their clerks. In most chambers, the clerks are, to use a favorite expression of Chief Justice Warren, not "unguided missiles." The Justices normally outline the way they want opinions drafted. But the drafting clerk is left with a great deal of discretion. The Justices may "convey the broad outlines," but they "do not invariably settle exactly how the opinion will be reasoned through."[180] The details of the opinion are left to the clerk, in particular the specific reasoning and research supporting the decision. The technical minutiae and footnotes, which are so dear to the law professor, are left almost completely to the clerks. Thus, footnote 11 of the *Brown* school segregation opinion[181]—perhaps the most famous footnote in Supreme Court history—was entirely the product of a Warren law clerk.

To be sure, the Justices themselves go over the drafts, and, said Justice Rehnquist, "I may revise it in toto." But, he also admits, "I may leave it relatively unchanged."[182] Too many of the Justices circulate drafts that are almost wholly the work of their clerks.

The growing number of law clerks has naturally led to an increase in the length, though plainly not the quality, of opinions. What

Douglas once wrote about Court opinions has become increasingly true: "We have tended more and more to write a law-review-type of opinion. They plague the Bar and the Bench. They are so long they are meaningless. They are filled with trivia and nonessentials."[183]

The product of the Douglas animadversion has been one result of the burgeoning bureaucratization of the Court. Law clerks have a similar academic background and little other experience. For three years they have had drummed into them that the acme of literary style is the law review article. It is scarcely surprising that the standard opinion style has become that of the student-run reviews: colorless, prolix, platitudinous, always erring on the side of inclusion, full of lengthy citations and footnotes—and above all dull.[184]

The individual flair that makes the opinions of a Holmes or a Cardozo literary as well as legal gems has become a thing of the past. There is all the difference in the world between writing one's own opinions and reviewing opinions written by someone else. It is hard to see how an editor can be a great judge. Can we really visualize a Holmes coordinating a team of law clerks and editing their drafts?[185]

According to a federal appellate judge, "We need to reduce our dependence on the system of judicial apprenticeships and on a mass production model that will soon swallow us up."[186] In the Supreme Court, as in most institutions, the balance of power has shifted increasingly to the bureaucrats and away from the nominal heads. Law clerks now have tremendous influence. All too often the clerk corps sets the tone in the Marble Palace. Asked about the shrillness that some observers perceived in Burger Court opinions, Rehnquist said, "It may reflect conflict among law clerks rather than acerbity or lack of civility among the judges."[187]

Chapter Two

Judicial Review in Operation

ITS ROLE as ultimate guardian of the constitutional ark makes the Supreme Court unique among judicial tribunals. The Court is primarily a political institution. Its task is to vindicate individual rights, strike down laws that are unconstitutional, and arbitrate between the states and the federal government and between the different branches of the federal government.[1]

A judge on such a tribunal has an opportunity to leave his imprint upon the life of the nation as no mere master of the common law possibly could. Only a handful of Americans have made so manifest a mark as did Justice Holmes.[2] The same cannot be said of even the greatest of English judges. To be a judge is certainly among life's noblest callings; but the mere common law judge, even in a preeminently legal polity such as Britain, cannot begin to compare in power and prestige with a Justice of the Supreme Court. A judge who is regent over what is done in the legislative and executive branches—the *deus ex machina* who has the final word in the constitutional system—has attained one of the ultimates of human authority.

"To argue," as an English observer recently wrote, "that [the Court's] task is somehow not political is naive."[3] But one must never forget that the Supreme Court follows the forms of a law court. The high bench does not exercise power that is directly political in form; its decisions must grow out of the traditional form of the lawsuit, August though its role may be in the constitutional sphere, it can only resolve actual cases brought before its bar by adverse parties.

JUDICIAL INDEPENDENCE

The fulcrum upon which the awesome power vested in the federal courts turns is the Article III guaranty of judicial independence. The Framers were well aware of the need for such independence. "He has made Judges dependent on his Will alone," declares the Declaration of Independence about George III, "for the tenure of their offices, and the amount and payment of their salaries." The Founders ensured that such a complaint could not arise in the governmental system they were creating.

In *Palmore v. United States*,[4] however, the defendant was convicted in a non-Article III court for a felony committed in violation of a law enacted by Congress. The court in question, the Supreme Court of the District of Columbia, was established by an act of Congress, which provided that its judges were to be appointed by the President for fifteen-year terms and might be removed during their terms by a five-member commission. Could Congress thus provide for trial and conviction by a court not protected by the Article III guaranty of life tenure?

The postargument *Palmore* conference was closely divided. The key issue was stated at the outset by Chief Justice Burger: "Does crime of D.C. have to be tried before Article III judge?" The Chief Justice answered in the negative. In his view, a "constitutional basis for this" was provided by the Article I provision vesting Congress with the power to "exercise exclusive Legislation in all Cases whatsoever, over" the District of Columbia.[5] A bare majority voted with the Chief Justice to affirm Palmore's conviction.

Justice Douglas led the argument the other way. His categorical view was that Congress "can't try crimes except in Article III courts." Douglas was supported by Brennan and Marshall, with the latter declaring flatly, "A felony can't be tried in an Article I court." Stewart also voted ("tentatively," he said) to reverse, but on the ground of an illegal search and seizure—a point not considered by the Court in its *Palmore* opinion.

Palmore was decided by an eight-to-one vote. Congress could authorize the trial and conviction in a court not protected by the Article III guarantees. Only Douglas dissented, writing a strong opinion asserting that "All the normal vices of a dependent, removable judiciary are accentuated in the District of Columbia."[6]

The *Palmore* decision appears unfortunate. The District of Columbia judges are made dependent on the congressional will alone for the tenure of their offices despite the fact that they sit in courts set up by Congress. In criminal prosecutions where the "judicial Power" of the United States is exercised, the Article III safeguard of an independent judiciary should also govern.

Closely related to the Article III provision for judicial tenure is the clause providing that federal judicial compensation "shall not be diminished during their Continuance in Office." At issue in *United States v. Will*[7] were salary increases for federal judges, under a law providing for annual cost-of-living increases. In four consecutive fiscal years (years 1, 2, 3, and 4) Congress enacted statutes to stop the increases. In years 2 and 3, the statutes became law before the start of the fiscal year, and in years 1 and 4 became law on or after the first day of the fiscal year. A number of federal judges brought actions challenging the validity of the statutes under the Compensation Clause, and the lower court had decided in their favor.

There were two questions before the Supreme Court in *Will:* (1) Were the Justices disqualified because of their financial interest in the case? (2) On the merits, did the statutes stopping the increases violate the Compensation Clause?

At the postargument conference, Chief Justice Burger set the theme for the Court's answer to the first question. "The Rule of Necessity," he declared, "governs and we are not disqualified. [*Evans v. Gore*][8] requires this." The *Evans* case involved the constitutionality of income taxes upon the salaries of federal judges. The Court recognized that its members each had a personal interest in the case, but "there was no other appellate tribunal to which under the law [plaintiff] could go."[9] Where disqualification would remove the only tribunal that has jurisdiction over a case, that tribunal may continue to sit.

All the Justices agreed on the disqualification issue, though Rehnquist and Stevens stated that they had doubts about the Rule of Necessity. On the merits, the Justices were more closely divided. The majority agreed with the Chief Justice, who had stated at the conference that, with regard to years 1 and 4 "there was a vested increase and the effort to divest was unconstitutional." But a different result was required for years 2 and 3; the statutes stopping the increases became effective before the increases could take effect.

A "Score Sheet" on *United States v. Will* lists varying votes.[10] The final decision was unanimous; the Justices agreed that, as Powell put it in a December 5, 1980, letter to Stewart, "there is considerable advantage in having a unanimous Court."

The statutes governing years 2 and 3 were ruled valid since they took effect before the pay increases and thus did not diminish the judges' compensation. On the other hand, the statutes for years 1 and 4 became law on or after the first day of the fiscal year and hence "'diminished' the compensation of federal judges"[11] in violation of the Constitution.

The Burger draft opinion in *Will* had contained a sentence to which Justice Stewart objected. In a December 11, 1980, "Dear Chief" letter, Stewart noted that the sentence "says, among other things, that § 455 [the statutory provision governing judicial disqualification] is totally inapplicable to a Justice of this Court." Such a statement, Stewart wrote, was "inadvertently inaccurate." The Chief Justice deleted the offending sentence from the *Will* opinion.

In a December 3, 1980, letter to the Chief Justice, Brennan objected to a statement in the Burger draft opinion that the Compensation Clause "embodies a practical balancing of the need to increase compensation . . . against the need for judicial independence." Brennan wrote, "I seriously question that the Compensation Clause contemplates a balancing of interests: did not the Framers rather construct the clause as a flat prohibition of diminution of judicial salaries? In other words, doesn't the clause reflect a judgment that the public interest in a strong and independent judiciary is to be preferred absolutely over the fiscal concerns on the opposite side of the 'balance'?" Here, too, the criticism led to the deletion of the offending statement.

To one interested in the operation of the Supreme Court, *Will* is of interest because of indications by the Justices that the case caused them embarrassment. After the Court had voted to grant appellees' motion for a divided argument in the case[12]—a motion designed to allow Judge Will, the lead plaintiff, to participate in the oral argument—Chief Justice Burger informed the others in an October 2, 1980, Memorandum to Conference that he would issue a "strong dissent," if not for the fact that "my going on the record would further compound the damage that Will's appallingly bad judgment creates."

"I am profoundly concerned that Will's bad judgment could well operate to damage our cause in Congress and negate some of the efforts already expended with the Salary Commission and the efforts of our supporters in the Bar." The Burger memo asserted that the Justices were "collectively damaged by having a United States Judge appear in this Court for a class of which we are certified as members. We have acquiesced in that certification and Hurbert [sic] Will at the lectern is bound to be perceived as *our* advocate. This bears on the public perception of our role."

The "only hope," Burger wrote, was "that some combination of the activities of Messrs. Carter, Reagan, and Anderson, along with Iran and Iraq, will preempt the news the day of the argument." The Court was saved the Chief Justice's feared embarrassment. Judge Will did not participate in the oral argument.

The Justices' uneasiness about the *Will* case may also be seen from a March 10, 1981, Memorandum to the Conference from Justice Stevens. This memo was occasioned by a memorandum circulated to the Justices by "certain judges . . . recommending that $850,000 be paid to counsel for their work in preserving the independence and the quality of the Federal Judiciary." Stevens asserted that the judges' "memorandum takes a position that is contrary to the best interest of the Federal Judiciary."

In fact, the Stevens memo declared of the *Will* case, "in my judgment history will prove that the harm done to the Federal Judiciary by this litigation far outweighs the minimal benefits that it produced." Stevens was also harsh in dealing with "the suggestion . . . that counsel should be given special credit for handling unpopular litigation." That, Stevens wrote, "is a little hard to swallow. There are quite a few lawyers who would have regarded the opportunity to represent the Federal Judiciary as a privilege. It sure is not quite like a march on Selma."

In the end, the Justices ignored the issue of counsel fees, following the view suggested by Justice Brennan in a March 10, 1981, Memorandum to the Conference: " . . . it would be inappropriate for us either to oppose or support the award of counsel fees in this case. In addition, I think it would be most unwise. Our friends of the media would have a field day. It is inevitable, I think, that the opposition would be distorted whether or not, as Bill suggests, we propose that any savings be donated to charity. In the end the whole business would be a great disservice to the institution."

CASES AND CONTROVERSIES: MOOTNESS

Justice Brandeis used to say that what the Supreme Court did not do was often more important than what it did do. The fact that the highest tribunal acts as a law court has been more important than any other factor in determining the things that it does not do. The Founding Fathers deliberately withheld from the Supreme Court purely political power, such as power to veto or revise legislation. Instead, they delegated to the Court "The judicial Power" alone—which, by the express language of Article III, extends only to "Cases" and "Controversies." This, the Burger Court said, "limits the 'judicial power of the United States to the resolution of 'cases' and 'controversies.'"[13] Judicial power, in Marshall's words in 1799, may operate only upon "a controversy between parties which had taken a shape for judicial decision."[14]

Thus the Court's only power is to decide lawsuits between opposing litigants with real interests at stake, and its only method of proceeding is by the conventional judicial process. In the Burger Court's words, "The power to declare the rights of individuals and to measure the authority of governments . . . 'is legitimate only in the last resort, and as a necessity in the determination of real, earnest and vital controversy.'"[15]

It has long been established that a case that has become moot does not present a "case" or "controversy."[16] For the Article III requirement to be met in the Supreme Court, there must not only be a real case at the time the complaint is filed, but the case must be alive when the Court reviews it.

In the Burger Court jurisprudence this principle is illustrated by *DeFunis v. Odegaard.*[17] DeFunis, a white graduate of a state university, was denied admission to the university's law school even though thirty-six minority applicants who had averages below DeFunis had been accepted under a separate admissions procedure. DeFunis brought suit in state court claiming that the law school had discriminated against him on account of his race in violation of the Equal Protection Clause. The trial court agreed, and DeFunis was admitted to the law school. On appeal, the state supreme court reversed and held that the law school's admissions policy did not violate the Constitution. DeFunis was by then in his second year at the law school.

When *DeFunis* was argued in the U.S. Supreme Court, February 26, 1974, DeFunis had completed all but his last term. After the argument ended, DeFunis' attorney sent a letter to the Chief Justice stating that DeFunis had filed his registration for his last term on February 26. In addition, counsel for the university had informed the Court that DeFunis would be given the opportunity to complete his final semester and graduate, regardless of how the Supreme Court decided his case.

Despite this, most of the *DeFunis* conference was devoted to the merits of the case. The Chief Justice did suggest that *DeFunis* could be disposed of on mootness grounds, and Stewart stated flatly, "The case is moot." This is "not a class action and not remotely akin to *Roe* or *Doe*"[18]—the two abortion cases where the Court had rejected the mootness argument. "DeFunis is in law school and will graduate." Blackmun also stated that he thought the case was moot.

In the weeks that followed the conference, Stewart was able to secure the votes of Rehnquist and Powell for disposition of *Defunis* on mootness grounds. Five Justices thus agreed to avoid the merits, and their decision that the case was moot was announced in a per curiam opinion authored by Stewart.

To be sure, the *DeFunis* decision did not enable the Justices permanently to avoid the crucial constitutional issues involved in the case. As Brennan put it in dissent, "Few constitutional questions in recent history have stirred as much debate, and they will not disappear. They must inevitably return to the federal courts and ultimately again to the Court."[19] The Brennan prophecy was borne out when the *Bakke* case,[20] raising the same issue as *DeFunis,* came before the Supreme Court.

There are, however, cases that, by their very nature, always become moot because of the time that elapses between filing of the original complaint and consideration of the case by the Supreme Court. The best example of a case of this type is *Roe v. Wade*[21]—perhaps the most controversial case decided by the Burger Court. *Roe* and a companion case, *Doe v. Bolton,*[22] arose out of constitutional challenges to state laws prohibiting abortions. The complaint in *Roe,* filed in a federal district court in March 1970, alleged that plaintiff was a single, pregnant woman who wished to terminate her pregnancy by abortion but was unable to get a "legal" abortion because of the state prohibitory law. At the time the complaint was filed, *Roe v. Wade* was certainly a live case, but by the time the case was decided by the Supreme Court almost three years had passed and plaintiff's pregnancy had terminated. Under the normal rules governing mootness, that would have ended the case, for plaintiff no longer had any more of a personal interest in the decision than DeFunis had in his case.

There is, however, a crucial difference between *Roe* and *DeFunis.* In *DeFunis* the decision of mootness merely postponed decision on the merits until another case presenting the same constitutional issue arose. In *Roe,* and in any subsequent case challenging the constitutionality of an abortion law, the physical nature of pregnancy made it impossible for the case to remain live until the Supreme Court decided it. Traditional mootness concepts would thus require the dismissal of all such challenges.

The key question was that stated in an eleven-page letter by Brennan, analyzing *Doe v. Bolton*: "Is the case moot because Mary Doe is no longer pregnant?" He referred to this and other "threshold issues," and concluded, "None, in my opinion, forecloses decision on the crucial questions here—the existence and nature of a right to an abortion."[23]

So far as can be seen from the available conference notes, all agreed at the first postargument conference with the Brennan conclusion. The theme on the point under discussion was set by the Chief Justice, who said, "The unmarried girl has standing. . . . She didn't lose standing through mootness." No one at the conference took a different position.

The manner in which the *Roe* opinion dealt with the mootness issue was contained in Blackmun's first draft opinion of May 18, 1972, which is substantially the same as the final *Roe* opinion on the issue.[24] The usual rule is that an actual controversy must exist at all stages of appellate review and not only at the date the action is initiated, but where pregnancy is a significant fact in litigation, the pregnancy will have terminated before the usual appellate process is completed. If that makes the case moot, pregnancy litigation can never survive beyond the trial stage.

According to Blackmun, however, "Our law is not that rigid."[25] Pregnancy may come more than once to the same woman and it is always with us. Hence, "Pregnancy provides a classic justification for a conclusion of nonmootness. It truly could be 'capable of repetition, yet evading review.'"[26] Thus, the termination of Roe's 1970 pregnancy did not render the case moot.

The *Roe* decision on mootness has been assumed to be an application of an established "repetition" exception to the mootness rule. But the prior cases on the exception—and particularly those cited in the *Roe* opinion—are based on their particular facts and do not lay down a broadly applicable "repetition" exception.

In a 1975 case, the Court stated that the "repetition" exception would apply whenever two conditions were met: "(1) the challenged action was in its duration too short to be fully litigated prior to its cessation or expiration, and (2) there was a reasonable expectation that the same complaining party would be subjected to the same action again."[27] In the case in question, the Court dismissed for mootness where the second condition was not met.

Yet the Court also held that the second condition need not be met if the plaintiff brings a class action. In *Sosna v. Iowa*[28] plaintiff brought a class action challenging Iowa's one-year residence requirement for bringing a divorce action. By the time the case reached the Supreme Court, plaintiff had long since satisfied the residence requirement. At the postargument conference, Brennan, White, and Marshall voted to vacate on mootness. Douglas said that the case was "not moot because there may still be rights to maintenance and support for children." But the prevailing view was stated by Rehnquist. "On mootness I am troubled, but think it's a matter of class action law. If there's such a person in Iowa, I think the case can go on." Hence, as Stewart put it, plaintiff could still sue "as [a] representative, with no present personal interest."

With White alone dissenting, the *Sosna* opinion of the Court followed the Rehnquist approach on the mootness issue. Though a live controversy is required, said the Court, "The controversy may exist . . . between a named defendant and a member of the class represented by the named plaintiff, even though the claim of the named plaintiff has become moot."[29]

In addition, the Burger Court relaxed the second condition—that the *same* party would be subjected to the same state action again. In *Nebraska Press Association v. Stuart*,[30] a court had issued an order restraining the news media from publishing or broadcasting accounts of confessions and facts implicating the defendant in a criminal trial. The order expired by its own terms when a jury was impaneled. Despite this, the Court held that an action attacking the order on First Amendment grounds was not moot. The case was held to come within the "repetition" exception because other restrictive orders might be issued in the future by courts in the state.

The same approach was followed in a case challenging a court order excluding the press and public from a pretrial hearing on a motion to suppress certain evidence. The Court ruled that the case was not moot even though the order had been lifted well before appellate review was completed.[31] The order was "by nature short-lived," and "it is reasonably to be expected that petitioner, as publisher of two New York newspapers, will be subjected to similar closure orders."[32]

Mootness was not found in these cases even though the contingency of future action involving the same plaintiff was almost as remote as that involving the *Sosna* plaintiff, given the rarity of suppression and exclusion orders in criminal cases. But that may well have been true in *Roe v. Wade* as well. The Court assumed that there was a reasonable expectation that Jane Roe would become pregnant again. But there were no findings to support that assumption. For all we know, if the matter had been explored, there would have been evidence to show that Roe would be most unlikely to become pregnant again.

All the record shows is that Roe was a pregnant woman at the time of filing her complaint: "for aught that appears in this record, she may have been in her *last* trimester of pregnancy as of the date the complaint was filed."[33] If that was the case, the *Roe* decision "that States may impose virtually no restrictions on medical abortions performed during the *first* trimester of pregnancy"[34] was only an advisory opinion as far as she was concerned.[35]

One may also wonder whether the "repetition" exception itself is sufficient justification for the Court to entertain an otherwise moot case. If plaintiff is no longer adversely affected, how can there still be an Article III "case" or "controversy"? Why should the fact that the issue is "capable of repetition" change the need for a live case in the current litigation?

STANDING: *DATA PROCESSING* CASE

The use of the "repetition" exception to mootness shows that it is not accurate to characterize the Burger Court as one that attempted "to close the courthouse doors to those trying to enforce their constitutional rights."[36] The same conclusion follows when we analyze the cases on "standing." There were some restrictive decisions, but the standing concept itself was substantially expanded.

Standing itself has always been a basic requirement of an Article III "case" or "controversy." The key question is whether the given action has been brought by a proper party plaintiff. As Justice Brennan tells us, this is the issue "whether the *particular* plaintiff then requesting review may have it."[37] This question is more commonly put in terms of *standing:* Does plaintiff have standing to bring the action? In the Burger Court's words, "this Court has always required that a litigant have 'standing' to challenge the action sought to be adjudicated in the lawsuit. . . . Of one thing we can be sure: those who do not possess Art. III standing may not litigate as suitors in the courts of the United States."[38]

No aspect of our public law changed more rapidly during the Burger tenure than the law governing standing. The restricted conception of standing has given way during the past two decades to an ever-broadening concept that has increasingly opened the courts to challenges against governmental action.[39]

It is the expansion of standing that has made possible the veritable revolutions that have occurred in such fields as environmental law and consumer protection. The narrow concepts of standing were appropriate to a legal system geared only to hearing private-law claims. If public interest claims are to be adequately considered, the concept of those able to protect the public interest must be accordingly broadened.

It was the Burger Court that was responsible for the decision in *Association of Data Processing Organizations v. Camp*[40]—the case that has served as the foundation for the expanded concept of standing that has increasingly prevailed in recent years. Unfortunately, *Data Processing* also shows Chief Justice Burger at his worst as a leader of the Court.

The problem arose from the fact that two standing cases were presented to the Court during the 1969 term—*Data Processing* and *Barlow v. Collins.*[41] Both cases involved the same issue of standing and the opinions in each should have been assigned to one Justice, who would articulate a uniform Court approach to the issue. Instead, Chief Justice Burger assigned *Data Processing* to Douglas and *Barlow* to Brennan. According to one Justice, "The separate assignment of the cases led to much confusion and turmoil, before the Court arrived at a single approach for use in both cases."

As it turned out, Brennan had the most liberal approach to standing among the Justices. His draft *Barlow* opinion[42] enunciated a simple standing test. "This test is satisfied when the plaintiff alleges, as petitioners' complaint alleged here, that the challenged action has caused him substantial injury in fact." Nor was more required than injury in fact to meet the "case" or "controversy" requirement. Plaintiff with such an injury, Brennan wrote, "may therefore be deemed to have the personal stake and interest that imparts the concrete adverseness required by Article III. Recognition of his standing is then consistent with the constitutional limitations of Article III."

The Brennan effort to state a simple injury-in-fact test as the sole standing criterion was frustrated by Justice Douglas's draft *Data Pro-*

cessing opinion. As Brennan put it in a January 20, 1970, Memorandum to the Conference, "Bill Douglas' circulation in No. 85 [*Data Processing*] and mine in No. 249 [*Barlow*] differ on a very narrow but important question concerning how judges are to determine the standing of plaintiffs who challenge administrative action. . . .

"Bill's approach has two stages: (1) Since Article III restricts judicial power to cases or controversies, the starting point is to ascertain whether 'the plaintiff alleges that the challenged action has caused him injury in fact' (*Data Processing* at page 2); (2) if injury in fact is alleged, the judge then ascertains 'whether the interest sought to be protected by the complainant is arguably within the zone of interests to be protected or regulated by the statute or constitutional guarantee in question' (Id., at page 3). Only if both appear may standing be found. On the other hand, my approach restricts standing to inquiry (1), the constitutional requirement. At page 7 *Barlow,* I conclude: 'Recognition of his standing is then consistent with the Constitution, *and no further inquiry is pertinent to its existence.*' . . . The Conference must decide the issue before either case can come down."

At the January 23 conference, the Justices supported the Douglas approach and *Barlow* was reassigned to Justice Douglas, who wrote the final opinions of the Court enunciating the standing test in both *Data Processing* and *Barlow* along the lines summarized in Justice Brennan's memo.

Under the Brennan *Barlow* draft's approach, all that would be needed to secure standing is to show injury in fact—some adverse effect from the governmental act plaintiff challenges. Under the Court's *Data Processing* opinion there is a bipartite-injury test, which adds an additional requirement. To satisfy the second prong of the test, plaintiffs must show that the relevant statutes were meant to protect them from the specific type of action they are challenging.

The bipartite injury test laid down by the Douglas opinions is needlessly complex and a backward step toward a stricter standing requirement. There is much to be said for state decisions rejecting the bipartite injury test in favor of a single "injury in fact" test.[43] If a challenged act does, in fact, cause injury to plaintiff, that should be enough to give him standing. A person who has suffered injury in fact meets both the Article III requirement and the need to ensure that plaintiff has a personal interest in the act that he challenges. The required interest exists when plaintiff alleges that he has suffered harm

as a result of the challenged action—that is, the test that would have
been adopted had the Brennan *Barlow* draft come down as the final
opinion of the Court.

It is, however, erroneous to think of *Data Processing* as a decision restricting standing. The Douglas opinion of the Court may
have been less favorable to standing than the Brennan *Barlow* draft,
but on its own terms it did make for a vital liberalization of standing law. It did this by eliminating the requirement of a "legal interest"
or "legal wrong." *Data Processing* confers standing upon an ag-
grieved plaintiff even if no legal wrong is suffered. The Court did
away with the requirement that a plaintiff allege invasion of a legally
protected interest. "The 'legal interest' test goes to the merits. The
question of standing is different." When standing is placed in issue,
the question is whether plaintiff is a proper party to seek review, not
"whether, on the merits, the plaintiff has a legally protected interest
that defendant's action invaded."[44] Whether the harm done comes
within the concept of "legal wrong" is irrelevant to the existence of
standing.

Data Processing recognizes that harm alone, not harm to a legally
protected interest, is what is required for standing. Parties harmed by
governmental action are permitted to challenge it although no legal
interest of theirs is found to have been invaded by the action.

STANDING: OTHER CASES

The concept of standing adopted in *Data Processing* led to an expansion of standing in the later Burger Court cases. Plaintiffs who would
previously have been denied standing were permitted to challenge
different types of governmental action. Thus, the cases used to hold
that plaintiff had to show a so-called pocketbook interest in the challenged governmental act. But now, Justice Powell tells us, "Non-
economic interests have been recognized."[45] Toward the end of the
Burger tenure, the Court reemphasized that standing is no longer
confined to those who can show economic harm.[46]

In addition, under the Burger Court jurisprudence, the fact that
many persons share the same injury does not constitute sufficient reason for denying standing to any person who has in fact suffered
injury.[47] "Aesthetic and environmental well-being, like economic
well-being, are important ingredients of the quality of life in our society, and the fact that particular environmental interests are shared

by the many rather than the few does not make them less deserving of legal protection through the judicial process."[48]

The expansion of standing to include aesthetic and environmental interests coincided with the elevation by Congress of the public interest in the environment to the status of a legally protected interest.[49] Individuals and organizations with environmental complaints were increasingly permitted to bring legal actions.

The most liberal Burger Court decision in favor of environmental standing was *United States v. Students Challenging Regulatory Agency Procedures (SCRAP).*[50] An environmental association formed by law students in the District of Columbia brought an action challenging Interstate Commerce Commission orders allowing railroads to collect a 2.5 percent surcharge on freight rates pending adoption of selective rate increases. SCRAP alleged that the higher rate structure would discourage the use of "recyclable" materials, causing further consumption of forests and other natural resources and resulting in more refuse and nondisposable materials to pollute the environment. The Court held that SCRAP had standing. Its members used forests, streams, mountains, and other resources for recreation and would be damaged by the adverse environmental impact caused by the nonuse of recyclable goods.

According to Justice Powell, in *SCRAP,* "The concept of particularized injury has been dramatically diluted."[51] The Court itself recognized that SCRAP's allegation reflected an attenuated line of causation but held that the harm alleged was specific and perceptible enough for standing. The *SCRAP* decision indicates that the Court was well on its way to holding that any identifiable "injury in fact" may be enough to confer standing.

But what about the Burger Court decisions denying standing that critics have characterized as a broadside "shutting [of] the courthouse doors. . . . to those seeking to enforce constitutional rights"?[52]

Discussion of those decisions should start with recognition that what Powell terms "[t]he revolution in standing doctrine that has occurred"[53] has not meant the elimination of the standing requirement. Nor could it be so, in view of Article III's incompatibility with unlimited notions of standing. The Court never broke with the traditional requirement that a plaintiff must still show that standing exists.[54]

The Supreme Court had consistently denied standing to a plaintiff who relies only on his interest as a federal taxpayer.[55] Toward the end of Chief Justice Warren's tenure, the Court modified this rule in *Flast v. Cohen.*[56] The standing of a federal taxpayer to challenge federal expenditures on the ground that they violated the Establishment Clause of the First Amendment was upheld.

For taxpayer standing to exist, two criteria must be met: (1) The taxpayer attack must be against an expenditure that is an exercise of power under the Taxing and Spending Clause. (2) The taxpayer must show that a challenged expenditure exceeds a specific constitutional limitation upon the taxing and spending power.

In *Valley Forge Christian College v. Americans United,*[57] the Burger Court held that when these two criteria are not met, the bar to tax- payer standing still continues. The case arose out of a federal statute authorizing the Secretary of Health, Education, and Welfare to trans- fer surplus government property to educational institutions. A former military hospital was conveyed to a church-related college. Respon- dents sued as taxpayers, challenging the conveyance as violative of the Establishment Clause.

The *Valley Forge* conference was closely divided. Brennan spoke strongly in favor of standing. He was supported by Marshall, Black- mun, and Stevens. The latter noted that "taxpayer standing isn't enough. But *Flast* said it plus the Establishment Clause [violation] gave it." According to Stevens, the "source of adversary interest in *Flast* was the same" as in this case. Stevens also dealt with a point usually raised by opponents of taxpayer standing. "Talk about the Establishment Clause and nothing else," he said, "wouldn't open the floodgates"—that is, of constitutional litigation.

The other five voted against standing. As the Chief Justice put it at the conference, "This is an effort to extend *Flast.*" The bare majority refused to vote for such an extension. "We're at a *Flast* crossroads," declared Justice O'Connor. "Either abandon it or, if [we] stick to it, I would reverse and limit it to the spending and tax clause."

Powell went further. "*Flast* is out of step," he asserted, "and ought to be overruled." White and Rehnquist agreed. But they could not secure a majority for overruling *Flast.* Instead the O'Connor ap- proach of refusing to extend *Flast* was adopted by the *Valley Forge* decision. The Court ruled that respondents failed the first prong of the *Flast* test. They were not attacking a congressional action, only a decision by HEW to transfer property. Even more important, the ac- tion they challenged was not an exercise of power under the Taxing and Spending Clause. The authorizing legislation was an exercise of

Congress's power to dispose of federal property under the Property Clause of Article IV.

At the *Valley Forge* conference, White conceded that "maybe [you] can't distinguish cash from property on a principled basis." But the majority feared that to recognize standing here would be to recognize it for all taxpayers. An affirmance in favor of respondents' standing, White stated, "wouldn't prevent any taxpayer from relying on some other constitutional provision." Or in Justice Rehnquist's conference words, "You can't say you have . . . standing for one but not other constitutional provisions."

It should be borne in mind that *Flast* itself carved out a narrow exception to the categorical federal rule against taxpayer standing. One may disagree with the Burger Court's refusal to broaden the exception, but the refusal scarcely justifies condemnation of the Court for its "cynical attempts" to bar access to the courts.[58] The same is true of the Court's refusal to accept the concept of citizen standing, which appears even more inconsistent with traditional standing concepts.

Citizen standing was relied upon by plaintiffs in *United States v. Richardson*[59] and its companion case, *Schlesinger v. Reservists Committee to Stop the War*.[60] Plaintiff in *Richardson* sued as a taxpayer and citizen to challenge a statute permitting the CIA to account for its expenditures "solely on the certificate of the Director." He alleged that the law violated the constitutional requirement for a regular statement and account of public funds. In *Schlesinger,* plaintiffs sued as citizens and taxpayers challenging the membership in the Armed Forces Reserve of members of Congress as contrary to the constitutional clause that prohibits members of Congress from holding any other office.

The same conference discussed both *Richardson* and *Schlesinger.* Much of the discussion was devoted to the question stated by Chief Justice Burger at the outset: "Does this taxpayer satisfy *Flast* criteria?" A majority agreed with the Chief Justice that the *Flast* criteria were not met in either case, and his opinion took that view.

The conference also discussed the question of citizen standing, since the lower court in *Schlesinger* had held that their status as citizens gave plaintiffs standing and one judge in the lower court in *Richardson* also held that plaintiff there had standing as a citizen. In the conference, the vote was against citizen standing in both cases. Interestingly, Marshall, who was ultimately to dissent, agreed with the conference majority, saying, "The fact one is a citizen doesn't give standing." Only Justice Douglas spoke flatly in favor of citizen standing. "I'd let a citizen have standing," he declared.

White asserted, with regard to *Richardson,* "This is a citizen and not a taxpayer case." Despite this, it was the *Schlesinger* opinion that was devoted primarily to the citizen-standing issue, while the *Richardson* opinion dealt with taxpayer standing. The *Schlesinger* opinion completely rejected the notion that an individual can have standing as a citizen to challenge a governmental act that does not cause him some particularized injury. All citizens may have an interest in having government act in observance of the law, but that does not mean that every citizen suffers the required direct personal injury from nonobservance.[61]

The argument against citizen standing is that it would virtually do away with the standing requirement altogether. As Blackmun stated at the *Richardson* conference, "This could mean a challenge by any citizen to any government expenditure." If any citizen can sue qua citizen, it would follow that almost anyone can challenge any governmental act even if it does not affect him directly. Even if that were desirable, it is hard to see how it would be consistent with Article III. Under its requirements, "plaintiff must allege some particularized injury that sets him apart from the man on the street."[62]

Even Brennan, who took the most expansive standing view in the Burger Court, agreed with the decision on citizen standing. In a May 31, 1974, "Dear Chief" letter on the Burger *Schlesinger* draft opinion, Brennan wrote, "I have considered your proposed opinion in the above and agree with most of your discussion of the citizen-standing question and the absence of sufficient allegations of injury-in-fact to respondents as representatives of the class of all citizens." Brennan did, however, object to the portion of the draft that dealt with taxpayer standing. "I have the other view, however, as to Part IIC, which goes beyond the injury-in-fact requirement and holds that respondents lack taxpayer standing because of failure to allege a 'logical nexus' between their taxpayer status and the claim sought to be adjudicated." The Chief Justice declined to delete the offending passage, despite Brennan's threat to dissent.[63]

The nexus requirement was applied in later Burger Court cases. In *Warth v. Seldin,*[64] an action was brought against the town of Penfield (a suburb of Rochester, N.Y.), claiming that Penfield's zoning ordinance excluded persons of low and moderate income. Plaintiffs were corporations and associations that built low-cost housing and minority groups from Rochester with low or moderate incomes. The conference agreed five to three, with Justice Douglas not participating, that plaintiff had no standing. The opinion by Justice Powell held that the required nexus was lacking: the harms suffered were not caused by defendant's allegedly unconstitutional acts, since "their inability to reside in Penfield [may be] the consequences of the economics of the area housing market, rather than of respondents' assertedly illegal acts."[65]

The requirement that plaintiff must assert a "'direct' relationship between the alleged injury and the claim sought to be adjudicated"[66] was also applied in *Simon v. Eastern Kentucky Welfare Rights Organization*.[67] Several indigents and organizations representing them brought suit against the Secretary of the Treasury and the Commissioner of Internal Revenue. They claimed that the IRS violated the Internal Revenue Code by issuing a Revenue Ruling allowing non-profit hospitals that offered only emergency service to indigents to qualify as "charitable" corporations, which resulted in exempting their income from taxation and making donations to them deductible. Plaintiffs claimed that they had been denied treatment at the hospitals because of their indigency and that the IRS ruling "encouraged" the hospitals to deny services to indigents.

At the *Simon* conference, all but Marshall agreed with the Chief Justice that there was no standing (Marshall said he thought that there was standing under *SCRAP*[68] but ultimately joined Brennan's opinion concurring in the judgment.) According to Stewart, "This is a stranger and not a taxpayer"; hence *Warth v. Seldin* governed. For Justice Rehnquist, "taxpayers not being taxed have no standing to attack taxes against other taxpayers."

The most detailed conference discussion of the standing issue was by Powell, who wrote the *Simon* opinion. "It's a suit only against the Treasury," Powell noted, "not any hospital." In the Justice's view, "The asserted injury is . . . speculative." He conceded that "Congress might confer standing. But, under classic standing doctrine, there's none here."

Simon has been criticized as unduly restricting standing, but on the facts of the case the decision appears correct. For standing to exist, the injury must be one that can fairly be traced to the challenged action of defendant, and not solely to some third party. In *Simon* the injury alleged was done to plaintiffs because of the denial of services to them by the hospitals, not by defendants. Injury at the hands of a hospital is not enough to establish a case or controversy where no hospital is a defendant. Plaintiffs did not demonstrate that the acts of the hospitals were caused by the IRS ruling or that the ruling altered the operation of the hospitals. The complaint failed to show a "fairly traceable" causal connection between the injury claimed and the conduct challenged,[69] so that if the relief sought was granted, the injury was likely to be redressed.[70]

POLITICAL QUESTIONS

The "case" or "controversy" limitation of Article III—barring consideration of constitutional issues unless they arise in the course of actual litigation between interested adverse parties—is but one of the limitations developed by the Supreme Court upon the exercise of its authority. Even in true cases presented to it for decision, not all constitutional issues will be determined by the Court. Political questions have, by their very nature, been considered unsuitable for decision. Such questions, the high Court has said, "are wholly confided . . . to the political departments of the government."[71]

Thus, as Justice Brennan explained it in a letter to Chief Justice Burger, "the test of political questions is not whether their subject matter is of 'political' interest, but whether the policies of the doctrine of separation of powers are implicated. . . . [It is] the separation of powers issues that are the real substance of political question law."[72]

The leading modern case on political questions is *Baker v. Carr,*[73] one of the most important Warren Court decisions. In his opinion, Justice Brennan stated that "a court will not ordinarily inquire whether a treaty has been terminated, since on that question 'governmental action . . . must be regarded as of controlling importance.'"[74] Whether a treaty has been terminated is to be determined by the political departments, not the courts. But which political department has the constitutional authority? Does the President alone possess the power or does Congress share in the power—at least to the extent of consent by two-thirds of the Senate, as is required for the making of a treaty?

No constitutional provision deals with these questions, and they were not presented to the Supreme Court until the 1979 case of *Goldwater v. Carter.*[75] Nine senators and sixteen members of the House sought declaratory and injunctive relief against President

Carter after he announced that he was going to terminate the mutual defense treaty with the Republic of China (Taiwan). The President recognized the Peking government as the legal government of China. He did give Taiwan the one-year notice that the termination clause of the treaty required.

A majority at the *Goldwater v. Carter* conference on December 7, 1979, agreed that the complaint should be dismissed. The Chief Justice and Justice Stevens thought that there was no standing; Powell urged that the case was not ripe for review; Rehnquist argued that the case presented a political question. Stewart also said that "the case is nonjusticiable."[76] In addition, Brennan would have decided in favor of the President under his authority to recognize foreign governments, while Blackmun and White would have set the case for oral argument and full consideration.

The consensus among the conference majority was to issue an order stating the holding of the Court in skeleton fashion and remanding for dismissal. After the conference, the Chief Justice and Justice Stevens circulated a proposed order. It was summarized in a "Dear Chief" letter the next day by Justice Powell:

"The order as now drafted holds that the petitioners have no standing. This theory reflects the Wright–Tamm concurrence which stated that a congressman is not injured unless Congress is injured, and that Congress is not injured unless its will has been ignored."

However, Powell wrote, "I am reluctant to go on record holding that individual congressmen (or a group of them) lack standing to raise a constitutional issue concerning the exercise of their official duties. To be sure, we would not be saying that there *never* could be standing. But with no explanation, a flat holding here on standing could create trouble for the future. . . .

"It seems to me that the problem is absence of ripeness rather than lack of standing."

Two days later, on December 10, the standing holding was given the *coup de grace* when Rehnquist pointed out that it was contrary to the leading case on the subject. In a December 10 Memorandum to the Conference, Rehnquist wrote, "as I read the case of *Coleman v. Miller,* 307 U.S. 433 (1939), five out of the nine Justices who participated in that case thought that the 20 Kansas state senators who voted against ratification of the Child Labor Amendment had standing in this Court sufficient for Article III case or controversy purposes to question the ratification by Kansas of that amendment."

Now the Burger–Stevens draft order contained a contrary hold-ing—and without any supporting reasoning or citation of authority. Such an order, Rehnquist wrote, troubled him. "It seems to me that a per curiam of this sort which not only does not cite the authorities upon which it relies for reversal, but seems (at least to me) to run counter to an authority of this Court which has never been overruled, might be thought to give the appearance of 'brute force' and would surely be subject to very valid criticism."

At the December 7 conference, several Justices had referred to the political question issue. The Rehnquist memo now proposed decision on that ground. "I would simply invert the language of the proposed per curiam, and assume that there is standing but hold that the issue decided by the Court of Appeals and by the District Court is a 'politi-cal' question. . . . at least in the field of foreign affairs, the authority of the President to act is a 'political' or 'non-justiciable' question, and Art. III courts are not empowered to pass judgment on it."

The proper posture for the Court here, according to Rehnquist, was to follow the general approach in cases where it was determined that "there was no case or controversy by the time the matter reached this Court even though there was one when the case commenced"—that is, "to vacate and wash out prior federal proceedings." Rehnquist cited the *Munsingwear* case,[77] which had followed his approach in a mootness case. According to the Justice, "I think it is even more im-portant that prior federal decisions be washed out in a case which has decided a political question, at least where the case seeks a decision as to the authority of the President in the field of foreign affairs where no cognizable injury in fact has occurred in the United States."[78]

"The most positive alternative, from my point of view," Rehnquist wrote, "is that if there are six votes to order dismissal of the case, a simple order to that effect be entered, and those of us who felt obliged to support our vote with writing, as I now feel I would, could file separate opinions supporting the order. There would be no Court opinion, even a per curiam, so that our action would have very much the 'one day excursion ticket' effect and would not bind future Courts even to the extent that a per curiam opinion would if and when the question arose again."

Despite the Rehnquist prophecy in his December 10 memo that the *Goldwater* decision "would not bind future Courts," most commen-tators have assumed that Rehnquist's own plurality opinion states the controlling rule and that termination of a treaty is a nonjusticiable political question.[79] In practice, of course, this means that the President does possess the authority to terminate treaties;[80] since presidential termination action is immunized from judicial review, such action can never be subjected to successful legal challenge.

CONGRESSIONAL INFRINGEMENT ON STATES

It should not be forgotten that the political question doctrine is an anomaly in a system in which governmental acts may ordinarily be weighed in the judicial balance and, if necessary, found constitutionally wanting. That is what led Justice Douglas, concurring in the already mentioned case of *Baker v. Carr,* to imply that the whole political question doctrine is one that should be applied most narrowly, if at all. "I feel strongly," he declared, "that many of the cases . . . involving so-called 'political' questions were wrongly decided . . . [T]he category of the 'political' question is in my view narrower than the decided cases indicate."[81]

Certainly, the trend during this century has been to narrow the political question doctrine. Indeed, the more recent Supreme Court jurisprudence has increasingly tended to restrict the political question doctrine to foreign affairs.[82] It is one thing to hold that there must be judicial self-limitation in cases bearing directly on the transaction of external relations. It is quite another to use the political question doctrine as a formula to avoid decision in cases involving only internal affairs. If there is one principle that is the keystone of the organic arch, it is that of having the judiciary as the ultimate arbiter on all domestic constitutional questions. That, indeed, is what Americans normally mean by the rule of law.

Despite this, the Burger Court ruled that an important constitutional issue having nothing to do with foreign affairs did not present any judicial question. *Garcia v. San Antonio Metropolitan Transit Authority*[83] upheld the application of the minimum-wage and overtime provisions of the Federal Fair Labor Standards Act to employees of the publicly owned mass transportation system in San Antonio.

The Court's reasoning bears directly on the political question doctrine. The *Garcia* opinion agreed that "the Constitution's federal structure imposes limitations on the Commerce Clause."[84] But it refused to define those limitations and, more importantly, held that the remedy for their violation was political, not judicial. *Garcia* expressly recognizes the emphasis of the Framers on the need "to ensure the role of the States in the federal system." But it breaks sharply with prior law by concluding that protecting the states from improper exertions of federal regulatory authority is no longer a judicial function. Instead, "the principal means . . . to ensure the role of the States in the federal system lies in the structure of the Federal Government itself." That structure "was designed in large part to protect the States from overreaching by Congress."[85] The states' representation in Congress and their role in the selection of both the executive and legislative branches of the federal government are to be relied on to shield their interests from undue federal invasion.

The Court's ultimate conclusion is that the states must look to the federal political process rather than to enforceable constitutional limitations to protect them against undue congressional encroachment. "State sovereign interests, then, are more properly protected by procedural safeguards inherent in the structure of the federal system than by judicially created limitations on federal power."[86]

Under *Garcia* the scope of Congress's authority over the states under the Commerce Clause no longer presents any judicial question.[87] This is true even though all the accepted requirements for justiciability were met in *Garcia*. There was plainly a "case" or "controversy" in the Article III sense and the plaintiffs had standing. Despite this, the Court held that the judiciary could not decide whether a federal law violated "the limits on Congress' authority to regulate the States under the Commerce Clause."[88] *Garcia* did not deny that there are constitutional limits on the Commerce Clause; it only denied the judicial role in determining those limits.

Such a holding is so "inconsistent with the fundamental principles of our constitutional system"[89] that more than a "modest doubt" may be expressed on both its correctness and durability. The sine qua non of our constitutional system is the rejection of the doctrine that "political officials . . . are the sole judges of the limits of their own power."[90] Yet that is exactly the result under *Garcia* in cases involving claimed infringements by federal action on the states. Instead of judicial review, the states are left only with the "safeguard" of congressional self-restraint.

Garcia makes the question of the constitutionality of congressional infringements upon the states a political question beyond the power of judicial review. It flouts the basic principles of our constitutional law. Those principles rest on the fundamental proposition that it is for "the federal judiciary 'to say what the law is' with respect to the constitutionality of acts of Congress."[91]

Garcia's judicial abnegation ignores the dangers involved in entrusting the political branches with the last word on the legality of their acts. Over a century and a half ago, Justice Story summed up the situation: "The universal sense of America has decided, that in the last resort the judiciary must decide upon the constitutionality of the acts and laws of the general and state governments, so far as they are capable of being made the subject of judicial controversy."[92] From the beginning, this has been particularly true when federal and state power conflict. Judicial review has, indeed, always been the fulcrum of the federal structure. "So long, therefore, as this Constitution shall endure, this tribunal must exist with it, deciding in the peaceful forms of judicial proceeding the angry and irritating controversies between sovereignties, which, in other countries have been determined by the arbitrament of force."[93]

One may expect that the *Garcia* abdication of review power will ultimately be repudiated and that judicial review will again take its place in cases involving federal infringements on the states, as it does in other cases. In these cases, as in others in which constitutionality is at issue, one may share the *Garcia* dissenters' belief "that this Court will in time again assume its constitutional responsibility"[94]—"to say what the law is."[95]

Chapter Three

Separation of Powers
and Presidential Power

"THE SEPARATION of powers is not a doctrinaire concept to be made use of with pedantic rigor," said Justice Cardozo in a passage that has become virtual gospel in our public law.[1] Nevertheless, it was precisely a doctrinaire approach to separation that was increasingly followed by the Burger Court. Indeed, in its most important case on the matter, *Bowsher v. Synar,*[2] the Court adopted a formalistic posture that might well have baneful consequences for the functioning of the American polity. But the impact of the case would have been even more drastic had Chief Justice Burger's draft opinion come down as the final opinion in the case.

BOWSHER V. SYNAR: CONFERENCE AND DRAFT

Bowsher v. Synar was decided on the last day of the final Burger term. During the oral argument, the Solicitor General told the Justices that counsel arguing in favor of the challenged statute were trying to "scare" them with the argument that invalidating the law would endanger the independent agencies, such as the Federal Trade Commission and the Federal Reserve Board.

At this, Justice O'Connor interposed, "They scared me with it."[3]

The *Bowsher* decision may, despite the Court's effort to indicate the contrary, have serious implications for the independent agencies. The years before *Bowsher* had seen a revival of the claim that the independent agencies were unconstitutional: they exercise "executive power" but are not subject to presidential control. Attorney General Meese himself went out of his way to question their constitutionality in a widely reported speech: ". . . [W]e should abandon the idea that there are such things as 'quasi-legislative' or 'quasi-judicial' functions that can be properly delegated to independent agencies. . . . [F]ederal agencies performing executive functions are themselves properly agents of the executive."[4]

The argument against the independent agencies has far-reaching implications. Its scope was pointed out in a case challenging the constitutionality of the Federal Trade Commission: "[Plaintiff] is asking us to adopt a principle that would make every independent federal administrative agency unconstitutional; for the logic of its argument is not limited to the Federal Trade Commission but extends to . . . the other well-known, long-established federal agencies whose members the President selects but cannot remove (before their terms expire) without cause. [Plaintiff] thus is asking us to decree a fundamental change in the structure of American government."[5]

In *Bowsher* the Court dealt with the duties of the Comptroller General under the 1985 Gramm–Rudman Act. The Comptroller General is appointed by the President but may be removed from office by a joint resolution of Congress. Gramm–Rudman was a drastic attempt by Congress to eliminate the now-endemic federal deficit. The Act set a maximum deficit for the fiscal years 1986 through 1991. If, in any fiscal year, the budget deficit exceeded the limit the Act required across-the-board cuts in federal spending. The Act's "reporting provisions" required the directors of the Office of Management and Budget and the Congressional Budget Office to submit deficit estimates and program-by-program reductions to the Comptroller General, who then was to report to the President. The President then had to issue a "sequestration" order mandating the spending reductions. The order became effective unless, within a specified time, Congress legislated reductions.

At the postargument conference, all except White and Blackmun were for invalidating the challenged statute. The Chief Justice stated, "Comptrollers have always thought they were Congressional aides and not independent. . . . The 1985 Act pointedly refused to give the President the powers vested here in the Comptroller General. He's required to decide and issue reports to the President that binds the latter. The implementing responsibility is in the Comptroller General."

Burger referred to the *Myers* case—which held that the President had unlimited removal power over officers appointed by him—and the *Humphrey* case—which ruled that Congress could limit the President's removal power over members of independent agencies to removal only for cause.[6] "*Myers* said the power of removal was crucial to the Presidency. But that power as to the Comptroller Gen-

eral rests with Congress without any meaningful review anywhere."
Burger concluded by asserting, "*Humphrey* did not overrule *Myers*."

The implication was that presidential removal power was a constitutional sine qua non for all officers executing laws. The further implication was that that was also true for the FTC-type independent
agency—which cast doubt on those agencies' constitutionality, as
well as on the *Humphrey* case, which had upheld their validity.

Brennan rejected the Burger implications: "[T]his case raises only
the concern with keeping basic governmental powers distinctly separate. . . . Gramm–Rudman . . . involves a blending of legislative and
executive functions."

"I do not believe," Brennan went on, "that there is any such thing
as 'inherently executive' activity. Rather, the executive function is
only that which Congress leaves to be done in order to carry out the
enforcement of laws it passes. If Congress establishes standards for
clean air in its enactment, establishing such standards is legislative; if
Congress delegates the establishment of standards to an agency, this
same task becomes executive. This is why the Framers feared Congress so much more than it feared the other branches of Government—because the legislative branch has the power to define the
duties and functions that will be left to the other branches. Thus, in
my view, 'execution'—properly understood—begins where the bill
passed by Congress leaves off. . . . Congress cannot keep the power
directly to supervise the officer it leaves with the task of administering
and executing a law. If Congress controls that officer, it controls
executive as well as legislative power. And such a blending of those
powers violates the fundamental principle of separation of powers in
the most literal sense."

Brennan then discussed removal power. "As I have explained, I do
not believe that the power to remove is somehow 'inherently executive.' But the power to remove is the power to *control*. Therefore, to
the extent that Congress asserts power to remove an executive officer,
Congress asserts a power to control that officer's execution. The Constitution does not permit Congress to do that."

Brennan interpreted *Myers* and *Humphrey* so as not to cast any
doubt on the latter's continuing validity. "I note," he told the others,
"that the law in *Myers* was unconstitutional for just this reason—
Congress required the President to obtain approval from the Senate
before allowing removal. I note also that, under this analysis, the law
in *Humphrey's* was *not* unconstitutional. In *Humphrey's*, Congress
did not attempt to retain power to participate in the removal process;

rather, Congress simply qualified the President's removal power. Thus, while *Humphrey's* did implicate the question whether the Constitution requires an absolutely unitary executive, it did not implicate separation of powers properly understood. Therefore, striking down Gramm–Rudman because Congress has retained the power to remove in no way draws *Humphrey's* into question. . . .

"I would make very clear that *Humphrey's* is still good law. The notion that Congress can limit the President's power to remove as long as Congress does not itself participate in the removal process is no longer open to question. Indeed, the First Congress limited the President's power to remove the Comptroller two weeks after it made the famous 'Decision of 1789.' In addition, the ICC and FTC long antedated the New Deal. . . . Moreover, a very large part of Government has been developed in reliance on *Humphrey's* and so the force of *stare decisis* is very powerful."

It was important, Brennan stressed, that *Humphrey* be confirmed because Judge Scalia (as he then was) in the lower court[7] had cast doubt on *Humphrey* as a precedent. "This dictum is wrong and unwarranted, and we should make this very clear."[8]

The other majority Justices agreed that, as Justice O'Connor put it, "The Act violates basic separation of powers concerns. . . . executive branch powers are given to the legislative and you can't do that—the Comptroller General is a legislative person." Justice Stevens stated the same view. "The Comptroller-General is an agent or arm of Congress. The decision by a legislative person is the flaw for me." To Justice Powell, the statute's defect was that "the delegation was to execute a substantial portion of law and Congress reserved the power to remove."

Rehnquist took a somewhat different approach. "Removal doesn't seem too important to me. It's lack of Presidential control rather than the Congressional power of removal that's the flaw." The question, as he saw it, was, "Can the Comptroller General participate in execution?"

Rehnquist's conference statement was consistent with the Burger implication that presidential power over officers vested with executive functions was crucial to constitutionality. But the inference here, too, was that "lack of Presidential control" might invalidate agencies like the FTC.

When the Chief Justice circulated his seventeen-printed-page May 31, 1986, draft *Bowsher* opinion, it became apparent that he had not felt bound by the conference consensus. The Burger draft expressed an expansive view of presidential power that did bring into question the constitutionality of the independent agencies.

The draft stated the truism that "The Constitution does not contemplate that the President alone will 'faithfully execute' the laws." The President is given the power to appoint officers to carry out executive functions and "the draftsmen of the Constitution recognized that a President could not fulfill his Constitutional duties without the power to remove any of his officers who failed to execute his policies faithfully. The commissions issued to many of the major executive officers have recited that the holder serves 'during the pleasure of the President.'"

As Burger summarized the *Myers* case, "this Court emphatically reaffirmed the sole power of a President to remove his officers even though their initial appointment was subject to the approval of the Senate." *Myers* was quoted to emphasize that the Constitution "grants to the President the executive power of the Government, i.e., the general administrative control of those executing the laws, including the power of appointment and removal of executive officers—a conclusion confirmed by his obligation to take care that the laws be faithfully executed."

The Burger draft referred to the *Humphrey* case only to assert that the holding there "is wholly consistent with the Court's holding in *Myers,* and the *Humphrey's Executors* Court took pains to distinguish the *Myers* decision." The draft did not mention the *Humphrey* holding limiting presidential removal power or the Court's emphasis there on the independence of the FTC-type agency. Instead, Burger quoted *Humphrey* on the need to maintain the independence of the three branches, including the *Humphrey* Court's assertion, "The sound application of a principle that makes one master in his own house precludes him from imposing his control in the house of another who is master there."

The Burger draft also noted that a more recent case had "reaffirmed the teaching of *Myers* that the President has 'supervisory and policy responsibilities of the utmost discretion and sensitivity . . . and management of the Executive Branch—a task for which "imperative" reasons requir[e] an unrestricted [presidential] power to remove the most important of his subordinates. . . .'"[9]

Burger concluded that, "from 1789 to the present, it has been recognized that the President's authority to direct his subordinates is enforced through the power of removal." That power, the draft asserted, is . . . even more crucial to the management of the government and execution of the law than it was . . . in 1789."

Next in the Burger draft came a paean to presidential removal power: "A modern President must depend upon literally thousands of subordinates to give effect to the President's policies with fidelity. A subordinate of the Executive Branch . . . must be subject to replacement promptly if a President's policies are to be given effect. . . . [B]ecause the power of removal over Executive Branch officers resides in the President, Congress may not retain the sole power of removal of an officer charged with the execution of the laws." To permit Congress to retain that power would be "precisely the type of aggrandizement by one branch of Government that our Constitutional scheme was designed to prevent."

The rest of the Burger draft found that the Comptroller General was entrusted with executive powers by the challenged statute and that "these functions of the Comptroller General constitute the performance of duties explicitly conferred by the Constitution on the President to execute laws enacted by Congress." The ultimate conclusion was "that the powers vested in the Comptroller General under § 261 violate the command of the Constitution that the President 'shall take Care that the Laws be faithfully executed.'"

BOWSHER V. SYNAR: OBJECTIONS TO DRAFT

The Burger *Bowsher* draft stated a far more expansive view of presidential power than the other Justices were willing to accept. The Chief Justice was stating that the President possessed complete removal power over all officers "charged with implementing a statute." The implication was that the FTC-type independent agencies were unconstitutional, since they were not subject to the President's unlimited removal power, even though they were plainly "charged with implementing a statute."

All of the members of the conference majority except Justice Rehnquist objected to Part III. The first to do so was Stevens. In a June 2, 1986, letter to the Chief Justice, he wrote, "I think your opinion casts substantial doubt on the legal status of independent agencies and that it would be a serious mistake for the Court to adopt this approach."

Stevens asserted "that the rationale of the decision was that the function performed by the Comptroller General could not be performed by an arm of the Legislature unless Congress itself performed that function by the normal process of legislating described in *Chadha*. In other words, the central rationale should rest on *Chadha* rather than *Myers*." Stevens was to state this view more fully in his *Bowsher* concurrence. Stevens issued his separate opinion (concurred in by Marshall) despite the fact that, as the Chief Justice's May 31 Memorandum to the Conference transmitting his draft stated, "There was some expression by those voting as to the importance of a single opinion."

Marshall sent a June 2 "Dear Chief" letter seconding the Stevens letter. Marshall declared, "Your current draft's focus on the need for the President to be 'master in his own house' raises a host of important issues—including the propriety of independent agencies—that we do not have to consider at this time."

In a "Dear Chief" letter the same day, O'Connor summarized the conference accord on the matter: "My review of the Conference notes indicates that, with the possible exception of Bill Rehnquist, those who voted to affirm hoped to make sure that the opinion not cast doubt on the constitutionality of independent agencies. . . . I fear that the opinion as now written, especially Part III, does just that. For example, the draft discusses *Myers* extensively, and suggests that it stands for the general proposition that the power to appoint carries with it the general power to remove. Yet, with the exception of quoting some general language about separation of powers, the draft disregards *Humphrey's Executor* almost entirely. As I read *Humphrey's*, it limits *Myers* considerably by suggesting that Congress can impose significant limitations on the President's removal power over executive officers *even if* they perform 'executive functions.'"

As O'Connor saw it, the draft was wrong in suggesting "that the constitutional infirmity of the Act lies in the fact that the President does not have the power to remove the Comptroller General. In my view, precisely the obverse is the problem: The infirmity lies in the fact the *Congress* does have the power to remove, not in the fact that the *President* does not."

To O'Connor, the basic principle was "that Congress may not both create laws and implement them." In her view, Gramm–Rudman was invalid because it violated this principle. "By giving itself the sole power to remove the Comptroller General, Congress has retained so much control over the office that it is, in effect, participating in the execution of the law it created. . . . This kind of aggrandizement, our cases make clear, is impermissible."

The next day, June 3, Justice Powell wrote to the Chief Justice: "I share generally the views expressed by other Justices who have written you. . . . I could not join an opinion that casts substantial doubt on the constitutionality of the independent agencies, and do not think the vote at Conference supports such a view."

The Chief Justice also received a longer June 3 letter from Justice Brennan. "I agree," Brennan's letter began, "with what has been said by Sandra, John and Thurgood that the reasoning of the opinion in this case must be that Congress cannot retain the power to remove an officer charged with executing the law, and that the opinion should not rely on the rationale that the President must have power to remove such officers. Moreover, I think it very important that the opinion explain the basis and importance of this distinction, since it is only by doing so that we shall make clear that we are not questioning the viability of independent agencies."

The Brennan letter then discussed the separation of powers and its application to the case. "Whether this separation has been observed does not depend upon the formal designation of an officer as being within one or another branch of Government. Rather, it depends upon which branch holds the power actually to *control* that officer. Congress cannot retain the power directly to control an officer to whom it has delegated the task of executing a law whether that officer is formally designated an officer of the legislature or of the executive branch. . . . [T]he power to control is conferred by the power to remove. Thus, to the extent that Congress retains the power to remove a particular officer, it possesses the power to control that officer's performance. It is for this reason, and not because the power to remove is somehow 'inherently executive' that the power to remove is entangled in separation of powers questions."

Brennan's letter stated that there was a difference between "qualifying the President's power to remove" and retention of the removal power itself by Congress. "*Myers* and *Humphrey's Executors* can be understood in light of this distinction. In *Myers* Congress retained power to participate in the removal of an officer performing executive functions. This gave Congress direct control over an officer executing the law and thus violated the fundamental precept that Congress not control execution in addition to legislation. In *Humphrey's Executors,* on the other hand, Congress did not itself participate in the removal process, but simply limited the President's power to remove at will. In upholding the provisions for removal of FTC Commissioners,

Humphrey's Executors made clear that the dictum in *Myers* suggesting that the President's removal power must remain unfettered was incorrect.

"My concern is that by not making the distinction between *Myers* and *Humphrey's Executors* express, the opinion will give credence to the view—strongly suggested by the District Court—that *Humphrey's Executors* was wrong and that the *Myers* dictum was correct. I think that the opinion in this case must expressly draw the distinction between Congress having the power to remove and the President not having that power, and must clearly explain that our decision is based solely on the fact that Congress has removal power (and thus control over) the officer charged with executing the Budget Deficit Act."

Brennan's letter concluded with a reaffirmation of the points he had emphasized at the conference on the need to "reaffirm the holding in *Humphrey's Executors* that Congress can create independent agencies (i.e., agencies staffed by officers not removable at the President's pleasure)."

On June 4, the Chief Justice sent around a Memorandum to the Conference that indicated that he did not think the objections to his draft opinion were really important: "After reviewing carefully the various comments and memos, I conclude the essence of the problem is whether we skin the tiger from the neck to the tail or vice versa. Either way suits me, and the printer is now turning the tiger around. The hide, however, will look the same—at least as I see it."

With an attempt at bonhomie, which, coming from him, too often struck a false note, the Chief Justice wrote at the bottom of the memo: "I'll try to have it around before your second martini!"

Burger did circulate a second draft on June 5, which substantially changed the Part III passages. Now, as in the final *Bowsher* opinion, the *Myers* case was stated only for the proposition that Congress might not directly participate in the removal power. As in the final opinion, too, more emphasis was placed on the *Humphrey* case. The draft stated specifically, "*Humphrey's Executors* involved an issue not presented either in the *Myers* case or in this case—i.e., the power of Congress to limit the President's power to remove an officer 'wholly disconnected from the executive department.' . . . At the same time, the Court cast no doubt on the specific holding of *Myers* dealing with an executive officer that a direct Congressional role in the removal of such an officer is improper." The revised draft supported this statement by the footnote also contained in the final opinion, which indicates that *Bowsher* does not involve "casting doubt on the status of 'independent' agencies because no issues involving such agencies are presented here."

The revised Part III was essentially similar to the final *Bowsher* opinion. But it did contain the statement that the *Humphrey* "Court characterized the Federal Trade Commissioner as an officer who 'occupies no place in the executive power vested by the Constitution in the President,' but acts only 'in the discharge and effectuation of . . . quasi-legislative or quasi-judicial powers, or as an [officer of an] agency of the legislative or judicial departments of the government.'"

In a June 6 letter, Brennan informed the Chief Justice, "Your second draft does indeed accommodate many of my concerns. However, I still have problems with sections of the opinion that, I am afraid, still may cast doubt upon the continuing viability of many—if not all—independent administrative agencies. . . .

"My concern is that reintroducing such notions as whether some function is 'quasi-legislative' or 'quasi-judicial' will encourage claims that all sorts of independent agency activity is neither, and that it must therefore be under the President's control. In other words, I am afraid that reintroducing this analysis will cast doubt upon the legality of much of the work of independent administrative agencies despite disclaimers that the question is presented. This problem can easily be avoided simply by not using this terminology in the discussion."

Brennan further suggested that "rather than quoting the language from *Humphrey's Executors,* I would simply describe the result in that case."

With the terminology changes suggested by Brennan, the Burger opinion was acceptable to the majority Justices (except for Stevens and Marshall, who concurred only in the judgment). The consensus was that stated by Justice Powell, in his June 12 letter joining Burger's opinion, "I certainly do not want to undercut the type of independence the great administrative agencies have enjoyed, and I do not think your opinion—as now drafted—does this."

BOWSHER V. SYNAR: DECISION AND IMPLICATIONS

The *Bowsher* decision held that the role of the Comptroller General in the deficit reduction process violated the separation of powers. As the decision was explained by the Chief Justice in a June 10, 1986, letter to Justice Stevens, "[T]he central point is that the Comptroller General is removable by Congress, and therefore may not be entrusted with executive powers. Part III states: 'In light of these precedents, we conclude that Congress cannot reserve for itself the power of removal of an officer charged with the execution of the laws except by impeachment.' Part IV states: 'Against this background, we see no escape from the conclusion that, because Congress has retained removal authority over the Comptroller General, he is not an officer of the Executive Branch.' Part V states: 'It is apparent then, that Congress has placed executive powers in the hands of an officer who is subject to removal by Congress. . . . The Constitution does not permit breaching the boundaries of separated powers in this fashion.'"

The Court found specifically that the powers assigned to the Comptroller General were, indeed, "executive powers." It rejected the contention that the duties were essentially ministerial and mechanical so that their performance would not constitute "execution of the law" in any meaningful sense. "On the contrary," declared the Court, "we view these functions as plainly entailing execution of the law in constitutional terms." The statute "gives the Comptroller General the ultimate authority to determine the budget cuts to be made and that is the type of decision typically made" by officers charged with executing a statute.

To sum up the *Bowsher* decision: Congress may determine the nature of the executive duty imposed by a statute. But once Congress passes a law, its role ends. Congress can thereafter control the execution of a law only by passing new legislation. By placing the responsibility for execution of the statute in an officer subject only to congressional removal, "Congress in effect has retained control over the execution of the Act and has intruded into the executive function. The Constitution does not permit such intrusion."[10]

In its rigid interpretation of the separation of powers, *Bowsher* ignores the fundamental truth contained in the famous Holmes statement: "The great ordinances of the Constitution do not establish and divide fields of black and white."[11] The separation of powers does not divide government into watertight compartments, with a bright line between the three branches. Here, as in other areas of our public law, the powers of each terminate in a penumbra that shades gradually into the powers of another. *Bowsher* forgets the great principle recognized by Marshall at the outset—that there are powers of doubtful classification in the penumbra that are for the legislature to classify.[12] Instead, the Burger Court increasingly adopted a simple (one is tempted to say simplistic) and "distressingly formalistic view of separation,"[13] which struck down a power whenever it did not fit into the Justices' rigid separation-of-powers classification. In *Bowsher,* for example, the Court invalidated a congressional attempt not to make the Comptroller General subservient to Congress, but to insulate a vital office from political pressures. The alternative left by the Court is to subject the Comptroller General to White House control—the very thing that would destroy the independence and integrity of such an office.

But *Bowsher* has broader implications than its impact upon Comptroller General independence. Most of the majority Justices wanted the opinion to indicate that their decision did not apply to the independent agencies. Because of their objections, Chief Justice Burger added a footnote that specifically distinguishes the FTC-type agencies from the Comptroller General. "Appellants . . . are wide of the mark in arguing that an affirmance in this case requires casting doubt on the status of 'independent' agencies because no issues involving such agencies are presented here." That is true because "statutes establishing independent agencies typically specify either that the agency members are removable by the President for specified causes . . . or else do not specify a removal procedure." There is "no independent agency whose members are removable by the Congress for certain causes short of impeachable offenses, as is the Comptroller General."[14]

The key to constitutionality for the independent agencies is consequently the absence of congressional power to remove their members. The fact that presidential removal power is limited is not enough to support a challenge to their validity; that this makes them independent of presidential control does not cast doubt upon their constitutionality.

In a June 6, 1986, letter to Justice Brennan, the Chief Justice referred to the *Bowsher* footnote and stated, "I think I've made it clear we are casting no doubt on the SEC, FTC, EPA, etc." Burger thus intended his footnote to inter the doctrine of the unconstitutionality of the independent agencies urged by Attorney General Meese. But there is, unfortunately, language in the Chief Justice's opinion that may indicate that its ghost may still walk. The reasoning in the opinion is fundamentally inconsistent with the attempt to seal the Pandora's box of independent agency unconstitutionality. If the power delegated to the Comptroller General had been exercised directly by

Congress through provision in the statute for the mandatory budget cuts, no one would doubt that the power in question was "legislative" in nature. Why then does the Court hold that it is not the same when exercised by the Comptroller General? The answer seems to be that that is the case because it has not been exercised by the legislature itself. The implication then, since the power is plainly not "judicial," is that any power giving effect to a statute that is not exercised by the legislature or the courts must be "executive."

Such an approach may be criticized as being like the familiar parlor game: "It is not animal. It is not vegetable. Therefore, it must be mineral." More important, however, is its implication, despite the *Bowsher* footnote, for the independent agencies. If the carrying out of a law by someone other than the legislature or the courts must be "executive," why is that not true of the powers delegated to the independent agencies? But if that is the case, under *Bowsher's* formalistic approach to the separation of powers, how can those powers be exercised by agencies which are independent of the President? Despite the *Bowsher* footnote, then, it may be doubted that the view that "It has in any event always been difficult to reconcile *Humphrey's Executor's*[15] 'headless fourth branch' with a constitutional text and tradition establishing three branches of government"[16] has finally earned a deserved repose—especially now that its most vigorous judicial proponent[17] has himself been elevated to Olympus.

LEGISLATIVE VETO

Bowsher ruled an Act of Congress invalid on the ground that it infringed upon "The executive Power" delegated to the President by the Constitution. In *Immigration & Naturalization Service v. Chadha*,[18] the Burger Court struck down a power exercised by Congress itself on the same ground. The law invalidated in *Chadha* provided for use of the so-called legislative veto technique. That technique is basically similar to the British practice of laying administrative regulations before Parliament, where they can be annulled by a resolution passed by either House.

In a comparative study of Anglo-American administrative law published in 1972, I noted that, though "Congress has not adopted anything like the British practice of laying regulations before Parliament," the technique of "laying" had been increasingly used under American law.[19] The next decade saw an even greater use of the technique. Over fifty statutes enacted by Congress during that period contained what came to be called "legislative veto" provisions; executive and administrative action could be annulled by resolution of either or both Houses of Congress.

It has been estimated that there were some 200 provisions for annulment by congressional resolution in the statute book at the time of the *Chadha* decision.[20] According to one court, "The increasing use of provisions allowing for legislative veto of administrative lawmaking is a direct reflection of the growing interest in more effective legislative supervision of agency activity."[21] In setting up such procedures for annulment by legislative resolution, an organization of American legislatures declared, "legislatures will be reasserting their legislative prerogatives and regaining the basic law-making authority granted to them."[22] In 1982 the Senate passed a bill providing for laying of all federal rules and regulations before Congress and annulment by resolution of both Houses.[23]

The *Chadha* case arose out of a challenge to the one-House veto of an Immigration and Naturalization Service determination that deportation of an alien should be suspended because of extreme hardship. The immediate issue was only the congressional power to disapprove an agency decision in a particular case. As Powell pointed out in a concurring opinion, "the House's action appears clearly adjudicatory" and the Court could have held that "Congress impermissibly assumed a judicial function."

Powell had taken the same approach at the *Chadha* postargument conference. "I'm inclined to agree . . . that Congress delegated a judicial type function to the Attorney General.[24] They can't delegate to the Executive a quasi-judicial [function] and take it back as they did here." Marshall and O'Connor agreed. According to the former, "Congress gave itself power to adjudicate and that they can't do." O'Connor took a similar position, saying, "Because this is an adjudicative type function, [it] violates the separation of powers."

The others, however, agreed with Chief Justice Burger, who stated to the conference, that "whether [there was an] executive or judicial function in the INS doesn't matter. Perhaps it's a bit of both." The conference also saw agreement on the seriousness of the decision the Court was to reach. "The President and Congress," said the Chief Justice, "have found it a useful tool for over fifty years." Powell also voiced the Justices' reluctance. "I hate to see us invalidate this useful practice," he averred. On the merits, the Chief Justice told the conference, the basic question was, "Can Congress exercise a legislative function using this tool or does it take the whole scheme—[passage by] both Houses and presentment to the President?"

Of course, the Burger question was relevant only if the legislative veto involved exercise of a "legislative" function. White, who was to dissent, questioned whether a legislative function was involved in the veto procedure. "I'm not sure," White told the others, "that presentment to Congress or its action in this context is legislative." Hence, as he saw it, there was "no invasion of any constitutionally assigned powers of the President." White's conclusion was, "I'd say the [legislative] veto is constitutional—this is only reverse legislation."

Powell indicated, "I might agree with Byron." But he voted the other way, saying "the presentment and separation of powers arguments point toward affirmance." Only Rehnquist voted with White to uphold the legislative veto. Rehnquist stressed that "there are some two hundred statutes worked out as a compromise. I don't favor tumbling down the whole structure in an abstract way."

Except for White and Rehnquist, the Justices agreed that the legislative veto was invalid. The consensus was that summarized by the Chief Justice: "If the veto is exercise of legislative power—it's action that alters the rights of an individual—[and they] can't do that without the presentment process."

The most forceful presentation against the veto was made by Brennan: "If this be the passage of a law, then there must be presentment and bicameral approval; if this be something else, then it is beyond the power of Congress—for example, if Congress was merely delegating to itself the powers of an administrative agency to apply the law, where is the judicial review?"

Nor, according to Brennan, was the result affected by the fact that the veto enabled Congress to annul power that it itself had delegated. "In any event, I believe that whatever Congress might assign to an executive branch official, it cannot assign the functions of the Executive Branch to *itself*. Because the bicameral and presentment clauses were designed to hold in check an 'overweaning' legislative branch, this attempt to extend Congress' power is justiciable, and unconstitutional." [25]

The Burger–Brennan presentation persuaded the conference that the legislative veto was invalid. But the majority were still reluctant to decide the far-reaching issue before them. As Justice Powell stated in a February 25, 1982, "Dear Chief" letter, "I share the concern expressed by you and others about having to decide the one-house veto issue. The Executive and Legislative Branches have lived with it for decades—even though uncomfortably at times. If there were a principled way to avoid the issue, I would welcome it." That was true, wrote Powell in a March 9 letter to the Chief Justice, because the issue was one "where the fundamental structure of our government is implicated."

Several Justices urged that, if the issue could not be avoided, it should at least be decided narrowly. "I'll likely affirm," O'Connor said. "But we should do it very narrowly." The approach she favored was stated in a March 11, 1982, letter to the Chief Justice: "The decision in this case would not necessarily resolve the issue in other cases involving different types of 'legislative vetoes.'"

But the majority recognized that a narrow decision, in Brennan's words in a February 25 letter to Justice Powell, "would not settle the persisting controversy between the Executive and the Congress concerning the lawfulness of these one-house veto provisions." Instead, the *Chadha* decision was a categorical invalidation of the legislative veto. Chief Justice Burger delivered a broadside opinion that placed all laws containing legislative-veto provisions beyond the constitutional pale. The exercise by Congress of power to annul executive or administrative action by resolution of one or both Houses was ruled a patent violation of the separation of powers. The Constitution requires "that the legislative power of the Federal government be exercised in accord with a single, finely wrought and exhaustively considered procedure." That procedure is by "bicameral passage followed by presentment to the President" for his signature or veto. "It is beyond doubt that lawmaking was a power to be shared by both houses and the President." [26] The legislative veto is invalid because it permits Congress alone to exercise what amounts to veto-proof lawmaking power.

"This opinion," the Chief Justice had written to Brennan in an April 17, 1983, letter, headed Personal, "will get microscopic—and not always sympathetic (!) scrutiny across the park." But criticism of *Chadha* is not necessarily limited to Capitol Hill. Despite the Court's decision, the Constitution has never been construed as setting up a rigid separation of powers. Indeed, the very power that the Court asserts was violated by the congressional action—the President's veto power—is a legislative power. The constitutional grant to the President illustrates a blending of power intended to enable a check to be imposed by another branch upon exercises of legislative power by the legislative branch. The key principle is a system of checks and balances.

The *Chadha* opinion is based upon the type of formalistic construction of the separation of powers doctrine that would have made the rise of modern administrative law impossible. As the dissent by Justice White points out, the Court's decision that all "lawmaking" must be shared by Congress and the President "ignores that legislative authority is routinely delegated to the Executive branch, to the independent regulatory agencies." [27] If congressional action under the legislative-veto technique is "lawmaking" that must be shared by Congress and the President, why is the same not true of the executive and administrative rulemaking that the technique attempts to control?

The key issue is, indeed, one of control. The great need in an era of expanding administrative authority is to establish effective safeguards outside the executive branch. Congress is the one organ of government both responsive to the electorate and independent of the administration. The legislative veto enabled the American legislature to assume an effective role as supervisor of administration. There is no more important role for the contemporary legislature. "The political philosopher," wrote Woodrow Wilson, "has something more than a doubt with which to gainsay the usefulness of a sovereign representative body which confines itself to legislation to the exclusion of all other functions." [28]

The Court's condemnation is in such sweeping terms that it leaves no room for any use of the legislative-veto technique. Yet the problem of control remains. As John Stuart Mill tells us, "the proper office of a representative assembly is to watch and control the government." [29] What tools are left to Congress, after this Supreme Court decision, to enable it to perform this function? None that is as effective as the legislative-veto technique.

Congress can, to be sure, enact laws limiting executive authority and overruling invalid administrative exercise of power. These will, however, be subject to presidential veto and the President will rarely agree to restrictions upon his own administration's authority. It is also unreal to assume that Congress will now impose detailed restrictions in laws delegating power to the executive. The modern trend has been all the other way. Congress has neither the time nor the expertise needed to draft detailed standards limiting delegated authority. In addition, Congress is too often unwilling to make the hard choices needed to set meaningful policies for the executive. It has always been easier to pass a statute with vague language about the "public interest"—high sounding and meaningless in terms of restricting executive power. With the negative resolution technique now gone, it will be all but impossible for Congress to exercise its vital role of what Wilson called "vigilant oversight of administration."[30] The *Chadha* decision will ensure that Americans realize more than ever that *oversight* is the noun of the verb *overlook* as well as *oversee*.

NIXON CASE: BURGER DRAFT

Students of the Burger Court have pointed out that, while the Court invalidated important congressional acts on the ground that they infringed upon executive powers, the Justices refused to hold unconstitutional any presidential act as an infringement of congressional authority.[31] In only one case did the Burger Court vote against the President in a separation-of-powers case, and there the President had interfered with the judicial process by denying evidence needed in a criminal trial.[32]

The case in question was *United States v. Nixon*[33]—in many ways the culmination of the Watergate scandal. The case itself arose from a motion filed by the Watergate Special Prosecutor for a subpoena duces tecum directing President Nixon to produce certain tape recordings and documents relating to his conversations with aides and advisers. Following the return of an indictment against top White House aides and others for crimes arising out of the scandal, the special prosecutor determined that the tapes and documents were relevant evidence and a subpoena was issued. The President moved to quash the subpoena, asserting that conversations between a President and his close advisers were privileged and that the doctrine of separation of powers precluded judicial review of his privilege claim. This view would have meant unqualified presidential immunity from judicial process.

The President's claim was later characterized by the Court as "a claim of absolute Presidential privilege against inquiry by the coordinate Judicial Branch."[34] On May 20, 1974, District Judge Sirica denied the motion to quash and ordered the President to deliver the tapes and documents. An appeal was filed in the U.S. Court of Appeals, but before that court could act the Supreme Court, on June 15, granted a petition by the special prosecutor, asking the highest tribunal to hear the case on an expedited basis.

The Justices had followed the unfolding scandal with increasing fascination, and by the time the *Nixon* case reached them, their views on most of the issues had already been formed.

The day after the oral argument, on Tuesday, July 9, 1974, eight Justices met in conference—Justice Rehnquist having disqualified himself. As Brennan told former Chief Justice Warren later that day, the Justices were united in holding that the President must turn over the subpoenaed tapes and other documents, although none disputed the existence of some executive privilege. The conference discussion in this respect was summarized in a July 12 "Dear Chief" letter circulated by Powell: "we were all in accord that there is a privilege of confidentiality with respect to presidential conversations and papers. We also agreed that it is a qualified privilege and not absolute or unreviewable; and, in this case, that the Special Prosecutor has made a showing which overcomes the privilege and justifies *in camera* review."

However, according to the Powell letter, "We were not entirely in agreement as to the standard to be met in overcoming the privilege. . . . [S]ome of us emphasized that a President of the United States (and it must be remembered that we are speaking not just of the present incumbent) must be entitled to a higher level of protection against disclosure than a citizen possessing no privilege who is charged with crime or who may be a witness in a criminal case." The opposing view was stated by White, who was to write the draft on the matter that formed the basis for the *Nixon* opinion.

Another matter on which there was some difference at the conference was that of the authorship of the opinion. Justice Brennan said that the Court should emphasize its decision by issuing the strongest opinion possible and this could be done if the Court delivered a joint opinion—in the name of each of the participating Justices. The Court had done so only once before—in the 1958 Little Rock school desegregation case,[35] where the joint opinion of the Justices dramatically underlined their unanimity.

Chief Justice Burger refused to go along. "The responsibility is on my shoulders," he said. He would prepare the opinion and would circulate its different parts as he finished them.

The Chief Justice circulated his draft *Nixon* opinion in five separate sections.[36] The heart of the Burger draft, as of the final *Nixon*
opinion, was its section on "The Claim of Executive Privilege." The
draft was more favorable to the presidential claims than the final
opinion.

As a starting point, the Burger draft, like the final opinion, rejected
the presidential claim of "an absolute privilege as against a subpoena
essential to enforcement of criminal statues [*sic*]." But the draft went
on to say, "Since we conclude that the legitimate needs of the judicial
process may outweigh presidential privilege when the privilege is
based solely on the generalized need for confidentiality, it is necessary, in a given case to resolve these competing interests in a manner
that preserves the essential functions of each branch."

The implication is that, where an "essential" function of the
President is involved, the privilege claim may prevail even over the
needs of the judicial process. This implication is strengthened by
the draft's later development of the notion of presidential "core
functions," which would also prevail in any privilege case. "Under
Article II a President, for example, exercising certain of his enumer-
ated war powers, as in repelling a hostile attack, or exercising the
veto power, or conducting foreign relations is exercising powers at
the very core of his constitutional role. The courts have shown the utmost deference to presidential actions in performance of these core
functions."

The draft discussed two cases involving foreign relations and military secrets[37] that "dealt with a presidential function lying at the core
of Article II authority. In the present case, however, the generalized
claim of confidentiality relates to none of the kinds of activities for
which courts have traditionally shown the utmost deference, but on
the contrary the claim is somewhat removed from the central or core
function of the chief executive." In this case, "the need for relevant
evidence in the conduct of a criminal trial lies at the very core of the
Article III function of a federal court." In such a situation, the Article
III function prevails. "Thus here the core function of Article III is
pitted against a generalized need for presidential confidentiality without a showing that such confidentiality is necessary to protect a core
function of Article II. Under these circumstances the generalized assertion of privilege must yield to the demonstrated, specific need for
evidence in a pending criminal trial."

The difficulty with the "core function" approach is indicated by the following queries written by a Justice on his draft copy: "What does this mean? May St. Clair[38] argue other core functions at stake? What is a core function?"

The Burger draft recognized foreign relations and military secrets as involving "core functions" of the President, but it also recognized that the "core function" concept is not limited to these matters. Instead, it stated that "by referring to the deference due to all discussions of military and foreign policy secrets, we intend to intimate no view that discussion of highly sensitive domestic policies, for example, devaluation of the currency, imposition or lifting of wage and price controls, would not be entitled to a very high order of privilege, since the economic consequences of disclosure of such discussions could well be as pervasive and momentous as the disclosure of military secrets."

If that was true of "highly sensitive domestic policies," the same might be true of other domestic acts involving presidential duties "lying at the core of Article II authority." The "core function" concept has what Justice Black once termed "accordion-like qualities."[39] It is capable of expansion or contraction in each individual case, since it is without any defined limits to ensure that it will be kept within proper bounds, and counsel for the President could argue in *Nixon* that "core functions [are] at stake." As the draft put it, "The courts have shown the utmost deference to presidential actions in the performance of . . . core functions." If a court finds that a "core function" is involved, under the Burger approach, the President's prerogative in the matter must remain untouched.

NIXON CASE: OPINION BY COMMITTEE

In discussing the final *Nixon* opinion, a Justice who took part in the case characterized it as "opinion by committee." His characterization is supported by a paper in his file on the case. Typed on one page and without any identification, it reads simply:

Opinion Outline

   I. Facts [HAB]
   II. Appealability [WOD]

III. Intra-branch dispute [WJB or beefed-up WEB version]
IV. Rule 17(c) [BRW]
 V. [Merits of executive privilege: WEB: LFP as revised by PS]
VI. Standards to be met before in camera inspection is ordered [LFP as revised by WJB]
VII. The Court's judgment and order [WJB]

When the Justices saw how weak the Burger draft was, especially the crucial section on executive privilege, they concluded that substantial revisions were necessary. Rather than wait for new drafts by the Chief Justice, they decided to send him their own drafts of the different sections for him to use in his redrafts. These sections were to be drafted primarily by the Justices whose initials appear next to them.

An important consequence of the *Nixon* drafting process was the absence of that primary ingredient of superior Supreme Court opinions—one strong hand. Instead, there was the "opinion by committee," and the committee had to use as its foundation the unsatisfactory Burger draft. To soften the rebuff to the Chief Justice the other Justices used his draft language as much as possible. The result was that much of the final opinion reads as though it was the work of at least two authors.

The other Justices were particularly unwilling to accept the Burger draft on executive privilege with its doctrine of "core functions," which they felt tilted the balance unduly in favor of the presidential claim. The executive-privilege section was redrafted by Stewart, who had prepared a draft on the subject even before the Chief Justice had sent around his draft. As far as possible, Stewart also used the Chief Justice's. language in his redraft; but he eliminated the "core function" analysis.

By this point, it had been made clear to Chief Justice Burger that he could not secure a majority (indeed, he would remain virtually alone) if he did not abandon his "core function" analysis, and he gave way. On July 23 he circulated a new draft of the executive-privilege section. It was a modified version of the Stewart redraft. The "core function" concept was now completely eliminated.

The Burger redraft and the opinion as a whole was approved at a conference which met at 1:30 P.M. on July 23. The final printed draft was sent around later that day and met no objection. The next day the decision was announced and the opinion summarized by the Chief Justice to a packed courtroom. Seventeen days later President Nixon resigned.

NIXON CASE: EXECUTIVE PRIVILEGE CONFIRMED

The best description of the end product in *Nixon* was Burger's description of the opinion in an earlier case. The final draft there, wrote the Chief Justice in a Memorandum for the Conference, "resembles the proverbial 'horse put together by a committee' with a camel as the end result. But then even the camel has proven to be useful"[40] That was also true of the final *Nixon* opinion. With all its faults, it did reject the extreme claim of absolute executive privilege and was the catalyst that forced Nixon from the White House.

One should not underestimate the importance of subjecting the President himself to the rule of law,[41] but those who look upon the *Nixon* decision as an unqualified triumph of the law over presidential power have not read the Court's opinion carefully enough. Although the Court held against the President on the case presented, it indicated that presidential claims of privilege would prevail in virtually all other cases.

The leading work on executive privilege, published just before the *Nixon* decision, termed executive privilege a "constitutional myth."[42] While *United States v. Nixon* rejected the presidential claim of absolute executive privilege, it was far from the repudiation of executive privilege for which many had hoped. Though it seemed to limit presidential power, the Court's decision held for the first time that executive privilege has a valid constitutional basis.

Chief Justice Burger later summarized the *Nixon* holding as follows: "In *United States v. Nixon* we unanimously concluded that private Presidential conversations are presumptively privileged and we acknowledged that the President has a legitimate expectation of privacy in his private conversations with close aides. . . . But we held that the President's 'generalized assertion of privilege must yield to the demonstrated, specific need for evidence in a pending criminal trial.'"[43]

The presumptive privilege recognized by *Nixon* has two aspects: (1) the privilege resulting from the need "to protect military, diplomatic, or sensitive national security secrets"; (2) the "claim of public interest in the confidentiality of [presidential communications]."[44]

The Court, in stating that the privilege for the latter is a qualified one,[45] intimated that the privilege for the former is broader. This interpretation was confirmed in a later case, in which the Court made reference to "the more particularized and less qualified privilege relating to the need 'to protect military, diplomatic, or sensitive national security secrets. . . .'"[46]

If the privilege for matters relating to national security and foreign affairs is indeed "less qualified," does that imply either that it is not subject to judicial control or that it is subject to less judicial scrutiny? Either implication is disturbing. If there is a "less qualified" privilege relating to security and diplomacy, what keeps a Chief Executive from claiming such a privilege in order to prevent disclosures that have nothing to do with security or foreign affairs? What, indeed, would have happened in *Nixon* itself if the presidential claim of privilege had been based upon the need to protect national security, rather than the more generalized need to protect the confidentiality of presidential communications?

While Nixon personally lost the battle, presidential power may still have won the war because of the Court's recognition of "a presumptive privilege for Presidential communications."[47] In *Nixon*, the Court held that the general privilege of confidentiality of presidential communications must be balanced against the effect of the privilege on the effective functioning of the judicial branch. The balance was struck against the claim of privilege in that case because the Court determined that the interest in presidential confidentiality was outweighed by the impediment to the fair administration of criminal justice.

It is questionable whether the balance would be tilted against the presidential claim of privilege in a case which did not present a comparable fact pattern. In the vast majority of situations in which executive privilege is asserted, the plaintiff's claim is not based upon the need for specific evidence required in a criminal trial. The *Nixon* opinion itself noted that there would be "infrequent occasions of disclosure because of the possibility that such conversations will be called for in the context of a criminal prosecution."[48]

United States v. Nixon thus may be more a moral than a material victory. Even though the Court ruled that in an appropriate case the highest executive officer is subject to judicial process, the immediate holding of *Nixon* is one that will rarely, if ever, be applied again. The

Court's recognition of presidential privilege could become the basis for expanded use of the executive-privilege doctrine.

PRESIDENTIAL APPOINTING POWER

Nixon was the only case lost by a President in the Burger Court. In all other cases, the Court took an expansive view of executive authority. In *Buckley v. Valeo,*[49] the Justices reaffirmed the President's position as administrative chief of the federal government. That position stems from the presidential appointing power. Because of it, all "Officers of the United States" are chosen by the Chief Executive. The policies of the executive branch are made and carried out by the President and his appointees. The power to create federal offices may be vested in Congress; but the power to appoint to those offices is vested exclusively in the President.[50]

In *Buckley,* Congress attempted to evade this basic principle by setting up a federal agency and providing for presidential appointment of only a minority of its members. The Federal Election Campaign Act, as amended in 1974, created the Federal Election Commission, charged with administering and enforcing the Act. The commission was composed of six voting members: two to be appointed by the president pro tempore of the Senate, two by the Speaker of the House, and two by the President, subject to confirmation by both houses of Congress. The lower court rejected the claim that the statute's appointment provision violated the constitutional requirement for presidential appointment of all federal officers.

Though their final decision on the appointment of FEC members was unanimous, the Justices were closely divided at the postargument conference. Chief Justice Burger began by pointing out, "Congress can delegate what it itself may do. But some of the things the Commission can do, Congress can't." Because the FEC had executive functions, Congress could not appoint its members. "That goes too far," Burger asserted, "and I'd have to reverse."

The Chief Justice was supported by Justices Blackmun and Rehnquist. Referring to the appointment provision, Blackmun declared, "I generally feel negative about the constitutionality of this. Maybe Senate confirmation is as much authority as Congress constitutionally can have." Rehnquist said that he took a "dimmer view" on the appointment provision than White and Brennan, who had spoken for affirmance. "Issuance of regulations," Rehnquist stated, "has been a function of *independent* agencies. But is this one?" He noted that there was "simply no law" on the matter and concluded that he would reverse.

As noted, Brennan and White had spoken in favor of the appointment provision. White said that the appointment was "troublesome, but I think I'd sustain the composition. . . . There's no question for me that Congress can authorize regulation power and that's not an executive function." White noted that the FEC doesn't "have power to prosecute criminally and, if it did, it's invalid. They can bring a civil enforcement proceeding, but the Commission eschews that and we ought to wait until they try it." Justices Marshall and Powell also made statements for affirmance. Since Justice Stewart passed on the issue, the conference vote was four to three in favor of the appointment provision.

The opinion in *Buckley,* like that in *Nixon,* was an "opinion by committee." Stewart urged that a committee of the Justices should draft a per curiam opinion. The Chief Justice reluctantly agreed and gave up his function of leading the Court in the case to a committee composed of Stewart, Brennan, and Powell. The committee divided the work among the various members of the Court. The final draft was reviewed by a committee of clerks from the different chambers; but, as Powell put it in a January 19, 1976, letter, it was the job of "the 'Clerks Committee' to harmonize stylistic and verbiage differences between the several Parts subject, of course, to review by each of us." [51]

The section on the appointment of FEC members was written by Rehnquist. His draft striking down the appointment provision was joined by the other Justices, including those who had voted the other way at the conference.

The *Buckley* opinion was based upon a straightforward reaffirmation of the exclusive presidential position in the appointment process. It held that the FEC appointment provision violated the constitutional provision for appointment of "Officers of the United States" by the President, subject to Senatorial confirmation. The Court construed the term "Officers of the United States" to "include 'all persons who can be said to hold an office under the government.' . . . its fair import is that any appointee exercising significant authority pursuant to the laws of the United States is an Officer of the United States." [52] Unless he is an "inferior officer" whose appointment Congress had by law vested in department heads or the courts or unless their selection is provided for elsewhere in the Constitution, *all* offi-- cers of the United States must be appointed by the President in accordance with the Appointment Clause of Article II.

Buckley v. Valeo lends emphasis to the constitutional role of the President as administrative head of the government. Its principle plainly applies to all federal agencies, even those with predominantly legislative and judicial functions. Though Congress may provide for the independence of such agencies from presidential control,[53] it may not do so through exclusion of the President from the selection process. Both *Buckley* and *Bowsher* confirm that the presidential duty to "take care that the Laws be faithfully executed" ensures a correlative power to appoint and remove those officers through whom the laws are, in practice, executed.

FOREIGN AFFAIRS: TREATIES AND EXECUTIVE AGREEMENTS

In a 1979 memorandum, Justice Rehnquist referred to a conference discussion on *Goldwater v. Carter*[54]: "I agree with the comments expressed at various points in the Conference discussion on Friday to the effect that, at least in the field of foreign affairs, the authority of the President to act is a 'political' or 'non-justiciable' question, and Article III courts are not empowered to pass judgment on it."[55]

The deferential attitude toward presidential action in cases involving foreign affairs is one that was consistently displayed by the Burger Court. In our discussion of *Goldwater v. Carter,* we saw that a challenge to the presidential termination of a treaty was rejected—with a four-Justice plurality, speaking through Rehnquist, holding that the issue presented was "nonjusticiable because it involves the authority of the President in the conduct of our country's foreign relations."[56]

The end result of the *Goldwater* decision was to uphold the exercise of presidential power, since the Court, in effect, immunized it from judicial review. In other cases in which presidential action dealing with foreign affairs was challenged, the action was expressly upheld.

A decision upholding an executive agreement was rendered in *Dames & Moore v. Regan.*[57] At issue was the constitutionality of President Carter's executive agreement with Iran to secure the release of Americans held hostage in that country. In response to the seizure of the hostages, the President, acting pursuant to the International

Emergency Economic Powers Act (IEEPA) froze all Iranian government assets. After lengthy negotiations, the United States and Iran signed an agreement in Algiers. In return for release of the hostages, the United States agreed to terminate all legal proceedings against Iran in American courts and "to nullify all attachments and judgments obtained therein, to prohibit all further litigation based on such claims" and, instead, to transfer all such claims for binding arbitration to a new Iran-United States Claims Tribunal. Presidents Carter and Reagan issued executive orders implementing the Algiers agreement. Among them was an order that "suspended" all "claims which may be presented to the . . . Tribunal."

Petitioner had sued Iran in a federal court over a year before the Algiers agreement, alleging that it was owed over $3 million by the Iran Atomic Energy Organization. The court issued orders of attachment against Iranian property to secure any judgment that might be entered in petitioner's favor. Just after the Algiers agreement, the court granted summary judgment in petitioner's favor. Because of the agreement and executive orders, however, the court stayed execution of its judgment and vacated all prejudgment attachments and stayed further proceedings. Petitioner then sued to prevent implementation of the agreement with Iran, claiming that the government's actions "were unconstitutional to the extent they adversely affect petitioner's final judgment . . . , its execution of that judgment . . . , its prejudgment attachments, and its ability to continue to litigate."

Did the President have the constitutional authority to negotiate changes in foreign policy through an executive agreement rather than a treaty? And could the President by executive agreement effectively nullify a court judgment and its enforcement through attachment and execution? Even if the President possessed the power, did not the suspension of petitioner's claim constitute a taking of property, in violation of the Fifth Amendment, in the absence of just compensation?

The Justices first had to consider the statutory background. IEEPA expressly empowered the President to "compel," "nullify," or "prohibit" any "transfer" with respect to, or transactions involving, any property in which any foreign country has any interest. Chief Justice Burger emphasized this point in his conference presentation, saying "IEEPA authorizes termination and transfer, so [the President] has express Congressional authority."

The others agreed with the Chief Justice. According to Brennan, "IEEPA expressly empowered the President to transfer free of liens."

Or as Blackmun concluded, "Attachment is easy. IEEPA confirms Presidential power." The basis for congressional power in this respect was stated by White: "Congress could say no attachments and, if it did, no one could get one. That's really what IEEPA does—it allows the President to immunize property of [a] foreign country from attachment." White recognized that "*Zittman* and *Orvis*[58] say some things to the contrary, but I'm prepared to eat those words."

Thus, as Chief Justice Burger put it, the suspension of claims was authorized by statute. "If not enough," Burger went on, the Court "could fall back on inherent power." The others agreed on this also. "Congress has acquiesced in this," said White. Yet "even without it I'd have no problem resting on constitutional power." Blackmun was also prepared to "go on inherent power." Rehnquist stated that IEEPA alone "doesn't [give the power to suspend] but inherent [power] sanctioned by Congress will do it."

On the "taking" issue, the Justices agreed that the claim was not yet ripe for review—that, in Brennan's words, though the "inherent power to settle [is] limited by the Bill of Rights," there was "no loss yet, therefore the taking claim[is] premature."

Rehnquist stated that the Court should write a narrow opinion. He was not completely satisfied with relying on congressional authorization and acquiescence, "but the alternative of constitutional power not subject to Congressional restraints [is] even worse."

In *Dames & Moore,* the Court adopted an expedited briefing and argument schedule, "Because the issues presented here are of great significance and demand prompt resolution."[59] The opinion was assigned to Rehnquist, who worked with unusual speed. His draft was circulated on June 26, 1981, only two days after the argument, and the final opinion of the Court was issued on July 2.[60]

It is somewhat ironical that Rehnquist should have played the key role in expediting *Dames & Moore.* In a Memorandum to the Conference while *Goldwater v. Carter* was pending, Rehnquist wrote that the possibility of accelerated briefing, argument, and decision "is the worst possible alternative. . . . I mentioned in Conference Friday the tremendously accelerated schedule of argument and decision in the *Steel Seizure Cases.*[61] . . . [T]his Court has been suffering for nearly 30 years from an opinion which much too casually brushed off serious collateral questions in a determined effort to reach and decide the merits of a very important constitutional question. It was undoubtedly a good faith effort by the Court to respond to an event of great public importance, but that is not necessarily the formula for a decision which makes good law."

There is also irony in the fact that the Rehnquist *Dames & Moore* opinion relied in large part on the *Steel Seizure* case to support the decision upholding the executive agreement and the orders enforcing it. Rehnquist based the holding upon congressional authorization and acquiescence, much as did the oft-cited *Steel Seizure* opinion of Justice Jackson.[62] As a Rehnquist letter explained it, "we have chosen to rest the 'suspension of claims' neither on the delegation contained in § 1732 nor in IEEPA, but simply refer to them along with a host of similar congressional instances of acquiescence in the exercise of Presidential power in a certain area." This, noted Rehnquist, was "consistent with Jackson's statement in *Youngstown*." [63]

In addition, the *Dames & Moore* opinion did expressly reaffirm presidential power to enter into executive agreements settling the claims of the respective nationals. The agreement between the United States and Iran was thus valid even though it was entered into without the advice and consent of the Senate.

The original *Dames & Moore* draft[64] contained a statement that gains particular interest because of Rehnquist's normally restrictive view on delegations of power to the President and other officials. In this case, the Rehnquist draft asserted, the failure of Congress specifically to delegate authority was not determinative. Instead, "When Congress has enacted legislation delegating broad authority to the President to act in certain circumstances, and the President takes action in a similar and analogous circumstance, though perhaps not precisely covered by the statute, it is reasonable to suppose similar congressional willingness that the President have broad authority. The enactment of legislation closely related to the question of the President's authority in a particular case which evinces legislative intent to accord the President broad discretion may be considered to 'invite' 'measures on independent presidential responsibility.' *Youngstown*, 343 U.S., at 637 (Jackson, J., concurring)."

This passage in the draft led to a "Dear Bill" letter from Justice Blackmun: "Given your views on the delegation doctrine in general, I was a little surprised by the presence of those sentences. More importantly, however, I have no idea where such a rule could lead. . . . I would be much happier if those sentences could be deleted." [65]

Rehnquist explained in a "Dear Harry" letter later the same day. "I think," Rehnquist wrote, "I have quite consistently maintained that the 'delegation doctrine,' as you refer to it, has a different reach in foreign affairs than it does in domestic affairs. I think the Court so stated in *United States v. Curtiss–Wright Export Corp.*, . . . while at the same time making it clear that such delegation might not be upheld in a purely domestic matter." [66] Ultimately Rehnquist did delete the second sentence in the offending passage. In the final opinion, the first sentence appears as originally drafted. [67]

Though the Justices did unanimously uphold the Algiers agreement as a valid exercise of the presidential power to enter into executive agreements, they, like the rest of the country, were unhappy at paying what amounted to ransom. Their attitude was well stated in a letter from Powell. "I must add, just for my own personal satisfaction, that if the *honor* of the United States had not been pledged, I would have had great difficulty in sustaining the validity of the Agreements of Algiers. Having been coerced by the terrorist conduct of Iran in seizing and holding American diplomats for ransom, the United States certainly was not *legally* bound by these agreements. They would have been voidable, I think, in the courts of any country that had a civilized legal system as well as before the International Court of Justice. Having said this, I agree that the President had authority to enter into these agreements." [68]

FOREIGN AFFAIRS: TRAVEL ABROAD

Even the Warren Court upheld the governmental power to restrict travel abroad where national security might be adversely affected. In *Zemel v. Rusk*, [69] where the Secretary of State's refusal to validate passports for travel to Cuba was sustained, Chief Justice Warren himself wrote a draft opinion that went even further by indicating that the Court was upholding the validity of prohibitions against travel to Cuba and not only refusals to validate passports for such travel. On the other hand, the Warren *Zemel* draft also asserted "that the Executive possesses no inherent power to inhibit the travel of American citizens." This assertion was, however, deleted at Justice Harlan's insistence. Harlan, for one, declared, "I am not prepared to hold that the President's power over foreign relations would not have supported what was done here." [70]

In two cases, the Burger Court also upheld restrictions on the right to travel abroad, but it did so in a manner that made deference to the political departments the dominant theme. The first case was *Haig v.*

Agee.[71] Agee, a former agent of the Central Intelligence Agency, was running a campaign to expose CIA officers, agents, employees, and sources. He traveled to different countries and trained collaborators who publicly identified individuals and organizations with CIA ties. According to the Court, the record revealed that those identifications divulged classified information, violated Agee's contract not to make uncleared statements about the CIA, prejudiced the ability to obtain intelligence, and resulted in violence against those identified.

After Agee had persisted in these actions for some years, the Secretary of State revoked his passport on the ground that Agee's activities "have caused serious damage to the national security and foreign policy of the United States." Agee sued, claiming that Congress had not authorized the revocation and that his constitutional rights had been violated. Agee moved for summary judgment, and the lower court ruled in his favor.

The Court was, of course, bound by the procedural rule requiring it to accept the government's factual allegations that Agee was causing serious damage to national security as true for purposes of the summary-judgment proceeding.[72] But it is important to realize that most of the Justices had no doubt that those allegations did, indeed, state the facts in the case. Their attitude was once again stated in a letter by Justice Powell: "None of the material facts in the affidavits is refuted or denied. Moreover, counsel for Agee conceded, in an exchange with the District Court, that 'Agee was causing or likely to cause serious damage to the national security,' and that 'there were no facts in dispute.' . . . The possibility of a trial resulting in Agee proving . . . that his conduct had not caused—and indeed was not intended to cause—serious damage to the foreign policy and national security of the United States, is so unlikely as to be deminimis. . . . The affidavits submitted for and against the summary judgment motion afford—at least for me—more than enough evidence to revoke Agee's passport."[73]

Except for Brennan and Marshall, the others agreed at the post-argument conference that Agee's passport was validly revoked. The narrowest view in favor of the government was stated by Chief Justice Burger. Agee's "acts were in violation of his own agreements and he'll continue as his speech shows. . . . I'd reverse on [the] narrow ground he openly violated his contract with [the] Government."

Agee had claimed that, since there was no express statutory authorization for passport revocation, the regulation providing for it had to be supported by a longstanding administrative practice. Brennan supported this contention. However, Stewart, who spoke next, said that he was "not convinced that [the] administrative practice test is [the] proper standard." White agreed. "The statute," he said, "doesn't authorize any cancellations, but it's conceded that passports may be revoked for the same reasons they may be [denied].[74] If that's so, whenever a [new] reason comes up, it's the first time and administrative practice isn't a controlling requirement." Stevens also touched on the point, saying that White was "correct that [there is] always a first time."

A number of Justices stressed what Stevens called the "delegation to [the] President of broad, indeed, complete discretion." The statute delegating the passport power, said Powell, had been "on [the] books a long time and [there had] never [been] an attempt to limit its broad authority to the President." Rehnquist went even further, stating that, while the "right to travel abroad . . . may be regulated or cancelled by Congress, I also doubt Congress can restrict [the] President's right to regulate passports."

The lower court had decided for Agee on the ground that Congress had not authorized the passport revocation. But Agee had also raised constitutional issues—in particular the claim that the revocation violated his First Amendment right to criticize government. "My notes" Powell later wrote, "indicate that five of us indicated at Conference that both the statutory and constitutional issues should be decided."[75] The five, as Blackmun put it at the conference, "would also decide [the] constitutional questions raised and find them without merit." The reason for such a finding was succinctly stated at the conference by Powell: the "First Amendment can't protect 'fingering' our agents." Rehnquist said it somewhat differently. "My view," he said, is "that [the] First Amendment [claim] fails for [the] same reason [the] revelation of troopship sailing dates in *Near v. Minnesota*[76] failed." White and Stevens also said they would decide the constitutional claim against Agee.

Chief Justice Burger's draft *Agee* opinion, circulated at the end of May, 1981, dealt only with the statutory issue. It was essentially similar to the final opinion in reversing the lower court on that issue. It found that Congress had adopted the executive interpretation that the statute conferred the passport revocation power, including the power to revoke for reasons of national security and foreign policy. Nor was it necessary for the Executive to show long-standing enforcement of the power. It was enough that the Executive had "openly asserted" the power.

Several Justices wrote to the Chief Justice, saying that they "had hoped you would also address the constitutional claims that Agee presents in support of the judgment."[77] On May 29, Burger sent around a Memorandum to the Conference: "Since Byron, Harry, Lewis, and Bill Rehnquist have expressed a preference that we dispose of the constitutional claims, I am preparing a short additional section doing so."[78]

On June 3, the Chief Justice circulated a new section III for the *Agee* opinion. It rejected the argument that the constitutional right to travel was invalidly restricted because Agee's travel had jeopardized national security or that the First Amendment had been violated. On the latter point, the Rehnquist conference approach was followed— that is, that Agee's disclosures of names of intelligence personnel were no more entitled to First Amendment protection than the publication of troopship sailings.[79]

The Burger draft had also relied upon Agee's contract with the CIA to decide the case against him. This led to a letter from Stevens: "You may well be correct that his admission of a breach of the agreement with the CIA would be sufficient, but I should think it would be much more appropriate to reserve judmgent [*sic*] on that issue until it has been argued and is necessary for decision."[80] The Stevens objection led to the deletion of the passage relying upon the CIA contract from the final *Agee* opinion.

At the *Agee* conference, Rehnquist had stated the broadest view of presidential power over passports. He was given the opportunity to elevate his view to the level of Court doctrine in *Regan v. Wald*,[81] which has been described as the decision in which the full import of *Agee* was made clear.[82] At issue in *Wald* was a regulation prohibiting most travel to Cuba, including general tourist and business travel. The Court upheld the regulation, finding that it had been authorized by Congress. Respondents in *Wald* had also raised the constitutional claim, urging that the regulation violated their right to travel guaranteed by due process.

The conference was closely divided. Four Justices (Brennan, Marshall, Blackmun, and Powell) voted for respondents on the statutory ground. In their view, as expressed at the conference by Justice Blackmun, who wrote the principal dissent, "The case is one of statutory construction" and "the legislation here seems to support the court of appeals." The government had argued that, on the statutory as well as the constitutional question, the Court should defer to the Executive. But, Blackmun declared, "The deference argument is not persuasive."

The other five voted to reverse on both statutory and constitutional grounds. They took a different approach to the deference issue. The Chief Justice asserted that he would "like to let the President do what he wants here. He has the responsibility." Similarly, White stated, "I'm very reluctant to interfere with Presidential exercises of powers unless Congress speaks more clearly than here."

O'Connor, who told the others that the case was "a close call," conceded that "the legislative history supports the court of appeals." Yet Rehnquist expressed the majority approach when he said, "I don't give much deference to legislative history" in such a case. Even Powell, who issued a brief dissent, was troubled by the need to overrule the Executive. "The legislative history," he said, "seems to require what the court of appeals held." Yet Powell confessed, "I'd be glad to be unhorsed from that view."

At the *Wald* conference, O'Connor had referred to the constitutional question and said, "I think *Haig v. Agee* decides it." Rehnquist's *Wald* opinion of the Court stated that the constitutional issue had been settled by the Warren Court decision in *Zemel v. Rusk*.[83] In doing so, Rehnquist treated the *Zemel* opinion as though it went as far as the original draft by Chief Justice Warren[84]—that is, as upholding the executive power to prohibit travel to Cuba. As he had indicated at the *Agee* conference, the Rehnquist *Wald* opinion found that no First Amendment rights were implicated by such a prohibition. The right to travel abroad had to give way to national security considerations.

Nor was the Executive required to show "a Cuban missile crisis in the offing" to make its restrictions on travel valid. On the contrary, the Court should adhere to the "classical deference to the political branches in matters of foreign policy." The State Department had indicated that Cuba used terrorism and force in support of objectives inimical to American foreign policy interests. "Given the traditional deference to executive judgment '[i]n this vast external realm,' . . . we think there is an adequate basis under the Due Process Clause of the Fifth Amendment to sustain the President's decision to curtail the flow of hard currency to Cuba—currency that could then be used in support of Cuban adventurism—by restricting travel."[85]

Chapter Four

Federalism and the Commerce Power

THE WANT of a national power to regulate commerce was perhaps the primary cause of the Convention of 1787.[1] No other federal power was so universally assumed to be necessary. In fact, the Commerce Clause was little illuminated by debate[2] and was reported in the first draft of the Constitution substantially as it now stands.[3]

Just as important, however, was the establishment of a federal system that contained both a strong national government and the states as coordinate autonomous units. The Framers sought to keep a significant place in the system they were creating for the states, whose delegates they were. They did not intend to reduce the states to mere administrative units. While acting to form the "more perfect Union," they were clearly determined that it should be a Union not only of "indestructible States,"[4] but of states that should retain as much of their sovereignty as would not conflict with the functions of the national government.

The Commerce Clause was not intended to alter the essential nature of the federal system. Congress was vested with the authority to regulate "Commerce . . . among the several States," but the states were left with broad powers over commerce, even that which was interstate in nature. Both federal and state powers over commerce coexist. While the former may be supreme under the Constitution, they were not intended to eliminate the latter and were certainly never intended to do away with the essential balance between states and nation.

NATIONAL LEAGUE OF CITIES:
STATE SOVEREIGNTY REDIVIVUS?

Like Hamlet's father, state sovereignty has been a ghost that refuses to remain in repose. Not too long ago, the concept of the states as independent sovereignties appeared to be an anachronism. There had occurred a dramatic shift in the federal system's constitutional center of gravity. As Justice Jackson said, it is "undeniable that . . . we have been in a cycle of rapid centralization, and Court opinions have sanctioned a considerable concentration of power in the federal government with a corresponding diminution in the authority and prestige of state governments."[5]

The Burger Court's decision in *National League of Cities v. Usery*[6] appeared to change all that. For the first time since 1936,[7] the Court struck down an exercise of congressional power under the Commerce Clause on the ground that the federal statute at issue invalidly impinged upon the states as coordinate independent governments. If anything seemed inconsistent with the prior four decades of concentration of authority in the federal government, it was the notion that the states still possessed the attributes of sovereignty. In *National League of Cities* the Supreme Court relied upon "traditional aspects of state sovereignty"[8] in invalidating a federal statute. This led Justice Brennan to refer to "the newly announced 'state sovereignty' doctrine."[9]

Before *National League of Cities,* the Supreme Court took an increasingly expansive view of the federal commerce power.[10] The crucial test became not the crossing of state lines but whether the activity affected commerce. Mines and mills, factories and farms—all theretofore excluded because they were engaged in production rather than commerce in the Court's previous restricted sense[11]—were brought within the sweep of the Commerce Clause, provided only that they exerted *some* effect upon interstate commerce. As the Burger Court itself put it, "there is no question of Congress' power under the Commerce Clause to include otherwise ostensibly local activities within the reach of federal economic regulation, when such activities sufficiently implicate interstate commerce."[12]

What happens if a federal law regulates an activity carried on by a state? The most important pre–Burger Court case on this question was *Maryland v. Wirtz,*[13] which upheld an amendment to the Fair Labor Standards Act extending federal wage and hour requirements to employees of state-operated schools and hospitals. The Court rejected the claim that the amendment interfered with sovereign state functions. "[V]alid general regulations of commerce do not cease to be regulations of commerce because a State is involved. If a State is engaging in economic activities that are validly regulated by the Federal Government when engaged in by private persons, the State too may be forced to conform its activities to federal regulation."[14]

The dividing line under *Wirtz* was between cases in which the states were performing functions that could only be performed by the states as states—"Only a State can own a Statehouse"[15]—and those where the states were engaged in activities not essential to government as we have traditionally known it. The distinction was developed in the cases on the constitutional immunity of state instrumentalities from federal taxation, where "we look to the activities in which the states have traditionally engaged as marking the boundary of the restriction upon the federal taxing power."[16]

The just-quoted statement is from the opinion in *United States v. California*,[17] where it was held that a state-operated railroad was subject to the Federal Safety Appliance Act. That case went even further than *Wirtz*. After noting the line drawn in the tax cases, the Court stated, "But there is no such limitation upon the plenary power to regulate commerce. The state can no more deny the power if its exercise has been authorized by Congress than can an individual."[18]

Like *Wirtz*, *National League of Cities* arose out of the Fair Labor Standards Act—particularly the 1974 amendments. The original Act of 1938 specifically excluded employees of the states and their political subdivisions. In 1974 Congress extended coverage to these employees. Appellants in *National League of Cities* challenged the 1974 amendments.

At the postargument conference, the first vote was five to four to affirm the lower court's decision in favor of the amendments. The bare majority agreed with the view expressed by Justice Stevens: "Congress always does things that impinge on state sovereignty. I don't think the requirement of minimum wages is that intrusive on state sovereignty." The most interesting statement the other way was by Justice Powell, who said that he "would draw an equal protection analogy to say that the implications of federalism require strict scrutiny of federal legislation that is a direct impingement on state personnel practices." Under this approach, Powell said, he would "introduce a principle of necessity." A federal regulation must be supported by a compelling necessity. Powell gave *Fry v. United States*,[19] which had upheld application of a federal freeze to the wages of states employees, as an "illustration of its operation."

The minority Justices said that they thought that *Wirtz* need only be partially overruled. Stewart asserted that, unless *Wirtz* was totally overruled, it was necessary to affirm. After the vote, Rehnquist, Powell, and Blackmun agreed with Stewart that *Wirtz* should be totally overruled. The Chief Justice agreed. That made a new majority, and the decision was to invalidate the 1974 amendments.

The *National League of Cities* opinion by Rehnquist recognized that the conditions of employment of the public employees covered by the 1974 amendments were not beyond the scope of the federal commerce power had those employees been employed in the private sector. But the decisions establishing the breadth of congressional authority under the Commerce Clause involved laws regulating private individuals and businesses. A different situation exists when Congress seeks to exercise the commerce power in a manner that infringes upon the states as essential elements of the federal system: "There are limits upon the power of Congress to override state sovereignty, even when exercising its otherwise plenary powers to tax or to regulate commerce which are conferred by Art. I of the Constitution." [20]

The Court recognized that *Wirtz* could be distinguished, saying, "there are obvious differences between the schools and hospitals involved in *Wirtz*, and the fire and police departments affected here." [21] The Court did not, however, base its decision on these "obvious differences." Instead, it overruled *Wirtz*, refusing to distinguish between federal regulation applicable to state and local agencies such as police and fire departments and those (as in *Wirtz*) applicable only to schools and hospitals.

As Justice Stewart had put it at the conference, the "sovereignty of the states is in the role of a brake on the Commerce Clause." In its opinion, the Court relied upon "traditional aspects of state sovereignty" to invalidate the statute and the Tenth Amendment was resurrected as "an express declaration of [a] limitation on federal sovereignty." [22] *National League of Cities* thus appeared to be a constitutional landmark that drastically altered the relationship between federal and state power. But the bare majority for overturning the federal infringement upon the states was to be converted toward the end of the Burger tenure into one the other way.

GARCIA: DECISION PROCESS

The *National League of Cities* dissenters were unwilling to allow it to become a settled precedent. In the years following, they worked to minimize its effect. Thus, in *EEOC v. Wyoming*, [23] they obtained a majority for a Brennan opinion holding that a state game warden was protected by the federal law prohibiting age discrimination. At the conference, Powell had asserted, "We would have to overrule *League of Cities* to sustain this. If anything, this is an even more intrusive assault on the state. More than mere money [is involved. Congress] says [the state] can't have its own personnel policies."

The *National League of Cities* dissenters were able to secure Blackmun's vote for a bare majority distinguishing the earlier case. Their true view was stated in a January 25, 1983, Brennan letter to Stevens. After discussing changes in the *EEOC* opinion to meet Stevens' concerns, Brennan concluded, "Finally, there may be no need to tell you that, in my heart of hearts, I agree with you that 'the Commerce Clause gives Congress ample authority to impose economic burdens on states as well as other employers in its regulation of the employment market.' I did not, however, see it as my mandate to overrule *National League of Cities*, and attempted instead simply to constrain its most pernicious implications."

The opportunity of the *National League of Cities* dissenters finally came in *Garcia v. San Antonio Metropolitan Transit Authority*.[24] The constitutional balance between federal and state power was drastically altered again—this time in favor of federal authority. The *Garcia* Court flatly overruled *National League of Cities*.

Blackmun begins his majority *Garcia* opinion by noting, "We revisit in these cases an issue raised in *National League of Cities v. Usery*."[25] The issue in *Garcia* was the application of the minimum-wage and overtime provisions of the Fair Labor Standards Act to employees of the publicly owned mass transportation system in San Antonio. The system had brought the action, seeking a determination that it was entitled to *National League of Cities* immunity from the federal statute. The district court found that "operation of a public transit system is a governmental function entitled to Tenth Amendment immunity."[26]

The post–*National League of Cities* cases had stressed that its holding applied when congressional commerce power legislation impaired state ability "to structure integral operations in areas of traditional governmental functions."[27] At the *Garcia* postargument conference, the division among the Justices centered on the question stated by Brennan: "The question presented in this case is whether the operation of a publicly owned and operated mass transit system is a 'traditional state function' for purposes of the Tenth Amendment. In my view, it is not."[28]

The Chief Justice began the conference discussion by asserting, "*National League* is at a cross-roads in this case. . . . Private mass transit has faded out and large cities have gone public." Despite federal subsidies, he stated, "transit systems are [still] essentially local. This is like water in that respect and is here to stay."

Powell, Rehnquist, and O'Connor agreed. "We're talking here," said Powell, "of moving people to and from their work—a service that it's essential to provide." O'Connor referred to the fact that transit systems had originally been privately operated. "I don't think," she stated, "history freezes traditional public service."

Brennan, who led the argument for reversal, had decided not to deliver a frontal attack on *National League of Cities*. Instead, he argued that operation of the municipal transit system was not a traditional state function. Brennan began by asserting the soundness of the traditional-function test as the criterion upon which *National League of Cities* turned. "Indeed," according to Brennan, "if the states have not traditionally performed a particular function, they have, of course, survived as independent entities without performing that function at all. It is, therefore, difficult to see how federal regulation of that function can threaten the states' independent existence. . . . In this case there is no question that the states have not traditionally operated mass transit systems. Until recently, these systems were largely privately operated. Thus, the history of private operation of mass transit strongly suggests that operation of a mass transit system is not a traditional state function."

Nor, in Brennan's view, did the "recent large scale entry of the states into the mass transit field . . . alter this conclusion." Brennan pointed to the massive federal subsidies that made it possible for the states to operate mass transit systems. This made it "difficult to conceive of mass transit as the kind of state function that must be free of federal regulation to preserve the independent existence of the states. To my knowledge, none of the other functions which we have previously identified as traditional state functions is characterized by an absence of historical state involvement *and* the presence of federal funding in the states' development of that function."

Since over 80 percent of publicly owned mass transit became public after the Fair Labor Standards Act was amended to apply to publicly owned mass transit, "these states acquired their mass transit operations knowing that the operations would be subject to federal regulation. . . . For these reasons, I believe that the operation of a mass transit system is not a traditional state function. As a result, the Tenth Amendment is not violated when the Fair Labor Standards Act is applied to state operated mass transit systems."

In some ways, the most important conference statement was by Blackmun, who was to cast the crucial swing vote in *Garcia*. Blackmun stated that this was a "tough case for me after my concurrence in *National League of Cities*. . . . Municipal mass transit reeks of localism, like police, fire, etc. . . . [A] good opinion can be written either way." However, Blackmun concluded, "I come down on the side that this is local and affirm."

A Justice's docket book indicates that the vote at the postargument *Garcia* conference was four to four (with Blackmun, Powell, Rehnquist, and O'Connor for affirmance and Brennan, White, Marshall, and Stevens for reversal). Despite his conference statement pointing toward affirmance, the Chief Justice passed, according to the docket book.

On the other hand, a June 11, 1984, Blackmun Memorandum to the Conference points out "that the conference vote in [*Garcia*] was 5–4 to affirm." In any event, Chief Justice Burger did cast the deciding vote in favor of immunizing the municipal transit system as a traditional state function from the federal regulation. The result was that, as Brennan pointed out in an April 2, 1984, "Dear Byron, Thurgood and John" letter, "We four are in dissent in the above. I'll be happy to try my hand at the dissent."

A Blackmun memo noted that "my own vote [was] shaky on the affirming side. I assume that it is because of this that the Chief Justice assigned the cases to me, on his frequently stated reference to the 'least persuaded.'"

Garcia illustrates the risk a Chief Justice takes in assigning an opinion to the "least persuaded." The hope is that the shaky vote will become increasingly firm as the Justice goes through the process of fashioning a reasoned opinion. But the opposite may well be the result. Justice Blackmun's became increasingly less certain, and ultimately he decided that an opinion in support of the decision for affirmance just would not "write." "I have," he wrote in his June 11 memo, "spent a lot of time on these cases. I have finally decided to come down on the side of reversal. I have been able to find no principled way in which to affirm. It seems to me that our customary reliance on the 'historical' and the 'traditional' is misplaced and that something more fundamental is required to eliminate the widespread confusion in the area."

Accompanying the Blackmun memo was a thirty-page printed "draft of a proposed opinion [which] reflects my views." According to the draft, "A review of the operation of the 'traditional governmental function' standard in this and other cases now persuades us that the attempt to draw the boundaries of state regulatory immunity in terms of 'traditional governmental function' is both unworkable and inconsistent with the principles of federalism on which *National League of Cities* rests. For the reasons given below, we conclude instead that the prerequisite for state immunity from Commerce Clause regulation must be a federal statutory scheme that singles out the States for unequal regulatory burdens. Because the FLSA imposes minimum-wage and overtime obligations evenhandedly on private as well as public employers, we hold today that its application to municipal mass-transit systems like that operated by appellee San Antonio Metropolitan Transit Authority (SAMTA) is within the power delegated to Congress by the Commerce Clause."

The draft itself took an entirely different approach than *National League of Cities* to the substantive restraints on the exercise of the commerce power vis-à-vis the states: "The only substantive restraint . . . , in our judgment, is a requirement that Congress not attempt to single out the States for special burdens or otherwise discriminate against them."

The result is a significant narrowing of *National League of Cities* by the Blackmun draft. "While we adhere to *National League of Cities'* premise that the Commerce Clause is subject to special limitations when Congress seeks to regulate the 'States as States,' we cannot accept its specific formulation of the rule of state immunity to the extent that it is inconsistent with the principles we announce today. Federal regulation that is otherwise within Congress' power under the Commerce Clause may extend to state functions as long as it applies uniformly to private as well as public activities and does not discriminate against the States and their subdivisions."

"Nothing in the statutory scheme of the FLSA discriminates against SAMTA or any other municipally operated mass-transit system. Instead, SAMTA faces the same minimum-wage and overtime obligations that hundreds of thousands of other employers, private as well as public, must meet."

In a July 3 letter to Powell, Blackmun denied that his draft had overruled *National League of Cities:* "In the opinion I prepared this Term," Blackmun wrote, "and as to which some took umbrage, it was not overruled." The concluding paragraph of Blackmun's draft began with a similar disclaimer: "Today we reaffirm the fundamental premise of *National League of Cities* that Congress' authority under the Commerce Clause must accommodate the special role of the States in the federal system." But the next sentence indicated clearly that the earlier decision was well on its way to jurisprudential limbo: "We hold, however, that the necessary accommodation between federal power and state autonomy is realized when Congress places no burden on the States that it has not placed on private parties as well." Thus *National League of Cities* was shorn of most of its constitutional force.

It is scarcely surprising that the quondam majority for affirmance were taken aback by the Blackmun draft. The Chief Justice sent a June 11 "Dear Harry" letter. "At this stage—almost mid-June—a 30-page opinion coming out contrary to the Conference vote on a very important issue places those who may dissent in a difficult position. . . . I think we should set the case over for reargument and so move."

On the same date, O'Connor circulated a Memorandum to the Conference: "Needless to say Harry's circulation today supporting a reversal of the judgment below and offering a significant change in our approach to the Tenth Amendment question is unexpected." She, too, urged that the case be reargued.

The reargument motion received a bare majority and the case was scheduled for reargument. In a July 3 letter to Blackmun, Justice Powell wrote, "Sandra and I thought, in view of your opinion critical of *National League of Cities,* that it was desirable to focus the attention of the parties broadly on the principles followed by the Court in that case."

At the same time, Powell sent a Memorandum to the Conference that contained the order setting the case for reargument and asked the parties to brief and argue the question, "Whether or not the principles of the Tenth Amendment as set forth in *National League of Cities v. Usery* . . . should be reconsidered?"

Blackmun himself voted against reargument. "I venture to say, he wrote in his July 3 "Dear Lewis" letter, "that if the question is to be presented, *National League of Cities* just might end up being over-ruled"—which is the way it turned out.

Garcia was reargued at the beginning of October 1984. Little was added at the session. As Blackmun said at the conference, it was a "disappointing argument from all." The conference once again saw a five-to-four division—but this time in favor both of reversal and a specific overruling of *National League of Cities*. Brennan, who saw complete victory within the grasp of the anti-*National League of Cities* Justices, abandoned his cautious approach. He argued not only that *National League of Cities* should be overruled but that the question of commerce power infringement upon the states was not one for judicial cognizance. The balancing was for Congress—not the courts. As Justice Stevens stated it to the conference, this was "indeed a classic case where it's wrong for the judiciary to intervene."

GARCIA: THE SHIFTING FEDERAL BALANCE

On November 23, 1984, Justice Blackmun circulated a new *Garcia* draft, essentially similar to his final opinion in the case. The Black-mun opinion, concurred in by a bare majority, followed the Bren-nan–Stevens conference approach. It was a broadside one overruling *National League of Cities*. The opinion gave two principal reasons: (1) "the attempt to draw the boundaries of state regulatory immunity in terms of 'traditional governmental function' is . . . unworkable" and (2) such an attempt is "inconsistent with established principles of federalism."[29]

It should, however, be pointed out that mere difficulty in applying legal principles has never been considered an adequate reason for abandoning those principles. Holmes's admonition against expecting legal rules to operate with the precision of mathematical formulae is particularly relevant in public law: "the luxury of precise definitions is one rarely enjoyed in interpreting and applying the general provisions of our Constitution."[30]

The fact that courts reached seemingly inconsistent results in applying *National League of Cities* was not by itself enough to warrant overruling that case. It is, after all, the job of the Supreme Court to reconcile differences in lower court results. Moreover, it is by no means as clear as the *Garcia* opinion asserts that the federal courts were hopelessly divided in their application of *National League of*

Cities. The Court's assertion is based on a list of cases that, in its view, reach inconsistent results. As Justice Powell points out in his dissent, the cases listed by the Court do not demonstrate the impossibility of definition.

More important was the second reason given by *Garcia,* for it involved rejection of the underlying premise of *National League of Cities*—that the principles of federalism impose restrictions on the Commerce Clause and hence on the scope of congressional regulatory authority vis-à-vis the states. *National League of Cities* assumed that there were limits on the federal government's power to interfere with state functions and that the courts had to enforce those limits. The *Garcia* opinion agreed that "the Constitution's federal structure imposes limitations on the Commerce Clause."[31] But it refused to define those limitations and, more important, held that the remedy for their violation was political, not judicial. In effect, as seen at the end of Chapter 2, *Garcia* holds that congressional infringements upon the states present only political questions not subject to judicial cognizance.

Where does this decision leave the states' relationship to federal regulatory authority? Even if the Constitution is inconsistent with state sovereignty, there is no doubt that federalism is based on the continuance of the states as fully independent and autonomous governments. State independence and autonomy are inconsistent with their complete subjection to federal regulatory power. The *Garcia* Court does not disagree with this; it expressly recognizes the emphasis of the Framers on the need "to ensure the role of the States in the federal system." But it breaks sharply with prior law by concluding that protecting the states from improper exertions of federal regulatory authority is no longer a judicial function. Instead, "the principal means . . . to ensure the role of the States in the federal system lies in the structure of the Federal Government itself." That structure "was designed in large part to protect the States from overreaching by Congress."[32] The states' representation in Congress and their role in the selection of both the executive and legislative branches of the federal government are to be relied on to shield their interests from undue federal invasion.

Under *Garcia* the scope of congressional authority over the states under the Commerce Clause no longer presents any judicial question. "Since *Garcia* . . . ," says a federal judge, "the Tenth Amendment has become a dead letter in constitutional law."[33]

Garcia may tell us more about the operation of the Supreme Court than about federalism. The difference in result between the *National League of Cities* and *Garcia* cases may be explained less by legal logic than by the changed vote of Justice Blackmun, who had concurred in *National League of Cities*.

STATE REGULATION AND BALANCING

The Commerce Clause is a grant of affirmative power to Congress to regulate interstate commerce. "The Commerce Clause," Justice Blackmun tells us, "does not state a prohibition; it merely grants specific power to Congress."[34] But the Commerce Clause also has a negative aspect. It not only serves as a positive affirmation of federal authority, it also cuts down state power by negative implication.[35] The Commerce Clause stripped the states of the ability to advance their own commercial interests at the expense of the nation. It "sought to put an end to the economic autarchy of the states"[36] and to set up instead what the Burger Court termed a "national 'common market.'"[37]

The bounds of the negative restraint appear nowhere in the words of the Commerce Clause. If the clause does limit state authority, the scope of the limitation lacks precise definition. The clause may be a two-edged sword, but the real question is the swath of the negative cutting edge.[38]

This question was answered in classic form in *Cooley v. Board of Port Wardens*[39] over 125 years ago, when the Court first determined the extent of state regulatory power over commerce. *Cooley* upheld a Pennsylvania law that required vessels using the port of Philadelphia to engage local pilots. According to the *Cooley* Court, the test to determine whether there is state power to enact such a law is whether the type of regulation at issue demands national uniformity: "Whatever subjects of this power are in their nature national, or admit only of one uniform system, or plan of regulation, may justly be said to be of such a nature as to require exclusive legislation by Congress."[40] On the other hand, where national uniformity is not necessary, the subject may be reached by state law, as in *Cooley*.

Almost two decades after *Cooley* the Court declared, "Perhaps no more satisfactory solution has ever been given of this vexed question than the one furnished by the court in that case."[41] Much the same comment can still be made. In *Ray v. Atlantic Richfield Co.*[42] the Burger Court applied the *Cooley* test to a Washington law requiring supertankers navigating Puget Sound to have a local pilot on board and to have tug escorts. The Court ruled that states are free to impose pilotage requirements on vessels. In addition, the Commerce Clause did not prevent the state from enacting the tug escort provision, which was similar to the local pilotage requirement in *Cooley* and thus was not the type of regulation that demands a uniform national rule.

The *Cooley–Ray* approach is a balancing test that makes the validity of a state regulation depend upon a weighing of national and local interests. The judicial inquiry, the Court stated in 1978, "involves consideration of the weight and nature of the states' regulatory concern in light of the extent of burden imposed on interstate commerce. . . . Where the statute regulates evenhandedly to effectuate a legitimate local public interest, and its effects on interstate commerce are only incidental, it will be upheld unless the burden imposed on such commerce is clearly excessive in relation to the putative local benefits."[43]

COOLEY LOST AND REGAINED

The Burger Court recognized that it "has employed various tests to express the distinction between permissible and impermissible impact [of state regulation] upon interstate commerce."[44] Attempts since *Cooley* to formulate other tests have proved unsatisfactory. The *Cooley* approach is still the most workable in cases involving the validity of state commercial regulations. This can be seen by comparing *Cooley* to the most significant case in which the Court departed from the *Cooley* balancing test.

In *South Carolina State Highway Department v. Barnwell Brothers* (1938),[45] the Court upheld a South Carolina statute banning from state highways trucks and "semi-trailer" trucks whose width exceeded ninety inches and whose weight, including load, exceeded twenty thousand pounds. The law was sustained despite the fact that it set stricter limitations on truck width and weight than the laws of surrounding states. There is language in *Barnwell* that might be read as applying a "rational relation" rather than a "balancing" test:

"[T]he judicial function, under the commerce clause as well as the Fourteenth Amendment, stops with the inquiry . . . whether the means of regulation chosen are reasonably adapted to the end sought."[46]

Relying on *Barnwell,* the states have subjected interstate motor carriers to a veritable code of regulations in areas not covered by the Federal Interstate Commerce Act and Interstate Commerce Commission regulations. The Supreme Court has used *Barnwell* to sustain state licensing requirements, holding that the states may require interstate motor carriers to obtain licenses.

The Court has also held that a state may impose reasonable license fees upon interstate motor carriers,[47] if they bear a rational relation to the cost of maintaining and policing the highways. As long as the fee is based upon some fair approximation of use and is neither discriminatory against interstate commerce nor excessive in comparison with the benefit conferred, it will pass constitutional muster.

Barnwell and its progeny left observers with the uneasy feeling that those decisions would permit the states to carry on the very restrictive practices that the Commerce Clause was intended to preclude. What the Court said in *Barnwell* was that the *Cooley* test should not be the determining factor in the motor-vehicle field because of the part the states play in providing road facilities. Certainly the furnishing of highways by the state differentiates road regulation from comparable train regulation.[48] At the same time, one cannot help but feel that separate regulation in each state may result in a "crazy quilt"[49] of state laws that may severely burden interstate motor transportation. Interstate commerce by motor may be faced with a rampart of economic barriers, which constitute a constant clog upon that mobility of commerce that the Constitution was designed to foster.

The situation was improved by the Burger Court decisions on the matter—though they did not mark a complete return to *Cooley.* The key case here was *Raymond Motor Transportation v. Rice.*[50] A Wisconsin statute prohibited trucks longer than fifty-five feet from using its highways. An interstate carrier operating sixty-five-foot, double-trailer units presented "a massive array of evidence"[51] to disprove the state's assertion that the prohibition contributed to highway safety. The state, "for reasons unexplained,"[52] made no effort to contradict this evidence. Instead, it relied on *Barnwell.*

At the *Raymond* conference, Justices Brennan and Stewart stressed that there was no evidence supporting the state claim that the pro-

hibition made a contribution to highway safety. It was "very tempt-
ing," said Stewart, "to rely on *Barnwell* and say the state can, on
safety agenda, do almost anything it wants. But the state's case for
safety was demolished at the trial when all that was proved was that
people didn't like big trailers." Most of the others agreed with the
Brennan–Stewart view.

Raymond was assigned to Powell. His opinion acknowledged that
Barnwell arguably indicated that state motor regulations should be
sustained despite showings of burdens on interstate commerce in the
absence of discrimination against interstate commerce. Powell refused, however, to carry this special deference to state highway regulations to the extent urged by Wisconsin. Instead, his opinion weighed
the state's asserted safety purpose against the degree of interference
with interstate commerce.

The statute forced truckers with double-unit trailers to either separate the units upon entering Wisconsin or avoid Wisconsin altogether. In addition, truckers were prevented from accepting interline
transfers of sixty-five-foot double units for movement through Wisconsin from carriers in the thirty-three states where the units were
legal. Hence, the burden on interstate commerce was substantial,
whereas the state regulation could not be said to make more than the
most speculative contribution to highway safety.

After he had read the *Raymond* draft, Justice Rehnquist sent a
January 23, 1978, letter to Justice Powell. Rehnquist wrote, "I think
the Chief and I were the only ones in this case who voted to dissent."
But the Powell opinion "has persuaded me" that, on the facts, the
decision in favor of the state should be reversed. This did not mean
that Rehnquist had abandoned his conference stance. "I am not quite
yet ready, however, to give up what I thought had been established as
a fairly strong presumption in *Barnwell*, in favor of state safety regulations at least where they pertain to state-owned roads rather than
privately owned railroad trackage. . . . If it turns out that I am alone
in my view, I may give up with only a 'graveyard' dissent."

But Rehnquist was not alone. The Chief Justice (who also had decided to join the decision striking down the truck limit law) and Justice Brennan, together with Rehnquist, joined a concurring opinion
by Justice Blackmun. The concurrence asserted that the *Raymond*
decision did not constitute a repudiation of the *Barnwell* deference to
state motor regulation. According to Blackmun, the decisive factor in
Raymond was the failure of the state to show that its length regula-

tion made any contribution to highway safety. Except in such a case, *Barnwell* would still control: "In other words, if safety justifications are not illusory, the Court will not second guess legislative judgment about their importance in comparison with related burdens on interstate commerce."[53]

It is unfortunate that the Burger Court, both in *Raymond* and in a later case that the Court characterized as "*Raymond* revisited,"[54] did not see fit completely to repudiate the *Barnwell* exception to the *Cooley* approach. Despite the Court's attempt to distinguish these motor regulation cases, separate regulation by each state is undesirable. In a country dominated by the free trade concept of the Commerce Clause, it is anomalous that interstate commerce by motor may require a carrier to obtain permits and pay tolls every time it crosses a new state line.

STATE BARRIERS TO IMPORTS

The Burger Court tended toward a strict approach to state power to prohibit importation of articles from other states or to enact embargo measures forbidding shipments to other states. The Court started with the recognition, which dates from Marshall's day,[55] of state power to enact reasonable quarantine laws, which are not forbidden protectionist measures even though they are directed against interstate commerce. There are dangers inherent in the very movement of quarantined articles, such as diseased livestock. "Those laws," as the Burger Court pointed out, "did not discriminate against interstate commerce as such, but simply prevented traffic in noxious articles, whatever their origin."[56]

The Burger Court, however, construed the exception narrowly and limited it to articles that are noxious in the quarantine sense. In *Philadelphia v. New Jersey,*[57] it struck down a New Jersey law that prohibited the importation of most "solid or liquid waste which originated or was collected outside the territorial limits of the State." The state court had found that the law had a legitimate environmental purpose—to continue using New Jersey's landfill sites would take a heavy environmental toll, both from pollution and loss of scarce open lands.

At the conference, Justice Stewart declared that the New Jersey law was a "clear, frank, gross bar against interstate commerce—precisely the kind of parochial legislation directly barring articles of commerce from entering the state." White agreed, saying, "at this time [there is] only the burden issue here and I think it is a clear discrimination without adequate justification." Only the Chief Justice and Brennan and Rehnquist refused to go along with the Stewart—White view (and Brennan was to change his vote and join the opinion of the Court). The dissenters' view was pithily expressed by Rehnquist's conference assertion: "New Jersey is now made a garbage heap for Pennsylvania and New York."

The *Philadelphia* decision refused to accept the state argument that waste was not protected by the Commerce Clause. This contention, resting on a two-tiered definition of commerce, was rejected by the Court. "All objects of interstate trade merit Commerce Clause protection; none is excluded by definition at the outset." [58]

The *Philadelphia* case presented the relatively rare situation of a state law that on its face contains a flat prohibition against importation of specified out-of-state articles. Normally, when a state employs its power to discriminate against interstate commerce, it seeks to disguise the true impact and put forth some legal pretext for what appears to be a state health regulation. The Supreme Court must then unmask the ruse.

In *Great Atlantic & Pacific Tea Co. v. Cottrell*,[59] a Mississippi statute provided that milk from another state might be sold in Mississippi only if the other state accepted Mississippi milk on a reciprocal basis. The statute was used to deny a Louisiana milk producer the right to sell milk in Mississippi solely because Louisiana had not signed a reciprocal agreement with Mississippi. The entire Court agreed with the view stated by the Chief Justice at the conference: "The Commerce Clause invalidates this economic regulation. This is not a health measure."

In the *A & P* case, Mississippi was imposing the kind of reciprocity that may exist between nations in international trade. Yet the Commerce Clause itself creates the necessary reciprocity in interstate commerce. It does not allow Mississippi to force its judgment as to proper level of milk sanitation on other states at the expense of an absolute ban on the interstate flow of milk. To allow Mississippi to insist that a sister state either sign a reciprocity agreement acceptable to Mississippi or be foreclosed from exporting its products to Mississippi would permit preferential state trade areas destructive of the very purpose of the Commerce Clause.

The North Carolina statute challenged in *Hunt v. Washington State Apple Advertising Commission*[60] was closer to the line. It required all containers of apples shipped into the state to bear the legend: "no grade other than the applicable United States grade or standard." Washington, the nation's largest apple producer, had established a stringent inspection program that required all apples shipped in interstate commerce to be tested under strict standards and graded accordingly. The Washington grades were the equivalent of, or superior to, those of the U.S. Department of Agriculture. The North Carolina law, in effect, prohibited the display of Washington grades in North Carolina.

The Court affirmed an injunction against prohibiting the display of Washington apple grades. Although neutral on its face, the law had the practical effect of discriminating against interstate sales of Washington apples. It increased the costs of doing business in the North Carolina market for Washington growers and dealers while leaving those of their North Carolina counterparts unaffected. In addition, the statute stripped away the competitive advantage that the Washington apple industry had earned for itself through its extensive inspection and grading system and had a "leveling effect which insidiously operate[d] to the advantage of local apple producers." Washington apples would have to be marketed under the inferior federal grades. "Such 'downgrading' offers the North Carolina apple industry the very sort of protection against competing out-of-state products that the Commerce Clause was designed to prohibit."[61]

If there is any difficulty with the *Hunt* decision, it stems from the fact that it may not give enough weight to what the Court concedes to be the states' "substantial interest in protecting their citizens from confusion and deception in the marketing of foodstuffs."[62] The states do possess prohibitory power to protect against fraud[63] and shield against contagion. Why is the state interest in protecting local purchasers from confusion not sufficient to sustain the North Carolina regulation? Under *Hunt,* must North Carolina now allow display of all state apple grades, even though the apple-producing states use different grading systems, or only of those state grades that are the equivalent of, or superior to, the federal grades?

EMBARGO LAWS

The Burger Court applied the principles governing state prohibitions on importation to embargo measures forbidding shipments outside the state. The premise is that the nation is a common market in which state lines cannot be made barriers to the free flow of both raw materials and finished goods. A state may exercise its quarantine power to bar shipments beyond its borders of articles that present immediate health hazards, such as dead animals,[64] but it may not forbid such shipments to promote its own economic interests.

In *Pike v. Bruce Church, Inc.*[65] the Burger Court ruled an Arizona prohibition against shipping uncrated cantaloupes out-of-state invalid. The prohibition served only to require growers to have their crating done in the state.

Pike reaffirms the lack of state power to prohibit shipments in order to further local interests. This approach is particularly significant in a period of resource shortages. As the Court said years ago in *Pennsylvania v. West Virginia*[66]—which invalidated a West Virginia law forbidding the export of natural gas until the reasonable requirements of its people were satisfied—otherwise "Pennsylvania might keep its coal, the Northwest its timber, the mining states their minerals. And why may not the products of the field be brought within the principle?"[67]

An important exception to *Pennsylvania v. West Virginia* was laid down almost a century ago in *Geer v. Connecticut.*[68] A law forbade the out-of-state shipment of game killed within the state. The law was sustained on the ground that the state has a peculiar property right in its wildlife. Until reduced to possession, said the Court, wildlife was not private property, but a natural resource. The Commerce Clause was held not to prevent the state from prohibiting the export of such a resource "which belongs in common to all the people of the State, which can only become the subject of ownership in a qualified way, and which can never be the object of commerce except with the consent of the State."[69]

The *Geer* principle was applied in the *Hudson County* case[70] to sustain a New Jersey prohibition against transporting any water out of its streams or lakes into any other state. On the other hand, *Pennsylvania v. West Virginia* refused to apply *Geer* to the embargo on natural gas. The Court stated that natural gas, unlike game, is privately owned: "Gas, when reduced to possession, is a commodity; it belongs to the owner of the land."[71]

This attempt to remove resources such as natural gas from the *Geer* principle is unsatisfactory. Wildlife and water, too, when reduced to possession, become individual property. The key factor is that stressed in *Pennsylvania v. West Virginia:* if *Geer* and *Hudson County* were extended to other resources, embargo might be met with embargo, and commerce among the states might dry up. From this point of view the *Geer* reasoning had, as Chief Justice Burger termed it, become a legal anachronism.[72]

In *Hughes v. Oklahoma*,[73] the Chief Justice's characterization was elevated to Burger Court jurisprudence. At issue was a state law prohibiting the interstate transfer of minnows. The state relied on *Geer* to sustain the law, but the time had come for *Geer* in the highest Court. At the conference, the majority agreed with Justice Stewart—this was a "clear interference with interstate commerce despite *Geer v. Connecticut*." Blackmun asserted, "The whole recent trend is against this. *Geer* is an anachronism." Powell noted that there were "lots of ways besides this to conserve resources."

Only the Chief Justice and Rehnquist voted to affirm. Logically, Rehnquist accepted the reasoning the other way. Referring to *Philadelphia v. New Jersey*,[74] he told the conference, "If garbage is subject [to Commerce Clause restraints], so too are minnows. But stare decisis requires me to follow *Geer* and affirm."

The Court struck down the Oklahoma law. According to the opinion of Brennan, the *Geer* theory of state ownership of wild game was "pure fantasy": "The 'ownership' language of cases such as [*Geer*] must be understood as no more than a 19th-century legal fiction."[75] *Hughes* expressly overruled *Geer* and concluded that Commerce Clause challenges to state regulations of wildlife should now be considered according to the same rules applied to other natural resources.

STATE-CREATED COMMERCE

Yet if the Burger Court recognized the *Geer* exception as an aberration, it also created a questionable exception to the bar of the Commerce Clause upon state prohibitory and embargo measures that may have even greater impact. *Hughes v. Alexandria Scrap Corp.*[76] held that the limitation on state prohibitory laws and embargo measures applies only to state restrictions on commerce that flourishes in a free market, not commerce that owes its existence to a state subsidy program.

In a March 25, 1976, Memorandum to the Conference, Powell described the statute at issue in *Alexandria Scrap* as "Byzantine in its intricacy." To deal with the growing problem of abandoned autos, a Maryland law provided for a "bounty" for destruction of any vehicle. To receive the bounty, local scrap processors needed only to submit an agreement with suppliers to indemnify the processors against third-party claims. Non-Maryland processors had to submit certificates of title to the autos. This gave Maryland processors a substantial competitive advantage.

According to the Powell memorandum, "The tentative vote at the Conference on this case was 6 to 3 to affirm the decision . . . invalidating the Maryland statute." Justice White said that Maryland was "protecting local business from outsiders. This case has that smell." Hence, Justice Blackmun summed it up, the law "runs afoul of the Commerce Clause—it's a burden. The milk cases[77] and *Pike*[78] are pertinent."

Stewart, Rehnquist, and Stevens disagreed. "I can't think," Rehnquist declared, "either the commerce or equal protection grounds wash. All the state did was to bounty local processors. It's a 'buy local' policy bidding up the price of scrap. This is not a prohibition or burden."

Powell was assigned the *Alexandria Scrap* opinion. "I undertook initially to write it in accord with the Conference vote," Powell's memo informed the others. Then he had the experience that not infrequently happens during the Court's decision process: "after spending considerable time on this case, I concluded that it simply 'would not write'—at least for me—in accord with my vote."

Powell then circulated a new draft which, his memo told the conference, "concludes that the Maryland statute, as amended in 1974, neither violates the Commerce Clause nor denies appellee equal protection of the laws." The new Powell draft was joined by the Chief Justice and Blackmun, as well as the three conference dissenters. This converted the six-to-three conference vote against the statute to a six-to-three majority in its favor.

According to the Powell opinion, the entry by the state itself into the market as a purchaser of a potential article of commerce does not create a burden upon that commerce if the state restricts its trade to local businesses. The decision, Stevens explained in a June 11, 1976, letter to Brennan, "rests on the factual judgment that the availability of the bounty payments resulted in an artificially enhanced value for abandoned hulks, which in turn created either a market for the hulks that did not previously exist, or alternatively, enlarged a preexisting market." The commerce that Maryland had "burdened" would not even exist if Maryland had not decided to subsidize this portion of the scrap-processing business.

In effect, *Alexandria Scrap* holds, as Brennan pointed out in an April 1, 1976, letter to Powell, "that state action of the kind here forecloses application of usual Commerce Clause principles." However, the holding that Commerce Clause restrictions apply only to commerce in a free market, not to commerce that owes its existence to the state, has disturbing implications. The result may be to exclude a growing area of commerce in an era of increasing state entry into the commercial arena—what Douglas referred to as the tendency of government to undertake nongovernmental functions: a railroad, a mill, an irrigation system, or bridges, street lights, and sewage disposal plants.[79]

Under *Alexandria Scrap*, are all these functions now removed from the reach of the Commerce Clause's restrictions on state power? If they are, how far does the exemption for state-created commerce extend? May a state, for example, limit its own purchases to goods produced in the state? In his dissent Brennan asserted, "state statutes that facially or in practical effect restrict state purchases of items in interstate commerce to those produced within the State are invalid unless justified by asserted state interests—other than economic protectionism—in regulating matters of local concern for which 'reasonable nondiscriminatory alternatives, adequate to conserve legitimate local interests, are [not] available.'"[80] If Brennan is correct, it is difficult to see why his conclusion should not also apply to the Maryland law in *Alexandria Scrap* itself.

TAXATION OF FOREIGN COMMERCE

The Constitution restricts not only state power to regulate commerce, but also state power to tax commerce. With regard to state taxing power, we must distinguish between interstate and foreign commerce. For the former, the Constitution left a permissive area to the states. But for foreign commerce, the Constitution left no leeway. The Import–Export Clause forbids the states to tax foreign trade. As the Court said almost half a century ago, "[t]he Import–Export Clause states an absolute ban, whereas the Commerce Clause merely grants power to Congress."[81]

From Marshall's day until the Burger Court, interpretation of the Import–Export Clause had been governed by the original-package doctrine laid down in *Brown v. Maryland*.[82] Brennan has called the Marshall opinion there the seminal opinion on forbidden state taxes on imports.[83] Maryland required all importers to obtain a $50 license. The Court ruled the tax on the importer was a tax on the imports themselves, which the Constitution absolutely prohibits.

Brown precludes the states from subjecting imports to even a general nondiscriminatory tax. This raises the further question of how long imported goods retain their immunity from state taxation. As Marshall put it, "[T]here must be a point of time when the prohibition ceases, and the power of the state to tax commences." This point of time occurs when the goods no longer retain their status as imports. In words grown familiar with judicial repetition, the *Brown* opinion stated the guide for determining when imported goods cease to be imports: "It is sufficient for the present to say, generally, that when the importer has so acted upon the thing imported, that it has become incorporated and mixed up with the mass of property in the country, it has, perhaps, lost its distinctive character as an import, and has become subject to the taxing power of the State; but while remaining the property of the importer, in his warehouse, in the original form or package in which it was imported, a tax upon it is too plainly a duty on imports to escape the prohibition in the constitution."[84]

The most controversial application of *Brown* was in *Low v. Austin* in 1871.[85] It held that the states were prohibited by the Import–Export Clause from imposing a nondiscriminatory ad valorem property tax on imports until they lost their character as imports and became incorporated into the mass of property in the state.

Low was followed until the Burger Court decision in *Michelin Tire Corp. v. Wages.*[86] A Georgia county assessed ad valorem property taxes against tires imported by Michelin that were included, on assessment dates, in an inventory maintained at its local warehouse. The Georgia court held that the tires had lost their status as imports. The Supreme Court ruled that the tires were subject to the tax regardless of whether the Georgia court was correct in holding that they had lost their status as imports, since the "assessment of a nondiscriminatory ad valorem property tax against the imported tires [was] not within the constitutional prohibition against laying 'any Imposts or Duties on Imports.' Insofar as *Low v. Austin* [was] to the contrary, that decision [was] overruled."[87]

At the conference following the *Michelin* argument, however, the Justices did not decide to overrule *Low v. Austin*. Instead the conference vote, as explained by Justice Brennan in his November 21, 1975,

Memorandum to the Conference, was "to affirm the holding of the Georgia Supreme Court that the tires had lost their status as imports by reason of the sorting, segregating by size and style and comingling of the tires with other shipments." This enabled the Georgia decision to be affirmed without any need to reconsider *Low* or the original-package doctrine.

The original draft opinion of the Court that Brennan circulated on November 21[88] was intended, in the words of the Brennan memo, "to reflect what I understand was the conference vote." The draft stated, "[W]e have no occasion in this case to reconsider *Low v. Austin* and its progeny." Instead, the draft applied the original-package doctrine and did not question *Low*'s continuing validity. On the contrary, the draft assumed that the prohibited "Imposts or Duties on Imports" in the Import Clause included local ad valorem property taxes such as those imposed by Georgia upon the Michelin tires.

The Brennen memo briefly reviewed the prior law on the question: "Marshall never said it was in *Brown v. Maryland*,[89] and Taney in the *License Cases*[90] said it was not. Research by some distinguished scholars has lead [sic] them unanimously to conclude that Taney was right and that the ad valorem tax is not an 'impost or duty.' But one decision of this Court a century ago, *Low v. Austin*, written by Mr. Justice Field, held squarely without any analysis or discussion, that it was an 'impost or duty.'"

The Brennan draft stated expressly that it was not questioning the authority of *Low v. Austin*, but in his covering memo he took a different approach. "For myself, I'd be willing to grapple with the question in this case and overrule *Low v. Austin*. . . . I don't see any reason for a reargument asking the parties to address that specific question since there is a very voluminous amicus brief from California that fully canvasses all the authorities."

Brennan was also willing to overrule *Low v. Austin* without further argument even though he recognized the impact of such a decision. "I agree that overruling *Low* will have far-reaching consequences particularly in this day when such an enormous quantity of goods marketed in this country is imported from Japan and West Germany. In its amicus brief Los Angeles County said it would make a difference of $15,000,000 annually to that county alone."

The Brennan memo was a bid for support for a more far-reaching decision. He concluded, "Unless there are four or more of the Brethren who feel as I do, I'll say no more about it."

Soon after they received Brennan's draft and covering memo, all except Justice White sent replies indicating their support for overruling *Low*. The developing consensus was well expressed by the Chief Justice in a December 3, 1975, "Dear Bill" letter: "I would like to see your full dress treatment of *Low*. Maybe it's time *Low* was laid low! Things have changed since John Marshall's time."

Justice Brennan then circulated a completely revised *Michelin* draft, which was quickly agreed to by the others, except for Justice White, who issued a short concurrence stating that there was no need to overrule *Low v. Austin*. In his December 22, 1975, letter Blackmun wrote, "I think this will clean away some of the cobwebs in this area." The *Michelin* opinion not only did that; it also completely changed the Court's approach to the Import–Export Clause. On its face, Brennan's *Michelin* opinion merely overruled the *Low v. Austin* holding that an ad valorem property tax came within the clause's prohibited "Imposts or Duties." But the *Michelin* opinion was actually far more sweeping. It repudiated the jurisprudence on the matter that had prevailed since the Marshall Court and all but eliminated one of the oldest doctrines—the original-package doctrine—from our constitutional law.

TAXATION OF INTERSTATE COMMERCE

"It is," the Burger Court tells us, "a truism that the mere act of carrying on business in interstate commerce does not exempt a corporation from state taxation."[91] Interstate commerce derives benefits from local government and should pay its fair share of the costs.[92] It also should not secure competitive advantage from tax immunity denied to local commerce. On the other hand, interstate commerce may not be taxed to the full limit by every state through which it passes. The interstate trader would then be at a tremendous disadvantage compared with local businessmen. In order to avoid this inequity, the tax situation must be equalized. In Justice Blackmun's words, "The Commerce Clause balance tips against the tax . . . when it unfairly burdens commerce by exacting more than a just share from the interstate activity."[93]

The Burger Court's most important decision on state power to tax interstate commerce was that in *Complete Auto Transit v. Brady*.[94] Before that decision, the Commerce Clause was construed to contain a prohibition against state taxation on the "privilege" of engaging in interstate commerce. The leading case was *Spector Motor Service v. O'Connor,*[95] where a franchise tax imposed upon a foreign corporation for the privilege of doing a wholly interstate business within the state was held invalid, even though the tax was apportioned to include only the business activities within the state. The constitutional infirmity of such a tax persists, said the Court, no matter how fairly it is apportioned.

Complete Auto overruled *Spector* and held that a state may tax directly the privilege of conducting interstate business. At issue in *Complete Auto* was a Mississippi tax of 5 percent of gross receipts imposed for the privilege of doing business in the state as applied to appellant, a Michigan motor carrier who transported into Mississippi motor vehicles manufactured outside the state. After the vehicles were shipped into Mississippi by railroad, appellant moved them by truck to Mississippi dealers.

At the *Complete Auto* conference, Stewart made perhaps the best overall presentation: "The first issue is whether this is a tax on 'interstate' commerce. It is, so we come to the second question." Stewart then noted that there were "two lines of authority. . . . Congress' exclusive power over interstate commerce precludes a state tax on privileges. The other line allows state taxes that don't discriminate against interstate commerce." However, Stewart concluded, "unless *Spector* is to be overruled, it controls and requires reversal."

White and Marshall agreed that *Spector* should be followed, but the others stated that it should be overruled. Ultimately, the conference dissenters went along and Blackmun delivered a unanimous opinion of the Court. The tax at issue was a privilege tax and it was imposed upon an interstate activity, but the Court refused to strike the tax down because it was applied to an interstate activity having a substantial nexus with the taxing state, was fairly apportioned to the business done in the state, and was fairly related to services, such as police protection, provided by the state. The *Spector* rule, that a state tax on the "privilege of doing business" is per se unconstitutional when applied to interstate commerce, was expressly overruled.

Spector had become a formalistic anachronism ripe for overruling. The immunity of a wholly interstate business from a privilege qua privilege tax is out of line with more recent notions of state taxing power, particularly those cases permitting the income from interstate commerce to be reached with a properly allocated tax. Although recognizing that interstate commerce could thus be taxed under those cases, the *Spector* Court held that a franchise or privilege tax was quite another matter.

The *Spector* distinction between franchise and other taxes has no relationship to economic realities, since it is interstate business that is burdened in both cases. Thus, an allocated tax "on" the income of a wholly interstate business is valid, but under *Spector,* a franchise or other privilege tax, though also measured by the income, might not be exacted from a company doing an entirely interstate business.

This point had been well made by several Justices at the postargument conference. "I must say," said Powell, "that we're at the point of total absurdity when Mississippi could have so easily avoided this defect." That could have been done by following the advice of White: "Don't be stupid and use the fatal words: tax on the 'privilege' of doing interstate business." As the *Complete Auto* opinion put it, the *Spector* "rule looks only to the fact that the incidence of the tax is the 'privilege of doing business'; it deems irrelevant any consideration of the practical effect of the tax."[96]

INCOME TAXES AND APPORTIONMENT

Complete Auto illustrates the Burger Court's tendency to uphold state taxes against Commerce Clause claims. This tendency is also illustrated by the Court's reception of similar claims against state income taxes. The starting point here was the Warren Court decision in *Northwestern States Portland Cement Co. v. Minnesota.*[97] It upheld a Minnesota tax on the income from sales of cement in the state of an Iowa corporation that manufactured the cement at its Iowa plant. The Minnesota law was set up to tax only that portion of the company's income reasonably attributable to business done in the state. To do so, the law utilized three ratios in determining the portion of net income taxable under state law: (1) the taxpayer's sales assignable to Minnesota to its total sales; (2) the taxpayer's property in Minnesota to its total property; and (3) the taxpayer's payroll in Minnesota to its total payroll. *Northwestern States* held that it is not an improper interference with interstate commerce to permit a state, within whose borders a foreign corporation engages in activities in aid of that commerce, to tax the net income derived from those activities on a properly apportioned basis.

The Burger Court decision in *Moorman Manufacturing Co. v. Bair*[98] went one step further and upheld an Iowa statute that prescribed a single-factor sales formula to "apportion" income of an interstate business for state income tax purposes. Moorman was an Illinois corporation that manufactured animal feeds in Illinois. It sold its products to Iowa customers through salesmen in Iowa and made deliveries from its warehouses in the state. Iowa sales accounted for about 20 percent of its total sales. Iowa imposed its income tax on companies selling tangible property in the state in the portion that the gross sales in Iowa bore to the total gross sales.

Moorman contended that the Iowa single-factor formula was invalid under the Commerce Clause. It argued that, since all other states taxing income, including Illinois, had come to use the three-factor formula upheld in the *Northwestern States* case, the Iowa single-factor formula inevitably led to multiple taxation. At the conference on the case, Brennan, Blackmun, and Powell agreed with the Moorman argument. "The trend toward the three-factors test," Blackmun asserted, "would be stopped by affirmance here. This disfavors out-of-state producers and favors in-state [producers]." In fact, said Blackmun, "I'd be inclined to constitutionalize a standard that would reverse." When Blackmun concluded, Powell declared, "Harry has made my speech and I'd reverse."

The six others spoke in favor of the state tax. The general approach in such a case was stated by the Chief Justice: "The cases add up to the requirement that there must be an egregious or gross distortion in result. . . . This doesn't add up to that." Stewart agreed: "It may be that, as an economic matter, sales as a [sole] factor is ill-advised." But that did not make the Iowa formula unconstitutional. Stewart also rejected the principal Moorman argument, saying, "The validity of what Iowa has done can't be measured by what other states have done."

The six-to-three conference vote was also the final vote in the case. The *Moorman* decision held that the Commerce Clause does not require computation of net income under the three-factor formula. While Moorman claimed that Iowa's formula was responsible for tax duplication, the Court asserted that the claim was not proven.

As already noted, Iowa was the only state that used the single-factor sales formula in imposing corporate income taxes. Other states used the three-factor formula: property, payroll, and sales. Hence, Iowa's formula posed what another case called "a credible threat of overlapping taxation." [99]

The Iowa practice ensured that out-of-state businesses selling in Iowa would have higher total tax payments than local businesses.

This was true because Iowa attributed to itself all the income derived from sales in Iowa, while other taxing states, where the taxpayer had property and employees, used the three-factor formula to tax some portion of the same income through attribution of property or payroll in those states. An interstate corporation thus faced an overall tax liability greater than that encountered by a corporation domiciled in Iowa with its total property and payroll located there.

The *Moorman* case illustrates the Burger Court's reluctance to bar states from sources of revenue in a period of perpetual financial crises. At the same time, *Moorman* is difficult to support on Commerce Clause grounds. Particularly disturbing is the invitation that the decision gives to other states to gain comparable advantages by returning to single-factor formulas. Blackmun noted in dissent that under the Iowa "formula now upheld by the Court, there is little reason why other States, perceiving or imagining a similar advantage to local interests, may not go back to the old ways. The end result, in any event, is to exacerbate what the Commerce Clause . . . was devised to avoid." [100] As the Court once said in another context, "[T]he sheer inconsistency of the [single-factor] formula with that generally prevailing may tend to result in the unhealthy fragmentation of enterprise and an uneconomic pattern of plant location." [101]

FEDERALISM, COMMERCE, AND THE COURT

The law, said Justice Cardozo,[102] has its periods of ebbs and flow. The same is true of federalism in operation. After years of seemingly irresistible centripetal flow, the federal tide may have begun to ebb. In the Burger Court, a centrifugal swing appeared to have started with the *National League of Cities* decision.[103] But that decision was overruled toward the end of the Burger tenure by *Garcia*.[104] That case indicates that the Burger Court did not significantly shift the balance in the federal system toward the states. Despite the fears expressed by commentators and political pressures from President Reagan's "new federalism," [105] the Burger Court jurisprudence did not provide a vehicle for the revival of the doctrine of dual federalism—under which states and nation were treated as equals.

On the other hand, the Commerce Clause decisions discussed in this chapter have been based on the need to permit the states to function as effective governments, endowed with the authority to tax and regulate businesses within their borders. This consideration was, however, more compelling in the cases involving taxation than in

those involving regulation. In a period of endemic economic crises
the Burger Court was unable to resist the demands of the states to tap
all possible sources of revenue. The dominant theme in the tax cases
was judicial willingness to uphold state taxes against claims based
upon the Commerce Clause and the Import–Export Clause. This was
true even when the cases involved taxes that had been ruled invalid
by prior Courts. Only one state tax was stricken by the Burger Court
on Commerce Clause grounds, and it involved a patently discriminatory tax,[106] which even the strongest exponent of state power in
this area would have to condemn if the Commerce Clause is to have
any meaning as a restraint on state power.

To reach its decisions in these cases, the Burger Court repudiated
two formalistic tests that imposed unwarranted obstacles to the legitimate exercise of state taxing power: that the property being taxed
was technically still in the package in which it had been imported[107]
and that the tax was on the *privilege* of doing interstate business measured by net income or gross receipts, rather than on the income itself.[108] These tests never should have determined the illegality of taxes
that were otherwise levied with an even hand and consistent with the
other requirements for valid state taxation. The shift in judicial emphasis from form to practical effect can only be commended.

Nevertheless, the Burger Court's Commerce Clause balance sheet
was not all in favor of state power. The Court continued to follow a
strict approach toward state attempts to impose regulatory barriers
upon commerce. State attempts to restrict importation of milk and
apples were sharply rebuffed,[109] as was New Jersey's effort to impose
the sole burden of conserving the state's landfill space on out-of-state
interests.[110] A state endeavor to create a local monopoly on fruit crating met a similarly hostile reception.[111] The Court even went further,
holding that the long-settled power of the states to embargo game
and water shipments may no longer exist.[112] All of these decisions
contribute to making a reality of the Commerce Clause's fundamental goal: "to create an area of free trade among the several States."[113]

The Burger Court's Commerce Clause jurisprudence appears in
favorable perspective, particularly when we compare its work in
other areas. The Court did not suffer from the internal atomization
that too often characterized its other decisions. Of course, it did not
always manage to speak with a unified voice; but it did so more often
than in most other fields. Where dissents were rendered, they were
less strident.

Most important, the decisions did not turn back the constitutional clock to the days of dual federalism. Under the Burger Court jurisprudence, the states and the federal government do not confront each other as equals. One may agree with the *National League of Cities* effort to preserve the states as independent governments, free from federal control in their integral operations. But its overruling and the other cases indicate that the Supreme Court by itself may not be relied upon to hold back the onrushing flood of federal power.

Chapter Five

First Amendment I: Freedom of Expression

A DOMINANT TREND in the Warren Court was a shift in emphasis from property rights to personal rights. The preferred-position theory—that the Constitution gives a preferred status to personal, as opposed to property, rights—became accepted doctrine. The result is a double standard in the exercise by the Supreme Court of its review function. The tenet of judicial self-restraint does not rigidly bind the judge in cases involving civil liberties and other personal rights.[1] The presumption of validity gives way far more readily in cases where life and liberty are restrained. In those cases, the legislative judgment must be scrutinized with much greater care.

Early in Chief Justice Burger's tenure, the Court stated "that the dichotomy between personal liberties and property rights is a false one. . . . In fact, a fundamental interdependence exists between the personal right to liberty and the personal right to property. Neither could have meaning without the other."[2]

But the Burger Court did not abandon the preferred-position approach; on the contrary, like its predecessor, it recognized that each generation must necessarily have its own scale of values. Nineteenth-century America was concerned with the economic conquest of a continent, and property rights occupied the dominant place. A century later, individuality was dwarfed by concentrations of power and concern with personal rights had become more important. With the focus of concern on the need to preserve an area for the development of individuality, the Justices were naturally more ready to find legislative invasion when personal rights were involved than in the sphere of economics.[3]

Both the Warren Court and the Burger Court were especially willing to recognize the rights guaranteed by the First Amendment as peculiarly suitable for inclusion in the preferred-position theory.

Countless cases have recognized the special constitutional function of the First Amendment—a function both explicit and indispensable.[4] The free society itself is inconceivable without what Justice Holmes called "free trade in ideas."[5] In the Burger Court, as in the Warren Court, governmental power over First Amendment freedoms was narrower than that permitted over property rights.

COMMERCIAL SPEECH

The Burger Court did more than confirm its predecessor's general approach in First Amendment cases. It also extended constitutional protection to types of speech previously held beyond the Amendment's reach—in particular, commercial speech. Whatever restrictions may otherwise be imposed on governmental power over expression, affirmed *Valentine v. Chrestenson,*[6] the leading pre–Burger Court case, "the Constitution imposes no such restraint on government as respects purely commercial advertising."[7]

The first indication that all was no longer well with *Valentine's* commercial-speech doctrine came in *Pittsburgh Press Co. v. Pittsburgh Commission on Human Rights.*[8] The commission held that petitioner newspaper had violated an ordinance prohibiting sex-designated employment advertisements. The paper claimed that the ordinance violated its First Amendment rights, since it interfered with editorial judgment as to the makeup of the help-wanted section of the paper. The commission's response was based upon the argument that the speech at issue was commercial speech unprotected by the First Amendment.

The Court agreed that "[t]he advertisements are thus classic examples of commercial speech."[9] But there were indications that *Valentine* might be overruled. Chief Justice Burger began his conference presentation by asserting that there was "no evidence the *Press* practice clearly aids discrimination. . . . I have trouble distinguishing a paid ad from the rest of the newspaper." He stated that the paper's "makeup, layout, etc." were beyond state control "and a statute that conflicts with it runs afoul of the First Amendment."

Justice Douglas spoke next against the *Valentine* doctrine itself. He said that he had "grave misgivings about *Valentine* and now think it should be overruled." Stewart did not go that far but indicated that he too favored a reversal. "I never thought *Valentine* meant the government could tell a newspaper what it could print or how it must print it. And this ordinance does just this and it's verboten under the First Amendment." Blackmun agreed, saying, "This is an intrusion into newspaper policy and close to a prior restraint."

The others were for affirmance. Rehnquist asserted, "*Valentine* is good law and does cover want-ads." Brennan, White, and Marshall also voted for affirmance. Powell, who was to write the opinion, made the most complete statement in favor of the ordinance. "I start from the premise that I'm not absolutist about freedom of the press. A newspaper ad as to availability of marijuana would not be protected. . . . This ordinance is not directed against the press; it's against employers and is simply an implementation of a state policy rested on the police power."

The *Pittsburgh Press* decision followed the conference view and affirmed the commission's action. Yet the Court did not completely reject the newspaper's claim that "commercial speech should be accorded a higher level of protection than [*Valentine v.*] *Chrestenson* and its progeny would suggest" and that, since "the exchange of information is as important in the commercial realm as in any other," the Court should "abrogate the distinction between commercial and other speech." Instead, the Court indicated that this contention might have "merits . . . in other contexts," but not in this case where not just commercial activity but illegal commercial activity was involved. The restriction on advertising here was "incidental to a valid limitation on economic activity." [10]

The implication that advertising of a legal activity might not be prohibited was borne out in *Bigelow v. Virginia*.[11] The Court reversed a conviction of a newspaper publisher for printing an advertisement that would "encourage or prompt the procuring of abortion." The opinion stated that *Valentine v. Chrestenson* was not "authority for the proposition that all statutes regulating commercial advertising are immune from constitutional challenge."[12] At the conference, Rehnquist had declared, "I can't distinguish *Pittsburgh Press*" and his dissent asserted that the advertisement was "a classic commercial proposition directed toward the exchange of services rather than the exchange of ideas."[13]

A year later, in *Virginia State Board of Pharmacy v. Virginia Consumer Council*,[14] the Court held squarely that commercial speech came within the protection of the First Amendment. A consumer group had brought an action challenging a state statute barring a pharmacist from advertising prescription drug prices. The conference consensus to strike the law was stated by Blackmun, the author of the opinion. "*Bigelow* is the only case really in point and [it] did restrict and confine [*Valentine v.*] *Chrestenson* to hold that some First Amendment protection applies to commercial advertising. The real emphasis is upon the free flow of information."

The two dissenters at the conference were Justices Stewart and Rehnquist. "Because," said Rehnquist, "I don't think there's a First Amendment right here, but only Fourteenth [Amendment] equal protection, I'd reverse."

Stewart's conference vote was based on a more flexible view of the First Amendment. He began by asserting, "There's no such thing as a constitutional 'right' to know. The Constitution only derivatively secures the opportunity to receive speech or writing. *Lamont* and *Mandel*[15] held that potential receivers or readers have standing to vindicate the pharmacists' right to speak or write." Stewart went on, "I have difficulty seeing how commercial price advertising is protected by the First Amendment. If it is, how [can government] prohibit false, misleading, and unfair advertising now regulated by federal and state laws?"

Powell told the others, "Potter's point has substance and if there were any doubt in my mind affecting the FTC power to regulate deceptive advertising, I'd take a second look," but, striking down the law here would not eliminate governmental power over deceptive advertising. Stewart ultimately agreed and issued a concurrence stressing that the decision against the statutory prohibition did not preclude regulation of false or deceptive advertising.

Virginia State Board of Pharmacy, with only Rehnquist dissenting, struck down the law restricting prescription price advertising. Speech "which does 'no more than propose a commercial transaction'"[16] was ruled squarely within the protection of the First Amendment. Society has a strong interest in the free flow of commercial information, even of advertisements.

But the Burger Court's protection of commercial speech did not stop with the prescription-price type of commercial advertising. The *Virginia State Board of Pharmacy* opinion distinguished regulation of commercial advertising by pharmacists from regulation of other professions, noting that "Physicians and lawyers, for example, do not dispense standardized products; they render professional *services* of almost infinite variety and nature.[17] In *Bates v. State Bar,*[18] the Court dealt directly with the barring of attorney advertising. Two Arizona attorneys had opened a "legal clinic" and advertised "legal services at very reasonable fees," listing fees for certain services.

As Chief Justice Burger put it at the conference, here were "only a couple of guys soliciting clients." But he was troubled by the extension of *Virginia State Board of Pharmacy* to lawyer advertising. "Lawyers for me are a special breed of officers of the court whose First Amendment rights are inhibited. If we're ready to extend *Virginia Pharmacy* to professional services, I'm not." However, he passed, saying that the rule might well be overbroad.

White agreed, but Blackmun, who authored the *Bates* opinion, said, "I prefer not to go on overbreadth theory, but go right to First Amendment." And Stevens stated the approach to be taken in the *Bates* opinion; he "wouldn't use overbreadth in the area of commercial advertising." Rehnquist also opposed applying the overbreadth doctrine. "If overbreadth is going to apply in the area of commercial speech [it] will open Pandora's Box in the area of bans on deceptive advertising."

On the First Amendment issue, five Justices (Brennan, White, Marshall, Blackmun, and Stevens) expressed the view that the Arizona rule invalidly restricted the free flow of commercial speech. As Blackmun put it, "*Bigelow* and *Virginia Pharmacy* go far to sustain the First Amendment attack here." However, Blackmun did say, "I'm not sure I'd go too far. Maybe we ought to stop with saying this ad is O.K."

The three dissenters at the conference (Stewart, Powell, and Rehnquist) agreed with the view urged in the American Bar Association amicus brief—that all lawyer advertising was deceptive. That was true even though, as Rehnquist conceded, it was "hard to say that, on the face of the record, these fellows were deceptive." Despite this, Rehnquist went on, "I'd say, treat this as if it were [deceptive]. You allow the state to legislate against that danger. I'd let the State Bar assume that as to price advertising."

Powell, a former ABA president and the only member of the Court appointed directly from private practice, expressed the greatest concern at the proposed majority decision. "Anything beyond *Martindale* [*–Hubbell Law Directory*[19]] is likely to be inherently deceptive and misleading. Once you let this genie out of the bottle, there will be hell to pay. A state is constitutionally free to decide that an ad like this is inherently deceptive."

The *Bates* decision, by a bare majority (the Chief Justice having joined the dissenters), struck down the Arizona rule. The state may not prohibit truthful advertisements concerning the availability and terms of routine legal services. Powell continued to express concern at *Bates*, and in the next case on lawyer advertising, *In re R.M.J.*,[20] he told the conference that they all knew "my *Bates* views. . . . It destroyed the essential character of our profession." Despite this, Powell delivered the *R.M.J.* opinion striking down a Missouri regulation that required lawyers to list areas of practice in the precise wording stated in the rule and prohibiting mailing of announcement cards to persons other than lawyers, friends, and relatives. At the *R.M.J.* conference Powell stated, "I'd reverse because everything the lawyer did was protected by *Bates*."

Powell did not participate in the last Burger Court decision on lawyer advertising, *Zauderer v. Office of Disciplinary Counsel*.[21] An Ohio attorney ran an advertisement offering to represent defendants in drunk driving cases and refund their fees if they were convicted and another that contained a drawing of a defective birth control device, the Dalkon Shield. He advised previous users of the device not to assume that it was too late to sue for their injuries and offered to represent them on a contingent fee basis. The state's Office of Disciplinary Counsel filed a complaint alleging that the first advertisement was deceptive in offering criminal representation on a contingent fee basis. The second advertisement violated rules regarding advertising that prohibited self-recommendation, accepting employment resulting from unsolicited legal advice, and the use of illustrations, and was deceptive in failing to disclose a losing client's liability for costs.

The Chief Justice told the postargument conference, "I think the Dalkon Shield [ad] was bait to get clients to let him bring a particular suit against a particular defendant." Burger also said that "*Ohralik*[22] [a lawyer solicitation case] used some strong language suggesting that this was misrepresentation." Burger indicated that he thought the state could bar both ads.

Brennan argued at the conference that the Dalkon Shield ad might not be the basis of attorney discipline. "May a State ban all discussion of truthful legal information in lawyer advertising? Under *Bates* analysis, I would think not. This is not an ad like the one discussed at argument—'The defendant is guilty as hell, see me for details'—that's at least potentially deceptive. A State has an interest in restricting deceptive information and *potentially* deceptive information, and this interest may justify a prophylactic rule in some circumstances. But in the absence of *any* indication that Zauderer's legal 'advice' comes close to the line of deception, isn't the sole reason for restricting it a matter of 'taste'? And doesn't the First Amendment prohibit such restrictions?"[23]

Brennan answered these questions in the affirmative. As he saw it, "in the absence of *any* indication that Zauderer's 'advice' even comes close to the line of deception, I believe the public's right to know outweighs the State's alleged need for an all-encompassing prophylactic rule."

Brennan went on, "I believe the State surely may require the affirmative disclosure of truthful information by a lawyer when he advertises that he takes cases for a contingent fee." However, Brennan questioned the application of the principle in this case. "While I believe," he said, "that Ohio can require a lawyer to qualify the statement 'you pay no legal fees if you lose,' there's a serious question here whether Zauderer received fair warning that his ad was proscribed"[24]—that is, the ground on which Brennan ultimately dissented in the case.

Zauderer was assigned to White, whose opinion followed his approach at the conference: "On the Dalkon Shield, this goes too far. But the discipline for the contingent fee is O.K. So also [there was] no due process violation on the drunk driving [ad]"—rejecting the Brennan argument in a February 28, 1985, "Dear Byron" letter, "that the procedures leading up to the State's reprimand for the drunk driving advertisement did not comport with due process."

O'Connor, who delivered a dissent on the Dalkon Shield ad, said, in a February 22 letter to Justice White: "Your opinion sweeps more broadly than I am presently able to join, particularly in Part III discussing Ohio's rule prohibiting the giving of unsolicited legal advice. I tend to think the dignity of the profession justifies a little more leeway in state regulation. The use of unsolicited professional advice to obtain business should be subject to greater regulation than other forms of commercial speech, in my view."

The Chief Justice joined the O'Connor dissent with a May 14 letter containing an animadversion against "the shysterism increasingly manifested by lawyers." Rehnquist also joined. "It seems to me," he wrote to White on February 25, "that Ohio may adopt the position that it does not wish attorneys . . . to 'stir up litigation,' and therefore I think this argument advanced by the state is entitled to more weight than you give it."

Except for *Zauderer,* the lawyer advertising cases were, in many ways, the culmination of the Burger Court jurisprudence extending First Amendment protection to commercial speech. Speech proposing a commercial transaction is within the constitutional guaranty. That is as true of professional advertisements, which were considered unprofessional conduct before *Bates,* as of other advertisements proposing commercial transactions.

At the *Bates* conference, Justice Blackmun had noted that "states are entitled to time, place, and manner regulations," so far as the commercial speech at issue was concerned. But the Burger Court also held that, while commercial speech is entitled to protection, the protection afforded it is "somewhat less extensive than that afforded 'noncommercial speech.'"[25] Thus, government remains free to prevent dissemination of commercial speech that is false, deceptive, or misleading or that proposes an illegal transaction. While the state may not, as seen, prohibit truthful lawyer advertising of the type at issue in *Bates,* it may restrain or bar in-person solicitation of clients even though the solicitation is carried out by speech.[26]

Powell was the primary author of the Burger Court jurisprudence covering commercial speech. The Powell approach was summarized in a Blackmun comment on the Powell draft in the case on lawyer solicitation of clients: "I read your opinion as centering between the more extreme views expressed at the conference of January 18. Although it does not express my precise position, any more than it does the positions of some of the others, it is a good middle-of-the-road opinion."[27]

The opinion lay between the *Valentine* extreme of no constitutional protection of commercial speech and the opposite extreme of treating commercial speech like other types of speech. While rejecting the *Valentine* holding, Powell and his colleagues did not discard "the 'common-sense' distinction" between commercial speech and other varieties of speech.[28] Under the Burger Court jurisprudence, there is no parity of constitutional protection between commercial and noncommercial speech. Instead, as Stevens put it in a May 16, 1980, letter to Powell, "there is a lesser First Amendment interest in protecting proposals to engage in commercial transactions than there is in more pure forms of communication."[29] Hence, commercial speech is placed in a subordinate position in the scale of First Amendment values, making it subject to regulation that might not be permissible in the realm of noncommercial expression.[30]

Government may control commercial speech that is false, deceptive, or misleading or proposes an illegal transaction. Commercial speech that does not come within these categories is governed by the test stated by Justice Powell in *Central Hudson Gas & Electric Co. v. Public Service Commission.*[31] The Court struck down a regulation banning public utility advertising promoting electricity use, which the commission found contrary to the national policy of conserving energy.

The Powell opinion—the culmination of his contribution to the Burger Court jurisprudence in this area—stated a four-part test for commercial-speech cases:

"At the outset, we must determine whether the expression is protected by the First Amendment. For commercial speech to come within that provision, it at least must concern lawful activity and not be misleading. Next, we ask whether the asserted governmental interest is substantial. If both inquiries yield positive answers, we must determine whether the regulation directly advances the governmental interest asserted, and whether it is not more extensive than is necessary to serve that interest."[32]

The first three parts were met: the promotional ads were lawful commercial speech; governmental interest in conservation was substantial; and it was advanced by the regulation. But the complete ban on promotional advertising was more extensive than necessary to further energy conservation. Thus, the state's interest did not justify suppression of information about devices or services that would cause no net increase in energy use. Nor had the state shown that its interest in conservation could not be protected by more limited regulation.

Powell defined commercial speech both as "speech proposing a commercial transaction" and as "expression related solely to the economic interests of the speaker and its audience."[33] In his concurring opinion, Justice Stevens asserted that the latter definition was "unquestionably too broad."[34] In a letter to Stevens, Powell stated that he believed it was entirely proper to rely on both formulations. The second definition was not at all intended to expand the scope of commercial speech. On the contrary, Powell wrote, "To me they [that is, both definitions] seem to have substantially the same reach."[35]

Stevens also asserted that the challenged regulation involved "total censorship" of more than only commercial speech. "Perhaps I miss your thought," Powell replied, "but I see no political content in the exhortation to purchase electricity. I have not thought there was any First Amendment distinction between the advertising of drugs by regulated pharmacists and the advertising of electricity by regulated power companies."

POLITICAL SPEECH

In a 1977 letter to Stewart, Powell referred to the view "that there can be no distinction in First Amendment analysis between, say, economic and political issues. In general theory, this may be true. But no First Amendment right is absolute, and in the balancing process that often must be applied I think we have weighted the scales more favorably where political speech is concerned."

Stewart wrote to Powell that "calling [expression] political rather than economic, philosophical, ethical, or social, does not lead to any difference under the First Amendment. . . . [T]he First Amendment protects the expression of *ideas,* not just those that can in one sense or another be characterized as 'political.'" The language in First Amendment cases "does not mean—and I know of no case holding—that the expression of ideas about art, literature, family life, religion, public morals, economic affairs, or other 'non-political' matters is not protected to exactly the same degree."

At the same time, there has never been any doubt that political speech is protected. Indeed, as Stewart put it to Powell, "our cases have on occasion suggested that speech about political matters could not be more central to the purposes of the First Amendment."[36]

In *First National Bank of Boston v. Bellotti,*[37] however, it was argued that, while the state might not prohibit the commercial speech of corporations, it might ban their political speech—at least where the speech did not affect the corporation's own property or business. At issue was a statute prohibiting corporations from making contributions or expenditures to influence voting "on any question submitted to the voters, other than one materially affecting any of the property, business or assets of the corporation." Under a proviso in the law, no question "concerning the income, property or transactions of individuals" was to be deemed one affecting a corporation's property or business. The bank wanted to publicize its views on a proposed constitutional amendment authorizing a graduated personal income tax. The state attorney general decided that would violate the statute. The state court upheld the statute.

At the conference on the case only Justice White thought that the statutory prohibition was clearly constitutional, though Brennan said that he was inclined to agree with him. The other seven Justices disagreed. The Chief Justice asked, "Can the First Amendment be limited to corporations in respect of materially affecting their interests?" Burger thought not. "I can't distinguish the *New York Times* from other corporations. The state can't attach unconstitutional limitations." Rehnquist asked, "Why should only *Time* and the *New York Times* have First Amendment protection?"

As Stewart expressed it, they should "reverse on the ground Massachusetts can't tell the corporation it can't express its views on a proposal to have a personal income tax." But the conference decided to avoid the constitutionality of the general ban and focused on the proviso that no question concerning the taxation of individuals was to be deemed to affect a corporation's property or business. Blackmun said that the proviso's "conclusive presumption is a content-related restriction" and, as such, violated the First Amendment. Brennan, Powell, Rehnquist, and Stevens agreed with the Blackmun approach.

The result was an eight-to-one (Justice White) vote at the conference to reverse, but only on the validity of the proviso. Brennan summarized his position in a December 1, 1977, Memorandum to the Conference: "My view at conference was that we should attempt to address only the statutory proviso and reverse on the ground of disagreement with the Supreme Judicial Court's view, implicit in its opinion, that the proviso may be constitutional. In such case, I would have reserved the question whether the First and Fourteenth Amendments invalidate the statute's provision that the only corporations that may advertise are those able to show that the referendum question is one 'materially affecting any of the property, business or assets of the corporation.'" Brennan was willing to go along with this approach even though at the conference he had agreed with White that the statute's general prohibition was constitutional.

In a December 6 "Dear Bill" letter, Chief Justice Burger explained why he assigned the opinion to Brennan. "I had assigned the case to you on the old English Judges' rule-of-thumb that when a case is to be narrowly written, it should be written by the judge 'least persuaded.'"

After considering the case, Brennan wrote (again in the December 1 memo), "I am not the one who should write the Court opinion. . . . I am satisfied that the opinion cannot be limited to the constitutionality of the 'conclusive presumption' and that the constitutionality of the general ban must also be decided." The corporation "have on this record demonstrated that they have a constitutional right to spend money to oppose referenda questions concerning the adoption of graduated income taxation solely for individuals" and had attacked both the proviso and the general ban. "Since it's clear that the general prohibition would remain in effect if we struck down only the proviso, a failure to decide the constitutionality of the general prohibition would be to deny appellants relief on a constitutional claim—which is ripe for review and not moot—without deciding any issue against them."

Brennan wrote that if he were to write an opinion on the general prohibition, "I presently feel that I would write to sustain its constitutionality." Hence, the opinion should be reassigned.

Brennan also noted his principal concern with striking down the general Massachusetts prohibition: "Corporate spending as a corrupting influence in the political process has long been a national concern. . . . It seems to me that a decision invalidating the rather narrow Massachusetts general limitation must inevitably call into question the constitutionality of all corrupt practices acts."

This view was shared by other Justices. The Chief Justice stated in his December 6 letter, "Many of us at the Conference expressed concern about taking any step which would undermine state and federal Corrupt Practices Acts." And in a March 11, 1978, letter to Powell he said, "I do not want corrupt practices statutes to be placed under a shadow."

Powell himself had replied to Brennan's anxiety over the corrupt practices laws in a December 6, 1977, Memorandum to the Conference: "I share Bill Brennan's concern that we not undercut the Corrupt Practices Acts. But I do not think a holding in appellant's favor on this issue would 'call into question' the constitutionality of those acts. In *Buckley v. Valeo*[38] we drew a distinction between contributions and expenditures. This case is a major step further removed even from expenditures. It involves only the expression of views on public issues; not views in support of or in opposition to a political candidate. (Even if the corporation made 'contributions' in order to pool its resources with others of like mind, the dangers inherent in *political* contributions would be absent.) No problem of 'corruption' is involved at all, using that term in the context of the Corrupt Practices Acts."

The Chief Justice now assigned the case to Powell, whose opinion held that the states may not prohibit corporations from spending money to express their views even on issues not related to their business interests. First Amendment rights are not limited to corporations engaged in the communications business. On the contrary, "the press does not have a monopoly on either the First Amendment or the ability to enlighten."[39]

Powell's view in this respect had been succinctly stated in his December 6 memo: "I think it is too late to hold that persons who elect to do business in the corporate form may not express opinions through the corporation on issues of general public interest. It seems to me that circumscribing speech on the basis of its source, in the absence of a compelling interest that could not be attained otherwise, would be a most serious infringement of First Amendment rights."

The state had argued in *First National Bank* that political speech by corporations was entitled to less constitutional protection than commercial speech. The Court said that this argument would invert the First Amendment balance "by giving constitutional significance to a corporation's 'hawking of wares' while approving criminal sanctions for a bank's expression of [political] opinion."[40]

The *First National Bank* holding was applied in *Consolidated Edison Co. v. Public Service Commission*[41] to strike down a commission order that prohibited the inclusion with monthly bills of inserts discussing controversial issues. Rehnquist had objected at the conference that, with the utilities' "complete monopoly, it's a too ready-made market for utility propaganda" and Stevens had said that the "captive audience problem here is disturbing." The Court nevertheless ruled the prohibition invalid (with only Blackmun and Rehnquist dissenting). The Powell opinion followed his conference statement "that this is regulation of speech content." As such it was subject to stricter scrutiny, but there was no compelling interest to support it. In Stevens' pithy conference comment, "this is prior restraint and offensiveness to recipient [is] not a compelling interest."

The Burger Court decisions on political speech were not limited to these cases involving corporations. The Court also gave an entirely new dimension to political speech in *Buckley v. Valeo*.[42] At issue was the Federal Election Campaign Act of 1971, as amended in 1974: (1) Individual political contributions were limited to $1,000 to any single candidate, with an overall annual limitation of $25,000; independent expenditures by individuals and groups "relative to a clearly identified candidate" were limited to $1,000 a year; campaign spending by candidates for various federal offices and spending for national conventions by political parties were subject to prescribed limits; (2) contributions and expenditures above certain threshold levels must be reported and publicly disclosed; (3) a system for public funding of presidential campaign activities was established; and (4) a Federal Election Commission was established to administer and enforce the legislation.

Our earlier discussion of *Buckley*[43] was concerned with the appointment of members of the Federal Election Commission, a minor part of the statutory scheme. The provisions dealing with political contributions and expenditures gave the Justices more difficulty and the conference was divided. The presidential campaign funding provision and the power of Congress to require reporting and disclosure presented no problem. For Chief Justice Burger, the disclosure provisions are "the heart of the whole thing for me. I think they are constitutional and highly desirable." But he and Brennan, Marshall, and Blackmun expressed doubts on the threshold limits of $10 and $100 that triggered the record-keeping and disclosure requirements. Ultimately, however, all but the Chief Justice went along with the decision to uphold the limits, agreeing with Justice Stewart—it was "for Congress to fix the limits and not for us to second guess."

The strongest conference statement against the law was made by Powell: "This statute is a revolutionary change in the system under which we've lived for 200 years. The entire Act, in purpose and effect, perpetrates the grossest infringement upon First Amendment rights. This Act, in effect, will advantage incumbents and disadvantage challengers. Instead of a system neutral on its face, where all scramble for all the money they can get, [they] rig the structure for the incumbent. . . . only guarantee greater concentrations of power to keep the 'ins' in office."

The *Buckley* decision upheld the limitations on contributions, following the view stated by Rehnquist, "It's an act, not speech." The decision was unanimous, although, at the conference, Blackmun had stated, "I lean to reverse on contributions," and the Chief Justice and Justice Stewart had had doubts.

With regard to the expenditure provisions, the Chief Justice set the conference theme when he said, "This is pure speech." Stewart, who was to write the portion striking down the expenditure restrictions, stated that they were "wholly unconstitutional under the First Amendment." Blackmun was of the opinion that "there's a serious First Amendment infringement, simply indefensible, in the expenditure provisions." And for Justice Powell the provisions were "the most drastic abridgements of political speech since the Alien and Sedition Acts." Brennan, White, and Marshall dissented from the conference consensus on the expenditure provisions (though Brennan ultimately agreed).

At Stewart's suggestion, the Chief Justice gave up his assigning function and reluctantly agreed to have Justices Stewart, Brennan, and Powell work as a committee to draft the per curiam opinion.

The portion dealing with expenditures was written by Stewart, who treated expenditures as a form of political speech. "A restriction on the amount of money a person or group can spend on political communication during a campaign necessarily reduces the quantity of expression by restricting the number of issues discussed, the depth of their exploration, and the size of the audience reached. This is because virtually every means of communicating in today's mass society requires the expenditure of money." [44] In effect, then, the statute infringed upon the First Amendment freedom to speak without legislative limits on candidacies for public office.

As restrictions on First Amendment rights of political expression, the challenged provisions had to satisfy the strict-scrutiny standard of review. [45] They would be valid only if supported by a *compelling* state interest. The *Buckley* opinion rejected the argument, accepted by the court of appeals, that the governmental interest in equalizing the relative ability of individuals and groups to influence elections justified the limitations. In a November 10, 1977, Memorandum to the Conference in a later case, Justice Rehnquist stated his impression of the court of appeals acceptance of this argument in *Buckley:* "The Court of Appeals there, it seemed to me, appeared to say that in order to achieve the 'compelling state interest' of allowing everybody to be heard to some extent, Congress did not abridge the First Amendment by preventing some people from talking as much as they wanted.

This seemed to me like something out of George Orwell, or like Rousseau's idea that people would be forced to be free."[46]

SYMBOLIC SPEECH

The cases just discussed show that the right of free speech is not limited to mere expression of words. Thus, campaign expenditures were treated in *Buckley v. Valeo* as a form of political speech protected by the First Amendment. The notion of nonverbal speech had, however, been used to protect symbolic speech well before the Burger Court. Over half a century ago, the Court ruled that display of a red flag as a symbol of opposition to organized government is covered by First Amendment protection.[47]

In *Spence v. Washington*,[48] the Burger Court held that the same is true of a display of the flag upside down with a peace symbol affixed. Defendant in *Spence* had been convicted under a state law forbidding the exhibition of the U.S. flag with figures, symbols, or other extraneous material attached. The conference agreed (Justices White and Rehnquist dissenting) to reverse, but different views were expressed on the rationale for the decision.

On May 29, 1974, the Chief Justice circulated a three-and-a-half page draft per curiam, which, he wrote in his covering memo, "does not fully satisfy me. We might perhaps better reverse in one line." The Burger per curiam held the state statute "to be unconstitutionally overbroad in its potential application to protected activity under the First Amendment. . . . The statute would forbid the publication of a picture or representation of the flag with any overwriting or other superimposition. The statute would make illegal, for example, the taking, developing, or printing for display of any photograph of a public official or war hero in front of a flag. The filming of a motion picture in which anyone or anything appeared 'in front' of the flag would be illegal, as would the exhibition in Washington State of any such film, since the flag and the superimposed person or object would be on the same plane as the covered flag on the celluloid print and on the screen. The Tomb of the Unknown Soldier as a printed or photographic overlay on the flag as part of a Memorial Day or Veterans' Day tribute would also appear to be condemned by the Washington statute. . . .

"Whatever interest the State may assert in attempting to regulate the placing of foreign matter on the body of a United States flag, there is no basis for such sweeping regulation of traditional modes of expression." However, Burger himself believed that the state interest was sufficient to sustain narrowly drawn regulation to protect the flag, and he dissented from the ultimate *Spence* decision.

White wrote to the Chief Justice on May 29, "I cannot agree with your *per curiam*" and either he or Rehnquist (both of whom had favored affirmance at the conference) would circulate a dissent. But the Burger per curiam was also unsatisfactory to those who had been for reversal. They wanted the conviction set aside because it violated the First Amendment. A new per curiam was circulated by Justice Powell essentially similar to the final plurality opinion. It was joined on June 12 by Justices Brennan and Stewart and on June 13 by Justice Marshall. Although Justice Brennan had written to Justice Powell, "I . . . suggest you make it a signed opinion,"[49] the Powell draft was issued as a per curiam for a plurality of the Court.

The *Spence* per curiam held that, in "the factual context and environment in which it was undertaken," defendant's action was protected symbolic speech: "there can be little doubt that appellant communicated through the use of symbols." Nor could the state justify its restriction of expression by any substantial state interest. On the contrary, there was "no interest the State may have in preserving the physical integrity of a privately owned flag [that] was significantly impaired on these facts."[50]

It should be stressed that *Spence* was not intended to indicate that flag desecration laws were, as such, violative of the First Amendment. On the contrary, as Powell had stated at the *Spence* conference, while he was for reversal here, "I have a different feeling as to a desecration statute. The physical integrity of the flag may be protected"—so that the 1989 flag burning case[51] would probably have been decided differently had Powell not retired.

A few years later, in *Wooley v. Maynard,*[52] the Chief Justice circulated a draft opinion of the Court that refused to apply the symbolic speech concept to the nonverbal expression at issue in the case. A New Hampshire law required motor vehicles to bear license plates embossed with the state motto, "Live Free or Die," and made it a misdemeanor to obscure the motto. Maynard and his wife, Jehovah's Witnesses, viewed the motto as repugnant to their moral, religious, and political beliefs and covered it up with tape. They were found guilty of violating the statute, but the district court granted an injunction against enforcement of the law.

The Chief Justice spoke at the conference in favor of affirmance. "The state can't compel me to convey its message on a picket sign." Justices Blackmun and Rehnquist were the only ones to speak the other way. In Rehnquist's words, "symbolic speech is not applicable."

In his draft opinion of the Court, circulated March 10, 1977, Chief Justice Burger expressly disagreed with the holding below "that by covering up the state motto . . . , Mr. Maynard was engaging in symbolic speech." Maynard's conduct was not similar to Spence's. "Unlike the prominently displayed flag in *Spence* . . . , it is doubtful that the strip of tape placed on the license plate would attract significant notice." Indeed, "the act of covering the motto was not itself intended to communicate, but rather was designed to attract attention of passers-by so that Mr. Maynard could then express his point of view. The symbolic speech doctrine does not reach so far. Under that rationale virtually any bizzare [*sic*] or illegal conduct would be deemed symbolic speech so long as it were likely to stimulate interest or integrity."

The view of the Justices who objected to the Burger refusal to recognize Maynard's conduct as symbolic speech was expressed by Justice Brennan in a March 11, "Dear Chief" letter: "I don't think I could agree with the resolution of the symbolic speech issue on the facts of this case; I would think that it is probably fairly clear to most people that Maynard's covering up the 'Live Free or Die' slogan is his way of communicating his disagreement with the slogan." Justice Stewart went further and prepared a short concurrence stating his disagreement with Burger.

In a March 16 Memorandum to the Conference, Burger agreed to delete the offending part, though he did write, "Those to whom that part appeals may want to say something separately." Only Rehnquist supported the Burger draft view on symbolic speech; he stated in his dissent "that there is no protected 'symbolic speech' in this case."[53]

The Burger opinion of the Court held that the New Hampshire law deprived the Maynards of their First Amendment right to refrain from speaking. Adopting an approach similar to the Burger conference approach, the opinion asserted that the "statute in effect requires that appellees use their private property as a 'mobile billboard' for the State's ideological message." Or as Justice Brennan summarized the Court's holding, "Maynard cannot be compelled by the state to disseminate a message with which he disagrees."[54]

Brennan appears to have been correct that Maynard's conduct did involve symbolic speech. Commentators have also treated *Wooley v. Maynard* as a symbolic speech case and concluded that "the Court applied settled symbolic speech principles."[55] Such an interpretation would be impossible if the Burger draft had come down in its original form, with its categorical rejection of the claim that symbolic speech was involved in the case.

It should, however, be stressed that neither *Spence* nor *Maynard* means that identifying nonverbal conduct as symbolic speech necessarily means the end of the First Amendment inquiry. As Stewart put it in an April 14, 1977, letter to the Chief Justice on *Wooley v. Maynard,* "sometimes interests in free expression must be subordinated to strong societal policies." The countervailing governmental interest may be sufficiently compelling to justify the given restriction on the First Amendment right.

This may be seen from a case like *Clark v. Community for Creative Non-Violence.*[56] The National Park Service issued a permit to respondent for a demonstration to call attention to the homeless. The permit authorized erection of symbolic "tent cities" in Lafayette Park and on the Mall in Washington, D.C. Permission was, however, refused for the demonstrators to sleep in the tents. The Service relied on a regulation that allowed "camping" (defined as including sleeping) only in designated campgrounds. The lower court ruled that the regulation violated the demonstrators' right of free expression.

Opening the *Clark* conference, the Chief Justice conceded that the demonstrators' goal was to make a 'statement' in this form." Despite this, the First Amendment claim was a "wholly frivolous claim, absolutely absurd." None of the others concurred in this characterization, but all except Justices Brennan and Marshall supported the Burger view that the decision below should be reversed. As Burger saw it, "*United States v. O'Brien*[57] supports this regulation." *O'Brien* was the case in which the Warren Court upheld a conviction for burning a draft card as an antiwar protest. The Court held that, even though the burning had a communicative element, restriction of that element was valid if it met a four-prong test: "[1] if it is within the constitutional power of the Government; [2] if it furthers an important or substantial governmental interest; [3] if the governmental interest is unrelated to the suppression of free expression; and [4] if the incidental restriction on alleged First Amendment freedoms is no greater than is essential to the furtherance of that interest."

The conference majority agreed that *O'Brien* required reversal. Their view was expressed by Rehnquist. After stating that he agreed with the Chief Justice, Rehnquist said, "I'd treat it as symbolic speech and apply the *O'Brien* test to come out on the side of the Government. This is speech-plus, subject to regulation as plain speech is not."

The *Clark* decision followed the conference approach. The opinion recognized that sleeping in connection with the demonstration was expressive conduct. The regulation and its application to prohibit the sleeping was nevertheless ruled valid, since the *O'Brien* test was met. The regulation was upheld as a time, place, or manner restriction regulating symbolic conduct.

SPEECH AND THE PUBLIC FORUM

Well before the Burger Court, the cases had developed the concept of the "public forum," giving a right of access to public places for First Amendment purposes. That concept was both applied and expanded during Chief Justice Burger's tenure. The earlier cases had upheld the right of individuals to use public places as forums for expression. The Burger Court also recognized, in *Kleindienst v. Mandel*,[58] a First Amendment right "to receive information and ideas," and that freedom of speech "'necessarily protects the right to receive.'"[59]

An action had been brought to compel the Attorney General to grant a temporary nonimmigrant visa to a Belgian journalist whom the American plaintiffs had invited to participate in academic conferences. The journalist himself—an unadmitted nonresident alien—had no constitutional right that had been violated. At the *Mandel* conference, however, Douglas focused upon the right of plaintiffs to hear the journalist's ideas: "Congress has been held to have broad exclusionary power, but it's not that problem but whether serious-minded people can have him. In terms of the philosophy of our Constitution, the First Amendment allows people to become educated."

The *Mandel* opinion accepted the Douglas view that the plaintiffs possessed a First Amendment right to receive ideas and information from the invited speaker. But the decision was based on the principle stated by the Chief Justice at the conference—that the exercise of the power to exclude aliens is "almost unreviewable." As Justice Stewart told the conference, the cases involving the right to receive information[60] "didn't involve people coming from abroad and, as to that, the power to exclude is absolute in the Congress. That overrides the First Amendment rights of Americans to have him brought in."

While speech may not be prohibited in a public place that comes within the public forum concept, it may be subjected to reasonable regulation; laws regulating the time, place, or manner of speech stand on a different footing from laws prohibiting speech altogether.[61] Thus, the Court held that reasonable time, place, and manner regulations, applicable to all speech irrespective of content, may be imposed.[62]

The Burger Court applied the principle just stated in *Grayned v. Rockford*.[63] An ordinance prohibited a person from willfully making a noise or diversion that disturbed the peace or good order of a school in session. At the conference, only Marshall voted to reverse the conviction. He subsequently changed his vote and was assigned the opinion upholding the ordinance as a constitutional regulation of activity around a school. The ordinance was aimed only at conduct disrupting normal school activities and, as such, was narrowly tailored to further the compelling interest in creating an atmosphere conducive to learning.

Also at issue in *Grayned,* as well as in the companion case of *Police Department v. Mosley*,[64] was an ordinance that prohibited picketing within specified distances of schools in session. Both ordinances did not apply to peaceful picketing of schools involved in labor disputes. At the conference, the Justices indicated that this ordinance, too, would have been upheld if it did not contain the exception for labor picketing. Even Douglas stated, "But for that I would think it valid. Black's separate opinion in *Cox v. Louisiana*[65] covers this." But the labor-picketing exception led the conference to vote to strike down the ordinance. As Douglas told the conference, "The exception for labor shows some other basis than peace, quiet, etc." And Justice Powell asserted, "I see no rationality for the labor union exception."

The key defect of the ordinances, according to the opinion of Marshall, was that they described "permissible picketing in terms of its subject matter,"[66] which based the application upon the content of the particular picketing. One thing is clear about the case law on the matter: regulation of speech cannot be valid if it is not content neutral. A content-based restriction will be upheld only if the Court can find that the content fits within a category of speech that is itself unprotected by the First Amendment.[67]

The principle barring content-based regulation was the basis of decision in *Southeastern Promotions v. Conrad.*[68] Petitioner had applied for use of a municipal theater for the showing of the controversial rock musical *Hair.* Although no other engagement for the theater was scheduled, the municipal board rejected the application. They determined that the production would not be "in the best interest of the community." The policy was to "allow those productions which are clean and healthful and culturally uplifting." The lower courts denied an injunction.

The *Southeastern Promotions* majority was disturbed by the board's action. A handwritten memorandum by one of the Justices asserts, "The holding below virtually annihilates much of modern theatre. The loss to culture and to First Amendment rights would be tragic."[69] The opinion of the Court compared the board's action to a censorship system. It was what Douglas termed "content screening"[70] based on the board members' judgment of the musical's contents. Such a content-based prohibition was in categorical conflict with the First Amendment.

Southeastern holds that the city was not free to deny use of the public forum on the basis of a production's content. But that holding depends in turn upon the holding that a municipal theater does come within the public forum concept. Establishment of that concept itself required rejecting the view originally stated by Holmes: "For the Legislature absolutely or conditionally to forbid public speaking in a highway or public park is no more an infringement of the rights of a member of the public than for the owner of a private house to forbid it in his house."[71]

According to the handwritten memo, the city could not argue "that as a proprietor it's in no different position than a private theatre. Rather, . . . because it is municipally owned, there are constitutional limitations upon the powers of the auditorium board to refuse to lease the theatre. They may not lease only to Protestants, to whites, and to men and refuse to lease to Catholics, to Blacks and to women solely because they are Catholics, Blacks or women. Nor may they refuse to lease to exhibitors of plays or movies if the refusal constitutes a denial of First Amendment rights."

The *Southeastern Promotions* opinion declared categorically that municipal theaters "were public forums designed for and dedicated to expressive activities."[72] Under the decision, "a community-owned theater [is treated] as if it were the same as a city park or city street."[73] For First Amendment purposes, a public auditorium is equated with streets, parks, and other public places that come within the public forum concept.

The mere fact that a place is owned by the public does not mean that it comes within the public forum concept. Public facilities not performing speech-related functions may be treated differently. The Warren Court ruled that jailhouse grounds might be closed to demonstrations,[74] and demonstrators might be convicted of trespass even though they were on public property. According to the dissenters, the Court was treating the public property in the case as though it were private property.[75] That was certainly the implication of the opinion of the Court—made even clearer by the last sentence in Black's draft opinion: "And there is no right to 'demonstrate' which is constitutionally paramount to an owner's right to use his property."[76]

The Burger Court applied the same approach to a military base in *Greer v. Spock*.[77] At issue were regulations that categorically banned partisan political speeches and demonstrations at Fort Dix. The lower courts had ruled against the regulations on First Amendment grounds.

Chief Justice Burger began the *Greer* conference by stressing, "It's not a public forum like a public park. *Lloyd v. Tanner* [the shopping center case discussed below] has much bearing." The Chief Justice also referred to the *Cafeteria Workers*[78] case, where the Court upheld the power of the military to bar entry to a base. Burger noted that the Hatch Act isolates civilian employees from politics. They "can also isolate the military, absolutely forbid political rallies." The conference notes used by me end the Burger presentation à la Gertrude Stein, with a "base is a base is a base is a base."

All the others agreed except for Douglas and Marshall. Brennan passed but ultimately joined Marshall in dissent. Douglas retired before the decision. "This is the military," said Stewart, who was to write the *Greer* opinion, "and our constitutional tradition to isolate the military from politics requires this. This is what *Cafeteria Workers* stands for."According to White, the decision below "crosses the line against involving the military in politics unnecessarily. This is military property, and if we allow this, I don't know where to stop."

The *Greer* opinion followed the conference consensus and upheld the challenged regulations. The Stewart opinion rejected "the principle that whenever members of the public are permitted freely to visit a place owned or operated by the Government, then that place becomes a 'public forum' for purposes of the First Amendment. Such a principle of constitutional law has never existed, and does not exist now."[79] The business of a military base like Fort Dix is to train soldiers, not to provide a public forum.

The Burger Court also refused to extend the public forum concept to a municipal rapid transit system. In *Lehman v. Shaker Heights,*[80] a candidate for state office was refused advertising space on the vehicles of a city transit system.

The conference was closely divided. The key question was whether, as Brennan urged, the city had created a public forum when it allowed advertisements on its vehicles. If it had, the First Amendment plainly barred it from discriminating on the basis of message content. White argued the other way. As he saw it, "advertising that they take is not First-Amendment protected and, if they don't want to infringe on passengers' rights as captives, the city can draw the line."

The White view prevailed, and the decision held that the political advertising ban was valid. The car advertising space was not a public forum; that being the case, even a content-based prohibition was valid.

To be sure, even if a public forum is involved in the given case, that does not mean that all regulations of speech in it are invalid. We have already seen that content-neutral reasonable time, place, and manner regulations will be upheld even though they regulate expression in a place coming within the public forum concept. In addition, not all public forums are alike for First Amendment purposes.

The Minnesota state fair, operated by a public corporation on state-owned land, prohibited sale or distribution of any merchandise except from a duly licensed and assigned location on the fairgrounds. Respondent, an organization espousing the Krishna religion, filed suit claiming that the rule violated their First Amendment rights. In *Heffron v. International Society for Krishna Consciousness,*[81] the respondent asserted that the rule suppressed the practice of Sankirtan, which enjoins its members to go into public places to distribute or sell religious literature and to solicit donations. The highest state court held that the rule unconstitutionally restricted the Krishnas' religious practice.

The conference majority was for reversal, agreeing with the Chief Justice that the fair "can't allow roaming at will." Stewart noted that it was "part of [Krishna] religious belief to pester people—give me money or give me back my flowers." But that did not mean the fair rule was invalid. On the contrary, said Stewart, "This is almost a paradigm of a time, place, and manner regulation and I'd reverse."

White, who was to deliver the Court's opinion, agreed. "If [we] address [the] case on the premise it wasn't Krishna," he pointed out, "you wouldn't let this sort of thing go on in art galleries. So why isn't the fair the same thing?" In fact, White asserted, in the fair situation, "the public interest becomes more important."

The other majority Justices took the same view. Justice Blackmun (though he later joined the dissenters with regard to literature distribution) stressed the "maintenance of order and prevention of fraud" and Rehnquist stated that the "crowd control problem here established a higher state interest than in door-to-door distribution."

Powell summed up the majority consensus by characterizing the rule as "a school book example of legitimacy." The decision of the Court (Brennan, Marshall, Blackmun, and Stevens dissenting on restricting literature distribution) upheld the challenged rule as a reasonable time, place, and manner regulation. The rule was content neutral and nondiscriminatory and served the significant state interest of order and crowd control at the state fair. Such a regulation might be too restrictive for a public street, but the state fair may be treated differently than a street, though both may come within the public forum concept. "The flow of the crowd and demands of safety are more pressing in the context of the Fair. As such, any comparisons to public streets are necessarily inexact."[82]

The Court also rejected a novel public forum claim in *Cornelius v. NAACP Legal Defense Fund.*[83] An Executive Order limited participation in the Combined Federal Campaign (CFC)—an annual fundraising drive aimed at federal employees—to charitable agencies that provided direct health and welfare services. Legal defense and political advocacy organizations, which were specifically excluded, claimed that their First Amendment right to solicit charitable contributions was violated. The lower court ruled in their favor.

Only seven Justices were present at the *Cornelius* conference (Marshall and Powell did not participate in the decision). The Chief Justice began by pointing out, "We have first to say whether or not [this is] a public forum. . . . This is not a public forum for me."

Brennan, Blackmun, and Stevens disagreed. "Fund raising per se is speech," stated Blackmun. "CFC is a limited public forum and a compelling state interest must be the justification." No such interest was shown here, said Blackmun. In addition, he noted, "Respondents are similar to those allowed access."

However, White, Rehnquist, and O'Connor voted with the Chief Justice for reversal. According to White, "This is a nonpublic forum and the limitation has a reasonable basis." O'Connor, the author of the opinion, said, "It's a First Amendment case, although CFC is not a public forum. . . . The Government has the right to limit participants in some degree." She voted not only for a reversal but for a remand on which the NAACP would have an opportunity to prove "invidious discrimination" because the Government disagreed with their viewpoints.

The O'Connor *Cornelius* opinion held that solicitation in the CFC was protected by the First Amendment. But the CFC was a nonpublic forum and the government's reasons for excluding respondents satisfied the reasonableness standard. The government could reasonably limit participation to those spending directly for food and shelter. In addition, it could conclude that "political" and "nontraditional" charities would hinder CFC's effectiveness.

Among the most criticized Burger Court decisions on the public forum concept were those dealing with privately owned shopping centers. In the 1946 case of *Marsh v. Alabama*[84] the Court applied the public forum concept to a company-owned town, which was ruled subject to the First Amendment and might not prohibit literature distribution by a Jehovah's Witness. The Warren Court extended *Marsh* to a shopping center in the *Logan Valley* case,[85] which held that the center was the functional equivalent of the business district of the company town. The *Logan Valley* doctrine was, however, reconsidered by the Burger Court in *Lloyd Corp. v. Tanner*.[86] The lower court there had ruled that a shopping center's policy of prohibiting distribution of handbills protesting the draft and the Vietnam War violated the First Amendment.

At the *Lloyd* conference, Douglas spoke most firmly in favor of affirmance. "Lloyd's Center," Douglas urged, "has all the signs of public domain. It's used as such by the American Legion,[87] the Red Cross, etc. Can this same public operation discriminate against some?"

Brennan, Stewart, Marshall, and Blackmun also spoke for affirmance. "I won't go beyond *Logan Valley*," said Stewart, "but this is a bigger part of the city than Logan Valley. Therefore, the subject-matter of the speech is none of our concern. Government can't pick or choose based on agreement or disagreement with what's said."

On the other side, White, Powell, and Rehnquist were for reversal. "This," stated White, "would take *Logan Valley* beyond my line of what's a public authority for all the purposes of the First Amendment." Powell, who was to write the *Lloyd* opinion, said, "I don't see *Marsh* here at all. This isn't a case where there's nothing except the company town. Nor do I see this as a *Logan Valley* case. It's a closed mall without vehicles, but pedestrian traffic." Rehnquist went even further, saying, "I don't think *Marsh v. Alabama* was rightly decided."

The conference voted five (Douglas, Brennan, Stewart, Marshall, and Blackmun) to three for affirmance (with Chief Justice Burger passing).[88] At the conference, Blackmun had declared, "This is a *Marsh* case, even if a close one." In his view, *Marsh* required affirmance, "even apart from *Logan Valley*." Blackmun, however, switched his vote and with the Chief Justice joining the dissenters, the final decision was for reversal. The decision declined to apply *Logan Valley*, emphasizing instead factual differences between the two cases. Although *Lloyd* did not overrule *Logan Valley*, its reasoning, as Stewart later pointed out, "cannot be squared with the reasoning of the Court's opinion in *Logan Valley*."[89] What was clear at any rate was that *Lloyd* refused to treat the shopping center as a public forum for First Amendment purposes.

The refusal became established Burger Court doctrine in *Hudgens v. National Labor Relations Board*.[90] The Court categorically ruled that the First Amendment does not apply to privately owned shopping centers. At issue was the right of strikers to enter an enclosed mall to picket their employer. The *Hudgens* decision followed the view expressed by the Chief Justice at the conference. "The mall or center is not public enough to allow this." As Burger saw it, there was "little left of *Logan Valley* and I'd expressly overrule it."

"For me," Stewart, who wrote the *Hudgens* opinion, told the conference, "*Logan Valley* was a company town case. *Lloyd v. Tanner* repudiated that. Therefore, [there is] no constitutional right to picket." *Hudgens* expressly overruled *Logan Valley* and settled the law against the public forum status of shopping centers.

But *Hudgens* was not the end of the Burger Court jurisprudence on the matter. A footnote was added in *Prune Yard Shopping Center v. Robins*.[91] At issue was the exclusion from a California shopping center of students distributing pamphlets and soliciting signatures for petitions against a United Nations resolution. The California Supreme Court held that the state constitution protected speech and petitioning in shopping centers. The center owner contended that a property owner's rights to exclude the students might not thus be restricted.

As Stewart put it at the conference, "The state law obligates the shopping center to permit distribution of leaflets." All the Justices voted for affirmance, following the lead of the Chief Justice. "This shopping center," Burger told the conference, "is essentially like that in *Lloyd v. Tanner*. But here it's state law that forces a balance between the constitutional right of speech and the property owner's right to use his property for its own purpose." In such a case the balance set by state law must prevail. Or as the Chief Justice wrote in his May 7, 1980, letter joining Rehnquist's opinion of the Court, "If this is what California wants to declare as California law, so be it."

The *Prune Yard* decision essentially followed Burger's approach. While a shopping center does not normally come within the reach of the First Amendment, the states may adopt in their constitutions a broader conception of freedom of expression. Under the Burger Court jurisprudence, a shopping center is not a public forum, but the states may make it one under their own constitutional provisions protecting speech.

Chapter Six

First Amendment II: Freedom of the Press

JUSTICE STEWART once observed that the press is "the only organized private business that is given explicit constitutional protection."[1] The press is, of course, more than a business. It is the very fulcrum upon which the First Amendment turns; speech, however free, has little impact if it reaches only those within earshot.

Our history is filled with struggle over the press, but the Supreme Court was seldom called upon to define its rights and responsibilities. All this has changed in recent years. Cases involving freedom of the press came before the Warren Court with increasing frequency, and they became one of the staples of constitutional jurisprudence during Chief Justice Burger's tenure. Most of them go beyond the guaranty of freedom of expression to aspects of press freedom that the Framers could never have imagined. We start with a classic case in the Burger Court involving prior restraint on expression—the *Pentagon Papers Case.*[2]

PENTAGON PAPERS AND PRIOR RESTRAINTS

In 1971 the government, for the first time, sought to use the courts to censor news before it was printed. This attempt might well have succeeded if one of the Justices' law clerks had not happened to turn on his radio one summer afternoon.

What was to become one of the most widely publicized court cases began without fanfare. On Sunday, June 13, 1971, a low-key headline appeared in the *New York Times:* Vietnam Archive: Pentagon Study Traces 3 Decades of Growing U.S. Involvement.[3] It was followed by long excerpts culled from a top secret forty-seven-volume history of American involvement in Indochina prepared within the Defense Department.

The study, which was dubbed *The Pentagon Papers,* "revealed a dismaying degree of miscalculation, bureaucratic arrogance and deception."[4] After a second installment appeared, the Attorney General went to court to suppress further publication. He contended that dissemination would cause "immediate and irreparable harm" to national defense and security.

The lower courts acted with unusual speed. The New York District Court hearing was held on Friday. The district judge who had issued a temporary restraining order against the *Times* on Tuesday lifted the order. Five days later, the court of appeals remanded for further hearing and continued the restraining order pending further decision.

On the day the case was being heard in Manhattan, the *Washington Post* went to press with its own version. Once again, the Justice Department sought an injunction, and the court of appeals in Washington held that the government was not entitled to any preliminary injunction.[5] It had, however, issued a temporary restraining order pending its decision, and it granted a stay so that the government could take the case to the Supreme Court. The restraining order was still in force when certiorari was sought.

Knowledge of the *Pentagon Papers Case* had, of course, penetrated the Marble Palace. In most chambers, discussion of the case began the day after the government filed its initial request for a temporary restraining order. There was substantial speculation about whether the case could be brought to the Supreme Court before the 1970 term ended. Although virtually everyone outside the Court assumed that the case would ultimately be decided by the Justices, in the Court there was a strong feeling that the best disposition might be a simple denial of certiorari—but that was possible only if both courts of appeals decided completely in favor of the newspapers.

While the case was pending, Justice Black's clerks, returning from dinner at his house, reported that he had said he "never was too fond of injunctions against newspapers." "Even when the national security is involved?" asked his wife. "Well, I never did see how it hurts the national security for someone to tell the American people that their government lied to them," said Black.

The *Times* and *Post* cases were both decided by the lower courts on June 23, 1971. Each of those courts knew what the other was doing; Chief Judges Bazelon and Friendly were in regular telephone communication between New York and Washington. Late in the morning of June 24, the *Times* filed its application for certiorari and interim relief. It was promptly sent by Justice Harlan to the full Court. The government's petition for certiorari and interim relief was filed at 7:15 that evening and sent by the Chief Justice to the Justices at their homes.

The next morning (Friday, June 25), the conference met to consider the applications. Black, Douglas (by proxy from Goose Prairie, Washington), Brennan, and Marshall were prepared to deny certiorari and vacate the outstanding stays. The Chief Justice and Harlan, White, and Blackmun wanted the cases set for argument the following week. Harlan had, indeed, circulated a proposed order that would have denied the *Times*'s application "pending further order of this Court." The issue was ultimately resolved in accordance with the view stated by Justice Stewart, who voted to grant certiorari and continue the stays, but to set argument for the following morning. An order to that effect was issued in the early afternoon. The order contained the notation that Black, Douglas, Brennan, and Marshall would vacate all temporary restraining orders and deny certiorari. The Chief Justice had strongly opposed these Justices' action, but they wanted their opposition to continuing the stays on the public record.

The record in the *Post* case had arrived shortly after the order issued; the record in the *Times* case, which included a complete copy of the secret study, arrived with armed guards about 8:00 P.M. Brennan and White stayed to look at the secret papers and did not leave until 10:30. Other members of the Court looked over the *Pentagon Papers* the next day—except for Black, whose absolutist view of the First Amendment made the documents' content immaterial.

As soon as Brennan arrived at the Court the next morning (Saturday, June 26), he drafted a brief per curiam affirming the lower court in the *Post* case and reversing it in the *Times* case. The oral argument took place from 11:00 A.M. to 1:00 P.M.

The most important exchange, which went almost unnoticed, took place between Brennan and Solicitor General Erwin Griswold. Brennan asked whether it was not "correct that the injunctions so far granted against the *Times* and the *Post* haven't stopped other newspapers from publishing materials based on this study or kindred papers?" Griswold replied that it was his understanding that everything published in other papers was based upon materials in the *Times* and *Post*.

Brennan then asked whether other papers did not have copies of the *Pentagon Papers* or access to the study. Grisworld answered that he did not know. But then he conceded, "There is a possibility that anybody has it."

Brennan said that, in view of this, "I've always thought that the rule was that equity has to be rather careful not to issue ineffective injunctions. And isn't that a rule to be, a factor to be considered in these cases?" Griswold, however, said "there is nothing in this record, or known outside the record, which would indicate that this injunction would be useless."[6]

The first hour of the conference was inconclusive—with a four-three-two lineup prevailing (Black, Douglas, Brennan, and Marshall for the newspapers, the Chief Justice and Harlan and Blackmun for the government, and Stewart and White in between).

At about 2:30, however, one of Black's clerks called the Brennan chambers. He had just heard on the radio that the government had obtained a temporary restraining order against the *St. Louis Post–Dispatch*.

This news was the catalyst for the final decision. The new restraining order had been issued while the Solicitor General was stating that, as far as he knew, no further orders would be necessary. Griswold clearly did not know what other papers had what materials. The likelihood that any injunction would be futile had become very real. White and Stewart quickly announced that they would vote for the Brennan-drafted per curiam, which now had a six-man Court behind it. The opinion was sent to the printer late that afternoon and announced on the afternoon of June 30.

By then Douglas had left again for Goose Prairie, but he had left behind his concurring opinion. Black concurred after Douglas's draft was revised to meet Black's objections to a section declaring the Vietnam War unconstitutional. Separate opinions were also issued by the other Justices. None of the majority opinions was concurred in by more than two Justices.[7]

The *Pentagon Papers* decision marks the most dramatic assertion of the principle against prior restraint of the press in American jurisprudence. It is also plain that the decision is not based upon an absolutist view of that principle. The newspapers concerned were subject to temporary injunctions that prevented them from publishing the *Pentagon Papers*. Even more important, six of the Justices would have upheld an injunction in certain circumstances. As stated in three of the concurring opinions,[8] there is a narrow class of cases in which the First Amendment's ban on prior judicial restraint may be overridden—where "disclosure . . . will surely result in direct, immediate, and irreparable damage to the Nation or its people."[9] The example given is that of publication that will imperil a troop transport. This exception provides the legal justification for wartime censorship.

It must, however, be emphasized that the question of whether the exception applies is one for judicial resolution. The majority rejected Harlan's contention that the judiciary may review only to the extent of satisfying itself that the subject matter of the dispute does lie within the foreign-relation power. If the Executive seeks a judicial remedy, it must submit the basis upon which that remedy is sought to full judicial scrutiny.

ACCESS TO NEWS

The *Pentagon Papers* case shows plainly that prior restraints bear a heavy presumption against their constitutional validity.[10] Yet the right to publish may be empty if the press does not have access to government information. Does the Constitution confer upon the press a judicially enforceable right of access to files, trials, and prisons?

The right of access to news was dealt with by the Warren Court in *Estes v. Texas*,[11] the first case involving the issue of television in the courtroom. The original draft opinions in *Estes* rejected the notion of a press right of access.[12] Both the draft opinion of the Court by Stewart and the draft dissent of Clark expressly denied that the First Amendment grants news media such a privilege. Had this remained in the final *Estes* opinions, it might have foreclosed fresh consideration by the Burger Court. Instead, the final Clark opinion of the Court in *Estes* stated only that the press was "entitled to the same rights as the general public,"[13] while the Stewart dissent contained an intimation that the First Amendment did support a right of access.[14]

These statements were the only ones by the Court on the matter when *Houchins v. KQED*[15] came before the Justices in the 1977 term. Houchins was the sheriff of Alameda County, California. KQED reported the suicide of a prisoner in the Greystone portion of the county jail and requested permission to inspect Greystone. After permission was refused, KQED filed suit, arguing that Houchins violated the First Amendment by refusing to provide any effective means by which the public could be informed of conditions at Greystone or the prisoners' grievances.

Houchins then announced regular monthly tours for twenty-five persons, to parts of the jail. But Greystone was not included and cameras, tape recorders, and interviews with inmates were forbidden. The lower court enjoined petitioner from denying responsible news media access to the jail, including Greystone, and from preventing their using photographic or sound equipment or from conducting inmate interviews.

The conference was closely divided. The case for reversal was stated bluntly by White: "I don't see any right of access for anyone or why, if [they] let the public in, [they] must let the press in with their cameras." On the other side, Stevens asked, "Can a policy denying all access be constitutional? I think not." Stevens emphasized the public interest "as to how prisons are run."

Of particular interest, in view of his position as the "swing vote," was the ambivalent statement of Stewart: "The First Amendment does not give [the press] access superior to that of the general public. Moreover, there is no such thing as a constitutional right to know." Nevertheless, the Justice concluded, "Basically, I think the injunction here does not exceed [the permitted] bounds." Stewart also noted, "If the sheriff had not allowed public tours, he did not have to allow the press in."

The conference, with Marshall and Blackmun not participating, divided four (Brennan, Stewart, Powell, and Stevens) to three (the Chief Justice and White and Rehnquist) in favor of affirmance. The opinion was assigned to Justice Stevens who circulated a draft opinion[16] essentially similar to the dissent ultimately issued by him. It contains a broad recognition of a constitutional right of access to information on the part of the press—a right that "is not for the private benefit of those who might qualify as representatives of the 'press' but to insure that the citizens are fully informed regarding matters of public interest and importance."[17]

Under the Stevens draft, "information gathering is entitled to some measure of constitutional protection,"[18] and had it come down as the *Houchins* opinion of the Court, it would have established a First Amendment right of access to news. But the Stevens draft was not able to retain its majority. On April 24, 1978, Stewart, whose vote had helped to make up the bare majority for affirmance, wrote to Stevens that "Try as I may I cannot bring myself to agree that a county sheriff is constitutionally required to open up a jail that he runs to the press and the public. . . . [I]t would be permissible in this case to issue an injunction assuring press access equivalent to existing public access, but not the much broader injunction actually issued by the District Court." This was essentially the view taken in Stewart's *Houchins* concurrence.[19]

Chief Justice Burger's draft dissent was explained in an April 25 Memorandum to the Conference, which said, "I have devoted a substantial amount of time on a dissent in this case with some emphasis on systems of citizen oversight procedures which exist in many states. . . . This approach, rather than pushy TV people interested directly in the sensational, is the way to a solution. . . . I agree with Potter's view that media have a right of access but not beyond that of the public generally."

But the Burger draft was not to be a dissent. Its holding for reversal received a majority when Justice Stewart concurred in the judgment for reversal. On May 23, the Chief Justice sent a "Dear Potter" letter that pointed out that any press right of access could hardly be limited to the news media: "[T]here are literally dozens of people . . . who tour prisons. . . . Many of them write books, articles, or give lectures or a combination. I'm sure you will agree they have the same rights as a TV reporter doing a 'documentary.' Can they have greater First Amendment rights than these others whose form and certainty of communications is not so fixed?

"I do not believe First Amendment rights can be circumscribed by the scope of the audience. If so, the early pamphleteers who could afford only 100 sheets were 'suspect.'" On the contrary, the Chief Justice noted, "a team of TV cameramen (camera-persons!) will tend to produce far more disruption than the serious student or judge, lawyer, or penologist who wants to exercise First Amendment rights with a somewhat different objective."

On June 9, Burger sent around a second draft. "As a legislator I would vote for a reasonably orderly access to prisons, etc., by media, because it would be useful. But that is not the issue. The question is whether special access rights are *constitutionally compelled*." He answered in the negative.

The Burger opinion was joined by only White and Rehnquist. This made it the plurality opinion of a seven-Justice Court, as Stewart's concurrence enabled the decision for reversal to come down as the majority decision. Stevens' affirmation of a First Amendment right of access became the dissenting view.

The Burger Court also rejected, in *Branzburg v. Hayes*,[20] the view that "[t]he right to gather news implies, in turn, a right to a confidential relationship between a reporter and his source."[21] Reporters had refused to testify before grand juries investigating drug dealers. To gather news, they had to protect their sources; otherwise, the sources would not furnish information, to the detriment of the free flow of information protected by the First Amendment.

At the *Branzburg* conference, the Chief Justice declared, "I reject categorically the suggestion that this is a specific constitutional right." He didn't "think anyone except the President of the U.S." was immune from a grand jury subpoena. "They must appear."

White, who wrote the opinion, agreed. "Presently, I don't think I'd establish any privilege at all. . . . I would not in any event allow a privilege to the extent of keeping confidential what [he] has seen as [an] actual crime."

Blackmun, Powell, and Rehnquist agreed with the Burger–White view. "It would be unwise," said Powell, "to give the press any constitutional privilege and we're writing on a clean slate, so we don't have to give constitutional status to newsmen. I'd leave it to the legislatures to create one."

The other four favored the claimed privilege, though Marshall did state, "I think the press exaggerates the importance of [confidentiality[22]]." The dissenters asserted the view that, as Stewart expressed it, "The First Amendment requires some kind of qualified privilege for confidences to reporters." Douglas based his vote for the reporters on a different theory. "The Ninth Amendment," he said, "stated the proper constitutional rule. It's in the realm of items of association, belief, etc."

The *Branzburg* decision held that reporters have the same obligation as other citizens to respond to grand jury subpoenas. The public interest in the investigation of crimes outweighs whatever interest there may be in protecting sources. Under *Houchins*, the press does not possess a constitutional right of access to information not available to the public generally; under *Branzburg*, it does not have any immunity from grand jury subpoenas not possessed by other citizens.

ACCESS TO COURT PROCEEDINGS

The Burger Court did confirm a press right of access in one important area—to court proceedings. But it did so hesitantly. Indeed, its first decision on the matter ruled against the press claim—although the first draft opinion would have given a broad right of access. But a Justice changed his vote six weeks later and that opinion became the dissent.

The difficult constitutional cases are not those in which the courts are asked to vindicate a given right, but those in which conflicting rights—each by itself deserving of judicial protection—are at issue. In *Gannett Co. v. DePasquale,*[23] defendants in a murder trial asserted their right to a fair trial required exclusion of the public and press from a pretrial hearing on a motion to suppress two crucial items of evidence—a confession and the murder weapon. A newspaper claimed that the press and the public had a right of access to judicial proceedings even though the accused, the prosecutor, and the trial judge all had agreed to closure. The closure order was upheld by the highest state court.

The claims of the press rested on both the Sixth Amendment guaranty of a public trial and the First Amendment guaranty of freedom of the press. At the postargument conference the Chief Justice indicated that neither amendment supported a reversal. In his view, the Sixth Amendment public trial right did not apply "because the motion to suppress [is] not part of the trial." And as for the "First Amendment argument, there isn't any for me."

Stewart, who ultimately wrote the *Gannett* opinion, also spoke for affirmance. "I don't think the First Amendment claim is valid, since the press has no greater rights than the public." On the Sixth Amendment issue, the Justice reached the same result as the Chief Justice but refused to follow his approach, saying, "I can't agree it's not part of the trial."

Stewart nevertheless reached the same result "because the right to a public trial is explicitly given to the accused; but there is a public interest and who but the accused can trigger that? I'm inclined to hold that only the prosecutor can speak for the public where a motion for closure is made by the defendant."

Rehnquist and Stevens also were in favor of affirmance. "The Sixth Amendment," said Rehnquist, "means for me only protection for the rights of the accused. . . . [T]he Framers didn't give the public a right to access." Stevens relied on "a critical difference between seeing a live hearing and reading a transcript of it. If the public has a right of access to the live performance, we'll be holding that the electronic media must be allowed."

The other five Justices spoke in favor of reversal. They were led by Brennan, who was for establishing a constitutional right of access for the press and the public. White and Marshall agreed that the suppression hearing was part of the trial. "The public," Marshall declared, "has a right because, if the accused is done dirt, the public interest is hurt. The public is entitled to know what happens when it happens."

Of particular interest were the statements of Blackmun, who wrote the first *Gannett* draft, and Powell, who was ultimately the "swing vote" in the case. Blackmun said that he agreed that the Sixth Amendment provided for the "public character of trial. . . . I think the public directly and the press indirectly have an interest in preventing the abuse of public business. I'd take the Sixth Amendment approach." Powell, who was to change his mind on this point, agreed. As he put it, "This is Sixth [Amendment] and not First." Powell also agreed that this "suppression hearing is part of a criminal trial." In his view, "the trial judge didn't do enough when he heard the accused and the prosecutor agreed to closure." The judge should also have allowed the press to be heard.

In a May 9, 1979, letter to Blackmun, Powell wrote that, at the *Gannett* conference, "I do not think a majority of the Court agreed as to exactly how the competing interests in this case should be resolved." On the other hand, the tally sheet of a Justice present at the conference indicates that a bare majority (Brennan, White, Marshall, Blackmun, and Powell) favored reversal.

The opinion was assigned to Blackmun, who circulated a draft opinion of the Court which was a broadside rejection of the decision below.[24] In his final *Gannett* dissent, Blackmun began by stating that he could not "join the Court's phrasing of the 'question presented.'"[25] How he saw that question was indicated by the first sentence of the Blackmun draft: "This case presents the issue whether, and to what extent, the First, Sixth, and Fourteenth Amendments of the Constitution restrict a State, in a criminal prosecution, from excluding the public and the press from a pretrial suppression-of-evidence hearing, when the request to exclude is made by the defendant himself."

Blackmun's draft was virtually the same as his *Gannett* dissent, with the omission of the statement of facts (which was to be used in the opinion of the Court) and changes made to convert the draft from a majority opinion to a dissent.[26] The Blackmun draft read a broad right of public and press access to all criminal proceedings into the Sixth Amendment's public trial guaranty: "The public trial guarantee . . . insures that not only judges but all participants in the criminal justice system are subjected to public scrutiny as they conduct the public's business of prosecuting crime."[27]

Had the Blackmun draft opinion come down as the final *Gannett* opinion, it would have completely resolved the issue of access to criminal proceedings in favor of a wide right on the part of the public and the press. But the Blackmun draft was not able to secure a majority. On April 5, 1979, Stewart sent a "Dear Harry" note: "I shall in due course circulate a dissenting opinion."

The Stewart draft dissent was an abbreviated version of his opinion of the Court. The Sixth Amendment public trial guaranty is one created for the benefit of the defendant alone and was personal to the accused. Even if the contrary were the case, the tentative decision was wrong; the public trial guaranty applies only to trials, not to pretrial proceedings. Nor does the First Amendment compel a different result, since it gives the press no right superior to that of the public. "If the public had no enforceable right to attend the pretrial proceeding in this case, it necessarily follows that the petitioners had no such right under the First and Fourteenth Amendments."[28]

Stevens also circulated a brief draft dissent, which asserted, "I do not believe the Court has the authority to create this novel remedy for a random selection of bystanders."

The general expectation in the Court was that the Blackmun draft would come down as the *Gannett* opinion. Then, on May 31, 1979, a month and a half after the drafts were circulated, Powell wrote to Blackmun: "I was inclined to view this case as presenting primarily a First Amendment rather than a Sixth Amendment issue. . . . I had become persuaded that my views as to the Sixth Amendment coincide substantially with those expressed by Potter. . . . I therefore will join his opinion." Powell also had written a draft, originally as a dissent, which would be issued as a concurring opinion, "in which I address the First Amendment issue. I am sorry to end up being the 'swing vote.' At Conference I voted to reverse. But upon a more careful examination of the facts, I have concluded that the trial court substantially did what in my view the First Amendment requires."

The case was now assigned to Stewart, whose revised version of his draft dissent was redrafted as the *Gannett* opinion of the Court. The most substantial change was pointed out in Stewart's June 7 covering memorandum. "You will note that I have unabashedly plagiarized Harry Blackmun's statement of facts in Part I and discussion of mootness in Part II. I offer two excuses: (1) the pressure of time, and (2) more importantly, I could not have said it better."

The *Gannett* decision did not finally resolve the issue of access to criminal proceedings. In 1980, the Justices were again presented with the issue in *Richmond Newspapers v. Virginia.*[29] A trial court had closed a criminal proceeding to the public and the press. The closure order was upheld by the highest state court.

According to Chief Justice Burger at the postargument conference, the fact that the case involved the trial and not a pretrial proceeding differentiated this case from *Gannett.* "*Gannett* didn't decide this case. . . . The assumption has been that trials must be public. They were taken for granted from 1787 to 1791"—i.e., from the drafting of the Constitution to the ratification of the Bill of Rights. "There's a common thread for public trials." But that still left the question: "What's the constitutional handle?"[30] The Chief Justice was "not persuaded it's in the First Amendment either as an access right or an association right. I would rely on the fact it was part of judicial procedure before adoption of the Bill of Rights. The Ninth Amendment is as good a handle as any."

Richmond Newspapers might have become a leading case in the revival of what used to be termed "the forgotten amendment,"[31] but the Chief Justice's suggestion was not supported by the others and the opinion does not discuss the Ninth Amendment beyond a brief reference in a footnote.[32]

Rehnquist, who alone spoke for affirmance, asserted, "There are tensions between *Gannett* and this case." At the argument, Professor Laurence Tribe had relied on the Sixth as well as the First Amendment. White alone said that the Court "might get some mileage out of the Sixth." The others who spoke on the matter agreed with Justice Stewart, "Tribe's Sixth Amendment argument is not appealing."

Instead, the others relied upon the First Amendment. Their view was best expressed by Stewart: "The Sixth was resolved against public trials in *Gannett.* The press has no right superior to the public of access to institutions like prisons which are traditionally closed." On the other hand, "trials have been open traditionally subject to time, place, and manner regulations. . . . I agree there is a First Amendment right, subject to the overriding interest in a fair trial."

The ultimate conference conclusion was, as stated by Justice Stevens, that "the First Amendment protected some right of access. . . . I'd be prepared to hold that, in the absence of any rational basis for denying access, the benefits of openness argue for it."

The opinions in *Richmond Newspapers*—both the plurality opinion of the Chief Justice and the concurring opinions of Stevens, Brennan, Stewart, and Blackmun—followed the Stewart conference approach. The Burger Court squarely held that access to court proceedings is protected by the First Amendment. This is a more satisfactory basis for decision than the Sixth Amendment route followed in the Blackmun *Gannett* draft.

Even after *Richmond Newspapers,* however, many assumed that the case held only that the First Amendment guaranteed access to trials, not to the *Gannett* type of pretrial proceedings. A case decided during the last Burger term—*Press-Enterprise Co. v. Superior Court*[33]—dealt specifically with a closed preliminary hearing in a California murder case. A newspaper sued to have the transcript of the proceedings released. The state court held that there was no First Amendment right of access to preliminary hearings.

At the *Press-Enterprise* conference, Brennan delivered the strongest statement in favor of reversal, saying "that there is a First Amendment right of public access to judicial proceedings" because "at its core, the First Amendment protects public debate about how government operates. The ultimate reason for protecting such speech is to facilitate the process of self-governance. . . . [T]he right to speak necessarily includes a corollary right to obtain the information necessary to speak; in other words, a 'right to know.'"

Brennan asserted that a right of access would not mean the "parade of horribles" urged by the state. It would not mean access to grand jury proceedings or police interrogations, which "must be private to work effectively. In fact, a First Amendment right of access is appropriate for only a very few government functions. Other than judicial proceedings, the only candidates I can think of are legislative debates and perhaps administrative hearings."

Brennan's conference conclusion was, "it is clear that there is a right of public access to preliminary hearings." That was true, in the Justice's view, because "The same considerations that led to the results in our earlier cases apply here with equal force. Historically, preliminary hearings have been open to the public in the same way and for the same reasons as trials. . . . [T]he preliminary hearing serves exactly the same sort of 'public show' purposes as the trial."

The crucial point was that "the preliminary hearing is really a part of the 'trial' for purposes of the right of public access. It is part of the state's official proceedings for dealing with criminals, part of the public show that—like the trial—reveals how we treat criminals. Consequently, the importance of public access in fulfilling the purposes of preliminary hearings and the public's need to be able to attend such hearings are the same as for the trial."[34]

The *Press-Enterprise* decision held that the First Amendment right of access to criminal proceedings applied to the preliminary hearing in the California criminal case. The same is presumably true of other pretrial proceedings, such as that in *Gannett*. But the Burger *Press-Enterprise* opinion was not as forthright as one would have wished. The Chief Justice stressed that the right of access applied to California, where there had been a tradition of public accessibility. There may be an implication that the same result might not be reached in a case from another state. Thus the question raised by *Richmond Newspapers* may not have been unqualifiedly answered in favor of a First Amendment right of access.

GAG ORDERS

Another controversial issue during the Burger years involved so-called gag orders—judicial attempts to censor the press by forbidding news media from publishing material that could impair the right to a fair trial. The conflict in these cases between the right of an accused to trial by an impartial jury and the right guaranteed by the First Amendment came before the Court in *Nebraska Press Association v. Stuart*.[35] A state judge in a murder trial had prohibited the press from publishing confessions or admissions and facts "strongly implicative" of the accused.

The Chief Justice began the conference by noting, "Issuance of prior restraints may in some cases be permissible." But that was not true here. In fact, the Court "decided this case when we decided the *Pentagon Papers* case."

All the Justices agreed that the lower court decision upholding the gag order should be reversed. But there was disagreement over whether such orders might ever be validly issued. Justice Brennan urged that the First Amendment be construed to bar all prior restraints. He was supported by Justices Stewart, White, Marshall, and Stevens. The latter asserted that there was "no clear and present danger found here, so [I would] reverse outright."

The others supported the Burger view on prior restraints. Justice Blackmun stated that he "could join an opinion that rated the First Amendment above the Sixth. But [there] should be no prior restraint on what has occurred in open court." Justices Powell and Rehnquist took the same approach. Rehnquist stressed, "[You] can't forbid the press to report what was said at [an] open preliminary hearing."

Powell said, "Courts can't impose prior restraints with respect to public hearing or [materials] that the press gets on its own, however shabbily it gets it." On the other hand, Blackmun stressed, "[I] don't want to close the door completely against some restraint."

When the Chief Justice sent around his typewritten draft opinion of the Court on June 7, 1976, he explained, in his covering Memorandum to the Conference, that "I have undertaken to express the views of all but those who would regard prior restraint barred in all cases and for whatever reason. My own reexamination of all the relevant cases suggests that, unlike the situation in England, such a showing is very difficult to make under the First Amendment as construed by the Court, but neither is it a total impossibility, as yet; and this case does not call for going that far."

The Burger memo and draft led Brennan to circulate his opinion concurring in the judgment the next day. As stated in Brennan's covering memo, "Its approach, in the Chief's words, is 'forever to bar prior restraint against pretrial publicity,' which I thought was the conference consensus."

The Chief Justice replied with a "Dear Bill" letter the same day. "If the Conference consensus was as you suggest, to 'forever bar prior restraint' on pretrial publicity, I would be prepared to articulate that, but this is not my recollection."

The Chief Justice then inquired "whether a majority of the Conference is willing in this case 'to forever bar prior restraint on pretrial publicity'." [36] The majority ultimately agreed with the Burger view that it was not. "In my view," Powell wrote back, "it is not necessary to go so far—certainly in the case before us. Nor did I understand that a majority of the Conference voted to hold that never, under any conceivable circumstances, would a court have the power to restrain prejudicial publicity even for the briefest period of time. I have not thought that our previous decisions justify such a sweeping final conclusion." [37]

Powell wrote that he "would simply decide the case before us and say that it is unnecessary to determine there never could be a prior restraint on pretrial publicity." The Burger opinion did not follow this advice. It indicated that prior restraint might sometime be permissible—though, as Powell had said, "the presumption is against any such restraint and one who asserts a need for it bears a heavy burden indeed."

As the Powell letter noted, the *Nebraska Press* opinion did indicate that, while the barriers to prior restraints were not insuperable, they remained high. The Burger opinion stated specifically that prior restraints came to court with a heavy presumption against their validity, which the order at issue failed to overcome, since there was no finding that measures short of prior restraint would not have protected the accused's rights.

Nebraska Press leaves the outer limits of the prior restraint prohibition unclear. Despite the contrary indication in the Burger opinion, one may question whether a gag order can ever overcome the presumption against prior restraints. Five Justices indicated that they doubted whether such orders would ever be justifiable.[38]

Yet even here we cannot be certain. Stevens, in his concurrence, indicated his agreement with the Brennan view that prior restraint was a constitutionally impermissible method for enforcing the right to a fair trial.[39] But Stevens also indicated that he might be troubled by certain cases.[40] He gave an example in a June 9, 1976, Memorandum to the Conference: "Consider, for example, the possibility of surreptitious recording of strategy conferences between the defendant and his lawyer. Perhaps there is a constitutional right to publish even that kind of information, but I hesitate to decide the most extreme cases in the abstract without the benefit of argument."

TELEVISION IN THE COURTROOM

During Chief Justice Warren's tenure the Supreme Court first dealt with television in the courtroom. In *Estes v. Texas*,[41] the Court decided that television of a notorious trial over defendant's objections was inconsistent with the fair trial guaranteed by due process. The Court originally voted the other way in *Estes*[42] and an opinion of the Court upholding TV in the courtroom had been drafted by Justice Stewart. The decision against TV came down after Justice Clark switched his vote.

Clark's *Estes* opinion had originally rejected the state's contention "that the television of portions of a criminal trial does not constitute per se a denial of due process." Indeed, Clark's draft had asserted flatly, "The facts in this case demonstrate clearly the necessity for the adoption of a *per se* rule" that TV by its very nature is constitutionally incompatible with the proper conduct of criminal trials. But these passages were watered down and nothing like a per se rule against TV was contained in the final *Estes* opinion.

Otherwise television in the courtroom might have been constitutionally doomed. Regardless of the circumstances and of any future improvements that might be made in television coverage, any televised trial would automatically violate due process.

The opening under the Burger Court for televising of trials came in *Chandler v. Florida*,[43] which upheld a Florida rule permitting television coverage of criminal trials, notwithstanding the objections of the accused. All the Justices agreed at the conference that the Florida rule did not violate due process, but there was disagreement over whether a holding to that effect could be made without overruling *Estes*. Chief Justice Burger pointed out that "this is like *Estes* in some respects. No prejudice is shown in either case and both were notorious cases." The basic question was: "Should the states be left to experiment? I think so, in general." On the other hand, "Anything that endangers a fair trial is suspect and must be justified on some ground." Burger concluded his presentation by stating that he agreed with Harlan, whose *Estes* concurrence had denied that the decision categorically prohibited any televised trials.

As Stewart saw it, *Chandler* was "indistinguishable from *Estes*, which I'd overrule and affirm." White was less categorical, saying, "I think [we] have to chop up *Estes* some to affirm, but I'd do that." Marshall, on the other hand, stated, "I'd leave *Estes* alone"; and Blackmun said, "I don't think this is *Estes*."

Powell indicated that he was troubled by televised trials and that there was "a substantial per se argument that ought to exclude TV from the courtroom." At the same time, "*Estes* can be read as you want. I'd leave it on the books and follow John Harlan's notion that TV is part of everyday life, like it or not."

In his *Estes* dissent, Stewart had deleted a statement that "the Court today holds that any television of a state criminal trial constitutes a *per se* violation of the Fourteenth Amendment."[44] In *Chandler*, however, Stewart asserted "that *Estes* announced a *per se* rule."[45] He said that a decision for the Florida rule would require the overruling of *Estes* and "I would now flatly overrule it."[46] The majority agreed with the Chief Justice and Powell, and their position was stated by Blackmun, who wrote to the Chief Justice, "I share your reading of *Estes*."[47]

The *Chandler* opinion of the Court was based upon a laborious effort to distinguish *Estes*, rather than overrule it. The *Chandler* opinion relies on Harlan's *Estes* concurrence to show that the statement of a per se rule in the Clark opinion of the Court received the support of only a plurality of four Justices. Yet the Clark *Estes* opinion did not announce a per se rule. And Harlan, in his *Estes* concurrence, did no more than stress what should have been obvious once Clark deleted the per se references from his draft—namely, that the *Estes* decision held that the televised trial deprived defendant of due process under the "facts in this case." [48] Despite the contrary assumption in the *Chandler* opinions, the Harlan *Estes* concurrence was not issued to demonstrate Harlan's refusal to subscribe to a per se rule, since the *Estes* opinion of the Court stated no such rule. Instead, Harlan was only stressing that, in an area of such rapid technological change, the decision was based upon "television as we find it in this trial." [49]

In these circumstances, whether the Burger or Stewart view on *Estes* was correct may be irrelevant. As Blackmun said in a "Dear Chief" letter, "I am not really sure that the ultimate disposition of *Estes v. Texas* by way of overruling it or not overruling it, is very important. Whether overruled or not, *Estes* now certainly fades into the background." [50]

At the same time, it should not be thought that the *Chandler* Court was laying down its own per se rule categorically affirming the validity of all televised trials. All *Chandler* held was that a state rule allowing television coverage of a criminal trial does not automatically violate the Constitution.

The Justices themselves were troubled at the notion of TV in every courtroom. Powell wrote in a letter of the "enduring concern . . . that the presence of the camera may impair the fairness of a trial, but not leave evidence of specific prejudice." Powell suggested that the *Chandler* opinion should be "clear as to the protection that the Constitution affords a defendant who objects to his trial being televised. . . . I am inclined to think it desirable that we make explicit that the defendant who makes a timely motion to exclude the cameras, and alleges specific harms that he fears will occur, is entitled as a matter of right to a hearing. We have precedent for such a requirement in *Richmond Newspapers* and in my concurring opinion in *Gannett*." [51]

Even though Blackmun made a similar suggestion, the hearing idea was not included in the Burger *Chandler* opinion. Yet Burger himself was far from approving television in every case. "For me there *may be* a risk of due process and equal protection violations in putting a few out of thousands of trials on TV or in a 'Yankee Stadium' setting." [52]

The others, too, were uneasy at what Blackmun called "the risk of adverse psychological impact on various trial participants." In criminal trials, Blackmun wrote, "any type of media coverage is capable of creating an impression of guilt or innocence. Assuming *arguendo* that more people are likely to watch the news than read about it, the incremental risk of juror prejudice seems to me a difference in degree rather than kind." [53]

TAXATION, CENSORSHIP, AND ACCESS TO THE PRESS

As a general proposition, freedom of the press means freedom from prior restraints upon publication. But it also must mean protection of the press from the governmental discrimination that arose in *Minneapolis Star & Tribune Co. v. Minnesota Commissioner of Revenue.*[54] Minnesota imposed a tax on the cost of the ink and paper used in producing newspapers, exempting the first $100,000, and the highest state court held that it did not violate freedom of the press.

The press is, of course, subject to tax laws. But the *Grosjean* case[55] had ruled invalid a Louisiana tax on the gross receipts from the sale of advertising imposed on newspapers with a circulation above 20,000. The Court held that the tax was an abridgement of the freedom of the press. But the Court also emphasized that the tax was intended to penalize the state's large newspapers, which had strongly opposed Senator Huey Long. In *Minneapolis Star,* there was no such invidious motive, but the Minnesota tax did single out newspapers.

The Chief Justice began the conference by pointing out that "a nondiscriminatory sales tax would be O.K. But this is a tax limited to newspapers." Burger came out for reversal, though he did say, "I reject the argument that the Stamp Tax history supports the newspaper." Burger also noted that he was "not sure that *Grosjean* is the complete answer. There Huey Long's vendetta was influential. I see no motive here to interfere with press freedom."

The absence of improper motive was considered irrelevant by the conference. The First Amendment, Blackmun declared, is a "prohibition [against] putting special burdens on the press and that's what this tax is." White said, "This singles out publications which turn out to be newspapers, and only a few of them." Or as Powell told the conference, "This singles out newspapers for special and discriminatory treatment."

Rehnquist alone spoke in support of the tax. "If a sales tax is O.K., I can't see why this tax isn't all right." Rehnquist also was not persuaded by the singling-out argument. The tax, he stated, "applies only to newspapers because [they] can't collect a sales tax as easily."

With only Rehnquist dissenting, the *Minneapolis Star* decision struck down the tax. The First Amendment does not permit a state to tailor a tax so that it singles out the press. This is particularly true where the burden is placed on large publications; such a tax begins to resemble a penalty for the largest newspapers.

In addition, the First Amendment means freedom of the press from censorship. The Burger Court was not confronted with the constitutionality of the traditional type of censorship. The Court did, however, deal with attempts to use the criminal law to accomplish some of the restraining effects of a censorship system.

In *Cox Broadcasting Co. v. Cohn*,[56] the Court had before it a statute making it a misdemeanor to publish the name or identity of a rape victim. A television reporter had learned the name of a rape victim from the indictment and had revealed it in a broadcast.

At the *Cox* conference, the Chief Justice indicated that he was troubled by the implications of striking down the statute. "If this statute is invalid, then aren't juvenile statutes also?" Stewart and Blackmun pointed out that a law prohibiting the report of juvenile proceedings was different because, in Blackmun's words, "Theoretically juvenile proceedings are not a public trial."

On the merits, the Justices (and even the Chief Justice) all agreed that the statute was invalid. "I think," said Stewart, "that on its face it's unconstitutional. . . . Here we have a truthful report of a public proceeding." Even Rehnquist, who ultimately dissented on other grounds, stated the same view. "On the merits," he told the conference, "I agree that you can't constitutionally [prohibit][57] the right of a newspaper truthfully to report a public proceeding."

The Court was thus unanimous on the statute's invalidity. As Blackmun put it, "You can't bridle the press constitutionally this way." The Justice recognized that there were dangers of abusive exercise of press power, but he concluded, "As a practical matter, we have to rely on the self-restraint of the press in these cases."

The *Cox* decision followed the conference and ruled that the statute violated the First Amendment. Under *Cox* and a later case[58] there is no power in government to suppress publication of the news, nor can the same result be accomplished by penalizing publication, which has the same effect as censorship. The converse of censorship (in effect, forcing the press to print copy) was presented in *Miami Herald Publishing Co v. Tornillo*.[59] At issue was a state law granting a political candidate a right to equal space in a newspaper to reply to criticism and attacks.

The advocates of such a law relied on the relative scarcity of media outlets to which members of the public (even those running for office) may have access. At the conference, Stewart noted that this claim did not have a physical basis, as it did in radio and television. "The spectrum of frequencies," he stated, "is not limited as claimed in [broadcasting]."[60] But Stewart asserted, "the monopoly of newspapers ironically is doing just that."

Despite the Stewart assertion, the *Miami Herald* decision unanimously struck down the right-to-reply law. As the Court saw it, the statute operated as a command in the same sense as a law forbidding a newspaper to publish specified matter. Government cannot take it upon itself to decide what a newspaper may or may not publish.[61] Under *Miami Herald,* the First Amendment erects a barrier between government and the print media.

BROADCAST MEDIA

The *Miami Herald* holding applies only to the traditional press. Any person can publish a newspaper without any license. But the same is not true of the broadcast media with their inherent physical limitation. Frequencies are scarce and must be portioned out among applicants.[62] Government allocation and regulation of broadcast frequencies are thus essential.[63] The Warren Court itself stated that there can be no First Amendment right to broadcast comparable to the right to speak, write, or publish.[64] Consequently its *Red Lion* decision[65] upheld the so-called fairness doctrine of the Federal Communications Commission, which required broadcasters to provide reply time to personal attacks or political editorials.

Red Lion was based on "the right of the public to receive suitable access to social, political, esthetic, moral, and other ideas and experiences."[66] The implication is that there may be a right of individual access to the airwaves to ensure that the public right to receive diverse materials is vindicated.

The Burger Court decisions, however, refused to recognize such a constitutional right of access to the broadcast media. In *Columbia Broadcasting System v. Democratic National Committee*,[67] CBS had refused to sell time to the Democratic National Committee for political advertising and to an organization for anti–Vietnam War announcements. It was claimed that the First Amendment barred a broadcaster from following a general policy of refusing to sell time for comment on controversial public issues. The lower court upheld the claim.

Chief Justice Burger began the *Democratic National Committee* conference by stating the issue: "Whether TV may have a policy not to sell advertising time to responsible advertisers with controversial messages to deliver." The Chief Justice stated that "the FCC relies on the fairness doctrine as sufficient." Judge McGowan, in his court of appeals dissent, had relied on that doctrine and urged that it imposed the only relevant obligation on broadcasters. Burger told the conference, "I think Judge McGowan was correct below."

Justice White also spoke for affirmance. Referring to the claim that the Communications Act required access, he declared, "The statutory argument is absurd." On the constitutional argument, White said, "The Constitution doesn't require FCC regulation. Even though *Red Lion* said TV must act as a spokesman for other voices, this doesn't go that far." Stewart, Blackmun, Powell, and Rehnquist agreed with the Burger–White approach.

There were thus six votes for the view stated by Blackmun: "I can't see the right of access as a constitutional right." Douglas (who was ultimately to concur with the decision reversing), Brennan, and Marshall were for affirmance. Their view, as put by Marshall, was that "the denial of controversial ads flies in the face of the First Amendment."

The *Democratic National Committee* decision followed the conference consensus that there is no constitutional right of individual access to the airwaves. The Court stressed that the primary responsibility over broadcasting was vested in Congress and the regulatory agency established by it. This means that a different result may be required where Congress requires broadcasters to grant access to their facilities. Such a congressional provision was at issue in *Columbia Broadcasting System v. Federal Communications Commission*.[68] The statutory provision there authorized the FCC to revoke a broadcast license because of the broadcaster's "failure to allow reasonable access to or to permit purchase of reasonable amounts of time by a legally qualified candidate for federal elective office." The broadcast networks challenged the statute on First Amendment grounds, claiming that it unduly circumscribed their editorial discretion. The networks had sought review of an FCC order that they had violated the statute by refusing to sell time to the Carter–Mondale Presidential Committee for December 1979, which they felt was too early for the 1980 campaign.

In effect, the statute provided an affirmative right of access to the broadcast media for individual candidates for federal office. And it was a new right created by Congress. As White put it at the conference, "Congress intended to change the law. The old law never allowed a candidate to do this."

The conference vote was five to four to reverse the decision below affirming the FCC order. The Chief Justice said that he had only a "skeptical confidence in the FCC." The issue was, "Could the networks' judgment as to when the campaign was in full swing be reviewed [by the FCC]? . . . I'd be inclined to sustain the networks' judgment unless clearly wrong. Even if the networks made the wrong decision, in my view, to avoid censorship I'd give them the benefit of the doubt."

The view of the majority was best stated by Justice White, who delivered the dissent. "I think the FCC put too tight a grip on the broadcasters—particularly on the threshold issue of when the campaign began. My standard would be something like, if reasonable men could differ, the networks' decision should be sustained." Powell, Rehnquist, and Stevens agreed with White. As Powell put it, "The Commission went beyond its authority in saying it decided when the campaign commenced."

Brennan, Stewart, Marshall, and Blackmun spoke for affirmance. Their opinion was that Congress could change the law to provide for the right of access and, in Blackmun's words, "I'd let the Commission decide when the campaign begins." Marshall's statement was pithy: "The networks are the biggest censors of all and I don't mind the FCC censoring the censors."

Since Chief Justice Burger and Justice Powell ultimately voted in favor of affirmance, the decision in *CBS v. FCC* was to uphold the statute and the FCC order. The result is consistent with the jurisprudence on the subject. As stated by the Chief Justice at the conference, "TV has large, but not as much as the print media, discretion in editing." Congress and the regulatory agency may impinge upon that discretion in a manner not permissible for the traditional press. They may impose upon broadcasters the kind of fairness requirement ruled unconstitutional for newspapers in *Miami Herald*. Congress may even create a right of access though none is otherwise demanded by the First Amendment.

But there are limits to the congressional power in this respect: Congress may not restrict broadcasters in a manner that restricts the public's access to ideas. The Court held that that limit had been exceeded in *Federal Communications Commission v. League of Women Voters.*[69] A federal statute prohibited any noncommercial broadcast station that received federally funded grants to "engage in editorializing." The lower court ruled that the statute violated the First Amendment. The court rejected the contention that the prohibition served a compelling government interest in ensuring that publicly funded broadcasters do not become propaganda organs for the government.

The Chief Justice, who passed at the conference, said that "whether public broadcasting is as different as the Solicitor General argues, and thus regulable this way, is troublesome." Burger did, however, indicate what his ultimate vote would be when he pointed out that the "strongest argument [to support the law] is the spending power one."

White, Rehnquist, and Stevens, who with the Chief Justice were to be the dissenters in the case, spoke in favor of the law. Rehnquist noted that "this is an act of Congress specifically prohibiting what's at issue here and [is] entitled to deference." Rehnquist also stressed that public spending was involved. "I'd tell people, you get the money on conditions and, if you want it, you must comply with the conditions." The Justice also made two other points: (1) "The Government has control over broadcasting beyond that over the press"; and (2) there was "very little restriction on speech any way." Justice White also made the latter point, saying that, under the law, there were "no programming limits and no restrictions on any news."

On the other side, Blackmun conceded that "limitations on broadcast speech have been upheld on the scarcity ground. But this prohibition is at the core of the First Amendment." O'Connor, who provided the fifth vote for affirmance, agreed. "A complete ban goes to the heart of the First Amendment. I don't think the government interest here is compelling."

Powell, who also spoke in favor of affirmance, stated, "This is regulation of speech content with a negligible state interest." Stevens answered Powell much as he was to do in his dissent. "True," said Stevens, "it's content regulation, but it's neutral—no bias at all." In addition, Stevens pointed out that publicly funded stations "give the impression it's the official view because of funding."

The *League of Women Voters* decision struck down the law prohibiting editorializing by public broadcasters. The broadcast industry
may operate under restraints not imposed upon the traditional press.
According to the opinion of the Court, however, the restrictions permitted are intended to secure the public's First Amendment interest in
receiving a balanced presentation of views, including those of broadcasters themselves. Preserving the free expression of editorial opinion
is an essential part of the First Amendment scheme. The interests
served by the ban on editorializing are not substantial enough to justify the abridgement of important journalistic freedoms.

LIBEL: PUBLIC INTEREST VERSUS PUBLIC FIGURES

One of the Warren Court's most important First Amendment decisions was in *New York Times v. Sullivan*.[70] That decision constitu-
tionalized the law of libel, holding that libel suits might not be
brought by public officials unless they could prove "actual malice"—
that the libel was published "with knowledge that it was false or with
reckless disregard of whether it was false or not."[71] In later cases, the
Warren Court applied the *New York Times* rule to libel suits by
"public figures," even though they were not government officials.[72]

Both the *New York Times* rule and its application to public figures
were the handiwork of Brennan.[73] The Justice continued his efforts to
expand the *New York Times* rule—this time to matters of "public
interest"—and he was successful in the first case on the subject in the
Burger Court: *Rosenbloom v. Metromedia*.[74]

Metromedia's radio station had broadcast news of Rosenbloom's
arrest for possession of pornography. The report said the police believed that they had hit the supply of a main distributor of obscene
material. Rosenbloom sued for libel. The jury awarded substantial
damages, but the court of appeals reversed, holding that the *New
York Times* standard applied even though "plaintiff was not a public
figure" and that plaintiff's evidence did not meet that standard.

Brennan was the key Justice in *Rosenbloom*. He was determined to
push *New York Times* even further, and he was given the opportunity when the conference voted five to three (Douglas not participating) to affirm and he was assigned the opinion. The majority
votes were cast by the Chief Justice and Black, Brennan, White, and
Blackmun. Since the votes of the Chief Justice and Blackmun seemed
to be based largely on their stated unwillingness to allow a "smut

peddler" any libel award, and since Black followed his consistent view that all libel statutes were unconstitutional, Brennan doubted that an opinion could be written that would command five votes.

Despite his doubt, Brennan decided to write an opinion discarding the focus of earlier cases on the plaintiff as a "public official" or "public figure" and applying the *New York Times* standard to all cases involving a subject of general or public interest. A draft to that effect was circulated on February 17, 1971. The draft was intended to ensure that within a sphere of public interest, the press's freedom to publish could not be abridged by libel judgments based on the uncertain line of a jury's determination of negligence. The main questions that the Justice had to decide in writing the draft were the wording of the "test" to be used to describe the extent of the constitutional protection—"legitimate public" or "general public" interest were the two main contenders—and whether the opinion should assert that "public figures and officials" also had areas of privacy. Brennan settled on "legitimate public interest" and the flat assertion that certain areas of the lives of even the most public men would be outside the constitutional requirement imposed.

On March 25, the Chief Justice wrote to Brennan that he had "considerable trouble" with the draft, although he "agreed with the general proposition that participation in any activity that is affected with an important public interest draws the participants somewhere in the 'target zone' the Court has given public officials and public figures." Almost a month later, on April 19, Brennan received a Burger letter joining the Brennan opinion, without any comment.

Blackmun sent Brennan a note[75] stating that he also would join if two changes were made in the draft: (1) Eliminate a reference to Professor Meiklejohn's article, The First Amendment Is an Absolute[76] (Blackmun had written, "I suspect I am not an absolutist so far as the First Amendment is concerned."); and (2) limit the holding to protection for "a genuine segment" of the media. Brennan dropped the cite to Meiklejohn and specified in the holding that the news medium involved was a "licensed radio station." The latter change was intended to avoid the implications of Blackmun's desire for an express limitation to "genuine" news media. Blackmun then joined Brennan's opinion and Justice Black circulated his concurrence in the result.

On May 19, almost three months after Brennan's circulation, the dissenting opinions of Harlan and Marshall—the latter joined by Stewart—were sent around. Brennan feared that the strong dissents might persuade Chief Justice Burger and Justice Blackmun to change their votes, but on May 24, the Chief Justice invited Brennan into his chambers and reaffirmed his support. Burger rejected the major argument of the Marshall–Harlan position that the Brennan opinion required too much attention by the Court to evaluations of the record—in effect, constitutionalizing the fact-finding process. The Chief Justice said that he, like Brennan, thought that the Marshall–Harlan approach involved as much scrutiny of the record.

White now circulated his concurrence, which took the more limited view that the *New York Times* rule had to apply to all reporting of "the official actions of public servants."[77] Brennan pointed out to him that his shift in focus from the person involved to the *issue,* really put him in the Brennan camp. But White remained firm on issuing his own opinion.

Brennan did, however, make an important change in his opinion that was a response to Justice Marshall's criticism that the Brennan opinion placed courts in the position of saying what it was legitimate for the public to know. The final Brennan draft changed the formulation of the governing test from "legitimate public interest" to "of public or general interest," borrowing the phrase from Warren and Brandeis's seminal law review article on The Right to Privacy.[78] The change was intended to make clear the thrust of the test—to divide the public from the private, and allow the press full play in the former area.

Despite the fragmented nature of the *Rosenbloom* decision and the fact that Brennan spoke for only a plurality of three, it was generally assumed that, as White specifically stated in his concurrence, "at least five members of the Court would support [the rule that] if the publication about them was in an area of legitimate public interest,"[79] the *New York Times* standard would apply. But the Brennan success in importing the public interest test into the Court's jurisprudence was to prove short lived. Three years after *Rosenbloom,* a new majority rejected the Brennan view that *New York Times* "should extend to the defamatory falsehoods relating to private persons if the statements concerned matters of general or public interest."[80]

The rejection came in *Gertz v. Robert Welch, Inc.*[81] A Chicago policeman named Nuccio was convicted of murder. The victim's family retained Gertz, "a reputable attorney," to represent them in civil litigation against Nuccio. An article appearing in the John Birch Society magazine alleged that Nuccio's murder trial was part of a Communist conspiracy to discredit the local police, and it falsely stated that Gertz had arranged Nuccio's "frame-up," implied that petitioner had a criminal record, and labeled him a "Communist-fronter." Gertz sued for libel. The jury returned a verdict for Gertz, but the lower courts decided that the *New York Times* standard should apply and set aside the verdict, relying on *Rosenbloom*.

At the *Gertz* conference, Brennan, of course, spoke strongly in favor of following *Rosenbloom*. But this time he was fighting a losing battle. Two new Justices, Powell and Rehnquist, had been appointed and they both voted against the Brennan position (Black, whom Powell had replaced, had concurred in *Rosenbloom*). In addition, Chief Justice Burger, who had joined Brennan's *Rosenbloom* opinion, indicated that he would vote to reverse.

The Chief Justice began his conference discussion by noting that the key question was "whether *Times* applies." Burger concluded that it did not. "I reject the idea" he said, that "a lawyer becomes a public figure because his client is. And he seems to be just another lawyer. That's different from Rosenbloom, who was a target among the law breakers."

Stewart, Marshall, Powell, and Rehnquist also rejected the *Rosenbloom* test. "I can't accept the 'public interest' standard," declared Powell, who was to write the *Gertz* opinion, "because it leaves the power to the press to determine what is 'public interest.'" That left the pre-*Rosenbloom* "public figure" standard as the relevant one and the consensus agreed with Stewart when he stated, "Gertz for me is not a public figure in the *Times* sense merely because he's a prominent and well-known lawyer. So I'd let him have a state remedy."

At the conference, Blackmun was ambivalent. He noted that he had joined *Rosenbloom* and still agreed with its test,[82] but indicated that he would reverse for a new trial. Ultimately, Blackmun joined the Powell *Gertz* opinion rejecting the *Rosenbloom* test. Blackmun did so, he wrote, in order to ensure that there was a Court for Powell's opinion, since it was "of profound importance for the Court . . . to have a clearly defined majority position that eliminates the unsureness engendered by *Rosenbloom*'s diversity."[83]

As it turned out, only the Brennan concurrence continued to adhere to the public interest standard in *Gertz*. The opinion of the Court flatly refused to apply *New York Times* to private individuals, as contrasted with public officials and public figures.[84] *Gertz* thus withdrew to the boundary fixed by the pre-*Rosenbloom* cases. As long as they did not impose liability without fault, the states were permitted to define for themselves the appropriate standard of liability for defamatory falsehoods.

Gertz is certainly less favorable to the press than the test urged by Justice Brennan. Yet *Gertz* hardly is enough to justify the conclusion that the Burger Court was hostile to the press. The decisions discussed here show the contrary. In *Gertz*, too, the Court did not repudiate the *New York Times* rule of press protection; it only refused to extend it beyond the public official–public figure test recognized by the Warren Court.

Even with regard to defamation suits by private individuals, it should be noted, *Gertz* laid down important limits that are protective of the press. Thus, the Powell opinion held specifically that though the states may fix the liability standard in such suits, they may not impose strict liability for defamatory speech; nor may punitive damages be permitted unless a plaintiff proves the *New York Times* type of "malice"—that is, "a showing of knowledge of falsity or reckless disregard for the truth."[85]

What these *Gertz* limitations mean was pointed out in a January 17, 1974, letter from White to Powell on the latter's draft *Gertz* opinion. Under the opinion, White wrote, "you still require fault beyond the damaging circulation of falsehoods. This pretty well forces the States to revise their libel laws substantially. Likewise, requiring that the private plaintiff prove actual injury to reputation imposes a substantial federal limitation on state libel laws, and pretty well scuttles the ingrained idea that there are certain statements that are per se libellous." In White's view, as stated in another letter,[86] there was no "satisfactory evidence or basis for further restricting state court power to protect private persons against reputation-damaging falsehoods published by the press or others."

As White shows in his *Gertz* dissent,[87] the restrictions on absolute liability and punitive damages imposed by *Gertz* do constitute substantial protections for the press. They may, in fact, be even more meaningful in terms of damage awards than the public interest test urged by Brennan.[88] From this point of view, *Gertz* was as much a victory as a defeat for the press and the vindication of its First Amendment rights.

Chapter Seven

Church and State

THE WARREN Court handed down many controversial decisions, but the one that was subjected to the greatest criticism was *Engel v. Vitale*[1]—striking down prayer in the public schools. The storm has still not subsided. Religious leaders throughout the country condemned the Court, and the mail attacking it was the largest in the Court's history. Chief Justice Warren later wrote, "I vividly remember one bold newspaper headline, 'Court outlaws God.'"[2]

The outcry at the school prayer decision points up the crucial position of the separation between church and state. Americans are, in the Supreme Court's phrase, "a religious people whose institutions presuppose a Supreme Being."[3] So many religious faiths coexist and form so important a part of the life of the community that few things that the Court does affect so intimately the daily lives of the people as its decisions on the permissible relationships between church and state.

Freedom of belief was, indeed, the very first basic freedom written into the Bill of Rights. Congress, the First Amendment categorically declares, "shall make no law . . . prohibiting the free exercise [of religion]." The religious freedom accorded by the First Amendment is, however, not exhausted by the right to practice one's religion, free from penalty or discrimination. The First Amendment also provides that Congress shall make no law "respecting an establishment of religion." The constitutional guaranty is thus divided into two parts: the state shall neither prefer nor penalize religion. As Justice Frankfurter said, "The essence of the religious freedom guaranteed by our Constitution is therefore this: no religion shall either receive the state's support or incur its hostility."[4]

FINANCIAL AID: TAX EXEMPTION

"Congress shall make no law respecting an establishment of religion." What exactly does this mean? "We are all agreed," Justice Frankfurter stated, "that the First and the Fourteenth Amendments have a secular reach far more penetrating in the conduct of Government than merely to forbid an 'established church.'"[5] The difficulty is in determining exactly how much further the amendments do reach.

In a leading case some years ago, the Court indicated that the constitutional division between church and state was sharper than many people had realized. In an oft-quoted statement, the Court concluded that, "In the words of Jefferson, the clause against establishment of religion by law was intended to erect 'a wall of separation between church and State.'"[6]

The "wall of separation" metaphor may be a striking image, but, as with all jurisprudential formulas, we must take care lest it serve as a substitute for reflection and reasoning. Even if we agree that the First Amendment was intended to erect a "wall of separation between church and State," that hardly tells us what it is that the wall separates.[7]

Direct money grants to churches and other religious institutions, common in many of the colonies, are categorically outlawed by the Establishment Clause.[8] In *Walz v. Tax Commission*,[9] it was claimed that the same should be true of the indirect financial aid provided by tax exemptions for religious organizations. The Court had on several occasions refused to deal with appeals raising the tax exemption issue, but the four votes for noting probable jurisdiction in *Walz* were obtained when Chief Justice Warren and Justice Fortas joined what had come to be known in the Court as the Black–Douglas Establishment Clause axis. With the departure of Warren and Fortas from the Court, however, the *Walz* result was virtually a foregone conclusion even before the argument took place. It, nevertheless, took almost half a year for the decision—a delay so lengthy that commentators concluded that *Walz* was a casualty of the absence of a ninth Justice[10] and that the Court was split four to four. But the delay was not caused by disagreement over the result. At the postargument conference, all except the Black–Douglas axis agreed with Chief Justice Burger's statement that the "exemptions haven't fostered a breakdown of the wall. It's a neutral [thing] which neither deters free exercise nor establishes a religion."

The *Walz* delay was caused by the weakness of the Burger draft opinion, which was circulated February 13, 1970. As one Justice put it, "The opinion in its original state, was lacking in any response to several of the major arguments against the exemptions."

On April 21, the Chief Justice sent around a revision, which incorporated much of the approach followed by Justice Brennan in his draft concurrence. Brennan analyzed religious tax exemptions in terms of their history, the governmental purpose behind them, and the effect of their existence on church–state relations—that is, their operation in practice. Burger not only adopted the history–purpose–operation framework, he also used several choice quotes[11] and Brennan's argument that religious organizations contribute to American pluralism.[12]

In his covering memo, the Chief Justice stated that the revisions in his April 21 redraft "make no change in my judgment, but were made to reflect emphasis on points raised by others." A Brennan law clerk wrote under this, "euphemism! He's *stolen* our opinion—down to the quotes!"

White joined the original Burger draft four days after it was circulated. His clerks said that he was pleased that the opinion was muddled; he could thus join it without committing himself to any precise position. A month later the Chief Justice received his third vote from a surprising source—Black, who was apparently influenced by Burger's strong reliance on what he called Black's "eminently sensible realistic" *Everson* opinion.[13] Stewart also joined the revised draft, as well as Marshall after Burger agreed to delete a reference to the possibility that the elimination of the exemptions might pose a free exercise problem.

Walz upheld the tax exemption, with only Douglas dissenting. The Burger opinion stressed two factors: (1) "The purpose and primary effect[14] . . . of tax exemption is not aimed at establishing, sponsoring, or supporting religion," and (2) "the end result—the effect—is not an excessive government entanglement with religion."[15]

We shall see that these were two of the factors included in the three-factor test to be adopted in *Lemon v. Kurtzman*.[16] Particularly significant was enunciation of the entanglement factor. The original Burger draft did not spell out that factor, though it did imply it: "The tax exemption affirmatively furthers the separation of church and state by eliminating the necessity for tax valuations, liens and foreclosures and the confrontations which often follow in the train of those processes."

Brennan's draft concurrence specifically referred to the entanglement factor, which he termed "extensive state involvement with religion."[17] Burger borrowed the concept, renaming it "excessive government entanglement with religion."[18]

The Court relied on the history of tax exemptions to buttress its decision that they did not violate the clause. Behind the scenes Justices Brennan and Douglas debated the nature of early Virginia practice regarding tax exemptions for churches. Brennan contended that the Virginia General Assembly, with Madison at times sitting as a member, had granted these exemptions from the 1770s on. Douglas stated, in his draft dissent, "The fact that churches in Virginia were not exempted from taxation until 1840, four years after Madison's death, had been attributed to 'the vigilance of men like Jefferson and Madison.'" The Virginia Code provisions appeared to support Brennan's conclusion. When he was shown them, however, Douglas would not give way, saying that there were gaps for some years. Douglas sent his law clerk to do research on the Virginia session laws in the Library of Congress. There he labored with some help from the Brennan clerks. No session law contradicting Brennan was found; indeed, more code provisions supporting him appeared. Douglas yielded and deleted the sentence.

FINANCIAL AID: SCHOOLS AND COLLEGES

The nonentanglement requirement enunciated in *Walz* became the basis of decision a year later in *Lemon v. Kurtzman*,[19] which arose out of companion cases involving challenges to Pennsylvania and Rhode Island laws. The Pennsylvania statute provided financial support to nonpublic schools by way of reimbursement for the cost of teachers' salaries, textbooks, and instructional materials. Under the Rhode Island statute the state paid teachers in nonpublic elementary schools a supplement of 15 percent of their annual salary. Both statutes required the subjects and teaching materials to be the same as in public schools or approved by the state and prohibited payment for religious teaching.

The Justices considered *Lemon* together with *Tilton v. Richardson*,[20] which dealt with federal construction grants for church-related colleges. The vote to take both the state and federal cases was what a Justice termed "predictably unanimous." The cases were argued early in March 1971.

The March 6 postargument conference first discussed the Pennsylvania and Rhode Island cases. The Chief Justice began the discussion by stating, "I don't see any difference between the Pennsylvania and Rhode Island plans"—a point on which all agreed. "Entanglement is the only problem I see here," Burger went on. He pointed out that "there's already a great deal in supervision of the secular activities. It's the crux of accreditation. But [here] we have direct payment."

Harlan spoke for the state laws. "If it's permissible, as I think it is, for public funds to be used for the 'public school' part of religious schools and we can protect against trespass of religion into the public part, then policing is not entanglement in the sense of inhibiting recipients from using it for religion."

White, ultimately the lone dissenter, was even firmer in favor of state aid. "The state can say, 'Wherever you want your secular education, we'll pay for it.' If there's also religious training, so be it." White took an entirely different view of entanglement than the others. "Entanglement is only another word for saying, as a matter of free exercise, government can't muffle or inhibit one's religion."

Black and Douglas reiterated their strong Establishment Clause position. Justice Stewart declared, "Here the grants are beamed directly at helping the parochial schools." Justice Blackmun was uncharacteristically forthright. "Here are outright grants, which means the schools may use their own funds for other purposes. . . . The logical end to these Pennsylvania and Rhode Island cases is complete support."

The conference vote was four to hold the state plans constitutional (the Chief Justice and White, Marshall, voting only on the Rhode Island plan, and Harlan) and four finding them unconstitutional (Black, Douglas, Stewart, and Blackmun). Brennan was undecided. The vote in the federal case was seven to two (Black and Douglas) to affirm, upholding the federal statute's grant of funds to sectarian colleges. Brennan, the deciding vote in the Pennsylvania and Rhode Island cases, was leaning toward holding them both unconstitutional but decided to wait until opinions both ways were prepared. Harlan called him to urge him to vote, at least tentatively, for upholding the state plans. He argued that if Brennan voted to strike down the plans, Marshall might also do so. Harlan also anticipated a move by the Chief Justice to be on the majority side. Brennan agreed to vote tentatively to uphold the state statutes and called the Chief Justice. He also requested that he not be assigned the opinion. Brennan told his clerks that he hoped that Harlan would be assigned the opinions.

Chief Justice Burger, however, assigned the opinions to himself. He circulated opinions on May 6 holding the two state statutes unconstitutional and the federal statute constitutional. Justice Stewart joined the next day.

On May 9, Douglas circulated his separate opinion in the state cases and his dissent in the federal case. Black joined the Douglas opinions May 25. At this point the Chief Justice spoke to Brennan about the federal case, referring to the federal statute's provision that prohibited religious use for twenty years of college structures erected with federal funds. Burger wanted to strike down the twenty-year limitation and hoped that this would convince Brennan to sustain the rest of the federal statute. But Brennan decided to issue his own opinion concurring in the state cases and dissenting on the federal statute.

On June 7, Brennan and Harlan discussed the cases at lunch. Harlan said he was having trouble distinguishing between the state and federal statutes. Brennan replied that all three must be struck down since they gave funds directly to sectarian institutions. Harlan indicated that he would not vote until he had read Brennan's opinion. Later that day, however, Harlan circulated a note to the conference that the Chief Justice had convinced him and he was joining the Burger opinions in both the state and federal cases. Blackmun also joined on June 9.

Brennan circulated his concurrence and dissent on June 10; the next day White circulated his opinion in favor of holding all three statutes constitutional. The final vote came when Marshall joined Douglas in both the state and federal cases. The result was that the state statutes were voted down, eight to one, and the grant of federal funds to sectarian colleges survived by a vote of five to four.

Lemon v. Kurtzman is known primarily for the three-factor test enunciated there. As stated in the Chief Justice's opinion, "First, the statute must have a secular legislative purpose; second, its principal or primary effect must be one that neither advances nor inhibits religion . . .; finally, the statute must not foster 'an excessive government entanglement with religion.'"[21]

As the Chief Justice had stated at the conference, the problem was "entanglement." The states had created statutory restrictions to guarantee the separation between secular and religious education and to ensure that state financial aid supported only the former. But the need to monitor the schools necessarily involved excessive entanglement between government and religion.

The law at issue in *Tilton v. Richardson* provided federal construction grants for college and university facilities, excluding "any facility used or to be used for sectarian instruction or as a place for religious worship, or . . . primarily in connection with any part of the program of a school or department of divinity." Four church-related colleges and universities in Connecticut received such grants.

The determinative factor in *Tilton* was that the aid was granted to institutions of higher education. This was the principal point made by the Chief Justice in his conference presentation. "This can be distinguished from aid to primary schools," Burger said. "The relationship between establishment and free exercise is different as to colleges from what it is as to primary schools." [22] There was less danger here than in church-related primary and secondary schools dealing with impressionable children. Religious indoctrination is not a substantial purpose or activity of these church-related colleges. In addition, there was a smaller risk of entanglement; only minimal inspection would be needed. Douglas had urged at the *Tilton* conference that, "Unless the Government inspects to be sure, then [it is] not doing its duty and, if it does, then [there is] the entanglement that separation was intended to [prohibit]." The conference majority, however, agreed with the Chief Justice. "Partial payment for [a] building on condition that no religion is taught in the building involves most minimal entanglement." Even Marshall told the conference, "Inspection is a normal governmental function and won't create improper intervention into religious institutions."

The *Lemon–Tilton* dichotomy between schools and colleges remained fundamental in the Burger Court jurisprudence. Aid to church-related schools was ruled invalid in *Levitt v. Committee for Public Education*.[23] A statute authorized reimbursement to private schools for performing services mandated by state law—in particular the cost of testing pupils. The Court had no difficulty in concluding that the direct payments violated the Establishment Clause. The dividing line here was stated by Justice Blackmun at the conference: "The states can require tests . . . but they [can't] subsidize it. . . . The state is covering the costs of part of the teaching process and [this is] a direct aid to religion in the parochial schools. To that extent this scheme is bad."

Nor did it make any difference that, as Blackmun pointed out, the tests were required by the state. The basic difference here is between regulation and funding of education. The distinction was pointed out in a letter by Douglas: the "service a state may 'mandate' a religious school to perform might include, for purposes of health, keeping room temperatures at 72. . . . But I doubt if the state could constitutionally take on the heating and sanitary services of a religious school." [24]

Any direct financial aid to religious schools is invalid. As Douglas said at the *Levitt* conference, "A school is an organic whole; its functions are inseparable." But, as *Tilton* indicates, the same is not necessarily true of colleges and universities.

In *Roemer v. Board of Public Works*,[25] for example, the state established a program of grants to all private colleges. Each year, the colleges were to receive for each student (excluding those enrolled in seminarian or theological programs) 15 percent of the amount spent for each student in the state college system. No funds could be "utilized by the institutions for sectarian purposes."

The Justices, by a bare majority, upheld the grant program. The predominant theme at the postargument conference was set by Blackmun, who was to deliver the plurality opinion. "These are general grants," said Blackmun. There was "no denomination support per se. This really calls only for application of settled principle. There's a secular purpose and I wouldn't upset the finding of no sectarian [purpose]. This is close to *Tilton* and I would hope the opinion would encourage plans like this."

The key distinction in the Burger Court jurisprudence was the line between *Lemon* and *Tilton*. As Powell put it at the *Roemer* conference, "Liberal arts colleges are not controlled or financially supported by the Church. Academic freedom is complete and colleges are different from primary or secondary schools."

INDIRECT AID TO SCHOOLS

With direct financial aid to sectarian schools thus outlawed, states sought to accomplish the same purpose with indirect aid. In *Committee for Public Education v. Nyquist*,[26] the state reimbursed low-income parents for part of the tuition paid to private schools and provided tax credits for higher-income parents. The Court struck down the tuition reimbursements on the ground that "the State seeks to relieve their [the parents'] financial burden sufficiently to assure that they continue to have the option to send their children to religion-oriented schools." The tax credits were held to have the same effect: "there would appear to be little difference for purposes of whether such aid has the effect of advancing religion, between the tax benefit allowed here and the tuition grant."[27]

In a later case, *Mueller v. Allen*,[28] a state provided tax deductions for "tuition, textbooks and transportation" for children attending any elementary or secondary school. Despite *Nyquist,* the conference divided five to four in favor of the state law.

"This is a deduction," the Chief Justice began the conference discussion. "*Nyquist* was a direct subsidy and this isn't. Yet this comes close." According to Burger, "The state has a legitimate secular purpose" because the law "(1) lifts a substantial burden off the public schools; (2) fosters diversity; and (3) private [schools] do a better education job."

White also spoke in favor of the law, conceding that, in the church–state cases, "I've been out of step with the court for years." Rehnquist and O'Connor, too, supported the law. According to the latter, "This is a true tax deduction and, while it's [a] form of subsidy, it's indirect and, on that ground, I'd affirm."

Powell's conference statement was of particular interest: "Can we say on this record that [this] 25-year-old statute has fostered the evils the Establishment Clause was designed to prevent? I don't think I can say so. If we strike this statute down, I can't think of any aid to parochial schools that can survive."

The dissenters, on the other hand, stressed the effect of the decision on public education. "An affirmance here," Justice Blackmun asserted, "goes a long way to killing off the public schools. . . . I don't agree parochial schools produce a superior product to public schools."

Mueller upheld the tax deduction. The Rehnquist opinion relied on the point made by the Justice at the conference: "This covered group is broader than that in *Nyquist.* . . . [U]nlike the assistance at issue in *Nyquist,* [the statute here] permits *all* parents—whether their children attend public schools or private—to deduct their children's educational expenses." The statute was treated as one "that neutrally provides state assistance to a broad spectrum of citizens" and, as such, "not readily subject to challenge under the Establishment Clause."[29]

The Rehnquist rationale, however, ignores reality in its assertion that *all* parents are really benefited by the tax deduction. Public schools do not charge tuition and normally furnish free books and transportation. Hence, as Marshall points out in his dissent, "Of the total number of taxpayers who are eligible for the tuition deduction, approximately 96 percent send their children to religious schools. Parents who send their children to public schools are simply ineligible to obtain the full benefit of the deduction."[30]

Despite the Rehnquist attempt at distinction, the *Mueller* deductions were similar to the *Nyquist* credits. The difference in result in the two cases indicates a changed attitude in the Burger Court to indirect aid to religious schools; but direct payments to religious schools continued to be invalidated by the Court. What about other forms of indirect aid, such as the furnishing of auxiliary support services in sectarian schools?

Meek v. Pittenger[31] arose out of a state program that provided three forms of aid for nonpublic schools: (1) loans of textbooks "acceptable for use in the public schools"; (2) loans of secular instructional materials (including projectors, recorders, periodicals, and laboratory equipment); and (3) provision of auxiliary services, including testing, remedial, and therapeutic services by public employees at the private schools.

At the *Meek* conference, with Douglas out and Marshall not voting, only Brennan spoke in favor of invalidating all three forms of aid, since in his view, no tax money could be spent, directly or indirectly, for religious schools. The others took the view that the textbook loans were valid under the *Allen* case[32] decided by the Warren Court. As far as the other parts of the state program were concerned, Brennan was supported by Stewart, Blackmun, and Powell. Stewart said that the "auxiliary teaching is unconstitutional." With regard to "the educational materials which are not covered by *Allen,*" he first said, "I'm not sure." But ultimately Stewart said, "Since they're given to the school, that's unconstitutional."

According to Powell, "The keystone in *Allen* was that identical services were provided children in both public and private schools. But when the state comes directly to the aid of parochial schools and gives them this, that takes the financial burden off their backs. That's as bad as the *Nyquist* situation under the Establishment Clause."

Powell concluded his conference presentation by anticipating his vote in *Mueller v. Allen:* "I would hope for an opinion that emphasizes that providing the same thing for everybody could pass muster."

The *Meek* conference vote was six to one to uphold the textbook loans (ultimately Douglas and Marshall, who had not voted at the conference, joined the Brennan dissent on this point) and four to three to strike down the instructional materials and auxiliary services programs. Since Chief Justice Burger was in the *Meek* minority, assignment of the case fell to Brennan, the senior member of the conference majority. Brennan, however, wrote to the Chief Justice on February 24, 1975, "I've decided that I should not assign the opinion in the above. . . . I'm alone in my conference vote that the text books statute should fall with the statutes on services, etc."

The Brennan letter also noted the close conference division on the other aspects of the case: "Thurgood's vote on services, etc. could make a difference I agree. If he agrees with Potter, Lewis, Harry and me, the majority will be 5–3 on that question. If he votes with you, Byron and Bill Rehnquist, there would be an affirmance by a 4–4 vote."

As it turned out, not only Marshall but also Douglas joined with Brennan, Stewart, Blackmun, and Powell to strike down the loan of instructional materials and the provision of auxiliary services. The loan of instructional materials had the impermissible effect of aiding religious activity; the materials assisted in the operation of schools performing a primarily religious role. Provision of auxiliary services involved excessive entanglement. To be certain that the auxiliary teachers remained religiously neutral, the state would have to engage in continuing surveillance.

Two years later, however, in *Wolman v. Walter,*[33] a divided Court sustained a state scheme that provided for diagnostic services (psychological, speech, and hearing) by public school personnel on religious school premises and therapeutic and remedial services for students needing specialized attention to be performed off the private school premises. The majority said that the state scheme here was different from that in *Meek* and did not suffer from its defects. As Chief Justice Burger put it at the conference on *Committee for Public Education v. Regan,*[34] the next case on the subject, "Did *Wolman* retreat from *Meek*? I don't think so."[35]

Regan itself arose out of a state law that reimbursed religious schools for the costs of administering and grading standardized educational achievement tests. The tests, unlike those invalidated in *Levitt,*[36] were not teacher-prepared tests but tests prepared by the state education authorities. The Court upheld the *Regan* test reimbursements, holding that *Wolman,* rather than *Levitt,* controlled the case.

"If you thought as Bill Brennan does, that any tax money is unconstitutional," said Justice Stewart at the *Regan* conference, "life would be easy. But that's not the Court's test since *Everson*[37] and so we must come down to specific details."

On the merits, the Chief Justice told the conference, "I don't see why compensation for doing the state's job can violate the religion clauses." Powell stated a similar position. "I'm going as far as I'm willing to go in saying the state can't pay religious schools for doing the state's job." Burger also saw a free-exercise aspect to the case. "Wouldn't denying compensation be a burden on free exercise?" the Chief Justice asked.

Regan upheld the test reimbursement—a decision confirming *Wolman*'s retreat, however brief, from *Meek* and *Levitt.* In a letter on *Regan,* Justice Rehnquist referred to "the various permutations and commutations of this issue at least since I have been on the Court."[38] What some consider another permutation in church–state jurisprudence took place in two cases during the 1984 term.

The first was *Grand Rapids School District v. Ball,*[39] which arose out of a program to provide supplementary classes in private schools, including religious schools, conducted by public school teachers. Among the courses were "remedial" and "enrichment" mathematics, reading, art, music, and physical education. A bare majority ruled the program invalid. The program, according to the Brennan opinion of the Court, impermissibly promoted religion in three ways. The state-paid teachers, influenced by the pervasively sectarian nature of the religious schools, indoctrinated the students in particular religious tenets. The symbolic union of church and state threatened to convey a message of state support for religion. The program in effect subsidized the religious functions of the schools by taking over a substantial portion of their responsibility for teaching secular subjects.

A companion case, *Aguilar v. Felton,*[40] involved a program funded by Title I of the Federal Elementary and Secondary Education Act of 1965. New York state sent public school teachers and other professionals into religious and other private schools to provide remedial instruction and clinical and guidance services. New York, unlike Grand Rapids, had adopted a system for monitoring the religious content of the classes. The program was held unconstitutional by the court of appeals. The opinion, by Judge Henry J. Friendly,[41] was praised by several Justices during the *Aguilar* postargument conference.

Chief Justice Burger began the conference discussion by asking, "Does the Title I program fail? Henry Friendly felt he had to strike it. I can't agree with it so far as it announces an absolute test." Burger also asked whether *Meek*[42] "can be distinguished because [there is] nothing in the record about advancing religion." The Chief Justice, however, was troubled by the "surveillance element."

Stevens told the conference, "The fact that this was remedial makes the argument [in favor of the program] stronger." Blackmun was even weaker in his conference support. "This case is indistinguishable from *Meek* and maybe we should overrule it. Until we do, I must affirm."

The conference voted five (Brennan, Marshall, Blackmun, Powell, and Stevens) to three, with the Chief Justice passing, to affirm. The Chief Justice ultimately joined the dissenters. The Brennan opinion stressed that the New York monitoring system created a danger of excessive entanglement: "Agents of the State must visit and inspect the religious school regularly, alert for the subtle or overt presence of religious matter in Title I classes."[43]

This led Rehnquist to assert in his dissent, that "the Court takes advantage of the 'Catch 22' paradox of its own creation . . . whereby aid must be supervised to ensure no entanglement but the supervision itself is held to cause an entanglement."[44]

Whether the Rehnquist animadversion is valid or not, *Grand Rapids* and *Aguilar* are clear in their confirmation of the *Meek* ban on state teaching assistance to religious schools. Government is prohibited from relieving religious schools of their task of secular education—at least where the assistance takes place in the religious schools themselves.

OTHER OFFICIAL SUPPORT

Other types of official support for religion met a mixed response from the Burger Court. A relatively easy case was presented by *Larkin v. Grendel's Den*.[45] A state law provided that premises within 500 feet of a church should not be licensed to sell liquor if the church objected. The court of appeals had held that the statute conferred a direct benefit upon religion by "the grant of a veto power over liquor sales."

Chief Justice Burger began the *Larkin* conference by declaring, "The statute is invalid on its face in delegating great power to a private party." Nor, in Burger's opinion, was it "important that it's a church. But the fact that it's a church makes it easier." The Chief Justice also stressed that there was "no review power over the church's decision, as I see it."[46]

The conference consensus supported the Burger view. In Powell's words, the statute "violates the Establishment Clause on its face." Justice Stevens pointed out that there were already 26 establishments[47] selling liquor within 500 feet of the church, which "shows that this is bad as applied to Grendel's."

Even White, who usually voted to uphold state action against Establishment Clause attacks, agreed with the conference, although "A flat ban,[48] however, would be constitutional in my view." Only Rehnquist voted at the conference to sustain the challenged law. O'Connor told the conference, "On the Establishment Clause, I'm not at rest, so I will pass." She ultimately voted with the majority. Rehnquist remained the only *Larkin* dissenter.

The church veto in *Larkin* so patently violated the Establishment Clause that it is scarcely surprising that it was stricken down by a near-unanimous Court. Just as easy have been cases in which the public schools are used directly for religious purposes.

Although striking down school prayers was the Warren Court's most criticized decision, it is difficult to see how any other decision would have been consistent with the Establishment Clause. School prayers "are religious exercises, required by the States in violation of the command of the First Amendment that the Government maintain strict neutrality, neither aiding nor opposing religion."[49]

The ban against school prayers was extended by the Warren Court to Bible reading[50] and by the Burger court to posting of the Ten Commandments.[51] More difficult was the "moment of silence"—at issue in *Wallace v. Jaffree*.[52] An Alabama statute authorized teachers in public schools to "announce that a period of silence not to exceed one minute in duration shall be observed for meditation or voluntary prayer." The sponsor of the law stated that it was an "effort to return voluntary prayer" to the schools.

The district court found that the Alabama law had been enacted "to encourage a religious activity." Nevertheless, it upheld the law since it had concluded that the Supreme Court decisions were errone-

ous. After reviewing what it perceived to be newly discovered historical evidence, the district court concluded that "the establishment
clause . . . does not prohibit the state from establishing a religion."[53]
Not surprisingly, the court of appeals rejected "the District Court's
remarkable conclusion that the Federal Constitution imposes no obstacle to Alabama's establishment of a state religion."[54]

Chief Justice Burger began the December 7, 1984, *Wallace* conference by speaking in favor of the Alabama law. "The moment of silence is completely neutral. The reference to 'prayer' in the statute
doesn't change this for me." The *Lemon* three-prong test was not
violated. "The statute serves a secular purpose, since a student can
use the moment for anything he pleases."

The opposition was led by Justice Brennan. "I would hold that the
moment of silence for meditation or voluntary prayer violates the Establishment Clause. . . . According to the legislative sponsors and the
governor of Alabama this statute was intended to bring back school
prayer. As such it was a clear effort to advance the practice of religion
in the public sphere."

Brennan referred to the fact that the statute had been amended
to permit meditation or prayer—"adding the words 'or voluntary
prayer' was intended to make clear to students that they could pray
during the moment of silence; the legislature showed no similar solicitude for any other type of thought or activity. . . . In the context of
the legislative purpose to thrust prayer back into the schools, this
amendment must be read as state endorsement of religious practice.
Certainly the young Jaffree children and others at their impressionable age, hearing each morning the authoritative voice of their teacher
instruct them that they must observe a moment of silence for voluntary prayer, would receive the message of official endorsement of the
religious practice. . . . [T]he clear purpose and effect of advancing religion compel invalidation under the *Lemon v. Kurtzman* approach.
As far as I am concerned, this statute cannot be squared with the crucial values of neutrality and separation that I have long thought the
Establishment Clause embodies. Though not specifically sectarian,
the statute is not neutral because it endorses the religious as opposed
to the nonreligious. And in purpose and effect the statute thrusts religion into the school. In essence the school house becomes each morning a house of worship for that moment."[55]

The conference vote was five (Brennan, Marshall, Blackmun,
Stevens, and O'Connor) to four (the Chief Justice and White, Powell,
and Rehnquist) to strike down the law. Powell told the conference

that the statute "promotes free exercise and that's enough to sustain it." But he later switched his vote and that made the final *Wallace* tally six to three to invalidate the statute.

The opinion was assigned to Stevens by Brennan, the senior majority Justice. The Stevens opinion of the Court followed the Brennan conference approach. The Alabama law was motivated by a purpose to advance religion and hence failed the first prong of the *Lemon* test—it did not "have a secular legislative purpose."[56]

Powell and O'Connor wrote concurrences in which they stated specifically that statutes providing only for a "moment of silence" in schools might be constitutional.[57] The opinion of the Court also suggested that "an appropriate moment of silence" law might be valid.[58] At the *Wallace* conference, Blackmun had stated that a "meditation statute is constitutional," and Brennan had said that, if it provided only for a minute of silence "for meditation," "the statute might pass muster."[59] The Burger Court did not deal with the validity of laws providing only for a moment of silence, but the statements at the conference and the *Wallace* concurrences indicate that it would have upheld them by a large majority.

It should, however, be noted that the Burger Court extension of the ban on school prayer in *Wallace* did not mean a watertight separation between the sectarian and the secular. Such a separation would invalidate prayers in legislative halls and invocations of divine protection in governmental organs, as well as references to God in laws and rituals. Indeed, "A fastidious atheist or agnostic could even object to the supplication with which the Court opens each session: 'God save the United States and this Honorable Court.'"[60]

In *Marsh v. Chambers*,[61] the Court refused to strike down a state legislature's practice of opening each day with a prayer by a chaplain paid by the state. The Burger opinion relied almost entirely on history, stressing the historical practice in this country—starting even before the first Congress in 1789—of utilizing this kind of legislative prayer.

The legislative prayer result can also be justified on the ground that legislators, unlike schoolchildren, are mature adults who may absent themselves from the proceedings without incurring any penalty.[62] In addition, legislative prayers and similar exercises, as a matter of practical reality, are more ceremonial than sectarian. American public life is permeated with references to God, but references of the type contained in the motto "In God We Trust" have become so interwoven into the fabric of our civil polity as not to present the type of involvement between church and state that the First Amendment forbids. Such references in maxims, oaths, exercises, and ceremonies, whatever may have been their origins, no longer have a primary religious purpose or meaning.

In *Lynch v. Donnelly,*[63] one of the Burger Court's more controversial decisions, a bare majority ruled that the same was true of a creche, placed at public expense, by a city in the heart of the shopping district. The lower court found that the display endorsed and promulgated Christian beliefs in violation of the Establishment Clause.

The Chief Justice began the *Lynch* conference by speaking in favor of reversal. "This has been a practice for over a century. . . . Whether it's part of a larger scene or separate, I see no First Amendment violation. It's not a secular activity, but it's no different from chaplains for me. . . . This would pass the [*Lemon v.*] Kurtzman[64] tests."

White, Powell, Rehnquist, and O'Connor agreed. "*Nyquist,*"[65] Powell said, "makes the primary test whether the purpose here is to advance religion. I can't see that here. The setting here has the creche in the middle of 4,000 square feet. It is primarily associated, not with Christian religion, but with a national holiday."

On the other side, Brennan made much the same argument that he was to make in his *Lynch* dissent. He was supported by Marshall, who said, "Christ is not like a Thanksgiving turkey," and Blackmun and Stevens. Blackmun in particular, was not happy about the case. This was "another case we can do without. . . . The crass commercialization of Christmas sickens me. Little is lost, I suppose, however we decide." As Blackmun saw it, "*Marsh* is not controlling; [there is] no similar history here. If we apply *Lemon,* affirmance is hard to avoid . . . public support leads me to affirm."

O'Connor began her conference presentation by conceding that *Lynch* was "not an easy case. . . . *Marsh* doesn't help—[there was] no significant history [here] at the time of drafting of the First Amendment. The *Lemon* tests then come into play. . . . But I'd acknowledge that purpose and effect are not to be treated separately—rather in tandem. Looking at them that way, the district court didn't view the whole setting and I'd, therefore, reverse."

The bare conference majority for reversal held firm. The Burger opinion paralleled his conference presentation. By considering the creche "in the context of the Christmas season," the Chief Justice was able to find a "secular purpose." It "depicts the historical origins of this traditional event long recognized as a National Holiday." There is a "primary effect" that does not benefit religion or Christianity, and there is no "entanglement." Hence the three-part *Lemon* test was met.

During the conference, Rehnquist asserted that the case was actually a "pee wee. People are not really bothered by this in its Christmas context." As a member of the religious majority, he was unaware that its tenets were not only not accepted by, but might also prove offensive to, those of other faiths.[66] The *Lynch* decision appears insensitive to the meaning of the nativity scene to non-Christians, particularly to Jews for whom the depiction of the birth of Christ may be offensive as a fundamental point of departure from Judaism.[67] As one commentator puts it, "To those who feel excluded because to them a government-funded nativity scene is either offensive or insulting, *Lynch v. Donnelly* conveyed a sad and disappointing message."[68]

The original Burger *Lynch* draft contained a reference to the "Vicar of Rome." This led to a March 7, 1984, Memorandum to the Conference from the Chief Justice: "An expert on canonical law alerted me to the fact that the common usage 'Vicar of Rome' is not accurate. The precise description is 'Vicar of Christ' or 'Bishop of Rome.' Absent dissent, I will correct my error in due course."

FREE EXERCISE

The constitutional guaranty of freedom of religion is based upon two First Amendment clauses, the Establishment Clause and the Free Exercise Clause. It is the Free Exercise Clause that guarantees freedom of religion itself. The clause secures the right of religious belief and the right to practice and propagate one's faith unrestricted by governmental action.

Yet the Free Exercise Clause gives us more than the right to have our own beliefs reign in the private kingdom of the individual mind. It ensures that we will not be penalized for the particular faiths that we follow or refuse to follow. Our forebears had too much experience—both in the Old World and the New—of what it means to be discriminated against for not being a member of the established church not to have intended wholly to outlaw all power in government to continue such discriminations. Eliminated by the First Amendment is the possibility of governmental power to restrain or penalize the free exercise of belief or nonbelief. The Protestant and the Catholic, the

Calvinist and the Greek Orthodox, the Jew and the Muslim, the agnostic and the atheist, all may sit down at the common table of our councils without an inquisition into their faiths or modes of worship, or their lack of same.[69]

The Free Exercise Clause received a new dimension in *Wisconsin v. Yoder*.[70] Respondents, members of the Amish religion, were convicted of violating Wisconsin's compulsory school attendance law by refusing to send their children to school after the eighth grade. The Amish provide a continuing informal vocational education designed for life in the rural Amish community. Respondents sincerely believed that high school attendance was contrary to their religion and way of life and that they would endanger their own salvation and that of their children by complying with the law.

The Chief Justice set the *Yoder* conference theme when he spoke in favor of affirming the lower court's ruling that application of the compulsory school-attendance law to respondents violated their rights under the Free Exercise Clause. He had "difficulty in finding a compelling state interest. . . . I agree with Jefferson that the kind of discipline and training these [children] get from their fathers is as good as anything they'd get in Wisconsin schools."

The conference consensus agreed that the decision should be affirmed—with only Douglas the other way. The Chief Justice wrote the opinion. As pointed out by Stewart, "the substantive reliance of the opinion is exclusively upon the right of free exercise of religion, conferred by the First and Fourteenth Amendments of the Constitution."[71] Burger's opinion stressed that the Amish mode of life and their refusal to submit their children to further secular education were essential parts of their religious beliefs; hence enforcement of the compulsory attendance law would gravely endanger the free exercise of those beliefs.

The original Burger draft indicated that parents had a constitutional right to direct their children's religious upbringing and education. In an April 10, 1972, "Dear Chief" letter, Stewart objected: "I am enough of a disciple of Hugo Black to be unable to agree that 'parental direction' is a constitutional right. To be sure, our society has long been organized in terms of the monogamous family structure, and this Court's cases make clear that the interests arising from that structure enjoy procedural due process as well as equal protection immunity from governmental interference. But it is something else to say that those interests are substantive constitutional rights."

The opinion was then changed in two places to refer to the "interest of parents" to guide the religious upbringing of their children—though it did retain "the right of parents to direct" their upbringing.[72]

Yoder does not mean that free exercise must always prevail over state law. While legislative power over beliefs alone is forbidden, it may reach actions that are in violation of social duties or subversive of good order, even when the actions are demanded by religion.[73] As the Court stated over a century ago: "Laws are made for the government of actions, and while they cannot interfere with mere religious belief and opinions, they may with practices. Suppose one believed that human sacrifices were a necessary part of religious worship, would it be seriously contended that the civil government under which he lived could not interfere to prevent a sacrifice?"[74]

Yoder was an exception to this general principle, but it applied only to a small religious community with an established separate way of life.[75] And even the Amish are not exempt from other valid laws. In the Burger Court jurisprudence, this was shown by *United States v. Lee,*[76] which denied an Amish employer of Amish workers an exemption from social security taxes. He believed that payment of taxes and receipt of social security benefits would violate the Amish faith. Congress had exempted self-employed Amish from the taxes, but not Amish who employed others. The lower court held that the requirement was an infringement upon free exercise.

The Chief Justice began the *Lee* conference by coming out for reversal. Referring to the Amish, he pointed out that "taking care of their own is a very important free exercise right." Yet this case was different from *Yoder* and other Free Exercise cases.[77] "Congress has gone far to help them. But I can't see how we can exempt them from social security taxes. This is a neutral statutory scheme."

All the others agreed on reversal, but "This isn't easy," Blackmun asserted. "Balancing takes us farther than we've gone before. The tax is minimal, but exemption would relieve them of taking care of other than their own." Blackmun concluded that "the governmental interest, while not for me compelling, is substantial enough to reverse."

Powell and O'Connor said that the governmental interest here in what Stevens termed "even-handed enforcement" was greater than Blackmun indicated. To Powell, "the governmental interest is very substantial, if not indeed compelling." And O'Connor stated, "I think there's a compelling state interest that requires the burden on free exercise to give way."

Even Rehnquist—increasingly the "odd man out" in freedom-of-religion jurisprudence—went along with the others in *Lee*. Rehnquist said that he was voting for reversal even though "reversal is inconsistent, I suggest, with *Sherbert* [*v. Verner*[78]] and *Thomas* [*v. Review Board*[79]]—but both were wrong anyway. So [I vote to] reverse." In the cases referred to by Rehnquist, the Court had invalidated denials of unemployment benefits to people who would not perform work counter to their religious beliefs.

Myriad exemptions flowing from religious beliefs would be difficult to accommodate with operation of the social security system or, indeed, of the general tax system. "When followers of a particular sect enter into commercial activity as a matter of choice, the limits they accept on their own conduct as a matter of conscience and faith are not to be superimposed on the statutory schemes which are binding on others in that activity."[80]

The *Lee* principle is the only one consistent with the orderly functioning of society. The contrary principle "would be to make the professed doctrines of religious belief superior to the law of the land, and in effect to permit every citizen to become a law unto himself."[81] Instead of the line between church and state drawn by the First Amendment, there would be the subordination of the state on any matter deemed within the sovereignty of the religious conscience.[82]

Bob Jones University v. United States[83] furnished the occasion for a striking application of the *Lee* principle. At issue was the refusal of the Internal Revenue Service to continue to grant tax-exempt status to private schools that practiced racial discrimination. The Internal Revenue Code provided tax exemption for corporations operated "for religious, charitable . . . or educational purposes." In 1971, the IRS issued a ruling providing that a school not having a racially nondiscriminatory policy is not "charitable" within the common law concepts reflected in the statute. The university and schools involved in the case believed that their racially discriminatory admissions policies were required by the Bible; the Free Exercise Clause thus barred application of the new IRS policy.

Most of the *Bob Jones* conference discussion was devoted to the question of whether the IRS had the power or whether Congress alone could end the tax exemption. The consensus was that the IRS action was valid, particularly in the light of congressional failure to act. As the Chief Justice told the others, "Congress has acquiesced in the exemption for at least twelve years." Justice Blackmun said, "Congress has ratified the [IRS] interpretation." Powell made the same point. "Although it hasn't ratified explicitly, Congress certainly hasn't overturned the IRS for 12 years. The 1976 § 501(i) implicitly approved it." The section referred to by Powell denied tax exemption status to social clubs that practiced racial discrimination.

Rehnquist, who was to be the sole dissenter, declared, "I don't understand how we can conclude [that there was] Congressional ratification, although I agree that's the strongest argument. Therefore I don't reach the First Amendment argument."

Several of the others also indicated that they preferred not to deal with the constitutional question. Brennan, however, urged that the Court had to reach the Free Exercise issue, and there was uniform agreement that there was no First Amendment violation. Powell declared that he saw "no difficulty with the constitutional issue. Bob Jones [University] is primarily a secular institution." Closer to the decision on the issue was O'Connor's conference comment: "I agree that compelling public policy [that is, against racial discrimination] overcomes the First Amendment." Even Rehnquist agreed on this point. After saying that he did not reach the First Amendment argument, Rehnquist went on to say, "though I wouldn't find it meritorious if I did."

The Burger opinion of the Court followed the *Bob Jones* conference consensus on the Free Exercise issue. It held that the governmental interest at stake—eradicating racial discrimination in education—was so compelling that it substantially outweighed whatever burden the denial of tax benefits placed on these schools' exercise of their religious beliefs.

It will be recalled that Rehnquist indicated that the *Sherbert* and *Thomas* cases were wrongly decided. In *Sherbert v. Verner*,[84] the Warren Court held that unemployment benefits might not be denied to a Seventh Day Adventist because she refused to work on Saturday. *Thomas v. Review Board*[85] extended that holding to a worker who quit his job when his employer required him to work in a department that made turrets for military tanks. As a Jehovah's Witness, he could not work on weapons without violating the principles of his religion. The Court, in an opinion by Chief Justice Burger, ruled that the denial of unemployment benefits violated the Free Exercise Clause.

In his lone dissent in *Thomas*, Rehnquist pointed out "that there is a 'tension' between the Free Exercise Clause and Establishment

Clause." For the state to require provision of financial assistance to persons solely on the basis of their religious beliefs was to "foster the 'establishment' of religion." Rehnquist posed the example of a law that required benefits to be granted to those who quit their jobs for religious reasons as one that "would plainly violate the Establishment Clause."[86]

A law comparable to that posited by Rehnquist was invalidated in *Estate of Thornton v. Caldor, Inc.*[87] A statute prohibited employers from dismissing workers who refused to work on their Sabbath. The Court held that the statute had "a primary effect that impermissibly advances a particular religious practice." Hence it violated the Establishment Clause. Free Exercise does not give anyone "the right to insist that in pursuit of their own interests others must conform their conduct to his own religious necessities."[88]

Perhaps the most striking application of the *Lee* principle occurred in *Goldman v. Weinberger*,[89] decided during the last Burger term. Petitioner, an Orthodox Jew and ordained rabbi, was an officer serving as a clinical psychologist at an air force base. He brought suit claiming that a regulation that prohibited him from wearing his yarmulke while on duty infringed upon his Free Exercise rights. The Court of Appeals for the District of Columbia held for the government, even though Judges Mikva and Edwards (two of the court's most liberal members) sat on the three-judge panel. The Supreme Court voted four (White, Blackmun, Powell, and O'Connor) to three (Brennan, Marshall, and Stevens) to grant certiorari. It is probable that Brennan and Marshall, who would vote to reverse, were against taking the case because they feared an affirmance if review were granted.

At the postargument conference, the Chief Justice spoke in favor of affirmance. "If Mikva, Edwards, and Swygert can hold no religious burden outweighing the military, [so][90] can I. Judges have no business second guessing the military."

Brennan delivered the strongest argument the other way. "We have reaffirmed repeatedly that service men and women do not lose their constitutional rights when they enter the military. I believe that military regulations which interfere with the free exercise of religion are subject to strict scrutiny. . . . The wearing of a yarmulke cannot, to my mind, interfere with discipline and Air Force identity any more than does the wearing of rings, medals, or undergarments with religious significance. The fact that the Air Force permits the wearing of such jewelry and undergarments suggests to me that it cannot rationally forbid the wearing of an unobtrusive religious head-covering that does not interfere with the wearing of the full uniform.

"I would decide this case narrowly, holding simply that the wearing of yarmulkes by Orthodox Jews cannot reasonably be said to pose a threat to the Government's asserted interests." The Court should "not address the question of the military's obligation to accommodate other, more obtrusive forms of religious apparel, such as turbans and saffron robes, which significantly interfere with the prescribed uniform. There is no need to answer these more difficult questions at this time. The Government has made no showing that there really are hordes of Sikhs and so forth lurking 'in the woodwork.' We cannot refuse Dr. Goldman his constitutional rights on the basis of an unsupported parade of potential horribles." [91]

White specifically disagreed with Brennan. "Even if they allow rings, etc., I don't see why they can't disallow this." Powell, Rehnquist, and Stevens also agreed with the Chief Justice, with Stevens saying, "I have to say the military can draw lines on visibility, as here." Blackmun, who ultimately dissented, agreed, but said, "Deferring to the military can be dangerous. . . . On balance, however, I'm inclined to affirm."

The final *Goldman* decision was to affirm by a bare majority. The opinion by Rehnquist rejected the Brennan strict-scrutiny approach and stressed instead the deferential nature of review. Rehnquist explained the decision in a memorandum on a case dealing with a prison hair-length regulation.[92] "The *Goldman* decision indicates that our review of military regulations on First Amendment grounds is far more deferential than constitutional review of similar laws or regulations designed for civilian society. . . . [T]he military is a specialized society separate from civilian society, that requires greater discipline and unity. The fact that prison life is similarly distinct . . . implies that a similar degree of deference is appropriate for review of prison regulations restricting First Amendment rights." [93]

According to a February 14, 1986, letter from Brennan to Rehnquist, the latter's draft opinion in *Goldman* contained "some language which I believe might inadvertently, but deeply, offend our Jewish friends. . . . the use . . . of the word 'idiosyncracies' to describe the practice of wearing yarmulkes. Could I suggest . . . a less judgmental term like 'such practices?'"

Rehnquist replied on February 18: "I think one of the reasons I used it was that the petitioner's brief itself . . . refers to 'his slightly idiosyncratic apparel.' But you may well be right that some orthodox Jews might be offended by the language, and so I am happy to substitute other language."

NEUTRALITY AND NONINTERVENTION

The First Amendment requires state neutrality between religious beliefs and between the sectarian and the secular. Thus, as *Sherbert* and *Thomas* show, when the state confers a benefit, it cannot deny it to a person for conduct conforming to his religious beliefs. Similarly, the state may not distinguish between religious and nonreligious groups with regard to meetings permitted on public facilities. In *Widmar v. Vincent*,[94] a state university routinely provided facilities for meetings of registered student organizations; but it refused to allow a registered student religious group to conduct its meetings in university facilities, relying on a regulation prohibiting use of university buildings "for purposes of religious worship or religious teaching." The lower court held that the regulation violated the First Amendment, rejecting the university's argument that its action was required by the Establishment Clause.

At the *Widmar* conference, all except White spoke in favor of affirmance. The Chief Justice noted that "the regulation applies to the content of the message. I don't see any conflict with the Establishment Clause. This is primarily a speech, not a religion case." On the other side, White asserted, "Compelling the university to allow the use of facilities raises Establishment [Clause] problems that the university should be allowed to avoid by this kind of regulation."

The basic conference theme was that stated by Powell, who was to author the *Widmar* opinion: "I agree that this is a public forum and [they] should not discriminate between recognized groups of students." Rehnquist made the same point, saying, "Although religious groups are not entitled to super access, but, if [they] open up to other groups, [they] can't discriminate against this one."

The conference was also with the Chief Justice on the Establishment Clause issue. "Allowing them to participate as others do," said Stevens, "it's neutral." O'Connor put it a little differently. "To the extent establishment is here, free exercise takes precedence." A decision for affirmance would be one "accommodating neutrality."

With only White dissenting, the *Widmar* decision invalidated the university refusal to provide the facilities. The opinion found that a policy of allowing access to university facilities by religious groups on the terms available to other groups would not violate the Establishment Clause. On the contrary, the state may not engage in content-based discrimination against religious speech. State neutrality, rather than establishment, is furthered when the open-forum policy is applied equally to both religious and nonreligious speech.

The principle of neutrality requires the state to follow a hands-off policy in religious disputes. Most of the cases applying that policy have involved contests for control of church property or other internal ecclesiastical disputes. The decisions in such cases, Brennan informs us, have "settled the proposition that in order to give effect to the First Amendment's purpose of requiring on the part of all organs of government a strict neutrality toward theological questions, courts should not undertake to decide such questions."[95]

The first case expounding the principle of official neutrality in religious disputes, *Watson v. Jones*,[96] developed from a split in the Presbyterian Church in Kentucky, arising out of conflicting Civil War loyalties. The plaintiffs broke away into a distinct religious body and sought a decree affirming that they were the true and only Presbyterian Church and ousting defendants from church property in Louisville. The Court stated that such a case should not be decided by the courts but by the established ecclesiastical authorities of the Church concerned. Judicial intervention in such a controversy would open up "the whole subject of the doctrinal theology, the usages and customs, the written laws, and fundamental organization of every religious denomination."[97]

The principle of nonintervention by the judiciary in religious disputes and internal ecclesiastical affairs was applied by the Warren Court in the *Hull* case.[98] Two local churches had withdrawn from the Presbyterian Church and sued the general church to enjoin it from trespassing on their property. Under state law, the right to the property turned on whether the general church had departed from the tenets of faith and practice it had held when the local churches had affiliated with it. The Court ruled that no court could inquire into whether the general church had deviated from its doctrine. Such an inquiry necessarily requires the courts to weigh the significance and meaning of disputed religious doctrine—something prohibited by the neutrality principle.

The Burger Court, however, indicated that *Hull* did not prohibit the courts from playing any role in resolving church property disputes. The *Sharpsburg* case[99] arose out of an action by a regional church against two withdrawing local churches to determine who should control the local churches and their property. The state court decided that the action taken by the local churches was valid since it was by a majority of the respective congregations in accordance with the state's General Religious Corporation Law.

The Supreme Court unanimously held that the regional church's appeal should be dismissed for want of a substantial federal question. The one-paragraph per curiam intimated that the state court might rely upon the statute governing the holding of property by religious corporations, where the court's resolution of the dispute involved no inquiry into religious doctrine.

Sharpsburg was unusual because Brennan wrote both the per curiam and the concurring opinion. Brennan issued the latter because he felt it important to express his view on the implications of the *Hull* decision.[100] After that decision, two polar misapprehensions had arisen. Some thought that *Hull* forbade the resolution of church property disputes by any method other than the application of secular property law. Others took the view that, under *Watson v. Jones*,[101] deference to the rulings of church authorities provided the only constitutional method of resolving such disputes, even after *Hull*. Brennan wanted to make clear that any method of dealing with the disputes was constitutional, as long as it did not involve the courts in the resolution of doctrinal issues.

Brennan's *Sharpsburg* concurrence also dealt with a point raised by White. He had indicated that he would join an opinion that stated that the *Watson* deference to the rulings of church authorities is acceptable only if the church authority "having power to decide property disputes is part of church polity." In other words, White wanted the courts, before deferring to the church authority, to investigate church polity to make certain that the authority was empowered under church law to resolve the property dispute. Brennan feared that such a civil inquiry into church polity would pose the same danger as civil inquiry into religious doctrine. In his *Sharpsburg* concurrence, he indicated that the *Watson* approach is proper only when the church governing bodies can be readily identified, and that it leaves determination of the jurisdiction of those bodies to the churches themselves. Thus the Brennan concurrence made plain a point not dealt with in *Hull*. The courts may not become involved in the resolution of church polity questions either.

Shortly after the *Sharpsburg* decision, a *Washington Post* article concluded that the per curiam and concurring opinions "suggested that church hierarchies will find it increasingly difficult in the future to protect themselves against rebellious congregations. . . . The practical effect of the Supreme Court action is likely to be a strengthened position for churchmen opposed to the trend toward church-sponsored social action and to the expression of liberal political and theological views by church leaders."[102]

This comment misconceived the intent of Brennan. A principal purpose of his concurrence was to reject the notion that *Hull* precluded further reliance on *Watson*, which remains the primary protection of those hierarchical churches, engaged in social action ventures, which have yet to get title to all church property placed in the name of the general church. *Sharpsburg*, accordingly, helped rather than hurt those churches, subject to the Brennan indication that general churches whose polity is genuinely a subject of controversy could not expect assistance under *Watson*.

Chapter Eight

Equal Protection I:
Classifications and Review Standards

E QUAL PROTECTION was made a constitutional right in 1868,[1] but it was not until the second half of the twentieth century that the Supreme Court, in W. H. Auden's phrase, first "found the notion of equality." The period of vigorous enforcement began with Earl Warren when the equal protection mantle began to be spread over an increasingly broad area. If one great theme has recurred in our public law since then, it has been that of equality, with the courts giving ever wider effect to the right to equality contained in the Fourteenth Amendment.

If the egalitarian revolution in American law began under Chief Justice Warren, it gained increasing impetus under his successor. In many respects, indeed, the Equal Protection Clause acquired its broadest connotation under the Burger Court. That was true because of the expansion of the standard of review in equal protection cases.

ECONOMIC REGULATION AND RATIONAL BASIS

In an October 21, 1977, Memorandum to the Conference[2] in the *Bakke* case,[3] his Court's most noted equal protection case, Chief Justice Burger stressed the importance of the standard of review. "The first question for the Court is what level of scrutiny should be applied in this case."

It is important to bear in mind that the Equal Protection Clause—as pointed out by Justice Stewart in an April 16, 1973, letter to Justice Blackmun[4]—"confers no substantive constitutional rights or liberties—with the exception of the right to vote on an equal basis with other qualified voters articulated in recent cases. This provision of the Constitution, rather, is concerned with classifications."

In addition, even as far as classifications are concerned, the Equal Protection Clause is, despite the popular conception, not a guaranty of absolute equality, requiring the law to treat all persons exactly alike.[5] It is based upon the assumption that government may recognize and act upon the factual differences that exist between individuals and classes. Hence, a mere showing that different persons are treated differently is not enough to show denial of equal protection.[6]

The Constitution does not require things different in fact to be treated in law as though they were the same.[7] The Equal Protection Clause permits states to write into law differences that exist in those areas in which public power is exerted. There is no doctrinaire requirement that legislation must be couched in all-embracing terms.[8] Statutes must, of necessity, be directed to less than universal situations.[9] Otherwise they would be ineffective, for they would fail to take account of factual diversity.[10]

The right to legislate implies the right to classify.[11] The Equal Protection Clause does not deny to states the power to treat different classes of persons in different ways nor deprive the states of their power to base action upon classifications that reflect factual differentiations that distinguish those classified from others.[12] Under traditional equal protection principles, incidental individual inequality does not contravene equal protection, provided it is based upon classification that has a reasonable basis in fact.[13]

A half century ago, when judicial scrutiny of governmental action challenged on equal protection grounds was governed entirely by this traditional rational-basis test, Holmes characterized the Equal Protection Clause as "the usual last resort of constitutional arguments."[14] That was true because review under the rational-basis test is an extremely deferential one. All it requires is that the classification at issue have a reasonable basis in fact and that it "rest upon some ground of difference having a fair and substantial relation to [the] object of the legislation."[15] The Court need only determine that the particular classification was the product of a rational legislative choice.[16] Under the rational-basis test, "it is only the invidious discrimination, the wholly arbitrary act, which cannot stand."[17] Virtually all laws emerge untouched from mere rationality scrutiny: "that test . . ., when applied as articulated, leaves little doubt about the outcome; the challenged legislation is always upheld."[18]

In theory, the normal standard of review in equal protection cases has remained the rational-basis standard. The Burger Court continued to apply that standard in cases involving property rights, particularly those dealing with economic regulation. Thus, Justice Marshall has referred to the "minimal standards of rationality that we use to test economic legislation that discriminates against business interests."[15]

The case that best exemplifies the Burger Court's approach to laws regulating business is *New Orleans v. Dukes*.[20] A New Orleans ordinance prohibited the selling of foodstuffs from pushcarts in the Vieux Carré, or French Quarter, but there was an exception for "vendors who have continually operated the same business within the Vieux Carré . . for eight years prior to January 1, 1972." Plaintiff, who had operated pushcarts in the Vieux Carré for only two years, claimed that the ordinance denied her equal protection.

The lower court had ruled the ordinance invalid, relying on *Morey v. Doud*.[21] An Illinois statute regulating currency exchanges barred them from selling money orders without a license, but excepted the American Express Company. The Court held that the exception resulted in a denial of equal protection. However, *Morey v. Doud* stands apart as the only modern case in which the Court has struck down an economic classification as irrational.[22]

Morey v. Doud had plainly become an anomaly, and the dominant question in the *New Orleans v. Dukes* conference was whether it should be overruled. Marshall and Powell said it should not, but Brennan, Stewart, and Rehnquist spoke strongly the other way and Blackmun said that he was inclined to overrule. The vote was six to two (Marshall and Powell) in favor of upholding the New Orleans ordinance, with Justice Douglas not participating.

Ultimately all of the Justices participating agreed to a reversal. The opinion was originally drafted as an opinion of the Court by Brennan. Both the original draft and the final opinion flatly overruled *Morey v. Doud*. However, the original draft was even more deferential in its review under what it termed "the test of minimum scrutiny." The dominant theme was that "The judiciary may not intrude into the realm of legislative value judgments." Indeed, according to the Brennan draft, the deferential approach should not be abandoned even in an extreme case: "even if the city did intend to create a permanent monopoly, that would not alter the applicable equal protection standard, or subject the discrimination to more careful scrutiny. . . . There is nothing in the Equal Protection Clause which denies the city the option of establishing a monopoly if the city rationally believes that reduced competition will benefit it economically by preventing an unsightly and bothersome proliferation of street vendors and thereby fostering increased tourism."

The quoted passages were omitted from the final *New Orleans v. Dukes* opinion. Brennan, its author, wrote in a June 16, 1976, Memorandum to the Conference that the case should "be the subject of a . . . 'bare-bones' per curiam disposition." This led to a "Dear Bill" letter the same day from Stewart. "I should think that this should continue to be a signed opinion . . . in that it squarely overrules *Morey v. Doud*."

The opinion was, nevertheless, issued as a per curiam, and it confirmed the deferential approach followed by the Burger Court in cases involving challenges to economic classifications. A good summary of that approach was contained in a one-paragraph draft *New Orleans v. Dukes* concurrence by the Chief Justice, which was circulated April 14, 1976, but withdrawn before the decision was announced: "The political branches of government must have wide scope in regulating commercial activity, and whether the choices made by the city government here are wise and sound, or the contrary, it is not the function of judges to reassess them on the basis of the Equal Protection Clause."

SUSPECT CLASSIFICATIONS

The most important thing about the Burger Court's equal protection jurisprudence was not its use of the rational-basis test but its expanded use of a stricter level of scrutiny. The notion that certain cases demand such a stricter level was first articulated in a footnote in the 1938 *Carolene Products* case.[23] *Carolene Products* itself dealt with economic regulation, then as now reviewed under the rational-basis test. However, in what has been called the "famous footnote four"[24] in his otherwise obscure opinion, Justice Stone questioned whether "more exacting judicial scrutiny" might not be appropriate in cases involving restrictions on the personal rights guaranteed by the Fourteenth Amendment—"whether prejudice against discrete and insular minorities . . . may call for a correspondingly more searching judicial inquiry."[25]

The second most celebrated footnote in Supreme Court history[26]— upon which the strict scrutiny review standard has been based—was actually conceived and drafted by a law clerk.[27] "The ideas originated with me," the clerk later recalled. Stone, he said, "adopted it almost as drafted." [28] "It seemed to me desirable," Stone wrote Chief Justice Hughes, "to file a caveat in the note," to the rational-basis standard applied in "the ordinary run of . . . cases" for "these other more exceptional cases." What he was trying to state, Stone said, was the "notion that the Court should be more alert to protect constitutional rights in those cases where there is danger that the ordinary political processes for the correction of undesirable legislation may not operate." [29]

Stone's singling out of "discrete and insular minorities" has been developed into the concept of "suspect" classifications. The starting point here was the statement made by the Court in *Korematsu v. United States.*[30] Though the decision upheld the exclusion of citizens of Japanese descent from the West Coast during World War II, the opinion also stated, "It should be noted, to begin with, that all legal restrictions which curtail the civil rights of a single racial group are immediately suspect. . . . [C]ourts must subject them to the most rigid scrutiny." [31]

The suspect classification concept is based on the proposition that, as Brennan once put it, the Equal Protection Clause's "assertion of human equality is closely associated with the proposition that differences in color or creed, birth or status, are neither significant nor relevant to the way in which persons should be treated." [32] These differences should all be constitutionally irrelevant; the law should remain blind to them, not distinguishing on the basis of who a person is or what he is.

When a suspect classification is at issue, the test of mere rationality gives way to one of strict scrutiny under which the classification will be held to deny equal protection unless justified by a "compelling" governmental interest. [33] Thus, racial and ethnic distinctions are inherently suspect and call for the most exacting judicial examination. [34] Governmental action that singles out members of a race for discriminatory treatment may not be justified upon the ground that it is reasonably related to maintenance of public order. [35] Similarly, a law that operates to curtail the legal activities of an organization formed to vindicate the rights of a racial minority may not be sustained, though it might otherwise be valid under the state's power to regulate the legal profession and improper solicitation of legal business. [36]

All the Burger Court Justices agreed that racial classifications are suspect and must be subject to strict scrutiny under the compelling interest test. Chief Justice Burger, who at times asserted that the emphasis on review standards was misplaced, conceded in his October 21, 1977, memo, "Although I have long been uneasy with the 'slogans' that have evolved in equal protection analysis, I think that the Court must give the very closest look possible—essentially 'strict scrutiny'—to any state action based on race. No member of this Court, so far as I recall, has ever had any question but that racial classifications are suspect under all circumstances."

Even Rehnquist, who accused his colleagues of importing the strict scrutiny approach into the Equal Protection Clause without any constitutional foundation, indicated that that approach was proper in racial classification cases. "I take it as a postulate," a November 11, 1977, Rehnquist memorandum[37] reads, "that difference in treatment of individuals based on their race or ethnic origin is at the bull's eye of the target at which the Fourteenth Amendment's Equal Protection Clause was aimed. . . . [C]ertainly the cases are too numerous to require citation that differentiation between individuals on this basis is 'suspect,' subject to 'strict scrutiny,' or whatever equivalent phrase one chooses to use."

If virtually all laws emerge untouched from rational-basis scrutiny, the opposite is true of laws subject to strict scrutiny. "If a statute is subject to strict scrutiny," Marshall tells us, "the statute always, or nearly always, . . . is struck down."[38] Or as Rehnquist succinctly stated to the conference,[39] "Strict [scrutiny] means nothing passes; rational [basis] means everything does."

What the compelling interest test means in practice was also pointed out in a February 8, 1973, letter from Stewart to Powell. "Application of the so-called 'compelling state interest' test automatically results, of course, in striking down the state statute under attack. . . . There is hardly a statute on the books that does not result in treating some people differently from others. There is hardly a statute on the books, therefore, that an ingenious lawyer cannot attack under the Equal Protection Clause. If he can persuade a court that [strict scrutiny][40] is involved, then the state cannot possibly meet its resulting burden of proving that there was a compelling state interest in enacting the statute exactly as it was written."

The great danger in the strict scrutiny approach is, as the Stewart letter asserted, "to return this Court, and all federal courts, to the heyday of the Nine Old Men, who felt that the Constitution enabled them to invalidate almost any state laws they thought unwise."

SEXUAL CLASSIFICATIONS: *FRONTIERO* CASE

All of the Justices have agreed that racial classifications must be treated as suspect, but are there other classifications that fall within the suspect classification category?

In his Powell letter, Justice Stewart gave an affirmative answer. "I fully agree that some few classifications are suspect, notably and primarily race, but also others, including alienage, perhaps sex, perhaps illegitimacy, and indigency."

In the law, as in the society, this century has seen a virtual transformation in the field of women's rights. According to the famous English epigram, "A woman can never be outlawed, for a woman is never in law."[41] Until recently, American law displayed a similar attitude. The first case under the Equal Protection Clause denied the right of women to practice law. "The paramount destiny and mission of woman," said Justice Bradley in his opinion, "are to fulfill the noble and benign offices of wife and mother. This is the law of the Creator."[42]

A century later, the law of the Creator was being construed differently. The common law jeremiad against women had been abandoned; virtually all legal disabilities based upon sex were being eliminated. Political rights, economic rights, the right to share in public services and benefactions were placed beyond governmental power to make sexual classifications.

The removal of sexual disabilities was almost entirely the work of the Burger Court. The first case striking down a sexual classification was *Reed v. Reed*,[43] decided during the second Burger term in 1971. A state statute provided that if persons were equally qualified to administer estates males must be preferred to females. The Chief Justice wrote a unanimous opinion holding that the statutory classification could not pass the test of reasonableness since "a difference in the sex of competing applicants for letters of administration" does not bear "a rational relationship to a state objective that is sought to be advanced by the operation of" the statute. "By providing dissimilar treatment for men and women who are thus similarly situated, the challenged section violates the Equal Protection Clause."[44]

In *Reed* the Court employed the test used in reviewing economic classifications. The sexual classification was invalidated only on the ground that it violated the rational basis test. There was no indication that any other standard of review might be appropriate. As far as we know, indeed, the propriety of a stricter review standard was not considered by the conference.

Two years after *Reed,* the validity of a sexual classification was again presented in *Frontiero v. Richardson.*[45] This time, however, the proper standard of review was discussed and reflected in the opinions ultimately issued.

The question in *Frontiero* concerned the right of Sharon Frontiero, an air force lieutenant, to claim her spouse as a "dependent" and obtain increased quarters allowances. Married men were automatically granted such benefits, but women had to prove that their husbands received more than half their support from them.

At the conference, Chief Justice Burger declared, "*Reed v. Reed* has nothing to do with this." There was no invidious discrimination here under the *Reed* test. He was supported only by Rehnquist. The others found the law invalid, with the consensus being stated by Stewart. The statute was "on its face grossly discriminatory against a readily identifiable class in a basically fundamental role of life." The statute, like that in *Reed,* had to fall under the rational-basis test.

Brennan drafted an opinion of the Court reflecting the conference consensus. "As you will note," the Brennan covering memorandum began, "I have structured this opinion along the lines which reflect what I understood was our agreement at conference. That is, without reaching the question whether sex constitutes a 'suspect criterion' calling for 'strict scrutiny,' the challenged provisions must fall for the reasons stated in *Reed.* . . . I do feel however that this case would provide an appropriate vehicle for us to recognize sex as a 'suspect criterion.' And . . . perhaps there is a Court for such an approach. If so, I'd have no difficulty in writing the opinion along those lines."

Brennan's draft opinion of the Court followed the *Reed v. Reed* standard of review, noting appellant's contention "that sex, like race, alienage, and national origin, constitutes a 'suspect criterion,' and that a classification based upon sex must therefore be deemed unconstitutional unless necessary to promote a compelling governmental interest." Use of the *Reed* standard of review made it unnecessary to deal with this contention. "We need not, and therefore do not, decide this question, however, for we conclude that the instant statutes cannot pass constitutional muster under even the more 'lenient' standard of review implicit in our unanimous decision only last term in *Reed v. Reed.*"

The Government had argued that the differential treatment in *Frontiero* was justified by considerations of efficient administration. The Brennan draft declared that, even under *Reed,* this was not enough to justify a law: "'administrative convenience' is not a shibboleth, the mere recitation of which dictates constitutionality. On the contrary, *Reed* establishes that any statutory scheme that draws a sharp line between the sexes, solely for the purpose of achieving administrative convenience" is based on arbitrary choice. "We therefore hold that, by according differential treatment to male and female members of the uniformed services for the sole purpose of achieving administrative convenience, the challenged statutes violate the Due Process Clause." [46]

Had the Brennan draft come down as the *Frontiero* opinion, it might well have aborted the substantial development in sex discrimination law that occurred in the Burger Court. The use of the rational-basis test in both *Reed* and *Frontiero* would probably have meant its adoption for all cases involving sexual classifications. That would, in turn, have meant the same narrow scope of review for such classifications as is available in review of economic classifications.

Some of the Justices, however, were not satisfied with only the *Reed* test as the governing criterion in sex discrimination cases. Justice White in particular wrote to Brennan, "I would think that sex is a suspect classification, if for no other reason than the fact that Congress has submitted a constitutional amendment making sex discrimination unconstitutional. I would remain of the same view whether the amendment is adopted or not." [47]

Interestingly, the White letter pointed out what opponents of strict scrutiny had urged—that it meant a return to the substantive due process approach used by the pre-1937 Court to invalidate economic regulation with which the Justices disagreed. "Of course," White's letter conceded, "the more of this we do on the basis of suspect classifications not rooted in the Constitution, the more we approximate the old substantive due process approach."

Two Justices wrote opposing the suspect classification approach. Powell stated, "I see no reason to consider whether sex is a 'suspect' classification in this case. Perhaps we can avoid confronting that issue until we know the outcome of the Equal Rights Amendment." [48]

Stewart, who turned out to be the key vote in the *Frontiero* decision, went even further. "I see no need to decide in this case whether sex is a 'suspect' criterion, and I would not mention the question in the opinion." He would "substitute a statement that we find that the classification effected by the statute is invidiously discriminatory. . . . I should suppose that 'invidious discrimination' is an equal protection *standard* to which all could repair." [49]

If Brennan could not obtain the votes of Stewart and Powell, it was most unlikely that he could secure a Court for a stricter standard of review than that applied in his draft opinion. Despite this, Brennan decided to rewrite his opinion to provide for strict scrutiny of sexual classifications. He circulated a redraft substantially similar to his final *Frontiero* opinion: "classifications based upon sex, like classifications based upon race, alienage, and national origin, are inherently suspect and must therefore be subjected to close judicial scrutiny." The *Frontiero* statutes were thus ruled invalid—not under the *Reed* rational-basis test, but under the strict-scrutiny requirement of compelling interest.

Powell characterized the redraft as one "in which you have now gone all the way in holding that sex is a 'suspect classification'." [50] It will be recalled that White favored the suspect classification approach because of the Equal Rights Amendment. Powell opposed it because of the amendment. He was concerned "about going this far at this time" because "it places the Court in the position of preempting the amendatory process initiated by the Congress."

An Equal Rights Amendment, Powell explained, would represent "the will of the people." "If, on the other hand, this Court puts 'sex' in the same category as 'race' we will have assumed a decisional responsibility (not within the democratic process) unnecessary to the decision of this case, and at the very time that legislatures around the country are debating the genuine pros and cons of how far it is wise, fair and prudent to subject both sexes to identical responsibilities as well as rights."

Powell urged that the original Brennan draft was "as far as we need to go." On the other hand, he concluded, "If and when it becomes necessary to consider whether sex is a suspect classification, I will find the issue a difficult one. Women certainly have not been treated as being fungible with men (thank God!). Yet, the reasons for different treatment have in no way resembled the purposeful and invidious discrimination directed against blacks and aliens. Nor may it be said any longer that, as a class, women are a discrete minority barred from effective participation in the political process."

Powell thus could not join Brennan's new opinion. And Justice Blackmun, in a "Dear Bill" letter, said, "I have now concluded that it is not advisable, and certainly not necessary, for us to reach out in this case to hold that sex, like race and national origin and alienage, is a suspect classification. It seems to me that *Reed v. Reed* is ample precedent here and is all we need and that we should not, by this case, enter the arena of the proposed Equal Rights Amendment."[51]

But Brennan received a letter from Justice Douglas agreeing with the redraft. "For purposes of employment I think the discrimination is as invidious and purposeful as that directed against blacks and aliens. I always thought our 1874 decision[52] which gave rise to the 19th Amendment was invidious discrimination against women which should have been invalidated under the Equal Protection Clause."[53] Justices White and Marshall also agreed to join the Brennan redraft.

Douglas had suggested that "There may be a way for you to sail between Scylla and Charibdis." But Brennan was unwilling to try. He replied to Justice Powell that he was "still of the view that the 'suspect' approach is the proper one and, further, that now is the time, and this is the case, to make that clear.[54] . . . [W]e cannot count on the Equal Rights Amendment to make the Equal Protection issue go away."

Brennan noted that eleven states had voted against ratification and several more were expected to do so shortly. "I therefore don't see that we gain anything by awaiting what is at best an uncertain outcome. . . . Congress and the legislatures of more than half the States have already determined that classifications based upon sex are inherently suspect."

Brennan's letter also suggested that the suspect classification approach was not as radical as it seemed to its opponents. The key step in applying that approach in sex discrimination cases had really been taken in *Reed.* Indeed, "the only rational explication of *Reed* is that it rests upon the 'suspect' approach."

Chief Justice Burger, the author of the *Reed* opinion, now wrote to Brennan. "I have watched the 'shuttlecock' memos on the subject of *Reed v. Reed* and the 'suspect' classification problem. . . . Some may construe *Reed* as supporting the 'suspect' view but I do not. The author of *Reed* never remotely contemplated such a broad concept." Burger would "join someone who expresses the narrow view expressed by Potter, Harry and Lewis."[55]

In early May, Powell circulated an opinion rejecting suspect classification in favor of that followed in *Reed,* which, he said, supported the decision invalidating the *Frontiero* statute. He was joined by Chief Justice Burger and Justice Blackmun. In a letter joining the Powell opinion, the Chief Justice suggested that Powell insert the word "every" or "all" before his statement that the Brennan opinion "would hold that classifications based upon sex . . . are 'inherently suspect and must therefore be subjected to close judicial scrutiny.' . . . With or without my puny effort to mute the outrage of 'Womens Lib,' I will join." [56]

Brennan's persistence was now to lose him his majority. Justice Stewart finally refused to join and instead issued a one-sentence concurrence in the judgment only, which agreed that the statute at issue worked an invidious discrimination under *Reed v. Reed.* Justice Brennan had to recirculate his opinion (which he did on May 9) as a plurality opinion only. Though his use of the suspect classification approach was joined by Douglas, White, and Marshall, it was rejected by Powell (joined by the Chief Justice and Blackmun) and Stewart, who issued their separate opinions concurring in the judgment on the *Reed* rational-basis approach, as well as by Justice Rehnquist, who dissented.

SEXUAL CLASSIFICATIONS: INTERMEDIATE STANDARD

Brennan's original draft would probably have confirmed the rational-basis test as the appropriate standard of review in sex discrimination cases. Had that standard been applied in the first two cases striking down sexual classifications, it is most unlikely that the Court would have rejected it in later cases. On the other hand, the Brennan plurality opinion in *Frontiero* opened the way to adoption of a stricter standard in *Craig v. Boren,* [57] decided in 1976.

Craig struck down an Oklahoma law prohibiting the sale of "non-intoxicating" 3.2 percent beer to males under the age of twenty-one and to females under the age of eighteen as denial of equal protection to males eighteen to twenty years of age. Brennan once again wrote the opinion, but he realized that he could not secure a Court for a *Frontiero*-type opinion that treated sex as a suspect classification subject to the compelling interest requirement. At the *Craig* conference, Brennan urged a review standard between that followed in

Reed and that advocated by him in *Frontiero*. At least three of the others (White, Marshall, and Stevens) agreed that, as Stevens put it, "some level of scrutiny above mere rationality has to be applied."

In his opinion, Brennan enunciated an in-between standard—stricter than the rational-basis test but not as strict as the compelling-interest requirement. "To withstand constitutional challenge, classifications by gender must serve important governmental objectives and must be substantially related to attainment of those objectives." [58] This test enabled the Burger Court to apply a stricter standard of review in sex discrimination cases than would have been permitted under the narrow review provided for in the Brennan original draft *Frontiero* opinion.

Brennan stated that the stricter standard enunciated by him was established by previous cases, particularly *Reed* and that he was only applying *Reed* in striking down the Oklahoma law. This led Chief Justice Burger to write to Brennan on November 15, 1976, "you read into *Reed v. Reed* what is not there. Every gender distinction does not need the strict scrutiny test applicable to a *criminal* case. *Reed* was the innocuous matter of who was to probate an estate." [59] As the Chief Justice noted in his earlier letter to Brennan, [60] "a lot of people sire offspring unintended!"

Craig v. Boren established an intermediate level of scrutiny for sexual classifications—between rational-basis and the strict scrutiny employed in review of suspect classifications—making them at least "quasi-suspect." [61] Sex became a disfavored classification subject to heightened scrutiny. [62]

Since *Craig v. Boren*, those seeking to uphold gender classifications have the burden of showing an "exceedingly persuasive justification" for the law. "The burden is met only by showing at least that the classification serves 'important governmental objectives and that the discriminatory means employed' are 'substantially related to the achievement of those objectives.'" [63] This version of the intermediate scrutiny test is taken from the opinion in *Mississippi University for Women v. Hogan*. [64]

Plaintiff in the case had applied for admission to the School of Nursing, but he was turned down because the university limited its enrollment to women. The lower court held that the exclusion was contrary to the Equal Protection Clause.

A bare conference majority voted to affirm, though they agreed with Brennan that the decision should be narrowly confined to the exclusion of males from the nursing school. The Brennan approach was tactically wise; a broader decision might not have retained the necessary five votes.

Justice O'Connor, who wrote the opinion, specifically stated, "I can't say no single-sex school [would be valid]." "I don't think," the Chief Justice declared, "all-women colleges must go down the drain." Blackmun affirmed, "I don't think everything has to be coed." Powell asserted that there was a "perfectly justifiable reason for one-sex schools. . . . I don't think he was a victim of sex discrimination. . . . [T]his guy could go to one of the coed nursing schools. They don't have to provide an all-male nursing school."

Rehnquist disagreed with the majority emphasis on a narrow decision. "You can't limit [the decision] to a nursing school. Strike it down there and soon it's the end of the women's university."

By the same bare majority as at the conference, the *Mississippi University for Women* decision held that the exclusion of males violated equal protection, since it could not meet the intermediate-scrutiny test. The primary justification had been that the policy compensated for discrimination against women. For Justice O'Connor, however, "Rather than compensate for discriminatory barriers faced by women, MUW's policy of excluding males from admission to the School of Nursing tends to perpetuate the stereotyped view of nursing as an exclusively woman's job." Hence the university had failed the second part of the *Craig v. Boren* test, since it had not shown "that the gender-based classification is substantially and directly related to its proposed compensatory objective."[65]

In *Roberts v. United States Jaycees*,[66] discrimination charges were filed against the Jaycees under the Minnesota Human Rights Act because of their exclusion of women from full membership. The Jaycees contended that requiring them to accept women would violate the male members' constitutional right of free association. The court of appeals agreed.

Chief Justice Burger began the *Roberts* conference by speaking for affirmance. "This is a public accommodation under Minnesota law, but doesn't freedom of association protected by the First Amendment prevail here? For me it does."

But the Chief Justice was alone; he was so isolated, indeed, that he ultimately chose to be listed as not participating in the decision. Brennan argued strongly that the Jaycees had not shown enough to bring themselves under the Court's privacy or associational right holdings. The Brennan view was accepted by the conference. Powell asked, "Do the Jaycees have any significant area of privacy? Isn't it a business—indeed a public business?" There were "no criteria of a private club. [There is] no selectivity of members." Powell did, however, stress, "We must save private clubs that are such."

For O'Connor, "The Jaycees are a speech-plus organization . . . and the statute only marginally affects First Amendment interests." Justice Stevens made a typically pithy conference comment: "Male chauvinists can't have protection unless they admit they are."

The *Roberts* decision unanimously ruled against the Jaycees. Striking down gender discrimination (except perhaps in a purely "private" club) does not infringe upon First Amendment rights. The Brennan opinion found that the Jaycees lacked the distinctive characteristics needed to bring an organization within the cases protecting privacy and freedom of association.

These Burger Court opinions indicated an acceptance of the middle-level standard of review for gender classifications. Such classifications would be upheld only if they bear a substantial relationship to an important governmental interest. However, the intermediate standard leaves much more room for individualized application by the Justices than either the rational-basis test or strict scrutiny under the compelling-interest test. The *Craig v. Boren* test allows the Justices to base their decisions upon their individual perceptions of the reasonableness of the sexual classification and the governmental interest asserted in each case.[67] Justices inevitably differ whether the asserted governmental interest is "important" enough to meet the *Craig* requirement. Hence it is not surprising that the cases are not completely consistent or that the Court sometimes follows the *Craig* test more as a matter of form than substance.

In *Michael M. v. Superior Court*,[68] the Court upheld California's "statutory rape" law, which defined unlawful sexual intercourse as "an act of sexual intercourse accomplished with a female not the wife of the perpetrator, where the female is under the age of 18 years." Petitioner was a seventeen-and-a-half-year-old male who had been convicted for sexual intercourse with a younger girl. He claimed that he had been denied equal protection because the statute made men alone criminally liable. The state court upheld the statute.

Chief Justice Burger began the postargument conference with a strong statement for affirmance, urging that "the state doesn't have to treat boys and girls alike for all purposes, at least in a sexual context. Protection against teen-aged pregnancy is a [valid] state interest even if protection [of][69] teen-age chastity is not. . . . Rationality alone suffices. He concluded, somewhat inconsistently, "The case really presents the question of what values the judicial system should support, and female chastity has always been regarded as a higher value than most."

Stewart, Blackmun, Powell, and Rehnquist also spoke in favor of affirmance. Stewart conceded that this was "intellectually a very puzzling case. . . . [M]ales and females are not similarly situated and therefore no equal protection violation is involved here. The statute is based on biological differences, contrary to all other equal protection cases." Rehnquist asserted, "This is [based] on the difference between men and women that provides a perfectly acceptable basis for the [statutory] difference." Justices Blackmun and Powell said that the Court could affirm "even under *Craig v. Boren.*"

The presentation on the other side was led by Brennan. He stressed that the asserted state interest could be achieved better by a gender-neutral statute. He was supported by White and Marshall, though the former stated that the statute should be ruled invalid only as applied in this case. "I couldn't reach the same result if the man was 50 and the girl 11." Stevens also voted for reversal, saying "[T]his is bad on its face and not only as applied." Stevens also asserted, "If the pregnancy basis is accepted, why say no punishment for a woman but punishment for a man? That's irrational under whatever standard you use."

Rehnquist wrote the plurality opinion upholding the California law. He started by recognizing "that the traditional minimum rationality test takes on a somewhat 'sharper focus' when gender-based classifications are challenged." The *Reed v. Reed* test was noted and Rehnquist then pointed out that, in *Craig v. Boren,* "[T]he Court restated the test to require the classification to bear a 'substantial relationship' to 'important governmental objectives.'"[70]

According to Rehnquist, however, the *Craig* test does not require statutes to be invalidated "where the gender classification is not invidious, but rather realistically reflects the fact that the sexes are not similarly situated in certain circumstances." More particularly, "a legislature may 'provide for the special problems of women.'" In this case, Rehnquist concluded, the state had an important interest in preventing illegitimate teenage pregnancies and the statutory classification was substantially related to that end: "the statute . . . reasonably reflects the fact that the consequences of sexual intercourse and pregnancy fall more heavily on the female than on the male."[71]

Blackmun wrote a December 17, 1980, "Dear Bill" note in which he stated his "concern that the opinion does not follow the analysis of *Craig v. Boren,* but has substituted a lower level of scrutiny." Blackmun wrote that he was thus reconsidering his conference vote to affirm. He ultimately did vote with the majority in favor of the California law, but he concurred in the judgment only, refusing to join the Rehnquist opinion.

The *Michael M.* case well illustrates the point already made—that the middle-level standard of review of sexual classifications leaves more room for individualized application by the given Justice than either the rational-basis or compelling-interest test.

The different approaches of different Justices to application of the *Craig* test may also be seen in *Rostker v. Goldberg.*[72] Rehnquist again wrote the opinion upholding a challenged law and Brennan was again on the other side. The Military Selective Service Act was challenged because it authorized the President to require the registration of males and not females for the draft. The exclusion of women from combat positions was not challenged in the case.

At the postargument conference not only were the Justices divided in the case but also there was a difference among them on the proper standard of review. The Chief Justice began by stating, "This action, right or wrong, satisfies *Craig v. Boren.*" Blackmun and Powell, too, said that they would come out in favor of the law under *Craig.* Brennan and Marshall also stated that they would apply *Craig* but used its test to urge the invalidity of the law.

Stewart declared, "I don't agree with tier tests—invidious is the only test." Such an approach would have meant an even more subjective review standard than that under the *Craig v. Boren* test. Stevens stated another point of view, saying, "On the level of scrutiny . . . I read *Boren* as describing the holding in *Reed v. Reed.*" The Stevens approach would have meant a return to the rational-basis test used in *Reed* or in the original Brennan draft *Frontiero* opinion.

Rehnquist, who wrote the *Rostker* opinion, indicated that the exclusion of women from draft registration was valid regardless of what review standard was used. "Equal protection says [you] can't treat similarly situated people differently. Since the prohibition against combat is not challenged here, they are not similarly situated." The statute passed muster under "either the heightened-scrutiny test or any other."

The conference vote was seven to one (Marshall) in favor of the challenged law. (Despite his conference statement, Brennan is listed in the docket book used by me as having passed.) The Rehnquist opinion professed to follow the *Craig v. Boren* test. First it rejected the government's argument that it "should not examine the Act under the heightened scrutiny with which we have approached gender-based discrimination." The opinion then found that the *Craig* test's first requirement had been met since "No one could deny that under the test of *Craig v. Boren, supra,* the Government's interest in raising and supporting armies is an 'important governmental interest.'" [73]

The exemption of women from registration was then found to be sufficiently related to Congress's purpose in authorizing registration. Justice Rehnquist stated, "Men and women, because of the combat restrictions on women, are simply not similarly situated for purposes of a draft or registration for a draft. . . . The fact that Congress and the Executive have decided that women should not serve in combat fully justifies Congress in not authorizing their registration, since the purpose of registration is to develop a pool of potential combat troops." [74]

One is left with the uneasy feeling that the Burger Court's use of the *Craig v. Boren* test in the cases involving gender-classifications too often depended upon the individual Justice's attitude toward sexual differentiations. The Court itself pointed out that "levels of 'scrutiny' which this Court announces that it applies to particular classifications made by a legislative body, may all too readily become facile abstractions used to justify a result." [75] As the cases we have been discussing show, this is particularly true of the intermediate standard laid down by *Craig v. Boren.*

ALIENAGE AS SUSPECT CLASSIFICATION

In his February 8, 1973,[76] letter to Powell, Stewart wrote that alienage is one of the "few classifications [which] are suspect. . . . A state law that makes such suspect classifications is, I think, presumptively invalid."

The notion of alienage as a suspect classification is a direct result of the Burger Court jurisprudence. Not too long ago, classifications based upon citizenship were ruled valid in most cases. As the Court summarized it, the alien is a "person" protected by the Fourteenth Amendment, but he "has never been conceded legal parity with the citizen."[77] The law in this area was justified by the fact that there is a fundamental difference between alienage and a characteristic such as race.

All this changed under the Burger Court. In *Graham v. Richardson,*[78] in 1971, the Court held that the Equal Protection Clause prevented states from conditioning welfare benefits upon citizenship. The Justices rejected the long-standing concept that the state had a "special public interest in favoring its own citizens over aliens in the distribution of limited resources such as welfare benefits." In Justice Cardozo's oft-quoted words, "In its war against poverty, the state is not required to dedicate its own resources to citizens and aliens alike."[79] *Graham v. Richardson* repudiates the "special public-interest" doctrine in the field of public benefits.

Two years after *Graham,* in the 1973 case of *Sugarman v. Dougall,*[80] the Court invalidated a New York law that provided that only U.S. citizens may hold positions in the competitive class of the state civil service. The Justices indicated that a state might restrict certain positions to citizens, but the New York law went too far. As Justice Blackmun said, it "is a complete bar," and Justice Powell called it "overbroad."

In the *Sugarman* conference,[81] Blackmun, the author of the *Graham* opinion, asserted that "the important thing about *Graham* was that welfare benefits were paid from funds to which aliens had contributed." But the *Graham* opinion had been broader in scope than this Blackmun statement indicates. The opinion did mention the fact that aliens contributed to the tax revenues from which welfare funds were drawn. But the opinion went much further and held that classifications based on alienage, like those based on nationality or race, "are inherently suspect and subject . . . to strict scrutiny under the compelling state interest test."[82] The state's concern for fiscal integrity was ruled not a compelling enough justification for the questioned classification.

Blackmun's *Sugarman* opinion stressed the "great breadth" of the statute's requirement: "Its imposed ineligibility may apply to the 'sanitation man, class B,' . . . to the typist and to the office worker, as well as to the person who directly participates in the formulation and execution of important state policy."[83] The opinion restated the *Graham* holding that classifications based on alienage are subject to strict scrutiny. The special public-interest doctrine, relied on by the state, to show the substantiality of its interest here, was not sufficient to meet the compelling-interest requirement: "We perceive no basis for holding the special-public-interest doctrine inapplicable in *Graham* and yet applicable and controlling here."[84]

Sugarman was the high-water mark in the Burger Court jurisprudence on alienage as a suspect classification. It did not, however, mean that aliens or anyone else had a constitutional right to work for the state. This was also pointed out in the April 16, 1973, letter,[85] in which Stewart stressed that the Equal Protection Clause conferred no substantive rights but was concerned only with classifications. Referring to *Sugarman*, Stewart wrote, "The present case would be the same, I think, if New York law provided that the 60 mile an hour speed limit should apply only to alien automobile drivers. Yet surely there is no constitutional right to drive one's car at an excessive speed."

ALIENAGE: GOVERNMENTAL FUNCTIONS

In a March 4, 1976, letter to Justice Brennan,[86] Chief Justice Burger wrote, "I cannot join saying that alienage is a 'suspect classification.' I can no longer go along with these 'litmus' words." The Chief Justice was not alone in his opinion. Both Stewart and Powell would indicate their agreement with his view during later conferences.

What was to look like a retreat from *Graham v. Richardson* was anticipated by the conference discussion in *Sugarman*. In the lower court in *Sugarman*, Judge Lumbard had written a concurring opinion that differentiated the decision invalidating the challenged New York law from other cases: "Nothing in our decision should be construed to mean that a state may not lawfully maintain a citizenship requirement for those positions where citizenship bears some rational relationship to the special demands of the particular position. There are some positions in the civil service, as in elective office, where broad policy decisions are made as a matter of course, and in such positions the state and the city, and their citizens, may properly require the officeholder to be a United States citizen."[87]

During the *Sugarman* conference, a number of Justices stated their agreement with Judge Lumbard. Chief Justice Burger would have applied the Lumbard analysis to *Sugarman* itself. "As applied here, I think *Graham* is not controlling. The jobs here are policy oriented and [the statutory] application is O.K., however doubtful a blanket exclusion" might otherwise be. Stewart, Blackmun, and Powell also agreed with Lumbard.

What these Justices' agreement with the Lumbard approach meant was shown in the 1978 case of *Foley v. Connelie*,[88] where (together with Justices White and Rehnquist) they made up the majority that voted in favor of a challenged New York law that required state police to be U.S. citizens. The conference majority was of the view that such a law was different from that in *Sugarman*.

"Police officers," the Chief Justice began the conference, "exercise very important powers and we ought to analyze the claims of aliens in that light." There was, said Burger, an "exception in *Sugarman* for employees exercising discretion in areas of public policy. . . . I'd exclude any job having an impact on important aspects of people's lives. . . . I'd sooner let an alien be a mayor before I'd let him be a policeman."

The Burger approach was followed by the other members of the conference majority. White stressed that "police forces are charged with maintenance of order and security." Blackmun said, "[O]n balance I come down with the state, even if that's a retreat from past cases. They are representatives of state authority—we call them officers." And Powell declared, "they participate in execution of public policy with broad authority and that's enough for me. If jurors enforce the law under the supervision of judges, how much more significant are the duties of police officers acting on their own."

In some ways, the most interesting statement in the *Foley v. Connelie* conference was made by Stewart. "We may have gone down the wrong path in this area. The Fourteenth Amendment suggests that citizenship has a superior status; yet we use the Fourteenth to give aliens special consideration." Despite this statement and his indication that he agreed with the Lumbard approach, Stewart voted to invalidate the New York law. He found "*Sugarman* controlling unless overruled."

The conference vote was to uphold the law by a bare majority (with Brennan, Stewart, Marshall, and Stevens dissenting), but Stewart reconsidered and the final *Foley* division was six to three. The opinion of the Court was by the Chief Justice and followed the essentials of his conference presentation. The cases "generally reflect a close scrutiny of restraints imposed by States on aliens," but the Court has not "held that all limitations on aliens are suspect." On the contrary, citizenship may be a relevant qualification for positions "held by 'officers who participate directly in the formulation, execution, or review of broad public policy.'" The Chief Justice stressed the authority of police officers "to exercise an almost infinite variety of discretionary powers." Hence they participate directly in the execution of public policy and the police function is consequently "one where citizenship bears a rational relationship to the special demands of the particular position."[89]

The public policy exception applied in *Foley* was expanded a year later in *Ambach v. Norwick*[90] to include positions involving significant governmental functions. New York prohibited the employment of an alien as a public school teacher unless that person had manifested an intention to apply for citizenship. The conference vote reflected the final five-to-four division in the Court in favor of upholding the law (with Brennan, Marshall, Blackmun, and Stevens dissenting). The most significant conference statement was that by Justice Powell, who was to deliver the *Ambach* opinion. He asserted that it was "hard to think of an alien as a member of a suspect class when he can so easily change his status."

The Powell *Ambach* opinion did not, however, completely reject the concept of alienage as a suspect classification. Instead it did so only in the *Foley–Ambach* type of case. At the *Ambach* conference, Blackmun said, "This case comes in between *Foley* and *Griffiths*." (In *Griffiths*,[91] a companion case to *Sugarman v. Dougall,* the Court struck down a requirement of citizenship for admission to the Bar.) To the *Ambach* majority, the case was closer to *Foley* and came within its holding "that some state functions are so bound up with the operation of the State as a governmental entity as to permit the exclusion from those functions of all persons who have not become part of the process of self-government." In a case involving "[t]he exclusion of aliens from such governmental positions,"[92] the strict-scrutiny standard of review would not be applied. In such a case, "the rational-basis standard" would be used.

Ambach found that "teaching in public schools constitutes a governmental function . . . public school teachers may be regarded as performing a task 'that go[es] to the heart of representative government.'"[93] That finding meant that only the rational-basis test need be met by the challenged law. That test was met here since the statute bore a rational relationship to the state's interest in furthering its educational goals.

During the conference on the next alienage case, *Cabell v. Chavez-Salido,*[94] Rehnquist noted, "There is much tension between *Foley* and

Ambach, on one hand, and *Graham, Sugarman,* and *Griffiths,* on the other." Justice Blackmun summarized the changing law in this area: "*Graham* said [alienage] was suspect. Then came *Foley* and *Ambach* that changed direction. The *Sugarman* exception was meant to be narrow, but isn't any more."

Cabell itself was, as Blackmun told the conference, "another alienage chapter." At issue was a California statute requiring "peace officers," including probation officers, to be citizens. The lower court held the statute invalid.

The Chief Justice began the *Cabell* conference by saying that he "read *Foley* as sustaining [this] classification [as] rationally based." With regard to probation officers, the "central-to-political-community test is satisfied here. [They] advise judges, wear sidearms, and can make arrests." Blackmun took issue on this point. "Parsing the duties of a probation officer," he said, "they're under direct supervision and have not much leeway." Therefore, the *Foley* exception should not apply.

Brennan, Marshall, and Stevens agreed with Blackmun. "What characteristic of class," asked Stevens, "justifies special treatment of aliens for this particular job? It's a *federal* interest to provide incentives to become citizens. The state can't rely on this. Another might be that a citizen would know more of local affairs than aliens. But that would apply to citizens of other states. Loyalty is no justification because [there are] other ways of testing that." Stevens also asserted, "I don't think *Foley* and *Ambach* control. The idea of jobs looked up to is not present as to probation officers. It's an irrational classification."

The other four were with the Chief Justice for reversal. Powell agreed with Rehnquist, saying that there was "tension among our cases as to the standard to be applied." But, Powell went on, "I think the *Foley* police officer is closest and should control here." White, who was to deliver the *Cabell* opinion, took the same position. The result here, White pointed out, "depends on how you assess the significance of probation officers' work. [It's] more like the police—indeed maybe even more important." Rehnquist put it somewhat differently. "Probation officers work closely in tandem with the police. Therefore . . . the same result follows."

Brennan, speaking for affirmance, had argued that probation officers were different because they dealt only with those on probation. O'Connor took direct issue with him. "A probation officer deals with all people in the community who have had contact with an accused or victim. His constituency is not limited to probationers."

O'Connor also said that the case was controlled by *Foley* and she would vote to reverse.

The O'Connor vote made for a bare majority in favor of reversal. The *Cabell* opinion followed the conference views expressed by the majority. Probation officers, like the police officers in *Foley,* exercise the sovereign's power to exert coercive force over individuals. Hence, they come within the governmental-function exception and a citizenship requirement may be imposed.

Perhaps Blackmun was correct that the governmental-function exception may originally have been "meant to be narrow, but isn't any more." Yet *Foley, Ambach,* and *Cabell* do not mean that the Burger Court abandoned the notion of alienage as a suspect classification. What the Court did with those cases was to establish a two-tier standard of review applicable to alienage classifications alone. Where alienage classifications are used by states in their police-power regulations or the grant of social-welfare benefits, such as welfare payments or education,[95] they are considered suspect and subject to strict-scrutiny review. "We have, however, developed a narrow exception to the rule that discrimination based on alienage triggers strict scrutiny. This exception has been labelled the 'political function' exception and applies to laws that exclude aliens from positions intimately related to the process of democratic self-government."[96]

Where public employment is concerned, the exclusion of aliens from positions that "are so closely bound up with the formulation and implementation of self-government that the State is permitted to exclude from those positions persons outside the political community" is subject only to the rational-basis review standard: "[W]e have concluded that strict scrutiny is out of place when the restriction primarily serves a political function."[97] In other cases, alienage classifications are still subject to strict scrutiny.

ALIENAGE: FEDERAL CLASSIFICATIONS

The two-tier review standard in alienage cases, with strict scrutiny except for public positions involving government functions closely related to self-governance, does not give a complete picture of the Burger Court jurisprudence on the subject—but only of the cases on alienage classifications in state laws. Two 1976 decisions indicate that a different approach was followed by the Court in cases in which federal classifications were challenged. Those decisions hold that *all* federal alienage classifications will be subject only to the deferential review permitted under the rational-basis test.

In *Mathews v. Diaz*,[98] the Court upheld a federal statute that made aliens eligible for enrollment in Medicare only if they had resided in this country for at least five years. The unanimous opinion focused upon the fact that Congress had conditioned eligibility for participation in the program, and Congress has broad constitutional power over immigration and naturalization. It can make rules that would be unacceptable if applied to citizens, and it has no constitutional duty to provide *all aliens* with the welfare benefits provided to all citizens. In determining whether the statutory discrimination between citizens and aliens is permissible, judicial review in the area of immigration and naturalization is narrow. Congress may decide that, as an alien's tie to this country grows stronger, so also does the strength of his claim to an equal share in its munificence. Hence the classification in this case is reasonable and that is all that is required for it to be upheld.

The distinction between state and federal power in this area was also crucial to the decision in *Hampton v. Mow Sun Wong*,[99] decided the same day as *Mathews v. Diaz*. A Civil Service Commission regulation barred all aliens from employment in the federal competitive civil service. *Hampton* was first argued in January 1975 and the conference then divided four to four, with Douglas unable to participate. At the conference, Stewart had stated the difficulty in the case. He conceded that "Congress can be as discriminatory as it pleases in admitting immigrants." Yet this did not mean that "the Fifth Amendment is wholly inapplicable. Congress can't say that no resident alien shall have a right of appeal, for example. Congress could condition admission to the country, but this Civil Service regulation isn't that kind of a statute."

On February 14, 1975, all the Justices voted to set *Hampton* for reargument.[100] At the postreargument conference, Chief Justice Burger repeated his disagreement with the notion of alienage as a suspect classification. "We can't say that aliens are discrete, insular classes for all purposes, though they may be for some." He was in favor of upholding the regulation, pointing to the "long period of legislative acquiescence in this regulation." Referring to the plaintiff aliens, Burger asserted that they "may have lots of rights, religion, etc., but [they have] no constitutional right to a job." The Chief Justice did, however, note, "If the opinion made clear that Congress had the power, I might go along."

Brennan, while emphasizing that "this is a regulation, not a statute," went on to indicate that, even if it were a statute, he would vote against it. As Brennan saw it, the Court could apply the suspect classification approach. Furthermore, he asserted, "I don't see any legitimate governmental interest."

Marshall and Powell also stated that they thought the classification would be bad even if enacted by Congress. *Sugarman* and *Graham*, according to Powell, are not irrelevant. "But it doesn't follow that aliens are a suspect class where federal government employment is concerned. . . . [The prohibition] sweeps so broadly . . . Congress ought to write a narrow statute limiting exclusion to sensitive jobs."

Stewart, White, and Blackmun spoke for the alien exclusion on the ground that it was a federal, not a state, classification. "Is this regulation," asked Stewart, "equivalent to an Act of Congress? I think it is in light of the legislative history." The Justice went on to say that *Graham* and its progeny "gave suspect classification status to aliens. It seems odd, but there it is as to *states* and can be explained away on that ground. But the Federal Government has broad and important interests in the regulation of aliens." White and Blackmun agreed that, in the latter's words, "Congress has immigration and naturalization powers and that should be enough."

Rehnquist's position was virtually dictated by his dissents in the cases striking down alienage classifications. As he put it at the conference, "This is a fortiori after my dissents in *Sugarman* [and *Graham*]."

The vote after the *Hampton* reargument reflected the same four-to-four division as the year before. That left the decision up to Stevens, whose first day on the bench had seen the *Hampton* reargument. Stevens told the conference, "There's a difference in equal protection between the Fifth and Fourteenth [Amendments]. The Government has the power to exclude or condition entry. . . . Both Congress and the President could do that. . . . But that's not the case here. Congress didn't decide to do this, nor the President." Stevens stated that he would vote against the regulation, but his rationale was different. "I would not do it on lack of power but that the decision was not made by the appropriate arm of government."

The Stevens vote had broken the *Hampton* deadlock and he was assigned the opinion even though his approach had been accepted by no other Justice. The Stevens *Hampton* opinion followed his conference presentation. As summarized in an April 14, 1976 "Dear John" letter from Stewart,[101] "[Y]our opinion ultimately rests upon a determination that the protection of the national interests relating to immigration and naturalization is entrusted to the Congress and the President by the Constitution and is not the concern of the Civil Service Commission unless made part of the Commission's responsibilities by an express delegation of that authority. Part III of the opinion demonstrates that there has not been such a delegation to the Commission of authority to consider immigration and naturalization interests in promulgating regulations governing eligibility for employment in the federal civil service."

It has been generally assumed that the Stevens *Hampton* opinion held that, if the challenged alien exclusion had been contained in a federal statute or presidential order it would have been valid.[102] Stevens himself rejected this interpretation of his *Hampton* opinion. In an April 22, 1976, Memorandum to the Conference, Stevens referred to Rehnquist's *Hampton* dissent. "Bill refers to a 'holding' that the regulation would have been valid if expressly mandated by Congress." Stevens conceded that this statement "correctly describes my own view, but because I know that view is not shared by Bill Brennan and perhaps others, I tried to write the opinion to avoid any such holding. Actually the portion of my opinion which Bill quotes merely states that if the rule were expressly mandated by Congress, 'we might presume that any interest which might rationally be served by the rule did in fact give rise to the adoption.' . . .

"There are two reasons why I think this statement does not amount to a holding. (a) What we might presume is not necessarily what we would in fact presume if the issue were squarely presented; (b) presuming a rational basis is not the same as presuming validity, because the Court might regard the classification as sufficiently invidious to require a stronger justification. . . . In all events, if anyone wants to write separately disclaiming any such holding, I surely would not object."

None of the Justices acted on the Stevens invitation, and the result has been the widespread assumption that *Hampton* upheld the federal power to impose such an exclusion where it was mandated by either Congress or the President. After *Hampton,* the President, by executive order, barred most aliens from employment in the federal civil service. This presidential order was upheld on the authority of the *Hampton* case.[103]

The Supreme Court itself indicated that *Hampton* did uphold federal power to impose the alien bar at issue there in *Nyquist v. Mauclet,*[104] decided in 1977. The Blackmun *Nyquist* opinion drew a sharp distinction between state and federal alienage classifications. The former, the opinion declared, "are inherently suspect and subject to close judicial scrutiny." Federal classifications are treated differently. Blackmun noted that, in *Mathews v. Diaz,* "the Court applied relaxed scrutiny in upholding the validity of [the] federal statute" at issue there. Then Blackmun pointed out that the state, seeking to have its alienage classification sustained in *Nyquist,* could "draw no solace" from this relaxed review standard "because the Court was at pains to emphasize that Congress, as an aspect of its broad power over immigration and naturalization, enjoys rights to distinguish among aliens that are not shared by the States."[105] *Hampton* was cited to support this statement.

The result is not only a two-tier review standard in cases involving state alienage classifications, but also a sharp distinction in the review standard applied to state and federal alienage classifications. The rule usually followed in review of state classifications is that stated in *Nyquist*—strict scrutiny: "Alienage classifications by a State that do not withstand this stringent examination cannot stand."[106] Where federal classifications are at issue, "relaxed scrutiny," as *Nyquist* terms it, is applied. The implication is that the Court will review only under the rational-basis test and defer to the Congressional judgment in both cases involving police-power regulations or dispensation of benefits and those involving governmental functions with policy-making powers.

One may question whether the use of two totally different tests to review state and federal classifications is justified. If aliens are protected by the Fifth and Fourteenth Amendments, why should the federal government be permitted to discriminate against them? As Justice Powell put it at the *Hampton* conference, "If we let them in, how can we not treat them as 'persons'? . . . I can't see how we can discriminate if we admit them unconditionally."

ILLEGITIMACY AND INCONSISTENCY

The Burger Court did not deal adequately with classifications based on illegitimacy. Such classifications appear to be peculiarly appropriate for the suspect-classification approach, which turns on recognition that the right to equal protection should not depend upon characteristics such as race, birth, or status, over which the individual has no control. From this point of view, the marital status of one's parents is something beyond the individual's control.

The Burger Court never followed this straightforward approach. Its decisions on illegitimacy classifications have a more or less ad hoc quality, in which particular fact patterns and the Justices' individual reactions to the purpose of the given classification are even more controlling than usual.[107] This can be seen from the disposition of *Labine v. Vincent*,[108] the first Burger Court case involving a statutory discrimination against illegitimate children.

A Louisiana law permitted inheritance by an illegitimate child from the father only if the child had been acknowledged by the father. At the conference, the argument in support of the law was led by Black: "There has always been a classification of legitimate and illegitimate and we can't hold that it denies equal protection." The vote was five to four to uphold the Louisiana law, and Black was assigned the opinion.

Black circulated a draft arguing that Louisiana was only attempting to follow the intent of its citizens in placing illegitimate children lower in the line of succession than legitimate children. In justifying the state's discrimination on the basis of intent, the draft emphasized that Louisiana allowed parents to inherit or disinherit legitimate children and to do generally with their estate what they desired. The Louisiana law was no more than an effort to give effect to parents' unarticulated desires, rather than to impose the state's own determination of the desirable order of succession.

Brennan soon circulated a draft dissent showing that Black was in error about Louisiana law on disinheritance. Louisiana had extensive restrictions on the rights of individuals to dispose of their estates without providing for their children. Thus the Black argument based on intent could not hold up. Hence, Brennan asserted, the discrimination between legitimate and illegitimate children was solely a decision by the state.

In joining the Brennan dissent, Douglas observed, in a March 9, 1971, note, "You certainly scalped Hugo." Black then deleted his inaccurate exposition of Louisiana law and the argument based on intent. The result was, as the Brennan dissent phrased it, "simply excluding such illegitimate children from the protection of the [Equal Protection] Clause."[109]

Brennan was so annoyed by the revised Black opinion that he wrote that "today's decision cannot even pretend to be a principled decision. This is surprising from Justices who have heretofore so vigorously decried decision-making rested upon personal predilections, to borrow the Court's words, of 'life-tenured judges of this Court.'"[110] The quote was from Black's *Labine* opinion and reflected Brennan's irritation at Black for constantly accusing colleagues who disagreed with him of voting their "personal predilections."[111]

In terms of equal-protection jurisprudence, the Black *Labine* opinion represented a step backward to what the law had been before the Warren Court's decision in *Levy v. Louisiana*.[112] Black had been the strongest opponent of the *Levy* decision at the 1968 conference on the case,[113] and the depth of his feelings on illegitimacy were shown when he added a passage to his *Labine* opinion during the last conference on the case, Friday, March 26, 1971. He asserted that the relationship between parent and illegitimate child was "illicit and beyond the recognition of the law."[114] For Brennan this was proof that the *Labine* decision was based upon "untenable and discredited moral prejudice."[115]

The *Labine* opinion held that "the choices reflected by the . . . statute are choices which it is within the power of the state to make."[116] Why this was so was not stated in terms of equal-protection analysis. Only a brief note was devoted to such analysis: "Even if we were to apply the 'rational basis' test to the Louisiana intestate succession statute, that statute clearly has a rational basis in view of Louisiana's interest in promoting family life and of directing the disposition of property left within the State."[117]

A year after *Labine,* the Court, in *Weber v. Aetna Casualty & Surety Co.,*[118] struck down a Louisiana law that limited recovery under workmen's compensation to legitimate children and acknowledged illegitimates. Unacknowledged illegitimates were relegated to the lesser status of "other dependents." The Court distinguished *Labine* on the ground that it reflected the "traditional deference" to the state's power over property disposition. Yet the *Weber* result and reasoning are plainly inconsistent with those in *Labine.* Most significant in this respect was *Weber*'s rejection of the Equal Protection approach followed in cases involving economic regulation.

Weber conceded that such cases are governed by the rational-basis test, but the Court declared that a "stricter scrutiny" must be exercised here because the statutory classification affected "sensitive and fundamental personal rights."[119] The inferior classification of unacknowledged illegitimates bore no significant relationship to the recognized purposes that workmen's compensation statutes served.

When *Weber* was decided, the Court had not yet developed the intermediate-scrutiny which it came to apply in sex classification cases.[120] In *Mathews v. Lucas*,[121] decided six months before *Craig v. Boren*[122] applied intermediate scrutiny to gender cases, the Court began to discuss more fully review standards to be applied in illegitimacy cases. At issue in *Lucas* was a Social Security Act provision that conditioned the eligibility of certain illegitimate children for survivor's benefits upon a showing that the deceased wage earner was both the child's parent and was supporting the child. Legitimate children and illegitimates who could inherit from the deceased under state law were entitled to a presumption of dependency.

Much of the conference discussion was devoted to the review standard. Several Justices stated that strict scrutiny was not the proper approach. "I wrote *Weber*," Powell noted, "but I didn't say there that illegitimates were always a suspect class." White said that it was "hard when you get a class like this, when the classification was not on an immutable characteristic, to apply strict scrutiny." Stewart pointed out that "social security legislation is full of all kinds of classifications, many of which are hard to support. But if you apply strict-scrutiny tests, the whole scheme becomes unravelled."

Stewart also indicated that, for him, *Lucas* was comparable to *Frontiero*.[123] The case, he stated, was "tough for me in light of *Frontiero*." But the *Lucas* opinion itself, delivered by Blackmun, rejected the gender-classification analogy. The opinion recognized that "illegitimacy . . . is, like race or national origin, a characteristic determined by causes not within the control of the illegitimate individual." But review here should be based "on less demanding standards" than those required for suspect classifications. As *Lucas* saw it, "because illegitimacy does not carry an obvious badge, as race or sex do, . . . the Act's discrimination between individuals on the basis of their legitimacy does not 'command extraordinary protection from the majoritarian political process' . . . which our most exacting scrutiny would entail."[124] Under the "less demanding" standard, the *Lucas* Court upheld the challenged social security provision.

Despite the fact that, in the Burger Court's own words, "illegitimacy is analogous in many respects to the personal characteristics that have been held to be suspect when used as the basis of statutory differentiations,"[125] *Lucas* refused to apply anything like strict scrutiny, which, as Justice Stewart noted in his conference presentation, would undoubtedly have resulted in the invalidation of the law. Indeed, in a June 7, 1976, letter to Blackmun, Rehnquist, indicated that "you are applying the so-called 'minimum rationality' standard to this case."

In the 1977 case of *Trimble v. Gordon*,[126] the challenged law was an Illinois statute that allowed illegitimate children to inherit by intestate succession only from their mothers; legitimate children might inherit from both parents. The lower court had upheld the law on the authority of *Labine v. Vincent*. Most of the *Trimble* conference discussion focused on whether *Labine* was controlling. The Chief Justice and Stewart, Blackmun, and Rehnquist stated that the case was controlled by *Labine,* whose holding was stated by Stewart as one "that intestacy laws are outside the limits of the Equal Protection Clause."

Brennan led the argument the other way, stressing in detail the differences between the statute here and that in *Labine*. White, Marshall, and Powell agreed. Stevens went further, agreeing with the dissenters that the statutes were really not distinguishable. However, Stevens went on, "Even if *Labine* is not distinguishable on a principled basis, the equal protection analysis there is out of step with current teaching. So I'd overrule *Labine*."

Powell also was "willing to overrule *Labine,* although we can distinguish the statutes as Bill Brennan does." The subsequent Powell *Trimble* opinion did not overrule *Labine,* but it did contain a footnote stating that "subsequent cases have limited [*Labine*'s] force as a precedent."[127] The *Trimble* opinion repeated what *Lucas* had said about the illegitimacy review standard. Once again it was said "that classifications based on illegitimacy fall in a 'realm of less than strictest scrutiny.'" However, "the scrutiny 'is not a toothless one.'"[128]

More than this *Trimble* did not say about the review standard. But the decision invalidated the Illinois law on the ground that it "bears only the most attenuated relationship" to any legitimate governmental purpose. From this point of view, the law failed even the minimum rational-basis test, since the "statutory classification [did not] bear some rational relationship to a legitimate state purpose."[129]

In the 1978 case of *Lalli v. Lalli,*[130] it was indicated that illegitimacy classifications should be reviewed under an intermediate-scrutiny standard. The challenged New York law in *Lalli* allowed an illegitimate child to inherit from his intestate father only if a court of competent jurisdiction had, during the father's lifetime, entered an order declaring paternity. At the conference, the Justices differed on the current status of *Labine*. Blackmun said that he thought that "*Labine* is more like this case" and, on its authority, would vote in favor of the law. Justice Stevens, on the other hand, declared, "I don't see how I can rely on *Labine* after *Trimble*."

Powell, who wrote the *Lalli* plurality opinion, told the conference, "I went so far as I can in *Trimble* and *Weber* for illegitimates, so I'm going to go against them here." He distinguished the *Trimble* statute from the New York law in *Lalli*. The Illinois statute invalidated in *Trimble* "eliminated 'the possibility of a middle ground between the extremes of complete exclusion [of illegitimates claiming under their father's estates] and case-by-case determination of paternity." [131] In contrast, the single requirement at issue under the New York law was an evidentiary one; the marital status of the parents was irrelevant. The *Lalli* statute was directly related to the state interest in the orderly disposition of property in an area involving unique and difficult problems of proof.

Powell in *Lalli* stated the review standard more specifically than had been done in the prior cases: "Although . . . classifications based on illegitimacy are not subject to 'strict scrutiny,' they nevertheless are invalid under the Fourteenth Amendment if they are not substantially related to permissible state interests." Powell's opinion also stressed that "the State's interests are substantial," "of considerable magnitude," and "important." [132]

The review standard thus stated by the Powell *Lalli* opinion is essentially similar to the middle-level scrutiny applicable in gender-classification cases, as originally articulated in *Craig v. Boren*. [133] Here, too, Powell is saying that the classification is invalid unless it is substantially related to important governmental interests. What is striking, however, is that in the case where this intermediate scrutiny was articulated as the proper standard for reviewing illegitimacy classifications, the statute was upheld. In *Trimble*, on the other hand, an essentially similar statute was invalidated even though the Court there seemed to be applying a narrower review standard.

In his *Lalli* concurrence, Blackmun declared that *Trimble* was "explainable only because of the overtones of its appealing facts." [134] It is more accurate to say that the difference in result in *Trimble* and *Lalli* is explainable by the switch in Powell's vote, which converted the four-Justice *Trimble* dissenters into the bare majority in *Lalli*. The Powell switch was explained by his statement that he had gone as far as he would for illegitimates in *Trimble* and *Weber;* he would now vote against them. His opinion upheld the New York law, despite his statement of a broader review standard than that in *Trimble,* where the statute was invalidated under the seemingly more deferential standard stated by the Powell *Trimble* opinion. *Trimble* and *Lalli,* as well as the other illegitimacy cases, lend weight to the Burger Court's comment that review standards "may all too readily become facile abstractions used to justify a result." [135]

In illegitimacy as in alienage cases, there may be a difference between state and federal power to make classifications. In *Fiallo v. Bell,*[136] the Immigration Act granted special preference to the children of citizens and resident aliens. The law excluded illegitimate children from the preference that would otherwise be granted because of their relationship to their fathers.

The *Fiallo* conference, like the opinion, focused upon congressional authority over immigration. "The broad powers of Congress in this field," declared the Chief Justice, "leave little room for equal-protection claims." If not for this, stated Stewart, "this would have to be reversed, because there's a wholly irrational distinction made between mothers and fathers."

Justice Blackmun asserted that this was a "nonreviewable area of Congressional power." Powell, on the other hand, said, "I wouldn't go far as to say never judicial review, but only that it's so limited in this area."

Powell's *Fiallo* opinion followed his conference approach. It emphasized "the limited scope of judicial inquiry" and "the need for special judicial deference to congressional policy choices" in the immigration field. Though *Fiallo* rejects the view that the government's power in this area is never subject to judicial review, it states expressly that "congressional determinations such as this one are subject only to limited judicial review." [137] Here, as in the alienage cases, the review standard for federal action in the immigration area is, as Stevens put it at the *Fiallo* conference, "rational basis even if it creates hardship."

POVERTY, AGE, AND MENTAL RETARDATION: DRAWING THE LINE

Attempts were made to have the Burger Court treat classifications based upon wealth and age as suspect classifications—or at least as semisuspect. But the Court refused to extend the broader standard of review beyond the classifications already discussed. The Burger Court decisions aborted what many had seen as a contrary trend in the Warren Court with regard to wealth classifications. That Court appeared increasingly to agree with Bernard Shaw that "the worst of crimes is poverty," as it tried to equalize criminal law between those with means and those without.[138] Outside the criminal justice field, it began to invalidate other laws that turned on the ability to pay, such as the poll tax.[139]

The Burger Court proved unwilling to extend this Warren Court jurisprudence. The Warren Court had broadened the right of indigents to assigned counsel to include appeals, as well as the criminal trial.[140] The evil in both cases, said the Court, "is the same: discrimination against the indigent." The Burger Court held that the right was limited to the first appeal as of right. An indigent defendant seeking discretionary review in the state supreme court was not denied equal protection by the denial of assigned counsel even though he was "somewhat handicapped in comparison with a wealthy defendant who has counsel assisting him . . . at every stage in the proceeding."[141]

In *Dandridge v. Williams*,[142] the Court upheld a state welfare law limiting the amount of a grant to families with dependent children to $250 per month. It was claimed that the limitation discriminated against plaintiffs as poor people because of the size of their families— a violation of equal protection.

The *Dandridge* Court indicated that the suspect-classification approach was not appropriate and that in both "the area of economics and social welfare," the challenged law would be upheld "[i]f the classification has some 'reasonable basis.'" To be sure, the Court noted that the cases applying that review standard had involved economic regulation. "The administration of public welfare assistance, by contrast, involves the most basic economic needs of impoverished human beings. We recognize the dramatically real factual difference between the cited cases and this one, but we can find no basis for applying a different constitutional standard." [143] Under the rational-basis standard the challenged law was easily upheld.

The Burger Court definitely rejected the notion of wealth as a suspect classification in the 1973 case of *San Antonio Independent School District v. Rodriguez.*[144] That case (to be discussed also in Chapter 10) arose out of a challenge to the financing of public school education by the property tax; equal protection was denied to children in poorer districts that had a low tax base. The lower court had held the rational-basis standard inappropriate: "More than mere rationality is required, however, to maintain a state classification . . . which is based upon wealth." That was true because "lines drawn on wealth are suspect." [145]

During the conference, Stewart stated the position that the Supreme Court would take on the suspect-classification approach. As Stewart saw it, such a classification might not be recognized, "until we can find a discrete class of people invidiously discriminated against. 'Poor' and 'pauper' are too general."

In his opinion for the Court, Justice Powell also found that there was no discrimination against any discrete class. Hence, the Court refused "to extend its most exacting scrutiny to review a system that allegedly discriminates against a large, diverse, and amorphous class, unified only by the common factor of residence in districts that happen to have less taxable wealth than other districts." [146] The fact that the law burdened poor persons in the allocation of educational benefits was held not enough to make the classification a suspect one.

The same approach was followed by the Burger Court to the claim that classifications based upon age should be treated as suspect. *Massachusetts Board of Retirement v. Murgia*[147] upheld a statute that provided for the mandatory retirement of state police officers at the age of fifty. The Court rejected the claim that strict scrutiny was the proper test for determining whether the law denied equal protection. The class of officers over fifty was found not to "constitute a suspect class for purposes of equal protection analysis." The Court's approach was similar to the Stewart–Powell position in *San Antonio*. According to Powell, who drafted the *Murgia* per curiam, "old age does not define a 'discrete and insular' group . . . in need of 'extraordinary protection from the majoritarian political process.' Instead, it marks a stage that each of us will reach if we live out our normal span." The fact that those over the stated age were singled out was not enough to require more than rational-basis review. "Even if the statute could be said to impose a penalty upon a class defined as the aged, it would not impose a distinction sufficiently akin to those classifications that we have found suspect to call for strict judicial scrutiny." [148]

In *Cleburne v. Cleburne Living Center*, [149] the Court refused to find that the mentally retarded were a "quasi-suspect" class. A zoning ordinance barred a home for the mentally retarded from the area. The court of appeals had ruled that mental retardation is a "quasi-suspect" classification and that, under heightened scrutiny, the ordinance was facially invalid because it did not substantially further any important governmental interests.

The *Cleburne* conference focused on the heightened scrutiny standard. Chief Justice Burger began the discussion by asking, "Are the mentally retarded a quasi-suspect class?" He gave a negative answer. "I can't agree," he asserted, "that the mentally retarded are a discrete insular minority. They are entitled to special attention, but not heightened scrutiny."

White, Rehnquist, and O'Connor agreed with Burger. Their dominant theme was a refusal to extend the quasi-suspect classification concept. "I wouldn't create another category of heightened [scrutiny]," stated White, "but [would] use rational basis." Rehnquist stated the same view, saying, "I agree with Byron that we ought not create quasi[-suspect classes]. We should rein in on that trend and create no more." O'Connor also affirmed, "I wouldn't create a new class."

The four who spoke against heightened scrutiny agreed that the rational basis test should be applied. As White put it, "That would mean a remand to the court of appeals [for it to] apply the correct standard." Stevens agreed that the rational-basis test should be applied, but, he urged, "There's no rational basis for the ordinance. I wouldn't see why we should send it back. I'd affirm."

Because of the split in the majority on the case's disposition, as well as the fact that Justice Powell did not participate in the conference, *Cleburne* was set for reargument. At the postreargument conference, Powell stated his agreement with the refusal to treat mental retardation as a quasi-suspect classification. "I hesitate to go to heightened scrutiny, which I've never favored. I'm not sure even race or gender needs more than rational [basis]. Anyway, I don't want to add another category of heightened scrutiny."

Powell also indicated that he would be willing to follow the Stevens approach. "I could join holding [the ordinance] facially invalid on the rational[-basis test]." The majority ultimately agreed, and struck down the ordinance because the record did not reveal any rational basis for believing that the proposed group home would threaten the city's legitimate interests in a way that permitted uses in the zoned area would not.

But the key element in the *Cleburne* decision was the majority's refusal to create another classification subject to broader review. There would be no further quasi-suspect classifications to which heightened scrutiny would be applied.

PARADISE LOST FOR AN EXTRA TIER?

The Equal Protection Clause is, in Justice Rehnquist's words, "undoubtedly one of the majestic generalities of the Constitution." [150] Furnished with no guide other than the skeleton language of the text, the Court has been completely free to mold its equal-protection jurisprudence in accordance with its own conceptions.

Rehnquist, indeed, goes further. While a member of the Burger Court, he declared that, "in providing the Court with the duty of enforcing such generalities as the Equal Protection Clause, the Framers of the Civil War Amendments placed it in the position of Adam in the Garden of Eden. . . . [U]nfortunately . . . the Court has indeed succumbed to the temptation." [151]

Certainly the standards of review that have been developed to deal with different types of classification have been the Justices' own handiwork. In fact, the levels of scrutiny discussed in this chapter have been almost entirely the product of the Burger Court. That has been especially true of the suspect-classification concept. Under Chief Justice Warren, as will be seen in Chapter 9, the Justices accepted the notion of race as a suspect classification. But it was under Warren's successor that stricter review standards were applied to gender, alienage, and illegitimacy classifications. According to Justice Rehnquist, "the expansive notions of judicial review" which result from these standards "require a conscious second-guessing of legislative judgment in an area where this Court has no special expertise whatever." [152]

Despite the Rehnquist animadversion, the Burger Court's refusal to adhere to the traditional rational-basis standard in all equal-protection cases can be justified. In practice, the traditional test of mere rationality means a flaccid standard of review: "For that test, too, when applied as articulated, leaves little doubt about the outcome; the challenged legislation is always upheld."[153] Indeed, as seen toward the beginning of this chapter, when the rational-basis test was the general review standard, Justice Holmes could characterize the Equal Protection Clause as "the usual last resort of constitutional arguments."[154]

Since Holmes's day, the law and the society's attitude toward the concept of equality has been completely altered. The Equal Protection Clause itself gives constitutional status to the view expressed by John Stuart Mill: "There ought to be no pariahs in a . . . civilized nation; no persons disqualified except through their own default."[155] We have come to see that the required default does not exist because the individual possesses characteristics over which he has no control, such as race, sex, birth, or status. These characteristics are "constitutionally an irrelevance."[156]

However, if the rational-basis test were inexorably applied as the only review standard, even classifications resting upon such a "constitutional irrelevance"[157] would almost always have to be upheld. That is why the Court had to develop an equal-protection standard of review with more than one tier: a bottom tier of rational basis and an upper tier of strict scrutiny.

Yet that two-tier model also proved inadequate. What was troublesome about the Burger Court's jurisprudence in this area was not its development of a third tier, or, perhaps more accurately, another half tier—the intermediate level of scrutiny first enunciated in *Craig v. Boren*[158]—but its failure to apply the new standard consistently. We have seen the inconsistency in the case law on alienage, illegitimacy, and, in practice, even gender. The result was what Justice Brennan once termed "the hassle we're now in as to what is proper equal protection analysis"[159]—with its consequence of a jurisprudence that too often depended on the individual Justice's attitude toward the particular statutory classifications.

It may be said that that is the inevitable result when judges are subjected to the temptation posed by a skeleton provision such as the Equal Protection Clause. It is the Justices who must fill out the bony structure with the flesh and the blood—not to mention the soul—that makes equal protection a living constitutional concept.[160] They have thus worked out review standards that may be intended to give a delusive appearance of certainty but that are, in reality, anything but mechanical in their operation.

This is particularly true of the intermediate level of scrutiny developed by the Burger Court. Yet even if that level is not as definite in its application as some might wish, it has meant an important practical change in equal-protection review. It tells us, at a minimum, that there will be heightened scrutiny[161] of a quasi-suspect[162] classification. The Court will take a hard look[163] at such a classification, approaching it skeptically[164] to ensure that valid and sufficiently substantial governmental interests justify the departure from equality. That is really the essence of the extra tier constructed by the Burger Court. Government is told that, when it discriminates against the previously stigmatized groups protected by intermediate-level review, its action will be subjected to the added skepticism of more heightened scrutiny.[165]

Chapter Nine

Equal Protection II:
Racial Classifications

IT IS constitutional cliché that, before the Warren Court decisions, the Fourteenth Amendment had not succeeded in securing legal equality for blacks. With *Brown v. Board of Education*[1]—in many ways the seminal constitutional law decision during the Warren years—the Equal Protection Clause became more than a paper protection against racial discrimination. Certainly the Warren Court decisions brought about a quantum change in American law and life. Chief Justice Warren recalled that, when he first arrived, the Supreme Court itself had a separate washroom for Negroes.[2] One of the first things he did was to eliminate discrimination that was taking place right in the Court building. By the end of his tenure, the Court had virtually rooted out segregation from American law.

But the Warren Court really had it relatively easy in *Brown* and its progeny. The blatant discrimination involved in segregation in education and other public programs made it a simple matter for the Warren Justices to decide the cases that came before them. "Civil rights in the [Warren Court] was a good guys/bad guys issue . . . and there was no doubt on which side the Court was on."[3]

The basic problem for the federal courts, once *Brown* had ruled in 1954 that school segregation was unconstitutional, was how to enforce the *Brown* principle. Resolution of that problem, too, was relatively straightforward. Once the Justices saw that the *Brown* "all deliberate speed"[4] formula was interpreted to countenance indefinite delay, they replaced it with the *Green* requirement of a desegregation "plan that promises realistically to work, and promises realistically to work *now*."[5]

Yet even *Green v. County School Board* was a relatively simple case. The school district involved in *Green* was a rural one with little residential segregation; half of its population was black. It contained two schools, one on the east side of the county (almost entirely white) the other on the west side (entirely black). The dual school system could thus be eliminated by the simple remedy of geographic zoning. The *Green* Court pointed out that this "could be readily achieved . . . simply by assigning students living in the eastern half of the county to the New Kent School and those living in the western half of the county to the Watkins School." [6]

This remedial suggestion provided for attendance under a modified "neighborhood school" concept. The same remedy would prove inadequate in urban areas with entirely different residential patterns—particularly in cities outside the South that had never had legally imposed segregation. Would neighborhood schools be sufficient to meet the constitutional standard, or would more drastic remedies be appropriate—for example, busing between white and black areas to ensure meaningful integration? [7]

SWANN, BUSING, AND REMEDIAL POWER

These questions were soon answered by the Burger Court, which had to deal with the segregation problem in urban school districts—first of all in the urban South and then in Northern cities containing large black "ghettoes." The Court's first major school case, decided in the second Burger term, gave rise to a serious conflict between the new Chief Justice and the majority. The latter was ultimately able to frustrate the Burger effort to weaken the remedial power of the federal courts in segregation cases.

The case in question was *Swann v. Charlotte–Mecklenburg Board of Education.* [8] The Court upheld the far-reaching desegregation order issued by the district court, which included efforts to reach a seventy-one to twenty-nine white–black ratio in the schools and provision for extensive busing to help attain that goal. About 10,000 students were involved—one-fourth of the school children in the district.

At the conference, Chief Justice Burger began his discussion on the merits of *Swann* by querying "whether any particular demands are either required or forbidden. *Brown I* said the right is a right to be free from discrimination–separation solely because of race was outlawed." This was the theme the Chief Justice was to repeat in the first drafts of his *Swann* opinion. Burger said the Court had "to look at the facts to see if there is evidence of discrimination. The rigidity of 71–29 by [District Judge] McMillan disturbs me. There must be some play in the joints—perhaps a 15 percent leeway?"

The Chief Justice was supported at the conference only by Justice Black. Here again, it was the "new" Black who spoke—not the Justice who had once been the leading liberal on the Court. "I have always had the idea that people arrange themselves often to be close to schools. I never thought it was for the courts to change the habits of the people in choosing where to live."

The other Justices expressed support for the district court. Harlan, who might normally have been expected to vote with the Chief Justice, indicated his strong agreement with the district court. "The neighborhood school is not a constitutional requirement if departure from it is necessary to disestablish a segregated system. . . . Busing is not an impermissible tool."

The majority disagreed with Burger on the requirements imposed by *Brown*. Their view was stated by Justice Stewart, whom the Chief Justice might also normally have hoped to rely upon. "Not only desegregation," Stewart asserted, "but affirmative integration is required." That was necessary to "convert to a unitary school system."

The conference discussion indicated a clear majority to affirm. Chief Justice Burger and Black were alone. Despite this, the Chief Justice himself prepared the draft *Swann* opinion, another violation of the established Court practice of having the Chief Justice assign the opinion only when he is a member of the majority.

The key issue in *Swann* was that of the remedial power of the courts in desegregation cases. As Douglas had stated at the conference: "The problem is what is the power of the court without the help of Congress to correct a violation of the Constitution." He then pointed to the broad remedial powers of the courts in other areas. "If there is an antitrust violation, we give a broad discretion." The same should be true here.

Even though the Douglas view on remedial power was supported by the conference majority, the Chief Justice circulated a draft *Swann* opinion[9] that stated a most restricted view of remedial power, which the draft contrasted with what it termed "a classical equity case"— for example, removal of an illegal dam or divestiture of an illegal corporate acquisition. "Here, however, we are not confronted with a simple classical equity case, and the simplistic, hornbook remedies are not necessarily relevant. Populations, pupils or misplaced schools cannot be moved as simply as earth by a bulldozer, or property by corporations."

According to the Burger draft, "the ultimate remedy commanded by *Brown II,* restated and reinforced in numerous intervening cases up to *Alexander,*[10] was to discontinue the dual *system.*" The judicial power was limited to measures aimed at "[d]iscontinuing separate schools for two racial groups." The consequence of such measures "would be a single integrated system functioning on the same basis as school systems in which no discrimination had ever been enforced." The implication was that federal courts could only act to bring about the situation that would have existed had there never been state-enforced segregation. This was virtually to give the Supreme Court imprimatur to the view that "the Constitution . . . does not require integration. It merely forbids discrimination"[11]—a view supposedly already repudiated.[12]

Chief Justice Burger's efforts to limit the remedial power of the district courts were frustrated by the other Justices. Their pressure led the Chief Justice to modify his restricted approach, and the final *Swann* opinion adopted a very broad conception of remedial power.

The final *Swann* opinion specifically rejected the view stated in the Burger draft that the remedial power in this type of case was somehow less than that in the classical equity case: "[A] school desegregation case does not differ fundamentally from other cases involving the framing of equitable remedies to repair the denial of a constitutional right. The task is to correct, by a balancing of the individual and collective interests, the condition that offends the Constitution.[13] . . . Once a right and a violation have been shown, the scope of a district court's equitable powers to remedy past wrongs is broad, for breadth and flexibility are inherent in equitable remedies." Remedial discretion includes the power to attempt to reach a goal of racial distribution in schools comparable to that in the community and to order extensive busing if that is deemed appropriate to "produce an effective dismantling of the dual system."[14]

The most important thing about the *Swann* decision was its recognition of broadside remedial power in desegregation cases—secured over the Chief Justice's vigorous opposition. *Swann* goes far beyond the no-segregation principle laid down in *Brown.* The federal courts do have the power to issue whatever orders may be necessary to bring about an integrated school system—the broad and flexible power traditionally exercised by courts of equity. This includes extensive busing if deemed appropriate to attain the goal "of insuring the achievement of complete integration at the earliest practicable date."[15]

DE JURE VERSUS DE FACTO SEGREGATION

Swann marks the culmination of the Supreme Court decisions on de jure segregation. If such segregation by law is proven, the question becomes solely that of remedy. The district court should order "whatever steps might be necessary to convert to a unitary system in which racial discrimination would be eliminated root and branch."[16] Once de jure segregation has "been shown, the scope of a district court's equitable powers to remedy past wrongs is broad, for breadth and flexibility are inherent in equitable remedies."[17]

Cases involving de jure segregation—segregation required by law— must be distinguished from cases involving de facto segregation, "where racial imbalance exists in the schools but with no showing that this was brought about by discriminatory action of state authorities."[18] In the de facto case, the Burger Court held that the courts might not act to remedy the situation; the segregation was caused, not by law, but by such factors as housing patterns.

De facto segregation occurs in every major metropolitan area; its "root cause" is essentially "one of segregated residential and migratory patterns."[19] As Powell points out, "This is a national, not a southern, phenomenon. And it is largely unrelated to whether a particular State had or did not have segregative school laws."[20]

In practice, the de jure–de facto distinction means that using *Green–Swann* to eliminate dual school systems is possible only in the South. *Brown, Green,* and *Swann* did lead to substantial progress in integration in southern states. "No comparable progress has been made in many nonsouthern cities with large minority populations primarily because of the de facto–de jure distinction nurtured by the courts."[21]

The key case in the Burger Court on segregation outside the south is *Keyes v. Denver School District.*[22] The Denver school system had never been operated under constitutional or statutory provisions which either mandated or permitted racial segregation. However, schools in one area of the city were overwhelmingly black or Hispanic. The district court had found that this was the result of intentional race-conscious decisions by the school board in constructing schools and drawing attendance zones. The district court had also found that all the segregated schools were educationally inferior to the predominantly white schools.

As in *Swann,* Chief Justice Burger did not play a leadership role in the *Keyes* decision. At the postargument conference, he stated only, "This is not the typical *Brown* case—66% white, 14% Negro, 20 % Chicano. . . . [N]o one was denied admission to school on racial grounds. . . . Plaintiffs have the burden to show discrimination" and, in his view, that burden had not been met.

Brennan, however, stated the rationale upon which *Keyes* was to be decided. De jure segregation could be shown not only when it was required or permitted by law, but also when segregated schools resulted from the intentional acts of the school board. The Denver board had followed a deliberate segregation policy. There thus could exist a predicate for a finding that the entire school system was segregated de jure. The burden was on the school board to prove that the deliberate segregation shown did not make the entire school system a dual school system.

Most of the others agreed, and the *Keyes* opinion was assigned to Brennan. The most interesting aspect of *Keyes,* however, was the Court's implicit resolution of the de jure–de facto issue. There had been some consideration of that issue in *Swann.* In Chief Justice Burger's early drafts, he stressed that the Court's objective was only school segregation: "it does not and cannot embrace all the problems of racial prejudice in residential patterns, employment practices, location of public housing, or other factors beyond the jurisdiction of school authorities, even when those patterns contribute to disproportionate racial concentrations in some schools."[23]

In a March 6, 1971, letter to the Chief Justice, Douglas objected that this "paragraph excludes from *de jure* segregation relevant to school problems both restrictive social covenants and racial public housing. . . . [S]uch state-sanctioned practices are included in *de jure* segregation for purposes of the public school problem." Douglas asked the Chief Justice "not [to] decide the scope of *de jure* segregation,"[24] and the final *Swann* opinion did not discuss it.

In the *Keyes* conference, Justice Douglas repeated his view on de facto segregation. "What has been called de facto is in most cases de jure—housing programs, restrictive covenants—lots of state and federal action." Hence, he "would just apply *Swann* and reverse."

But it was Justice Powell who stated the strongest disagreement with the de jure–de facto distinction. "The distinction between de jure and de facto can't be defended constitutionally or logically. The Court has worked itself into a position that ignores that population trends have been the product of state action of all sorts."

Powell urged the abandonment of the de jure–de facto distinction. But the others, except for Douglas, refused to take that step—though Brennan did state that the distinction troubled him also. The prevailing view was stated by Rehnquist: "It never occurred to me to reject the distinction between de jure and de facto."

Powell's separate *Keyes* opinion concurred in part and dissented in part. He expanded on his view that the de jure–de facto distinction should not be perpetuated. In its place there should be "a uniform national rule."[25] If segregated schools exist, the courts may order whatever steps may be necessary to secure an integrated system. However, the Justice strongly questioned "any remedial requirement of extensive student transportation solely to further integration.[26] . . . There is nothing in the Constitution, its history, or—until recently—in the jurisprudence of this Court that mandates the employment of forced transportation of young and teenage children to achieve a single interest, as important as that interest may be."[27]

On April 3, 1973, soon after he had read the Powell *Keyes* draft, Brennan sent around a Memorandum to the Conference. "At our original conference discussion of this case, Lewis first expressed his view that the de jure–de facto distinction should be discarded. I told him then that I too was deeply troubled by the distinction." Nevertheless, the majority "was committed to the view that the distinction should be maintained, and I therefore drafted *Keyes* within the framework established in our earlier cases." While he was "still convinced that my proposed opinion for the Court is, assuming the continued vitality of the de jure–de facto distinction, a proper resolution of the case, I would be happy indeed to recast the opinion and jettison the distinction if a majority of the Court is prepared to do so."

But there was an internal inconsistency in the Powell approach that made it unacceptable. While it would have meant the end of the de jure–de facto division, it would also have meant the virtual end of busing as a desegregation remedy. Segregation would have been subjected to uniform treatment throughout the country; but the courts would have been divested of the power to order transportation to further integration—even in the *Swann*-type case where dismantling of the dual system could not be accomplished without busing.

Brennan made this point in his April 3 memo: "Although Lewis and I seem to share the view that de facto segregation and de jure segregation (as we have previously used those terms) should receive like constitutional treatment, we are in substantial disagreement, I think, on what that treatment should be. Unlike Lewis, I would retain the definition of the 'affirmative duty to desegregate' that we have set forth in our prior cases, in particular *Brown II, Green,* and *Swann.* Lewis's approach has the virtue of discarding an illogical and un-workable distinction, but only at the price of a substantial retreat from our commitment of the past twenty years to eliminate all ves-tiges of state-imposed segregation in the public schools. . . . In my view, we can eliminate the distinction without cutting back on our commitment and I would gladly do so." To go along with Justice Powell, however, might lend weight to his view on busing. Thus it might be better to treat *Keyes* as a de jure case and avoid the de facto issue.

Blackmun was also dissatisfied with the distinction. In a January 9, 1973, letter to Brennan, he stated, "I am not at all certain that the de jure–de facto distinction in school segregation will hold up in the long run. Segregation may well be segregation, whatever the form." And in a May 30, 1973, letter to Justice Brennan, he wrote, "I retain some unease about the situation, for I am persuaded, as Lewis and Bill Douglas appear to be, that the de jure–de facto distinction even-tually must give way. Lewis' opinion—both parts of it—is, for me, forceful and persuasive. I take it . . . that you also are inclined to the view Lewis entertains except for the question of remedy. I feel, how-ever, as apparently you do, that we need not meet the de jure–de facto distinction for purposes of the Denver case."

As it turned out, the *Keyes* opinion did not discuss the de jure–de facto distinction. Only Douglas, in his separate concurrence, publicly supported the Powell view that the distinction should be abandoned. Both Brennan and Blackmun ultimately decided not to deal with the issue in *Keyes.* Instead, the Brennan opinion of the Court treated the Denver segregation as de jure; the segregated schools in a substantial part of the city resulted from the purposeful acts of the school board.

SEGREGATION AND THE SUBURBS

There have been no cases since *Keyes* raising the de jure versus de facto segregation issue. Hence, the de jure–de facto distinction has continued as the dividing line in desegregation jurisprudence. The mere fact that segregated schools exist in a district is not enough.

Only where de jure segregation is shown may the *Green–Swann* remedial power be used to do away with a dual school system.

However, *Keyes* shows that de jure segregation may be shown from the intentional acts of the school authorities that contributed to the existence of segregated schools. Those acts are just as unconstitutional as the segregation laws invalidated in *Brown*. Thus, as Brennan pointed out in a June 13, 1973, Memorandum to the Conference on *Keyes*, "the threshold question [was] simply whether the evidence of actions by the respective School [Board] supported the findings of the respective . . . Courts of unconstitutional actions constituting *de jure* segregation." If there was such evidence, the absence of state laws requiring segregation became irrelevant. "Indeed," notes the Brennan memo, "this is true even if the School Board's actions are in derogation of state law forbidding segregation, as does Colorado's Constitution." All that would be necessary was, in the words of another Brennan note, "a finding of purposeful discrimination . . . sufficient to support the remedial order."[28]

The question of the extent of remedial power in cases involving de jure segregation had not, however, been fully settled where a remedy confined to the school district concerned would prove ineffective. This became clear when the Court was confronted with a case arising out of a city with a black majority, surrounded by white suburbs. A racial mix could be secured only from the white children who lived in the suburbs.

Milliken v. Bradley[29] arose out of an action seeking relief from segregation in the Detroit school system. The district court concluded that the Detroit Board of Education had created and perpetuated school segregation in Detroit. Under the principles laid down in the prior cases, this was de jure segregation. But since two out of three pupils in Detroit were black a *Swann*-type order confined to the city would not remedy the problem. A Detroit-only plan, the district court found, "would not accomplish desegregation . . . within the corporate geographical limits of the city." Instead, it only "would make the Detroit school system more identifiably Black . . . thereby increasing the flight of Whites from the city and the system."

The district court concluded that it "must look beyond the limits of the Detroit school district for a solution to the problem." It then ordered preparation of a desegregation plan covering the city and fifty-three suburban school districts. The plan was based on fifteen clusters, each containing part of the Detroit system and two or more suburban districts. Extensive school busing was ordered within the clusters. The district court acted without evidence that the suburban school districts had committed acts of de jure segregation. The court of appeals affirmed the decision.

As the Brennan June 13, 1973, memorandum noted, the district court could find that there were "constitutional violations resulting in system-wide racial segregation of the Detroit public schools" and that a "constitutionally adequate system of desegregated schools can-[not] be established within the geographical limits of the Detroit school district." The key question then became that of "whether 'the district judge's order requiring preparation of a metropolitan plan for cross-district assignment and transportation of school children throughout the Detroit Metropolitan area represents a proper exercise of the equity power of the District Court.'"

The Chief Justice circulated a May 31, 1974, draft *Milliken* opinion of the Court, which tried to regain part of the ground lost when the majority refused to accept his draft opinion in *Swann*. In addition to its restricted view of the scope of remedial power, the Burger *Swann* draft stressed what it called the district court's attempt to establish as "the 'norm' . . . a fixed mathematical racial balance reflecting the pupil constituency of the system." Such an attempt was beyond judicial power: "Neither the Constitution nor equitable principles grants to judges the power . . . to order the individual schools to reflect the [racial] composition of the system."[30]

The refusal of the other Justices to accept this draft language led the Chief Justice to drop it. Instead, the final *Swann* opinion indicated that racial balance might be used as a starting point and expressly conceded that "the very limited use made of mathematical ratios was within the equitable remedial discretion of the District Court."[31]

Now, in his *Milliken* draft, the Chief Justice's major emphasis was on the racial balance issue, rather than on the question of cross-district remedies that, as the Brennan June 13 memo stated, was the principal issue in the case.

According to the *Milliken* draft, "[I]t seems clear that the District Court and the Court of Appeals placed the primary focus on the desire to achieve 'racial balance' in a city predominantly composed of Negro students, and this approach plainly equated desegregation with racial balance as a constitutionally mandated remedy. . . . [T]he District Court expressly and frankly directed the use of a 'fixed mathematical racial balance' which was to be based on the 'overall pupil racial composition' of Detroit and the 53 outlying school districts . . . to the end that, upon implementation, *no school, grade or classroom* [would be] substantially disproportionate *to the overall pupil racial composition. . . .* This is far from the use of the total racial composition as a 'starting point' in the analysis of possible violations as envisioned in *Swann.*"

The Burger draft conceded that the presence of racially identifiable schools might shift the burden of proof to the school authorities. "However, the use of significant racial imbalance in schools within an autonomous school district as a signal which operates simply to shift the burden of proof, is a very different matter from equating racial imbalance with a constitutional violation calling for a remedy in the form of an order for some fixed racial balance accomplished by enlarging the relevant area until the hypothetically 'desirable' racial mix is achieved." [32]

Racial balance, the Chief Justice wrote, made the cross-district remedy invalid. According to the *Milliken* draft, "to approve the remedy imposed by the District Court on these facts would make racial balance the constitutional objective and standard; a result not even hinted at in *Brown I* and *Brown II* which held that the operation of dual school systems, not some hypothetical level of racial imbalance, is the constitutional violation to be remedied. Unlike *Swann,* this case did not involve a 'very limited use . . . of . . . mathematical ratios' as a 'starting point,' but, on the contrary, the finding of racial imbalance became the controlling standard for determining the existence of a violation. This misread the explicit guidelines of *Swann* that 'to require, as a matter of substantive constitutional right, any particular degree of racial balance or mixing' would be reversible error."

Almost all of these portions of the *Milliken* draft were removed from the final *Milliken* opinion. Instead the opinion stresses that the de jure segregation was limited to the city of Detroit. Hence, the judicial remedial power might not extend to the suburbs, and there was no legal basis for including them in the desegregation plan.

The *Milliken* approach is thus consistent with the *Keyes* refusal to abandon the de jure–de facto distinction. It is true, as *Keyes* shows, that a de jure situation in a substantial part of a school district may permit the court to order comprehensive desegregation throughout the district. As Stevens was to sum it up during the conference on a later school desegregation case,[33] "I've been under the impression that proof of de jure justified a system-wide remedy."

But that does not mean that a desegregation plan may include outlying school districts. As the Chief Justice stated in his *Milliken* draft, "Federal authority to impose cross-district remedies presupposes a fair and reasoned determination that there has been a constitutional violation by all of the districts affected by the remedy."

IMPACT VERSUS INTENT

The Burger Court has been criticized for holding that proof that a government act has a disproportionate impact upon racial minorities is not enough to show a violation of equal protection. Yet such a holding follows logically from the *Keyes* refusal to eliminate the de jure–de facto distinction. In a de facto segregation situation, the students attend schools that are predominantly black or white. Still that is not enough to make for a constitutional violation. In the absence of racially discriminatory intent or purpose, the mere fact that black and white children are treated differently does not prove a denial of equal protection.

The same approach was applied in *Washington v. Davis*,[34] the leading Burger Court case on disproportionate impact. At issue was the validity of a qualifying test given to applicants for positions as police officers in the District of Columbia. The test was developed by the U.S. Civil Service Commission and used throughout the federal service. Four times as many black applicants failed the test than did whites. It was claimed that this disproportionate impact standing alone was sufficient to establish a constitutional violation. The court of appeals agreed. Defendants denied discriminatory intent. They had systematically sought to enroll black officers and, since 1969, 44 percent of new police recruits had been black—a figure roughly equivalent to the percentage of 20- to 29-year-old blacks within the fifty-mile radius in which recruiting efforts had been concentrated. The court of appeals found the lack of discriminatory intent irrelevant where the racially differential impact of the test was so great.

The discussion at the *Washington v. Davis* conference reflected the final decision and division in the Court. Chief Justice Burger began by noting, "The Negro failure rate was four times that of whites and that triggers a hard look at the test. . . . The district court found [the test] job related. . . . The court of appeals reversed because of the fail rate of Negroes. I would feel inclined to agree with [District Judge] Gesell."

Stewart also spoke in favor of reversing the court of appeals. He stated the approach that the Court was to follow. "The test at most when racially discriminatory impact is shown is that the city had the burden of showing only that there was no discriminatory intent. There was none shown here and I'd reverse."

White, author of the opinion, agreed with Justice Stewart. Only Brennan and Marshall disagreed. The majority was plainly impressed by the defendants' efforts to recruit blacks. White stressed that the evidence showed "they went out to hire blacks" and Justice Blackmun stated, "The recruiting practices in evidence dispel any intent to discriminate."

The opinion of the Court for reversal followed the conference discussion. Disparate effect alone was not enough to show a violation of equal protection. A discriminatory racial purpose must be shown. On the other hand, disproportionate impact may be relevant and call for further inquiry. But here the affirmative efforts to recruit black officers negated any inference of discriminatory purpose.

The same approach was followed a year later in *Arlington Heights v. Metropolitan Housing Development Corp.*[35] The Court held that the refusal of a Chicago suburb to rezone to permit construction of a multiracial apartment complex did not violate equal protection, even though there were almost no blacks in the suburb and 40 percent of those eligible to become tenants in the new apartments were black. Once again the Court ruled that the fact that the refusal to rezone resulted in a racially disproportionate impact was not enough. Proof of racially discriminatory purpose was required and none was shown.

AFFIRMATIVE ACTION OR REVERSE DISCRIMINATION?

In many ways the most difficult equal protection cases in the Burger Court were those challenging preferences for minorities. These programs were established because other measures proved inadequate to eliminate racial discrimination. Previous attempts had focused upon the formal equality before the law established by the Equal Protection Clause. Now the concept of legal equality, presented in traditional negative terms, was said to be inadequate to deal with the factual inequalities caused by racial discrimination. Instead, ensuring equality to white and black alike may require more than adherence to formal equality in the application of legal precepts and doctrine. The evidence of true equality between the races may depend, not only on the absence of disabilities, but also on the presence of abilities.

During the 1960s society had begun to recognize the claim that there is a social duty to make "compensation" for the inequalities under which racial minorities have had to live. Racially neutral programs were giving way to programs that gave a preference to members of minority groups that had been the victims of racial discrimination.

However, these new programs posed a new dilemma. In *Brown* and the later desegregation cases the courts were confronted with school systems that violated the Equal Protection Clause, but judicial enforcement did not deprive anyone else of the right to an equal education. Yet such a result was precisely that with which the decision in a case like *Regents of the University of California v. Bakke*[36] had to deal. As Justice Marshall expressed it in an April 13, 1978, memorandum on the *Bakke* case, "[T]he decision in this case depends on whether you consider the action of the Regents as *admitting* certain students or as *excluding* certain other students."

The real problem was that the special admissions program at issue in *Bakke* did provide both for admitting a specified number of minority students and for excluding others who might have been admitted had there been no special program. During the oral argument, Marshall was to put his finger on the case's dilemma in this respect, when he told Bakke's counsel, "You are arguing about keeping somebody out and the other side is arguing about getting somebody in."[37] A decision for the university would keep Bakke and others like him out of medical school; a decision for Bakke would prevent minority applicants from "getting in" under the special program.

In the April 13, 1978, memo, Marshall also noted that the manner in which a program with racial preferences was labeled would depend on whether the "getting in" or the "keeping out" was emphasized: "If you view the programs as admitting qualified students who, because of this Nation's sorry history of racial discrimination, have academic records that prevent them from effectively competing for medical school, then this is affirmative action to remove the vestiges of slavery and state imposed segregation by root and branch. If you view the program as excluding students, it is a program of quotas which violates the principle that the Constitution is color-blind."

To those who favored racial preferences, *affirmative action* would correct centuries of racial discrimination by positive measures aimed at moving minorities into the mainstream. To opponents, racial preferences were *reverse discrimination,* which, however benign in intention, replaced discrimination against minorities with discrimination against whites who were themselves wholly innocent in the matter. A year before *Bakke,* Brennan attempted to soften the discriminatory connotation by calling the *Bakke*-type program *benign discrimination.*[38] But semantics could not disguise the impact of the special admissions program. In a pre-*Bakke* case, the state court dealt with the claim that "because the persons normally stigmatized by racial classifications are being benefited, the action complained of should be considered 'benign.'" According to the court, "the minority admissions policy is certainly not benign with respect to nonminority students who are displaced by it."[39]

BAKKE AND AFFIRMATIVE ACTION

In the *Bakke* case,[40] the Court dealt squarely with the validity of special programs involving racial preferences. The University of California at Davis Medical School alloted 16 of the 100 places in the entering class to minority applicants. The admissions criteria were also considerably less demanding than those of the regular admissions program. Bakke, a white applicant, had been rejected by Davis even though his admissions scores were higher than those of the minority applicants accepted under the special program. He brought an action to compel his admission to the medical school. The complaint alleged that, because of defendants' action "in excluding plaintiff from the first-year Medical School class under defendants' minority preference admission program plaintiff has been invidiously discriminated against on account of his race in violation of the Equal Protection Clause."

The decision in the *Bakke* case and the process by which it was reached well illustrates the manner in which the Burger Court operated. Instead of a flat decision upholding or striking down racially preferential programs, the Court handed down a fragmented decision that mirrored the internal atomization of the Court. *Bakke* again illustrates the essential failure of Chief Justice Burger to assume an effective leadership role in the molding of his Court's jurisprudence.

In *Bakke,* the lead in the decision process was assumed by other members of the Court—notably by Justices Brennan and Powell.

It should be stressed that the *Bakke* decision was really two decisions—each decided by a five-to-four vote. The first decision was that the Davis special admissions program was invalid and that Bakke should be admitted to the medical school. Powell joined the Chief Justice and Stevens, Stewart, and Rehnquist to make up the majority. The second decision was that race was a factor that might be considered in an admissions policy without violating the Constitution. Powell joined Brennan, White, Marshall, and Blackmun to make up the bare majority here.

The unifying factor behind both *Bakke* decisions was Justice Powell's vote, which—though it was fully endorsed by no other Justice—spoke for the bare majorities on each of the major issues.

The result has been that commentators, courts, and admissions officers have treated Powell's opinion as the authoritative opinion in the *Bakke* case. The Davis program was invalidated, but admissions officers are permitted to operate programs that grant racial preferences—provided that they do not do so as blatantly as was done under the sixteen-seat "quota" provided at Davis.

Powell's crucial part in the *Bakke* decision process began with his circulation of a draft opinion on November 22, 1977—two weeks before the *Bakke* conference on the merits. The draft contained a constitutional discussion essentially similar to that in the Justice's *Bakke* opinion. It began with a treatment of the proper standard of review. To Powell, strict scrutiny[41] was required and the Davis program could not pass the test, since it was not supported by any "compelling interest."

The Powell draft rejected the view that allotting places for preferred racial groups was the only effective means to secure diversity in the student body. But the draft went on to give the example of Harvard to show how an admissions program, which considers race among other factors, might be "designed to achieve meaningful diversity in the broad sense of this term." Such a program permits race to be considered but, at the same time, "specifically eschews quotas."

Powell's reference to race as a factor that may be considered by an admissions program turned out to be crucial to the *Bakke* case. It was to serve as the bridge between the initial Powell rejection of the Davis program and the final decision, which enabled the four pro-Davis Justices to join a significant portion of the ultimate opinion.

The November 22 Powell draft ended with a categorical rejection of the Davis program: "When a State's distribution of benefits or imposition of burdens hinges on the color of a person's skin or on his ancestry, he is entitled to a demonstration that the challenged classification is necessary to promote a substantial state interest. Petitioner has failed to carry this burden."

At the December 9, 1977, *Bakke* conference on the merits, Powell repeated the views expressed in his draft. "I can't join Thurgood, Byron, and Bill in their holding that 16 or 84 or any quota was okay. . . . [T]he effect of the Fourteenth [Amendment] is completely lost. . . .While admissions policy should be left to the university, the colossal blunder here was to pick a number. Diversity is a necessary goal to assure a broad spectrum of Americans an opportunity for graduate school. . . . Each applicant should be able to compete with others and taking race into account is proper—but never setting aside a fixed number of places."

Powell thus said that he would vote to affirm the California decision in Bakke's favor. Justice Brennan interjected that he thought that, under the approach to the case he had just stated, Powell should vote to affirm in part and reverse in part. The judgment of the lower court seemed to require that Davis adopt a colorblind admissions system for the future. Powell went along with Brennan's approach, saying, "I agree that the judgment must be reversed insofar as it enjoins Davis from taking race into account."

In a December 19, 1978, Memorandum to the Conference, Justice Powell summarized the concession. "As I stated at Conference (when Bill Brennan put the question as to the form of a judgment under my view), I had not considered the scope of the trial court's injunction. If it can be read as enjoining Davis from ever including race or ethnic origin as *one* element, to be weighed *competitively* with all other relevant elements in making admissions decisions (i.e., from adopting what I shall refer to herein as the 'Harvard'-type admissions policy), then—as I stated—I would certainly favor a modification of that injunction. . . . [I]n the unlikely but welcome event that a consensus develops for allowing the competitive consideration of race as an element, I think we should affirm as to the Davis program, but reverse in part as to the scope of the injunction."

The Powell concession was the key that led to the ultimate compromise resolution of the *Bakke* case. Under the Court's decision, the Davis program itself was ruled violative of equal protection; but the decision specifically held that race might be considered as a factor in admissions programs. This has permitted the use of race in a flexible admissions policy designed to produce diversity in a student body. Minority students may be admitted even though they may not fully measure up to the academic criteria.

FULLILOVE AND CONTRACT PREFERENCES

There has not been another *Bakke*-type university admissions case in the Supreme Court despite the fact that it was widely predicted that *Bakke* would spawn a series of similar challenges to special admissions programs.

On the other hand, there have been cases involving the problem of racial preferences outside the field of university admissions. The first such post-*Bakke* case, *Fullilove v. Klutznick*,[42] involved a federal statute that provided that at least 10 percent of the grants for public works be spent for minority business enterprises (MBE).

On its face the MBE provision seems similar to the Davis program condemned in *Bakke*. A fixed proportion of the benefits is reserved for members of racial minorities, and whites are completely excluded from competing for that proportion. But there were significant differences. The *Fullilove* program had been set up by Congress, and the legislative history showed that Congress had concluded that discrimination had contributed to the negligible percentage of public contracts awarded minority contractors.

In his conference presentation, Chief Justice Burger stressed that the MBE preference was established by Congress. The Court should "give more latitude to Congress than [to] administrative or state action." *Bakke* was not "as pertinent as *Katzenbach v. Morgan*"[43]— the leading case upholding the broad power of Congress to enact laws protecting minorities under the Enforcement Clause of the Fourteenth Amendment. The dominant theme should be "deference to Congress."

The strongest view against the validity of the MBE preference was stated by Justice Stewart. Under "the Constitution as I understand it, the Fifth and Fourteenth [Amendments] must mean you can't predicate exclusions on race. It's per se invidious however loftily motivated."

Rehnquist and Stevens voted with Stewart, but the others supported MBE's constitutionality. Of particular interest was the view expressed by Powell, the author of the *Bakke* swing opinion. "I'd have agreed with Potter twenty years ago, but *Brown* and *Green*,[44] Congress in VII [of the Civil Rights Act of 1964], in the Voting Rights Act— all have led me to assume that . . . a substantial or compelling state interest permits classifications on race. The governmental interest here is very substantial." Powell then went into what he considered a key distinction between *Fullilove* and *Bakke*. "I wouldn't accept [that] historic discrimination [that is, that alleged in *Bakke*] is enough. I'd want definitive findings and there is an adequate record here." Powell also stated that he "wouldn't second guess the choice of means."

The vote at the *Fullilove* conference was six to three to uphold the MBE provision. Chief Justice Burger assigned the opinion to himself. His draft, like his final opinion, focused on the point he had made at the conference—the MBE program had been set up by Congress and the Court should defer to the congressional judgment. Congress had acted under two of its broadest powers: the spending power and the power to enforce the Fourteenth Amendment.

Neither the Burger draft nor his final opinion contained any discussion of the standard of review in such a case. Indeed, the Chief Justice's draft stated specifically, "This opinion does not adopt, either expressly or implicitly, the formulas of analysis articulated in . . . *University of California Regents v. Bakke*." Brennan and Marshall objected, and on June 17, 1980, they wrote to the Chief Justice, "we believe that some standard of review is necessary, and we intend to circulate a concurring opinion that articulates our view of the correct standard and explains how that standard is implicit in the analysis you apply to this case."

Burger replied in a June 18 Memorandum to the Conference saying that "it seems to me there is a 'tempest in a saucer' aspect as to terms. I frankly believe that adopting a magic 'word-test' is a serious error and I will neither write nor join in these 'litmus' approaches." This led Marshall, joined by Brennan and Blackmun, to issue a concurrence stating that the proper standard of review was articulated in the Brennan *Bakke* opinion and the MBE provision was valid under that standard.

Powell wrote a concurrence in *Fullilove,* which followed his *Bakke* approach on the review standard. In a June 13, 1980, Memorandum to the Conference, he said, "I have applied . . . the strict scrutiny analysis to the racial classification incorporated in § 103(f) (2)."

How could Powell vote to uphold the MBE provision when he had been the decisive vote to invalidate the Davis program because it had provided for a racial quota? "Like *Bakke*," the Powell memo conceded, "this is a quota system case." To Powell, however, this case was different from *Bakke*, where the Powell opinion had noted, "In this case . . . there has been no determination by the legislature or a responsible administrative agency that the University engaged in a discriminatory practice requiring remedial efforts." [45]

Fullilove "differs from *Bakke* in that the congressional record makes clear—at least for me—that Congress made appropriate findings of racial discrimination against minority contractors." Powell also stressed the congressional power to enforce the Fourteenth Amendment. "Moreover," stated the June 13 memo, "as the opinion of the Chief Justice properly emphasizes, Congress has a unique responsibility under § 5 of the 14th Amendment. Accordingly, I conclude that the set-aside is constitutional."

MORE RECENT CASES

The *Fullilove* decision does not conflict with *Bakke*. If there had been a legislative or administrative finding that the challenged program was necessary to remedy past discrimination by the university, the Davis special admissions program might have been valid. In *Fullilove*, the legislative history demonstrated that Congress had made such a finding. *Fullilove* is thus consistent with *Bakke* and particularly the Powell *Bakke* opinion.

The same is true of the more recent Burger Court cases involving racial preferences under affirmative action. Like *Fullilove*, they involve employment, not university admissions. Most of them were decided under Title VII of the Civil Rights Act, in which Congress prohibited racial discrimination in employment. Hence, they do not bear directly upon the constitutional status of *Bakke*, but they may still be relevant to discussions of that subject.

The one post-*Fullilove* case not decided under Title VII was *Wygant v. Jackson Board of Education*.[46] The issue was whether a school board, consistent with the Equal Protection Clause, might extend preferential protection to teachers because of their race or national origin. The board had entered into a collective bargaining agreement under which lay-offs were to be in reverse order of seniority, "except that at no time will there be a greater percentage of minority personnel laid off than the current percentage of minority personnel employed at the time of the layoff." Under this provision, white teachers were laid off, while black teachers with less seniority were retained. Displaced white teachers brought suit claiming that they had been discriminated against. The lower court held that equal protection had not been violated; racial preferences were ruled permissible as an attempt to remedy "societal discrimination."

The Chief Justice began the *Wygant* conference by stating, "Societal discrimination never commanded a Court here. Close scrutiny, a searching examination, is the test. A compelling state interest must be shown and the court of appeals said 'reasonableness'" was the test. "Without a finding of actual discrimination, [we] can't sustain the contract. [Moreover] A school board is not like Congress or a state legislature to decide these questions."

The case for affirmance was led by Brennan. The case was governed by *Weber,*[47] where "an affirmative action plan that was the product of a collectively bargained agreement was upheld by a majority of this Court. . . . While there are some differences between the factual circumstances in *Weber* and those involved here, these are not 'differences that make a difference.' A comparison of the cases makes clear, I believe, that *Weber* controls this case."

In *Wygant* as in *Weber,* the contract was "voluntarily entered into." Brennan also pointed out that, "In *Wygant,* (a) the school board is of course aware of its own course of conduct over the years, and it engaged in numerous inquiries throughout the years which confirmed the fact that its poor record regarding minorities required redress (b) we have been presented with the figures indicating that black teachers had never been hired until relatively recently, and (c) the fact of segregation and discrimination in American school[s] is thoroughly documented. In *Weber,* despite the lack of 'case specific' judicial findings, we accepted that the plan was remedial in nature."

Brennan also dealt with the question of whether the means chosen were acceptable. "I think they are. . . . [T]he state has a compelling interest in remedying past discrimination and creating a diverse faculty."[48]

The Chief Justice was supported by White, Powell, and Rehnquist. "The desire to have a diverse faculty," said White, "doesn't, without more, justify what's done here. . . . I don't find any concession of discrimination—societal or otherwise." Powell stressed, "The classification is based solely on race. It must be justified on compelling state interest grounds. . . . [There was] no showing here that meets even the intermediate level of scrutiny."

The vote was four to four (Brennan, Marshall, Blackmun, and Stevens), when O'Connor, the junior Justice, spoke. She agreed with the Burger approach on standard of review, saying, "The Court has fashioned a standard of scrutiny in racial discrimination—strict scrutiny. The Sixth Circuit was wrong in applying a standard of reasonableness. . . . Remedying this has been held not compelling."

Despite her statement, O'Connor did not vote with the Chief Justice. Instead, as explained by Brennan in a November 20, 1985, "Dear Thurgood, Harry, and John" letter, "the vote at Conference was four to reverse (the Chief, Lewis, Byron and Bill), and we four to affirm, with Sandra voting to vacate." Noting that the Chief Justice had assigned the *Wygant* opinion to Justice Powell, Brennan said, "I must assume that since the Conference Sandra has joined the Chief, et al."

O'Connor did ultimately vote with the Burger bloc to make a bare majority for reversal. Powell, who delivered the plurality opinion, followed the essentials of his *Bakke* approach. The racial classification at issue, like that in *Bakke,* must be subjected to strict scrutiny. It may be upheld only if justified by a compelling state interest and only if narrowly tailored to the achievement of the state's goal. According to Powell, the racial classification in *Wygant* was not justified by a compelling state interest because no evidence existed in the record that the school board had ever discriminated in hiring on the basis of race.[49]

Here Powell repeated his *Bakke* view that societal discrimination alone (upon which both Davis Medical School and the board of education in *Wygant* had relied) was not enough to justify a racial classification designed to remedy such discrimination: "Societal discrimination, without more, is too amorphous a basis for imposing a racially classified remedy."[50] Instead, there must have been specific prior discrimination warranting remedial action.

O'Connor, the one member of the *Wygant* Court who had not participated in *Bakke,* subscribed to the Powell approach "because it mirrors the standard we have consistently applied in examining racial classifications in other contexts."[51] She noted, citing Powell's *Bakke* opinion, that "a state interest in the promotion of racial diversity has been found sufficiently 'compelling,' at least in the context of higher education, to support the use of racial considerations in furthering that interest." [52] But that would not justify race as the sole determining factor in *Wygant,* any more than it justified race as the sole factor in determining eligibility for the sixteen seats set aside under the Davis special admissions program.

To be sure, the more recent cases have involved more than mere applications of *Bakke*. In *Firefighters Local Union v. Stotts,*[53] the Court had indicated that a racially preferential program similar to that in *Wygant* was invalid unless it was necessary "to provide make-whole relief only to those who have been actual victims of illegal discrimination."[54] In a March 7, 1984, letter to Justice White, after he had read White's draft *Firefighters* opinion, Brennan asserted that such a holding "would cast considerable doubt on . . . race-conscious affirmative remedies." But the *Firefighters* implication that preferential treatment may not be given to nonvictims was repudiated both in *Wygant* and other cases. No Justice in *Wygant* asserted the view that affirmative action plans are limited to benefiting identifiable victims of past discrimination.

It is true that, as pointed out in a Powell memorandum, "*Wygant* only speaks directly to the use of layoffs; its discussion of hiring practices is dicta."[55] Soon after *Wygant,* however, in *Local 28, Sheet Metal Workers v. Equal Employment Opportunity Commission,*[56] six Justices specifically agreed that preferential relief may be granted benefiting individuals who are not actual victims of discrimination as a remedy for past discrimination. Among them was Powell who stated expressly that he, too, agreed that preferential relief need not be limited to actual victims of discrimination. (At the conference, he had said, "I don't agree the bar [is] only for victims.") This Powell view was consistent with what the Justice had said in *Bakke*. The use of race as a factor in admission decisions gives a preference to minority applicants who had not themselves been actual victims of discrimination.

It is true that, in both the *Sheet Metal* case and a companion case, *Local Number 93 v. Cleveland,*[57] the Court upheld plans that required fixed goals and numbers for hiring and promotion of blacks. This may seem inconsistent with *Bakke* because it assigned a fixed number of seats to racial minorities. In *Sheet Metal,* however, there was, as Powell stated, in a March 6, 1986, "Dear Chief" letter, "the undisputed record of gross discrimination by the union over a period of at least two decades, and its intransigence in resisting every effort (including court orders) to implement appropriate remedies."

(At the conference, Marshall had asserted, "*Sheet Metal Workers* [are] the most racially biased union today.") For Powell, the finding that the union had committed egregious violations clearly established a governmental interest sufficient to justify the imposition of a racially classified remedy.

In the *Cleveland* case, the plan upheld had been adopted in a consent decree. The Court treated such a plan as one entered into voluntarily by the parties. Voluntary action by employers and unions seeking to eliminate race discrimination may include race-conscious relief that may not be subject to the *Bakke*- or *Wygant*-type limitations.

To be sure, the Court has not been united in its post-*Bakke* approach to programs providing for racial preferences. But none of its decisions has been inconsistent in important respects with *Bakke* and its interpretation in the field of educational admissions. Like *Bakke*, the cases uphold the validity of well-tailored affirmative action programs. That is true even though, as in *Bakke* itself, the Justices have not agreed on the results or even on the appropriate standard of review. Yet, in practice, as O'Connor points out, "the distinction between a 'compelling' and an 'important' governmental purpose may be a negligible one. The court is in agreement that, whatever the formulation employed, remedying past or present racial discrimination by a state actor is a sufficiently weighty state interest to warrant the remedial use of a carefully constructed affirmative action program."[58]

This, after all, is the most important thing when we consider the Burger Court jurisprudence on the subject. "Despite the Court's inability to agree on a route, we have reached a common destination in sustaining affirmative action against constitutional attack."[59]

RACIAL DISCRIMINATION AND THE BURGER COURT

The Burger Court's decisions on racial classifications form a logically consistent corpus. Crucial to those decisions was the Court's refusal to discard the de jure–de facto distinction. Where de jure segregation was found, the decisions simply built on the Warren Court caselaw, particularly *Green*.[60] The courts have the duty to take action to correct the situation and their remedial power in this respect is as broad as the constitutional violation itself.[61] It includes the authority to order any "plan that promises realistically to work, and promises realistically to work *now*."[62] The courts may take any and all measures, including racial rezoning and extensive busing, that may be deemed appropriate to attain the desired goal.

In *Keyes*,[63] however, the Burger Court declined the Douglas–Powell invitation to apply the *Green–Swann* approach to all segregation cases, regardless of whether they were de jure or only de facto. The remedial power has remained limited to cases where the segregation was required by law or a result of purposeful intent that could be proved.[64] Therefore exercise of the *Green–Swann* remedial power has been largely confined to the southern states. The constitutional obligation to operate integrated systems has thus been one of regional rather than national application.[65] The pervasive school segregation found in major urban areas outside the South has been left all but untouched.[66] Even where purposeful intent may be found in a city with a black majority, such as Detroit, the remedy must be confined to the city itself even though it would not prove effective to secure the proper racial mix. Since the de jure element was lacking in the surrounding white suburbs, they might not be included in any desegregation plan.[67]

The holding that disproportionate effect upon racial minorities is not enough by itself to show a denial of equal protection[68] is also a logical extension of the Court's refusal to do away with the de jure–de facto distinction. The mere fact that black and white children are treated differently where there is de facto segregation does not prove a constitutional violation. The same is true when there is disparate impact without proof of discriminatory intent.

The decisions on affirmative action programs have also been logically consistent. The key decision here was, of course, that in *Bakke*.[69] Its "central meaning" was stated in Brennan's opinion: "Government may take race into account when it acts not to demean or insult any racial group, but to remedy disadvantages cast on minorities by past racial prejudice, at least when appropriate findings have been made by judicial, legislative, or administrative bodies with competence to act in this area."[70]

Powell had written to Brennan on June 23, 1978, "If your statement is read literally, I doubt that it does reflect accurately the judgment of the Court. In terms of 'judgment,' my opinion is limited to the holding that a state university validly may consider race to achieve diversity. . . . This holding could be stated more broadly in one simple sentence as follows: 'Government validly may take race into account in furthering the compelling state interest of achieving a diverse student body.'

"Despite the foregoing, I have not objected to your characterization of what the Court holds as I have thought you could put whatever 'gloss' on the several opinions you think proper." The Brennan statement thus appeared virtually without contradiction from the other Justices. The result has been that the Brennan version has been taken as the "central meaning" of *Bakke* by most commentators and has molded the post-*Bakke* law on the subject.

Bakke has consequently meant anything but the end of programs providing for racial preferences. On the contrary, the later Burger Court decisions built upon *Bakke* in dealing with such programs. Unless there was proof of purposeful discrimination or a legislative or administrative finding to that effect, race as the sole determining factor in employment decisions was ruled invalid, as it was in *Bakke* itself. But properly tailored affirmative action programs were upheld when they were entered into voluntarily by the parties or used in "remedying past or present racial discrimination by a state actor."[71] And the Court rejected the view that affirmative action plans must be limited to benefiting identifiable victims of past discrimination; preferential treatment may be given to minority members who had not themselves been victims of discrimination.

These cases also support the view that, except for *Swann*, Chief Justice Burger did not really attempt to lead the Court in its decisions in the racial-classification cases. And in that one case his efforts were rebuffed by the other Justices. He ultimately had to redraft his opinion (six drafts in all were necessary) so that it reflected the views of the majority, rather than his own restricted view of the scope of remedial power in segregation cases.

If anyone can be characterized as the Court's leader in the racial discrimination cases, it was Brennan. He was the Justice most active in ensuring that the *Swann* decision and opinion would be a resounding reaffirmance, and even extension, of the broad remedial power recognized in his own *Green* opinion. Brennan was also responsible for the broadest application of the de jure concept in *Keyes*, as well as the refusal in that case to do away with the de jure–de facto distinction. It is true that the Brennan view did not prevail in *Milliken;* yet the decision there was a logical consequence of the continued adherence to the de jure–de facto line.

But Justice Brennan's most significant victory was in the affirmative action cases. If not for Brennan, indeed, it is probable that the Burger Court would have ruled all racial preferences unconstitutional. He saw the opportunity to change the Powell unqualified vote against the Davis special admissions program to one that reversed the lower court's refusal to allow race to be considered at all in admission decisions. That, in turn, led the way to the *Bakke* decision that race may be considered as a factor, which, in turn, has permitted the continuance of affirmative action programs.

The racial cases show that it is mistaken to think of Brennan as engaged in only a holding action in the Burger Court—seeking only to preserve the essentials of the Warren Court jurisprudence against the Burger "counterrevolution." It was the Brennan lead, as much as anything, that molded the jurisprudence of the Burger Court, which went well beyond anything done by Chief Justice Warren and his colleagues in enforcing the organic ban against racial discrimination.

Chapter Ten

Fundamental Rights:
Equal Protection and Due Process

IN HIS February 8, 1973,[1] letter to Justice Powell on *San Antonio Independent School District v. Rodriguez*,[2] Justice Stewart asserted, "After much consideration, . . . I have decided I cannot subscribe to an opinion that accepts the 'doctrine' that there are two separate alternative tests under the Equal Protection Clause, and that the necessary first step in any equal protection case is to decide which test to apply, and therefore first to decide whether a 'fundamental interest' is affected."

Stewart was willing to apply a strict-scrutiny approach in cases involving a "suspect classification," but he was not willing to use the compelling-interest requirement in other cases. "I have become convinced . . . that the theory that there is a 'compelling state interest' test and a quite different 'rational basis' test under the Equal Protection Clause is wholly spurious and unsound, in the absence of a 'suspect' classification."

SHAPIRO V. THOMPSON

Stewart recognized, however, that the strict-scrutiny approach that he was rejecting had been followed by the Court in recent years. "I do not for a moment," Stewart wrote Powell, "criticize you for embracing this analysis. It is the analysis adopted by the district court in this case, the analysis briefed and argued before us, and the analysis that finds support in several of our recent cases."

It was in the Warren Court that the strict-scrutiny standard of review began to be applied, both in cases involving suspect classifications and fundamental rights. The landmark case in this respect was *Shapiro v. Thompson*.[3] In terms of legal impact, no Warren-Court decision was more far-reaching than *Shapiro*. For it articulated an approach that, in Justice Harlan's dissenting phrase, "creates an exception which threatens to swallow the standard equal protection rule."[4] More than that, the *Shapiro* approach has been applied in both due process and equal protection cases. This has meant what critics have contended amounts to a revival of the substantive due process jurisprudence practiced in what Stewart's letter called "the heyday of the Nine Old Men."

The Connecticut Welfare Department denied assistance to a woman under the Program for Aid to Families with Dependent Children. She had not lived in the state for a year, as required by Connecticut law. The lower court held the state residence requirement unconstitutional.

The case originally came before the Court during the 1967 Term. At the May 3, 1968, conference, Chief Justice Warren focused upon the Social Security Act, which permitted state statutes that "limited this particular kind of relief to residents of a year or more. . . . I can't see," he declared, "how I can say that the federal statute is unconstitutional." After the argument, the conference voted six to three to reverse and uphold the residence requirement. Chief Justice Warren took the opinion himself and circulated a draft opinion of the Court on June 3, 1968. The Warren draft rejected the claims that the residence requirement restricted the constitutional right to travel and that equal protection had been denied.

Most important, in view of the different approach ultimately followed by the Court in the case, Warren applied the "rational basis test" to the equal protection claim. Stricter review was required only "when the statutory classification is drawn along lines which are constitutionally impermissible or 'suspect,' . . . or when the classification is invidious or wholly arbitrary. . . . [T]here is nothing inherently suspect, arbitrary or invidious about the durational residence requirements challenged in these cases to warrant the application of the stricter equal protection test advanced by appellees."

A thirty-page draft dissent was circulated on June 13 by Justice Fortas that concluded that "the durational residence requirement is unconstitutional as an impermissible and unjustified burden on the right to travel." The Fortas draft dissent, like the Warren draft opinion of the Court employed the rational-basis test in its equal protection review. The constitutional guaranty, wrote Fortas, "insists upon reasonable defensible classifications and denies governmental power otherwise to distinguish between the treatment accorded citizens."[5]

After he had read the Fortas dissent Brennan told him that he was joining his opinion. At the next conference, on June 13, Justice Stewart refused to cast a vote. With Brennan's switch, that made for a four-to-four division. It was now almost the end of the term, and it was decided to set the case for reargument in the 1968 term.

At the conference after the reargument, Stewart was now in favor of affirmance. The new vote was five to three to strike down the residence requirement, with White passing. Brennan was assigned the opinion. Despite the closeness of the vote he wrote a broad opinion expanding the scope of judicial review in equal protection cases. Brennan adopted the compelling-interest test as the review standard. Since the classification between new and old residents served to penalize the exercise of the fundamental right to interstate travel, it had to be justified by a compelling governmental interest. This extended the compelling-interest standard to cases involving "fundamental rights," such as the right to travel.

The Brennan opinion striking down the residence requirement under the compelling-interest test won the speedy agreement of Douglas, Marshall, Fortas, and Stewart. But then Stewart expressed hesitation about the compelling-interest analysis to Brennan, saying that the case should be decided on the traditional rational-basis standard of equal protection. Stewart told Brennan that "we should reserve the compelling interest approach for cases involving the First Amendment or racial discrimination." Brennan answered this in a memo: "[F]reedom of *interstate* movement is as fundamental as first amendment freedoms. Freedom of speech is at the core of our concept of a free society; freedom of interstate movement is at the core of our concept of a Federal *Union*. They are essentially the same kind of right—they provide the basis for our whole system of economic, social and political interchange. Furthermore, both are rights which are particularly vulnerable to restrictive legislation, since with each we cannot satisfactorily identify the group which may be chilled in the exercise of the right."

A few days later, Stewart told Brennan that he had been mistaken, and he now agreed that the compelling-interest analysis was appropriate because the right of interstate travel was a constitutional right. White also joined the Brennan opinion—making the final vote six to three.

The use of the compelling-interest test in *Shapiro v. Thompson* was entirely Brennan's handiwork. It illustrates once again Brennan's key role in fashioning the jurisprudence of both the Warren and Burger Courts. Even more important was *Shapiro*'s extension of strict-scrutiny review to cases involving fundamental rights—crucial to the expansion of review power that occurred under the Burger Court. It may be doubted that a decision like *Roe v. Wade*[6] would have been handed down had *Shapiro v. Thompson* not laid the doctrinal foundation. From this point of view, it is of fundamental importance that the draft opinion of the Court by Chief Justice Warren did not come down as the final *Shapiro* opinion. If it had, the rational-basis test would have been confirmed as the standard of review in equal protection cases in a case where the fundamental right of interstate movement was involved. The compelling-interest test would not have become "an increasingly significant exception to the long-established rule that a statute does not deny equal protection if it is rationally related to a legitimate governmental objective."[7] Nor would the test have encroached upon the due process area as it did in *Roe v. Wade*. Some of the most controversial Burger Court decisions might never have been made.

OTHER FUNDAMENTAL RIGHTS

Justice Harlan delivered a strong *Shapiro* dissent, calling "this branch of the 'compelling interest' doctrine particularly unfortunate and unnecessary."[8] The compelling interest approach could take over the major part of equal protection jurisprudence. Harlan referred to the cases applying "the traditional equal protection standard . . . to statutory classifications affecting such fundamental matters as the right to pursue a particular occupation, the right to receive greater or smaller wages or to work more or less hours, and the right to inherit property."[9]

"Rights such as these are in principle indistinguishable from those involved here, and to extend the 'compelling interest' rule to all cases in which such rights are affected would go far toward making this Court a 'super-legislature.'"[10]

Certainly, an expansive view of the fundamental rights protected by the compelling-interest test would go far to support the Harlan animadversion. But the Burger Court did not take the expansive approach. Instead it limited itself to the main strands of fundamental-rights analysis that had become established in the Warren Court and, even with regard to them, it tended to assume a narrower posture.

The Warren Court had used the compelling-interest standard in reviewing classifications that restricted the following fundamental rights: (1) the right to vote;[11] (2) the right of access to the judicial process;[12] and (3) the right to travel involved in *Shapiro v. Thompson*. In cases involving those three fundamental rights, the Burger Court also employed the strict-scrutiny standard in reviewing the challenged laws.

The Burger Court cases declare flatly that the right to vote is a fundamental right.[13] Hence, "burdens on the right to vote . . . are constitutionally suspect and invalid . . . under the Equal Protection Clause unless essential to serve a compelling state interest."[14] Using the strict-scrutiny standard, the Court invalidated various restrictions on the franchise and on the correlative right to become a candidate.[15]

The right of access to the courts was also treated as a fundamental right for purposes of equal protection analysis. The key case here was *Boddie v. Connecticut*.[16] The Court held it unconstitutional for a state to deny indigents the right to bring divorce proceedings because they could not pay court fees or the cost of service of process. As Brennan put it, "A State may not make its judicial processes available to some but deny them to others simply because they cannot pay a fee."[17]

The Burger Court continued to follow the *Shapiro v. Thompson* approach and treat the right to travel as a fundamental right with its corollary of strict-scrutiny review. In *Memorial Hospital v. Maricopa County*,[18] for example, one-year residence in a county as a condition for receiving nonemergency hospitalization or medical care at the county's expense was invalidated. The residence requirement penalized persons who exercised their right to engage in interstate travel "by denying newcomers 'basic necessities of life.'" As such, it "must be justified by a compelling state interest." Fiscal integrity or administrative efficiency were found not sufficient enough to meet this "heavy burden of justification."[19]

To a limited extent, the Burger Court expanded the strict-scrutiny approach to fundamental rights in equal protection cases. Thus it applied strict scrutiny to infringements upon the right to marry or to dissolve that relationship. Though not expressly articulated, the *Boddie* decision[20] turned, in part, upon the state law's infringement upon this fundamental right. Without access to the state courts, petitioner was completely barred from exercising his right to dissolve his marriage.

In *Zablocki v. Redhail*,[21] the Court struck down a state law that imposed a direct restriction upon the right to marry. Any resident having minor issue not in his custody but whom he was required to support might not marry without court permission, which could be granted only upon a showing that the support order had been met and that the children were not likely to become public charges.

In the postargument *Zablocki* conference, a good part of the discussion was devoted to whether the federal courts should abstain and give the state courts the initial opportunity to deal with the constitutional claim. Except for the Chief Justice, all the Justices agreed that abstention was not required and that issue was disposed of briefly in a *Zablocki* footnote.[22] On the merits, all except Rehnquist voted against the challenged law. But they were divided on whether the decision should be based upon due process or equal protection. White urged, "Substantive due process is the rationale." But the others agreed with Justice Blackmun, who stated, "I prefer equal protection to substantive due process."

All but Rehnquist agreed that equal protection was violated. "The state," said Stewart, "can prohibit all sorts of people from getting married." He gave as examples laws covering "consanguinity, [those] already married, age, etc." "But," Stewart concluded, "there is a limit and this exceeds it." Powell declared that the statutory classification "flunks the means–end test. . . . [The state] can deal with this problem by other means and, in that sense, it's irrational." The statute was really an attempt to ensure the enforcement of support orders and that could not be done through the restriction upon the right to marry. It was, to Stevens, "too questionable that this kind of collection device is permissible." Even Rehnquist called the law "screwy."

The conference notes used by me do not indicate any discussion of the review standard, which was, however, dealt with in Marshall's opinion of the Court striking down the law. "Since . . . the right to marry is of fundamental importance and since the classification at issue here significantly interferes with the exercise of that right, we believe that 'critical examination' of the state interests advanced in support of the classification is required."[23] Though the Court found that there were "legitimate and substantial [state] interests,"[24] the means selected for achieving those interests were held to impinge unnecessarily upon the fundamental right to marry.

The Burger Court followed its predecessor in treating the right to vote, of access to the courts, and to travel as fundamental rights triggering strict-scrutiny review, and even extended the fundamental-rights concept in *Zablocki v. Redhail*. But it also narrowed the rights protected as fundamental by the Warren Court. In *Ross v. Moffitt*[25] it refused to extend the holding that there was a right to court-appointed appellate counsel beyond the first appeal given by state law. Similarly, the Court declined to follow *Boddie v. Connecticut*[26] in cases that seemed to involve comparable fee restrictions on access to judicial remedies.

In *United States v. Kras,*[27] a law requiring a $50 filing fee to obtain a discharge in bankruptcy was upheld under the rational-basis test. The Court distinguished *Boddie* on the ground that access to the courts was absolutely essential to exercise the fundamental right to dissolve the marriage relationship. Elimination of the debt burden did not rise to the same constitutional level. Thus, strict scrutiny over restrictions on the right of access to the courts was limited to restrictions on access in order to protect fundamental rights. "There is no constitutional right to obtain a discharge of one's debts in bankruptcy."[28]

There are also Burger Court decisions that appear to take a narrow approach to the right to vote and to travel, upholding laws that do not appear supported by the "compelling interest" required to abridge those rights.[29] However, despite these cases and cases like *Kras,* the overall Burger Court theme in the equal protection field was recognition of the fundamental rights recognized by the Warren Court and application of the strict-scrutiny standard in cases involving classifications restricting them. At the same time, except for a case like *Zablocki v. Redhail,* the Burger Court refused to extend the fundamental-rights approach beyond those rights recognized as fundamental by its predecessor.

ENTITLEMENTS: DRAWING THE LINE AGAIN

One of the most important accomplishments of the Burger Court was its rejection of "the wooden distinction between 'rights' and 'privileges'"[30] that had been of crucial importance in administrative law.[31] The Court did so by developing the concept of "entitlements." Even though there is no preexisting right to a particular governmental benefit, if a statute provides for dispensation of the benefit those who meet the statutory conditions have an entitlement to it. Thus welfare recipients had an entitlement to their welfare payments (where the payments were provided to those coming within the conditions laid down by the legislature[32]) and students had an entitlement to their education (where the state had undertaken to provide an educational system[33]).

The Burger Justices held that such entitlements were protected by procedural due process; hence they might not be terminated without notice and hearing, including the essential procedural protections developed in our administrative law. Yet they refused to treat the entitlements as fundamental rights which triggered strict scrutiny in equal protection cases. The key cases here are *Dandridge v. Williams*[34] and *San Antonio Independent School District v. Rodriguez,*[35] which have already been discussed for their refusal to treat classifications based on wealth as suspect classifications.[36]

Dandridge declined to find that there was any fundamental right to welfare payments. The welfare recipients had argued that their "fundamental rights" were infringed by the maximum-grant regulation at issue in the case. The Court rejected the argument, adopting instead what Marshall's dissent termed "equal protection analysis . . . on the basis of a closed category of 'fundamental rights.'"[37] The majority recognized that "The Constitution may impose certain procedural safeguards upon systems of welfare administration."[38] This did not mean that there was a "fundamental right" to welfare. Since the plaintiffs' fundamental rights had not been violated, review was governed by the rational-basis test.

The most important case drawing the line between fundamental rights and other rights and refusing to treat entitlements as fundamental rights was the *San Antonio* case. As seen previously, it arose out of a challenge to the financing of public school education by the property tax, on the ground that equal protection was denied to children in districts having a low tax base. The lower court had subjected the challenged law to strict scrutiny, holding that there was a fundamental right to education, because of the "crucial nature of education for the citizenry."[39]

The discussion at the postargument *San Antonio* conference resulted in the same five-to-four vote to uphold the school financing system that ultimately decided the case. Several of the majority Justices stressed the far-reaching impact of a decision the other way. As the Chief Justice put it, the district court, which had invalidated the financing scheme, "has overhauled the whole fiscal and taxation structure of the state." Powell was even more emphatic, asserting, "The position of the district court would necessitate a complete restructuring of local and state government, particularly taxation."

Several Justices questioned the direct relationship between the amounts spent and the quality of education. "The basic premise," stated Chief Justice Burger, "is that the amount of dollars available determines the quality of education—that education can't be a function of wealth. . . . I don't see any thoughtful analysis here." He also doubted that one could "equate equal advantages with equal protection as exactly the same." Two of the dissenters expressed the same doubt. "Money alone doesn't answer this," stated Douglas. Similarly, Justice White said that he thought that "inequality of input of dollars would not alone make a case." Blackmun went further, declaring, "I don't think we can effectively legislate quality education."

The most important conference statement on the standard of review was made by Powell, who wrote the *San Antonio* opinion. "Education is not a fundamental interest requiring application of the compelling-interest test."

The opinion of the Court followed the same approach. Strict scrutiny is required where a law "operates to the disadvantage of some suspect class or impinges upon a fundamental right explicitly or implicitly protected by the Constitution."[40] The *San Antonio* Court refused to find that, even if the challenged classification turned upon wealth, it was suspect. But the Court also found that no fundamental right was implicated in the case.

The question on the latter issue was "whether education is a fundamental right, in the sense that it is among the rights and liberties protected by the Constitution." The Court stressed that its role in this area must be borne in mind: "It is not the province of this Court to create substantive constitutional rights in the name of guaranteeing equal protection of the laws." Thus the key to discovering whether education is "fundamental" is not to be found in the relative societal significance of education—as by weighing whether education is as important as the right to travel. "Rather, the answer lies in assessing whether there is a right to education explicitly or implicitly guaranteed by the Constitution."[41]

Education is not among the rights expressly protected by the Constitution. Nor is there "any basis for saying it is implicitly so protected."[42] Even if education is essential to effective exercise of First Amendment freedoms and the right to vote, there is no indication that the present levels of educational expenditure fall short of providing for meaningful exercise of those rights. Instead, as Blackmun expressed it at the conference, the Court should "review on the assumption that the Texas scheme provides basic minimum education."

Only a constitutional right comes within the fundamental-right concept for purposes of Equal Protection analysis. Since no one has a constitutional right to education,[43] infringements upon that right are reviewable only under "the usual standard for reviewing a State's usual social and economic legislation"[44]—that is, the rational-basis test.

What the *San Antonio* drawing of the line means is that only rights protected by the Constitution itself are protected by strict-scrutiny review. This narrow approach loses sight of the fact that the concept of "rights" has expanded drastically. Thus, the entitlements to welfare and education are plainly not "rights" recognized by the Constitution. Yet the Burger Court decisions themselves acknowledge that these entitlements are "today . . . more like 'property' than a 'gratuity.'"[45] Those meeting the relevant statutory conditions are *entitled* to the benefits; hence they have at least a statutory right to them.

Since the Burger Court has held that these "rights" are protected by procedural due process, it is anomalous to hold that they are not "fundamental" rights. There is a suggestive analogy in the jurisprudence of the California Supreme Court that the Burger Court might well have followed. The normal rule in our administrative law is that judicial review of administrative decisions is a limited one, intended essentially to ensure that those decisions are reasonable.[46] The California court has, however, ruled that this version of the rational-basis test gives way in cases where the challenged administrative decision "substantially affects a fundamental vested right."[47] In such a case there is to be full review, with the reviewing court exercising its independent judgment on the weight of the evidence.

The California court has held that, for purposes of such broad review, a right may be "fundamental" even if it is not a constitutional right. The standard used when determining which rights are "fundamental" for administrative-review purposes is whether the right or interest at stake "is important enough 'to individuals in their life situations' to require an independent judicial review."[48] The California courts have decided that fundamental rights are involved in death benefits,[49] disability payments,[50] and welfare benefits.[51] Thus the California concept of fundamental rights includes mere economic benefits; as such, it is as broad as the concept of "entitlements" developed by the Burger Court itself.

The California concept of fundamental (even if not constitutional) rights is thus of an encroaching nature.[52] The same is plainly not true of the Burger Court's notion of fundamental rights for purposes of strict scrutiny in equal protection cases. That notion was essentially limited to the rights deemed fundamental by the Warren Court. Cases like *Dandridge* and *San Antonio* draw the line at those rights and refuse to extend strict scrutiny to rights not protected by the Constitution—which, of course, includes the statutory rights that come within the Burger Court's own entitlement concept. As far as those rights were concerned, review was conducted only under the rational-basis test, which meant that classifications which impinged upon them were almost always upheld by the Burger Court.

FUNDAMENTAL RIGHTS AND DUE PROCESS

We now come to an area of constitutional law where the Burger Court was even more activist than its predecessor. The Warren Court had subjected laws impinging upon fundamental rights to strict scrutiny when they were challenged under the Equal Protection Clause. Yet the Court's approach was also subject to expansion; it might be applied to other constitutional challenges, particularly those made under the Due Process Clause.

The potential for expansion here may be seen from the Warren Court's 1967 decision in *Loving v. Virginia*.[53] Loving was white; his wife was black. They were convicted of violating the Virginia miscegenation law. The highest state court affirmed.

The Justices agreed without dispute that the constitutional time had come for state miscegenation laws. Chief Justice Warren assigned the opinion to himself, thinking that the Chief Justice should take responsibility for a decision that would offend many Southerners. Virginia had argued that the statute was not discriminatory, since it applied equally to whites and blacks. Warren considered this argument nonsense; the law had been passed to ensure white supremacy, and the legislative history showed that. Warren told Benno Schmidt, the law clerk who was drafting the opinion, to emphasize that point.[54]

Schmidt tells how, when Warren read over the *Loving* draft, he saw that the 1923 case of *Meyer v. Nebraska*[55] was cited to show that there were fundamental freedoms connected with the family that the states could not restrict. Warren chuckled and said that *Meyer* had been written by Justice McReynolds back in the heyday of substantive due process and had been singled out by Justice Black as an example of the "old" Court's acting without any basis in the constitutional text. Citing *Meyer* would be like waving a red flag in front of Black. Despite this, he left the *Meyer* cite in, and Black let it pass.

Black's hackles were, however, raised by something else. The Chief Justice stressed that the statute was dealing with a major aspect of the individual's life—whom to marry. As Schmidt recalls, "Justice Black blew up because we were referring to the right to marry, which is nowhere mentioned in the Constitution. . . . [H]e didn't want any sort of natural law notion creeping into the opinion."[56] Warren toned down the right to marry language, and Black withdrew his objection.

The *Loving* opinion shows the interrelationship between equal protection and due process review. Since the miscegenation law was based upon a suspect classification, it had to "be subjected to the 'most rigid scrutiny.'"[57] But the Warren opinion stressed that the freedom to marry was a "fundamental freedom"[58] and the Virginia law violated due process. The state could not restrict the fundamental right without compelling reasons.[59] The implication was that restrictions of fundamental rights were to be subjected to strict scrutiny when they were challenged under the Due Process Clause.

It was in *Shapiro v. Thompson*[60] that the Warren Court adopted the "fundamental rights" branch of the strict-scrutiny standard under the Equal Protection Clause. Harlan, who dissented, asserted, "This branch of the doctrine is also unnecessary. When the right affected is one assured by the Federal Constitution, any infringement can be dealt with under the Due Process Clause."[61]

Harlan was given the opportunity to apply his approach when he was assigned the opinion in *Boddie v. Connecticut.*[62] We have already discussed *Boddie* as an equal protection case,[63] but the Harlan opinion disposed of the case upon due process grounds. The Due Process Clause requires that access to the courts to obtain a divorce "may not be placed beyond the reach of any individual. . . . [T]his right is the exclusive precondition to the adjustment of a fundamental human relationship."[64] Once again, the implication is that the law restricting the fundamental interest is subject to strict scrutiny, even when the law is challenged on due process rather than equal protection grounds.

In the Burger Court, this implication became accepted doctrine. In his dissent in *Roe v. Wade,* Rehnquist referred to the compelling interest test used in review of classifications infringing upon fundamental rights. "But the Court adds a new wrinkle to this test by transposing it from the legal considerations associated with the Equal Protection Clause of the Fourteenth Amendment to this case arising under the Due Process Clause of the Fourteenth Amendment."[65] The privacy cases, culminating in *Roe v. Wade* itself, best illustrate the Court jurisprudence in this respect.

GRISWOLD AND PRIVACY

Roe v. Wade[66] is, in many ways, the paradigmatic Burger Court case. It is clearly the most controversial decision rendered by that Court, and no Court decision has been more bitterly attacked. "It is hard to think of any decision in the two hundred years of our history," declared Cardinal Krol, the President of the National Conference of Catholic Bishops, "which has had more disastrous implications for our stability as a civilized society."[67] Condemnatory letters were sent to the Justices in unprecedented volume, particularly to Blackmun, the author of the opinion. Antiabortion pickets continue to show up at his speeches.[68]

The right of privacy is the fundamental right upon which the *Roe* decision was based. It is most unlikely that the men who drew up the Constitution and the Bill of Rights intended to confer, as against government, a right of privacy in the sense in which that term is used today. But there are indications that the Founders did intend to include within the sphere of constitutional protection matters that the present-day observer would classify as coming under an overall right of privacy. The Framers first recognized the right of privacy in the Fourth Amendment's prohibition against unreasonable searches and seizures.

The Fourth Amendment conception of privacy was, nevertheless, rudimentary compared to the right of privacy recognized in our law during the past quarter century. The Framers could think of a sphere peculiar to the individual in his home, his papers, his effects—a sphere that the Bill of Rights rendered immune from governmental encroachment. But the right to privacy in its present-day constitutional connotations is nothing less than the right of the individual to be protected from any wrongful intrusion into his private life.[69] "Liberty in the constitutional sense must mean more than freedom from unlawful governmental restraint; it must include privacy as well, if it is to be a repository of freedom. The right to be let alone is indeed the beginning of all freedoms."[70]

When Warren and Brandeis wrote their seminal 1890 article first asserting a legal right of privacy,[71] the great need was to protect the privacy of the individual against intrusions by other private individuals, particularly the press. That need has certainly not diminished in an age in which excesses in prying have become more or less commonplace. But important though the right of privacy vis-à-vis other private individuals has become, it is overshadowed by the overriding necessity to protect privacy against both society and government.

It was the Warren Court that first recognized the right to privacy as a basic constitutional right, "no less important than any other right carefully and particularly reserved to the people."[72] *Griswold v. Connecticut*,[73] decided in 1965, was the first case confirming the existence of a broad right of privacy against government. And the right is a constitutional one, unlike that advocated in the Warren–Brandeis article and since accepted by the law as a right enforced by the private law of torts. As Black put it, *Griswold* elevated "a phrase which Warren and Brandeis used in discussing grounds for tort relief, to the level of a constitutional rule which prevents state legislatures from passing any law deemed by this Court to interfere with 'privacy.'"[74]

A Connecticut law prohibited the use of contraceptive devices and the giving of medical advice in their use. Griswold was the director of the Planned Parenthood League and Dr. Buxton was the medical director of the League's New Haven Center. They gave advice to married persons on preventing conception and prescribed contraceptive devices for the wives. They were convicted of violating the birth control law, and their conviction was affirmed by the state's highest court.

The *Griswold* conference found a seven-to-two majority in favor of striking down the Connecticut law, but the majority Justices did not articulate a clear theory on which to base the decision. Justice Douglas stated the simplest rationale. The law violated the defendant's First Amendment right of association, which was more than a right of assembly. Thus, he reasoned, the right to send a child to a religious school was "on the periphery" of the right of association. He cited the *Pierce* case.[75] He also used the analogy of the right to travel, which the Court had said "is in radiation of First Amendment and so is this right." There was nothing more personal than this right and it too was "on the periphery" and within First Amendment protection.

Black was the strongest conference opponent of this Douglas approach. "The right of association is for me a right of assembly and the right of the husband and wife to assemble in bed is a new right of assembly for me."

Only Stewart supported Black's view. He stated that he could not "find anything [against this law] in the First, Second, Fourth, Fifth, Ninth or other Amendments. So I'd have to affirm." The others agreed that the law should be ruled unconstitutional, but differed in their reasoning. Clark declared, "There's a right to marry, maintain a home, have a family. This is in an area where we have the right to be let alone." Goldberg said that "the state cannot regulate this relationship. There's no compelling state reason in that circumstance justifying the statute."

Chief Justice Warren assigned the opinion to Justice Douglas, who had expressed the clearest theory upon which the Connecticut law might be invalidated. Douglas quickly prepared a draft opinion. The draft based the decision on the First Amendment, likening the husband–wife relationship to the forms of association given First Amendment protection. The draft did not mention, much less rely upon, a constitutional right of privacy, and had the draft come down as the *Griswold* opinion, the right of privacy might never have been recognized as a constitutional right by the Warren Court.

The Douglas draft was changed because of an April 24, 1965, letter from Brennan. He wrote that the "association" of married couples had little to do with the advocacy protected by the First Amendment and urged that the *Griswold* decision be based upon the right of privacy. He suggested that the expansion of the First Amendment to include freedom of association be used as an analogy to justify a similar approach in the area of privacy. The final *Griswold* opinion of the Court stated that the "specific guarantees in the Bill of Rights have penumbras, formed by emanations from those guarantees that help give them life and substance." A constitutional right of privacy was included in these penumbras. The right of marital privacy—"older than the Bill of Rights—older than our political parties, older than our school system" [76]—was violated by the Connecticut law.

Griswold holds squarely that the Bill of Rights does establish a constitutionally protected zone of privacy. This *Griswold*-created right has served as the foundation for some of the most controversial Burger Court decisions. By 1977, the Court could state, "*Griswold* may no longer be read as holding only that a State may not prohibit a married couple's use of contraceptives." [77] The right of privacy recognized in *Griswold* is not one that inheres only in the marital relationship. Instead, "If the right of privacy means anything, it is the right of the *individual*, married or single, to be free from unwarranted governmental intrusion into matters so fundamentally affecting a person." [78]

The *Griswold* decision process shows once again the key role played by Justice Brennan in both the Warren and Burger Courts. The change in the Douglas opinion, from the draft relying on freedom of association to the circulated draft and final *Griswold* opinion establishing a Bill of Rights—created "regime of privacy," was of fundamental significance.

ROE V. WADE: CONFERENCE AND ASSIGNMENT

During the *Griswold* conference Chief Justice Warren had stated that he could not say that the state had no legitimate interest, noting that that could apply to abortion laws—implying that he thought such laws were valid. Those who expected the Burger Court to be less activist than its predecessor relied upon false hopes. It was under Chief Justice Burger that the right of privacy was extended to include the right to an abortion. As Burger put it, "This is as sensitive and difficult an issue as any in this Court in my time." [79]

Roe v. Wade[80] came before the Court with a companion case, *Doe v. Bolton*.[81] In both cases, pregnant women sought relief against state abortion laws, contending that they were unconstitutional. At issue in *Roe* was a Texas statute that prohibited abortions except to save the mother's life. The statute in *Doe* was a Georgia law that proscribed an abortion except as performed by a physician who felt, in "his best clinical judgment," that continued pregnancy would endanger a woman's life or injure her health; the fetus would likely be born with a serious defect; or the pregnancy resulted from rape. In addition, the Georgia statutory scheme posed three procedural conditions: (1) that the abortion be performed in an accredited hospital; (2) that the procedure be approved by the hospital staff abortion committee; and (3) that the performing physician's judgment be confirmed by independent examinations by two other physicians.

The final *Roe v. Wade* opinion contrasted the Texas and Georgia statutes as follows: "The Texas statutes under attack here are typical of those that have been in effect in many States for approximately a century. The Georgia statutes, in contrast, have a modern cast and are a legislative product that, to an extent at least, obviously reflects the influences of recent attitudinal change, of advancing medical knowledge and techniques, and of new thinking about an old issue."[82]

Roe v. Wade and *Doe v. Bolton* were both discussed at the same postargument conference in December 1971. The Chief Justice devoted much of his *Roe v. Wade* discussion to the question of standing. On the merits, Burger said, "The balance here is between the state's interest in protecting fetal life and the woman's interest in not having children." In weighing these interests, the Chief Justice concluded, "I can't find the Texas statute unconstitutional, although it's certainly archaic and obsolete."

Douglas, who spoke next, declared categorically, "The abortion statute is unconstitutional. This is basically a medical and psychiatric problem"—and not only to be dealt with by prohibitory legislation. Douglas also criticized the statute's failure to give "a licensed physician an immunity for good faith abortions." Brennan, who followed, stressed even more strongly the right to an abortion, which should be given a constitutional basis by the Court's decision.

Stewart, next in order of seniority, stated, "I agree with Bill Douglas." He did, however, indicate that there might be some state power. "The state can legislate, to the extent of requiring a doctor and that, after a certain period of pregnancy, [she] can't have an abortion."

White said, "On the merits I am on the other side. They want us to say that women have a choice under the Ninth Amendment." White said that he refused to accept this "privacy argument." Marshall, on the other hand, declared, "I go with Bill Douglas, but the time problem concerns me." He thought that the state could not prevent abortions "in the early stage [of pregnancy]. But why can't the state prohibit after a certain stage?" In addition, Marshall said that he would use "liberty" under the Fourteenth Amendment as the constitutional base."

Blackmun, then the junior Justice, spoke last. Blackmun displayed an ambivalence that was to be reflected in his draft *Roe v. Wade* opinion. "Can a state properly outlaw all abortions? If we accept fetal life, there's a strong argument that it can. But there are opposing interests: the right of the mother to life and mental and physical health, the right of parents in case of rape, the right of the state in case of incest. I don't think there's an absolute right to do what you will with [your] body." Blackmun did, however, say flatly, "This statute is a poor statute that . . . impinges too far on her."

The discussion of *Doe v. Bolton* paralleled that in *Roe v. Wade*. The Chief Justice asserted, "I do not agree with this carving up of the statute by the three-judge court. . . . The state has a duty to protect fetal life at some stage, but we are not confronted with that question here. . . . I would hold this statute constitutional."

The Georgia statute "is a much better statute than Texas," Justice Douglas declared. But he had doubts on the statute's practical effects. "We don't know how this statute operates. Is it weighted on the side of only those who can afford this? What about the poor?" Douglas said that he was inclined "to remand to the district court to find out."

Brennan had no doubts. He would affirm the decision below "as far as it goes" but would also "go further to strike down the three-doctor thing as too restrictive." Stewart agreed with the last point. But Justice White again spoke in favor of the state. As he saw it, "The state has power to protect the unborn child. This plaintiff didn't have trouble [taking] advantage of procedures. I think the state has struck the right balance here."

Once again Blackmun's position was ambivalent. "Medically," he pointed out, "this statute is perfectly workable," but he emphasized the competing interests at stake. "I would like to see an opinion that recognizes the opposing interests in fetal life and the mother's interest in health and happiness." Blackmun also indicated interest in Douglas's approach. "I would be perfectly willing to paint some standards and remand for findings as to how it operates: does it operate to deny equal protection by discriminating against the poor?"

The conference outcome was not entirely clear; the tally sheets of different Justices do not coincide.[83] What was clear, however, was that a majority were in favor of invalidating the laws: in *Roe v. Wade*, it was five (Douglas, Brennan, Stewart, Marshall, and Blackmun) to two (the Chief Justice and Justice White) according to one tally sheet, and four to three (with Blackmun added to the dissenters) according to a December 18, 1971, Douglas letter to the Chief Justice. Despite the fact that he was not part of the majority, Chief Justice Burger assigned the opinions to Blackmun.

Though the majority may have disapproved of the Burger assignment, only Douglas (whose tally sheet showed four votes for invalidating the laws, with himself as senior Justice in the majority) protested, in his December 18 "Dear Chief" letter: "As respects your assignment in this case, my notes show there were four votes to hold parts of the . . . Act unconstitutional. . . . There were three to sustain the law as written. I would think, therefore, that to save future time and trouble, one of the four, rather than one of the three, should write the opinion."

The Chief Justice replied with a December 20 "Dear Bill" letter. "At the close of the discussion of this case I remarked to the Conference that there were, literally, not enough columns to mark up an accurate reflection of the voting in either the Georgia or the Texas cases. I therefore marked down no votes and said this was a case that would have to stand or fall on the writing, when it was done. That is still my view of how to handle these two . . . sensitive cases, which, I might add, are quite probably candidates for reargument."

According to a *Washington Post* report, Douglas sent his letter "asserting his prerogative to assign the case, but Burger held fast to his position."[84] Douglas and Brennan, who had led the proabortion bloc at the conference, decided to wait to see the Blackmun drafts before doing anything further. Though Douglas had tallied Blackmun with the minority, others had noted his vote with the majority. This might well mean Blackmun opinions agreeable to Douglas and Brennan, and make either a confrontation with the Chief Justice or a separate majority draft unnecessary.

ROE V. WADE: BLACKMUN DRAFT

Justice Blackmun has termed *Roe v. Wade* "a landmark in the progress of the emancipation of women."[85] That could hardly have been said had his original draft become the final opinion of the Court. The draft did strike down the abortion statute, but it did so on the ground of vagueness—not because it restricted a woman's right to have an abortion. The draft expressly avoided the issue of the state's substantive right to prohibit abortions or "imply that a State has no legitimate interest in the subject of abortions or that abortion procedures may not be subject to control by the State."[86]

The abortion opinion had been assigned in December 1971. Blackmun was the slowest worker on the Court, and the abortion cases were his first major assignment. He worked at them mostly alone.

Finally, on May 18, 1972, Blackmun sent around his draft *Roe v. Wade* opinion. "Herewith," began the covering memo, "is a first and tentative draft for this case. . . . [I]t may be somewhat difficult to obtain a consensus on all aspects. My notes indicate, however, that we were generally in agreement to affirm on the merits. That is where I come out on the theory that the Texas statute, despite its narrowness, is unconstitutionally vague.

"I think that this would be all that is necessary for disposition of the case, and that we need not get into the more complex Ninth Amendment issue. This may or may not appeal to you. . . . I am still flexible as to results, and I shall do my best to arrive at something which would command a court."

In *United States v. Vuitch*,[87] decided the year before, the Court had upheld a similar District of Columbia abortion law against a vagueness attack. The Blackmun draft distinguished *Vuitch* on the ground that the statute there prohibited abortion unless "necessary for the preservation of the mother's life or health," while the Texas statute only permitted abortions "for the purpose of saving the life of the mother." Thus *Vuitch* "provides no answer to the constitutional challenge to the Texas statute."

In the Texas statute, "Saving the mother's life is the sole standard." This standard is too vague to guide physicians' conduct in abortion cases. "Does it mean that he may procure an abortion only when, without it, the patient will surely die? Or only when the odds are greater than even that she will die? Or when there is a mere possibility that she will not survive?"

"We conclude that Art. 1196, with its sole criterion for exemption as 'saving the life of the mother,' is insufficiently informative to the physician to whom it purports to afford a measure of professional protection but who must measure its indefinite meaning at the risk of his liberty, and that the statute cannot withstand constitutional challenge on vagueness grounds."

Blackmun's vagueness analysis was extremely weak. If anything, the "life saving" standard in the *Roe v. Wade* statute was more definite than the "health" standard upheld in *Vuitch*. But the draft's disposition of the case on vagueness enabled it to avoid the basic constitutional question. As the Blackmun draft stated, "There is no need in Roe's case to pass upon her contention that under the Ninth Amendment a pregnant woman has an absolute right to an abortion, or even to consider the opposing rights of the embryo or fetus during the respective prenatal trimesters."

Indeed, so far as the draft contained intimations on the matter, they tended to support state substantive power over abortions. "Our holding today does not imply that a State has no legitimate interest in the subject of abortions or that abortion procedures may not be subjected to control by the State. . . . We do not accept the argument of the appellants and of some of the amici that a pregnant woman has an unlimited right to do with her body as she pleases. The long acceptance of statutes regulating the possession of certain drugs and other harmful substances, and making criminal indecent exposure in public, or an attempt at suicide, clearly indicate the contrary." This was, of course, completely different from the approach ultimately followed in the *Roe v. Wade* opinion of the Court.

The *Roe v. Wade* draft did not deal at all with the right of privacy. It was, however, discussed in Blackmun's *Doe v. Bolton* draft, which he circulated on May 25, 1972. As summarized in the covering memo, his draft "would accomplish . . . the striking of the Georgia statutory requirements as to (1) residence, (2) confirmation by two physicians, (3) advance approval by the hospital abortion committee, and (4) performance of the procedure only in [an] accredited hospital."

Blackmun's *Doe* draft[88] dealt specifically with the claim that the law was an "invalid restriction of an absolute fundamental right to personal and marital privacy. . . . The Court, in varying contexts, has recognized a right of personal privacy and has rooted it in the Fourteenth Amendment, or in the Bill of Rights, or in the latter's penumbras." The draft flatly rejected the assertion "that the scope of this right of personal privacy includes, for a woman, the right to decide unilaterally to terminate an existing but *unwanted* pregnancy without any state interference or control whatsoever." As the draft put it, "Appellants' contention, however, that the woman's right to make the decision is absolute—that Georgia has either no valid interest in regulating it, or no interest strong enough to support any limitation upon the woman's sole determination—is unpersuasive."

The draft rejected as "unfair and illogical" the argument that "the State's present professed interest in the protection of embryonic and fetal 'life' is somehow to be downgraded. That argument condemns the State for past 'wrongs' and also denies it the right to readjust its views and emphases in the light of the more advanced knowledge and techniques of today."

The *Doe* draft, utterly unlike the final Blackmun opinions, stressed the countervailing interest in fetal life. "The heart of the matter is that somewhere, either forthwith at conception, or at 'quickening,' or at birth, or at some other point in between, another being becomes involved and the privacy the woman possessed has become dual rather than sole. The woman's right of privacy must be measured accordingly." That being the case, "The woman's personal right . . . , is not unlimited. It must be balanced against the State's interest." Hence, "we cannot automatically strike down the remaining features of the Georgia statute simply because they restrict any right on the part of the woman to have an abortion at will."

The implication here was that substantial state power over abortion existed. Under the *Doe* draft, as the Blackmun covering memo pointed out, the state may provide "that an abortion may be performed only if the attending physician deems it necessary 'based upon his best clinical judgment,' if his judgment is reduced to writing, and if the abortion is performed in a hospital licensed by the State through its Board of Health." This was, of course, wholly inconsistent with the Court's final decision in *Roe v. Wade*.

ROE V. WADE: REARGUMENT AND SECOND CONFERENCE

It soon became apparent that the Blackmun drafts were not going to receive the five-Justice imprimatur needed to transform them into Court opinions. On May 18 and 19, 1972, Brennan and Douglas sent "Dear Harry" letters urging, in Brennan's words, "a disposition of the core constitutional question. Your circulation, however, invalidates the Texas statute only on the vagueness ground. . . . I think we should dispose of both cases on the ground supported by the majority." Douglas agreed. "That was the clear view of a majority of the seven who heard the argument. . . . So I think we should meet what Bill Brennan calls the 'core issue.'" Douglas also referred to the fact that, at the conference, "the Chief had the opposed view, which made it puzzling as to why he made the assignment at all."

The conference minority now sought to delay—and perhaps reverse—the abortion decisions. *Roe* and *Doe* had come before a seven-Justice Court. The two vacancies were not filled until Powell and Rehnquist took their seats in January, 1972. After the Blackmun drafts were circulated in May, the Chief Justice directed his efforts to securing a reargument in the cases, arguing that the decisions in such important cases should be made by a full Court.

At this point White sent around a brief draft dissent.[89] Circulated May 29, it effectively demonstrated the weakness of the Blackmun vagueness approach in striking down the Texas law. Referring to the *Vuitch* decision that a statute that permitted abortion on "health" grounds was not unconstitutionally vague,[90] the White draft declared, "If a standard which refers to the 'health' of the mother, a referent which necessarily entails the resolution of perplexing questions about the interrelationship of physical, emotional, and mental well-being, is not impermissibly vague, a statutory standard which focuses only on 'saving the life' of the mother would appear to be a fortiori acceptable. . . . [T]he relevant factors in the latter situation are less numerous and are primarily physiological."

On May 31, Chief Justice Burger circulated a Memorandum to the Conference favoring reargument—"[T]hese cases . . . are not as simple for me as they appear to be for others. The states have, I should think, as much concern in this area as in any within their province; federal power has only that which can be traced to a specific provision of the Constitution. . . . I want to hear more and think more when I am not trying to sort out several dozen other difficult cases. . . . I vote to reargue early in the next Term."

The Burger move to secure reargument was opposed by the Justices who favored striking down the abortion laws. They feared that the two new Justices would vote for the laws. In addition, the White draft dissent might lead another Justice to withdraw his support from the Blackmun *Roe* draft—maybe even Blackmun himself whose position had been none too firm. Indeed, he had become convinced that the cases should be reargued and circulated a May 31 Memorandum to the Conference to that effect. "Although it would prove costly to me personally, in the light of energy and hours expended, I have now concluded, somewhat reluctantly, that reargument in *both* cases at an early date in the next term, would perhaps be advisable. . . . I believe, on an issue so sensitive and so emotional as this one, the country deserves the conclusion of a nine-man, not a seven-man court, whatever the ultimate decision may be."

Douglas replied to Justice Blackmun the same day, "I feel quite strongly that they should not be reargued." The next day, June 1, an angry Douglas wrote to the Chief Justice, "If the vote of the Conference is to reargue, then I will file a statement telling what is happening to us and the tragedy it entails."

The Douglas statement was never issued even though the Justices did vote to set the abortion cases for reargument. Only Douglas was listed as dissenting.[91]

As it turned out, Douglas and the others who favored invalidating the abortion laws gained the most from the reargument. Had Douglas prevented reargument, the original Blackmun drafts might have remained the final *Roe* and *Doe* opinions. They would have dealt narrowly with the issues before the Court and have been anything but the ringing affirmation of the constitutional right to abortion contained in the final opinions. Chief Justice Burger had hoped to secure the votes of the two new Justices and then persuade Justice Blackmun himself to switch. Instead, he got a split vote from the new Justices and a vastly stronger *Roe* opinion.

The abortion cases were reargued on October 11, 1972. At the conference, the Justices who had participated in the earlier conference took the same positions as before. The two new Justices took opposing positions. Powell said that he was "basically in accord with Harry's position," while Justice Rehnquist stated, "I agree with Byron" White—who had declared, "I'm not going to second guess state legislatures in striking the balance in favor of abortion laws."

Several Justices agreed with Justice Stewart when he stated, "I can't join in holding that the Texas statute is vague." Stewart was for striking that law, but urged a different approach. He said that he would "follow John Harlan's reasoning in the Connecticut case[92] and can't rest there on the Ninth Amendment. It's a Fourteenth Amendment right, as John Harlan said in *Griswold*."

ROE V. WADE: SECOND DRAFT AND FINAL OPINION

The most important part of Blackmun's postreargument conference presentation was his announcement, "I am where I was last Spring." However, he made a much firmer statement this time in favor of invalidating the abortion laws. He also said, "I'd make Georgia the lead case." But he was opposed on this by several others, particularly Powell, who felt that "Texas should be the lead case."

Most important of all, during the summer, Blackmun had completely rewritten the abortion opinions. On November 21, he circulated the revised draft of his *Roe v. Wade* opinion. "Herewith," began the covering memo, "is a memorandum (1972 fall edition) on the Texas abortion cases."

He expressly abandoned the vagueness holding. The holding on the constitutional merits "makes it unnecessary for us to consider the attack made on the Texas statute on grounds of vagueness."

The new Blackmun draft contained the essentials of the final *Roe v. Wade* opinion, including its lengthy historical analysis. In particular, Blackmun now grounded his decision upon *Griswold v. Connecticut*.[93] According to Blackmun, "the right of privacy, however based, is broad enough to cover the abortion decision." In addition since the right at issue was a "fundamental" one, the law at issue was subject to strict-scrutiny review: the state regulation of the fundamental right of privacy "may be justified only by a 'compelling state interest.'"[94]

The Blackmun privacy–strict scrutiny approach was substantially influenced by a Douglas draft opinion in *Doe v. Bolton,* which had been prepared in January, 1972. The Douglas draft[95] had expressly invalidated the abortion law as violative of the right of privacy and adopted the strict-scrutiny review standard. There is a note in Douglas's hand, dated March 6, 1972, indicating that a copy of his draft had been "sent . . . to HB several weeks ago."

At the postargument conference, the Chief Justice had asked, "Is there a fetal life that's entitled to protection?" Justice Stewart said that the Court should deal specifically with this issue, saying, "it seems essential that we deal with the claim that the fetus is not a person under the Fourteenth Amendment." The *Roe v. Wade* opinion met this Stewart demand with a statement that the word "person" in the Fourteenth Amendment does not include a fetus[96]—a point that is said to have been added at Justice Stewart's insistence.[97]

The second draft also adopted the time approach followed in the final opinion. However, it used the first trimester of pregnancy alone as the line between invalid and valid state power. "You will observe," Justice Blackmun explained in his covering memo, "that I have concluded that the end of the first trimester is critical. This is arbitrary, but perhaps any other selected point, such as quickening or viability, is equally arbitrary."

The draft stated that, before the end of the first trimester, the state "must do no more than to leave the abortion decision to the best medical judgment of the pregnant woman's attending physician." However, "For the stage subsequent to the first trimester, the State may, if it chooses, determine a point beyond which it restricts legal abortions to stated reasonable therapeutic categories."

Later drafts refined this two-pronged time test to the tri-partite approach followed in the final *Roe* opinion. In large part, this was in response to the suggestion in a December 12 letter from Justice Marshall: "I am inclined to agree that drawing the line at viability accommodates the interests at stake better than drawing it at the end of the first trimester. Given the difficulties which many women may have in believing that they are pregnant and in deciding to seek an abortion, I fear that the earlier date may not in practice serve the interests of those women, which your opinion does seek to serve."

The Marshall letter stated that his concern would be met "If the opinion stated explicitly that, between the end of the first trimester and viability, state regulations directed at health and safety alone were permissible."

Marshall recognized "that at some point the State's interest in preserving the potential life of the unborn child overrides any individual interests of the women." However, he concluded, "I would be disturbed if that point were set before viability, and I am afraid that the opinion's present focus on the end of the first trimester would lead states to prohibit abortions completely at any later date."

Blackmun adopted the Marshall suggestion, even though Douglas and Brennan wrote expressing their doubts about the "viability" approach.

In a December 14, 1972, letter, Stewart delivered a more fundamental criticism of the Blackmun approach: "One of my concerns with your opinion as presently written is the specificity of its dictum—particularly in its fixing of the end of the first trimester as the critical point for valid state action. I appreciate the inevitability and indeed wisdom of dicta in the Court's opinion, but I wonder about the desirability of the dicta being quite so inflexibly 'legislative.'" This is, of course, the common criticism that has since been directed at *Roe v. Wade*. The high bench was acting like a legislature; its drawing of lines at trimesters and viability was, in the Stewart letter's phrase "to make policy judgments" that were more "legislative" than "judicial." Stewart worked on a lengthy opinion giving voice to this criticism, but in a December 27 letter he informed Blackmun that he had decided to discard it and "to file instead a brief monograph on substantive due process, joining your opinions."

ROE V. WADE: DUE PROCESS REGAINED AND LOST

According to Justice Blackmun's November 22, 1972, covering memorandum transmitting his second *Roe v. Wade* draft, "As I stated in conference, the decision, however made, will probably result in the Court's being severely criticized." Just before he circulated the final *Roe v. Wade* draft, Blackmun sent around a January 16, 1973, Memorandum to the Conference, which began, "I anticipate the headlines . . . when the abortion decisions are announced." Blackmun understated the outcry. The scare headlines and controversy were far greater than anything anticipated by the Court. Almost all the criticism was directed to the question of whether abortion should be permitted or prohibited. To one interested in Supreme Court jurisprudence, of even greater interest is the constitutional approach followed in striking down the state abortion laws. It applied the compelling-interest standard in reviewing those laws; but it did so in cases involving due process, not equal protection, challenges.

The Blackmun *Roe* opinion was based upon two essential holdings: (1) "the right of privacy, however based, is broad enough to cover the abortion decision." It follows from this that there is a "fundamental right" to an abortion; (2) "Where certain 'fundamental rights' are involved, the Court has held that regulation limiting these rights may be justified only by a 'compelling state interest.'" [98]

The state interest in protecting the health of the woman does not become "compelling" until the end of the first trimester of pregnancy. The interest in protecting "the potentiality of human life" [99] becomes "compelling" only after viability. Hence, state laws restricting the "fundamental right" to an abortion before that time are invalid.

Rehnquist, in his dissent, points out what the Court had done in its *Roe* opinion. *Roe* was a due process, not an equal protection case. "The test traditionally applied in the area of social and economic legislation is whether or not a law such as that challenged has a rational relation to a valid state objective." [100] But that was not the review standard applied in *Roe*. The abortion laws were subjected to strict scrutiny under the compelling-interest test.

According to Rehnquist, "The Court eschews the history of the Fourteenth Amendment in its reliance on the 'compelling state interest' test." [101] The strict scrutiny–compelling interest approach had been developed to deal with equal protection claims. When the Court applied the test that had been used in suspect-classification cases to cases involving fundamental rights, those cases were also equal protection cases. Now, in *Roe*, the Court held that the compelling-interest test should be used when a statute infringing upon fundamental rights was challenged on due process grounds. As Rehnquist put it, in *Roe*, "the Court adds a new wrinkle to this test by transposing it from the legal considerations associated with the Equal Protection

Clause of the Fourteenth Amendment to this case arising under the Due Process Clause of the Fourteenth Amendment." [102]

In Rehnquist's view, "the Court's sweeping invalidation of any restrictions on abortion during the first trimester is impossible to justify under that standard, and the conscious weighing of competing factors that the Court's opinion apparently substitutes for the established test is far more appropriate to a legislative judgment than to a judicial one." [103]

Certainly, there is danger that the importation of the compelling-interest standard into the Due Process Clause will lead to a revival of the substantive due process approach that prevailed in what Stewart termed, "the heyday of the Nine Old Men, who felt that the Constitution enabled them to invalidate almost any state laws they thought unwise." [104]

From this point of view, there is validity to the Rehnquist charge that *Roe* marked a return to the substantive due process approach followed in cases such as *Lochner v. New York*,[105] "when courts used the Due Process Clause to strike down state laws . . . because they may be unwise, improvident, or out of harmony with a particular school of thought." [106] According to Justice Rehnquist, the *Roe* adoption of the compelling-interest standard in due process cases will inevitably require the Court once again to pass on the wisdom of legislative policies in deciding whether the particular interest put forward is or is not "compelling." As Rehnquist put it in a 1977 memorandum, "the phrase 'compelling state interest' really asks the question rather than answers it, unless we are to revert simply to what Holmes called our own 'can't helps.'" [107] Just as important, the determination of what are and what are not "fundamental rights" is also left to the unfettered discretion of the individual Justices.[108]

The Rehnquist animadversion is not as valid today as it may have been when *Roe* was decided. The Burger Court later drew the line at what rights may be considered "fundamental" for the purposes of strict scrutiny under the Due Process Clause. This substantially narrowed the scope of its revival of substantive due process.

It should also be borne in mind that there are due process cases where review less flaccid than that under the rational-basis standard is plainly appropriate. The rights guaranteed by the First Amendment are fundamental rights, made applicable to the states by the Due Process Clause of the Fourteenth Amendment.[109] When a state burdens the exercise of First Amendment rights, there is a violation of due process, and most observers would agree that the state law should be subjected to strict scrutiny under the compelling-interest test. The entire Burger Court expressly stated that that is the case.[110]

Presumably even Chief Justice Rehnquist would agree with this strict-scrutiny posture in cases involving the fundamental rights guaranteed under the First Amendment. His criticism of the *Roe v. Wade* approach was thus more a criticism of degree than one of kind and was presumably answered by the later cases to be discussed, which limit the applicability of the strict-scrutiny approach by restricting the rights deemed fundamental for purposes of the more exacting review standard. As we shall see, those cases prevented the *Roe* approach from being extended much beyond the abortion cases themselves. For those favoring an even broader judicial role in protecting privacy, the *Roe* substantive due process revival was to become essentially a lost opportunity.

OTHER ABORTION DECISIONS

According to a December 30, 1971, letter from Brennan to Douglas, "The decision whether to abort a pregnancy obviously fits directly within each of the categories of fundamental freedoms I've identified and, therefore, should be held to involve a basic individual right. . . . [T]he crucial question is whether the State has a compelling interest in regulating abortion that is achieved without unnecessarily intruding upon the individual's right."

In its post–*Roe–Doe* abortion decisions the Burger Court continued to apply the compelling-interest test to laws regulating abortion procedures. Toward the end of the Burger tenure, six Justices[111] remained committed to the *Roe* "principle that a woman has a fundamental right to make the highly personal choice whether or not to terminate her pregnancy" and that "restrictive state regulation of the right to choose abortion, as with other fundamental rights subject to searching judicial examination, must be supported by a compelling state interest."[112]

Under this approach, some regulations were upheld. Thus as the Brennan letter conceded, "I would, of course, find a compelling State interest in requiring abortions to be performed by doctors," and the Court did indicate that laws limiting abortions to licensed doctors were valid.[113] Similarly, the Court upheld a requirement that abortions be performed in licensed "hospitals," when the term included outpatient hospitals and clinics.[114] But a law requiring abortions to be performed in full-service hospitals was invalidated as imposing undue cost burdens on those seeking abortions, when their health could be fully protected on an out-patient basis in appropriate nonhospital facilities.[115]

The Burger Court also upheld some limitations that might make it more difficult to exercise the right. Some of the issues that might arise after the *Roe* decision were pointed out in a "Dear Harry" letter from the Chief Justice. "I have more 'ploughing' to do on your memo but one thing that occurs to me is the possible need to deal with whether husbands as such or parents of minors have 'rights' in this area."[116] The Court invalidated statutes giving spouses and parents an absolute veto over abortions.[117] But it indicated that it would uphold a requirement of parental consent unless the pregnant minor showed that she was mature enough to make the decision herself.[118] A statute requiring either parental or judicial consent was ruled valid toward the end of the Burger tenure,[119] as was a law requiring the giving of notice to parents before an abortion was performed.[120]

These decisions were made by a closely divided Court. Indeed, in the last case cited, *H. L. v. Matheson*,[121] the Justices originally voted to strike down the notice requirement. An opinion of the Court to that effect was circulated by Justice Marshall. Justices Stewart and Powell, however, switched their votes and the Marshall draft became his dissent in the case.

The Court's decisions upholding some of the requirements governing minors were justified by Powell's conference comment: "The incapacity of minors [has been] a fact of life and law for thousands of years, and we ought not strike down these requirements for a . . . structured consent."[122] Thus, as Powell explained in a later Memorandum to the Conference,[123] "These cases recognized that the state has a legitimate interest in assuring a parental role in the abortion decision, subject to judicial review." Adhering to this view, the Court rejected the "argument that a pregnant minor, regardless of age or circumstances and without notice to parents, has a constitutional right to decide for herself, in consultation with a physician, whether to have an abortion."[124]

While the Burger Court continued to adhere to the *Roe* principle that a woman had a right to choose to have an abortion, it rejected governmental attempts to assert a societal interest in preservation of the fetus that would limit the woman's freedom of choice.[125] In this respect, the majority of the Justices remained true to the view originally stated in Brennan's December 30, 1971, letter to Douglas: The *Roe* opinion should deal "with the material interest in the life of the fetus and the moral interest in sanctifying life in general. [But] I would deny any such interest in the life of the fetus in the early stages of pregnancy."

Yet the right to an abortion did not include the right to public funding for abortions. In two cases, the Court upheld state and federal refusals to fund abortions for indigent women.[126] "I see nothing," asserted Justice Stewart, at the conference on one case, "in the burden on constitutional right argument, for however fundamental [the right] the state has no duty to subsidize [it]." According to Justice Powell, this was very different from *Roe v. Wade*. "*Roe*," he told the same conference, "dealt with an absolute deprivation. Although the refusal to fund burdens *Roe*'s fundamental right, what's the end of the road to require funding?"

Several Justices said that there was no more of a duty to subsidize abortion than other rights that were constitutionally protected. "I don't think the failure to subsidize is a deprivation," Stevens said to the conference. "In *Meyer*[127] [they] can't forbid teaching of German, but need not subsidize it." To Rehnquist, the proper analogy was the right to counsel on discretionary appeals. "*Ross v. Moffitt,*[128] means the state doesn't have to fund a lawyer even though he can't be prohibited."

As Stewart summarized these cases: "although government may not place obstacles in the path of a woman's exercise of her freedom of choice, it need not remove those not of its own creation. Indigency falls in the latter category."[129]

The outcome in these cases has been consistent with the Burger Court's posture in other cases involving wealth distinctions.[130] But it has made the *Roe* right an unenforceable one for those who cannot pay for abortions. To some, this has made for a significant retreat from the cases enforcing abortion rights. "I need not say," wrote Blackmun in 1980, "how disappointed I have been in what I perceive to be the Court's noticeable withdrawal in recent cases from the more positive position taken in *Roe, Doe* and *Danforth*. I fear that the forces of emotion and professed morality are winning some battles. That 'real world' continues to exist 'out there' and I earnestly hope that the 'war,' despite these adverse 'battles,' will not be lost."[131]

PRIVACY: DRAWING THE LINE

In his *Roe v. Wade* concurrence, Douglas listed three groups of rights that "come within the meaning of the term 'liberty' as used in the Fourteenth Amendment."[132] The list was based upon a suggestion contained in the December 30, 1971, ten-page letter sent to Douglas by Brennan after he had read Douglas's draft opinion in *Doe v. Bolton*.[133]

The Brennan letter noted his agreement "that the right [of privacy] is a species of 'liberty' (although, as I mentioned yesterday, I think the Ninth Amendment . . . should be brought into this problem at greater length), but I would identify three groups of fundamental freedoms that, 'liberty' encompasses: *first,* freedom from bodily restraint or inspection, freedom to do with one's body as one likes, and freedom to care for one's health and person; *second,* freedom of choice in the basic decisions of life, such as marriage, divorce, procreation, contraception, and the education and upbringing of children; and, *third,* autonomous control over the development and expression of one's intellect and personality."

As a general proposition the Burger Court did not extend protection to these "fundamental freedoms" much beyond those recognized by the Warren Court and its own *Roe* and *Doe* abortion decisions. The Court did extend the right (first recognized in *Griswold*[134]) to use contraceptives. *Eisenstadt v. Baird*[135] invalidated a statute that prohibited distribution of contraceptives to single persons. The *Eisenstadt* opinion noted that *Griswold* had based the right of privacy violated there upon the marital relationship, but it stressed that that relationship was based upon an association of two individuals. "If the right of privacy means anything, it is the right of the *individual,* married or single, to be free from unwarranted governmental intrusion into matters so fundamentally affecting a person as the decision whether to bear or beget a child."[136]

The Court later stated that the right of privacy protects personal decisions relating to marriage, procreation, contraception, family relationships, and child rearing.[137] According to a more recent case, "Protecting these [decisions] from unwarranted state interference . . . safeguards the ability independently to define one's identity that is central to any concept of liberty."[138]

But these words were written by Brennan, who took the broad view of privacy. The Burger Court majority did not construe the right to personal autonomy (third in the Brennan list) as broadly as Brennan.

The Court's approach here is illustrated by *Kelly v. Johnson*,[139] which upheld a regulation limiting the length of a policeman's hair. The lower courts had invalidated the regulation. At the postargument conference, the Chief Justice said that they were "dead wrong." Except for Brennan (who passed but ultimately joined the dissent) and Justice Marshall, the others agreed. Plaintiff here was a police officer, and as Stewart saw it, "the uniform includes hair dress." Hence, there was "no personal liberty interest if [you] join the police department."

The other majority Justices took the same approach, which was summed up by Rehnquist, "I'd like to see it said that, whatever liberty interest a civilian may have, it's lesser here and [there is a] legitimate [state] interest here."

This was the core of the reasoning used in the Rehnquist opinion of the Court. Though the opinion left open the question of "whether the citizenry at large has some sort of 'liberty' interest within the Fourteenth Amendment in matters of personal appearance,"[140] it may be assumed that the decision was mainly limited to the police officer, who had (in Rehnquist's conference phrase) a "lesser liberty interest" than an ordinary civilian. This point was the basis for Justice Powell's concurrence, which indicated expressly that what might be a "reasonable regulation to a uniformed police force . . . would be an impermissible intrusion upon liberty in a different context."[141] And, even with regard to the police officer, as Powell expressed it at the conference, "the state can't arbitrarily tell him how to groom his personal appearance." As an example, Powell said, there was "no legitimate interest of the state to satisfy the [police] chief's personal ideas."

The most controversial Burger Court decision narrowing the Brennan conception of privacy was *Bowers v. Hardwick*.[142] An action was brought by a homosexual who challenged a Georgia statute criminalizing consensual sodomy. The court of appeals held that the statute violated plaintiff's fundamental rights because his homosexual activity was a private association beyond the reach of state regulation.

There is no doubt that the lower court decision was consistent with the Brennan concept of privacy. As already seen, within the "fundamental freedoms" encompassed by "liberty," the Brennan letter included "freedom of choice in the basic decisions of life" and "autonomous control over the development and expression of one's intellect and personality." To support the autonomy notion, Brennan wrote, "I'd rely on *Stanley v. Georgia*[143] and its quotation from the Brandeis opinion in *Olmstead v. United States*."[144] (*Stanley* had held that the state might not criminalize the private possession of obscene material; the Brandeis quote was his famous statement of the right of privacy as "the right to be let alone—the most comprehensive of rights and the right most valued by civilized man."[145])

The *Bowers* majority refused to follow the *Stanley* approach and reversed the lower court. At the conference on the case, however, the vote was five to four the other way. The Chief Justice began the conference by stressing that "only homosexual activities" were involved in the case—"no marital privacy. Georgia agrees that an expansion to marital would get them in trouble." Burger's conference statement came down strongly in favor of reversal. "Our society has values that should be protected. The teachings of history and custom frown on this and the sanction is prohibition."

Brennan led the argument the other way. As he saw it, "the case implicates two firmly established lines of our cases, namely, the right to privacy . . . and secondly, those cases which recognize that the home remains a sort of a castle within our legal system." Brennan rejected the view that the statute must be reviewed only under a rational-basis test. "Because of the two interests implicated in this action—the privacy right and the sanctity of the home—I am convinced that heightened scrutiny is required."

Brennan was careful to point out that "a decision sustaining the lower court will not mean the end of adultery and incest laws. I have no doubt but that a State would be able to show sufficient interest to defend these statutes. The point is only that the State must be made to articulate its reasons, beyond saying merely that they do not like oral sex, or sodomy, or homosexuals.

"I want to emphasize that to me, this is a case involving certain sexual conduct engaged in between consenting adults, regardless of their marital status, regardless of their gender. It is not about homosexuality, it is not about single persons. It is about sexual privacy in the home between consenting adults. The statute purports to make none of these distinctions.

"Thus, I would hold that an act such as this which seeks to criminalize certain sexually intimate conduct between consenting adults, regardless of the marital status or gender of the adults, within the privacy of the home, must be defended by the state under a heightened standard of review. I simply cannot believe that this would be a controversial result."[146]

Brennan's conference view was supported by Marshall, Blackmun, and Stevens. Blackmun emphasized, "This isn't public conduct. It's limited to the home and reaches the marital situation. . . . [M]uch of the state's argument reminds [me] of *Loving*[147] and efforts to regulate prohibition." The Justice also said that "privacy and association were upheld in *Stanley*" and he asserted that "thought control and religion [were the] underpinning here."

Stevens declared, "This is a liberty interest case." It was not enough that the "condemnation was made by a majority. If it was correct, [they could] enforce this against married people. Isn't it part of liberty for everyone?"

The Chief Justice was supported at the conference by White, Rehnquist, and O'Connor. Rehnquist said, "I can't say substantive due process supports attack on the statute as limited to the home." O'Connor noted, "The right of privacy is a Fourteenth Amendment personal liberty." But "the right is not absolute and doesn't extend to private consensual homosexuality. State legislative power to enact this is not unconstitutional as exercised."

At the conference, the key vote was Justice Powell, who started by urging, "We ought to decriminalize this conduct. The statute [has] not [been] enforced for 50 years." He then stated a view of the case that differed from the approach of the other Justices. "*Robinson v. California*,[148] [invalidating a law] mandating the criminal status of drug addiction, may be relevant. It rested on the Eighth Amendment [prohibiting cruel and unusual punishment]. . . . If [we] accept the allegation that only acts of sodomy can satisfy this fellow, isn't that pertinent? I'd treat it as such and hold that, in the context of the home," the statute is invalid.

Powell's stand against the statute made the conference vote five to four for affirmance. On April 8, 1986, however, a few days after the conference, Powell circulated a Memorandum to the Conference telling the others that he had changed his vote.

"At Conference last week, I expressed the view that in some cases it would violate the Eighth Amendment to imprison a person for a private act of homosexual sodomy. I continue to think that in such cases imprisonment would constitute cruel and unusual punishment. I relied primarily on *Robinson v. California*.

"At Conference, given my view as to the Eighth Amendment, my vote was to affirm but on this ground rather than the view of four other Justices that there was a violation of a fundamental substantive constitutional right—as [the lower court] held. I did not agree that there is a substantive due process right to engage in conduct that for centuries has been recognized as deviant, and not in the best interest of preserving humanity. I may say generally, that I also hesitate to create another substantive due process right.

"I write this memorandum today because upon further study as to exactly what is before us, I conclude that my 'bottom line' should be to reverse rather than affirm. The only question presented by the parties is the substantive due process issue, and—as several of you noted at Conference—my Eighth Amendment view was not addressed by the court below or by the parties.

"In sum, my more carefully considered view is that I will vote to reverse but will write separately to explain my view of this case generally."

With Powell's switched vote, the bare majority became one in favor of the statute. Powell issued a separate concurrence, which indicated that, while he joined the Court's opinion, he might vote differently in a criminal case in which someone had been sentenced to prison for sodomy. "In my view a prison sentence for such conduct . . . would create a serious Eighth Amendment issue"—that is, might well constitute "cruel and unusual punishment."[149]

The *Bowers* opinion of the Court, by White, was based upon a simple drawing of the line comparable to that in the *San Antonio* case.[150] The sodomy statute did not violate the fundamental rights of homosexuals. As explained in a White memo just before the decision was announced, "[H]omosexual conduct is not a constitutionally protected liberty interest, and that homosexuality is not a suspect or quasi-suspect classification entitled to heightened scrutiny."[151]

The right of privacy, in the *Bowers* Court's view, did not extend to homosexual sodomy. The right of privacy was limited to the categories covered by prior cases: child rearing and education,[152] family relationships,[153] procreation,[154] marriage,[155] contraception,[156] and abortion.[157]

For our purposes *Bowers v. Hardwick* is significant as a valedictory summation of the Burger Court posture on fundamental rights and review standards. In *Roe v. Wade*,[158] the Court extended the fundamental-rights–compelling-interest approach to cases involving violations, not of equal protection, but of due process. There were strong objections by Rehnquist to the "transposing [of the compelling state interest test] from the legal considerations associated with the Equal Protection Clause of the Fourteenth Amendment to this case arising under the Due Process Clause of the Fourteenth Amendment."[159] Rehnquist charged that the *Roe* result was a revival of the now-discredited doctrine of *Lochner v. New York*.[160] "As in *Lochner* and similar cases applying substantive due process standards to economic and social welfare legislation, the adoption of the compelling state interest standard will inevitably require this Court to examine the legislative policies and pass on the wisdom of these policies in the very process of deciding whether a particular state interest put forward may or may not be 'compelling.'" [161]

To the dissenting Justices of an earlier day, *Lochner* and its progeny enabled the Court to exercise the functions of a "super-legislature." [162] To Rehnquist, the same was true of *Roe.* "The decision here," the Justice asserted, "to break pregnancy into three distinct terms and to outline the permissible restrictions the State may impose in each one, for example, partakes more of judicial legislation than it does of a determination of the intent of the drafters of the Fourteenth Amendment." [163]

The Rehnquist animadversion was elevated to the status of Court doctrine in *Bowers v. Hardwick,* which stressed the Court's reluctance "to discover new fundamental rights imbedded in the Due Process Clause." In the majority's view, "Judge-made constitutional law having little or no cognizable roots in the language or design of the Constitution" made the Court "most vulnerable and . . . nearest to illegitimacy." The example given was that "of the substantive gloss that the Court had placed on the Due Process Clause" when the *Lochner* approach was in its heyday. The moral of the earlier experience was that "There should . . . be great resistance to expand the substantive reach of [due process], particularly if it requires redefining the category of rights deemed to be fundamental. Otherwise, the Judiciary necessarily takes to itself further authority to govern the country without express constitutional authority." [164]

From this point of view, *Bowers,* like *San Antonio,* [165] is a crucial case in the Burger Court jurisprudence. *San Antonio* drew the line for the recognition of new fundamental rights under the Equal Protection Clause. *Bowers* does the same under the Due Process Clause. In both cases, since the laws at issue were found not to infringe upon fundamental rights, they were subject to review only under the narrow rational-basis standard.

Though *Roe v. Wade* did apply the fundamental right–compelling interest approach to due process challenges, the Burger Court aborted its own developing law in this respect by its later decisions, particularly that in *Bowers.*

Yet, even in its own terms, the Court's later approach appears unduly narrow. Perhaps there is no fundamental right of homosexuals to engage in acts of sodomy, but there is a fundamental right to privacy in the home.[166] Or so we thought after *Stanley v. Georgia*.[167] Just as significant as its narrowing of the review standard was the *Bowers* Court's restricted conception of the right of privacy. Certainly, the majority's conception of the rights included in privacy was narrower than that urged by Justice Brennan.

Chapter Eleven

Criminal Procedure I: Identification, Arrest, and Fair Trial

D URING THE 1968 presidential election, Richard M. Nixon had run against Chief Justice Warren and his Court as much as he had run against his Democratic opponent, Hubert H. Humphrey. He accused the Court of "seriously weakening the peace forces and strengthening the criminal forces in our society."[1] Nixon pledged that his Court appointees would be different.

When Nixon's appointee, Warren E. Burger, took his place in the Court's center chair, it was widely expected that he would implement what Warren himself called Nixon's "law and order" issue.[2] Many feared that the Burger Court would soon relegate the criminal-law landmarks of the Warren Court's constitutional-law "revolution" to legal limbo. But the anticipated reversals of the key Warren Court precedents did not materialize. Instead, the essentials of the Warren jurisprudential edifice were preserved. *Gideon*,[3] *Mapp*,[4] and *Miranda*[5]—the great Warren Court trilogy on the procedural rights of criminal-law defendants—all survived. To be sure, they were modified—even narrowed and blunted—in important respects.

IDENTIFICATION

Mistaken identification has probably been the single greatest cause of conviction of the innocent.[6] The Warren Court attempted to deal with the problem by its decisions in a 1967 trilogy of cases that the Justices themselves referred to as the Lineup Cases.[7] The most significant of these was the *Wade* decision that there was a Sixth Amendment right to counsel at a pretrial lineup: "police conduct of such a lineup without notice to and in the absence of his counsel denies the accused his Sixth Amendment right to counsel and calls in question the admissibility at trial of the in-court identifications of the accused by witnesses who attended the lineup." [8]

Wade was, however, all but overruled by one of the Burger Court's early criminal law decisions—*Kirby v. Illinois* [9]—though the Justices originally voted to treat *Kirby* as a case calling for the simple application of *Wade*. *Wade* itself involved a postindictment lineup, but that was not a crucial factor in the Court's decision. As Justice Brennan pointed out in his draft *Kirby* opinion, the same "hazards to a fair trial that inhere in a post-indictment" lineup are also present in a lineup before indictment. [10]

Kirby involved just such a preindictment situation. Kirby had been arrested for robbery and taken to a police station, where the victim positively identified him. The lower court held that the admission of testimony about the identification was not error; *Wade* was not applicable to preindictment identifications.

Only seven Justices were present at the *Kirby* postargument conference (Black and Harlan had resigned just before the 1971 term). Chief Justice Burger started the discussion by indicating that he favored affirmance. "I don't have trouble with a preindictment and postindictment dichotomy" and *Wade* should be ruled applicable only to lineup-type identifications after indictment. Burger was supported by Stewart and Blackmun, though the latter did say, "This leaves me with a bad taste."

Douglas, Brennan, White, and Marshall favored a reversal. They were led by Brennan, who strongly urged that the *Wade* reasoning applied equally to pre- and postindictment identifications. The four-man majority agreed that the opinion should be written by Brennan, since he had written the *Wade* opinion.

The Brennan draft opinion contains a simple and straightforward rejection of the pre- and postindictment dichotomy as the criterion upon which the *Wade* lineup right to counsel turns. "*Wade* did not turn on the circumstance that the lineups conducted were postindictment without notice to counsel who represented the accused." Instead, the test for *any* pretrial confrontation of the accused is "whether the presence of his counsel is necessary to preserve the defendant's basic right to a fair trial."

Such a test required a decision in Kirby's favor. "There plainly inheres in a showup after arrest and before indictment the hazards to a fair trial that inhere in a post-indictment confrontation." In this respect, "the confrontation after arrest differs not at all from the confrontation after indictment."

The draft's conclusion was "that the principles of . . . *Wade* apply to showups conducted after arrest." Hence, Kirby's conviction must be reversed because he "had not been advised that he had the right to have counsel present at the showup."

When Powell and Rehnquist were sworn in on January 6, 1972, there was now a full Court and it was desirable to have *Kirby* decided by a majority rather than only a four-Justice plurality.

On January 24, the Court issued an order restoring *Kirby* to the calendar for reargument.[11] At the postreargument conference, the seven who had participated in the original *Kirby* conference took their same positions.

The Chief Justice again urged affirmance. "Does *Wade* . . . apply to a preindictment confrontation?" he said. "No and we don't have to overrule *Wade*." He went further and said, "I'd overrule if it were the only way to decide." But that was unnecessary here if the Court simply refused to "extend" *Wade* to this case.

The two new Justices were for affirmance. Powell indicated that he "would not apply *Wade* to preindictment. Per se exclusionary rules should be developed with great restraint. . . . So I won't extend *Wade*." Justice Rehnquist agreed. "On the basis of no extension to punishment and that only I'd affirm."

The original four-to-three decision in Kirby's favor became a five-to-four decision the other way. Justice Stewart's draft dissent[12] became the plurality opinion. It distinguished between pre- and postindictment identifications and held that there was no right to counsel until the postindictment stage.

Had the Brennan draft come down as the final *Kirby* opinion, it would have made a substantial difference to the rights of criminal defendants. Identification of suspects through confrontation with their victims is most often a part—and a vital part—of the investigative stage. It usually occurs after the suspect is arrested and brought in for questioning. Postindictment lineups are relatively rare. To guarantee the right to counsel only for them, as the final *Kirby* decision does, is, in effect, to take away that right in most lineups.

The Burger Court also changed the law on other types of identification. In *Stovall v. Denno,*[13] the Warren Court ruled that, where the circumstances showed that an identification procedure was "unnecessarily suggestive," admission of testimony concerning the identification denied defendant due process. *Stovall* had been interpreted as laying down "a strict rule barring evidence of unnecessarily suggestive confrontations."[14] The lower court in *Manson v. Brathwaite*[15] had followed such a per se rule. An undercover police officer, who had given a description of a narcotics vendor, was shown a photograph of defendant whom he identified as the vendor. The court of appeals, in an opinion by Judge Henry J. Friendly, held that evidence as to the photo should have been excluded because the examination of the single photo alone was unnecessary and suggestive. *Stovall,* wrote Friendly, laid down a flat rule "requiring the exclusion of identifications resulting from 'unnecessarily suggestive confrontation.'"[16]

Judge Friendly had long followed a per se rule in these cases, and the Chief Justice began the *Manson* conference by noting, "Henry has carried this torch for years." Burger advocated instead, a "totality of circumstances" approach; identification evidence would not be excluded as long as, under the totality of circumstances, the identification was deemed reliable. Stewart, White, Blackmun, Powell, and Rehnquist agreed. "I think," Powell declared, "only the totality rule makes sense . . . that standard brings me out to reverse." Blackmun, who was to write the opinion, stated, "I don't buy per se. 'Totality' protects the defendant from unreliable evidence." Blackmun also urged that the Court "shouldn't constitutionalize it." Here Blackmun was following what Stewart had previously told the conference, "If this is only a sufficiency of evidence problem, that's not constitutional for me."

The *Manson* decision followed the conference approach by a seven-to-two vote (Stevens, who had been with the dissenters at the conference, concurred). Blackmun's opinion of the Court rejected the per se view in favor of the totality approach advocated at the conference. In place of the *Stovall* strict rule excluding all suggestively obtained identification evidence, *Manson* provided for a balancing process under which the circumstances indicating the reliability of the evidence would be weighed against "the corrupting effect of the suggestive identification itself."[17] In *Manson* itself, the identification was held, under the totality of circumstances in the case, to possess "sufficient aspects of reliability"[18] to be admissible without violating due process.

Manson narrowed the *Stovall* rule, making it most difficult to challenge suggestive identification procedures. Under *Manson*, a violation will not be found "except in outrageous situations"; consequently a variety of very suggestive identification procedures have been upheld.[19]

ARREST AND PRELIMINARY HEARING

The Fourth Amendment erects a buffer against arbitrary treatment of citizens by government.[20] It includes a categorical prohibition against "unreasonable searches and seizures," which is more than a bar against unlawful search for evidence. The amendment is a circumscription of power over the person, as well as over his "houses, papers, and effects."[21]

The Fourth Amendment interposes a magistrate between the citizen and the police.[22] While it rests upon the desirability of having magistrates rather than police officers determine when arrests are permissible,[23] public interest does require recognition of some power to arrest without a warrant. The Fourth Amendment is only a bar against "unreasonable" arrests and is construed in light of what was deemed unreasonable at common law.[24]

The common law permitted arrest without a warrant of any person who had committed a felony in the arresting officer's presence or, if the felony was committed out of his presence, where he had "probable cause"—that is, reasonable grounds—to believe both in the commission of the crime and the guilt of the arrested party.

In the Burger Court, the common law rule was elevated to the constitutional plane in *United States v. Watson*[25] and *United States v. Santana.*[26] In *Watson,* postal inspectors, acting on information from a reliable informant that defendant was in possession of stolen credit cards, arrested him in a restaurant without first obtaining a warrant. In *Santana,* acting on probable cause that a narcotics offense had been committed, police officers attempted a warrantless arrest of defendant while she was standing in her doorway. She retreated into the vestibule and was arrested there. The lower courts ruled that the arrests violated the Fourth Amendment.

At the *Watson* conference, Stewart stated the view that "an arrest in a public place can be made on probable cause without more." White, who was to write the opinion, noted, "The historic rule is arrest without a warrant even in houses."[27] All except Brennan agreed that the warrantless arrest was valid. Even Marshall, who ultimately delivered the *Watson* dissent, agreed with the majority at the conference. "The crime was committed in the presence of the arresting officers[28] and that's enough to reverse without getting to other questions."

The *Watson* decision held that the common law rule on warrantless arrests was included in the Fourth Amendment. Hence the amendment was not violated by the warrantless arrest, and it was immaterial that there were no exigent circumstances, so that the officers could have first obtained a warrant. In Blackmun's words at the *Santana* conference, "[You] don't need a warrant at common law to arrest a felon" and, under *Watson,* the same was true under the Fourth Amendment.

At the *Santana* conference the majority took the view that the open doorway was a public place. "Standing in a doorway," said Stewart, "is the same as on the sidewalk." Or as Powell put it, "The lady was at least in plain view and arguably in a public place."

At the *Santana* conference the Justices disagreed on whether the arrest had to be limited to the public place or could be made by a warrantless entry into the house itself. White said, "I'd let them go in after announcing [their] presence." Stewart said, "I'd not go so far as Byron and allow entry [into the house] to arrest if [they] have probable cause." Rehnquist stated that he could subscribe to the White view if it got a majority, but Powell said that he could not join "Byron's broad view."

In *Santana* all the majority Justices agreed that the fact that the arrest was actually made in the vestibule did not change the result. "There was an entry into the house after her retreat inside," White told the conference. But legally that was the same as the doorway. She "may not defeat an arrest which has been set in motion in a public place . . . by the expedient of escaping to a private place." [29] This was particularly true in this case where defendant was in possession of money and drugs and, in the Blackmun conference characterization, the "likelihood of destruction of the evidence was reasonably believed by the officers." In these circumstances, Stevens asserted at the conference, "Here there was money and drugs and the chance that something would be done with [the evidence] was good. . . . [I]t was not unreasonable to do what they did."

Watson and *Santana* allow warrantless arrests in felony cases where the probable cause requirement is met.[30] According to *Tennessee v. Garner,*[31] however, *Watson* does not mean that if this requirement is satisfied the Fourth Amendment has nothing to say about *how* the seizure is made. *Garner* tells us that the reasonableness of an arrest depends not only on when and where an arrest is made, but also on how it is carried out. In *Garner* a state statute provided that if, after a police officer had given notice of an intent to arrest a suspect, the suspect fled or forcibly resisted, "the officer may use all the necessary means to effect the arrest." Acting under this statute, a police officer shot and killed respondent's son. The son had fled at night over a fence behind a house he was suspected of burglarizing. The lower court held the statute invalid.

At the *Garner* conference, the Chief Justice stressed, "Burglary is a violent crime under Tennessee law. . . . [The officer] knew a felony had been committed and that a felon was fleeing. I'd give officers wide latitude."

The conference notes of a Justice indicate, however, that Burger passed at the conference (though he ultimately joined the *Garner* dissent). Rehnquist and O'Connor urged that the statute as applied was valid. "The Tennessee statute," said Rehnquist, "may be unacceptably applied." He gave the example of cases involving minor crimes. "But this is burglary at night time, with a potential for personal violence. I can't find anything in the Fourth Amendment that makes apprehending a balancing question."

The others at the conference, led by Brennan, voted for affirmance. The majority approach was summarized by Blackmun: "It comes down to balancing life against life. Decide the statute as applied [is invalid] and affirm." Marshall summarized the rationale to be stated in the *Garner* opinion: "You can shoot only when your life or someone else's is in danger. No one's life was in danger at any time in this case." The statute in operation was pithily characterized by Stevens: "This is almost a statute authorizing execution if [you] don't stop on command."

The *Garner* decision held the statute invalid insofar as it authorized deadly force against an apparently unarmed, nondangerous fleeing suspect. Apprehension by use of deadly force was ruled a seizure subject to the Fourth Amendment reasonableness requirement. It was constitutionally unreasonable to use deadly force against fleeing suspects who did not pose a threat of serious physical harm to others.[32]

Watson and *Santana* permit warrantless arrests under the common law rule, but they do draw the line against warrantless arrests made without probable cause. Yet even the Warren Court recognized that, in appropriate circumstances, police officers may stop and search persons suspected of criminal activity.[33] The Burger Court continued to recognize this "stop and frisk" exception.[34] It also read in another exception to the probable cause requirement in border searches. The key case here was *United States v. Martinez–Fuerte*.[35] A vehicle was stopped at a fixed checkpoint sixty-six miles from the Mexican border and its occupants briefly questioned even though there was no reason to believe the vehicle contained illegal aliens. The lower court reversed a conviction based upon the testimony of those questioned at the checkpoint. The Supreme Court had held that roving patrols might stop motorists in the general area of the border if there was a reasonably warranted suspicion that a vehicle contained illegal aliens.[36] They might not stop a vehicle merely because of the apparent Mexican ancestry of its occupants.[37]

At the conference on the second of those cases, the *Brignoni–Ponce* case,[38] Rehnquist had asserted, "Since you're looking for aliens, and particularly Mexicans, there's a founded suspicion justifying a stop and search." Justice Powell stated the majority consensus when he said that in the prior cases, starting with the Warren Court "stop and frisk" case,[39] "a particularized reason was shown. Here, to stop just because he looks like a Mexican, goes beyond those cases."

At the *Martinez–Fuerte* conference only Brennan and Marshall were in favor of affirmance. White passed, but ultimately joined the majority decision for reversal. "I think," said Stewart, "stops to interrogate without reasons at all are O.K., just as checks for driving licenses, fruit fly, weighing trucks." The difference between check points and roving patrols was stressed by Powell. He would sustain the "stop at a fixed check point, which unlike a roving patrol, is created by higher authority." Also, in the check point situation, "The intrusion is drastically different also."

The *Martinez–Fuerte* decision recognized that checkpoint stops are "seizures" under the Fourth Amendment, but they do not violate the amendment even in the absence of any individualized suspicion that the particular vehicle contains illegal aliens. The Powell opinion, like his conference statement, stressed that the intrusion here was minimal. Nor was the procedure invalid because secondary inspections were made largely on the basis of apparent Mexican ancestry. The Rehnquist position at the *Brignoni–Ponce* conference apparently prevailed.

Under *Martinez–Fuerte,* and even more so under *Watson* and *Santana,* "seizures" may be made without first obtaining a warrant. Still, the Burger Court limited the seizure power to the power to hold the individual only briefly. *Watson* and *Santana* may hold that the police officer's assessment of probable cause provides legal justification for arresting a person, even without a warrant. But the Burger Court cases justified only the seizure itself and "a brief period of detention to take the administrative steps incident to arrest."[40] After that period, there is no power to continue the detention; instead, the individual is entitled to a timely preliminary examination for a "judicial determination of probable cause as a prerequisite to extended restraint of liberty following arrest."[41]

The holding to this effect was made in *Gerstein v. Pugh*.[42] Under Florida law, prosecutors might charge all noncapital crimes by information, without any prior preliminary hearing. Respondents, who had been arrested and held for trial, brought a class action, claiming a constitutional right to a judicial hearing on the issue of probable cause. The lower court agreed, holding that the Florida procedure, under which a person arrested and charged by information, might be jailed pending trial without any judicial probable cause determination, violated the Fourth Amendment.

At the *Gerstein* conference, the Chief Justice noted that "the Federal Rules [of Criminal Procedure] provide no probable cause hearing on informations." Stewart also made this point, saying, "This attack, if it succeeds, will invalidate Rule 5 [of the Federal Rules], which denies a preliminary hearing if [it's an] information."

Despite the Burger–Stewart point, the conference was of the unanimous opinion that the Florida procedure was invalid. The prevailing view was stated by White: "In principle, I agree [one] ought not stay in jail very long without at least an ex parte determination of probable cause by a magistrate." Powell repeated the same thought: "In principle, [it's] impossible to resist the idea that [one] can't hold people in jail without a judicial test of probable cause." Rehnquist stressed that "there's no historical sanction for this and, if [there is] not, I agree with Byron."

The unanimous *Gerstein* decision elevated the right to a preliminary examination to the constitutional plane: The Fourth Amendment requires a timely judicial determination of probable cause as a requisite to extended detention following arrest. The disagreement among the Justices was over what White termed the "real issue" at the conference—that is, "what kind of hearing [is required] at an early date? . . . I wouldn't say an evidentiary hearing" was necessary. Powell said that he, too, "wouldn't require an adversary hearing. I agree with Byron." The Powell opinion of the Court followed the same approach. Though it stated the right to a preliminary examination as a constitutional right, it held expressly that the probable cause issue could be determined without "the full panoply of adversary safeguards."[43]

FAIR TRIAL: COUNSEL

The overriding constitutional concern in criminal cases is defendant's right to a fair trial.[44] A fair trial presupposes certain constitutional requirements. In the first place, there is the right to counsel. The Warren Court, in one of its most celebrated decisions—*Gideon v. Wainwright*[45]—held that the Sixth Amendment right of counsel is incorporated in the Fourteenth Amendment's Due Process Clause. A state conviction was consequently invalid because the accused's request to have a court-appointed lawyer had been denied.

But the *Gideon* Court, following the conference suggestion of Chief Justice Warren, limited the decision to the felony case at hand, without addressing the question of how far the new right to assigned counsel extended.[46] That question was presented to the Burger Court in *Argersinger v. Hamlin*.[47] Defendant was charged in Florida with carrying a concealed weapon, an offense punishable by imprisonment up to six months, a $1,000 fine, or both. Unrepresented by counsel, he was sentenced to ninety days in jail. He challenged his conviction, alleging a *Gideon* right to counsel. The Florida court held that the right to court-appointed counsel extends only to trials for offenses punishable by more than six months' imprisonment.

Argersinger was originally argued before a seven-Justice Court, but because of its importance the case was scheduled for reargument after Powell and Rehnquist took their seats.[48] At the conference after the reargument, the Chief Justice asserted, "The question is really not whether but when we'll grant this right." He worried about the effect of a decision extending *Gideon*. "What we need is a lot more information. . . . I'd set it for reargument next term and solicit from the states what the impact would be."

The others, however, voted to decide the case now in favor of a broad extension of *Gideon*. There was, nevertheless, a difference of opinion on the proper dividing line in such cases. Douglas spoke in favor of the line that governed in cases on the right to trial by jury— that is, *Gideon* should apply to "anything above a petty offense, carrying no more than six months." Powell agreed. He indicated (as he was to do in his *Argersinger* concurrence) that he was disturbed by the practical implications of a broader right. "I don't see how [you] can administer a rule requiring a lawyer if as much as an hour's imprisonment is involved. I think Bill Douglas' six months may be best, with a *Betts v. Brady*[49] test for less than that."

Blackmun, on the other hand, stated, "I don't think [it is] necessary to equate six months [for the right to a] jury with lawyers." And Stewart asserted the view that was ultimately to prevail: "[You] can't imprison at all without a lawyer; so no lawyer, no jail." The Stewart approach was countered by Rehnquist, who declared, with regard to so broad a right of counsel, that "openly to recognize it is to act like a legislature rather than a court."

The conference's close division on the proper line may be seen from a March 2, 1972, "Dear Chief" letter from Blackmun. . . . "[M]ine seems to be the swing vote, and at the moment I feel I could draw the line either at imprisonment or at the six-month mark." The majority went along with the six-month line. The Chief Justice, who had not voted at the conference, sent around a March 6 Memorandum to the Conference: "I am now persuaded that Bill Douglas' approach presents an acceptable solution, even assuming that at some future date the Court would have a different view such as 'no counsel no confinement' and a new look at the jury problem."

The opinion was assigned to Douglas, who now adopted the imprisonment line stated by Stewart at the conference. This led to a March 28 letter from the Chief Justice: "I have your proposed opinion to reverse. Since the original assignment was predicated on your vote to affirm I cannot join in a reversal. . . . The event will now await the votes on this disposition. I assume some of the Brethren may wish to wait until a writing is ready on the original vote to affirm."

None of the others persisted in their votes to affirm (though Powell did write a concurrence adhering to the six-month line) and even Burger finally concurred in the decision and the imprisonment test. However, Stewart, who had stated the categorical "no lawyer, no jail" rule, indicated in an April 12 letter to Douglas that the draft was unnecessarily broad. The Douglas draft had held that counsel was constitutionally required "if the offense is in the imprisonable class— that is to say if the statute makes any imprisonment a permissible penalty." Stewart wrote that he could not agree with this statement. "There are undoubtedly a myriad of statutes and ordinances that make imprisonment 'a permissible penalty,' but for whose violation imprisonment is virtually never imposed—spitting on the sidewalk, jaywalking, smoking in the subway, etc." The correct standard (and the one ultimately adopted) "is . . . that a person cannot be actually sentenced to imprisonment unless he had a lawyer at his trial."

The Douglas draft also indicated that the right to counsel had a wide reach not limited to the case before the Court or even to criminal cases. To this Stewart wrote, "I could not join an opinion that seems to decide in advance that a lawyer is also required in various other criminal, quasi-criminal, civil, and administrative proceedings—whether involving the loss of a driver's license, revocation of parole or probation, the attachment of 'stigma,' or whatever."

As it finally came down, *Argersinger* held "that absent a knowing and intelligent waiver, no person may be imprisoned for any offense, whether classified as petty, misdemeanor, or felony, unless he was represented by counsel at his trial."[50]

Yet even as finally limited in accordance with the Stewart view, *Argersinger* did make for a substantial broadening of *Gideon*. The right to counsel was also broadened by *Coleman v. Alabama*[51]—though the decision process started out with anything but that result as its goal. *Gideon* and *Argersinger* had dealt with the right to counsel at the criminal trial. But the need for counsel exists even before formal accusation and trial. In *Coleman*, petitioners, arrested on a charge of assault with intent to murder, were taken before a judge for preliminary examination. They were bound over to the grand jury, though the state had not provided them with counsel. The preliminary hearing is not a required step in an Alabama prosecution.[52] When it is held, however, its purposes are to determine whether there is sufficient evidence against the accused to warrant presenting the case to the grand jury and to fix bail. The Alabama court affirmed the convictions.

According to one Justice, "*Coleman v. Alabama* had a curious progress through the Court." There were four votes to grant certiorari (Black, Douglas, Marshall, and Fortas). Despite this, at the postargument conference, there were seven votes to affirm; Harlan alone voted the other way. "With *Miranda*[53] on the books," Harlan asserted, "[we] can't say this isn't a stage at which he's entitled to a lawyer."

The Chief Justice was delighted with Brennan's vote to affirm the convictions and assigned him the opinion. Before the case came down, however, Brennan changed his mind, a majority to vacate formed behind him, and the eight Justices participating in the case produced seven opinions.

Brennan, at first, circulated an affirming opinion of the Court, which was joined by Douglas, Stewart, White, and the Chief Justice. But the apparent majority could not hold. Justice Black had voted to affirm at the conference, but as he pointed out, "The preliminary [hearing] is a very vital part of criminal procedure in Alabama. Its use is to get the evidence and it's a real knock-down fight." Now Black reconsidered his conference vote and circulated a draft dissent. He explained his changed view in a letter to the Chief Justice: "Where is there anything in the Constitution that says that although a man has the right at the time of prosecution, he cannot claim that help the first time he needs counsel?"[54]

Douglas also switched his vote and joined the Black dissent. Harlan circulated his own dissent. At this point, the Chief Justice circulated a January 9, 1970, memorandum indicating support for the Brennan draft and stating that he might add a concurrence attacking the Black reading of the Sixth Amendment as insufficiently strict and literal. Two weeks later, Burger formally joined the Brennan opinion, which still also had the votes of Stewart and White.

After he had studied Harlan's draft dissent, Brennan found it very persuasive on the right to counsel. He decided to change his vote. His opinion was redrafted to reflect the change. It was soon joined by Marshall, Douglas, and White. The holding that there was a right to counsel at the preliminary hearing now had a majority. *Coleman* thus came down as an extension of the *Gideon–Argersinger* right to counsel—the first decision holding the right applicable before formal proceedings against the accused.

The right to counsel does not override the right of the accused to conduct his own defense. The right of self-representation was confirmed in *Faretta v. California.*[55] The accused, charged with grand theft, requested that he be permitted to represent himself. The judge, after questioning him on the hearsay rule and the law governing the challenge of potential jurors, ruled that the accused had not made an intelligent and knowing waiver of his right to counsel and that he had no constitutional right to conduct his own defense. The judge appointed a public defender to represent the accused. The conviction was affirmed by the state appellate court.

The Chief Justice began the *Faretta* conference by framing the issue: "Does the accused have a constitutional right to represent him-

Fair Trial: Other Aspects 333

self derived from his Sixth Amendment right to be present at his trial[?]" Burger answered in the negative. "I'd rely on the Sixth [Amendment], 'the accused shall have the assistance of counsel for his defence.' I think this should be left to the discretion of the trial judge, subject to review for abuse of discretion."[56]

Blackmun and Rehnquist also voted to affirm. But the others spoke in favor of the accused's right to represent himself. Stewart, who was to author the *Faretta* opinion, best stated their view. "If the accused has knowingly and intelligently waived the right to counsel must the state honor that request?" The Justice pointed out that "historically [he] couldn't have a lawyer. The Sixth [Amendment] simply said he could have one if he wanted one." Stewart noted that he was "influenced in this by the federal statute and the practice of many states allowing the accused to represent himself."

The other majority Justices agreed with Stewart. According to Justice White, "The accused has a right to waive counsel." Powell said, "The federal statute has given this right since 1789. If the Constitution gives the right of presence and confrontation, [we] can't deny him the right to say, 'I don't trust lawyers.'" Douglas stressed the fact that Faretta had been represented by the public defender. "The public defender system gives the accused the feeling that government is on both sides of the case against him."

Several of the Justices told the conference that the right to self-representation did not mean that a lawyer might not be appointed to aid defendant in his conduct of the trial. Thus, Justice Marshall said that he "would require a lawyer to be there to be consulted." Justice White agreed. "The state may require the presence of a lawyer—although that puts the lawyer in a hell of a spot." The *Faretta* opinion recognized state power to aid defendant in this respect. While it categorically confirmed the Sixth Amendment right of self-representation, it also stated that the state "may . . . appoint a 'standby counsel' to aid the accused."[57]

FAIR TRIAL: OTHER ASPECTS

Another essential element of a fair trial is the right to a speedy trial guaranteed by the Sixth Amendment. In *Klopfer v. North Carolina*,[58] the Warren Court had held that that guaranty is binding on the states under the Fourteenth Amendment. In *Dickey v. Florida*,[59] decided during the new Chief Justice's first term, the Burger Court enforced the guaranty in favor of a prisoner who was confined because of his conviction on unrelated federal charges. He had not been tried on the state robbery charge until over seven years after his arrest, even though he had been available to the state during that time and had made repeated efforts to secure a prompt trial. In the interval two witnesses had died, others had become unavailable, and police records had been lost.

At the *Dickey* conference, Chief Justice Burger declared, "I can't see any defense for the state in this Court. It's almost a per se denial to keep him in the 'cooler' for eight years." The conference agreed and voted unanimously to hold that Dickey had unconstitutionally been denied a speedy trial. The Chief Justice however, prepared a skeletal opinion that was clear only as to result. The Burger opinion did not tell whether it had applied *Klopfer* retroactively (Dickey's prosecution began seven years before the *Klopfer* decision) and thus rested on the Sixth Amendment right to speedy trial, or whether it assumed that *Klopfer* was not retroactive and thus rested on Fourteenth Amendment "fundamental fairness."

The ambiguity in the Burger opinion led Justice Brennan to circulate a brief concurrence stating that he viewed the Court's decision as an application simply of the "fundamental fairness" requirement of the Fourteenth Amendment. The factors mentioned by the Chief Justice to show that Dickey had established his claim could not be read as establishing the factors that must be shown to support a Sixth Amendment claim. Brennan later expanded the concurrence to treat in some detail the issues that must be met in defining the Sixth Amendment right to speedy trial. The Brennan purpose was to expose the basic problems yet to be met in defining the Sixth Amendment right. The concurrence was intended to show that these issues had been ignored by the Court, that they posed basic constitutional questions, and that lower court precedent in point was not dispositive.

Harlan, in a one-page concurrence, stated that "whether it be the Due Process Clause or the Sixth Amendment that is deemed to apply, I fully agree that petitioner's federal constitutional rights were violated." But in Harlan's view, the decision should have been under "the historic meaning of the Due Process Clause of the Fourteenth Amendment."[60]

Another aspect of a fair trial is that it be held in "a fair tribunal."[61] In *North v. Russell*,[62] defendant had been convicted in a state police court for drunk driving and sentenced to thirty days in jail, a $150 fine, and revocation of his driver's license. The judge was a coal miner without any legal training or education. An appeal of right was provided to the circuit court, where all the judges were lawyers and where a trial de novo might be had. Instead of appealing, defendant sought habeas corpus, challenging his conviction before a lay judge. The highest state court rejected the challenge.

At the *North* conference, Stewart made a strong argument for reversal: "It seems to me that, given *Gideon* and *Argersinger,* the presumption must be, despite the history of lay judges, that [he] should have a lawyer judge—at least when it's a one-judge court." In *Ward v. Monroeville,*[63] the Court had ruled that trial before a biased judge was not constitutionally acceptable even though there was a later trial de novo before an impartial tribunal. According to *Ward,* "Petitioner is entitled to a neutral and detached judge in the first instance." As Stewart put it, "The *Ward v. Monroeville* requirement that [you] must have a constitutional court is here, and, since I say it's an unconstitutional court, *Ward* applies."

Stewart stood alone at the conference in his stand for reversal (though he was to be joined in his *North* dissent by Marshall). Several Justices took issue with the Stewart position on the unconstitutionality of lay judges. Powell asserted that it was "hard to find anything in the Constitution that proscribes lay judges. . . . An opinion that talks of 'competent' judges would be unfortunate." Justice Rehnquist agreed, saying that his "first preference would be to say no constitutional right to a lawyer judge."

Instead of deciding on the constitutionality of lay judges, the conference voted to follow the approach put forward by White: The Court should "affirm solely on the ground that the de novo trial removes any basis for the constitutional claims. . . . The right to a de novo trial before a lawyer judge gives him everything he wants."

The *North* opinion followed the White conference approach. The provision for a trial de novo removed any possible deficiency in the trial court. This made it unnecessary to reach the question of whether there could be a valid conviction when the only trial was before a lay judge.

It is unfortunate that *North* avoided the issue of the constitutionality of lay judges presiding over criminal trials. It is anomalous that North had a *Gideon–Argersinger* right to counsel, but that the presentation and arguments by his lawyer could be before the coal miner without any legal training who decided the case. It would have been preferable for the Court to have followed the Stewart view on the constitutional right to be tried before a judge trained to understand the legal issues and arguments of the *Gideon*-required counsel. But at least the decision did mean that no legal currency was given to the Powell–Rehnquist assertion that nothing in the Constitution proscribed lay judges in such a case.

The Burger Court also diluted other aspects of the fair trial requirement. When the Warren Court held that the Fourteenth Amendment guarantees a right to jury trial in serious criminal cases,[64] there is little doubt that the Court meant a traditional twelve-person common law jury with a unanimous verdict. In *Williams v. Florida*,[65] on the other hand, the Burger Court upheld conviction for robbery by a six-member jury. At the conference presentation Chief Justice Burger said, "on the six-man jury, I can't see a constitutional question." Black followed his literal approach to the Constitution and stated, "Nothing says [you] can't have less than twelve." But there is still a line of reasonableness in lowering jury membership—a line illustrated by the Burger hypothetical at the *Williams* conference: "If we get a three-man jury case."

In a case after *Williams*, the Court ruled that a state that dispensed with the requirement of jury unanimity did not violate due process.[66] In *Batson v. Kentucky*,[67] decided during the last Burger term, the Court held that the Equal Protection Clause prohibits a prosecutor from using peremptory challenges to exclude blacks from the jury. The lower court had held that the Sixth Amendment right to a jury drawn from a cross-section of the community had not been violated, relying on *Swain v. Alabama*.[68] That case had also held that racial discrimination might not be inferred merely from the prosecutor's use of peremptory challenges to dismiss blacks from the jury.

At the *Batson* conference, the Justices agreed that the case should be decided on equal protection rather than the Sixth Amendment. Chief Justice Burger spoke for affirmance. Unlike the others, he said that the case should be decided "only [on] the Sixth Amendment cross-section" argument. With regard to it, Burger asserted, "Our Sixth Amendment decisions don't suggest a different result from *Swain*."

The case the other way was, as was usual by then, led by Brennan: "I think that we should overrule *Swain* and hold that a black defendant can establish an equal protection violation based on the prosecutor's racially motivated use of peremptory challenges to eliminate a significant number of blacks from the venire in the individual defendant's case. We should treat racial equal protection claims in the petit jury context basically the same way we treat other kinds of racial discrimination claims."

Brennan stated the view accepted by the *Batson* majority. "I think that equal protection grounds are far preferable here to a 6th Amendment fair cross-section approach. . . . An equal protection approach to the problem would be narrower and more closely tailored to the problem. It would also avoid potentially serious difficulties in defining what groups should be cognizable under the fair cross section requirement. Because an equal protection theory would be available only to the singularly disadvantaged and distinct groups that receive special scrutiny, that approach should limit the number and types of challenges to the prosecution's use of peremptories."[69]

Only Rehnquist supported the Chief Justice at the conference. The others agreed with Brennan—rejection of the Sixth Amendment approach and reversal on equal protection. "I'd revisit *Swain*," said White, "and say here that, contrary to *Swain*, if defendant can prove there's a striking [from the jury] on account of race, [he] can require the prosecutor to justify." Blackmun declared, "It's discriminatory to assume blacks are acquittal-prone." Stevens summed up the conference consensus: "The courts that have assumed *Swain* held [they] could use peremptories on racial [grounds are] wrong. We should say it's constitutionally impermissible."

The *Batson* opinion by Powell followed the conference view. The use of peremptory challenges to exclude blacks from the jury violated equal protection. Once a defendant shows such exclusion, the burden shifts to the prosecutor to come forward with a neutral explanation for challenging black jurors. Repeating the conference point made by Blackmun, the opinion states that the prosecutor does not meet this burden by stating that he challenged the jurors on the assumption that they would be partial to defendant because of their shared race.

At the *Batson* conference, Powell had asserted, "We have to overrule *Swain*'s holding that won't permit inferences that striking causes an inference to arise of a racial basis." Despite this, Powell's draft opinion did not specifically overrule *Swain*. This was pointed out by Brennan in a January 23, 1986, "Dear Lewis" letter. "I feel strongly that the opinion must say expressly that to the extent *Swain* can be so read, it is overruled. Perhaps this could be done in a footnote." Powell added a footnote overruling *Swain*.

In his *Batson* conference statement, Brennan had noted, "The question whether the prosecutor may challenge the defendant's racially motivated use of peremptories is not before us in this case. . . .

I believe we should wait for another case to answer that question."

The *Batson* opinion followed the Brennan advice and did not deal with the issue. It is, however, of interest that Blackmun told the conference that, in his view, the *Batson* holding would also apply to use of peremptories by the defense. "I'm inclined to make it two-way," Blackmun said.

Marshall went even further. "I'd take peremptories away from both sides. [You] can't ever decide whether a strike [of a juror] is racially motivated." Marshall issued his *Batson* concurrence urging that peremptory challenges be banned entirely.

Marshall explained his position in a February 28, 1986, note to Brennan: "I continue to believe that the majority's approach will by its nature be ineffective in ending racial discrimination in the use of peremptories. I see no reason to be gentle in pointing that out, and I doubt that pulling my punches would make the situation any better."

In a February 24 letter to Marshall, Brennan had written, "You may well be right that the goal the Court seeks to achieve by allowing defendants to challenge the race-based use of peremptories can be circumvented by prosecutors and lower courts. . . . I am not yet ready to decide that peremptory challenges must be eliminated in order to cure the discriminatory use of those challenges and and [*sic*] for that reason do not join you."

The Burger Court also dealt with the manner in which the criminal trial is conducted. In *Estelle v. Williams*,[70] the accused, who had been held in custody pending trial, wore prison issue clothing during his trial. He had asked an officer at the jail for his civilian clothes, but the request was denied. The accused's attorney expressly referred to the jail clothing at voir dire, but neither the accused nor his counsel objected to the trial judge. After his conviction, the accused sought federal habeas corpus relief. The court of appeals held that the trial in jail clothing was inherently unfair.

At the *Estelle* conference, all but Brennan and Marshall were in favor of reversal. The Chief Justice said that he could not agree with the court of appeals ruling. "I would go with a supervisory rule in federal court that [you] can't try in jail garb over objection. But I see no basis for a constitutional rule. . . . [T]he failure to object ends the case for me."

The others in the majority also emphasized the defendant's failure to object. The most important statement to that effect was made by White. He urged the conference to "define the right as arising only on request . . . and I'd write it that way." White conceded that "this disagrees with the court of appeals analysis that the Constitution requires the state affirmatively to try in civilian clothes unless the prisoner requests otherwise." White said, "I don't agree with that. I can perhaps forgive the failure to make a request in some circumstances, but doubt this is one."

The *Estelle* decision followed the White conference approach, reversing the judgment below because, since no objection had been made, it could not be concluded "that respondent was compelled to stand trial in jail garb or that there was sufficient reason to excuse the failure to raise the issue before trial."[71] Such a decision appears unduly narrow. At the conference, Powell had declared, "If one requests not to be tried in prison garb, a denial would for me deny due process." But trial in prison garb is so prejudicial that it should be deemed inherently unfair and hence violative of due process[72] in all circumstances.

Illinois v. Allen[73] dealt with disruptive tactics by defendants at criminal trials. In two *causes célèbres*—the trial of antiwar demonstrators in Chicago (the so-called Chicago Seven trial) and the trial of Black Panthers in New York—the defendants had repeatedly disrupted the proceedings.

Allen had been convicted of robbery. During his trial, he engaged in persistent unruly conduct. He talked and argued with the judge, saying, "When I go out for lunchtime, you're going to be a corpse here." A statement by the judge, "One more outbreak of that sort and I'll remove you from the courtroom," had no effect. Allen said, "I'm going to start talking and I'm going to keep on talking all through the trial. There's not going to be no trial like this." The judge then ordered Allen removed.

The Illinois Supreme Court held that Allen had waived his constitutional right to be present at the trial. In a habeas corpus proceeding, the federal court of appeals disagreed. It held that a defendant's Sixth Amendment right to be present at his own trial was so "absolute" that, no matter how unruly or disruptive the defendant's conduct might be, he could never be held to have lost that right as long as he continued to insist upon it.

At the *Allen* conference, the Chief Justice also disagreed with the notion that defendant had waived his constitutional right to be present at his trial. "I don't like the concept of waiver. The key was the Illinois Supreme Court holding that his right to be present could be forfeited. . . . The alternatives of contempt, or gagging, or closed circuit TV are matters of discretion."

The conference focused on the holding below that the right to be present at trial could never be lost. The conference agreed that this holding was wrong and unanimously voted for reversal. The issue then became: What means are available to a trial court to prevent obstruction of its proceedings?

Allen itself was a rather odd vehicle for deciding this issue. The case had been tried more than a dozen years previously, and Allen's outbursts had been the result, most probably, of mental illness. Yet after an initial finding of incompetency, there had been a finding of competency to stand trial, and so the mental illness issue was eliminated from the case, so that it could serve as a broad treatment of defenses against disruptive behavior.

Three weeks after *Allen* was argued Justice Black circulated a March 17, 1970, draft opinion of the Court. The draft, like the final opinion, made a broad survey of the problems presented by disruption. Brennan, in particular, was dissatisfied. First, Black used the concept of "waiver," and Brennan agreed with the Chief Justice that what had occurred in the case should be called a "forfeiture." Brennan feared that use of "waiver" would undermine the strict standards that the Court had developed on waivers.

In addition, Black's draft hinted that there might be some constitutional infirmity in a civil contempt order issued without a jury trial. This was one of Black's pet theories and Brennan refused to go along with it. Brennan also wanted the opinion to make what he regarded as the fundamental point in the case: the safeguards of the Bill of Rights presuppose that government has the power to put a person on trial. This was the point that Brennan was to stress at the outset of his *Allen* concurrence.

After Brennan had drafted his concurrence, he conferred with Black on March 20. Black wanted, after all, to hold his unanimous Court and was willing to make changes. However, he objected to the word "forfeiture" as opening up a wholly unexplored avenue for deprivation of constitutional rights. A Black redraft, like the final opinion, used neutral words—"relinquished," "lost"—which implied no theory behind the deprivation. Brennan himself then abandoned "forfeiture" and substituted "surrender," in his concurrence, because he thought it was closer in implications to Black's terms.

At this point, the Court was pressing for an early announcement of the case. Apparently several trials in New York were being held up because of the disruptive activities of defendants, and trial judges were waiting for guidance. However, Douglas now added an element of uncertainty. At a conference on March 20, Douglas said that the case was a hard one for him and that he would probably join in the denial of relief, but was not sure. The Chief Justice then circulated a letter trying to speed up the writing of what he indicated would be a Douglas dissent, despite the fact that Douglas had voted to reverse and had reaffirmed that view, though with hesitation, at the most recent conference. Douglas then became quite peeved at the Chief Justice and suggested to Brennan that he would hold the case up until he was good and ready to let it come down. He was somewhat mollified when Burger circulated an apology on March 24.

Douglas circulated his own opinion on March 30, stressing that Allen was mentally ill. Yet Douglas also pointed out in a footnote[74] that Allen had ultimately been found competent to stand trial— which undercut his treatment of the case in his opinion.

The *Allen* decision itself held categorically that a disruptive defendant could be removed from the courtroom. Such a removal does not violate the right to be present, because defendant loses his right by his disruptive behavior. The Black opinion also indicated, following the Burger conference approach, that the trial judge had the discretionary alternatives of binding and gagging defendant or citing him for contempt.

Allen has been criticized,[75] but it must be conceded that it seems to have achieved its purpose of settling the problem of the disruptive defendant.

JUVENILE PROCEEDINGS

In re Gault[76] was the first major effort to define the constitutional rights of juveniles. The Warren Court held that juvenile defendants were entitled to most of the rights of adult criminal defendants. The second major effort in this area came in *In re Winship,*[77] decided during Chief Justice Burger's first term.

Winship was important not only for its precise holding, but also as an indication of the manner in which the Burger Court would apply *Gault.* More specifically, it would show whether *Gault* signaled the introduction into juvenile proceedings of all the traditional safeguards of criminal due process, or whether it marked a process of ensuring "fundamental fairness" to children without insisting that due process for juveniles must in all respects parallel that accorded adults.

In *Winship,* the New York Family Court had found a twelve-year-old to be a juvenile delinquent because he had stolen money from a woman's pocketbook. The judge acknowledged that the proof might not establish guilt beyond a reasonable doubt. He acted under a statute authorizing decision in such juvenile proceedings to be based on a preponderance of the evidence. The highest state court affirmed, holding that the Constitution did not require proof beyond a reasonable doubt in a juvenile delinquent case.

Chief Justice Burger began the *Winship* conference by asserting, "I don't think this is a constitutional problem. [You] could have all trials by [the] preponderance test if the legislature said so." Foreshadowing his *Winship* dissent, the Chief Justice declared, "I think everything this Court has done in the juvenile field has been a step backward." Burger concluded that no federal question was involved and voted to dismiss.

At the *Gault* conference, Justice Black had been the foremost advocate of treating the juvenile like an adult defendant. As he put it then, "whether or not he's a juvenile, he's being restrained of his liberty. Thus, he's entitled to *all* the guarantees."[78] At the *Winship* conference, however, Black spoke in support of the Chief Justice, stating that "whether the Constitution requires reasonable doubt is not an easy question. Whatever I've written to suggest it was, I depart [from] now and say [there is] no constitutional requirement." Black also would "dismiss as presenting no federal question."

However, Burger and Black stood alone. Stewart, who passed at the conference, would later join the Burger dissent. Douglas started the presentation for reversal by stating, "Since a crime is charged, it's a criminal case under the Fifth [Amendment] and within the Sixth [Amendment]—it's punishment. Beyond a reasonable doubt is the standard constitutional rule." Harlan agreed. "Since we've got into the juvenile field, I can't see how punishment for conduct [that is] a crime when committed by an adult can be tried except by the reasonable doubt standard." And White asserted, "Without cutting back on *Gault,* I see no way to deny application of the reasonable doubt standard."

Douglas, the senior majority Justice, assigned the *Winship* opinion to Brennan, who had strongly supported the majority view. He had urged that, of all the criminal due process safeguards, proof beyond a reasonable doubt was both the most fundamental and the one that could be introduced into juvenile proceedings with the least disruption.

The *Winship* drafting process illustrates once again the need to compromise. In order to hold his Court, Brennan had to write more narrowly than he might otherwise have wished. At one extreme, there was the need to appease Justice Harlan: No suggestion could be made that the right to jury trial for children flowed from proof beyond a reasonable doubt; nor could there be any indication that the decision applied to juveniles not charged with crime (specifically, PINS—that is, a "person in need of supervision—a category in New York law for "incorrigible, ungovernable or habitually disobedient and beyond . . . lawful control" youth, without being found a "juvenile delinquent").

Brennan told his law clerks that he had no qualms about avoiding the jury issue; its proper resolution was a complex and difficult question, best considered in a case actually raising the issue. On the other hand, PINS and juvenile delinquents were not two significantly different groups—both were stigmatized by their "conviction" and both were subject to loss of liberty. But Brennan was willing to leave the equation of PINS and delinquents to cases in which the issue was squarely presented.

At the other extreme was Justice Douglas. It was necessary to avoid any statement that the due process to be accorded children may differ from that given adults. The *Winship* opinion carefully avoided such a declaration, though the unstated assumption of the opinion was that juvenile and adult due process are not necessarily identical in their content.

The necessity not to offend Douglas prevented Brennan from trying to use *Winship* to formulate explicitly a process for determining the content of juvenile due process. Brennan had prepared the following, which he did not insert into his opinion only because of the need to humor Douglas: "We recognize that the 'condition of being a boy' may have a bearing on the nature of the due process to which a child is entitled. As a result of their youth, children are generally less responsible for their conduct than adults, just as they are more in need of guidance and more susceptible to its influence. In order to serve their special needs and to take advantage of their special abilities, the juvenile process appropriately differs from the criminal process in many respects. The possibility exists, accordingly, that 'the denial of rights available to an adult may be offset, mitigated or explained by action of the Government, as parens patriae, evidencing solicitude for the juveniles.' *Kent*.[79] Thus, when children are denied a criminal due process safeguard given to adults, courts must determine whether granting the children that right would destroy any characteristic of the juvenile process beneficial to them. If no such characteristic would be impaired, no constitutional ground exists for denying them the safeguard. If, however, the introduction of the right into the juvenile process would destroy or lessen any of its beneficial aspects, the question becomes whether the harm to children from that loss would outweigh that suffered as a result of the safeguard's absence."

The Brennan *Winship* opinion did, in actuality, follow the process outlined above. First, it was determined that no significant harm would be done to any beneficial aspect of the juvenile process by adoption of the reasonable-doubt standard. Hence, there was no constitutional ground for denying a juvenile a safeguard sufficiently fundamental to fair trial to be a part of criminal due process. A more difficult question would be presented with jury trial, to be sure, since its introduction might well weaken some of the beneficial characteristics of the juvenile process. Accordingly, under the projected Brennan test, it would be necessary to weigh the harm to children likely to result from the introduction of juries against the harm caused by their absence.

Of course, before *Winship* could turn to the juvenile due process issue, the Court had to decide that proof beyond a reasonable doubt is a requirement of criminal due process. Though this standard's status as a basic element of fundamental fairness had long been assumed, the Court had never directly so held prior to *Winship*. Brennan's opinion categorically affirms the constitutional status of the standard—and it was on this that Brennan lost Justice Black. He could not find "proof beyond a reasonable doubt" in "the words" of the Constitution, and thus was driven to dissent on this point. Despite his earlier adherence to Justice Frankfurter's statement in *Leland v. Oregon*[80] that proof beyond a reasonable doubt is "a requirement and safeguard of due process of law in the historic, procedural content of 'due process,'" Black was not to be moved. He had become wedded to his fundamentalist approach.

A week after Brennan circulated his *Winship* draft, the Chief Justice sent around a draft dissent. He charged that the Court was "straitjacketing" the juvenile process and that the decision "turns the clock back to the pre-juvenile-court era. . . . It is not necessary to dissent to that portion of the majority opinion which purports to decide for all time to come the due process rights of all accused persons of any age on the standard of proof since dissent is not necessary once the material is identified as dicta wholly unnecessary to the disposition of the case. As to that part of the Court's opinion, I need to express no views."

It is hard to see how the Chief Justice could treat the holding on standard of proof as dictum, since it was an essential part of the *Winship* decision. Stewart, who joined the Burger dissent, persuaded him on this point and a redraft of the dissent was circulated, omitting it.

Brennan then sent around a revised draft, which replied to Burger with a sentence, at the beginning of note 1, which was devoted to limiting the scope of the decision: "We do not understand how the Chief Justice can assert in dissent that this opinion 'rests entirely on the assumption that all juvenile proceedings are criminal prosecutions, hence subject to constitutional limitations.'"

Since there were now three dissents (Burger, Stewart, and Black), Harlan's vote was crucial if the Brennan opinion (joined by Douglas, Marshall, and White) was to speak for a majority. In a letter of March 19, 1970, Harlan asked for two changes. First, he wanted the sentence in note 1, "We do not understand how the Chief Justice" to be replaced with "We do not see how it can be said." Brennan readily complied, though he commented to his law clerks on how classically Harlanesque the request was, involving as it did an alteration of phrasing of de minimis import on all scores save that of getting the Justice's vote.

Harlan's second request was more important. He wanted Brennan to eliminate much of the draft's rationale for the proposition that the reasonable doubt standard plays a vital role in the American scheme of criminal procedure. Thus, Brennan omitted "The burden of proof is closely related to the privilege against self-incrimination as a device to offset the adverse effect of a defendant's failure to defend himself. It also compensates for lack of discovery proceedings and disclosure devices traditionally available to ordinary civil litigants." Harlan then joined Brennan's opinion. He also issued his own concurrence, which expressly differentiated PINS from juvenile delinquents. Brennan's opinion simply indicated that no view was expressed on PINS.

It is unfortunate that Brennan eliminated his test for determining the content of juvenile due process from his *Winship* opinion; it might have avoided the fragmented majority that decided *McKeiver v. Pennsylvania*.[81] The request of appellants there for a jury trial had been denied, and they were adjudged juvenile delinquents under Pennsylvania law. Appellants argued for a right to a jury because they were tried in proceedings "substantially similar to a criminal trial." But the state supreme court held that there is no constitutional right to jury trial in juvenile court.

The conference voted six to three (Black, Douglas, and Marshall) to affirm. The opinion was assigned to Justice Blackmun on December 29, 1970. His draft, circulated May 12, 1971, contained a suggestion that use of the reasonable doubt standard might obviate the need for jury trials even in adult criminal cases. This suggestion was fortunately omitted from the final opinion, largely (I have been told) at the instance of Justice White.

Chief Justice Burger joined the Blackmun opinion with a May 26, 1971, Memorandum to the Conference: "I join the Court's opinion for it marks a pause, at least, in the dismantling of the juvenile court system." Attached to the memo was a one-page concurrence (later withdrawn), which stressed the Chief Justice's dissatisfaction with the *Gault–Winship* line of cases: "The whole concept of juvenile courts rested on an agreed premise that youthful offenders ought to be shielded from the trauma of a criminal trial with its panoply of indictment, preliminary hearings, jury selection, and the contention and tension of the adversary process.

"Step by step the Court has abandoned these concepts while wistfully professing to cling to them. And step by step we have moved the juvenile into the very atmosphere society thought to spare him.

"It remains to be seen whether we can salvage the hopes for special treatment for youth offenders."

Burger also argued that it was unfair to judge the juvenile-court system by its failure to measure up to "its extravagant 'advance billing.' . . . If we measured the whole spectrum of criminal justice by its 'success,' it would indeed be in grave jeopardy—as perhaps it is."

As it turned out, Blackmun's *McKeiver* opinion spoke only for a four-Justice plurality. It affirmed the holding that jury trial was not constitutionally required in juvenile cases, but its reasoning was not as clear as it would have been had Brennan's omitted *Winship* approach been followed.

The *Gault–Winship* approach to juvenile rights may become a two-edged sword. It may serve as the foundation for the extension to juveniles of rights guaranteed to adult criminal defendants. But it may also lead to dilution of the rights of adults. In his *McKeiver* draft, Blackmun had indicated that the use of the reasonable-doubt standard might obviate the need for jury trials even in adult criminal cases—a statement that might well have had a baneful effect on the rights of defendants generally had it not been omitted from the final opinion.

The point just made can be seen even more clearly in *Schall v. Martin*,[82] decided toward the end of the Burger tenure. A New York preventive-detention law authorized pretrial detention of an accused juvenile delinquent because there was a "serious risk" that the juvenile "may before the return date commit an act which if committed by an adult would constitute a crime." Under the statute, notice, a hearing, and a statement of facts and reasons were given to the juvenile prior to any detention, and a formal probable-cause hearing was held shortly thereafter. Juveniles who had been detained under the statute brought an action claiming that their due process rights were violated. The lower court ruled in their favor, holding that since the vast majority of juveniles detained under the statute either had their cases dismissed before an adjudication of delinquency or were released after adjudication, the statute was administered not for preventive purposes, but to impose punishment for unadjudicated criminal acts.

At the *Schall* conference, the Chief Justice and Justice White passed. Burger asserted, "I have always thought *Gault*[83] would destroy the juvenile [justice] system. There are terrible problems of juvenile delinquency." White told the others, "My problem is that there's no record of the statute's application to the named plaintiffs or any other specific persons."

Brennan, Marshall, and Stevens voted to affirm. Their view was succinctly stated by Marshall: "The finding below was that the statute was used to punish delinquents and that's enough to affirm."

The other four voted to uphold the statute. Rehnquist alone indicated that the case was a simple one, saying, "as to the named plaintiffs, the charge of denial of due process is simply frivolous." Blackmun voiced the general feeling, even of those for reversal, when he said, "I share everyone's discomfort with this case. . . . [P]ublic interest is very strong in it, but prediction of future dangerousness is always troublesome." Blackmun stressed that "the judge here does provide a statement of reasons and the time of detention is not great." Powell also pointed out the state interest and short detention period. "The state certainly has a substantial interest in keeping [these] people off the street for a short time until the hearing. Those time spans are certainly reasonable."

"This type of statute," stated O'Connor, also speaking for reversal, "is prevalent in most states and, if we throw it out, we create a serious situation. What the statute requires, while slim, is enough to avoid constitutional difficulty. . . . I'd allow more of this for juveniles than adults."

The four-to-three *Schall* conference vote became six to three in favor of the law when the Chief Justice and White joined the majority. The Rehnquist opinion of the Court followed the conference consensus and held that the statute authorizing pretrial detention of juveniles did not violate due process. "The 'legitimate and compelling state interest' in protecting the community from crime"[84] was ruled sufficient to support the preventive detention law, given the regulatory purpose for detention and the procedural protections in the law.

In spite of O'Connor's statement, *Schall* plainly had implications for adult preventive-detention laws. As the *Schall* opinion emphasizes, "The harm suffered by the victim of a crime is not dependent upon the age of the perpetrator."[85] The clear inference is that crime prevention through preventive detention also does not depend upon age. It is, therefore, scarcely surprising that later the Court, under Chief Justice Rehnquist, relied on *Schall* in upholding the constitutionality of an adult pretrial-detention statute.[86]

Chapter Twelve

Criminal Procedure II: *Mapp* and *Miranda* in the Burger Court

M*app v. Ohio*[1] and *Miranda v. Arizona*[2] were the Warren Court's paradigmatic criminal procedure decisions. They were also among the most criticized cases decided by that Court, and it was widely expected that they would be among the jurisprudential casualities of the Burger Court. Yet, while their rules were narrowed in significant respects by the Burger jurisprudence, they have continued as foundations of the law of criminal procedure. Indeed, at the end of the Burger tenure, the Court declared that *Miranda* struck the proper balance between the competing interests of society and those accused of crime.[3]

SEARCHES FOR EVIDENCE

The Fourth Amendment is more than a buffer against arbitrary arrests; it is also a bar against unlawful searches for evidence. There is the question of what constitutes a "search" within the meaning of the amendment. It has been said that the Burger Court took a "grudging view" in its answers to this question,[4] particularly in the decisions holding that police use of a pen register[5] and a "beeper"[6] were not "searches" governed by the amendment.[7]

In the "beeper" case, *United States v. Knotts*,[8] the police had installed an electronic tracking device inside a chloroform container. When a suspect bought the container, they followed his car by monitoring the beeper. They then secured a search warrant and discovered illegal drugs in his cabin. The lower court held that the warrantless beeper monitoring was a "search" prohibited by the Fourth Amendment. It violated the individual's reasonable expectation of privacy.

The Chief Justice set the *Knotts* conference theme when he asserted that "the beeper surveillance didn't violate the Fourth"; there was no "search" and hence no warrant requirement. The most important conference statement was, however, made by Justice White, who declared that this was "a new Fourth Amendment claim that [they] have a reasonable expectation of privacy in the use here of public streets. [This] argument leaves me cold. They could have followed him about and can therefore do this. So I agree that the Fourth Amendment was not implicated up to the point the beep got to the house and was kept there. But they had probable cause when they got the warrant and entered the house."[9]

Rehnquist, author of the *Knotts* opinion, agreed. "This was nothing but an extension of the visual, no 'search.'" His opinion took essentially the same approach. What happened here "amounted principally to the following of an automobile on public streets." There was no expectation of privacy from visual surveillance in such a case and "scientific enhancement of this sort raises no constitutional issues which visual surveillance would not also raise."[10]

The *Knotts* opinion also relied on the "open fields" rule laid down over half a century earlier in the *Hester* case.[11] Under it, "the special protection accorded by the Fourth Amendment . . . is not extended to the open fields."[12]—that is, land outside the house itself and the surrounding curtilage.

The Burger Court also applied the "open fields" rule in *Oliver v. United States.*[13] Acting on reports that marijuana was being raised on petitioner's farm, police officers found a field of marijuana over a mile from petitioner's house. The district court suppressed evidence of the discovery of the field. It applied *Katz v. United States,*[14] which had laid down an "expectation of privacy" test to govern the reach of the Fourth Amendment. The district court held that petitioner had a reasonable expectation that the fields would remain private and that these were not "open" fields. The court of appeals reversed.

"The case for me," the Chief Justice began the *Oliver* conference, "is whether *Hester* makes these searches valid because the Fourth [Amendment] doesn't apply. Does the effort at privacy [a locked gate and a "No Trespassing" sign] change things?" Burger asserted that it did not. "I think *Katz* is the governing analysis—but under an objective, not subjective test." (Justice Harlan, concurring in *Katz,* had stated the test as one under which "a person [had] exhibited an actual [subjective] expectation of privacy."[15]) "'Open fields' for me are undeveloped plots and the number of trees can't change that. So I'd apply *Hester* here and affirm."

Brennan, Marshall, and Stevens disagreed with the Burger approach. Their view was succinctly stated by Marshall: "I wouldn't extend *Hester* to a plot where the owners did as much as was done here to shut people out."

The others voted with the Chief Justice to affirm. White stressed the Fourth Amendment's language and asked, with regard to "fields": "Is it a person, house, or effect? It hardly fits any of these and that's what *Hester* held, I think. . . . *Katz* doesn't mean we have roving authority to protect privacy whenever it's claimed. Anyway, *Katz* didn't overrule *Hester*."

Blackmun also relied on the constitutional wording. "The language of the Fourth Amendment doesn't reach fields." Powell referred to "John Harlan's concurrence in *Katz*," which, Powell said, included "only expectations society could recognize as reasonable. . . . That and the language of the Fourth excludes open fields." Rehnquist asserted a similar view: "An open field is not the same thing as the interior of a building."

In his *Oliver* opinion of the Court, Powell followed his conference approach, stressing that the "explicit language of the Fourth Amendment" did not include fields. Powell also followed Blackmun's conference suggestion: "I'd choose a bright line. . . . I'd go for a per se open fields exception." At the conference Powell had said, "I'd go with Harry's bright line." In his opinion, Powell did adopt the bright line—per se posture: "an individual may not legitimately demand privacy for activities conducted out of doors in fields, except in the area immediately surrounding the home."[16] Hence open fields are not free from warrantless intrusion by government officers.

The application of modern technology to the "open fields" rule was involved in *California v. Ciraolo*.[17] The police had received a tip that marijuana was growing in respondent's backyard, hidden behind two fences. Officers trained in marijuana identification flew over respondent's house and readily identified marijuana plants growing in the yard. A search warrant was obtained and the marijuana plants were seized. But the state court held that the warrantless aerial observation violated the Fourth Amendment.

At the *Ciraolo* conference, the Chief Justice urged reversal. "Aerial observation by the naked eye from an airplane is the issue here," he said. "Did respondent have a reasonable expectation of privacy that society is prepared to accept? . . . [I]n 1787 and 1791, [there were] no airplanes and the Framers didn't anticipate them." Perhaps, Burger conceded, "[We] could assume a violation if [there were] deliberate photos of sunbathing. But flying is so routine that people can't say they have an expectation of privacy."

The argument for affirmance was led by Justice Brennan. "In this case, because the parties agree that the police searched the area immediately surrounding his home, respondent was entitled to a reasonable expectation of privacy. . . . The police circumvented respondent's legitimate expectation of privacy by observing his property from the air. To allow . . . this type of surveillance would effectively eliminate any privacy interest in the area surrounding the home. . . . I cannot understand how the aerial surveillance that took place here can be considered anything but a 'search' of respondent's property."

Brennan was troubled by intrusive technologies. In a companion case, he noted at the conference, "The government used both an airplane and special photographic equipment to observe what could not be seen from the ground with the naked eye. . . . If we were to sanction the use of such measures here, I am afraid that there would be no limit on the type of intrusive technology the government could employ." [18]

The *Ciraolo* conference divided six to three (Brennan, Blackmun, and Powell, who asserted, "If we start down the road of cutting back on the Fourth [Amendment], we won't know where to stop"). The decision became one by a bare majority, when Marshall joined the dissenters. The Court opinion, by the Chief Justice, followed his conference approach; observation from public airspace in a physically nonintrusive manner does not violate the Fourth Amendment.

Powell, who wrote the dissent, indicated that the majority had acted in ignorance of the reality involved in air reconnaissance. In a December 13, 1985, letter to Brennan headed *Personal,* he referred to their World War II experience; "after all, certainly you and I know more about reconnaissance aircraft (for which the P-38 also was used) than some of our other friends!"

Where a "search" is involved within the meaning of the Fourth Amendment a warrant is normally required. Long before the Burger appointment, however, the Court recognized two major exceptions to the warrant requirement. A critic claims that the Burger Court's treatment of (1) the search incident to a lawful arrest and (2) the automobile exception "illustrates how it has cut down the protections provided by the Fourth Amendment." [19]

The Burger Court itself referred to the "long line of cases recognizing an exception to the warrant requirement when a search is incident to a valid arrest."[20] That exception had been recognized in an important Warren Court decision.[21] That decision did not, however, indicate whether the right to search the person flowed automatically from the fact of arrest or whether searches might be undertaken only when there was a likelihood that evidence or weapons would be found.[22] The Burger Court ruled that the former and broader approach was the correct one in two companion cases—*United States v. Robinson*[23] and *Gustafson v. Florida*.[24]

In *Robinson*, an officer had searched respondent after arresting him for driving after his license had been revoked. He found a package of heroin, which was introduced in evidence at the criminal trial. In *Gustafson*, petitioner had been searched after being arrested for driving without a license. Marijuana was found and used in evidence against petitioner. The court of appeals held that the evidence in *Robinson* had been obtained as a result of a search which violated the Fourth Amendment. The state court in *Gustafson* reached the opposite result.

The issue here, Chief Justice Burger began the conference, "was whether the search was within the proper scope as an incident of an arrest. . . . [I]f an arrestee is going to be taken into custody, the officer may go further than just a protective search—at least it may be more extensive than a *Terry*[25] frisk. . . . So long as there are grounds for arrest, a full search of the person may be made."[26]

Douglas, Brennan, and Marshall disagreed. Their view was succinctly stated by Douglas: "A search is limited to protection of the officer, and [it] goes way beyond that range here." The others supported the Chief Justice. The most influential conference statement was made by Stewart, who declared that he "would resent gradations in permissible scope. What's necessary here is ascertainable working rules." Several others agreed with Stewart. White said, "The forthright rule suggested by Potter is the only sensible one."

Stewart went on to tell the conference, "It's established that, where there's a constitutional custodial arrest, there can be a search of the whole person, or anything within his reach. . . . I'm bothered that cops often hustle and harass arrests. But that's not this case. Since [you] can have an inventory search at the station, why not at the scene of arrest?"

Rehnquist, who was to author the *Robinson* and *Gustafson* opinions, said, "[N]ot only precedent, but the Framers of the Fourth [Amendment] thought a full search in connection with a valid arrest was O.K." The Rehnquist opinions followed this view and stated the categorical rule that Stewart had urged: "in the case of a lawful custodial arrest a full search of the person is not only an exception to the warrant requirement of the Fourth Amendment, but is also a 'reasonable' search under that Amendment."[27]

The Warren Court recognized the search-incident-to-arrest exception to the warrant requirement but limited the exception to "a search of the arrestee's person and the area 'within his immediate control'—construing that phrase to mean the area from which he might gain possession of a weapon or destructible evidence."[28] The limitation was applied by determining whether and to what extent it was *possible* for the person arrested to reach the place that was searched notwithstanding his arrest.[29]

The need for a case-by-case assessment was largely eliminated by the Burger Court in *New York v. Belton.*[30] A policeman had stopped a speeding auto. The officer smelled burnt marijuana and saw an envelope on the floor of the vehicle that he associated with marijuana. He arrested the occupants of the car for unlawful possession of marijuana and searched them and the car. In a jacket on the back seat he found cocaine. A motion to suppress the cocaine was denied. The highest state court reversed; the warrantless search of the jacket pockets was invalid.

Once again, the most important conference statement was made by Stewart. "The issue here is the permissible geographic scope of a lawful custodial arrest. I'd hold that when the occupants of a car are lawfully arrested, the permissible geographic scope is the automobile."

The majority at the *Belton* conference agreed. The prevailing view was expressed by Powell. The search was valid because when you are "dealing with a passenger car, the interior of the car is a finite space normally under the control of the passengers in it."

Stewart's *Belton* opinion of the Court ruled that the search was a valid incident to a lawful custodial arrest. It laid down what Powell termed "a 'bright-line' rule"[31]—that is, the type of rule Stewart had urged in *Robinson* and *Gustafson:* "when a policeman has made a lawful custodial arrest of the occupant of an automobile, he may, as a contemporaneous incident of that arrest, search the passenger compartment of that automobile [including] the contents of any containers found within the passenger compartment."[32]

At the *Belton* conference, several of the Justices asserted that the case was indistinguishable from *Robbins v. California,*[33] decided the same day. In *Robbins,* the Court held that police officers, who had stopped a station wagon for driving erratically and who smelled marijuana, might not validly search the trunk and open and seize two packages of marijuana wrapped in opaque plastic. At the *Belton* conference, White had said, "I can't see how this can be distinguished from *Robbins.* If the package [were] on the back seat with the jacket, how can [you] say a warrant [is required] for one and not another?" Stevens had also asked, "[Is there] any difference between the back seat and the trunk? I don't think so. This [that is, *Belton*] has to be affirmed if *Robbins* is reversed."

Robbins was, however, different from *Belton.* It did not involve a search incident to arrest, but an automobile search, where no arrest had been made. Over half a century earlier, the *Carroll* case[34] had laid down the automobile exception to the warrant requirement. Federal agents had stopped a car they had probable cause to believe contained illegal liquor and subjected it to a warrantless search. Under *Carroll,* the reasonableness of the search of vehicles is judged differently from the search of homes. Probable cause alone may not be enough to justify search of a home without a warrant. But the mobility of automobiles makes rigorous enforcement of the warrant requirement impossible.[35] A valid search of a vehicle moving on a public highway may be made without a warrant, if probable cause for the search exists.

The *Carroll* doctrine permitted warrantless searches of cars only when there were both probable cause to believe the car contained evidence of crime and "exigent circumstances" making the warrant requirement impractical[36]—such as in the case of a moving vehicle. The Burger Court substantially lessened these restrictions.

In *Chambers v. Maroney,*[37] the police had probable cause to believe that a car was carrying robbers, guns, and the fruits of a crime. They arrested the occupants and then searched the car at the police station. The Court upheld the warrantless search. Under *Chambers* and later cases, the Burger Court virtually did away with the requirement of exigent circumstances justifying the search—at least when the nonmoving vehicle is in police custody.

In *South Dakota v. Opperman,*[38] respondent's car had been impounded for parking violations. The police found marijuana in the glove compartment. A motion to suppress the marijuana as evidence was denied. Stewart, who passed at the conference (though he later joined the four dissenters) expressed an interesting conference approach, in which he analogized the case to administrative inspection cases.[39] "Probable cause is an irrelevant concept here, perhaps as in *Camara* and *See*"[40]—the leading cases on administrative inspections. In those cases, "the substitute for probable cause was, that [they] get an order—an administrative one should suffice[41]—to regularize the procedure."

None of the others followed Stewart's approach. Instead, a five-to-three majority (which became a bare majority when Stewart joined the dissenters) agreed with Justice Rehnquist: "A search in these circumstances can't be discussed in terms of probable cause, since [the police were] not looking for evidence of crime. So the argument is over reasonableness and I think this was [reasonable]."

Opperman held that the Fourth Amendment permits a routine police inventory of an impounded auto. This ruling, together with the other Burger Court cases on auto searches, virtually removes the Fourth Amendment as a barrier to searches of vehicles in police custody.

This broadening of search power accorded with the views of both Chief Justice Burger and his successor. At the *Chambers* conference, the Chief Justice declared, "I have never been able to see why [you] need a warrant to search a car." And, at the *Robbins* conference, Justice Rehnquist told his colleagues, "I'd adopt the automobile exception as a bright line. If [the police] have probable cause to search for an object in an automobile, [they] don't need a warrant."

In *Robbins,* the majority did not accept the Rehnquist approach, holding instead that the police might not search a closed car trunk and seize wrapped packages there. However, the broader Burger–Rehnquist view was accepted in *United States v. Ross.*[42] Police officers, acting on information from a reliable informant, stopped a car and opened its locked trunk. They found a sealed bag of heroin. An officer drove the auto to headquarters and searched the car, finding a zippered pouch containing cash. The driver was convicted of possession of heroin with intent to distribute. The court had denied his motion to suppress the heroin and currency. The court of appeals reversed; the police should have first obtained a warrant.

"We need a bright line," declared the Chief Justice at the *Ross* conference—a point concurred in by several of the others, notably Powell, who stressed "[We] ought to have a bright line for the benefit of the police." The Court should allow this search, Burger asserted—what he termed "a 'French connection' search," which was "a complete exception from the warrant requirement. . . . I can't see how [we can] distinguish kinds of containers either."

Brennan, White, and Marshall spoke for affirmance. White said flatly that he would "stick to *Robbins*. I don't see [why they] have to have a warrant to open a suitcase in a hotel, but not in a car."

The others voted with the Chief Justice for reversal. The prevailing conference view was stated by Rehnquist. "The best chance for a bright line is the Government's . . . position—[allow] a search for anything in the car on probable cause to search the car." Thus, as Stevens, the author of the *Ross* opinion, put it to the conference, "the auto exception contains everything in the car. [The police] can make as much of a search as [they] could with a warrant."

Ross extended the "automobile exception." Whenever police have probable cause to believe that contraband may be found within an auto, they may search the entire car and any container found inside it. The scope of the search is as broad as a magistrate could authorize in a warrant to search the auto. In Powell's words to the *Ross* conference, "An automobile is very different from a residence."

There is, of course, no Fourth Amendment problem if the individual has given consent to what might otherwise be an illegal search and seizure. But what must be shown to establish "consent"? The Burger Court answered that question in *Schneckloth v. Bustamonte*.[43] A police officer had stopped an auto with a burned-out headlight and license plate light. When the officer asked if he could search the car, the driver replied, "Sure, go ahead" and opened the trunk and glove compartment. The officer found three stolen checks. The state court held that the search and seizure were valid, applying the standard previously formulated by Justice Traynor, one of the best judges never to sit on the Supreme Court: "Whether in a particular case an apparent consent was in fact voluntarily given or was in submission to an express or implied assertion of authority, is a question of fact to be determined in light of all the circumstances."[44] A federal appellate court disagreed in a habeas corpus proceeding: The state had to show not only that the consent had been uncoerced, but that it had been given with an understanding that it could be freely withheld.

The Chief Justice began the *Schneckloth* conference by saying that he "wouldn't require warnings" by the police that consent could be refused. He would accept "Traynor's totality [test which] adds up to reasonable under all the circumstances." According to Burger, that test was met here.

The opposition was led by Brennan; the state had to prove consent and part of the burden was showing that there was knowledge of the right to refuse. Justice Stewart, who was to deliver the Court's opinion, countered, "I would agree with [Bill Brennan] that the state has to prove consent, though not that the burden included knowledge that he didn't have to agree to the search. . . . I'd reverse."

Brennan was supported at the conference by Douglas and Marshall. The others agreed with the Burger–Stewart view. As Justice White put it, the Court "can infer from the request to search, and the consent thereto, that one knew that he could refuse." Blackmun stated his support for the Traynor approach in terms of state autonomy. "I always read *Ker*[45] as giving the states latitude to develop their own standards [as] California did here as to its voluntariness standard."

The *Schneckloth* decision followed the majority conference approach. The Traynor "totality of circumstances" test was adopted and, under it, valid consent had been given. The Court rejected the Brennan view that the state had to prove that the one giving consent knew that he had a right to withhold it. It was a factor to be taken into account; but the state did not have to establish it as a prerequisite to a valid consent.

EXCLUSIONARY RULE

"To me," Justice Fortas once told this writer, "the most radical decision in recent times was *Mapp against Ohio*."[46] *Mapp* held that the exclusionary rule, which forbids the admission of illegally obtained evidence, was applicable to the states under the Fourteenth Amendment. The theory behind *Mapp* was succinctly stated in a letter by Justice Clark, the author of the opinion. If the right guaranteed by the Fourth Amendment "is really to be enforceable against the states. . . , then we cannot carve out of the bowels [of] that right the vital part, the stuff that gives it substance, the exclusion of evidence."[47] The Constitution's ban against unreasonable searches and seizures is enforced by the exclusionary rule. Evidence obtained in violation of the Fourth Amendment may not be used in any way against the victim of the search.

Chief Justice Burger was anything but a partisan of the exclusionary rule. During his second term, he used *Bivens v. Six Unknown Named Agents*[48] to attack the rule. *Bivens* held that federal agents could be sued for damages for injuries resulting from their Fourth Amendment violations. The case apparently had nothing to do with the exclusionary rule. During the postargument conference, however, the Chief Justice, while opposing the decision on the ground that "courts [should not] create a cause of action for constitutional violations," also stated, "I agree that it's a good first step toward abolishing the exclusionary rule." Then, in his *Bivens* dissent, Burger delivered a broadside assault on the rule "as an anomalous and ineffective mechanism with which to regulate law enforcement." The Court should not continue "clinging to an unworkable and irrational concept of law."[49]

In *Coolidge v. New Hampshire*,[50] decided the same day as *Bivens*, the Chief Justice's dissent referred to "the monstrous price we pay for the exclusionary rule in which we seem to have imprisoned ourselves."[51] Burger was not alone. In their *Coolidge* opinions, Harlan asserted that *Mapp* should be overruled and Black and Blackmun stated specifically that "the Fourth Amendment supports no exclusionary rule."[52]

The expressions of discontent with the exclusionary rule led White to note, in a June 17, 1971, Memorandum to the Conference, "With the publication of *Coolidge* and *Bivens*, four Justices (CJ, JMH, HLB and HAB) will have stated for the record their dissatisfaction with *Mapp v. Ohio* insofar as the exclusionary rule is based on the Fourth Amendment."[53] White also pointed out that "although I do not presume to indicate Potter's present views, I note that he did not join the Court in *Mapp*. . . . My present view is that the exclusionary rule should at least be narrowed." White recommended a reexamination of *Mapp*. "I suggest we consider whether we should call for reargument in *Coolidge* limited to the single question whether *Mapp v. Ohio* should be overruled."

White did not obtain the votes needed to secure a *Coolidge* reargument on the *Mapp* issue, but it was clear that a majority of the Justices were dissatisfied with the exclusionary rule. The Burger Court was thus close to a majority for overruling *Mapp*. Soon after the 1970 term, however, Black and Harlan retired. They were replaced by Powell and Rehnquist. The latter proved even more firm than Black in his opposition to the exclusionary rule. But Powell, in line with his general views on stare decisis, was not ready to overrule *Mapp*, though he was willing to narrow the exclusionary rule. The subsequent Burger Court theme was stated by Justice Blackmun in the later *Janis* conference:[54] "Confine the exclusionary rule as narrowly as possible and never extend it." The later Burger years saw a progressive narrowing of the rule, culminating in the good-faith exception and cost–benefit cases.

A good-faith exception to the exclusionary rule had been urged in the Court almost a decade before it was established in the Burger Court jurisprudence. In the *Janis* conference, Powell stressed that "the police acted in good faith" and Rehnquist spoke in favor of a "good-faith exception in both civil and criminal cases." And in *Stone v. Powell,*[55] White's dissent urged that the exclusionary rule "should be substantially modified so as to prevent its application in those many circumstances where the evidence at issue was seized by an officer acting in the good-faith belief that his conduct comported with existing law and having reasonable grounds for this belief."[56]

Until 1984, the narrowing of the exclusionary rule was limited to settings that are "peripheral" or "collateral" to criminal procedure, such as grand jury proceedings[57] and civil tax proceedings,[58] as well as the use of illegally obtained evidence for impeachment purposes.[59] Burger Court jurisprudence had not affected the rule in its central application: the prosecution's case against a defendant whose Fourth Amendment rights had been violated. This was changed when, in the *Leon* and *Sheppard* cases, the Court adopted a good-faith exception to the exclusionary rule.

In *United States v. Leon,*[60] a police officer, acting under a search warrant issued by a state judge, seized large quantities of drugs. The lower court recognized that the police officer in question had acted in good-faith reliance on the warrant, but ruled that the evidence should be suppressed because the affidavit on which the warrant had been issued was insufficient to establish probable cause. *Massachusetts v. Sheppard*[61] involved a similar situation, except that the warrant was defective because it did not particularly describe the items to be seized. The *Sheppard* lower court also refused to recognize a good-faith exception.

Leon and *Sheppard* were discussed at the same postargument conference. The Chief Justice began the discussion by telling the others, "I'd adopt a good-faith exception and reverse." He did, however, advise the Court to go no further than that. "I would be dissatisfied to write anything that might be read as wiping out the exclusionary rule. We must write tightly to avoid that."[62]

Brennan, who strongly opposed a good-faith exception, realized that the votes were the other way. He, therefore, urged that the good-faith issue be avoided. "In this case [*Leon*], I fail to see why the proper disposition is not simply to vacate and remand in light of *Gates*.[63] . . . [T]he lower court, if given the opportunity to consider the warrant application in light of *Gates*, might well find a sufficient showing of probable cause to support the issuance of the warrant." However, "if there are five to reach the good-faith issue . . . then I will be in dissent."[64]

Brennan was supported by Marshall and Stevens, with the latter contending that it was "unwise to reach good faith here. . . . The reasonableness standard of the Fourth Amendment itself suffices."

The others agreed with the Chief Justice that a good-faith exception should be adopted, though Blackmun and Powell conceded that the cases could be decided without it. Powell also declared, "I wouldn't abandon the exclusionary rule as such under any circumstances." White, Rehnquist, and O'Connor, as well as Blackmun and Powell, spoke in favor of adopting a good-faith exception. According to O'Connor, it was "time to restrict the scope of the exclusionary rule. . . . the Framers relied on tort law, as the English did. . . . [G]ood-faith exception will require an adjustment of tort remedies to replace the exclusionary rule."

Several of the Justices urged that the Court adopt an objective good-faith exception. As Rehnquist put it, "I would not allow a subjective good-faith standard—only a wholly objective standard." Similarly Powell said, "I could perhaps go with an objective, reasonable good-faith test."

The *Leon* decision did enunciate an objective good-faith exception. As explained in the *Sheppard* opinion, "[T]he exclusionary rule should not be applied when the officer conducting the search acted in objectively reasonable reliance on a warrant issued by a detached and neutral magistrate that subsequently is determined to be invalid."[65] Since the officers in both *Leon* and *Sheppard* had acted in good-faith reliance upon search warrants, the lower court decisions in both cases were reversed.

There is still the question of whether *Leon* and *Sheppard* laid down a general good-faith exception or are limited to cases where a warrant has been obtained. The opinions are not clear, but the conference discussion indicates that the Justices did intend to confine the good-faith exception to the warrant setting. Even Rehnquist and O'Connor, perhaps the strongest opponents of the exclusionary rule, stressed such a limitation. Rehnquist told the conference, "I would adopt good faith, limited to a warrant situation." O'Connor also said, "I can go along with [a good-faith] exception, but only if it's . . . limited to warrant cases."

ILLEGAL EVIDENCE AND COST–BENEFIT ANALYSIS

Even more important regarding *Leon* and *Sheppard* was the use of cost–benefit analysis by the Court to buttress its conclusion that a good-faith exception to the exclusionary rule was warranted. In *Leon,* the Court stated, "Whether the exclusionary sanction is appropriately imposed in a particular case . . . must be resolved by weighing the costs and benefits of preventing the use of [the illegally obtained] evidence."[66] It was, however, in *Immigration & Naturalization Service v. Lopez-Mendoza,*[67] decided the same day as *Leon* and *Sheppard,* that the Burger Court elevated cost–benefit analysis (CBA) to the top of the Bill of Rights agenda. *Lopez-Mendoza* arose out of a deportation proceeding. The alien had contended that evidence introduced at the hearing should have been suppressed as the fruit of an unlawful arrest. The INS held that the evidence was admissible because the exclusionary rule did not apply to deportation proceedings. The court of appeals reversed.

The *Lopez-Mendoza* conference was closely divided. The crucial question was stated by the Chief Justice: "Should the exclusionary rule be extended to civil deportation proceedings?" Burger answered in the negative, saying, "I reject the argument that this is more like a criminal case, despite the hardship incident to deportation."

The conference focused on *Janis,*[68] which had held that the exclusionary rule did not bar the federal government from using evidence illegally obtained by state law enforcement officers in a civil tax proceeding. The *Janis* Court found that the "marginal deterrence provided by forbidding a different sovereign from using the evidence . . . does not outweigh the cost to society of extending the [exclusionary] rule to that situation."[69] The lower court in *Lopez-Mendoza* interpreted this to mean CBA: "in *Janis,* the Court balanced the deterrent benefit to be gained against the social cost of invoking the rule."[70]

At the *Lopez-Mendoza* conference, all the Justices assumed that CBA was appropriate to determine whether the exclusionary rule should be applied in a given case. Even Brennan, who led the argument in favor of affirmance, did not dispute the application of CBA. However, Brennan's use of CBA differed from that by the majority. "I would conclude that the balance of costs and benefits that we considered in *Janis* tips decisively in favor of applying the Rule to deportation hearings. I would therefore affirm."[71]

Brennan gave three reasons to support his conclusion: "*First,* here, unlike in *Janis,* there is a direct connection between the conduct of INS agents and the application of the Exclusionary Rule in deportation proceedings. . . . *Second,* the fact that the INS is a single, integrated federal agency actually weighs in favor of applying the Rule here." That was true "because here we can be especially confident that applying the Rule will yield substantial benefits in terms of deterring unconstitutional law-enforcement activity." Finally, "despite Andy Frey's[72] protestations, the evidence that we have suggests that the Exclusionary Rule has been thought for many, many years to apply in deportation proceedings. . . . Consequently, we have direct evidence of the kind that we rarely have in this area that a law-enforcement regime which applies the Exclusionary Rule is able to function smoothly and without substantial problems."

Brennan was supported by White, Marshall, and Stevens. The others voted to reverse. "Although I wrote *Janis,*" said Blackmun, "this for me is civil and I won't extend [this] judge-made rule to it." Blackmun stated the CBA conclusion of the conference majority: "The societal costs greatly exceed the benefits here." Rehnquist went further: "Don't let the exclusionary rule spread is my base belief." Powell and O'Connor agreed. "Even though [the agency] has applied the rule," asserted O'Connor, "we should not mandate it—at least in non-egregious situations that [do not] amount to due process violations."

The *Lopez-Mendoza* decision, like the conference vote, reversed by a bare majority. The O'Connor opinion followed a CBA approach that weighed the benefits secured from the exclusionary rule in the deportation case against the costs of applying the rule. The deterrent value was seen to be its primary benefit. O'Connor found the benefit to be significantly reduced in the deportation case. She then concluded that the social costs of applying the exclusionary rule in deportation proceedings "are both unusual and significant,"[73] and these costs, particularly in terms of delay and the increased burden on the agency, outweigh the benefits. White, who delivered the principal dissent, did not disagree with the cost–benefit approach. He simply appraised the costs and benefits differently, concluding that the Court had unduly minimized the benefits and exaggerated the costs.

Lopez-Mendoza may signal a fundamental change in the judicial approach to claimed violations of procedural rights. Before that case, the Court asked only: Has a procedural right guaranteed by statute and/or due process been violated in the given case?

Under *Lopez-Mendoza,* an affirmative answer is not enough to lead to a decision in favor of the individual. Instead, CBA must be applied to determine whether the right itself is guaranteed in the particular proceeding. If the CBA balance tilts against the right in the given case, the government will be upheld even though it has violated the right concerned.

CBA has about it a delusive aura of scientific objectivity that may be justified in the field of economics in which it began and has increasingly been used. As a constitutional law tool, however, it is as subjective as the Benthamite "felicific calculus"[74] that was its primitive progenitor. Just as each utilitarian would apply the "greatest happiness of the greatest number"[75] principle according to his own subjective judgment of the pains and pleasures involved, so each judge employing CBA will use his own calculus in weighing the procedural rights at issue. What appears as objective analysis is really Benthamism in modern dress—and with a subjective vengeance.

There is another factor that may be even more important in considering whether the *Lopez-Mendoza* type of CBA is appropriate. When we deal with an individual right such as that protected by the exclusionary rule, it is much easier to quantify costs than benefits. It is, indeed, all but impossible to measure most procedural rights in monetary terms, though it is not difficult to do so as far as the costs of protecting those rights in given cases are concerned. How much is freedom from illegally seized evidence worth? If the procedural right cannot be quantified in monetary terms, the cost–benefit approach will always tend to a weighting of the balance on the cost side of the scale. The result, in a case such as *Lopez-Mendoza,* is that the law is "drawn into a curious world where the 'costs' of excluding illegally obtained evidence loom to exaggerated heights and where the 'benefits' of such exclusion are made to disappear with a mere wave of the hand."[76]

A system that values basic rights in more than dollars-and-cents terms should hesitate before following an approach in which the end result is one in which *priceless* may too often mean *worthless.*[77]

MIRANDA AND POLICE INTERROGATION

Miranda v. Arizona[78] "was the centerpiece of the Warren Court's 'revolution in American criminal procedure.'"[79] While the Burger Court may have blunted *Miranda*,[80] as the Chief Justice himself said in 1980, "I would neither overrule *Miranda,* disparage it, nor extend it at this late date."[81]

Harris v. New York,[82] dealt with the question of whether a statement obtained in violation of *Miranda* could be used to impeach petitioner's testimony at trial. The state courts had held that the confession could be so used.

The Court was closely divided on the granting of certiorari, with Douglas, Harlan, Brennan, and White voting to grant. Despite this, the conference did not dispute the Chief Justice's assertion, "*Walder*[83] controls and requires affirmance." Burger was referring to a case in which physical evidence, inadmissible because seized illegally, was permitted to be used to impeach the accused's testimony. The conference vote was unanimous in favor of affirmance. The Chief Justice assigned the case to himself.

The Burger first draft concluded that, although "some comments in the *Miranda* opinion can be read as indicating a bar to use of an uncounseled statement for any purpose," those comments were dicta and "In our view the holding in *Walder v. United States* . . . is dispositive." The next day Black wrote to the Chief Justice that he agreed that *Walder* was indistinguishable but that since he had dissented in *Walder,* he wished to be noted as dissenting. Douglas also wrote that he was "doubtful" and wished to be noted as dissenting.

A day later Brennan sent a "Dear Chief" letter, saying that *Walder* did not control the result, and that, so far as it was relevant, *Walder* supported a dissent. He wrote that he would change his vote and circulate a dissent.

The Brennan dissent, first circulated January 29, 1971, distinguished *Walder* as involving only impeachment as to collateral matters unrelated to the crime presently charged. It stressed the language of *Miranda* that statements taken without warnings could not be used "in *any* manner."[84] Brennan's draft dissent concluded with the statement that "it is monstrous to aid the law-breaking policeman."[85]

The Brennan dissent was joined by Douglas and Marshall, with Justice Black listed as dissenting separately. Thus, instead of the unanimous conference decision, the *Harris* modification of *Miranda* was a bare majority decision. However, *Harris* was an early indication that the Burger Court would take a more restrictive approach to *Miranda*. Chief Justice Warren, in *Miranda*, had stated categorically that statements without the required warnings might not be used "in any manner" and had given the example of statements used for impeachment purposes.[86] Chief Justice Burger, in *Harris*, held specifically that such a use could be made of statements inadmissible under *Miranda* as part of the state's direct case.

In *Michigan v. Mosley*,[87] defendant had been arrested in connection with certain robberies. He exercised his right to remain silent after a police officer advised him of his *Miranda* rights. More than two hours later, another police officer also advised him of his *Miranda* rights and questioned him about an unrelated holdup–murder. He obtained an incriminating statement from defendant, who neither asked to consult with a lawyer nor indicated that he did not want to discuss the homicide. The lower court held that the second interrogation was a per se violation of the *Miranda* doctrine.

The *Mosley* conference was closely divided. Douglas, Brennan, White, and Marshall were for affirmance. The others voted to reverse. The Chief Justice said that here there was "no occasion to overrule *Miranda*. [We] can go along with a narrow basis" of decision. Such a basis was best indicated by Powell, who said, "[We] can decide the case within the framework of *Miranda*, without overruling or qualifying that decision." Powell's narrower approach was summarized by Justice Rehnquist: "I can go for Lewis's position that the question, after the warnings, is whether there was a voluntary waiver of *Miranda* rights."

Stewart, author of the *Mosley* opinion, stressed the fact that defendant had only said that he did not want to answer questions about the robberies. "It would have been proper," Stewart told the conference, "for the first detective to question [him] about the murder after stopping questions about the robberies."

The *Mosley* decision did not go as far as this Stewart conference approach. It rejected the lower court's per se approach and stressed the defendant's "right to cut off questioning."[88] That right, according to the Stewart opinion, was fully respected. After receiving the warnings again, defendant freely answered questions about the homicide during the second interrogation. The emphasis was on the voluntary nature of defendant's answers after the second warnings had been given.

Mosley did involve a dilution of *Miranda*,[89] but it left the essentials of the Warren Court landmark untouched. But the same was not true of three cases decided toward the end of the Burger tenure. The first was *New York v. Quarles*.[90] A police officer pursued a rape suspect into a supermarket. He caught the suspect, who was reportedly armed, and frisked him. After discovering an empty shoulder holster, the officer asked where the gun was. The suspect nodded toward some empty cartons and responded, "The gun is over there." The officer retrieved the gun from one of the cartons, formally arrested the man, and read him his *Miranda* rights. The state court excluded the statement and the gun because the suspect had not been given the *Miranda* warnings at the beginning.

The *Quarles* issue was stated by the Chief Justice at the beginning of his conference presentation: "Can exigent circumstances excuse [lack of] *Miranda* warnings and, in any event, can physical evidence as here be excluded?" Burger pointed out that "respondent was in custody, but, in that setting, it was natural for the officer to ask where the gun was. . . . I think we should craft an exception to *Miranda* for exigent circumstances, but I wouldn't overrule *Miranda*."

A bare majority at the conference (the Chief Justice and Justices White, Blackmun, Powell, and Rehnquist) agreed that the decision below should be reversed. "The public safety interest is compelling here," stated Blackmun. "This 'custody' was not the *Miranda* type. This was a spontaneous question incident to arrest." The bare majority concurred in the establishment of a "public safety" exception to *Miranda*.

Powell went further in his conference presentation. "I would have a per se rule that a cop learning a weapon is in the vicinity should be *required* to ask this question. [It would be] gross negligence on his part not to ask the question in his own interest and the safety of the public. We don't have to cut back on *Miranda* to do that."

The five-to-four division in *Quarles* was only on the admission of the statement made by the suspect. O'Connor joined to make up a majority of six on admission of the gun in evidence. As summarized by Brennan, "Sandra voted to affirm as to suppression of the statement but to reverse as to suppression of the gun."[91]

O'Connor herself explained her split vote in a letter to Rehnquist, author of the *Quarles* opinion: "I continue to believe that if we are to adhere to *Miranda*, a clear, bright line will serve us better than a blurring of the rule for a 'public safety' exception. What I believe is more important in the case is to determine that failure to properly administer *Miranda* warnings is not in itself justification for suppression of the nontestimonial fruits, i.e., the gun." [92]

The Rehnquist *Quarles* opinion established a "public safety" exception. *Miranda* should not "be applied in all its rigor to a situation in which police officers ask questions reasonably prompted by a concern for the public safety." [93]

Moran v. Burbine [94] also narrowed *Miranda*. After respondent was arrested by the police in Cranston, Rhode Island, in connection with a burglary, the police obtained evidence suggesting that he might be responsible for a murder in Providence. He was then questioned by Providence police about the murder. That same evening his sister, who was unaware that respondent was under suspicion of murder, telephoned the Public Defender's Office to obtain legal assistance for her brother on the burglary charge. An assistant public defender volunteered to act as respondent's counsel, but, when she phoned the police, she was told that he would not be questioned further until the next day. The attorney was not informed that the Providence police were there or that respondent was a murder suspect.

Less than an hour later, the Providence police began a series of interviews with respondent, giving *Miranda* warnings before each session and obtaining three signed waivers from him prior to eliciting three signed statements admitting to the murder. Respondent was unaware of his sister's efforts to retain counsel and of the attorney's telephone call, but at no time did he request an attorney. A federal appeals court held that the police, in failing to inform respondent of the attorney's call, had fatally tainted his waivers of his Fifth Amendment privilege against self-incrimination.

The Chief Justice began the *Moran* conference by speaking in favor of reversal. "The *Miranda* goal was to let the accused know his rights and, once done, the police can listen if he talks. The court of appeals was just wrong in trying to choke off his confession. It was for him to decide that he wouldn't exercise his right of silence."

Except for Brennan, Marshall, and Stevens, the others agreed with the Burger view. "It's a question," stated White, "only of voluntariness, after the *Miranda* warnings, which he was given." Since "*Miranda* was complied with," Rehnquist asserted, the statements were admissible even though there was "an element of deception here." O'Connor was of the same view, saying that, on the facts presented, "a waiver was binding even if he didn't know all the facts."

The *Moran* opinion of O'Connor followed the majority consensus and held that respondent's statements were admissible. *Miranda* procedures were followed and respondent's waivers were not invalidated by the failure to inform him of the attorney's call. As explained by O'Connor a week after the decision, "*Moran* holds that the failure to inform a suspect of events occurring out of his presence does not vitiate an otherwise valid waiver." [95]

Oregon v. Elstad [96] was more far-reaching in its implications for *Miranda*. Elstad had been implicated in a burglary. Police officers went to his home, and without advising him of his rights, an officer said he felt that Elstad was "involved" in the crime. Elstad answered, "Yes, I was there." Later, at the police station, an officer read him his *Miranda* rights. He waived them and made a full confession. The state court held that the second confession was the "tainted fruit" of the statement made in his home, which had been obtained in violation of *Miranda*.

The state court had relied on the "cat-out-of-the-bag" analysis of an earlier case, *United States v. Bayer*. Speaking for the Court there, Jackson had asserted, "Of course, after an accused has once let the cat out of the bag by confessing, no matter what the inducement, he is never thereafter free of the psychological and practical disadvantages of having confessed. He can never get the cat back in the bag. The secret is out for good. In such a sense, a later confession always may be looked upon as fruit of the first." [97]

At the *Elstad* conference, all but Brennan, Marshall, and Stevens were in favor of reversal. The Chief Justice stressed that "the Constitution forbids only 'compelled' [confessions]. Anyway, there was no real 'fruit' here. More broadly, fruits are admissible if [the] first [is] not exploited. . . . I would not overrule *Miranda*, but I won't expand it."

White, agreeing with the Chief Justice, referred to the *Bayer* approach and said " 'The cat-out-of-the-bag' rationale doesn't automatically apply. It's not a per se rule that makes the second a fruit of the first—maybe when the first was covered, but not here." Rehnquist made the point that " 'cat out of the bag' is useful only if there is some evidence of a connection"—that is, between the first and second statements.

The majority Justices emphasized the voluntary nature of the *Elstad* confession. As Blackmun pithily put it at the conference, "The second [statement] was voluntary and that's enough." The O'Connor opinion of the Court also stressed the voluntariness of the confession, as well as the lack of coercion in obtaining the first statement, which was "freely given in response to an unwarned but noncoercive question." A suspect who had responded to such questioning was ruled "not thereby disabled from waiving his rights and confessing after he has been given the requisite *Miranda* warnings." [98]

As one commentator points out, "[I]t is difficult to get agitated about the particular facts of this case." [99] If *Elstad,* like *Quarles,* reads an exception into *Miranda,* it does not seem like a very important one. But the *Elstad* implications for *Miranda* are more far-reaching than the immediate holding. During the *Elstad* conference, White had affirmed, "*Miranda* is a constitutional rule." In her *Elstad* opinion of the Court, however, O'Connor indicated that the *Miranda* safeguards are not themselves rights guaranteed by the Fifth Amendment.[100] "The *Miranda* exclusionary rule . . . sweeps more broadly than the Fifth Amendment itself. It may be triggered even in the absence of a Fifth Amendment violation. . . . [A] simple failure to administer *Miranda* warnings is not in itself a violation of the Fifth Amendment." [101]

At the *Elstad* conference, Stevens had said, "*Miranda* is a mirage." The assertion goes too far. Even with the Burger Court modifications, *Miranda* remained good law during the Burger tenure. But the *Elstad* "deconstitutionalization" of *Miranda* will make it easier for post-Burger Justices, not only to read new exceptions into *Miranda,* but even ultimately to abolish it.[102] Court observers were mistaken when they expected *Miranda* to be a casualty of the Burger Court jurisprudence. But the narrowing of the Warren Court landmark may have laid the foundation for a future overruling of its doctrine.

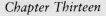

Chapter Thirteen

Administrative Power and Its Control

I T I S perhaps paradoxical that the one area of public law in which the Warren Court did not make any fundamental contributions is that of administrative law. A concern for individual rights that does not focus on the rights of the individual vis-à-vis the administrative process is bound to be only partially effective. In our evolving society, the relationship between administrative power and individual rights is becoming increasingly important, particularly in the burgeoning area of social welfare law.

As a court of appeals judge, Warren E. Burger made important contributions to administrative law. Indeed, two of his opinions rank as landmarks in the movement to broaden the due process rights of individuals dealing with administrative agencies.[1] It is therefore scarcely surprising that the Burger Court focused upon administrative law to a much greater extent than its predecessor.

ADMINISTRATIVE AGENCIES
AND ADMINISTRATIVE POWER

Appointments and Composition: Even though the Burger Court sat almost a century after the first modern administrative agency was created, it still had to confront fundamental issues concerning agencies and their powers.

In *Buckley v. Valeo*,[2] the Court, as seen in Chapter 3, confirmed the exclusive power of the President to appoint the members of federal administrative agencies. Congress may not assume any share in the appointing process. As Justice Blackmun put it at the *Buckley* conference, "Maybe Senate confirmation is as much authority as Congress can have."

Just as important as the appointing power is the manner in which agencies are constituted. Indeed, few questions are as crucial to administrative law as the composition of the administrative agency. This is particularly relevant because of the prevalence of state agencies whose members are chosen from the ranks of the regulated interests. More often than not, the result has been agencies that equate the "public interest" with the interest of those being regulated. For the age-old question of political science, *Quis custodiet ipsos custodes?* ("Who will regulate the regulators?"), our system has supplied a new answer: those who are regulated themselves.

In *Friedman v. Rogers*,[3] the Burger Court declined an invitation to strike a blow against agencies composed of members drawn from those regulated. A Texas law required that four of the six members of the Texas Optometry Board, which regulates the practice of optometry, be members of the Texas Optometric Association, the organization of professional optometrists (independent practitioners not employed by others). The constitutionality of the statute was attacked by an optometrist who practiced commercially (as a salaried employee) and was therefore ineligible for membership in the Association. He claimed that the statute violated his rights by subjecting him to regulation by the professional optometrists. The statute was also attacked by the Texas Senior Citizens Association, which claimed that its members had a right to representation of the general public on the Board.

The Court unanimously rejected the challenge: "[I]t was reasonable for the legislature to require that a majority of the Board be drawn from a professional organization that had demonstrated consistent support for the rule that the Board would be responsible for enforcing." Plaintiff had "no constitutional right to be regulated by a Board that is sympathetic to the commercial practice of optometry"; nor was there a constitutional basis for a "due process claim that the legislature is required to place a representative of consumers on the Board."[4]

Delegations of Power: During the past half century, a prime task of administrative law has been to legitimize the vast delegations of power given to agencies. In the *Panama* and *Schechter* cases[5] in 1935, the Court sought to control excessive delegations by requiring that Congress establish standards to limit administrative discretion. More recently the opinions in those cases have seemed written in another era as the courts all but abandoned the view expressed in them. Wholesale delegations became the rule: the new touchstone was the "public interest." As one observer summarized this trend, "The basic theme [is] simple: economic power . . . must be subjected to the 'public interest'"[6]—as defined by the administrator.

The statute involving the broadest delegation during the Burger years was the Gramm-Rudman Act at issue in *Bowsher v. Synar*.[7] As we saw in Chapter 3, the Supreme Court ruled Gramm-Rudman violative of the separation of powers. Plaintiffs had, however, also contended that "the Act's delegation to administrative officials of the power to make the economic calculations that determine the estimated federal deficit and hence the required budget cuts violates the constitutional provision vesting 'all legislative power' in the Congress."[8] The Court did not deal with the delegation issue; it held the statute invalid on other grounds. The delegation question was, however, discussed at the *Bowsher* conference—notably by Justice Brennan. His statement contains the only indication by a member of the highest Court on the Gramm-Rudman delegation:

"On the merits, my view is that the statute does not violate the delegation doctrine as developed in the case law. . . . Although it seems to me abundantly clear that the law was passed because Congress knew that it would be incapable of balancing the budget unless it created a mechanism which in effect forced it to do so."

Brennan made three main points: "First of all Congress has made the hard choices here. It has, after all, made the decision that cuts shall be imposed across the board. . . .

"Second, although much was made at argument of the discretion that vests in the . . . Comptroller General with respect to the calculations that must be made in order to determine deficits, the fact is that the Federal Reserve exercises just as much discretion on a daily basis as it seeks to regulate the supply of money. We were told that Congress could not choose between smaller budgets and more bombers and more social welfare programs, and so they shunted the problem over to the Comptroller. Well, when, for example, Congress is torn between clean air and a healthy automobile industry, it turns to an agency to determine the appropriate balance of the two. This is the reality of the administrative state.

"Third, there are standards to guide the Comptroller General. He is instructed, for example, as to many of the economic assumptions that must underlie his calculations." Hence, Brennan concluded, "given how far we have already come, and the fact that the delegation is not, to my mind, great in this case, I have no trouble saying that the statute does not violate the delegation doctrine."[9]

But the Burger Court also went out of its way to indicate that the old law on delegation may not be entirely passé. In a 1974 case[10] the Court indicated that "the requirements of *Schechter*" were still hurdles for statutes to overcome. During the conference on the case, Justice Douglas, who wrote the opinion, had gone further. Congress, he said, may act directly. "But if it's going to pass out to [administrative] agencies, it ought to give a specific standard." In this case, Douglas asserted, there was an "inadequate standard for delegation." In two later cases, the Court expressly restated the standards requirement as a limitation upon delegations. In both cases, the opinions declared that a delegation of power must be accompanied by discernible standards.[11]

More recently, the Court had before it the Occupational Safety and Health Act's delegation of authority to the Secretary of Labor to promulgate standards to ensure safe and healthful working conditions. Where toxic materials or harmful physical agents are concerned, a standard must comply with section 6(b)(5), which directs the secretary to "set the standard which most adequately assures, to the extent feasible, on the basis of the best available evidence, that no employee will suffer material impairment of health or functional capacity."

The plurality opinion by Justice Stevens in the case under discussion held that a challenged standard which limited exposure to benzene was invalid because it was not supported by adequate findings. As explained by Justice Marshall in a May 6, 1980, Memorandum to the Conference, "John contends that the 'reasonably necessary or appropriate' clause precludes the Secretary from taking regulatory action unless he has been able to establish that the risk he seeks to regulate 'threatens a significant number of workers.' Memo. at 28. To perform this task, the Secretary must be able to satisfy the 'requirement that the risk be quantified sufficiently to characterize it as significant in an understandable way.'" Under the Stevens opinion, before the Secretary can promulgate a standard, he must make a threshold finding that the place of employment is unsafe; significant risks are present.

In his opinion Stevens also referred to the delegation problem. He asserted that, if the government was correct in arguing that the statute did not require that the risk from a toxic substance be quantified sufficiently to enable OSHA "to characterize it as significant in an understandable way, the statute would make such a 'sweeping delegation of legislative power' that it might be unconstitutional under the Court's reasoning in"[12] the *Schechter* and *Panama* cases.

Even more significant was Rehnquist's concurring opinion. He would invalidate the statute as an invalid delegation of legislative power to the Secretary. Under the requirement of definable standards in enabling legislation this legislation "fails to pass muster. [Section 6(b)(5)] is completely precatory, admonishing the secretary to adopt the most protective standard if he can, but excusing him from that duty if he can't. In the case of a hazardous substance for which a 'safe' level is either unknown or impractical, the language of Section 6(b)(5) gives the secretary absolutely no indication where on the continuum of relative safety he should draw his line. Especially in light of the importance of the interests at stake, I have no doubt that the provision at issue . . . would violate the doctrine against uncanalized delegations of legislative power."[13] A year later, Rehnquist (this time joined by the Chief Justice) repeated his view that the statute exceeded Congressional power to delegate legislative authority.[14]

The Rehnquist opinions may sound like a voice from the past in its reliance upon doctrine so seemingly outmoded. Yet, as Rehnquist points out, "a number of observers have suggested that this Court should once more take up its burden of ensuring that congress does not unnecessarily delegate important choices of social policy to politically unresponsive administrators."[15] Calls for revitalization of the delegation doctrine have been heard from the entire political spectrum. The Rehnquist opinions indicate that such calls have started to be sounded within the Marble Palace itself. They acquire special significance since Rehnquist's own elevation to the Chief Justiceship.

Adjudicatory Authority: It is unquestionable that administrative agencies may be delegated the power to decide contested cases. Delegation of adjudicatory authority does not conflict with Article III's grant of the "judicial power" to the federal courts.[16] Administrative law assumes that not all adjudication must be judicial. Instead the power to decide cases—even those involving only private rights—may be vested in agencies as well as courts.

The Burger Court confirmed this established principle in *Commodity Futures Trading Commission v. Schor.*[17] At issue was the power of the CFTC to assume jurisdiction over common law counterclaims in a case brought before it by a private party. The Court held that the agency's interpretation of the statute as giving it jurisdiction over counterclaims was reasonable and well within the scope of its delegated authority. The lower court had ruled, however, that Congress did not possess the constitutional authority to vest the power to adjudicate a traditional contract action in a non–Article III court.

According to the Supreme Court, Article III does not confer an absolute right to the plenary consideration of every claim by an Article III court. Instead, Congress may authorize adjudication of Article III business in a non–Article III tribunal, such as an administrative agency.

Schor confirms the movement away from the notion that judicial power may not be delegated to agencies—that administrative adjudicatory power must be "softened by a quasi"[18] before it may be validly exercised. The courts have come to recognize that agency adjudicatory authority is analytically exactly like the power to decide cases possessed by the courts. *Schor* confirms that it is too late in our administrative law for there to be any question of the power to delegate adjudicatory power. Adjudications of both public and private rights may be committed to administrative agencies, as long as their decisions are subject to judicial review.

In *Atlas Roofing Co. v. Occupational Safety & Health Review Commission,*[19] the Burger Court dealt with the relationship between administrative adjudicatory authority and the constitutional right to jury trial in civil cases. Under the Occupational Safety and Health Act penalties up to $10,000 may be imposed by the Commission upon employers who violate the statutory duty to maintain safe working conditions. Petitioner employers contended that the imposition of penalties of $5,000 and $600 upon them violated their Seventh Amendment right to jury trial "in suits at common law."

At the *Atlas* conference only Justice Stevens spoke against the statute. "The penalty area is always for the judiciary." There was no room for an exception. "If you allow the nose in the tent, you can't contain it. This statute is a monster."

The others rejected the Seventh Amendment claim. The basic approach was stated by the Chief Justice. Referring to the Seventh Amendment's guaranty that the jury right "shall be preserved," he noted, "*Preserved* meant didn't create new right." The cause of action here was a new right created by Congress. As Justice White put it, it was "hard to say this resembles much in the way of common law as known in 1791." Justice Stewart suggested that the case was "akin to an equitable proceeding"—where no jury was constitutionally required. "Admiralty does without juries."

Although at the conference he was "firm to reverse," Stevens ultimately went along with the holding that the Seventh Amendment does not prevent Congress from giving an agency the task of adjudicating employment safety violations: "When Congress creates new statutory 'public rights,' it may assign their adjudication to an administrative agency with which a jury trial would be incompatible, without violating the Seventh Amendment's injunction that jury trial is to be 'preserved' in 'suits at common law.'" [20]

The easy answer to the Seventh Amendment claim is that the constitutional right to jury trial in civil cases exists only, as the amendment expressly indicates, in cases where the right was recognized at common law. As the conference discussion indicated, it has no application in noncommon law cases, such as equity, admiralty, and bankruptcy. Administrative proceedings did not exist at common law; they involve statutory requirements and procedures and may be litigated by the administrative machinery prescribed by the legislature without reference to the jury requirement.

At the *Atlas* conference, Powell had expressed concern about the agency procedure under which there was a hearing before an administrative law judge, whose decision became final unless a commissioner directed that it be reviewed by the Commission. "The case troubles me," he had said, "in the context of a hearing before an administrative law judge and [the ability to] go before the Board only with its consent." In a February 11, 1977, letter to Justice White, the author of the *Atlas* opinion, Powell noted, "You may recall my concern, expressed at Conference, with the procedure prescribed in this Act that forecloses any meaningful right to appeal a decision and findings by a single Commissioner. . . . The net effect of the procedure under this Act is to vest enormous power in a single individual, who may or may not be well qualified, without the procedural and other protections that are available in a court or in most administrative agencies."

INVESTIGATORY POWER

The Burger Court made a logical corpus out of the case law on one of the most significant administrative investigatory powers, the power of inspection. Inspection has been a significant governmental tool since colonial times, but it was not until the tenure of Chief Justice

Warren that the Supreme Court was presented with cases challenging administrative inspection power. The Warren Court decided that administrative inspections were subject to the search warrant requirement of the Fourth Amendment.[21] The requirement applied to business as well as residential premises.[22]

The power of inspection is so vital in meeting health, housing, safety, and other needs that an unqualified warrant requirement for all inspections might do more harm than good. In businesses subject to the kind of broadside regulatory authority that has become common, the widest inspection power is needed to make regulation effective. The Burger Court was aware of the need for such power and recognized exceptions to the warrant requirement for inspection of certain business premises.

The general Burger Court approach in the inspection cases was stated by Justice White during the decision process in *Donovan v. Dewey*.[23] "As I understand our cases, the general rule is that warrants are required before business premises may be invaded for purposes of searching for contraband or evidence of crime. I also think that the ultimate test of reasonableness is applicable to warrantless searches of both kinds of property but that in applying that test, warrantless searches of business premises will be permitted in many circumstances that would not excuse securing a warrant to search a home."[24]

The Court upheld exceptions to the warrant requirement for inspection of businesses selling liquor and firearms.[25] In such businesses the legislature has broad authority to fashion standards of reasonableness for searches and seizures, including authorizing warrantless inspections.

These early Burger Court decisions did not, however, make clear the basis and extent of the warrantless inspection exception. Did it apply to all regulated businesses or only to those subject to pervasive regulation? Or could the legislature authorize warrantless inspections wherever there was a direct public interest?

Marshall v. Barlow's, Inc.[26] partially answered these questions when it struck down warrantless inspections by OSHA of an electrical and plumbing installation business. An individual in the liquor or firearms business "has voluntarily chosen to subject himself to a full arsenal of governmental regulation."[27] Barlow's involvement in interstate commerce did not make it subject to the same degree of close supervision; nor did this imply constructive consent to inspections. Since few businesses operate without having some effect on interstate commerce, a contrary approach would remove the Fourth

Amendment requirement and permit warrantless inspections of almost all business premises. For the exception to apply, the business must be under the jurisdiction of an agency vested with pervasive regulatory authority over the specific industry.

The last Burger Court decision on the subject further clarified the distinction between the *Barlow's*-type case and the earlier cases. At issue in *Donovan v. Dewey*,[28] was a warrantless inspection of a stone quarry by mine inspectors. The lower court found for the quarry owner, ruling that *Barlow's* governed.

At the *Donovan* conference, the theme was set by the Chief Justice when he said, "This is not like Barlow's factory." All but Stewart agreed that reversal was required. "I was in dissent in *Barlow's*," Blackmun pointed out. "But, accepting it, the importance of the governmental interest and of warrantless inspections carry the day for me." Powell stressed that "here we have inspection of a particular kind of mine and findings why warrantless inspections are necessary in the interest of health and safety."

Rehnquist took a different approach. As he saw it, "The open fields doctrine is the only basis for sustaining this. The expectation of privacy was very limited here. I'd reverse on that narrow ground."[29]

Stewart alone, who was ultimately to dissent, voted the other way. He declared, "I can't distinguish [this case] from *Barlow's*. . . . This is *Barlow's* for me." In the most interesting part of his conference presentation, Stewart called into question the whole line of administrative inspection cases. "We may," he asserted, "have been wrong in *Camara*[30] and *See*[31] overruling *Frank v. Maryland*.[32] Perhaps these [inspections] should not be subject to the Fourth Amendment at all."

The *Donovan* decision followed the conference consensus and held that the warrantless inspection exception did apply. The key to the holding was the finding that the mining industry was as comprehensively regulated as the liquor and firearms businesses. As characterized by Rehnquist, "The Court holds that warrantless searches of stone quarries are permitted because the mining industry has been pervasively regulated."[33]

GOLDBERG V. KELLY

Perhaps the most important case on administrative procedure in American law was decided by the Burger Court—*Goldberg v. Kelly*.[34] Before *Goldberg*, it was settled law that the right to notice and hearing guaranteed by due process applied only in cases in which personal or property "rights" were adversely affected by administrative action. "Due process of law is not applicable unless one is being deprived of something to which he has a right."[35] If the individual was being given something by government to which he had no preexisting "right," he was being given a mere "privilege." Such a privilege "may be withdrawn at will and is not entitled to protection under the due process clause."[36]

This privilege concept was applied to licenses to sell liquor, operate billiard parlors, and to engage in other occupations deemed of little social value.[37] But its broadest application was in the burgeoning field of social welfare. During this century, government has become a gigantic fount that pours out largess on which an ever-increasing number of people depends. Under the traditional approach, all this public largess involves mere privileges.[38] In consequence, an ever-larger area of administrative power was being insulated from the safeguards of due process.

All this was changed by *Goldberg v. Kelly.*[39] At issue was whether welfare payments could be terminated without any pretermination hearing. The lower court held that a pretermination hearing was required by due process. In a companion case the lower court had reached the opposite result.[40]

At the postargument conference, October 13, 1969, Chief Justice Burger and Justices Black and Stewart favored upholding the state procedures. The question was, the Chief Justice said, "Is due process satisfied by a procedure which allows an appearance before termination, but also a full hearing afterward?" He urged that the states should be allowed to experiment: "perhaps we should let it alone for now." Justice Black agreed, saying, "I think the procedures are okay so long as later there is a full hearing." Black did not explain why he adopted this view, but his later discussion indicated that he felt that welfare payments are a "gratuity," not "property" protected by the "words" of the Due Process Clause. No other Justice expressed that view. Justice Stewart, who voted with Burger and Black, went out of his way to state his disagreement with the privilege concept. "I don't think the distinction between vested right and gratuity is significant to what requirements of due process obtain." On the other hand, Stewart said, "the totality of procedures here for me satisfies due process."

The other five at the conference voted to affirm. Douglas strongly rejected the Black notion of welfare as a privilege not protected by due process. "Can a state," he asked, create these things and withdraw them without the kind of due process we required in *Willner [v. Committee on Character & Fitness*[41]—a case barring disbarment of an attorney without notice and hearing]? Aren't they a species of property?" Brennan spoke even more strongly along similar lines, summarizing the view he was to take in his opinion.

Harlan also declared categorically, "This is not a gratuity. It's an entitlement or right . . . a vested right so long as the state chooses to give it." Harlan adopted a flexible approach to the type of hearing required: the "full panoply of a trial type hearing is not required." As he saw it, "Confrontation, cross-examination, etc., [are needed] where termination turns on questions of fact. Where other things are involved maybe more flexibility is required."

White said that he was "more with John than with the two Bills." Though, in other cases the government may cut off benefits before a full hearing, "the impact here is so severe that the balance should be cast for a full hearing before termination." White was not, however, sure whether the hearing would have to be held before "an independent judge."

The conference vote was five (Douglas, Brennan, Harlan, White, and Marshall) to three (Burger, Black, and Stewart) to affirm. Douglas, senior in the majority, assigned the opinion to Brennan. Brennan's main problem was to keep the votes of Harlan and White, who did not go so far as those who had urged a more sweeping view of due process. Thus, the Brennan opinion went out of its way to indicate reliance on the opinion of the lower court. Harlan had suggested that he would have been content to affirm on the basis of that opinion had Court practice permitted that and Harlan was, of course, crucial to a majority. Not too long before, the Court did at times affirm on the opinion below. However, Frankfurter had succeeded in ending the practice on the ground that it hurt the egos of those lower court judges whose decisions were affirmed, but not on the basis of their opinions.

The Brennan opinion-writing process in *Goldberg* well illustrates the need to compromise in order to hold votes. In Part I of his opinion, Brennan enunciated a rationale rejecting the privilege concept that had previously barred welfare recipients from procedural protection. Brennan stated that the constitutional claim could not be answered by the argument that "public assistance benefits are 'a privilege' and not a 'right.'" The opinion then characterized welfare benefits as a "matter of statutory entitlement" and added in a note that it "may be realistic today to regard welfare entitlements as more like 'property' than a 'gratuity.'"

The Justice himself would have preferred to go further and hold that welfare payments in today's economic and social setting constitute "property"—in the same sense that land ownership constitutes property. Brennan, however, felt that he had to write narrowly, for fear of losing Harlan and White. The latter was particularly concerned that the opinion not reach the interest in government employment. The result was that the *Goldberg* opinion replaced the privilege concept with that of "entitlement"—"more like 'property' than a 'gratuity'," but not "property" itself.

The original Brennan draft, circulated November 24, contained a different approach to the role of welfare than that stated in the final opinion. The key draft passage read as follows: "Whatever may have been true in the past, today we cannot confidently saddle the poor with the blame for their poverty. It has become increasingly clear that indigency is now largely a product of impersonal forces. . . . In other words, welfare is not charity but a means for treating a disorder in our society. Government, accordingly, has an overriding interest in providing uninterrupted assistance to the eligible, both to help maintain the dignity and well-being of a large segment of the population and to protect against the societal malaise that may flow from a widespread sense of unjustified frustration and insecurity."

White refused to accept this passage. He told Brennan that society had always been committed to spreading as widely as possible the opportunities to participate fully in economic, social, and political life—witness universal free public schools, universal suffrage, and so on. He thought it wrong to suggest that people in this country had once blamed the poor for their poverty and wrong to say that today welfare is given because society is responsible for poverty. Welfare is given to enable people to maintain their dignity and to participate in and contribute to society. Welfare functions to enable people to stand on their own feet and get off the dole.

Brennan replied that White failed to recognize endemic poverty, but, to hold White's essential vote, he revised the statement on poverty, and White joined the Brennan opinion on December 2. He provided the fourth vote. Douglas had joined the first draft on November 24. Marshall had joined the next day; the Chief Justice and

Black had announced that they would dissent. Harlan and Stewart were still to be heard from.

On December 11, Harlan sent Brennan a letter indicating general agreement with the opinion, but requesting that the term "trial-type hearing" be replaced by "evidentiary hearing." The use of the latter term in the final Brennan opinion has led to its employment during recent years as the generic administrative law term for what used to be called "trial-type hearings."

Harlan also wanted Brennan to add a clear statement that there was no right to an evidentiary hearing when the only issues were legal. Here, however, Brennan refused to yield. If he was not to decide that a hearing was necessary when only legal issues were presented, he was not going to decide that question the other way. The result was the addition of a footnote[42] that reserved the issue. Harlan then joined the opinion.

Black circulated his dissent on January 29, 1970, and Chief Justice Burger on February 12. The Chief Justice suggested in his first draft that the cases should be dismissed as improvidently granted—overlooking the fact that each was an appeal and that the two lower courts had reached contrary conclusions. Burger himself came to realize that the cases could not be avoided as improvident grants and the suggestion does not appear in his final dissent. However, at Harlan's suggestion, the Brennan opinion did point out that a decision by the Supreme Court was necessary since the courts below were in direct conflict.

Stewart also circulated a brief dissent on February 17. He had indicated that he was favorably disposed toward the Brennan opinion, but in the end he adhered to his initial statement at the conference—under the circumstances, due process was satisfied by the state procedures.

The dissents did not detract from the force of the *Goldberg* opinion. Compromise or not, it repudiated the notion that welfare payments were a mere "privilege" or "gratuity" that might be taken away without compliance with procedural due process. From this point of view *Goldberg* was a seminal decision: It worked what a federal judge terms a "due process" explosion under which "we have witnessed a greater expansion of due process . . . than in the entire period since ratification of the Constitution."[43] The post-*Goldberg* cases extended its hearing requirement to virtually all the cases that

used to be treated as involving only privileges not protected by procedural due process.[44]

EXPECTATIONS AND ENTITLEMENTS

The hallmark of due process protection under the Burger Court jurisprudence is an entitlement grounded in federal or state law. What
that means was shown by *Board of Regents v. Roth*[45] and *Perry v.
Sindermann*[46]—two companion cases decided in 1972. Roth had
been hired as assistant professor at a state university for one year. He
was not rehired. He claimed that, though he had no tenure rights, the
failure of university officials to give him a hearing violated due process. Sindermann had also been a professor in a state college system.
He had been employed for ten years under a series of one-year contracts. He was then not rehired for the next year without any explanation or hearing.

At the conference on the two cases, all but Douglas and Marshall
voted against Roth. In *Sindermann,* the majority consensus was the
other way. Marshall disagreed with the majority approach in *Roth*
and condemned the university's summary action. Roth "has a right
to say to the university that you let me out because I made a speech—
if not give me a reason."

In *Sindermann,* the Chief Justice asserted, "A naked claim does not
trigger a right to a university hearing." And Rehnquist stated, "The
institution ought not to be required to hold a hearing unless it wants
to." He also said that he "wouldn't put teachers in a special class."

Stewart, who was assigned both opinions, summarized "My
understanding of the Conference discussion" in a June 6, 1972,
"Dear Chief" letter: "[A] majority of us agreed that a state university faculty member . . . has no due process right to a hearing if he is
not reemployed, unless he can show that he has somehow been deprived of liberty or property." With regard to *Roth,* the Stewart approach was simple. As he had put it at the conference, "A nontenured
teacher with a one-year contract means just that." The situation in
Sindermann was different. The university teacher would "have a right
to a hearing if the university had deprived him of property because, in
fact, by reason of the actual 'policies and practices of the institution,'
he was entitled to continued employment, in the absence of 'cause' to
terminate it."

The Stewart conception of the "entitlement" protected by due process was stated in his draft *Roth* opinion, circulated on May 23, 1972. To have the required entitlement, "a person clearly must have more than an abstract need or desire for it. He must, instead, have a claim to it or a legitimate expectation of it. It is a purpose of the ancient institution of property to protect such claims and expectations upon which people rely in their daily lives, reliance that must not be arbitrarily undermined."

The Stewart draft led to a June 6 letter from Chief Justice Burger in which he asserted that examination of the draft "suggests that unilateral 'expectations' are perhaps being given a status never before acknowledged." Stewart replied in his June 6 letter to the Chief Justice, "I do not think the Due Process Clause entitles a person to a hearing simply because his 'unilateral' expectations have been defeated." The final *Roth* opinion contained "language modifications designed to eliminate any misapprehension on that score." The draft language on entitlements was changed to read: "He must have more than a unilateral expectation of it. He must, instead have a legitimate claim of entitlement to it."[47]

It may, however, be doubted that the Justices intended to remove "a legitimate expectation" from the area of protected entitlements. What *Roth* holds is that an entitlement protected by due process exists whenever the individual has a "legitimate expectation" that is defeated by the challenged administrative act. A legitimate expectation is one that is "reasonable" under the circumstances of the case. Sindermann had a reasonable expectation of a new contract; he had been given a contract ten previous times. Decisions that hold that such an administrative renewal practice is not enough, since the entitlement must be based upon the state constitution or a statute, are based upon a complete misunderstanding of the Stewart *Roth* opinion.[48]

The lower courts have also misread another aspect of the *Roth* opinion, which states another basis for requiring due process procedural rights—when the administrative action "imposed on him a stigma or other disability that foreclosed his freedom to take advantage of other employment opportunities."[49] Most lower courts have interpreted this to mean that both "stigma" *and* "foreclosure" must be present in the given case.[50] But in his letter to the Chief Justice, Stewart summarized his understanding that "a majority of us agreed" that a plaintiff "would, therefore, have such a [due process] right if the university had impaired his liberty by (1) personally stigmatizing him, or (2) foreclosing substantial employment opportunities elsewhere." Hence, under *Roth*, a deprivation of liberty triggering due process occurs when there is *either* a stigma *or* a foreclosure of employment opportunity.

APOGEE AND THERMIDOR

The culmination of the post-*Goldberg* due process expansion in the Burger Court was the decision in *Goss v. Lopez.*[51] A statute gave school principals authority to suspend pupils for up to ten days without any hearing. Six students had been summarily suspended from high school for ten days for disruptive conduct, during a student demonstration.

The Justices were sharply divided at the *Goss* conference. The view in favor of the students was stated succinctly by Stewart: "There's an entitlement to attend school and [they] can't suspend without a hearing of some kind."

Powell, who was to deliver a strong dissent, disagreed. "We are injecting the Court into an area far more extensive than any that *Goldberg* has got us into." The sanction here was not expulsion. "This is only suspension for ten calendar days and that's not harmful to children." On the other hand, Powell conceded, "If the suspension overlapped an exam period so that the child was really hurt, I'd be with the majority. But ten days can't be faulted as beyond legislative determination."

In many ways, the most interesting conference statement was by Rehnquist: "A non-monetary entitlement should have different protections from a monetary entitlement. The entitlement here is the right to education and graduation." Rehnquist drew the following distinction: "If [they're] going to keep a record of his infraction, [there] may be a stigma which requires a prior hearing. But if [it's] only internal discipline and record keeping, I see no reason to require a hearing."

The *Goss* decision followed the conference vote. By a bare majority (the Chief Justice and Blackmun, Powell, and Rehnquist, dissenting) the Court held that the pupils might not be suspended without any hearing. Due process prohibits exercise of summary suspension power. Adversary process is the constitutional means by which suspension cases must be resolved.

However, if the *Goldberg v. Kelly* revolution reached its apogee in *Goss v. Lopez,* it may have met its Thermidor in *Mathews v. Eldridge.*[52] The issue was whether due process required that the recipient of social security disability payments be afforded an evidentiary hearing prior to termination of those benefits. The statute and regulations provided that after the Social Security Administration terminated payments, the recipient could seek reconsideration and then an evidentiary hearing. If the recipient prevailed at the reconsideration, hearing, or a later agency appeal, he would be entitled to retroactive payments. The lower courts ruled that the "interest of the disability recipient in uninterrupted benefits [was] indistinguishable from that of the welfare recipient in *Goldberg*" and held that due process required a pretermination hearing.[53]

The conference majority (Douglas, Brennan, and Marshall, dissenting[54]) were in favor of reversal. "We've retreated from *Goldberg* as to the nature of hearing," stated Justice White. "I think there can be a paper determination now." Powell, who was to write the opinion, said, "I agree we've withdrawn somewhat from *Goldberg.*"

Powell ultimately focused on another aspect of *Eldridge,* pointing out that "the Social Security Act gives the citizen carefully-tailored safeguards beyond anything in *Goldberg.*" Because of that, he would distinguish the case from *Goldberg.*

Eldridge held that due process was satisfied by the post-termination procedures provided by the agency. The decision was based upon Powell's distinction between *Eldridge* and *Goldberg.* Welfare benefits involved the "brutal need" of persons on the very margin of subsistence, where termination "may deprive an eligible recipient of the very means by which to live while he waits."[55] In contrast, eligibility for disability benefits was not based upon financial need.

All the same, *Eldridge* appears inconsistent with *Goss,* which held that school pupils must be afforded presuspension hearings. The Court in *Eldridge* noted that *Goldberg* illustrates how "the degree of potential deprivation that may be created by a particular decision is a factor to be considered in assessing the validity of any administrative decisionmaking process." If that is determinative, who suffers the greater deprivation: the pupil subject to a short suspension or the disabled worker whose disability payments are ended?

According to Rehnquist at the *Goss* conference, a monetary entitlement should be treated differently from a nonmonetary entitlement.[56] *Eldridge* involved monetary benefits, and retroactive back payments can theoretically restore the recipient to his pretermination position; but in *Goss,* the effects of the suspension could not be so readily undone. If that is the key factor, does it mean that *Goldberg* now stands alone and that, if a post-termination hearing is enough in disability cases, the same is true in other monetary benefit cases other than welfare cases? *Eldridge* may permit summary action in non-emergency cases, where deprivation of the monetary entitlement occurs immediately, even though the post-termination hearing and decision may not occur, as *Eldridge* concedes, for a year.

Although *Goldberg v. Kelly* will probably continue to be followed, its effect will be confined to the welfare termination case. In cases involving other types of monetary largess, *Mathews v. Eldridge* will set the procedural theme. This does not mean that there will be no due process protection, but merely that a pretermination hearing is not necessary, only a post-termination hearing.

COST–BENEFIT ANALYSIS AND PROCEDURE

The Burger Court elevated cost–benefit analysis (CBA) to the top of the administrative law agenda. In the first place, the Court used CBA to deal with the consequences of the "due process explosion"[57] caused by *Goldberg v. Kelly.*[58] Hearings required by due process are no longer limited to cases concerning preexisting "rights." The pre-*Goldberg* "privileges" (such as welfare payments), removed from the reach of procedural due process, were transformed by *Goldberg* into entitlements, fully qualified for due process protection. The right to be heard as a matter of due process has been extended en masse to all the benefactory areas of administrative power, from the welfare benefits involved in *Goldberg* itself to disability, medicare, unemployment, and veterans' benefits, as well as education and housing.[59]

The *Goldberg* requirement of a judicial-type evidentiary hearing may, however, pose a serious dilemma for a system of administrative law which has extended procedural requirements from the traditional regulatory area to the expanding field of social welfare. Fully judicialized procedure may frustrate effective administration in fields such as welfare and social security—not only because of the nature of the cases but also because of their number. When we move from the older regulatory agencies to those administering benefactory statutes such as the Social Security Act, cases number in the millions. A full trial in every such case would make the system unworkable.

To resolve the problem, the Burger Court followed what amounts to a CBA approach in determining what type of administrative hearing due process requires in a given case. The Court developed a flexible due process concept that calls only for what it termed a hearing "appropriate to the nature of the case."[60]

Due process, in the Burger Court jurisprudence, demands only "some form of hearing,"[61] and the Court followed a simple cost–benefit test for deciding what kind of hearing is required in a given case. The test requires "comparing the benefit of the procedural safeguard sought . . . with the cost of the safeguard."[62]

Under this approach, the administrative hearing required depends upon a balancing of the costs and benefits involved in each additional procedure required. Fully judicialized procedure may be demanded in cases with the most serious consequences, such as welfare terminations.[63] In other cases, due process may demand less burdensome alternatives, where the benefits from the full evidentiary hearing would be outweighed by the costs involved.

The CBA approach is illustrated by *Ingraham v. Wright*,[64] where the issue was whether notice and hearing were constitutionally required before imposition of corporal punishment in public schools. The conference voted four (Brennan, White, Marshall, and Stevens) to three (Blackmun, Powell, and Rehnquist) in favor of a notice and hearing requirement—with the Chief Justice and Stewart passing. The most interesting conference statement was by White, who was to deliver the *Ingraham* dissent. *Goss,* he said, did not answer the due process issue here. "I wouldn't say that the mere fact corporal [punishment] was to be imposed automatically triggers some due process requirement. Maybe so if 'severe' punishment [is] planned; then 'liberty' would be invaded."

At the conference, Powell, who was to author the *Ingraham* opinion, took a categorical position against the procedural demand. "As to procedural due process I see nothing." . . . The courts are too deep already into schools."

The Chief Justice and Stewart ultimately joined the three-man conference minority, so that *Ingraham* was decided by a bare majority against the procedural claim. But the opinion of the Court did not limit itself to the holding that due process did not require notice and hearing prior to corporal punishment. Instead, it went on to say that "even if the need for advance procedural safeguards were clear, the question would remain whether the incremental benefit could justify the cost." Prior hearing in corporal punishment cases would unduly burden school discipline. "At some point the benefit of an additional safeguard to the individual affected . . . and to society in terms of increased assurance that the action is just, may be outweighed by the cost. . . . We think that point has been reached in this case."[65]

Previously *Goss v. Lopez*[66] itself had recognized that, even where due process is held to require a hearing, the hearing requirement itself may still be flexible. *Goss,* we saw, held that due process prohibited the summary suspension of school pupils. *Goss,* however, stopped "short of construing the Due Process Clause to require, countrywide, that hearings in connection with short suspensions must afford the student the opportunity to secure counsel, to confront and cross-examine witnesses . . . or to call his own witnesses."[67]

More formal procedures may be required for longer suspensions or expulsions. The hearings demanded for them should approach trial-type proceedings. In other cases, due process requirements should depend upon the CBA approach. Since there are alternatives less burdensome than fully judicialized hearings, the law should choose the less burdensome alternatives, where the incremental gain in the more burdensome procedure would be outweighed by the marginal costs, as in time and expense.[68]

This aspect of the Burger Court's CBA approach to administrative procedure is one with which most observers would agree. Toward the end of the Burger tenure, however, the Court placed CBA in administrative law in a new perspective, with its decision in *Immigration & Naturalization Service v. Lopez-Mendoza*[69] (see Chapter 12).[70] The Court there ruled that the exclusionary rule, which bars illegally seized evidence in a criminal case, does not apply in an administrative deportation proceeding. Evidence obtained as a result of an unlawful arrest is admissible in a deportation hearing because deportation is a purely civil proceeding. Its purpose is to determine eligibility to remain in this country, not to punish for a crime. The purpose of the exclusionary rule is to deter violations of the Fourth Amendment, which are less significant in deportation cases. On the other side of the balance is the cost involved in applying the rule. CBA leads to the conclusion that the exclusionary rule should not be applied in deportation proceedings.

Before *Lopez-Mendoza,* the cases had held that the exclusionary rule is a due process requirement in administrative proceedings ranging from Federal Trade Commission hearings[71] to deportation cases themselves.[72] The cases had assumed the *Mapp v. Ohio*[73] thesis that the exclusionary rule is included in the requirements of due process. They had asked only whether the exclusionary rule had been violated.

This is, of course, the question that must normally be asked in cases involving alleged violations of procedural rights by administrative agencies: Has a procedural right guaranteed by statute and/or due process been violated in the given case?

Under *Lopez-Mendoza,* an affirmative answer is not enough to lead to a decision against the agency. Instead, CBA must be applied to determine whether the right itself is guaranteed in the particular administrative proceeding. If the CBA balance tilts against the right in the given case, the agency will be upheld even though it has violated the right concerned, and even where the right is so fundamental as that embodied in the exclusionary rule.

NARROWING THE VIRES

Perhaps the most significant aspect of the Burger Court's administrative law jurisprudence was the restrictive view it demonstrated toward the scope of administrative power. The principal administrative law function of the courts is to keep agencies within their statutory limits. Legal rules do not have fixed areas of strains and stresses. There is an all-too-common administrative tendency to stretch legal rules to the breaking point, even at the risk of illegality. "You cannot blame the Minister for trying it on," said an English official to counsel at an administrative hearing over half a century ago.[74]

The Burger Court was readier than its predecessors to curb administrative attempts at "trying it on." During the previous quarter century the Court had taken a more hospitable posture toward the scope of agency authority and had been willing to apply a broad doctrine of implied agency powers. Justice Frankfurter's rationale explains the underlying premise: "[I]n enacting [delegating] legislation Congress is not engaged in a scientific process which takes account of every contingency. Its laws are not to be read as though every *i* has to be dotted and every *t* crossed."[75] Administrative powers were not to be construed in a niggardly manner; agencies were to be permitted to exercise not only authority expressly delegated, but also such powers as could reasonably be implied from the enabling legislation.

This administrative law counterpart of the *McCulloch v. Maryland*[76] implied-powers doctrine was applied in a more constricted manner by the Burger Court. It tended to narrow the vires of delegating statutes and refused to read in authority not specifically conferred unless it was *necessary*, as well as *proper*, to exercise the delegated power. Thus, in *NAACP v. Federal Power Commission*[77] the issue was whether the FPC, which had regulatory jurisdiction over electric utilities and gas companies, was authorized to issue a rule prohibiting racial discrimination in employment by those it regulated. At the postargument conference, with Justice Marshall not participating, all the others said that the proposed rule went too far. Stewart, who wrote the opinion, said, "I would analogize this to the National Labor Relations Board area and say the FPC . . . can't be asked to decide whether an unfair labor practice was committed. That's the NLRB job."

The Court held that the Commission did not have authority to issue the rule. The principal purpose of the Federal Power Act was to encourage the orderly development of plentiful supplies of electricity and gas at reasonable prices. The words "public interest" in the statutes were a charge to promote this purpose, not a directive to eradicate racial discrimination by regulated companies.

Other Burger Court decisions also refused to allow agencies to exercise powers not specifically delegated by Congress. At issue in *Federal Communications Commission v. Midwest Video Corp.*[78] were FCC rules requiring cable television operators to allow free access to certain channels by public, educational, governmental, and leased-access users. The conference voted five to three (Brennan, Marshall, and Stevens dissenting) to strike down the rules. The FCC had relied on an earlier *Midwest Video* case[79] that had upheld rules that required cable TV systems to originate a significant number of local programs. The Chief Justice told the conference, "My vote in *Midwest I* was shaky in sustaining the origination rules. This time the Commission has gone beyond what Congress intended." The others in the majority agreed that, in White's words, "There's a substantial difference between access and origination" and that the FCC had exceeded its statutory authority.

The *Midwest Video* decision held that the rules were not reasonably necessary to the effective performance of the FCC's responsibility for television regulation and thus were not within the

Commission's authority. In effect, the rules imposed common-carrier obligations on cable operators. Absent specific authority, the FCC may not regulate cable systems as common carriers any more than it may impose such obligations on broadcasters. Authority to compel cable operators to provide common carriage must come specifically from Congress.

A similar decision restricting administrative power was rendered in *National Labor Relations Board v. Catholic Bishop of Chicago.*[80] The Board had certified unions as bargaining agents for lay teachers in Catholic high schools. The Church claimed that teachers in church-operated schools were not within the Board's jurisdiction and that, if they were, the guarantees of the Religion Clauses of the First Amendment were violated.

At the conference the Chief Justice emphasized the constitutional issue. The Board had relied on the *Associated Press* case,[81] which had held that the First Amendment did not immunize the press from the requirements of federal labor law. But Burger said, "I think *Associated Press* is readily distinguishable. The religion clauses protect commerce before speech." Blackmun, on the other hand, stated, "*Associated Press* is in point. [There is] no violation of Free Exercise and Establishment [Clauses]."

The others decided not to rule on the constitutional issue. Stewart pointed out the way in which the issue could be avoided. "I don't think Labor Board jurisdiction can be maintained. I would prefer to follow *McCulloch,*"—a 1963 case, where the NLRB had asserted jurisdiction over foreign seamen.[82] The Court there declined to read the National Labor Relations Act so as to give rise to a question that "would have implicated sensitive issues of the authority of the Executive over relations with foreign nations."[83] Instead, the Court avoided the issue by holding that Congress had not intended to give the Board jurisdiction in such a case.

Under *McCulloch,* Stewart urged, the Court would "hold that the National Labor Act was not intended to apply to religious schools. We don't reach the constitutional questions in such a case." The majority agreed; as Rehnquist put it, "*McCulloch* offers the best way for me." Looking at the statutory intent, Justice Stevens asserted that it was "hard to think that Congress ever thought in 1935 that it was exercising jurisdiction over parochial schools."

Powell stated, "I think [there is] probably serious danger of a burden on free exercise at least down the road when unions get the bit in their teeth. The vitality of religious schools could be undermined to the point of extinction. . . . I hadn't thought of the *McCulloch* argument and would prefer it."

The conference voted six to three (Brennan, White, and Marshall the other way[84]) to follow the *McCulloch* approach and decide against the NLRB on nonconstitutional grounds. The Court held that, under the Labor Act, the Board had no jurisdiction over lay teachers in church-operated schools. In the absence of a clear expression of congressional intent to bring teachers in church-operated schools within NLRB jurisdiction, the Court would not construe the enabling statute to give the Board such jurisdiction.

The decisions discussed in this section were directly related to the law on delegation of powers. As seen, the Burger Court articulated doubts about the demise of the standards requirement.[85] But the Court's statements on delegation were only in the nature of obiter and did not affect the outcome in specific cases. One result of the decline of a meaningful standards requirement has been a growing ineptitude in the drafting of delegating statutes. Instead of drafting detailed standards, the legislature tends to leave it to the administrator. As Judge Wright has noted, it is so much "easier to pass an organic statute with some vague language about the 'public interest' which tells the agency, in effect, to get the job done."[86] Prior Courts were willing to look beyond the explicit statutory language and find implied authority in light of what the Court referred to as "'the mischief to be corrected and the end to be attained.'"[87] The Burger Court was no longer willing to assume implied power from the inadequate draftsmanship that is all too common in laws containing wholesale delegations.

A dominant theme in the Burger Court's administrative law jurisprudence was thus the restricted view it took with regard to delegated powers: statutes that relate to agencies must be strictly interpreted. The result was a substantial change in the Supreme Court's posture toward agencies. While earlier Courts would go beyond the black letter of delegating statutes and read in implied powers in the light of presumed congressional intent to confer broadside authority, the Burger Court adopted a narrower approach. It was more reluctant to go beyond the legislative language and read in powers not expressly conferred.

This changed attitude of the Court was also a direct response to the growing distrust of agencies. The crisis in confidence that has infected governmental institutions has had particular impact on perceptions of the administrative process in operation. Not long before his elevation to the highest bench, Warren Burger referred to the theory that an agency such as the FCC effectively represents the public interest as "one of those assumptions we collectively try to work with so long as they are reasonably adequate. When it becomes clear, as it does to us now, that it is no longer a valid assumption which stands up under the realities of actual experience, neither we nor the Commission can continue to rely on it."[88] It is hardly surprising that this skeptical attitude had its effects on the tribunal over which its author presided.

In 1971, Judge Bazelon asserted, "We stand on the threshold of a new era in the history of the long and fruitful collaboration of administrative agencies and reviewing courts."[89] The Burger Court may have started another crucial swing of the administrative law pendulum. The swing appears likely to increase as the Justices, like the citizenry generally, become increasingly disenchanted with claims of administrative expertise. If it culminates in a retreat from the past generation's reconciliation between administrative and judicial power, we may ultimately see a drastic alteration in traditional restrictions on the scope of judicial power in administrative law cases. If administrative agencies prove increasingly unable to meet societal needs, we can expect the courts to play a more activist role. The Burger Court's more constricted view of agency authority may foreshadow a broadening of the judicial role in administrative law, or it may be only a temporary manifestation of the current distrust of agencies.

Chapter Fourteen

Strands and Patterns

T HE HISTORY of an institution such as the Supreme Court, like a tapestry, is made up of many strands that, interwoven, make a pattern; to separate a single one and look at it alone not only defaces the whole but gives the strand itself a false value.[1] All too many studies of the Supreme Court, or of its individual members, concentrate upon single strands of the Court's work, emphasizing, more often than not, those aspects that diverge most sharply from the overall pattern. Such an approach is bound to give a distorted picture. Not infrequently, in truth, the reaction of writers about the Court is akin to that of the blind men from Hindustan when first confronted with an elephant. The aspect of the Court's work emphasized by the particular author tends to dominate his conception of the Court as a whole; yet he almost never comes to picture the Court as the institutional entity that it is. Small wonder, then, that the public, both legal and lay, has no clear picture of the working of our unique judicial organ and its proper place in a constitutional democracy.

Not long ago Chief Justice Rehnquist recalled his first visit to the Court after his appointment as a Justice: "We came over here, and it was kind of a grey afternoon. . . . And I just felt, literally, like I'd entered a monastery when I came over."[2] Neophytes on the high bench—even the strongest of them—are immediately aware of the overpowering institutional traditions. Such awareness continues throughout the Justices' Court tenure and, more than is generally realized, molds into the Court's pattern all but the most eccentric of its members. It has been said of one of the greatest Justices, Louis D. Brandeis, that he had an almost mystic reverence for the Court, whose tradition seemed to him not only to consecrate its own members, but to impress its sacred mission upon all who shared in any measure in its work.[3] Few members of the high tribunal may be capable of penetrating into its mystique with the perception of a Brandeis; still, "Everybody who comes here," says Rehnquist, "probably feels the constraints of the place."[4]

This book has been written upon the assumption that the pattern of the tapestry is more important than the single strands. Similarly, the Supreme Court as an institution is more significant than the individual Justices who make up its membership. Undoubtedly, the development of the Court's institutional traditions has been not dissimilar to the manner in which Topsy described her own developmental process. By the time of the Burger Court, nevertheless, the Court as an institution had all but fully "growed."

To be sure, to treat the Burger Court as an institutional entity may seem outdated in an age when even the law has succumbed to our society's preoccupation with the behavioral sciences. Judges are only men, we are told[5]—which is, of course, an indisputable observation. All the same, it hardly follows from this that only study of the psychological makeup of the individual Justices is now worthwhile. The state of a man's mind is as much a fact as the state of his digestion, according to a nineteenth-century English judge. Now, however, we are told that the two are intimately related and that the state of a judge's mind can hardly be known without some knowledge of the state of his stomach. To advocates of this sort of gastrological jurisprudence, all attempts to describe the Court as an institutional entity are fundamentally naive, and this is particularly true of the Burger Court, when the institutional ethos of the Court often seemed at a low ebb. At such a time, it is said, it is only the makeup of the individual Justice that is important if we are to understand the decisions of a fragmented Court.

No one not blind to the facts of legal life can deny that the Burger Court too often presented a far from edifying spectacle of internal atomization. But even that did not prevent that tribunal from functioning as an institutional entity. The Supreme Court had been splintered before (dissents and five-to-four decisions are not recent inventions of law professors); still, the Court's work as a governmental organ had to go on, as, indeed, it had to during the Burger years as well. This is, in fact, a basic difference between an ultimate judicial tribunal and commentaries upon its work. The Court cannot adopt an *either—or* approach. It *must* decide the case before it, even though the decision requires it to choose between two conflicting truths. The theorist need wholly reject neither, where neither states an exclusive verity; the Court *must* choose between them. Yet it is a mistake to assume that, because, in such cases, the individual members of the tribunal are sharply divided, the Court has ceased to function as an institution. On the contrary, even amid a plethora of such cases, the institutional pattern continues to be woven. It may be harder to determine the boundary at which the Burger Court balanced conflicting interests than it was to make a similar determination with regard to its predecessor. Still, the Burger Court, like its predecessor, was engaged in drawing the line between conflicting interests. While we may not be able to determine it by a general formula, points in the line were fixed by decisions that this or that concrete case fell on the nearer or farther side.

PRAGMATISM VERSUS PRINCIPLE

Before Chief Justice Burger's tenure, all Supreme Court documents were typed with as many carbon copies as needed. Thus, the memoranda on *in forma pauperis* (or Miscellaneous Docket) petitions sent to each Justice required many copies. Because it was necessary to use very thin paper, these memoranda were called flimsies. The junior Justices, who received the last copies, often had difficulty reading them.

This was changed when Chief Justice Burger sent around an August 7, 1969, memorandum: "The necessary steps are now being taken toward acquiring a Xerox machine in the building." The new copiers "will be utilized primarily in preparation and distribution of the Miscellaneous Docket memoranda ('flimsies' as they are commonly called.)"[6] Since that time, ample copiers have been provided for the Justices and Court staff, and word processors and a computer have been introduced.[7]

But the availability of copiers and the other communications devices had a baneful, though unintended, effect upon the operation of the Burger Court. One privy to the working of the Warren Court quickly notes the crucial importance of personal exchanges among the Justices—both in conference discussions and, even more so, in the postargument decision process. Such exchanges became less significant in the Burger Court. This has been noted by the Justices themselves. Conference notes during the Burger tenure show less an interchange of views than flat statements of each Justice's position in the case. "Not much conferencing goes on" at the conference, a Justice recently confirmed. "In fact, to call our discussion of a case a conference is really something of a misnomer, it's much more a statement of the views of each of the nine Justices, after which the totals are added and the case is assigned."[8]

"When I first went on the Court," writes Chief Justice Rehnquist, "I was both surprised and dismayed at how little interplay there was between the various justices."[9] Rehnquist, too, was referring to the conference, but his remark is equally applicable to the entire decision process. The constant personal exchanges in the Warren Court (much of it one-on-one lobbying by the Chief Justice and his allies or by opponents intended to influence votes) gave way to mostly written contacts through notes and memoranda. It is after all so much easier to make copies and send them around than to engage in protracted personal efforts to persuade others to change their positions. In the Court, as in other institutions, technology intended to facilitate communication has made for less personal interchange.

It was, however, more than the photocopier that made for the difference between the Burger and Warren Courts. A few years ago, the present Chief Justice compared the two tribunals. Rehnquist stated that the impact of the Court had been diminished under Chief Justice Burger. "I don't think that the Burger Court has as wide a sense of mission. Perhaps it doesn't have any sense of mission at all."[10]

Certainly the Warren Court did have Rehnquist's "sense of mission" when it virtually rewrote the corpus of our constitutional law; concepts and principles that had appeared unduly radical became accepted rules of law. The Warren Court led the movement to remake constitutional law in the image of an evolving society. In doing so, the Justices had to perform the originative role that the jurist normally is not called upon to exercise in more stable times—a role usually considered more appropriate for the legislator than for the judge.

From this point of view, the Warren Court was the paradigm of the "result-oriented" court, which used its power to secure the result it deemed right in the cases that came before it. Employing the authority of the ermine to the utmost, Warren and his colleagues never hesitated to do whatever they thought necessary to translate their own conceptions of fairness and justice into the law of the land. The same was plainly not true of the Burger Court. Although the Burger Court did not have any "sense of mission" comparable to its predecessor, that was not true of the entire Court—only of the centrist majority that pointed the way during most of the Burger tenure.

Rehnquist, who also said, "I don't know that a court should really have a sense of mission,"[11] clearly was a Justice who did, and that was true of some of the others as well. We can refer once again to the analysis by Justice Blackmun of the tripartite division within the Court. Blackmun said that he had always put "on the left" Brennan and Marshall and "on the right" Chief Justice Burger and Justice Rehnquist. "Five of us," Blackmun concluded, were "in the middle"— Stewart, White, Powell, Stevens, and himself.[12]

There is no doubt that the two Justices at each of the Burger Court's polar extremes were judges with an agenda. Stated broadly, Brennan and Marshall, those "on the left," saw it as their duty to preserve and, if possible, extend the Warren Court's liberal jurisprudence. To them the primary role of the courts was to serve as protectors of individual rights, and they consistently voted to ensure the effectiveness of that role. At the other pole, Burger and Rehnquist had the opposite judicial agenda. They sought what Rehnquist called "a halt to . . . the sweeping rules made in the days of the Warren Court"[13]—and not only a halt, but a rollback of much of the Warren jurisprudence. The Burger–Rehnquist conservative program included enlargement of government authority over individuals, a check to the expansion of criminal defendants' rights, and limitations on access to federal courts.

The actions of the polar Justices were based upon more or less fixed juristic principles that served as the foundation for the jurisprudential edifices they sought to construct. They adhered rigidly to those principles in most cases, which enabled Court-watchers to state with confidence how they would vote in almost all cases. Since their positions were normally fixed, it was rash to predict that they would vote differently in any important case. I was once told that the Brennan law clerks had confidently predicted that Rehnquist would vote with their Justice in the *Bakke* case.[14] One finds it hard to see the basis for their belief, given Rehnquist's reflex toward the right in cases involving racial classifications. At any rate, the Court community quickly saw where Rehnquist stood when, in line with his consistent position in such cases, he circulated a lengthy memorandum asserting that the special-admissions program at issue in *Bakke* was invalid.[15]

But if the four polar Justices habitually cast their votes in accordance with their basic liberal or conservative principles, that was not true of the Justices "in the middle." They were essentially pragmatists who considered cases on their individual facts and voted now with one polar core, now with the other. In certain fields, to be sure, the center Justices had a defined position. Thus, White and Powell more often voted with the conservative bloc in criminal cases, while Blackmun and Stevens were to be found with Brennan in many cases involving infringements upon personal rights—particularly those growing out of the right of personal autonomy that Blackmun had enshrined in his *Roe v. Wade* opinion.[16]

Despite these tendencies, the center Justices did not have anything like a defined juristic *Weltanschauung*. And that was true as well of the Burger Court as an institution. As its decisions oscillated between the polar blocs, or somewhere between the two extremes, the Justices in the middle held the balance—tilting it at times in one direction, at times in the other, ensuring that the Court would not be a mere reflection of either polar bloc. "I, with others," said Blackmun, "have been trying to hold the center. I think we've been fairly lucky in how we've come out."[17]

THE COUNTER-REVOLUTION THAT WASN'T

In 1983, a book was published entitled *The Burger Court: The Counter-Revolution That Wasn't*.[18] The subtitle is a succinct summary of the Burger Court in operation.

"When Warren E. Burger succeeded Earl Warren as chief justice of the United States in 1969," Anthony Lewis has written, "many expected to see the more striking constitutional doctrines of the Warren years rolled back or even abandoned. . . . In these, it was often said, the Warren Court had made a constitutional revolution. Now a counter-revolution was seemingly at hand."[19]

There is no doubt that Chief Justice Burger came to the Court with an agenda that included some dismantling of the jurisprudential structure erected under his predecessor, particularly in the field of criminal justice. Similarly, Burger's strongest supporter, Justice Rehnquist, took his seat with a desire to correct some of the "excesses" of the Warren Court[20]—to, as he put it, see that the "Court has called a halt to a number of the sweeping rulings that were made in the days of the Warren Court."[21]

The Burger–Rehnquist agenda was not carried out in the Burger years. Instead, the intended counter-revolution served only as a confirmation of most of the Warren Court jurisprudence. It can, indeed, be said that no important Warren Court decision was overruled during the Burger tenure. Some of them were narrowed by Burger Court decisions; others were, however, not only fully applied but even expanded.

We can see this even in the field of criminal justice, where Burger and Rehnquist were most eager to disown the Warren heritage—in Rehnquist's phrase, to make "the law dealing with the constitutional rights of accused criminal defendants . . . more even-handed now than it was when I came on the Court." It was, after all, to "the area of the constitutional rights of accused criminal defendants" that Rehnquist primarily referred when he referred to the "sweeping rulings of the Warren Court." [22]

The transformation of constitutional law in the criminal justice field during the Warren years culminated in the celebrated *Gideon, Mapp,* and *Miranda* trilogy. [23] The latter two in particular were decisions for which the Warren Court was widely criticized—denounced for putting "another set of handcuffs on the police." [24] Testifying before a Senate subcommittee just after *Miranda,* Truman Capote plaintively asked, "Why do they seem to totally ignore the rights of the victims and potential victims?" [25]

Though the Warren criminal cases became a major issue of Richard Nixon's presidential campaign, the Justices appointed by Nixon did not tilt the Court to the point of repudiating them. In fact, one of the Warren criminal trilogy was substantially expanded by the Burger Court. In *Gideon,* Chief Justice Warren had told the conference that it was "better not to say [the right to counsel applies in] 'every criminal case,' if we don't have to here." Warren told the others, "maybe it's best just to decide this case." [26] The Court followed Warren's suggestion to limit the *Gideon* decision to the case at hand and held only that there was a right to assigned counsel in the felony case at issue, without addressing the question of how far the new right extended.

The Burger Court not only followed *Gideon,* it expanded it to every case in which imprisonment may be imposed as a penalty, regardless of whether the crime involved is classified as a felony, misdemeanor, or even petty offense. [27] *Gideon* also only upheld the right to counsel at the criminal trial. [28] The Burger Court extended the right to counsel to preliminary hearings [29]—that is, before any formal accusation and trial—and gave practical effect to the right of the accused to represent himself if he so chose and knowingly and intelligently waived the right to counsel. [30]

Chief Justice Burger and Justice Rehnquist were both opposed to *Mapp* and *Miranda;* but they were not able to secure the votes needed to overrule those cases. Early in the Burger tenure, indeed, a majority of the Justices indicated that they were dissatisfied with the *Mapp* exclusionary rule. Before a majority could act on the dissatisfaction, however, two of the *Mapp* opponents retired. Justice Powell, one of the replacements, was not prepared to overrule *Mapp*, though he was willing to narrow the exclusionary rule. *Mapp* was not overruled; but the later Burger years saw a narrowing of the exclusionary rule, culminating in the good-faith exception and cost–benefit cases toward the end of Burger's tenure.[31]

Miranda had a similar fate in the Burger Court. The Chief Justice himself was anything but a partisan of *Miranda*. In a 1977 case where the Court refused to act on the request of twenty-two states to overrule *Miranda*'s procedural ruling,[32] the Chief Justice circulated a memorandum stating, "I will probably write separately focusing on the utter irrationality of fulfilling Cardozo's half-century old prophecy—which he really made in jest—that some day some court would carry the Suppression Rule to the absurd extent of suppressing evidence of a murder victim's body."[33]

Despite his disapproval of *Miranda*, in which he was joined by Rehnquist, the Chief Justice never succeeded in overruling that decision. The most the Burger Court did was to narrow *Miranda*, though that hardly affected the essentials of its doctrine. In the end, Burger himself realized that *Miranda* still remained as a pillar of defendants' rights.[34]

The other Warren Court landmarks also served as foundations of the Burger Court jurisprudence. *Griffin v. Illinois*[35]—in many ways the Warren watershed case in the Court's effort to ensure economic equality in the legal process—was extended to include the right of an indigent defendant to the psychiatric assistance needed for an effective defense[36] and even, outside the criminal law field, to invalidate court fees that prevented indigents from bringing divorce proceedings.[37]

Brown v. Board of Education[38] and its Warren Court progeny were applied in the *Swann* and *Keyes* cases[39] and held to vest broad remedial power in the courts to ensure desegregation, including extensive busing. The *Brown* principle was expanded to uphold affirmative action programs to aid minorities. No Justice, not even Rehnquist, who had once probably taken a different view,[40] questioned the antidiscrimination premise that underlay *Brown.* In fact, bearing in mind the efforts of the Chief Justice to frustrate the ultimate decisions in *Swann* and *Bakke,* the most important thing about the Burger Court decisions in this area was that, as one of Burger's principal adherents was to conclude in the Chief Justice's last term, "we have reached a common destination in sustaining affirmative action against constitutional attack."[41]

The same was true in the other areas of Warren Court jurisprudence, including the First Amendment, reapportionment, other aspects of equal protection, and judicial review in operation. In all these areas, the central premises of the Warren Court decisions were not really challenged by its successor. The core principles laid down in the Warren years remained as securely rooted in our public law as they were when Burger first took his seat.

At times, the Chief Justice and Rehnquist did succeed in securing modifications of Supreme Court doctrine. Even then their successes were either minor or transitory. Both Burger and Rehnquist had strong views on the relationship between federal and state power, and they constantly expressed concern about infringements on state prerogatives. Until O'Connor was appointed, Burger and Rehnquist were far more willing than any of their colleagues to leave questions to the states in which they might act free of federal interference. The Burger view on the subject of state power was satirically expressed in a letter on a pending case: "the question is one for the State. (States, unlike Federal agencies and this Court, are not infallible!)"[42]

The Burger–Rehnquist view of state power prevailed in the *National League of Cities* case,[43] where the Court held for the first time in years that the states were immune from federal regulatory power. The Rehnquist opinion resurrected the Tenth Amendment as a rampart behind which state sovereignty might remain unimpaired. As such, it appeared to signal a wholly new balance between federal and state power. But the Burger–Rehnquist victory proved short-lived. *National League of Cities* itself was overruled, and the Court adopted a far more deferential approach to federal power vis-à-vis the states.[44]

ACTIVISM AND THE WARREN COURT

There is an antinomy inherent in every system of law: the law must be stable and yet it cannot stand still.[45] It is the task of the judge to reconcile these two conflicting elements. In doing so, jurists tend to stress one principle or the other. Stability and change may be the twin sisters of the law, but few judges can keep an equipoise between the two.

Chief Justice Warren never pretended to try to maintain the balance. He was firmly on the side of change, leading the Supreme Court's effort to enable public law to cope with rapid societal change. Before then the Court had been divided between two antagonistic judicial philosophies, which differed sharply over the proper role of the judge. In simplified terms, the division was between judicial activism and judicial self-restraint.

The rule of restraint had been the handiwork of that seminal figure of modern American law, Justice Oliver Wendell Holmes. The Holmes philosopher's stone was "the conviction that our constitutional system rests upon tolerance and that its greatest enemy is the Absolute."[46] It was not at all the judicial function to strike down laws with which the judge disagreed. "There is nothing I more deprecate" asserted Holmes in a 1921 dissent, "than the use of the Fourteenth Amendment . . . to prevent the making of social experiments that an important part of the community desires . . . even though the experiments may seem futile or even noxious to me."[47] Not the judge but the legislator was to have the primary say on the policy considerations behind a regulatory measure. The judge's business, wrote Holmes in 1910 to his noted English correspondent, Sir Frederick Pollock, was to enforce even "laws that I believe to embody economic mistakes."[48]

By the 1940s, the Holmes approach of judicial self-restraint had become established doctrine. By then, the at-first lonely voice had become the new dispensation, which had now written itself into our law.[49] But the issues confronting the Supreme Court had also begun to change over the years, and judges like Black and Douglas had come to feel that even the Holmes canon could not suffice as the "be all and end all" of judicial review. These judges were willing to follow the rule of restraint in the economic area. But they believed that the protection of personal liberties imposed on the Court more active enforcement obligations. When a law allegedly infringed upon the personal rights guaranteed by the Bill of Rights, they refused to defer to the legislative judgment that the law was necessary.

Chief Justice Warren was soon drawn to the Black–Douglas activist approach. As a judge, Warren strongly believed that the law must draw its vitality from life rather than precedent. What Holmes termed "intuitions" of what best served the public interest[50] played the major part in Warren's jurisprudence. He did not sacrifice good sense for the syllogism. Nor was he one of "those who think more of symmetry and logic in the development of legal rules than of practical adaptation to the attainment of a just result."[51] When symmetry and logic were balanced against considerations of equity and fairness, he normally found the latter to be weightier.[52] In the Warren hierarchy of social values, the moral outweighed the material.[53]

Throughout his tenure on the Court, Chief Justice Warren tended to use "fairness" as the polestar of his judicial approach. Every so often in criminal cases, when counsel defending a conviction would cite legal precedents, Warren would bend his bulk over the bench to ask, "Yes, yes—but were you fair?"[54] The fairness to which the Chief Justice referred was no jurisprudential abstraction. It related to such things as methods of arrest, questioning of suspects, and police conduct—matters that Warren understood well from his earlier years as district attorney in Alameda County, California. Decisions like *Miranda v. Arizona*[55] were based directly upon the Warren fairness approach.

The Chief Justice's emphasis upon fairness and just results led him to join hands with Black and Douglas and their activist approach. Warren rejected the philosophy of judicial restraint because he believed that it thwarted effective performance of the Court's constitutional role. Judicial restraint, in the Warren view, all too often meant judicial abdication of the duty to enforce constitutional guarantees. "I believe," Warren declared in an interview on his retirement, "that this Court or any court should exercise the functions of the office to the limit of its responsibilities. . . . [F]or a long, long time we have been sweeping under the rug a great many problems basic to American life. We have failed to face up to them, and they have piled up on us, and now they are causing a great deal of dissension and controversy of all kinds." It was the Court's job "to remedy those things eventually," regardless of the controversy involved.[56] The Warren approach left little room for deference to the legislature, the core of the restraint canon.

The crucial question in constitutional cases, according to Frankfurter, the leading advocate of judicial restraint, was "[W]ho is to judge? Is it the Court or Congress? Indeed, more accurately, must not the Court put on the sackcloth and ashes of deferring humility in order to determine whether the judgment that Congress exercise[s] . . . is so outside the limits of a supportable judgment by those who have the primary duty of judgment as to constitute that disregard of reason which we call an arbitrary judgment[?]"[57]

To Warren and his supporters, Frankfurter had posed the wrong questions. Their view was well expressed by Black, replying to a letter asking whether the Court should defer to congressional judgment on constitutional issues. "The question just does not make sense to me. This is because if the Court must 'defer' to the legislative judgment about whether a statute is constitutional, then the Court must yield its responsibility to another body that does not possess that responsibility. If, as I think, the judiciary is vested with the Supreme, constitutional power and responsibility to pass on the validity of legislation, then I think it cannot 'defer' to the legislative judgment 'without abdicating its own responsibility. . . .'"[58]

"I think it is the business and the supreme responsibility of the Court to hold a law unconstitutional if it believes that the law is unconstitutional, without 'deference' to anybody or any institution. . . . I believe it is the duty of the Court to show 'deference' to the Constitution only."[59]

Chief Justice Warren and his activist supporters on the Court fully shared Black's view on deference. Detailed analysis of conference notes, memoranda, draft opinions, and extensive interviews reveal that Warren never considered constitutional issues in the light of any desired deference to the legislature.

For Warren, the issue on judicial review was not *reasonableness* but *rightness*. If the law was contrary to his own conception of what the Constitution demanded, it did not matter that a reasonable legislator might reach the opposite conclusion. When Warren decided that the Constitution required an equal population apportionment standard for all legislative chambers except the United States Senate,[60] the fact that no American legislature had followed the new requirement did not deter him from uniformly applying the standard. Harlan's dissent may have demonstrated that the consistent state practice was, at the least, reasonable.[61] For the Chief Justice, however, legislative reasonableness was irrelevant when the practice conflicted with his own interpretation of the Constitution. Hence, as a much-quoted statement by Anthony Lewis has it, "Earl Warren was the closest thing the United States has had to a Platonic Guardian, dispensing law from a throne without any sensed limits of power except what was seen as the good of society."[62]

WE ARE ALL ACTIVISTS NOW

According to one commentator, "[T]he entire record of the Burger Court . . . is one of activism."[63] Yet the Justices now "decide without much self-conscious concern for whether this is a proper role for the Court. We are all activists now."[64] At least so the history of the Burger Court tells us. One thing to be learned from the Burger years "is that the great conflict between judicial 'restraint' and 'activism' is history now."[65]

The statistics bear out the conclusion that the Burger Court record was, indeed, one of judicial activism. One measure was its willingness to strike down legislative acts. The Warren Court invalidated 21 federal and 150 state statutes; the Burger Court struck down 31 federal and 288 state laws.[66] The laws invalidated were at least as significant as those ruled unconstitutional by the Warren Court. The federal statutes that failed to pass constitutional muster in the Burger years included laws governing election financing and judicial salaries,[67] granting eighteen-year-olds the vote in state elections,[68] establishing bankruptcy courts,[69] as well as laws based on gender classifications in the military[70] and in various social security programs.[71] In addition, the Burger Court struck down the legislative veto, a method used by Congress to control executive action in nearly 200 statutes,[72] and a law designed to deal with the endemic budget deficit.[73] "If deference to Congress be the acid test of judicial restraint, the litmus of the Burger Court comes out much the same color as that of its predecessor."[74]

But it is not numbers alone than mark the Burger Court as an activist one. More important than quantity was the quality of the decisions rendered. The Burger Court was as ready as its predecessor to resolve crucial constitutional issues and to do so in accordance with its own conceptions of what the law should be. *United States v. Nixon*[75] brought the Court into the center of the Watergate vortex and its decision led directly to the first resignation of a President. Nor was there any doubt among the Justices on the propriety of their exercise of power to resolve the crisis. The *Nixon* decision process demonstrates the willingness of the Justices to mold the crucial constitutional principles to accord with their individual policy perceptions. The impact of judicial review was definitely broadened by *Nixon* and the Burger Court's other separation-of-powers decisions.

The Warren Court's activism was manifested in the number of new rights recognized by it, but the "rights explosion" was more than equaled by that under his successor. Few decisions were more far-reaching in their recognition of new rights than *Roe v. Wade*.[76] The right of privacy had first been ruled a constitutional right by the Warren Court in *Griswold v. Connecticut*.[77] It may be doubted, however, that the *Griswold* Court would have included the right to an abortion within this new right. At the *Griswold* conference, Chief Justice Warren had stated, "I can't say . . . that the state has no legitimate interest (that could apply to abortion laws)"[78]—implying that he thought such laws were valid.

In *Roe*, however, the majority had no hesitation in extending the right of privacy to include the right to choose to have an abortion. More than that, the *Roe* decision process and opinion lend substance to Stewart's criticism in a letter to Blackmun,[79] author of the *Roe* opinion, of "the specificity of its dictum—particularly in its fixing of the end of the first trimester as the critical point for valid state action. I appreciate the inevitability and indeed wisdom of dicta in the Court's opinion, but I wonder about the desirability of the dicta being quite so inflexibly 'legislative'." One familiar with the interchanges between the Justices on the line between valid and invalid state action in abortion cases—with the Blackmun drafts moving from a two-pronged time test to the tripartite approach followed in the final opinion—cannot help but feel that the Justices were acting more like a legislative committee than a court. Their drawing of lines at trimesters and viability was, for Stewart, "to make policy judgments" that were more "legislative" than "judicial."

The decision in *Roe v. Wade* may be taken as the very paradigm of the activist decision: the decision was not based upon principles worked out in earlier cases, but upon "policy judgments" made upon an ad hoc basis which led to recognition of a new right. Even here the Justices were influenced more by pragmatism than principle. "Too many wealthy women were flouting the law to get abortions from respected physicians. Too many poor women were being injured by inadequately trained mass purveyors of illegal abortions. Concerns of that sort, rather than issues of high principle, are what appeal to the centrist activists of the Burger Court."[80]

The hallmark of the activist Court is the *Roe*-type decision that creates a new right not previously recognized in law. The Burger Court recognized new rights for women and those dependent on

public largess. During the Burger years the law on sexual classifications was completely changed.[81] Though the Court did not go as far
as Justice Brennan had wished, virtually all legal disabilities based
upon sex were placed beyond the legal pale.

Even more significant in some respects was the recognition of legal
rights in the field of government largess. Until the Burger Court, no
one had any "right" to the largess dispensed by government. This
was true regardless of the nature of the given largess—whether it was
a job, a pension, welfare aid, veterans' or disability benefits, a government contract, or any other benefit to which the individual had no
preexisting "right."[82] The result was to place those dependent on
public largess in a legal status subordinate to that of others in the
community. If the governmental benefaction was a mere "gratuity"
or "privilege," it could be withheld or revoked without adherence to
the procedural safeguards that would otherwise be required by the
Due Process Clause.[83]

Such a legal approach may have been rendered obsolete by the reality of twentieth-century society. But it was not until the Burger
Court that the law started to make the welfare state itself a source of
new "rights" and to surround the "rights" in public benefactions
with legal safeguards comparable to those enjoyed by the traditional
rights of property. The landmark case was *Goldberg v. Kelly*,[84] where
due process was held to require "a full 'evidentiary hearing'" before
welfare benefits might be terminated. "It may be more realistic today
to regard welfare entitlements as more like 'property' than a 'gratuity.' . . . Such benefits are a matter of statutory entitlement for persons qualified to receive them."[85]

Goldberg v. Kelly was soon applied to other cases involving government largess: unemployment compensation, public housing, public employment, and government contracts.[86] In all these cases, the
"privileges" of not too long ago were transformed into virtual
"rights" entitled to the full procedural protection afforded to traditional property rights. Because of the Burger Court, the law was beginning to resolve the basic issue of fair dealing by government with
those dependent on it.

ROOTLESS ACTIVISM

The Burger Court opinions are full of essays on the virtues of judicial
restraint.[87] Typical is an oft-quoted statement of the Chief Justice:
"[T]he Constitution does not constitute us as 'Platonic Guardians'

nor does it vest in this Court the authority to strike down laws because they do not meet our standards of desirable social policy, 'wisdom,' or 'common sense.' . . . We trespass on the assigned function of the political branches under our structure of limited and separate powers when we assume a policymaking role, as the Court does today."[88] There are similar statements in the opinions of other Justices.

Despite this, we have just seen that the Burger Court was definitely an activist Court. But there was a fundamental difference between the activism of the Burger Court and that of its predecessor. Chief Justice Warren and his supporters (notably Justice Brennan) acted on the basis of overriding principles derived from their vision of the society the Constitution was intended to secure.

In particular the Warren Court acted on the basis of two broad principles: nationalism and egalitarianism. It preferred national solutions to what it deemed national problems and, to secure such solutions, was willing to countenance substantial growth in federal power.[89] Even more important was the Warren Court's commitment to equality. If one great theme recurred in its jurisprudence, it was that of equality before the law—equality of races, of citizens, of rich and poor, of prosecutor and defendant. The result was what Justice Abe Fortas once termed "the most profound and pervasive revolution ever achieved by substantially peaceful means."[90] More than that, it was the rarest of all political animals: a judicially inspired and led revolution. Without the Warren Court decisions giving ever-wider effect to the right to equality before the law, most of the movements for equality that have permeated American society would never have gotten off the ground.

Yet the Warren Court was more than the judicial counterpart of the Platonic philosopher–king. To Warren and his supporters, the Supreme Court was a modern Court of Chancery, a residual "fountain of justice" to rectify individual instances of injustice, particularly where the victims suffered from racial, economic, or similar disabilities. The Warren Justices saw themselves as present-day Chancellors, who secured fairness and equity in individual cases, fired above all by a vision of the equal dignity of man, to be furthered by the Court's value-laden decisions.[91]

No similar vision inspired the activism of the Burger Court. Instead of consciously using the law to change the society and its values, it rode the wave, letting itself be swept along by the consensus it perceived in the social arena—moving, for example, on gender discrimination when it became "fashionable" to be for women's rights.[92] From this point of view, the Burger Court's activism has been well termed a "rootless activism,"[93] which dealt with cases on an essentially ad hoc basis, inspired less by moral vision than by pragmatic considerations.[94]

The rootless activism of the Burger Court was a direct consequence of the divisions already stressed between the Justices. Because of it, "the hallmark of the Burger Court has been strength in the center and weakness on the wings."[95] The balance of power was held by the Justices "in the middle."[96] In Burger's last terms, however, the center's grip started to weaken. As Blackmun put it just after Burger retired, "I think the center held generally. .·. . [but] it bled a lot. And it needs more troops. Where it's going to get them, I don't know."[97]

The shift toward the right did not occur until the end of the Burger years. Before that, the balance was with the pragmatic Justices who did not decide cases in accordance with a preconceived ethical philosophy. This was particularly true when Justices Stewart and Powell were the key swing votes. The Stewart reply, when he was asked whether he was a "liberal" or a "conservative," bears repeating. "I am a lawyer," Stewart answered. "I have some difficulty understanding what those terms mean even in the field of political life. . . . And I find it impossible to know what they mean when they are carried over to judicial work."[98]

Justices who felt this way had the lawyer's aversion to making fundamental value choices. Judicial policy making was as frequent a feature during the Burger years as in the Warren years. But the policy choices were, in the main, made by Justices who, as relatively moderate pragmatists, were motivated by case-by-case judgments on how to make a workable judicial accommodation that would resolve a divisive public controversy. Inevitably, their decisions did not make for a logically consistent corpus such as that constructed by the Warren Court. In most areas of the law, the Burger Court decisions reflected less an overriding calculus of fundamental values than lawyerlike attempts to resolve the given controversy as a practical compromise between both sides of the issues involved.[99]

In the Warren Court, the leadership had come from the left; and constitutional doctrine was, in the important cases, made by Chief Justice Warren and his liberal supporters, notably Justice Brennan. Under Warren's successor, Brennan was shunted to one of the extremes that now more often played a lesser role. The Burger Court's activism was molded more by the moderate Justices "in the middle." As such, it was "inspired not by a commitment to fundamental constitutional principles or noble political ideals, but rather by the belief that modest injections of logic and compassion by disinterested, sensible judges can serve as a counterforce to some of the excesses and irrationalities of contemporary governmental decision-making."[100]

Thus judicial activism itself became a centrist philosophy, primarily practical in nature, without an agenda or overriding philosophy. Its essential approach was to adapt the answer of Diogenes, *Solvitur gubernando*[101]—and more or less on a case-by-case basis. Fundamental value choices were more often avoided than made. In its operation, "the Burger Court has exhibited a notable determination to fashion tenuous doctrines that offer both sides of a social controversy something important."[102]

The Burger years appear to have marked a legal watershed. After the Warren Court's rewriting of so much of our public law, the Burger Court was bound to be primarily a Court of consolidation. Transforming innovation, in the law as elsewhere, can take place only for so long. In historical terms, indeed, the Burger Court's main significance was its consolidation and continuation of the Warren heritage. Its role in this respect seems all the more important now that the Burger Court itself has given way to the Rehnquist Court.

In William H. Rehnquist, the Court once again has a strong Chief Justice. The Rehnquist Court, too, will be an activist Court, but its activism will be tilted toward the right. More than that, under the leadership of the conservative activist who now sits in the center chair, it may shape a new constitutional case law that could be the reverse image of that fashioned under Chief Justice Warren. The law, like other institutions, has its epochs of ebbs and flow.[103] In face of the probable Rehnquist flood tide, critics of the Burger Court may yet look back upon its receding period with more than a little nostalgia.

WARREN EARL BURGER
AND HIS COURT—
A CHRONOLOGY

1907	Born
1925–27	Student, U. of Minnesota
1931	LL.B. magna cum laude, St. Paul College of Law
1931	Member, Minnesota Bar
1931–53	Partner, Faricy, Burger, Moore & Costello
1931–46	Faculty, Mitchell College of Law
1953–56	Assistant Attorney General, U.S.
1956–69	Judge, U.S. Court of Appeals, District of Columbia
1969	Appointed Chief Justice of the U.S.
1970	Justice Harry A. Blackmun appointed *Coleman v. Alabama* *Goldberg v. Kelly* *Illinois v. Allen* *Walz v. Tax Commission* *In re Winship*
1971	Justices Hugo L. Black and John M. Harlan retire *Coolidge v. New Hampshire* *Graham v. Richardson* *McKeiver v. Pennsylvania* *New York Times v. United States* (Pentagon Papers Case) *Rosenbloom v. Metromedia* *Swann v. Charlotte-Mecklenburg Board of Education*
1972	Justices Lewis F. Powell and William H. Rehnquist appointed

Argersinger v. Hamlin
Board of Regents v. Roth
Branzburg v. Hayes
Kirby v. Illinois
Wisconsin v. Yoder

1973   *Frontiero v. Richardson*
Keyes v. Denver School District
Lemon v. Kurtzman
San Antonio School District v. Rodriguez
Roe v. Wade

1974   *Gertz v. Robert Welch, Inc.*
Lehman v. Shaker Heights
Miami Herald Publishing Co. v. Tornillo
Milliken v. Bradley
Spence v. Washington
United States v. Nixon

1975   Justice William O. Douglas retires
Justice John P. Stevens appointed
Goss v. Lopez
Southeastern Promotions, Ltd. v. Conrad

1976   *Buckley v. Valeo*
Craig v. Boren
Estelle v. Williams
Hampton v. Mow Sun Wong
Hudgens v. NLRB
Kelly v. Johnson
Mathews v. Eldridge
National League of Cities v. Usery
Nebraska Press Assn. v. Stuart
New Orleans v. Dukes
United States v. Santana
United States v. Watson
*Virginia State Board of Pharmacy v. Virginia Consumer
    Council*
Washington v. Davis

1977   *Ingraham v. Wright*
Trimble v. Gordon
Wooley v. Maynard

1978   *Foley v. Connelie*
        Houchins v. KQED
        Lalli v. Lalli
        Regents of the University of California v. Bakke
        Zablocki v. Redhail

1979   *Gannett Co. v. DePasquale*
        Goldwater v. Carter

1980   *Fullilove v. Klutznick*
        Richmond Newspapers v. Virginia

1981   Justice Potter Stewart retires
        Justice Sandra Day O'Connor appointed
        Chandler v. Florida
        Dames & Moore v. Regan
        Donovan v. Dewey
        H. L. v. Matheson
        New York v. Belton

1982   *United States v. Lee*

1983   *Bob Jones University v. United States*
        INS v. Chadha
        Mueller v. Allen
        United States v. Knotts

1984   *INS v. Lopez-Mendoza*
        Lynch v. Donnelly
        New York v. Quarles
        Oliver v. United States
        Schall v. Martin
        United States v. Leon

1985   *Cleburne v. Cleburne Living Center*
        Cornelius v. NAACP Legal Defense Fund
        Garcia v. San Antonio Metropolitan Transit Authority
        Oregon v. Elstad
        Tennessee v. Garner
        Wallace v. Jaffree

1986   Chief Justice Burger retires
        Batson v. Kentucky
        Bowers v. Hardwick
        Bowsher v. Synar

California v. Ciraolo
Goldman v. Weinberger
Moran v. Burbine
Press-Enterprise Co. v. Superior Court
Wygant v. Jackson Board of Education

NOTES

ABBREVIATIONS USED IN NOTES

BRW	Byron R. White	**JPS**	John Paul Stevens
FF	Felix Frankfurter	**LFP**	Lewis F. Powell
FFLC	Felix Frankfurter Papers, Library of Congress	**PS**	Potter Stewart
		SR	Stanley Reed
FMV	Fred M. Vinson	**TM**	Thurgood Marshall
HAB	Harry A. Blackmun	**WEB**	Warren E. Burger
HHB	Harold H. Burton	**WHR**	William H. Rehnquist
HLB	Hugo L. Black	**WJB**	William J. Brennan
JMH	John Marshall Harlan	**WOD**	William O. Douglas
JMHP	John Marshall Harlan Papers, Mudd Manuscript Library, Princeton University		

CHAPTER ONE

1. See FF-HHB, Jan. 31, 1956. FFLC: "The Chief Justice . . . is not the head of a department; not even a quarterback."

2. Quoted in B. Schwartz, A Basic History of the U.S. Supreme Court 172 (1968).

3. FF-WJB, March 27, 1958. FFLC.

4. See F. Frankfurter, Of Law and Men 133 (1956).

5. FF–FMV, n.d. FFLC.

6. 1 J. Bryce, The American Commonwealth 274 (1917).

7. FF–SR, April 13, 1939. FFLC.

8. N.Y. Times, Dec. 14, 1969, § 4, p. 9.

9. Gonzalez v. Freeman, 334 F.2d 570 (D.C. Cir. 1964).

10. N.Y. Times, Feb. 20, 1983 (Magazine), p. 20.

11. H. Black & E. Black, Mr. Justice and Mrs. Black: The Memoirs of Hugo L. Black and Elizåbeth Black 226 (1986). Compare W. Douglas, The Court Years 1939–1975, 232 (1980).

12. Washington Post, July 7, 1986 (national weekly edition), p. 8.

13. N.Y. Times, Feb. 22, 1988, p. A16. This statement was made in 1986, when Burger was still Chief Justice.

14. 1970 WEB file. JMHP.

15. Washington Post, *supra* note 12.

16. N.Y. Times, March 13, 1986, p. A24.

17. WEB, Memorandum to the Conference, March 25, 1971.

18. WHR, Re: *Goldwater v. Carter.* Memorandum to the Conference, Dec. 10, 1979.

19. L. Caplan, The Tenth Justice 162 (1987).

20. See C. Warren, The Supreme Court in United States History 48 (1924).

21. L. Caplan, *supra* note 19, at 162.

22. WEB-JMH, n.d., 1971 WEB file. JMHP.

23. WOD-WJB, April 24, [1972].

24. WEB, Re: No. 73-5772—*Faretta v. California,* Memorandum to the Conference, Nov. 29, 1974.

25. WEB, Re: No. 73-1573—*Withrow v. Larkin,* Memorandum to the Conference, March 13, 1975.

26. Fuentes v. Shevin, 407 U.S. 67 (1972).

27. WEB-BRW, Re: 75-746, 748 *Atlas Roofing Co., Inc.; Frank Irey, Jr., Inc. v. Occupational Safety & Health Review Commission et al.,* March 14, 1977.

28. WEB, No. 299—*Cohen v. California,* Memorandum to the Conference, May 25, 1971.

29. Mapp v. Ohio, 367 U.S. 643 (1961); Miranda v. Arizona, 384 U.S. 436 (1966).

30. Washington Post, *supra* note 12.

31. United States v. Nixon, 418 U.S. 683 (1974), discussed *infra* Chapter 3.

32. 478 U.S. 714 (1986), discussed *infra* 64.

33. Swann v. Charlotte-Mecklenburg Board of Education, 402 U.S. 1 (1971), discussed *infra* 256.

34. 404 U.S. 802 (1971).

35. 425 F.2d 630, 632 (9th Cir. 1970).

36. 404 U.S. 802 (1971).

37. See 20 Wall. x (U.S. 1874) (Justice Campbell).

38. W. Douglas, supra note 11, at 222.

39. D. O'Brien, Storm Center: The Supreme Court in American Politics 189 (1986).

40. N.Y. Times, Dec. 13, 1987, p. 37.

41. See 20 Wall. x (U.S. 1874).

42. See G. Haskins & H. Johnson, Foundations of Power: John Marshall 1801–15, 385–386, 384 (1981).

43. C. Fairman, Reconstruction and Reunion 1864–1888, 66 (1971).

44. In a May 26, 1984, letter to the author, Fairman indicates that he "spoke

quite incautiously" and that the practice under Chase may have been more "in doubt" than his quoted statement indicates.

45. C. Hughes, The Supreme Court of the United States 58–59 (1928).

46. The Economist, July 4, 1987, p. 26.

47. Swann v. Charlotte-Mecklenburg Board of Education, 402 U.S. 1 (1971), discussed *infra* 256.

48. 410 U.S. 113 (1973), discussed *infra* 297. For another illustration not discussed in this book, see B. Schwartz, The Unpublished Opinions of the Burger Court 284 (1988).

49. The Douglas Letters 185 (M. Urofsky ed. 1987).

50. B. Woodward & S. Armstrong, The Brethren: Inside the Supreme Court 180 (1979). The other case referred to was Lloyd Corp. v. Tanner, 407 U.S. 551 (1972).

51. United States v. Nixon, 418 U.S. 683 (1974), *infra* 81.

52. *Infra* 257.

53. Griswold v. Connecticut, 381 U.S. 479 (1965).

54. Bell v. Maryland, 378 U.S. 226 (1964).

55. See B. Schwartz, *Swann*'s Way: The School Busing Case and the Supreme Court 178 (1986).

56. 403 U.S. 217 (1971).

57. Bush v. Orleans Parish School Board, 365 U.S. 569 (1961).

58. G. Dunne, Hugo Black and the Judicial Revolution 85 (1977).

59. 400 U.S. 112 (1970).

60. 163 U.S. 537 (1896).

61. TCC–JMH, Sept. 12. Tom C. Clark Papers, Tarlton Law Library, University of Texas.

62. JMH-WEB, June 9, 1970. JMHP.

63. JMH-FF, Aug. 21, [1963]. FFLC.

64. 399 U.S. 1 (1970), *infra* 331.

65. Miranda v. Arizona, 384 U.S. 436 (1966).

66. Rowan v. Post Office Department, 397 U.S. 728 (1970).

67. N.Y. Times, March 8, 1986, p. 7.

68. The Douglas Letters, *supra* note 49, at 44.

69. Id. at 106–107.

70. Washington Post, Oct. 19, 1987 (National weekly edition), p. 36.

71. Id.

72. F. Frankfurter, *supra* note 4, at 133.

73. Regents v. Bakke, 438 U.S. 265 (1978), *infra* 269.

74. *Infra* 226.

75. N.Y. Times, Feb. 20, 1983 (Magazine), p. 20.

76. Brown v. Board of Education, 347 U.S. 483 (1954).

77. TVA v. Hill, 437 U.S. 153 (1978).

78. Regents v. Bakke, 438 U.S. 265 (1978), *infra* 269.

79. B. Schwartz, Behind *Bakke:* Affirmative Action and the Supreme Court 13–14 (1988).

80. See The Warren Liberals, *supra* this chapter.

81. J. Clayton, The Making of Justice: The Supreme Court in Action 217 (1964).

82. Swann v. Charlotte–Mecklenburg Board of Education, 402 U.S. 1 (1971), United States v. Nixon, 418 U.S. 683 (1974).

83. B. Schwartz, *supra* note 55, at 178.

84. California v. Byers, 402 U.S. 424 (1971).

85. PS-WEB, 75-1453—*Wooley v. Maynard*, April 14, 1977.

86. Jacobellis v. Ohio, 378 U.S. 184, 197 (1964).

87. JMH-HAB, Re: No. 108—*Richardson v. Perales*, April 21, 1971.

88. 410 U.S. 113 (1973), *infra* 297.

89. United States v. Nixon, 418 U.S. 683 (1974), discussed *infra* 81.

90. B. Woodward & S. Armstrong, *supra* note 50, at 322.

91. N.Y. Times, Feb. 20, 1983 (Magazine), p. 20.

92. Id.

93. B. Schwartz, *supra* note 48, at 487.

94. Milliken v. Bradley, 433 U.S. 267 (1977).

95. B. Schwartz, *supra* note 79, at 88.

96. Board of Education v. Pico, 457 U.S. 853 (1982).

97. See *supra* note 29.

98. Guardians Association v. Civil Service Commission, 463 U.S. 582 (1983).

99. Lau v. Nichols, 414 U.S. 563 (1974).

100. 411 U.S. 677 (1973), *infra* 221.

101. Atlas Roofing Co. v. Occupational Safety & Health Review Commission, 430 U.S. 442 (1977).

102. LFP-BRW, Feb. 11, 1977.

103. N.Y. Times, March 8, 1986, p. 7.

104. Id.

105. B. Schwartz, Super Chief: Earl Warren and His Supreme Court 429 (1983).

106. Swann v. Charlotte-Mecklenburg Board of Education, 402 U.S. 1 (1971), *infra* 256.

107. Regents v. Bakke, 438 U.S. 265 (1978), *infra* 269.

108. On Communist Party v. Whitcomb, 414 U.S. 441 (1974).

109. B. Schwartz, *supra* note 48, at 412.

110. B. Schwartz, *supra* note 79, at 53.

111. N.Y. Times, July 23, 1984, p.8.

112. Galloway, Who's Playing Center?, 74 American Bar Association Journal 42 (1988).

113. The Burger Court: The Counter-Revolution That Wasn't 252 (V. Blasi ed. 1983).

114. Rhodes v. Chapman, 452 U.S. 337 (1981).

115. N.Y. Times, Jan. 17, 1986, p. A14.

116. Newsweek, July 23, 1979, p. 68.

117. N.Y. Times, July 12, 1981, §4, p. 22.

118. N.Y. Times, Feb. 28, 1988, §4, p. 1.

119. N.Y. Times, March 3, 1985 (Magazine), p. 33.

120. Id. at 31.

121. Brown v. Board of Education, 347 U.S. 483 (1954).

122. Plessy v. Ferguson, 163 U.S. 537 (1896).

123. The Rehnquist memo is reprinted in Nomination of Justice William Hubbs Rehnquist, Hearings before the Senate Judiciary Committee, 99th Cong., 2d Sess. 324 (1986).

124. Washington Post, July 28, 1986 (national weekly edition), p. 8.

125. Brown v. Board of Education file. Robert H. Jackson papers, Library of Congress.

126. N.Y. Times, *supra* note 119, at 32.

127. WHR-WJB, Re: No. 75-1064 *Kremens v. Bartley,* March 8, 1977.

128. Time, Oct. 8, 1984, p. 28.

129. Rummell v. Estelle, 445 U.S. 263 (1980).

130. WHR, Memorandum to the Conference, Feb. 21, 1980.

131. 424 U.S. 1 (1976).

132. B. Schwartz, *supra* note 79, at 192.

133. Time, Oct. 8, 1984, p. 28.

134. N.Y. Times, Oct. 8, 1986, p. A32.

135. Regents v. Bakke, 438 U.S. 265 (1978), *infra* 269.

136. B. Schwartz, *supra* note 79, at 53.

137. This was, of course, a take-off on A. E. Housman, "To An Athlete Dying Young."

138. WHR, Memorandum to the Chambers of All Active and Retired Justices, June 12, 1973. Earl Warren papers, Library of Congress.

139. Washington Post, July 28, 1986, (national weekly edition), p. 8.

140. W. Rehnquist, The Supreme Court: How It Was, How It Is 301 (1987).

141. Time, Oct. 5, 1981, p. 22.

142. See E. Witt, A Different Justice: Reagan and the Supreme Court 29 (1986).

143. Time, Oct. 8, 1984, p. 28.

144. Time, April 19, 1982, p. 49.

145. N.Y. Times, March 8, 1986, p. 7.

146. Galloway, *supra* note 112, at 45.

147. Miranda v. Arizona, 384 U.S. 436 (1966).

148. Moran v. Burbine, 475 U.S. 412 (1986); Oregon v. Elstad, 470 U.S. 298 (1985).

149. Garcia v. San Antonio Metropolitan Transit Authority, 469 U.S. 528, 580 (1985) (dissent).

150. Metropolitan Life Insurance Co. v. Ward, 470 U.S. 869, 884 (1985) (dissent); Akron v. Akron Center for Reproductive Health, 462 U.S. 416, 453 (1983) (dissent).

151. Mississippi University for Women v. Hogan, 458 U.S. 718 (1982).

152. Wygant v. Jackson Board of Education, 476 U.S. 267, 284 (1986).

153. Minnesota Star Co. v. Commissioner of Revenue, 460 U.S. 575 (1983).

154. McKaskle v. Wiggins, 465 U.S. 168, 187–88 (1984).

155. Garcia v. San Antonio Metropolitan Transit Authority, 469 U.S. 528, 580 (1985).

156. 410 U.S. 113 (1973), *infra* 297.

157. Akron v. Akron Center for Reproductive Health, 462 U.S. 416, 455 (1983).

158. Id. at 458.

159. Id. at 459.

160. See E. Witt, *supra* note 142, at 52.

161. The Douglas Letters, *supra* note 49, at 146.

162. Wyzanski, Whereas—A Judge's Premises: Essays in Judgment, Ethics, and the Law 61 (1985).

163. W. Rehnquist, *supra* note 140, at 261.

164. N.Y. Times, April 21, 1962, p. 17.

165. Rehnquist, Who Writes Decisions of the Supreme Court?, U.S. News & World Report, Dec. 13, 1957, p. 74.

166. N.Y. Times, April 17, 1958 (Magazine), p. 16.

167. The Times (London), July 11, 1986.

168. N.Y. Times, Sept. 20, 1987 (Book Review), p. 40.

169. J. P. Stevens, Madison Lecture at NYU Law School, Oct. 27, 1982.

170. Miky, Mike, & Ricki–WJB, Monday 11/23 [19   ].

171. W. Rehnquist, *supra* note 140, at 263.

172. Justice O'Connor also joined the cert pool, so it ultimately consisted of six Justices.

173. The Douglas Letters, *supra* note 49, at 141.

174. FF-PS, April 29, 1960. FFLC.

175. W. Douglas, *supra* note 11, at 173.

176. R. Posner, The Federal Courts: Crisis and Reform 106 (1985).

177. Harvard Law School Bulletin, Winter 1986, p. 28.

178. W. Rehnquist, *supra* note 140, at 298.

179. Id. at 299–300.

180. Id. at 300.

181. Brown v. Board of Education, 347 U.S. 483, 494 n.11 (1954).

182. Harvard Law School Bulletin, *supra* note 177.

183. WOD, Memorandum to the Conference, Oct. 23, 1961. HLBLC.

184. Compare R. Posner, *supra* note 176, at 106–107.

185. Compare id. at 111.

186. A Dialogue about Legal Education as It Approaches the 21st Century 29 (J. Kelso ed. 1987).

187. Harvard Law School Bulletin, *supra* note 177, at 29.

CHAPTER TWO

1. The Economist, July 4, 1987, p. 14.

2. F. Rodell, Nine Men: A Political History of the Supreme Court from 1790 to 1955, 179 (1955).

3. The Economist, *supra* note 1.

4. 411 U.S. 389 (1973).

5. See id. at 397.

6. Id. at 419.

7. 449 U.S. 200 (1980).

8. 253 U.S. 245 (1920). The conference notes I have used read "Gore v. Evans."

9. 253 U.S. 248.

10. The "Score Sheet" reads as follows:

Score Sheet on *United States v. Will*

	YEAR I	YEAR II	YEAR III	YEAR IV
Justice STEVENS	Affirm	Reverse	Reverse	Affirm
Justice REHNQUIST	Affirm(?)	Reverse	Reverse	Affirm
Justice POWELL	Reverse	Reverse	Reverse	Affirm
Justice BLACKMUN	Affirm	Affirm	Affirm	Affirm
Justice MARSHALL	Affirm	Affirm	Affirm	Affirm
Justice WHITE	Affirm(?)	Reverse	Reverse	Affirm
Justice STEWART	Reverse	Reverse	Reverse	Affirm
Justice BRENNAN	Affirm	Affirm	Affirm	Affirm
The CHIEF JUSTICE	Affirm	Reverse	Reverse	Affirm
Totals:	7–2(?)	6–3	6–3	6–3
	Affirm	Reverse	Reverse	Affirm

Though it is stated, 449 U.S. at 231, that Justice Blackmun "took no part in the decision," he did participate in the conference and voting.

11. 449 U.S. at 225.

12. 449 U.S. 813 (1980).

13. Valley Forge Christian College v. Americans United, 454 U.S. 464, 471 (1982).

14. 2 A. Beveridge, The Life of John Marshall 468 (1916).

15. Valley Forge Christian College v. Americans United, 454 U.S. 464, 471 (1982).

16. Iron Arrow Honor Society v. Heckler, 464 U.S. 67, 70 (1983).

17. 416 U.S. 312 (1974).

18. Roe v. Wade, 410 U.S. 113 (1973); Doe v. Bolton, 410 U.S. 179 (1973), *infra* notes 21, 22.

19. 416 U.S. at 350.

20. Regents v. Bakke, 438 U.S. 265 (1978), *infra* 269.

21. 410 U.S. 113 (1973).

22. 410 U.S. 179 (1973).

23. WJB-WOD, Dec. 11, 1971.

24. The Blackmun draft is reprinted in B. Schwartz, The Unpublished Opinions of the Burger Court 103 (1988).

25. Id. at 108.

26. 410 U.S. at 125.

27. Weinstein v. Bradford, 423 U.S. 147, 149 (1975).

28. 419 U.S. 393 (1975).

29. Id. at 402.

30. 427 U.S. 539 (1976).

31. Though Justice Stevens did state at the conference, "Mootness troubles me."

32. Gannet Co. v. DePasquale, 443 U.S. 368, 378 (1979).

33. Rehnquist, J., dissenting, in Roe v. Wade, 410 U.S. at 171.

34. Id. at 171–72.

35. Compare id. at 172.

36. The Burger Years 3 (H. Schwartz ed. 1987).

37. Association of Data Processing Organizations v. Camp, 397 U.S. 150, 169 n.2 (1970).

38. Valley Forge Christian College v. Americans United, 454 U.S. 464, 471, 475 (1982).

39. Kaufman, C. J., dissenting in Evans v. Lynn, 537 F.2d 571, 610 (2d Cir. 1976), certiorari denied, 429 U.S. 1066 (1977).

40. 397 U.S. 150 (1970).

41. 397 U.S. 159 (1970).

42. Reprinted in B. Schwartz, *supra* note 24, at 33.

43. See B. Schwartz, Administrative Law 471 (2d ed. 1984).

44. 397 U.S. at 153, 171.

45. United States v. Richardson, 418 U.S. 166, 194 (1974).

46. Valley Forge Christian College v. Americans United, 454 U.S. 464, 486 (1982).

47. United States v. Students Challenging Regulatory Agency Procedures, 412 U.S. 669, 686 (1973).

48. Sierra Club v. Morton, 405 U.S. 727, 734 (1972).

49. Environmental Policy Act, 83 Stat. 852 (1970).

50. 412 U.S. 669 (1973).

51. United States v. Richardson, 418 U.S. 166, 194 (1973).

52. The Burger Years, *supra* note 36, at xiii.

53. United States v. Richardson, 418 U.S. 166, 194 (1973).

54. Compare id. at 191, 194.

55. See B. Schwartz, *supra* note 43, § 8.13.

56. 392 U.S. 83 (1968).

57. 454 U.S. 464 (1982).

58. The Burger Years, *supra* note 36.

59. 418 U.S. 166 (1974).

60. 418 U.S. 208 (1974).

61. Id. at 217.

62. 418 U.S. at 194.

63. Justice Brennan did dissent on the ground stated in his letter. 418 U.S. at 235.

64. 422 U.S. 490 (1975).

65. Id. at 506. Compare Brennan, J., dissenting, id. at 525.

66. Linda R. S. v. Richard D., 410 U.S. 614, 618 (1973).

67. 426 U.S. 26 (1976).

68. *Supra* note 50.

69. Watt v. Energy Action Foundation, 454 U.S. 151, 161 (1981).

70. Valley Forge Christian College v. Americans United, 454 U.S. 464, 472 (1982).

71. Chicago & Southern Air Lines v. Waterman Steamship Co., 333 U.S. 103, 111 (1948).

72. WJB-WEB, Re: *House of Representatives v. INS*, Nos. 80-2170, 80-2171, and 80-1832, April 7, 1983.

73. 369 U.S. 186 (1962).
74. Id. at 212.
75. 444 U.S. 996 (1979).
76. See PS-WEB, Dec. 11, 1979.
77. United States v. Munsingwear, 340 U.S. 36 (1950).
78. The Rehnquist memo added the following parenthetical comment: "(This would distinguish the *Steel Seizure Cases,* where although one of the grounds upon which President Truman relied was his power over foreign affairs, steel mills located in the United States had been seized pursuant to that order.)"
79. See Finzer v. Barry, 798 F.2d 1450, 1459 (D.C. Cir. 1986); 1 R. Rotunda, J. Nowak, & J. Young, Treatise on Constitutional Law 187 (1986).
80. See *infra* 90.
81. Baker v. Carr, 369 U.S. at 241, 246.
82. E.g., Baker v. Carr, *supra* note 73; Powell v. McCormack, 395 U.S. 486 (1969).
83. 469 U.S. 528 (1985).
84. Id. at 547.
85. Id. at 550, 551.
86. Id. at 552.
87. Id. at 547–48.
88. Id.
89. Powell, J., dissenting, id. at 567.
90. Id.
91. Id. at 567, quoting from Marbury v. Madison, 1 Cr. 137, 177 (U.S. 1803).
92. 3 J. Story, Commentaries on the Constitution of the United States § 1570 (1833).
93. Ableman v. Booth, 21 How. 506, 521 (U.S. 1859).
94. *Garcia,* O'Connor, J., dissenting, 469 U.S. at 589.
95. Marbury v. Madison, 1 Cranch 137, 177 (U.S. 1803).

CHAPTER THREE

1. Panama Refining Co. v. Ryan, 293 U.S. 388, 440 (1935).
2. 478 U.S. 714 (1986).
3. 54 U.S. Law Week 3710 (1986).
4. Quoted in B. Schwartz, Administrative Law: A Casebook (3d ed. 1988).
5. Hospital Corp. v. FTC, 807 F.2d 1381, 1392 (7th Cir. 1986).
6. Humphrey's Executor v. United States, 295 U.S. 602 (1935); Myers v. United States, 272 U.S. 52 (1929).
7. Though it is headed "per curiam," Justice Scalia undoubtedly wrote the opinion of the lower court in the case.
8. A typed version of the Brennan conference statement, headed *Bowsher v. Synar* No. 85-1377, -1378, -1379.
9. Quoting from Nixon v. Fitzgerald, 457 U.S. 731, 749, 750 (1982).
10. 478 U.S. at 734.
11. Springer v. Philippine Islands, 277 U.S. 189, 209 (1928).
12. Wayman v. Southard, 10 Wheat. 1, 43 (U.S. 1825).
13. White, J., dissenting, 478 U.S. at 759.

14. Id. at 725 n.4.

15. *Supra* n.6.

16. Synar v. United States, 626 F. Supp. 1374, 1398 (D.C. 1986).

17. *Supra* n.7.

18. 462 U.S. 919 (1983).

19. B. Schwartz & H. Wade, Legal Control of Government 90 (1972).

20. See White, J., dissenting, 462 U.S. at 967.

21. Opinion of the Justices, 431 A.2d 783, 786–87 (N.H. 1981).

22. National Conference of State Legislatures, Legislative Review of Administrative Regulations 4 (1977).

23. S. 1080, 97th Cong., 2d Sess.

24. The INS was in the Department of Justice, so the delegation was technically to the Attorney General. It should be noted that I have used extracts from notes of the conferences after argument and after reargument interchangeably.

25. The Brennan quotes are from a document headed *I.N.S. v. Chadha* No. 80-1832. It appears to be a memo summarizing the Justice's conference statement.

26. 462 U.S. at 951, 947.

27. Id. at 984.

28. W. Wilson, Congressional Government 270 (10th ed. 1894).

29. Quoted in Study on Federal Regulation, Congressional Oversight of Regulatory Agencies IX (1977).

30. W. Wilson, *supra* note 28.

31. See Chemerinsky, A Paradox without Principle: A Comment on the Burger Court's Jurisprudence in Separation of Powers Cases, 60 Southern California Law Review 1083 (1986).

32. Compare id. at 1084.

33. 418 U.S. 683 (1974).

34. Nixon v. Administrator of General Services, 433 U.S. 425 (1977).

35. Cooper v. Aaron, 358 U.S. 1 (1958).

36. These are reprinted in B. Schwartz, The Unpublished Opinions of the Burger Court 202 (1988).

37. Chicago & Southern Airlines v. Waterman Steamship Corp., 333 U.S. 103 (1948); United States v. Reynolds, 345 U.S. 1 (1953).

38. Counsel for the President in the case.

39. Rochin v. California, 34 U.S. 165, 177 (1952).

40. Quoted in B. Schwartz, *Swann*'s Way: The School Busing Case and the Supreme Court 85 (1986).

41. In July 1974, when *Nixon* was decided, this writer was directing a seminar in Jerusalem on recent developments in American law. The participants were lawyers, law professors, and government officials who came primarily from African countries. When the Supreme Court decision was announced, it had a dramatic effect at the seminar. The African jurists were all but overwhelmed by the spectacle of a court bringing the nation's highest officer to heel. Such a thing, they asserted, would have been impossible in their countries.

42. R. Berger, Executive Privilege: A Constitutional Myth (1974).

43. Re: 76-944 *Nixon v. Warner Communications, Inc.*, Memorandum to the Conference, Dec. 6, 1977.

44. 418 U.S. at 706.

45. Id. at 705–06.

46. Nixon v. Administrator of General Services, 433 U.S. 425, 447 (1977).

47. 418 U.S. at 708.

48. Id. at 712.

49. 424 U.S. 1 (1976).

50. Scully v. United States, 193 Fed. 185, 187 (D. Nev. 1910).

51. LFP-WJB, PS, WHR, *Buckley.*

52. 424 U.S. at 126.

53. Humphrey's Executor v. United States, 295 U.S. 602 (1935).

54. 444 U.S. 996 (1979), *supra* 58.

55. Re: *Goldwater v. Carter,* p. 3, Memorandum to the Conference, Dec. 10, 1979.

56. 444 U.S. at 1002.

57. 453 U.S. 654 (1981).

58. Zittman v. McGrath, 341 U.S. 446 (1951); Orvis v. Brownell, 345 U.S. 183 (1953).

59. Id. at 668.

60. The Chief Justice wrote to Rehnquist, "I will place ten Brownie points in your personnel file." Re: No. 80-2078—*Dames & Moore v. Regan, Secretary of the Treasury,* June 26, 1981.

61. Youngstown Sheet & Tube Co. v. Sawyer, 343 U.S. 579 (1952).

62. Id. at 637.

63. WHR-HAB, Re: No. 80-2078 *Dames & Moore v. Regan,* June 29, 1981.

64. Circulated June 26, 1981.

65. HAB-WHR, Re: No. 80-2078 *Dames & Moore v. Regan,* June 29, 1981.

66. *Supra* note 63.

67. 453 U.S. at 678.

68. LFP-WHR, 80-2078 *Dames & Moore v. Regan,* June 29, 1981.

69. 381 U.S. 1 (1965).

70. See B. Schwartz, Super Chief: Chief Justice Warren and His Supreme Court—A Judicial Biography 564–65 (1983).

71. 453 U.S. 280 (1981).

72. Id. at 287.

73. LFP-WEB, No. 80-83 *Muskie v. Agee,* June 5, 1981.

74. The conference notes used by me read "issued," but this seems an error.

75. LFP-WEB, 80-83 *Haig v. Agee,* May 29, 1981. See similarly BRW-WEB, Re: 80-83 *Haig v. Agee,* May 29, 1981.

76. 283 U.S. 697 (1931).

77. BRW-WEB, Re: 80-83—*Haig v. Agee,* May 29, 1981.

78. 80-83, *Haig v. Agee.*

79. 453 U.S. at 308, citing Near v. Minnesota, *supra* note 76.

80. JPS-WEB, Re: 80-83—*Haig v. Agee,* June 1, 1981.

81. 468 U.S. 222 (1984).

82. The Burger Years 53 (H. Schwartz ed. 1987).

83. *Supra* note 69.

84. *Supra* 94.

85. 468 U.S. at 243.

CHAPTER FOUR

1. Gibbons v. Ogden, 9 Wheat. 1, 224 (U.S. 1824).
2. Hood & Sons v. DuMond, 336 U.S. 525, 533–34 (1949).
3. J. Story, Commentaries on the Constitution of the United States § 1055 (1833).
4. Texas v. White, 7 Wall. 700, 725 (U.S. 1868).
5. R. Jackson, The Supreme Court in the American System of Government 65–66 (1955).
6. 426 U.S. 833 (1976).
7. Carter v. Carter Coal Co., 298 U.S. 238 (1936).
8. 426 U.S. at 849.
9. Dissenting in Hughes v. Alexandria Scrap Corp., 426 U.S. 794, 822 n.4 (1976).
10. Starting with NLRB v. Jones & Laughlin Steel Corp., 301 U.S. 1 (1937).
11. See B. Schwartz, Constitutional Law: A Textbook § 4.2 (2d ed. 1979).
12. Gulf Oil Corp. v. Copp Paving Co., 419 U.S. 186, 196–97 (1974).
13. 392 U.S. 183 (1968).
14. Id. at 196–97.
15. New York v. United States, 326 U.S. 572, 582 (1946).
16. United States v. California, 297 U.S. 175, 185 (1936).
17. 297 U.S. 175 (1936).
18. Id. at 185.
19. 421 U.S. 542 (1975).
20. 426 U.S. at 842.
21. Id. at 855.
22. Id. at 849, 842.
23. 460 U.S. 226 (1983).
24. 469 U.S. 528 (1985).
25. Id. at 530.
26. 557 F. Supp. 445, 446 (W.D. Tex. 1983).
27. Hodel v. Virginia Surface Mining Association, 452 U.S. 264, 288 (1981).
28. The Brennan conference quotes are from a document headed Garcia v. San Antonio Metropolitan Transit Authority Nos. 82-1913 and 82-1951. It appears to be a statement used by the Justice at the conference.
29. 469 U.S. at 531.
30. Powell, J., dissenting in *Garcia,* 469 U.S. at 561 n. 4. The Holmes reference is to O. Holmes, The Common Law 1 (1881).
31. 469 U.S. at 547.
32. Id. at 550–51.
33. Michigan v. Meese, 666 F. Supp. 974, 977 (E.D. Mich. 1987).
34. Department of Revenue v. Association of Washington Stevedoring Cos., 435 U.S. 734, 749 (1978).
35. W. Rutledge, A Declaration of Legal Faith 33 (1947).
36. Panhandle E. Pipe Line Co. v. Michigan Public Service Commission, 341 U.S. 329, 339 (1951).
37. Hunt v. Washington State Apple Advertising Commission, 432 U.S. 333, 350 (1977).

38. W. Rutledge, *supra* note 35, at 45.

39. 12 How. 299 (U.S. 1851).

40. Id. at 319.

41. Crandall v. Nevada, 6 Wall. 35, 42 (U.S. 1868).

42. 435 U.S. 151 (1978).

43. Raymond Motor Transportation v. Rice, 434 U.S. 429, 441 (1978).

44. Id. at 440–41.

45. 303 U.S. 177 (1938).

46. Id. at 190.

47. See, e.g., Dixie Ohio Express Co. v. State Revenue Commission, 306 U.S. 72, 76 (1939); Morf v. Bingaman, 298 U.S. 407, 412 (1936).

48. See *Barnwell*, 303 U.S. at 187.

49. Frankfurter, J., concurring, in Morgan v. Virginia, 328 U.S. 373, 388 (1946).

50. 434 U.S. 429 (1978).

51. Id. at 444.

52. Id. at 437.

53. Id. at 449.

54. Kassell v. Consolidated Freightways Corp., 450 U.S. 662, 671 (1981).

55. Gibbons v. Ogden, 9 Wheat. 1, 203 (U.S. 1824).

56. Philadelphia v. New Jersey, 437 U.S. 617, 629 (1978).

57. 437 U.S. 617 (1978).

58. Id. at 622.

59. 424 U.S. 366 (1976).

60. 432 U.S. 333 (1977).

61. Id. at 351

62. Id. at 353.

63. Plumley v. Massachusetts, 155 U.S. 461 (1894).

64. Clason v. Indiana, 306 U.S. 439 (1939).

65. 397 U.S. 137 (1970).

66. 262 U.S. 553 (1923).

67. Id. at 599.

68. 161 U.S. 519 (1896).

69. Id. at 535.

70. Hudson County Water Co. v. McCarter, 209 U.S. 349 (1908).

71. 262 U.S. at 599.

72. Baldwin v. Fish & Game Commission, 436 U.S. 371, 392 (1978).

73. 441 U.S. 322 (1979).

74. *Supra* note 57.

75. 441 U.S. at 334–35.

76. 426 U.S. 794 (1976).

77. Great Atlantic & Pacific Tea Co. v. Cottrell, *supra* note 59; Dean Milk Co. v. Madison, 340 U.S. 349 (1951).

78. Pike v. Bruce Church, Inc., *supra* note 65.

79. Dissenting in New York v. United States, 326 U.S. 572, 591 (1946).

80. 426 U.S. at 823.

81. Richfield Oil Corp. v. State Board of Equalization, 329 U.S. 69, 75 (1946).

82. 12 Wheat. 419 (U.S. 1827).

83. Michelin Tire Corp. v. Wages, 423 U.S. 276, 282 (1976).
84. 12 Wheat. at 441–42.
85. 13 Wall. 29 (U.S. 1871).
86. 423 U.S. 276 (1976).
87. Id. at 279.
88. Reprinted in B. Schwartz, The Unpublished Opinions of the Burger Court 326 (1988).
89. *Supra* note 82.
90. 5 How. 504 (U.S. 1847).
91. Colonial Pipeline Co. v. Traigle, 421 U.S. 100, 108 (1975).
92. Western Live Stock v. Bureau of Revenue, 303 U.S. 250 (1938).
93. Department of Revenue v. Association of Washington Stevedoring Cos., 435 U.S. 734, 748 (1978).
94. 430 U.S. 274 (1977).
95. 340 U.S. 602 (1951).
96. 430 U.S. at 288 n.15.
97. 358 U.S. 450 (1959).
98. 437 U.S. 267 (1978).
99. Japan Line v. County of Los Angeles, 441 U.S. 434, 455 (1979).
100. 437 U.S. at 292.
101. General Motors Corp. v. District of Columbia, 380 U.S. 553, 560 (1965).
102. Cardozo, a Ministry of Justice, 35 Harvard Law Review 113, 126 (1921).
103. *Supra* note 6.
104. *Supra* note 24.
105. N.Y. Times, Jan. 26, 1983, pp. A14, A17.
106. Boston Stock Exchange v. State Tax Commission, 429 U.S. 318 (1977).
107. *Supra* 121.
108. *Supra* 123.
109. *Supra* 115.
110. *Supra* 114.
111. *Supra* 117.
112. *Supra* 118.
113. McLeod v. J. E. Dilworth Co., 322 U.S. 327, 330 (1944).

CHAPTER FIVE

1. Letter of Justice Stone, April 12, 1941, quoted in Mason, The Core of Free Government, 1938–40: Mr. Justice Stone and "Preferred Freedoms," 65 Yale Law Journal 597, 626 (1956).
2. Lynch v. Household Finance Corp., 405 U.S. 538, 552 (1972).
3. Compare Kovacs v. Cooper, 336 U.S. 77, 95 (1949).
4. Dissenting, in Greer v. Spock, 424 U.S. 828, 852 (1976).
5. Dissenting, in Abrams v. United States, 250 U.S. 616, 630 (1919).
6. 316 U.S. 52 (1942).
7. Id. at 55.
8. 413 U.S. 376 (1973).
9. Id. at 385.

10. Id. at 388, 389.

11. 421 U.S. 809 (1975).

12. Id. at 820.

13. Id. at 831.

14. 425 U.S. 748 (1976).

15. Kleindienst v. Mandel, 408 U.S. 753 (1972); Lamont v. Postmaster General, 381 U.S. 301 (1965).

16. 425 U.S. at 762.

17. Id. at 773 n.25.

18. 433 U.S. 350 (1977).

19. Martindale-Hubbell Law Directory, which lists lawyers throughout the country.

20. 455 U.S. 191 (1982).

21. 471 U.S. 626 (1985).

22. Ohralik v. Ohio State Bar, 436 U.S. 447 (1978).

23. *Zauderer v. Office of Disciplinary Counsel,* No. 83–2166, Post-Argument Discussion, which contains a summary of Justice Brennan's argument at the conference.

24. Conference Memorandum, *Zauderer v. Office of Disciplinary Counsel,* No. 83–2166, apparently the memo on which the Brennan conference presentation was based.

25. Zauderer v. Office of Disciplinary Counsel, 471 U.S. at 637.

26. Ohralik v. Ohio State Bar, 436 U.S. 447 (1978).

27. HAB-LFP, May 12, 1978.

28. Ohralik v. Ohio State Bar, 436 U.S. 447, 455–56 (1978).

29. JPS-LFP, May 16, 1980.

30. *Ohralik,* 436 U.S. at 456.

31. 447 U.S. 557 (1980).

32. Id. at 566.

33. Id. at 562, 561.

34. Id. at 580.

35. LFP-JPS, May 17, 1980.

36. The quotes are from LFP-PS, Jan. 18, 1977; PS-LFP, Jan. 14, 1977. Both letters are headed No. 75-1153 *Abood v. Detroit Board.*

37. 435 U.S. 765 (1978).

38. *Infra* n.42.

39. Id. at 782.

40. 435 U.S. at 784 n.19.

41. 447 U.S. 530 (1980).

42. 424 U.S. 1 (1976).

43. *Supra* 88.

44. 424 U.S. at 19.

45. *Infra* 219.

46. See B. Schwartz, Behind *Bakke:* The Supreme Court and Affirmative Action 192 (1988).

47. Stromberg v. California, 283 U.S. 359 (1931).

48. 418 U.S. 405 (1974).

49. WJB-LFP, June 12, 1974.

50. Texas v. Johnson, 109 S. Ct. 2533 (1989).

51. 418 U.S. at 410, 415.

52. 430 U.S. 705 (1977).

53. Id. at 720.

54. Ibid.

55. 3 R. Rotunda, J. Nowak & J. Young, Treatise on Constitutional Law 270 (1986).

56. 468 U.S. 288 (1984).

57. 391 U.S. 367 (1968).

58. 408 U.S. 753 (1972).

59. Kliendienst v. Mandel, 408 U.S. 753, 762–63 (1972).

60. Stewart cited Lamont v. Postmaster General, 381 U.S. 301 (1965).

61. Linmark Associates v. Willingboro, 431 U.S. 85, 93 (1977).

62. Hudgens v. National Labor Relations Board, 424 U.S. 507, 520 (1976).

63. 408 U.S. 104 (1972).

64. 408 U.S. 92 (1972).

65. 379 U.S. 536, 581 (1965).

66. 408 U.S. at 95.

67. See R. Rotunda, J. Nowak, & J. Young, *supra* note 55, at 237.

68. 420 U.S. 546 (1975).

69. A typed version is headed No. 73-1004 *Southern* [sic] *Promotions v. Conrad.* It was apparently not circulated.

70. Concurring, 420 U.S. at 563.

71. Commonwealth v. Davis, 162 Mass. 510, 511 (1895). The Supreme Court affirmed, largely on the Holmes rationale. Davis v. Massachusetts, 167 U.S. 43 (1897).

72. 420 U.S. at 555.

73. Rehnquist, J., dissenting, id. at 570.

74. Adderley v. Florida, 385 U.S. 39 (1966).

75. Douglas, J., dissenting, id. at 52.

76. This sentence was deleted at Justice Clark's insistence. See B. Schwartz, Super Chief: Earl Warren and His Supreme Court—A Judicial Biography 631 (1983).

77. 424 U.S. 828 (1976).

78. Cafeteria Workers Union v. McElroy, 367 U.S. 886 (1961).

79. 424 U.S. at 836.

80. 418 U.S. 298 (1974).

81. 452 U.S. 640 (1981).

82. Id. at 651.

83. 473 U.S. 788 (1985).

84. 326 U.S. 501 (1946).

85. Amalgamated Food Employees Union v. Logan Valley Plaza, 391 U.S. 308 (1968).

86. 407 U.S. 551 (1972).

87. The record showed that the center had allowed the American Legion to sell poppies on Veterans Day.

88. There is a different vote count in B. Woodward & S. Armstrong, The Brethren: Inside the Supreme Court 179 (1979), but it is erroneous according to the docket book I have used.

89. Hudgens v. National Labor Relations Board, 424 U.S. 507, 518 (1976).

90. 424 U.S. 507 (1976).

91. 447 U.S. 74 (1980).

CHAPTER SIX

1. Stewart, Or of the Press, 26 Hastings Law Journal 631, 633 (1975).

2. New York Times Co. v. United States, 403 U.S. 713 (1971).

3. N.Y. Times, June 13, 1971, p. 1.

4. Time, June 28, 1971, p. 11.

5. The lower court decisions are reported in 444 F.2d 544 (2d Cir. 1971); 446 F.2d 1327 (D.C. Cir. 1971).

6. 71 Landmark Briefs and Arguments of the Supreme Court of the United States: Constitutional Law 222–23 (P. Kurland & G. Kasper eds. 1975).

7. Justice Harlan's dissenting opinion was concurred in by Burger, C. J., and Blackmun, J.

8. Those of Justices Brennan, Stewart, and White.

9. 403 U.S. at 730, per Stewart, J. This has been characterized as "the sole possible exception to the prohibition against prior restraints," Brennan, J., concurring, in Nebraska Press Association v. Stuart, 427 U.S. 539, 593 (1976).

10. New York Times Co. v. United States, 403 U.S. at 714.

11. 381 U.S. 532 (1965).

12. B. Schwartz, The Unpublished Opinions of the Warren Court 222 (1985).

13. 381 U.S. at 540.

14. Id. at 614–15.

15. 438 U.S. 1 (1978).

16. The Stevens draft is reprinted in B. Schwartz, The Unpublished Opinions of the Burger Court 349 (1988).

17. Also in 438 U.S. at 32.

18. Id.

19. Id. at 16.

20. 408 U.S. 665 (1972).

21. Id. at 728 (1972) (dissent).

22. The conference notes I have used contained the word "confidence" here.

23. 443 U.S. 368 (1979).

24. The Blackmun draft is reprinted in B. Schwartz, *supra* note 16, at 418.

25. 443 U.S. at 406.

26. E.g., changing "we" in the draft opinion of the Court to "I."

27. Also in 443 U.S. at 412.

28. This statement is not contained in the final Stewart opinion.

29. 448 U.S. 555 (1980).

30. I have changed the order of the Burger statements as they are contained in the conference notes made available to me.

31. Griswold v. Connecticut, 381 U.S. 479, 490 n.6 (1965).

32. 448 U.S. 579, n.15.

33. 478 U.S. 1 (1986).

34. Brennan's conference statement, headed *Press-Enterprise Co. v. Superior Court* No. 84-1560.

35. 427 U.S. 539 (1976).

36. LFP-WEB, June 8, 1976.

37. Id.

38. Justices White, Brennan, Stewart, Marshall, and Stevens.

39. 427 U.S. at 572.

40. Id. at 617.

41. 381 U.S. 532 (1965).

42. B. Schwartz, *supra* note 12, at 192.

43. 449 U.S. 560 (1981).

44. The Stewart draft is reprinted in B. Schwartz, *supra* note 12, at 195.

45. 449 U.S. at 583.

46. Id.

47. HAB-WEB, Dec. 29, 1980.

48. 381 U.S. at 550.

49. Id. at 588.

50. HAB-WEB, Jan. 19, 1981.

51. LFP-WEB, Dec. 30, 1980. On his suggested hearing, Powell wrote, "the purpose of a hearing would be (i) to enable a defendant to advance at the outset whatever grounds he may have as to why he thinks electronic media coverage would affect the fairness of his trial, (ii) to enable the court to prescribe in advance appropriate protective measures, and (iii) to facilitate the post-trial evaluation of untoward events that may occur."

52. WEB-PS, Jan. 12, 1981.

53. HAB-WEB, Dec. 29, 1980.

54. 460 U.S. 575 (1983).

55. Grosjean v. American Press Co., 297 U.S. 233 (1936).

56. 420 U.S. 469 (1975).

57. The conference notes used by me contained the word "enforce" here.

58. Landmark Communications v. Virginia, 435 U.S. 829 (1978).

59. 418 U.S. 241 (1974).

60. The conference notes I have used contained the word "we" here.

61. Compare Landmark Communications v. Virginia, 435 U.S. 820, 849 (1978).

62. Columbia Broadcasting System v. Democratic National Committee, 412 U.S. 94, 102 (1973).

63. Federal Communications Commission v. National Citizens Committee, 436 U.S. 775, 795 (1978).

64. Red Lion Broadcasting Co. v. Federal Communications Commission, 395 U.S. 367, 388 (1969).

65. Id.

66. Id. at 390.

67. 412 U.S. 94 (1973).

68. 453 U.S. 367 (1981).

69. 468 U.S. 364 (1984).

70. 376 U.S. 254 (1964).

71. Id. at 280.

72. Curtis Publishing Co. v. Butts and Associated Press v. Walker, 388 U.S. 130 (1967).

73. B. Schwartz, Super Chief: Earl Warren and His Supreme Court 531–40, 650–52 (1983).

74. 403 U.S. 29 (1971).

75. HAB-WJB, March 22, 1971.

76. 1961 Supreme Court Review 245.

77. 403 U.S. at 62.

78. 4 Harvard Law Review 193, 214 (1890).

79. 403 U.S. at 59. See also Gertz v. Robert Welch, Inc., 418 U.S. 323, 377 (1974) (state and federal courts felt obliged to follow *Rosenbloom* plurality opinion).

80. Id. at 337.

81. 418 U.S. 323 (1974).

82. Compare Blackmun, J., concurring, at 353.

83. Id. at 354.

84. The Court held that Gertz was not a public figure within its test.

85. 418 U.S. at 349.

86. BRW-LFP, Jan. 10, 1974.

87. 418 U.S. at 349.

88. Justice Brennan disagreed with this conclusion. Id. at 367.

CHAPTER SEVEN

1. 370 U.S. 421 (1962).

2. See B. Schwartz, Super Chief: Earl Warren and His Supreme Court—A Judicial Biography 441 (1983).

3. Zorach v. Clauson, 343 U.S. 306, 313 (1952).

4. West Virginia Board of Education v. Barnette, 319 U.S. 624, 654 (1943).

5. McCollum v. Board of Education, 333 U.S. 203, 213 (1948).

6. Everson v. Board of Education, 330 U.S. 1, 16 (1947).

7. Compare *McCollum, supra* note 5, at 213.

8. See Walz v. Tax Commission, 397 U.S. 664, 690 (1970).

9. 397 U.S. 664 (1970).

10. Justice Blackmun did not take the oath until June 9, 1970, after *Walz* was decided.

11. Particularly the Holmes quotations, 397 U.S. at 675, 678.

12. 397 U.S. at 689.

13. Everson v. Board of Education, 330 U.S. 1 (1947).

14. This part of the quote is from the Burger first draft.

15. 397 U.S. at 674.

16. 403 U.S. 602 (1971), *infra* note 20.

17. 397 U.S. at 690.

18. Id. at 674.

19. 403 U.S. 602 (1971).

20. 403 U.S. 672 (1971).

21. Id. at 612–13.

22. See id. at 685.

23. 413 U.S. 472 (1973).

24. WOD-WEB, June 14, 1973, in The Douglas Letters 203 (M. Urofsky ed. 1987).

25. 426 U.S. 736 (1976).

26. 413 U.S. 756 (1973).

27. Id. at 783, 790–91.

28. 463 U.S. 388 (1983).

29. Id. at 398–99.

30. Id. at 409.

31. 421 U.S. 349 (1975).

32. Board of Education v. Allen, 392 U.S. 236 (1968).

33. 433 U.S. 229 (1977).

34. 444 U.S. 646 (1980).

35. Justice Blackmun made a similar statement at the Regan conference.

36. *Supra* note 23.

37. *Supra* note 13. According to Justice Blackmun at the Regan conference, "*Everson* created the problem."

38. WHR-BRW, June 1, 1979.

39. 473 U.S. 373 (1985).

40. 473 U.S. 402 (1985).

41. 739 F.2d 48 (2d Cir. 1984).

42. *Supra* note 31.

43. 473 U.S. at 413.

44. Id. at 420–21.

45. 459 U.S. 116 (1982).

46. Justice O'Connor disagreed on this point. She told the conference, "I read the statute as saying there could be review of the church veto."

47. The conference notes used by me say "sixteen," but this is erroneous.

48. Presumably meaning the prohibition of any liquor store within 500 feet of a church.

49. Abington School District v. Schempp, 374 U.S. 203, 225 (1963).

50. Abington School District v. Schempp, 374 U.S. 203 (1963).

51. Stone v. Graham, 449 U.S. 39 (1980).

52. 472 U.S. 38 (1985).

53. 554 F. Supp. 1104, 1128 (S.D. Ala. 1983).

54. 472 U.S. at 48.

55. The Brennan quotes are from *Wallace v. Jaffree, Smith v. Jaffree,* Nos. 83-812, 83-929 Argued Tuesday December 4, 1984 For Conference Friday December 7, 1984. This was apparently Brennan's statement prepared for the conference.

56. 403 U.S. at 612, quoted 472 U.S. at 55.

57. Id. at 62, 84.

58. Id. at 59. See Powell, J., id. at 62.

59. See also Brennan, J., in Abington School District v. Schempp, 374 U.S. 203, 281 (1963), quoted 472 U.S. at 72–73.

60. Zorach v. Clauson, 343 U.S. 306, 313 (1952).

61. 463 U.S. 783 (1983).

62. See *Abington, supra* note 59, at 299–300.

63. 465 U.S. 668 (1984).

64. *Supra* note 19.

65. *Supra* note 26.

66. See Redlich, in The Burger Years 75 (H. Schwartz ed. 1987).

67. Compare id. at 76.

68. Id. at 77.

69. Compare J. Story, Commentaries on the Constitution of the United States § 1873 (1833).

70. 406 U.S. 205 (1972).

71. PS-WEB, April 10, 1972.

72. 406 U.S. at 232, 233.

73. Compare Reynolds v. United States, 94 U.S. 145, 164 (1879).

74. Id. at 166.

75. Compare United States v. Lee, 455 U.S. 252, 262 (1982).

76. 455 U.S. 252 (1982).

77. The Chief Justice referred specifically to Sherbert v. Verner, *infra* note 84, and Thomas v. Review Board, *infra* note 85.

78. *Infra* note 84.

79. *Infra* note 85.

80. 455 U.S. at 261.

81. Reynolds v. United States, 94 U.S. 145, 167 (1879).

82. Compare West Virginia Board of Education v. Barnette, 319 U.S. 624, 654 (1943).

83. 461 U.S. 574 (1983).

84. 374 U.S. 398 (1963).

85. 450 U.S. 707 (1981).

86. Id. at 720, 724, 726.

87. 472 U.S. 703 (1985).

88. Id. at 710. Somewhat surprisingly, Justice Rehnquist dissented without any opinion.

89. 475 U.S. 503 (1986).

90. The conference notes used by me has "neither" here.

91. The Brennan quotes are from *Goldman v. Weinberger,* No. 84-1097 Conference Date: January 17, 1986, apparently the Brennan conference memo.

92. Wilson v. Schillinger, 475 U.S. 1096 (1986).

93. WHR, Re: Case held for No. 84-1097, *Goldman v. Weinberger* No. 85-5699 *Wilson v. Schillinger,* Memorandum to the Conference, March 26, 1986.

94. 454 U.S. 263 (1981).

95. *Abington, supra* note 59, at 243.

96. 13 Wall. 679 (U.S. 1872).

97. Id. at 733.

98. Presbyterian Church v. Mary Elizabeth Blue Hull Presbyterian Church, 393 U.S. 440 (1969).

99. Maryland & Virginia Eldership v. Church of God at Sharpsburg, 396 U.S. 367 (1970).

100. *Supra* note 98.

101. *Supra* note 96.

102. I have not been able to trace this quotation, which I found, with the *Washington Post* attribution, in the notes of a Justice.

CHAPTER EIGHT

1. When the Fourteenth Amendment was ratified.

2. The memo was headed Confidential and titled Re: No. 76-811 *Regents of the University of California v. Allan Bakke.* It is reprinted in B. Schwartz, Behind *Bakke:* Affirmative Action and the Supreme Court 167 (1988).

3. Regents of the University of California v. Bakke, 438 U.S. 265 (1978).

4. Headed Re: No. 71-1222, *Sugarman v. Dougall.*

5. Tigner v. Texas, 310 U.S. 141, 147 (1940).

6. See Griffin v. County School Board, 377 U.S. 218, 230 (1964).

7. Tigner v. Texas, 310 U.S. 141, 147 (1940).

8. See West Coast Hotel Co. v. Parrish, 300 U.S. 370, 400 (1937).

9. See Frankfurter, J., dissenting, in Morey v. Doud, 354 U.S. 457, 472 (1957).

10. Compare Black, J., dissenting, id. at 471.

11. Brandeis, J., dissenting, in Quaker City Cab Co. v. Pennsylvania, 277 U.S. 389, 405 (1928).

12. Reed v. Reed, 404 U.S. 71, 75 (1971); Atchison, Topeka & Santa Fe Railroad Co. v. Matthews, 174 U.S. 96, 106 (1899).

13. Graham v. Richardson, 403 U.S. 365, 371 (1971); Phelps v. Board of Education, 300 U.S. 319, 324 (1937).

14. Buck v. Bell, 274 U.S. 200, 208 (1927).

15. Reed v. Reed, 404 U.S. 71, 76 (1972).

16. Alexander v. Fioto, 434 U.S. 634, 640 (1977).

17. New Orleans v. Dukes, 427 U.S. 298, 303–04 (1976).

18. Massachusetts Board of Retirement v. Murgia, 427 U.S. 307, 319 (1976) (dissent).

19. Id. at 321.

20. 427 U.S. 298 (1976).

21. 354 U.S. 457 (1957).

22. Massachusetts Board of Retirement v. Murgia, 427 U.S. 307, 320 (1976) (dissent).

23. United States v. Carolene Products Co., 304 U.S. 144 (1938).

24. So characterized in Mason, The Core of Free Government, 1938–40, 65 Yale Law Journal 597, 598 (1956).

25. 304 U.S. at 152 n.4.

26. The most celebrated footnote was in Brown v. Board of Education, 347 U.S. 483, 494 n.11 (1954).

27. The *Brown* footnote 11 was also drafted by a law clerk. See B. Schwartz, Super Chief: Earl Warren and His Supreme Court—A Judicial Biography 107 (1983).

28. A. Mason, Harlan Fiske Stone: Pillar of the Law 513 (1956).

29. Id. at 514.

30. 323 U.S. 215 (1944).

31. Id. at 216.

32. Regents of the University of California v. Bakke, 438 U.S. 265, 355 (1978).

33. Massachusetts Board of Retirement v. Murgia, 427 U.S. 307, 318 (1976) (dissent); Shapiro v. Thompson, 394 U.S. 618, 658 (1969) (dissent).

34. Regents of the University of California v. Bakke, 438 U.S. 265, 291 (1978).

35. Wright v. Georgia, 373 U.S. 284, 293 (1963); Cooper v. Aaron, 358 U.S. 1, 16 (1958).

36. See, e.g., *supra* 137.

37. Headed Memorandum to the Conference Re: No. 78-811 *Regents of the University of California v. Allen Bakke*. It is reprinted in B. Schwartz, *supra* note 2, at 173.

38. Dissenting, in Massachusetts Board of Retirement v. Murgia, 427 U.S. 307, 319 (1976).

39. Cabell v. Chavez-Salido, *infra* note 94.

40. The original reads "fundamental interest."

41. Frederic William Maitland Reader 134 (V. Delaney ed. 1957).

42. Bradwell v. Illinois, 16 Wall. 130, 141 (U.S. 1873).

43. 404 U.S. 71 (1971).

44. Id. at 76.

45. 411 U.S. 677 (1973).

46. Since the challenge was to a federal statute, the Due Process Clause of the Fifth Amendment, not the Equal Protection Clause of the Fourteenth, came into play. The Brennan draft is reprinted in B. Schwartz, The Unpublished Opinions of the Burger Court 70 (1988).

47. BRW-WJB, Feb. 15, 1973.

48. LFP-WJB, Feb. 15, 1973.

49. PS-WJB, Feb. 16, 1973.

50. LFP-WJB, March 2, 1973.

51. HAB-WJB, March 5, 1973.

52. Justice Douglas was probably referring to Bradwell v. Illinois, 16 Wall. 130 (U.S. 1873).

53. WOD-WJB, March 3, 1973.

54. WJB-LFP, March 6, 1973.

55. WEB-WJB, March 6, 1973.

56. WEB-LFP, May 8, 1973.

57. 429 U.S. 190 (1976).

58. Id. at 197.

59. WEB-WJB, Nov. 15, 1976.

60. *Supra* note 55.

61. Cleburne v. Cleburne Living Center, 473 U.S. 432, 442 (1985).

62. Craig v. Boren, 429 U.S. 190, 217 (1976) (dissent).

63. Mississippi University for Women v. Hogan, 458 U.S. 718, 723, 724 (1982).

64. 458 U.S. 718 (1982).

65. Id. at 729, 730.

66. 468 U.S. 609 (1984).

67. Compare 2 R. Rotunda, J. Nowak & J. Young, Treatise on Constitutional Law 523–24 (1986).

68. 450 U.S. 464 (1981).

69. The conference notes used by me use the word "against," but this seems an error.

70. 450 U.S. at 468, 469.

71. Id. at 469, 476.

72. 453 U.S. 57 (1981).

73. Id. at 69.

74. Id. at 78, 79.

75. Id. at 69–70.

76. *Supra* 215.

77. Harisiades v. Shaughnessy, 342 U.S. 580, 586 (1951).

78. 403 U.S. 365 (1971).

79. People v. Crane, 214 N.Y. 154, 164 (1915), affirmed, 239 U.S. 195 (1915).

80. 413 U.S. 634 (1973).

81. Ibid.

82. 403 U.S. at 372, 376.

83. Id. at 643.

84. Id. at 645.

85. *Supra* 215.

86. Headed Re: 74-775—*City of New Orleans v. Dukes*.

87. Dougall v. Sugarman, 339 F. Supp. 906, 911 (S.D.N.Y. 1971).

88. 438 U.S. 291 (1978).

89. Id. at 294, 296, 297, 300.

90. 441 U.S. 68 (1979).

91. In re Griffiths, 413 U.S. 717 (1973).

92. 441 U.S. at 73–74, 74.

93. Id. at 75–76.

94. 454 U.S. 432 (1982).

95. Graham v. Richardson, *supra* note 78; Nyquist v. Mauclet, 432 U.S. 1 (1977); Plyler v. Doe, 457 U.S. 202 (1982).

96. Bernal v. Fainter, 467 U.S. 216, 220 (1984).

97. Cabell v. Chavez-Salido, 454 U.S. 432, 439 (1982).

98. 426 U.S. 67 (1976).

99. 426 U.S. 88 (1976).

100. 420 U.S. 959 (1975).

101. Headed Re: No. 73-1596, *Hampton v. Mow Sun Wong*.

102. See, e.g., R. Rotunda, J. Nowak & J. Young, *supra* note 67, at 495; B. Schwartz, Constitutional Law: A Textbook 387 (2d ed. 1979).

103. Mow Sun Wong v. Hampton, 435 F. Supp. 37 (N.D. Cal. 1977), affirmed, 626 F.2d 739 (9th Cir. 1981), cert. denied, 450 U.S. 959 (1981).

104. 432 U.S. 1 (1977).

105. Id. at 7.

106. Id.

107. Compare R. Rotunda, J. Nowak & J. Young, *supra* note 67, at 503.

108. 401 U.S. 532 (1971).

109. Id. at 541.

110. Ibid.

111. Id. at 539.

112. 391 U.S. 68 (1968).

113. See B. Schwartz, Super Chief: Earl Warren and His Supreme Court—A Judicial Biography 715 (1983).

114. 401 U.S. at 538.

115. Id. at 541.

116. Id. at 537.

117. Id. at 536 n.6.

118. 406 U.S. 164 (1972).

119. Id. at 173.

120. *Supra* 226.

121. 427 U.S. 495 (1976).

122. *Supra* note 57.

123. *Supra* note 45.

124. 427 U.S. at 505, 506.

125. Trimble v. Gordon, 430 U.S. 762, 767 (1977).

126. 430 U.S. 762 (1977).

127. Id. at 767 n.12.

128. Id. at 767.

129. Id. at 768, 766.

130. 429 U.S. 259 (1978).

131. Id. at 266.

132. Id. at 265, 271, 268, 275.

133. *Supra* note 57.

134. 429 U.S. at 277.

135. Rostker v. Goldberg, 453 U.S. 69–70.

136. 430 U.S. 787 (1977).

137. Id. at 792, 793, 796.

138. E.g., Griffin v. Illinois, 351 U.S. 12 (1956); Gideon v. Wainwright, 372 U.S. 335 (1963).

139. Harper v. Virginia State Board of Elections, 383 U.S. 663 (1966).

140. Douglas v. California, 372 U.S. 353 (1963).

141. Ross v. Moffitt, 417 U.S. 600, 616 (1974).

142. 397 U.S. 471 (1970).

143. Id. at 485.

144. 411 U.S. 1 (1973).

145. Rodriguez v. San Antonio Independent School District, 337 F. Supp. 280, 282 (W.D. Tex. 1971).

146. 411 U.S. at 28.

147. 427 U.S. 307 (1976).

148. Id. at 313–14.
149. 473 U.S. 432 (1985).
150. Dissenting, in Trimble v. Gordon, 430 U.S. at 777.
151. Id. at 779.
152. Id. at 783.
153. Marshall, J., dissenting, in Massachusetts Board of Retirement v. Murgia, 427 U.S. at 319.
154. *Supra* note 14.
155. Mill, Representative Government, 43 Great Books of the Western World 382 (1909).
156. Jackson, J., concurring, in Edwards v. California, 314 U.S. 160, 185 (1941).
157. Marshall, J., dissenting, in Cleburne v. Cleburne Living Center, 473 U.S. 432, 469 (1985).
158. *Supra* note 57.
159. WJB-LFP, April 1, 1976, headed, Re: No. 74-1607 *Hughes v. Alexandria Scrap Corporation.*
160. Compare C. Allen, Law and Orders 122 (1945).
161. See Cleburne v. Cleburne Living Center, 473 U.S. 432, 443 (1985).
162. Id. at 442.
163. Compare Greater Boston Television Corp. v. FCC, 444 F.2d 841, 851 (D.C. Cir. 1970).
164. Compare Cleburne v. Cleburne Living Center, 473 U.S. 432, 440–441. (1985) (dissent).
165. Compare ibid.

CHAPTER NINE

1. 347 U.S. 483 (1954).
2. B. Schwartz, Super Chief: Earl Warren and His Supreme Court 127 (1983).
3. The Burger Court: The Counter-Revolution That Wasn't 113 (V. Blasi ed. 1983).
4. Brown v. Board of Education, 349 U.S. 294, 301 (1955).
5. Green v. County School Board, 391 U.S. 430, 439 (1968).
6. Id. at 442 n.6.
7. Compare J. Wilkinson, From *Brown* to *Bakke*—The Supreme Court and School Integration 1945–1978, 117 (1979).
8. 402 U.S. 1 (1971).
9. The Burger draft is reprinted in B. Schwartz, *Swann*'s Way: The School Busing Case and the Supreme Court 208 (1986).
10. Alexander v. Holmes County Board of Education, 396 U.S. 19 (1969).
11. Briggs v. Elliott, 132 F. Supp. 776, 777 (E.D.S.C. 1955).
12. Particularly by Green v. County School Board, *supra* note 5. See B. Schwartz, *supra* note 9, at 60.
13. 402 U.S. at 15–16.
14. Id. at 15, 30.

15. United States v. Montgomery County Board of Education, 395 U.S. 225, 231 (1969).

16. Green v. County School Board, 391 U.S. at 437–38.

17. Swann v. Charlotte-Mecklenburg Board of Education, 402 U.S. at 15.

18. Id. at 17–18.

19. Powell, J., in Keyes v. Denver School District, 413 U.S. 189, 222–23 (1973).

20. Id. at 223.

21. Id. at 218–19.

22. 413 U.S. 189 (1973).

23. See B. Schwartz, *supra* note 9, at 149.

24. Id.

25. 413 U.S. at 232.

26. Id. at 248.

27. Id. at 250–51.

28. WJB-WHR, Re: No. 16-539, *Dayton Board of Education v. Brinkman,* June 1, 1977.

29. 418 U.S. 717 (1974).

30. See B. Schwartz, *supra* note 9, at 217–18.

31. 402 U.S. at 25.

32. In the final opinion, this passage was placed in a footnote, with its last portion omitted. 418 U.S. at 740 n.19.

33. Columbus Board of Education v. Penick, 443 U.S. 449 (1979).

34. 426 U.S. 229 (1976).

35. 429 U.S. 252 (1977).

36. 438 U.S. 265 (1978).

37. Quoted in B. Schwartz, Behind *Bakke:* Affirmative Action and the Supreme Court 54 (1988).

38. UJO v. Carey, 430 U.S. 144, 170 (1977).

39. De Funis v. Odegaard, 507 P.2d 1169, 1182 (Wash. 1973).

40. I have discussed the *Bakke* case in much greater detail in B. Schwartz, *supra* note 37.

41. *Supra* 219.

42. 448 U.S. 448 (1980).

43. 384 U.S. 641 (1966).

44. Brown v. Board of Education, *supra* note 1; Green v. County School Board, *supra* note 5.

45. 438 U.S. at 305.

46. 476 U.S. 267 (1986).

47. United Steel Workers v. Weber, 443 U.S. 193 (1979).

48. *Wygant v. Jackson Board of Education,* No. 84-1349. Argued Wednesday, November 6, 1985 (apparently a typed version of the Brennan conference statement).

49. 476 U.S. at 278.

50. Id. at 276.

51. Id. at 285.

52. Id. at 286.
53. 467 U.S. 561 (1984).
54. Id. at 580.
55. LFP, Re: Hold for *Wygant v. Jackson Board of Education,* No. 84-1340, Memorandum to the Conference, May 21, 1986.
56. 478 U.S. 421 (1986).
57. 478 U.S. 501 (1986).
58. Wygant v. Jackson Board of Education, 476 U.S. at 286.
59. Id. at 302, Marshall, J., dissenting.
61. *Supra* note 5.
62. Swann v. Charlotte-Mecklenburg Board of Education, *supra* note 8.
63. *Supra* note 22.
64. *Supra* note 22.
65. Compare Powell, J., in Keyes v. Denver School District, 413 U.S. at 219.
66. Compare id. at 236.
67. *Supra* note 29.
68. *Supra* note 34.
69. *Supra* note 36.
70. 438 U.S. at 325.
71. O'Connor, J., in Wygant v. Jackson Board of Education, 476 U.S. at 286.

CHAPTER TEN

1. *Supra* 215.
2. 411 U.S. 1 (1973).
3. 394 U.S. 618 (1969).
4. Id. at 661.
5. The Warren draft is reprinted in B. Schwartz, The Unpublished Opinions of the Warren Court 308 (1985). The Fortas draft is reprinted, id. at 357.
6. 410 U.S. 113 (1973), *infra* 297.
7. Harlan, J., dissenting, in Shapiro v. Thompson, 394 U.S. at 658.
8. Id.
9. Id.
10. Id.
11. E.g., Harper v. Virginia Board of Elections, 383 U.S. 663 (1966).
12. E.g., Burns v. Ohio, 360 U.S. 252 (1959).
13. Dunn v. Blumstein, 405 U.S. 330 (1972).
14. Storer v. Brown, 415 U.S. 724, 729 (1974).
15. E.g., Bullock v. Carter, 405 U.S. 134 (1972).
16. 401 U.S. 371 (1971).
17. Id. at 389
18. 415 U.S. 250 (1974).
19. Id. at 269, 258, 263.
20. *Supra* note 16.
21. 434 U.S. 374 (1978).
22. Id. at 379 n.5.
23. Id. at 383.

24. Id. at 388.

25. 417 U.S. 600 (1974).

26. *Supra* note 16.

27. 409 U.S. 434 (1973).

28. Id. at 446. See similarly Ortwein v. Schwab, 410 U.S. 656 (1973) (filing fee for judicial review of administrative decision reducing welfare payments).

29. E.g., Sosna v. Iowa, 419 U.S. 393 (1975); Vlandis v. Kline, 412 U.S. 441 (1973); Salyer Land Co. v. Tulare Water District, 410 U.S. 719 (1973).

30. Barry v. Barchi, 443 U.S. 55, 71 (1979).

31. See B. Schwartz, Administrative Law §§ 5.11–5.13 (2d ed. 1984).

32. Goldberg v. Kelly, 397 U.S. 254 (1970).

33. Goss v. Lopez, 419 U.S. 565 (1975).

34. 397 U.S. 471 (1970).

35. 411 U.S. 1 (1973).

36. *Supra* 249–250.

37. 397 U.S. at 521 n.14.

38. Id. at 487.

39. Rodriguez v. San Antonio Independent School District, 337 F. Supp. 280, 283 (W.D. Tex. 1971).

40. 411 U.S. at 17.

41. Id. at 29, 33, 33–34.

42. Id. at 35.

43. At least under the federal Constitution.

44. 411 U.S. at 35.

45. Goldberg v. Kelly, 397 U.S. 254, 262, n.8 (1970).

46. See B. Schwartz, *supra* note 31, §§ 10.8, 10.37.

47. Strumsky v. San Diego Employees Retirement Association, 520 P.2d 29, 31 (Cal. 1974).

48. Berlinghieri v. Director of Motor Vehicles, 657 P.2d 383 (Cal. 1983).

49. *Strumsky, supra* note 47.

50. Frink v. Prod, 643 P.2d 476 (Cal. 1982).

51. Id. at 484.

52. Madison's phrase in The Federalist No. 48.

53. 388 U.S. 1 (1967).

54. Schmidt, Oral History Research Office, Columbia University (1977).

55. 262 U.S. 390 (1923).

56. Schmidt, *supra* note 54.

57. 388 U.S. at 11.

58. Id. at 12.

59. Compare 2 R. Rotunda, J. Nowak & J. Young, Treatise on Constitutional Law 563 (1986).

60. *Supra* note 2.

61. 394 U.S. at 661.

62. *Supra* note 16.

63. *Supra* 286.

64. 401 U.S. at 382–83.

65. 410 U.S. 113, 173 (1973).

66. 410 U.S. 113 (1973).

67. B. Woodward & S. Armstrong, The Brethren: Inside the Supreme Court 238 (1979).

68. Washington Post, Oct. 1, 1984 (national weekly edition), p. 33.

69. McGovern v. Van Riper, 43 A.2d 514, 518 (N.J. 1945).

70. Douglas, J., dissenting, in Public Utilities Commission v. Pollak, 343 U.S. 451, 467 (1952).

71. Warren & Brandeis, The Right to Privacy, 4 Harvard Law Review 193 (1890).

72. Mapp v. Ohio, 367 U.S. 643, 656 (1961).

73. 381 U.S. 479 (1965).

74. Dissenting, id. at 510 n.1.

75. Pierce v. Society of Sisters, 281 U.S. 370 (1925).

76. 381 U.S. at 484.

77. Carey v. Population Services International, 431 U.S. 678, 687 (1977).

78. Eisenstadt v. Baird, 405 U.S. 438, 453 (1972).

79. Re: *Abortion Cases*, Memorandum to the Conference, May 31, 1972.

80. *Supra* note 66.

81. 410 U.S. 179 (1973).

82. Id. at 116.

83. See B. Woodward & S. Armstrong, *supra* note 67, at 170.

84. July 4, 1972, p. 1.

85. N.Y. Times, March 8, 1986, p. 7.

86. The draft is reprinted in B. Schwartz, The Unpublished Opinions of the Burger Court 103 (1988).

87. 402 U.S. 62 (1971).

88. Reprinted in B. Schwartz, *supra* note 86, at 120.

89. Reprinted id. at 141.

90. *Supra* note 87.

91. 408 U.S. 919 (1972).

92. Poe v. Ullman, 367 U.S. 497 (1961).

93. *Supra* note 73.

94. 410 U.S. at 155.

95. Reprinted in B. Schwartz, *supra* note 86, at 93.

96. 410 U.S. at 155.

97. B. Woodward & S. Armstrong, *supra* note 67, at 233.

98. 410 U.S. at 155.

99. Id. at 162.

100. Id. at 173.

101. Id.

102. Id.

103. Id.

104. *Supra* 220.

105. 198 U.S. 45 (1905).

106. Ferguson v. Skrupa, 372 U.S. 726, 731 (1963).

107. Re: No. 76-811 *Regents of the University of California v. Allen Bakke*, Memorandum to the Conference, Nov. 11, 1977.

108. Compare Rehnquist, J., dissenting, in Weber v. Aetna Casualty & Surety Co., 406 U.S. 164, 179 (1972).

109. Gitlow v. New York, 268 U.S. 652 (1925).

110. Buckley v. Valeo, 424 U.S. 1, 64 (1976).

111. Chief Justice Burger and Justices Brennan, Marshall, Blackmun, Powell, and Stevens.

112. Akron v. Akron Center for Reproductive Health, 462 U.S. 416, 420 n.1 (1983).

113. See R. Rotunda, J. Nowak & J. Young, *supra* note 59, at 576.

114. Simopoulos v. Virginia, 462 U.S. 506 (1983).

115. Akron v. Akron Center for Reproductive Health, 462 U.S. 416 (1983).

116. Re: *Abortion Cases,* Dec. 13, 1972.

117. Planned Parenthood v. Danforth, 428 U.S. 52 (1976).

118. Bellotti v. Baird, 443 U.S. 622 (1979).

119. Kansas City, Missouri, Inc. v. Ashcroft, 462 U.S. 476 (1983).

120. H.L. v. Matheson, 450 U.S. 398 (1981).

121. 450 U.S. 398 (1981).

122. Conference notes, Belloti v. Baird, 428 U.S. 132 (1976).

123. 78-329 *Bellotti v. Baird* 78-330 *Hunerwadel v. Baird,* June 3, 1979.

124. LFP-TM, 79-5903 *HL., etc. v. Matheson,* Nov. 12, 1980.

125. Compare R. Rotunda, J. Nowak & J. Young, *supra* note 59, at 590.

126. Harris v. McRae, 448 U.S. 297 (1980); Maher v. Roe, 432 U.S. 464 (1977).

127. Meyer v. Nebraska, 262 U.S. 390 (1923).

128. 417 U.S. 600 (1974), *supra* 287.

129. Harris v. McRae, 448 U.S. 297, 316 (1980).

130. *Supra* 289.

131. HAB-TM, Re: No. 79-5903—*H.L. v. Matheson,* Nov. 12, 1980.

132. 410 U.S. at 211.

133. *Supra* note 81.

134. *Supra* note 73.

135. 405 U.S. 438 (1972).

136. Id. at 453.

137. Carey v. Population Services International, 431 U.S. 678, 685 (1977).

138. Roberts v. United States Jaycees, 468 U.S. 609, 619 (1984).

139. 425 U.S. 238 (1976).

140. Id. at 244.

141. Id. at 249.

142. 478 U.S. 186 (1986).

143. 394 U.S. 557 (1969).

144. 277 U.S. 438 (1928).

145. Id. at 478.

146. From what seems to be a typed version of Brennan's conference statement, headed 85-140 *Bowers v. Hardwick.*

147. Loving v. Virginia, 388 U.S. 1 (1967) (miscegenation law invalidated).

148. 370 U.S. 660 (1962).

149. 478 U.S. at 197.

150. San Antonio Independent School District v. Rodriguez, 411 U.S. 1 (1973), *supra* note 35.

151. BRW, Holds for *Bowers v. Hardwick,* No. 85-140, Memorandum to the Conference, June 25, 1986.

152. Pierce v. Society of Sisters, 268 U.S. 510 (1925); Meyer v. Nebraska, 262 U.S. 390 (1923).

153. Prince v. Massachusetts, 321 U.S. 158 (1944).

154. Skinner v. Oklahoma, 316 U.S. 535 (1942).

155. Loving v. Virginia, 388 U.S. 1 (1967).

156. Griswold v. Connecticut, *supra* note 73; Eisenstadt v. Baird, 405 U.S. 438 (1972).

157. Roe v. Wade, *supra* note 66.

158. *Supra* note 66.

159. 410 U.S. at 173.

160. 198 U.S. 45 (1905).

161. 410 U.S. at 174.

162. The famous phrase of Brandeis, J., dissenting, in Burns Baking Co. v. Bryan, 264 U.S. 504, 534 (1924).

163. 410 U.S. at 174.

164. 478 U.S. at 195.

165. *Supra* note 150.

166. Compare Bowers v. Hardwick, 478 U.S. at 195, 206.

167. *Supra* note 143.

CHAPTER ELEVEN

1. See B. Schwartz, Super Chief: Earl Warren and His Supreme Court—A Judicial Biography 763 (1983).

2. Id. at 763.

3. Gideon v. Wainwright, 372 U.S. 335 (1963).

4. Mapp v. Ohio, 367 U.S. 643 (1961).

5. Miranda v. Arizona, 384 U.S. 436 (1966).

6. Kamisar, in The Burger Years 145 (H. Schwartz ed. 1987).

7. United States v. Wade, 388 U.S. 218 (1967); Gilbert v. California, 388 U.S. 263 (1967); Stovall v. Denno, 388 U.S. 293 (1967).

8. Id. at 272.

9. 406 U.S. 682 (1971).

10. The Brennan *Kirby* draft is reprinted in B. Schwartz, The Unpublished Opinions of the Burger Court 54 (1988).

11. 404 U.S. 105 (1972).

12. Reprinted in B. Schwartz, *supra* note 10, at 60.

13. 388 U.S. 293 (1967).

14. Neil v. Biggers, 409 U.S. 188, 199 (1972).

15. 432 U.S. 98 (1977).

16. 527 F.2d 363, 368 (2d Cir. 1975).

17. 432 U.S. at 114.

18. Id. at 106.

19. See 1 W. LaFave & J. Israel, Criminal Procedure 584–85 (1984).

20. Brennan, J., dissenting, in United States v. Martinez-Fuerte, 428 U.S. 543, 578 (1976).

21. Cohen v. Norris, 300 F.2d 24, 28 (9th Cir. 1962); Wrightson v. United States, 222 F.2d 556, 559 (D.C. Cir. 1955).

22. McDonald v. United States, 335 U.S. 451, 455 (1948).

23. Trupiano v. United States, 334 U.S. 699, 705 (1948).

24. Carroll v. United States, 267 U.S. 132, 147, 149 (1925).

25. 423 U.S. 411 (1976).

26. 427 U.S. 38 (1976).

27. The conference notes used by me has "[?]" here.

28. This statement appears based on a misconception of the facts.

29. 427 U.S. at 43.

30. This is true only if the arrest is in a public place. Payton v. New York, 445 U.S. 573 (1980).

31. 471 U.S. 1 (1985).

32. Id. at 11.

33. Terry v. Ohio, 392 U.S. 1 (1968). Suspicion alone, of course, is not enough to constitute the probable cause needed for an arrest. Henry v. United States, 361 U.S. 98, 100, 104 (1959).

34. Adams v. Williams, 407 U.S. 143 (1972).

35. 428 U.S. 543 (1976).

36. Almeida-Sanchez v. United States, 413 U.S. 266 (1973).

37. United States v. Brignoni-Ponce, 422 U.S. 873 (1975).

38. Id.

39. Terry v. Ohio, 392 U.S. 1 (1968).

40. Gerstein v. Pugh, 420 U.S. 103, 114 (1975).

41. Id.

42. 420 U.S. 103 (1975).

43. Justices Stewart, Douglas, Brennan, and Marshall dissented on this. Id. at 119.

44. In re Murchison, 349 U.S. 133, 136 (1955).

45. 372 U.S. 335 (1963).

46. B. Schwartz, *supra* note 1, at 460.

47. 407 U.S. 25 (1972).

48. 404 U.S. 999 (1971).

49. 316 U.S. 455 (1942).

50. 407 U.S. at 37.

51. 399 U.S. 1 (1970).

52. The prosecutor may seek an indictment directly from the grand jury without a preliminary hearing.

53. Miranda v. Arizona, 384 U.S. 436 (1966).

54. B. Woodward & S. Armstrong, The Brethren: Inside the Supreme Court 70 (1979).

55. 422 U.S. 806 (1975).

56. In a November 29, 1974, Memorandum to the Conference, the Chief Jus-

tice repeated his view on the matter: "In my view the Constitution gives no right to a *pro se* defense; rather, it is a matter of discretion in the trial judge to be exercised most sparingly in cases with a potential of significant imprisonment. That, I had thought, was what *Gideon* and *Argersinger* were really all about."

57. 422 U.S. at 834, n.46. See also McKaskle v. Wiggins, 465 U.S. 168 (1984).
58. 386 U.S. 213 (1967).
59. 398 U.S. 30 (1970).
60. Id. at 39.
61. In re Murchison, 349 U.S. 133, 136 (1955).
62. 427 U.S. 328 (1976).
63. 409 U.S. 57 (1972).
64. Duncan v. Louisiana, 391 U.S. 145 (1968).
65. 399 U.S. 78 (1970).
66. Apodaca v. Oregon, 406 U.S. 404 (1972).
67. 476 U.S. 79 (1986).
68. 380 U.S. 202 (1965).
69. *Batson v. Kentucky,* No. 84-6263 Conference Date: Dec. 13, 1985 (apparently a typed version of Brennan's conference statement).
70. 425 U.S. 501 (1976).
71. Id. at 512.
72. Despite Justice Brennan's statement, id. at 521, it is hard to see how defendant can even consent to be tried while so clothed.
73. 397 U.S. 337 (1970).
74. Id. at 357 n.5.
75. See 3 W. LaFave & J. Israel, *supra* note 19, at 6.
76. 387 U.S. 1 (1967).
77. 397 U.S. 358 (1970).
78. B. Schwartz, *supra* note 1, at 673.
79. Kent v. United States, 383 U.S. 541 (1966).
80. 343 U.S. 790, 803 (1952). B. Schwartz, The Unpublished Opinions of the Warren Court 286 (1985).
81. 403 U.S. 528 (1971).
82. 467 U.S. 253 (1984).
83. *Supra* note 76.
84. 467 U.S. at 264.
85. Id. at 264–65.
86. United States v. Salerno, 481 U.S. 739 (1987).

CHAPTER TWELVE

1. 367 U.S. 643 (1961).
2. 384 U.S. 436 (1966).
3. Moran v. Burbine, 475 U.S. 412, 424 (1986).
4. *Kamisar,* in The Burger Years 157 (H. Schwartz ed. 1987).
5. That records numbers dialed from a given phone. Smith v. Maryland, 442 U.S. 435 (1979).
6. United States v. Knotts, 460 U.S. 276 (1983).

7. *Kamisar, supra* note 4, at 158.

8. 460 U.S. 276 (1983).

9. The original notes used by me read, "when entered house and got warrant."

10. 460 U.S. at 281, 285.

11. Hester v. United States, 265 U.S. 57 (1924).

12. Id. at 59.

13. 466 U.S. 170 (1984).

14. 389 U.S. 347 (1967).

15. Id. at 361.

16. 466 U.S. at 176, 178.

17. 476 U.S. 207 (1986).

18. The Brennan quotes are from what appear to be typed versions of the Justice's conference statements. They are headed *California v. Ciraolo* No. 84-1513 Argued Tuesday, December 10 For conference Friday, December 13; *Dow Chemical Co. v. United States* No. 84-1259 Argued Tuesday, December 10 For conference Friday, December 13. The companion case referred to is Dow Chemical Co. v. United States, 476 U.S. 227 (1986).

19. *Kamisar, supra* note 4, at 158–59.

20. Cupp v. Murphy, 412 U.S. 291, 295 (1973).

21. Chimel v. California, 395 U.S. 752 (1969).

22. See 1 W. LaFave & J. Israel, Criminal Procedure 246 (1984).

23. 414 U.S. 218 (1973).

24. 414 U.S. 260 (1973).

25. Terry v. Ohio, 392 U.S. 1 (1968).

26. The quotes are from *Gustafson* conference notes, but they are plainly applicable to *Robinson* as well.

27. 414 U.S. at 235.

28. Chimel v. California, 395 U.S. 752, 763 (1969).

29. See W. LaFave & J. Israel, *supra* note 22, at 275.

30. 453 U.S. 454 (1981).

31. Robbins v. California, 453 U.S. 420, 430 (1981).

32. 453 U.S. at 460.

33. 453 U.S. 420 (1981).

34. Carroll v. United States, 267 U.S. 132 (1925).

35. South Dakota v. Opperman, 428 U.S. 364, 367 (1976).

36. See *Kamisar, supra* note 4, at 159.

37. 399 U.S. 42 (1970).

38. 428 U.S. 364 (1976).

39. *Infra* 377.

40. Camara v. Municipal Court, 387 U.S. 523 (1967); See v. Seattle, 387 U.S. 541 (1967).

41. Under Marshall v. Barlow's, Inc., 436 U.S. 307 (1978), a judicial warrant would be necessary.

42. 456 U.S. 798 (1982).

43. 412 U.S. 218 (1973).

44. People v. Michael, 290 P.2d 852, 854 (Cal. 1955).

45. Ker v. California, 374 U.S. 23 (1963).

46. B. Schwartz, Super Chief: Earl Warren and His Court—A Judicial Biography 391 (1983).

47. Id. at 397.

48. 403 U.S. 388 (1971).

49. Id. at 420.

50. 403 U.S. 443 (1971).

51. Id. at 492.

52. Id. at 490, 498–99, 510.

53. Justice Blackmun also wrote, "I am not now prepared to commit myself to the exclusionary rule, even by the Fifth Amendment." HAB-HLB, June 16, 1971.

54. *Infra* note 68.

55. 428 U.S. 465 (1976).

56. Id. at 538.

57. United States v. Calandra, 414 U.S. 338 (1974).

58. United States v. Janis, *infra* note 68.

59. Harris v. New York, *infra* note 82. See Kamisar, *supra* note 4, at 164.

60. 468 U.S. 897 (1984).

61. 468 U.S. 981 (1984).

62. My quotes are taken together from the conference notes in both cases.

63. Illinois v. Gates, 462 U.S. 213 (1983).

64. These quotes are from a document headed *United States v. Leon* No. 83-1771. It seems to be the note prepared for Brennan's conference statement.

65. 468 U.S. at 987–88.

66. Id. at 906–07.

67. 468 U.S. 1032 (1984).

68. United States v. Janis, 428 U.S. 433 (1976).

69. Id. at 453–54.

70. 705 F.2d 1059, 1067 (9th Cir. 1983).

71. The Brennan quotes are from a document headed *I.N.S. v. Lopez-Mendoza* No. 83-491, apparently the conference statement prepared by Brennan.

72. Frey argued the case for the government.

73. 468 U.S. at 1046.

74. 3 Encyclopedia Brittanica 486 (1969).

75. 10 Works of Jeremy Bentham 142 (J. Bowring ed. 1962).

76. Brennan, J., dissenting, in *Leon,* 468 U.S. at 929.

77. Compare Comment, A Federal Question: Does Priceless Mean Worthless?, 14 St. Louis University Law Journal 268 (1969).

78. 384 U.S. 436 (1966).

79. *Kamisar,* in The Burger Court 82 (V. Blasi ed. 1983).

80. *Funston,* in 1 Encyclopedia of the American Judicial System 189 (R. Janosik ed. 1987).

81. Rhode Island v. Innis, 446 U.S. 291, 304 (1980).

82. 401 U.S. 222 (1970).

83. Walder v. United States, 347 U.S. 62 (1954).

84. 384 U.S. at 476 (emphasis added).

85. See the slightly changed version, 401 U.S. at 232.

86. 384 U.S. at 476–77.

87. 423 U.S. 96 (1975).

88. Id. at 104.

89. Particularly of the *Miranda* statement, 384 U.S. at 473–74.

90. 467 U.S. 649 (1984).

91. WJB-TM, JPS, Jan. 23, 1984.

92. The date is missing from my copy of this letter.

93. 467 U.S. at 656.

94. 475 U.S. 412 (1986).

95. SDO, Re: Cases Held for No. 84-1485, *Moran v. Burbine*, Memorandum to the Conference, March 17, 1986.

96. 470 U.S. 298 (1985).

97. United States v. Bayer, 331 U.S. 532, 540 (1947).

98. 470 U.S. at 312, 318.

99. *Kamisar, supra* note 4, at 155.

100. Compare Brennan, J., dissenting, 470 U.S. at 348.

101. Id. at 306.

102. *Kamisar, supra* note 4, at 168.

CHAPTER THIRTEEN

1. Office of Communication of the United Church of Christ v. FCC, 359 F.2d 994 (D.C. Cir. 1966); Gonzalez v. Freeman, 334 F.2d 570 (D.C. Cir. 1964).

2. 424 U.S. 1 (1976).

3. 440 U.S. 1 (1979).

4. Id. at 18.

5. Schechter Poultry Corp. v. United States, 295 U.S. 495 (1935); Panama Refining Co. v. Ryan, 293 U.S. 388 (1935).

6. C. Reich, The Greening of America 45 (1970).

7. 478 U.S. 714 (1986).

8. Synar v. United States, 626 F. Supp. 1374, 1398 (D.C. 1986), the lower court decision in *Bowsher*.

9. The typed version of Brennan's conference statement, headed *Bowsher v. Synar* No. 85-1377, -1378, -1379.

10. National Cable Television Association v. United States, 415 U.S. 336, 342 (1974).

11. Eastlake v. Forest City Enter., 426 U.S. 668, 675 (1976); FEA v. Algonquin SNG, Inc., 426 U.S. 548, 559 (1976).

12. Industrial Department v. American Petroleum Institute, 448 U.S. 607, 646 (1980).

13. Id. at 675.

14. Dissenting, in American Textile Manufacturers Institute v. Donovan, 452 U.S. 490, 543 (1981).

15. Concurring in Industrial Department v. American Petroleum Institute, 448 U.S. 607, 686 (1980). See, e.g., W. Douglas, Go East Young Man 217 (1974); Wright, Beyond Discretionary Justice, 81 Yale Law Journal 575, 582–86 (1972).

16. This was established by Crowell v. Benson, 285 U.S. 22 (1932).

17. 478 U.S. 833 (1986).

18. Springer v. Philippine Islands, 277 U.S. 189, 210 (1928).

19. 430 U.S. 442 (1977).

20. 430 U.S. at 455.

21. Camara v. Municipal Court, 387 U.S. 523 (1967).

22. See v. Seattle, 387 U.S. 541 (1967).

23. 452 U.S. 594 (1981).

24. BRW-TM, Re 80-901—*Donovan v. Dewey*, May 29, 1981.

25. Colonnade Catering Corp. v. United States, 397 U.S. 72 (1970); United States v. Biswell, 406 U.S. 311 (1972).

26. 436 U.S. 307 (1978).

27. Id. at 313.

28. *Supra* note 26.

29. The same approach was taken in Justice Rehnquist's concurring opinion. 452 U.S. at 608.

30. *Supra* note 21.

31. *Supra* note 22.

32. 359 U.S. 360 (1959).

33. 452 U.S. at 608.

34. 397 U.S. 254 (1970).

35. Bailey v. Richardson, 182 F.2d 46, 58 (D.C. Cir. 1950), affirmed by equally divided Court, 341 U.S. 918 (1951).

36. Gilchrist v. Bierring, 14 N.W.2d 724, 730 (Iowa 1944).

37. The cases are summarized in B. Schwartz, Administrative Law 227–28 (2d ed. 1984).

38. Id. at 230.

39. *Supra* note 34.

40. Montgomery v. Wheeler, 397 U.S. 280 (1970).

41. 373 U.S. 96 (1963).

42. Note 15 of the Goldberg v. Kelly opinion.

43. Friendly, Some Kind of Hearing, 123 University of Pennsylvania Law Review 1267, 1268, 1271 (1975).

44. The one exception is alien entry, which is still treated as a privilege. Landon v. Plasencia, 459 U.S. 21 (1982).

45. 408 U.S. 564 (1972).

46. 408 U.S. 593 (1972).

47. Id. at 577.

48. For an egregious example of such judicial misunderstanding, see B. Schwartz, Administrative Law Cases during 1987, 40 Administrative Law Review 139, 144 (1988).

49. 408 U.S. at 573.

50. See, e.g., the example referred to *supra* note 48.

51. 419 U.S. 565 (1975).

52. 424 U.S. 319 (1976).

53. Eldridge v. Weinberger, 361 F. Supp. 520, 523 (W.D. Va. 1973), affirmed per curiam, 493 F.2d 1230 (4th Cir. 1974), reversed, 424 U.S. 319 (1976).

54. Justice Douglas resigned before the decision, so that only Justices Brennan and Marshall ultimately dissented.

55. 397 U.S. at 261, 264.
56. *Supra* 386.
57. *Supra* note 43.
58. *Supra* note 34.
59. See B. Schwartz, *supra* note 37, § 5.16.
60. United States v. Raddatz, 447 U.S. 667, 677 (1980).
61. Logan v. Zimmerman Brush Co., 445 U.S. 422, 433 (1982).
62. Sutton v. City of Milwaukee, 672 F.2d 644, 645 (7th Cir. 1982).
63. E.g., Goldberg v. Kelly, *supra* note 34, itself.
64. 430 U.S. 651 (1977).
65. Id. at 680, 682.
66. *Supra* note 51.
67. 419 U.S. at 583.
68. For a fuller discussion, see B. Schwartz, *supra* note 37, § 5.31.
69. 468 U.S. 1032 (1984).
70. *Supra* 362.
71. Knoll Associates v. FTC, 397 F.2d 530 (7th Cir. 1968).
72. Navia-Duran v. INS, 568 F.2d 803 (1st Cir. 1977).
73. 367 U.S. 643 (1961).
74. Committee on Ministers Powers, Minutes of Evidence 75 (1932).
75. Dissenting, in United States ex rel. Knauff v. Shaughnessy, 338 U.S. 537, 548–49 (1950).
76. 4 Wheat. 316 (U.S. 1819).
77. 425 U.S. 662 (1976).
78. 440 U.S. 689 (1979).
79. United States v. Midwest Video Corp., 406 U.S. 649 (1972).
80. 440 U.S. 490 (1979).
81. Associated Press v. National Labor Relations Board, 301 U.S. 103 (1937).
82. McCulloch v. Sociedad National, 372 U.S. 10 (1963).
83. 440 U.S. at 500.
84. Justice Blackmun joined the dissent in the final decision.
85. *Supra* 374–375.
86. Wright, Book Review, 81 Yale Law Journal 575, 585 (1972).
87. NLRB v. Hearst Publications, 322 U.S. 111, 124 (1944).
88. Office of Communication of United Church of Christ v. FCC, 359 F.2d 994, 1003–04 (D.C. Cir. 1966).
89. Environmental Defense Fund v. Ruckelshaus, 439 F.2d 584, 597 (D.C. Cir. 1971).

CHAPTER FOURTEEN

1. Compare Judge Learned Hand, in 317 U.S. xi (1942).
2. N.Y. Times, March 3, 1985 (Magazine), p. 100.
3. L. Hand, *supra* note 1.
4. N.Y. Times, *supra* note 2.
5. 1 J. Bryce, The American Commonwealth 274 (1917).
6. JMHP.

7. N.Y. Times, Dec. 14, 1969, § 4, p. 9; Washington Post, Jan. 2, 1984 (national weekly edition), p. 24.

8. Justice Scalia, N.Y. Times, Feb. 2, 1988, p. A16.

9. W. Rehnquist, The Supreme Court: How It Was, How It Is 290 (1987).

10. N.Y. Times, March 3, 1985 (Magazine), p. 35.

11. Id.

12. N.Y. Times, March 8, 1986, p. 7.

13. N.Y. Times, *supra* note 10.

14. *Supra* 269.

15. See B. Schwartz, Behind *Bakke:* Affirmative Action and the Supreme Court 71 (1988).

16. *Supra* 297.

17. N.Y. Times, March 8, 1986, p. 7.

18. The Burger Court: The Counter-Revolution That Wasn't (V. Blasi ed. 1983).

19. Id. at vii.

20. N.Y. Times, Feb. 28, 1988, § 4, p. 1.

21. N.Y. Times, *supra* note 10.

22. Id. at 34, 35.

23. Miranda v. Arizona, 384 U.S. 436 (1966); Gideon v. Wainwright, 372 U.S. 335 (1963); Mapp v. Ohio, 367 U.S. 643 (1961).

24. B. Schwartz, Super Chief: Earl Warren and His Supreme Court 593 (1983).

25. J. Weaver, Warren: The Man, The Court, The Era 233 (1967).

26. B. Schwartz, *supra* note 24, at 460.

27. *Supra* 329–331.

28. The Warren Court had also extended the right to counsel to criminal appeals. Douglas v. California, 372 U.S. 353 (1963); However, according to Ross v. Moffitt, 417 U.S. 600 (1974), the right only extends to the first appeal as of right, not to further appellate proceedings.

29. *Supra* 331–332.

30. *Supra* 332.

31. *Supra* 360, 362.

32. Brewer v. Williams, 430 U.S. 387 (1977).

33. WEB, Memorandum to the Conference, Dec. 29, 1976. A toned-down version of this statement is contained in the Burger dissent in Brewer v. Williams, 430 U.S. 387, 416 (1977).

34. *Supra* 365.

35. 351 U.S. 12 (1956).

36. Ake v. Oklahoma, 470 U.S. 68 (1985).

37. Boddie v. Connecticut, 401 U.S. 371 (1971).

38. 347 U.S. 483 (1954).

39. *Supra* 256, 259.

40. *Supra* 29–30.

41. *Supra* 278.

42. WEB-HLB, Re: No. 60—*Evans v. Abney*, Dec. 10, 1969.

43. *Supra* 100.

44. *Supra* 103.

45. R. Pound, Interpretations of Legal History 1 (1923).

46. Frankfurter, The Early Writings of O. W. Holmes, Jr., 44 Harvard Law Review 717, 724 (1931).

47. Truax v. Corrigan, 257 U.S. 312, 344 (1921).

48. 1 Holmes–Pollock Letters: The Correspondence of Mr. Justice Holmes and Sir Frederick Pollock, 1874–1932, 167 (M. de Wolfe Howe ed. 1961).

49. Compare B. Cardozo, The Nature of the Judicial Process 79 (1921).

50. O. Holmes, The Common Law 1, (1881).

51. Id. at 1, 35–36.

52. Compare Jacobs & Youngs v. Kent, 230 N.Y. 239, 242–43 (1921).

53. Compare B. Cardozo, The Paradoxes of Legal Science 57 (1927).

54. A. Lewis, Portrait of a Decade: The Second American Revolution 139 (1964).

55. 384 U.S. 436 (1966).

56. U.S. News & World Report, July 15, 1969, pp. 62, 64.

57. FF-JMH, May 9, 1957. FFH.

58. HLB-Fred Rodell, Sept. 5, 1962. HLBLC.

59. Id.

60. Reynolds v. Sims, 377 U.S. 533 (1964).

61. Id. at 602–15.

62. 4 Justices of the United States Supreme Court 1789–1969, 2726 (L. Friedman & F. Israel eds. 1969).

63. The Burger Years: Rights and Wrongs in the Supreme Court 1969–1986, xx (H. Schwartz ed. 1987).

64. The Burger Court, *supra* note 18, at ix.

65. Id.

66. L. Caplan, The Tenth Justice 268 (1987).

67. United States v. Will, 449 U.S. 200 (1980); Buckley v. Valeo, 424 U.S. 1 (1976).

68. Oregon v. Mitchell, 400 U.S. 112 (1970).

69. Northern Pipeline Construction Co. v. Marathon Pipe Line Co., 458 U.S. 50 (1982).

70. *Supra* 221 *et seq.*

71. The cases are listed in The Burger Court, *supra* note 18, at 306 n.14.

72. Immigration & Naturalization Service v. Chadha, 462 U.S. 919 (1983).

73. Bowsher v. Synar, 478 U.S. 714 (1986).

74. The Burger Court, *supra* note 18, at 200.

75. *Supra* 81.

76. *Supra* 297.

77. 381 U.S. 479 (1965).

78. B. Schwartz, *supra* note 24, at 577.

79. *Supra* 307.

80. The Burger Court, *supra* note 18, at 212–13.

81. *Supra* 380.

82. The cases are summarized in B. Schwartz, Administrative Law § 5.12 (2d ed. 1984).

83. See, e.g., Cafeteria Workers Union v. McElroy, 367 U.S. 886, 896 (1961); Bailey v. Richardson, 341 U.S. 918 (1951).

84. 397 U.S. 254 (1970), *supra* 380.

85. Id. at 262.

86. The cases are summarized in B. Schwartz, *supra* note 82, § 5.16.

87. The Burger Court, *supra* note 18, at 198.

88. Plyler v. Doe, 457 U.S. 202, 242 (1982).

89. R. Funston, The Burger Court and Era, 1 Encyclopedia of the American Judicial System 190 (R. Janosik ed. 1987).

90. Fortas, in The Fourteenth Amendment Centennial Volume 34 (B. Schwartz ed. 1970).

91. Compare The Burger Court, *supra* note 18, at 212.

92. Compare 55 U.S. Law Week 2225 (1986).

93. The Burger Court, *supra* note 18, at 198.

94. Compare id., at ix.

95. Id. at 211.

96. *Supra* 400.

97. N.Y. Times, Sept. 25, 1986, p. B10.

98. *Supra* 22.

99. Compare the Burger Court, *supra* note 18, at 216.

100. Id. at 211.

101. Compare R. Pound, Administrative Law 56 (1942).

102. The Burger Court, *supra* note 18, at 216.

103. B. Cardozo, A Ministry of Justice, 35 Harvard Law Review 113, 126 (1921).

TABLE OF CASES

INDEX